GW00644933

Semantics Engineering with PLT Redex

Semantics Engineering with PLT Redex

Matthias Felleisen
Robert Bruce Findler
Matthew Flatt

The MIT Press
Cambridge, Massachusetts
London, England

For information about special quantity discounts, please email special_sales@mitpress.mit.edu.

This book was set in Charter and Avant Garde by the authors.

Printed and bound in the United States of America.

Library of Congress Cataloging-in-Publication Data

Felleisen, Matthias.
Semantics engineering with PLT Redex / Matthias Felleisen, Robert Bruce Findler, and Matthew Flatt.
    p.   cm.
Includes bibliographical references and index.
ISBN 978-0-262-06275-6 (hardcover : alk. paper)
1. Redex (Computer program language)   2. Domain-specific programming languages.   3. Programming languages (Electronic computers)—Semantics I. Findler, Robert Bruce.   II. Flatt, Matthew.   III. Title.
QA76.73.R227F45 2009
005.1'1—dc22

                                                                    2008053213

10 9 8 7 6 5 4 3 2 1

To Helga, Christopher, and Sebastian,
Hsing-Huei, ZC, and Emily,
Wen, Oliver, and Sophia

Contents

Preface

Working programmers engineer software systems. The typical engineering process consists of a number of phases, including the collection of requirements, the creation of a specification, the design of the architecture, the design of the modules, the maintenance of the system, and so on. In many cases, the engineering process involves iterative approaches, with repetitions across various phases in the process.

Working semanticists engineer models of programming languages. Such models almost always include at least one semantics, often several. Like the engineering of a software system, the creation of a semantics requires many different steps, including the formulation of a model, its exploration with test cases, example-based validation of invariants, theorem-proving, typesetting, and more. Also like the engineering of software systems, the engineering of a semantics is an iterative process, not a linear one.

This text is addressed to the working semantics engineer who needs a lightweight modeling tool. Typically these are graduate students and working programmers who find themselves engineering the semantics of a programming language or, more likely, an extension of a programming language. An ideal reader knows the functional programming language Scheme and has significant experience with representing information via S-expressions. A regular reader has a working knowledge of some functional language (Erlang, Haskell, ML) or has extensive experience programming functionally in a conventional language. In our experience, the key is a familiarity with programming over algebraic data types.

O**rganization.** We have organized the text into three parts. Part I presents a framework for the formulation of language models, focusing on *equational calculi* and *abstract machines*. Roughly speaking, a minimal model of a language requires the specification of the core of the syntax and its meaning. This book uses a *syntactic approach* to the formulation of meaning. Put differently, the meaning of the core syntax is mostly formulated through binary relations on itself. We illustrate the approach and its major ideas with several small programming languages inspired by Church's λ-calculus.

Part II introduces *software tools* for expressing the models from part I as PLT Redex programs. In principle, Redex is just a small domain-specific programming language, hosted in PLT Scheme. A typical Redex model consists of two parts: a grammar for the language syntax and a binary relation on the syntax. Put differently, formulating a language model in Redex requires as little effort as writing it down with paper and pencil. One immediate advantage of Redex programs is that these models are executable. It is thus possible to explore the models with examples; to create and run test suites that are also useful for an eventual implementation; to check whether examples satisfy some invariant; to typeset the model. Because Redex is an embedded programming language, semantics engineers may also use plain Scheme functions for the model and may even import their own tools. Part II explains how to do all this with examples from part I and more.

Part III collects seven contributions on a wide range of models, all formulated in Redex. In the first contribution, Carl Eastlund explains an intermediate point in the design of a variant of ACL2 with modules; the Redex model is used to explore how to map modules to ACL2's evaluator and, separately, to the theorem prover. Martin Gasblicher, in the second contributed article, presents the first rewriting model of macro expansion for the R^5RS version of Scheme; the Redex model allows programmers to step through the expansion of macro expressions. For the third article, Kathryn Gray extends her work on interoperability between untyped programming languages and typed ones; her Redex model combines the semantics of two distinct languages in one in order to investigate soundness issues. Joe Hallet, Eric Allen, and Sukyoung Ryu use a Redex model to explain one intricate part of Fortress's type system. The fifth article continues George Kuan's series of articles on type checking as a reduction system; thus, his Redex model uses reductions for modeling both the type checking process and for the evaluation process. With the penultimate contribution, Jacob Matthews describes his development of a web-based interview specification language. Last but not least, Mike Rainey demonstrates how Redex models are helpful for developing scheduling algorithms for a multi-core world.

To the Instructor. We have used the first two parts in graduate courses on topics in programming languages. A typical course covers the first two parts in four to eight weeks, depending on the familiarity of students with Scheme and/or functional programming. While we assign weekly homework projects for this period, we also ask students to work out Redex models for papers we pick. Students present the results of these projects in class. Equipped with this background, the course tackles additional topics. Sometimes students develop Redex models for papers of their choice; at other times, we jointly investigate historical developments of ideas.

To the Student. In addition, we have used the notes to train individual PhD students with a self-study plan. These students typically work through parts I and II in parallel so that they can immediately use the theoretical lessons to build practical models. Since most of our students end up extending a programming language, and since most of these designs are long-term efforts with many iterations, we consider it critical that students become intimately familiar with Redex (and other lightweight modeling tools).

Many times, our students iterate the model development to the point where we can reuse the test suites from the model for an actual implementation of a language extension. Our paper at the 2007 International Conference on Functional Programming on engineering functional and delimited continuations for a realistic programming system is a particularly good example of this kind of language development. We conjecture that all students of programming languages will benefit from such work flows.

Software. PLT Redex comes with the PLT Scheme implementation, which is available for free at

<code>http://www.plt-scheme.org/</code>

A Redex program is just a Scheme module that imports the Redex language. We urge you to download the software before you start reading so that you can experiment with Redex as you work your way through the book.

Programmers do not have to know much about Scheme to use Redex. Programmers who do know Scheme, especially PLT Scheme, can easily escape into the host language and build their own extensions. Jacob Matthew's contribution, for example, is the specification of a domain-specific web programming language; his model's reduction relations open a web browser to interact with the user.

Like all software, Redex isn't perfect. For that reason, DrScheme comes with a Help Desk facility and an error reporting interface. The former explains our intent and contains details that are beyond the scope of a text like this one. We intend to continue the development of Redex, and you will be able to find the documentation for these extensions and revisions in Help Desk. The error reporting interface is useful both for contacting us concerning failures and for requesting additional features.

In addition to Redex, our web site also hosts the models in this book, additional examples, and future contributions. Visit

<code>http://redex.plt-scheme.org/</code>

and also use it to share your favorite Redex models with others.

Acknowledgments. We thank Daniel P. Friedman for inspiring the exploration of reduction semantics and for pushing us to implement our ideas. Lambda, lambda, and once more, lambda.

Robert Hieb (1953–1992) and Matthias jointly worked out the style of reduction semantics used in part I in 1989 and 1990. Their collaboration was tragically shortened by a traffic accident; Bob is dearly missed.

Thanks to Robby's Tutu for the use of her lānai, where he built the first version of Redex. And thanks to Jacob Matthews and Casey Klein for numerous hours of work on Redex.

Over the past decade, many people have read drafts of part I and have used early versions of Redex. Three stand out for their use of our work and their feedback: Olivier Danvy, Johnathan Edwards, and Bill Richter. In addition, the book has benefited from the feedback of several generations of students who took our courses. They are too numerous to enumerate here, but we certainly we owe them a big "thank you."

Finally, we wish to thank our editors at the Press. Bob Prior encouraged us for years to turn these notes into a book, and Ada Brunstein took us over the final hurdles to make it happen. Mel Goldsipe helped us polish our writing and that of our contributors.

Of course, the remaining errors are all ours.

Matthias Felleisen, Robby Findler, Matthew Flatt

Part I

Reduction Semantics

Contents, Part I

1 • Semantics via Syntax

The specification of a programming language starts with its syntax. As every programmer knows, the syntax of a language comes in the shape of a variant of a BNF (Backus-Naur Form) grammar, which enumerates the grammatically legal vocabulary and sentences. The difficult part is the specification of the meaning of programs, i.e., how a program computes.

In this first part of the book, we develop a syntax-based approach to the specification of semantics. We start with the observation that computation generalizes calculations and that a child's training in calculations starts with phrases such as "1 plus 1 is 2." The trick is to see that such forms of calculation also apply to programs.

Calculating with programs means looking at the syntax of an expression or a statement and relating it to some other—presumably simpler—expression or statement. For the expression $1 + 1$, this claim is easy to understand; it is equal to 2, i.e., $1 + 1$ is related to 2. Even the application of a function to argument values can be expressed in this manner:

$$f(4) = 2 * 4 + 55 \qquad \text{if} \quad \textbf{define } f(x) = 2 * x + 55.$$

Mathematically put, we are specifying *the semantics of a programming language with a relation on its syntax.* For students of functional programming languages, this claim does not come as a surprise. They know that functional programming is little more than seventh grade algebra turned into a programming language, and the laws of algebra are equations that relate algebraic expressions to each other. What may come as a surprise is the possibility of specifying the semantics of (almost) all programming languages in this manner, including languages with imperative effects.

Here we introduce the idea, the minimal mathematical meta-knowledge, starting with syntax definitions as sets.

1·1 **Defining Sets.** A BNF grammar is used for several different purposes. One meaning is a set of strings. Another interpretation is a set of "trees," often called **abstract syntax** (trees). In this book, we always adopt the second perspective.

For this chapter and the next, we use the following BNF grammar as a running example:

$$
\begin{array}{rcl}
B & = & \mathtt{t} \\
  & | & \mathtt{f} \\
  & | & (B \bullet B)
\end{array}
$$

We take it as a short-hand for following constraints on the set B of abstract syntax trees:

$$
\mathtt{t} \in B
$$
$$
\mathtt{f} \in B
$$
$$
a \in B \text{ and } b \in B \;\Rightarrow\; (a \bullet b) \in B
$$

Technically, B is the *smallest* set that obeys the above constraints. To construct this set, we first include the basic elements $\mathtt{t}$ and $\mathtt{f}$, and then inductively combine those into compound elements.

Notation: we sometimes use "B" to mean "the set B," but sometimes "B" will mean "an arbitrary element of B." The meaning is always clear from the context. Sometimes, we use a subscript or a prime on the name of the set to indicate an arbitrary element of the set, such as "B_1" or "B'." Thus, the above constraints might be written as

$$
\mathtt{t} \in B \qquad\qquad \text{[a]}
$$
$$
\mathtt{f} \in B \qquad\qquad \text{[b]}
$$
$$
(B_1 \bullet B_2) \in B \qquad\qquad \text{[c]}
$$

Enumerating all of the elements of B in finite space is clearly impossible in this case:

$$
B = \{\mathtt{t},\ \mathtt{f},\ (\mathtt{t} \bullet \mathtt{t}),\ (\mathtt{t} \bullet \mathtt{f}),\ \ldots\}
$$

Given some tree, however, we can demonstrate that it belongs to B by showing that it satisfies the constraints. For example, $(\mathtt{t} \bullet (\mathtt{f} \bullet \mathtt{t}))$ is in B:

1. $\mathtt{t} \in B$ by [a]

2. $\mathtt{f} \in B$ by [b]
3. $\mathtt{t} \in B$ by [a]
4. $(\mathtt{f} \bullet \mathtt{t}) \in B$ by 2, 3, and [c]

5. $(\mathtt{t} \bullet (\mathtt{f} \bullet \mathtt{t})) \in B$ by 1, 4, and [c]

Usually, such arguments are arranged in the shape of a so-called proof tree:

$$\dfrac{\texttt{t} \in B \; [\text{a}] \qquad \dfrac{\texttt{f} \in B \; [\text{b}] \qquad \texttt{t} \in B \; [\text{a}]}{(\texttt{f} \bullet \texttt{t}) \in B} \; [\text{c}]}{(\texttt{t} \bullet (\texttt{f} \bullet \texttt{t})) \in B} \; [\text{c}]$$

Most of the time, proof trees come without labels that justify each step, because the steps are typically obvious:

$$\dfrac{\texttt{t} \in B \qquad \dfrac{\texttt{f} \in B \qquad \texttt{t} \in B}{(\texttt{f} \bullet \texttt{t}) \in B}}{(\texttt{t} \bullet (\texttt{f} \bullet \texttt{t})) \in B}$$

Exercise 1.1. Which of (1) $\texttt{t}$, (2) $\bullet$, (3)$((\texttt{f} \bullet \texttt{t}) \bullet (\texttt{f} \bullet \texttt{f}))$, (4) $((\texttt{f}) \bullet (\texttt{t}))$, or (5) "hello" are in B? For each member of B, provide a proof tree.

$1 \cdot 2$ **Relations.** A **relation** is a set whose elements consist of ordered pairs. For example, we can define the $\mathbf{R}$ relation to match each element of B with itself:

$$a \in B \;\Rightarrow\; \langle a, a \rangle \in \mathbf{R}$$

For binary relations such as $\mathbf{R}$, instead of $\langle a, a \rangle \in R$, we usually write $a \, \mathbf{R} \, a$:

$$a \in B \;\Rightarrow\; a \, \mathbf{R} \, a$$

or even simply

$$B_1 \, \mathbf{R} \, B_1$$

as long as it is understood as a definition of $\mathbf{R}$. As it turns out, the relation $\mathbf{R}$ is reflexive, symmetric, and transitive; that is, it satisfies the following three constraints:

        a relation $\mathbf{R}$ is **reflexive**   iff $a \, \mathbf{R} \, a$ (for any a)
        a relation $\mathbf{R}$ is **symmetric** iff $a \, \mathbf{R} \, b \Rightarrow b \, \mathbf{R} \, a$
        a relation $\mathbf{R}$ is **transitive**   iff $a \, \mathbf{R} \, b$ and $b \, \mathbf{R} \, c \Rightarrow a \, \mathbf{R} \, c$

If a relation is reflexive, symmetric, and transitive, then it is an **equivalence**. Certain names for a relation, such as $=$, suggest that the relation is an equivalence.

    The following defines a relation $\mathbf{r}$ that is neither reflexive, symmetric, nor transitive.

$(\texttt{f} \bullet B_1)$	$\mathbf{r}$	B_1	[a]
$(\texttt{t} \bullet B_1)$	$\mathbf{r}$	$\texttt{t}$	[b]

In the context of a reduction semantics, such relations are known as **notions of reduction.** A minor modification of this definition yields a relation $\asymp_\mathbf{r}$ that is reflexive:

$$
\begin{array}{rcl}
(\mathbf{f} \bullet B_1) & \asymp_\mathbf{r} & B_1 \qquad [\text{a}] \\
(\mathbf{t} \bullet B_1) & \asymp_\mathbf{r} & \mathbf{t} \qquad [\text{b}] \\
B_1 & \asymp_\mathbf{r} & B_1 \qquad [\text{c}]
\end{array}
$$

An alternative way of defining $\asymp_\mathbf{r}$ is to extend $\mathbf{r}$ and explicitly constrain the new relation to be reflexive:

$$
\begin{array}{rcl}
B_1 & \asymp_\mathbf{r} & B_2 \text{ if } B_1 \, \mathbf{r} \, B_2 \qquad [\text{ab}] \\
B_1 & \asymp_\mathbf{r} & B_1 \qquad [\text{c}]
\end{array}
$$

The relation $\asymp_\mathbf{r}$ is therefore called the **reflexive closure** of the $\mathbf{r}$ relation. We define yet another relation by adding symmetry and transitivity constraints:

$$
\begin{array}{rcl}
B_1 & \approx_\mathbf{r} & B_2 \text{ if } B_1 \, \mathbf{r} \, B_2 \qquad [\text{ab}] \\
B_1 & \approx_\mathbf{r} & B_1 \qquad [\text{c}] \\
B_2 & \approx_\mathbf{r} & B_1 \text{ if } B_1 \approx_\mathbf{r} B_2 \qquad [\text{d}] \\
B_1 & \approx_\mathbf{r} & B_3 \text{ if } B_1 \approx_\mathbf{r} B_2 \qquad [\text{e}] \\
& & \text{and } B_2 \approx_\mathbf{r} B_3
\end{array}
$$

The $\approx_\mathbf{r}$ relation is the **symmetric-transitive closure** of $\asymp_\mathbf{r}$, and it is the **reflexive-symmetric-transitive closure** or **equivalence closure** of $\mathbf{r}$.

1·3 Semantics as an Equivalence Relation.

The running example of B and $\mathbf{r}$ suggests how a programming language can be defined through syntax and relations on syntax—or, more specifically, as a set B of abstract syntax trees and a relation $\mathbf{r}$ on this set. In fact, an alert reader might begin to suspect that B is a grammar for boolean expressions with $\mathbf{t}$ for true, $\mathbf{f}$ for false, and $\bullet$ as the "or" operator. The relation $\approx_\mathbf{r}$ equates pairs of B expressions that have the same (boolean) value.

Indeed, using the constraints above, we can show that $(\mathbf{f} \bullet \mathbf{t}) \approx_\mathbf{r} (\mathbf{t} \bullet \mathbf{t})$, just as false $\vee$ true = true $\vee$ true:

$$
\dfrac{(\mathbf{f} \bullet \mathbf{t}) \approx_\mathbf{r} \mathbf{t} \ [\text{a}] \qquad \dfrac{\dfrac{(\mathbf{t} \bullet \mathbf{t}) \approx_\mathbf{r} \mathbf{t} \ [\text{b}]}{\mathbf{t} \approx_\mathbf{r} (\mathbf{t} \bullet \mathbf{t})} \ [\text{d}]}{}}{(\mathbf{f} \bullet \mathbf{t}) \approx_\mathbf{r} (\mathbf{t} \bullet \mathbf{t})} \ [\text{e}]
$$

It does not follow, however, that $\bullet$ is exactly like a boolean "or". If we wished to establish this connection, we would have to prove general claims about $\bullet$, such as $(B_1 \bullet \mathbf{t}) \approx_\mathbf{r} \mathbf{t}$ for any expression B_1.

Put differently, there is generally a gap between the semantics of a programming language and properties of this semantics language that we might like to know. For various purposes, the properties of a semantics are as important as the values it relates to expressions or programs. For example, if • really satisfied the laws of "or", then a compiler might safely optimize $(B_1 • \mathtt{t})$ as $\mathtt{t}$. Similarly, if the semantics of the language guaranteed that a number can never be added to anything other than another number, the implementation of the semantics need not check the arguments of an addition operation to ensure that they are numbers.

1·4 Semantics via Reduction.

The $\approx_\mathbf{r}$ relation should remind the reader of $=$ from arithmetic and algebra in primary school. Just like we teach students in this setting to use such equational reasoning for all kinds of purposes, we can use the $\approx_\mathbf{r}$ relation to prove the equivalence of certain expressions. In general, though, the relation does not suggest how to get from an arbitrary B to either $\mathtt{t}$ or $\mathtt{f}$—which is what we really need to build an interpreter for a semantics.

In this sense, the $\mathbf{r}$ relation is actually more useful than $\approx_\mathbf{r}$. Both cases in the definition of $\mathbf{r}$ relate an expression to a smaller expression. Also, for any expression B, either B is $\mathtt{t}$ or $\mathtt{f}$, or $\mathbf{r}$ relates B to at most one other expression. As a result, we can think of $\mathbf{r}$ as a **single-step reduction**, corresponding to the way that an interpreter might take a single evaluation step in working towards a final value.

Using $\mathbf{r}$, it is then possible to define $\leadsto_\mathbf{r}$ as the reflexive-transitive closure of $\mathbf{r}$:

$$
\begin{array}{lll}
B_1 & \leadsto_\mathbf{r} & B_1 \\
B_1 & \leadsto_\mathbf{r} & B_2 \ \text{ if } \ B_1 \ \mathbf{r} \ B_2 \\
B_1 & \leadsto_\mathbf{r} & B_2 \ \text{ if } \ B_1 \leadsto_\mathbf{r} B_3 \text{ and } B_3 \leadsto_\mathbf{r} B_2
\end{array}
$$

This yields a **multi-step reduction** relation. In particular, the multi-step relation $\leadsto_\mathbf{r}$ maps a single expression to many other expressions but to at most one of $\mathtt{t}$ or $\mathtt{f}$.

The relations $\mathbf{r}$ and $\leadsto_\mathbf{r}$ are intentionally asymmetric, emphasizing that evaluation should proceed in a specific direction towards a value. For example, given the expression $(\mathtt{f} • (\mathtt{f} • (\mathtt{t} • \mathtt{f})))$, we can show that there exits a sequence of **reduction**s from it to $\mathtt{t}$:

$$
\begin{array}{lll}
(\mathtt{f} • (\mathtt{f} • (\mathtt{t} • \mathtt{f}))) & \mathbf{r} & (\mathtt{f} • (\mathtt{t} • \mathtt{f})) \\
& \mathbf{r} & (\mathtt{t} • \mathtt{f}) \\
& \mathbf{r} & \mathtt{t}
\end{array}
$$

Each blank line in the left column is implicitly filled by the expression in the right column from the previous line. Each line is then a step in an argument that $(\mathtt{f} • (\mathtt{f} • (\mathtt{t} • \mathtt{f}))) \leadsto_\mathbf{r} \mathtt{t}$.

Exercise 1.2. Show that $(f \bullet (f \bullet (f \bullet f))) \leadsto_r f$ by constructing a reduction sequence based on the **r** one-step relation.

1·5 Reduction in Context.

How does the expression $((f \bullet t) \bullet f)$ reduce? According to **r** or $\leadsto_r$, it does not reduce at all. Intuitively, $((f \bullet t) \bullet f)$ should reduce to $(t \bullet f)$, by simplifying the first sub-expression according to $(f \bullet t) \, \mathbf{r} \, t$. Nothing in the definition of **r** matches $((f \bullet t) \bullet f)$ as the source expression, however. That is, we can only reduce expressions of the form $(f \bullet B)$ and $(t \bullet B)$. While the expression on the right-hand side of the outermost $\bullet$ can be arbitrary, the expression on the left-hand side must be f or t.

If we wish to reduce such B expressions to answers, we must extend the **r** relation to a relation that supports the reduction of sub-expressions.

$$
\begin{array}{llll}
B_1 & \rightarrow_r & B_2 & \text{if } B_1 \, \mathbf{r} \, B_2 & \text{[a]} \\
(B_1 \bullet B_2) & \rightarrow_r & (B_1' \bullet B_2) & \text{if } B_1 \rightarrow_r B_1' & \text{[b]} \\
(B_1 \bullet B_2) & \rightarrow_r & (B_1 \bullet B_2') & \text{if } B_2 \rightarrow_r B_2' & \text{[c]}
\end{array}
$$

The $\rightarrow_r$ relation is the **compatible closure** of the **r** relation. Like **r**, $\rightarrow_r$ is a single-step reduction relation, but $\rightarrow_r$ allows the reduction of any sub-expression within an expression. The reducible expression is called the **redex**, and the text surrounding a redex is its **context**.

In particular, the $\rightarrow_r$ relation includes $((f \bullet t) \bullet f) \rightarrow_r (t \bullet f)$. We can demonstrate this inclusion with the following proof tree:

$$
\cfrac{\cfrac{(f \bullet t) \, \mathbf{r} \, t}{(f \bullet t) \rightarrow_r t} \text{ [a]}}{((f \bullet t) \bullet f) \rightarrow_r (t \bullet f)} \text{ [b]}
$$

Continuing with $\rightarrow_r$, we can reduce $((f \bullet t) \bullet f)$ to t:

$$
\begin{array}{lll}
((f \bullet t) \bullet f) & \rightarrow_r & (t \bullet f) \\
& \rightarrow_r & t
\end{array}
$$

Finally, if we define $\rightarrow\!\!\!\rightarrow_r$ to be the reflexive–transitive closure of $\rightarrow_r$, then we get $((f \bullet t) \bullet f) \rightarrow\!\!\!\rightarrow_r t$. Thus, $\rightarrow\!\!\!\rightarrow_r$ is the natural **reduction relation** generated by **r**.

In general, the mere reflexive closure $\asymp_r$, equivalence closure $\approx_r$, or reflexive-transitive closure $\leadsto_r$ of a relation **r** is uninteresting. What we are most often interested in is the compatible closure $\rightarrow_r$ and its reflexive-transitive closure $\rightarrow\!\!\!\rightarrow_r$. Those two correspond to typical notions of expression evaluation and interpretation. In addition, the equivalence closure $=_r$ of $\rightarrow_r$ is interesting because it relates expressions that produce the same result.

Exercise 1.3. Explain why $(f \bullet ((t \bullet f) \bullet f)) \not\twoheadrightarrow_r t$.

Exercise 1.4. Show that $(f \bullet ((t \bullet f) \bullet f)) \twoheadrightarrow_r t$ with a reduction sequence based on $\rightarrow_r$.

$1 \cdot 6$ Evaluation Functions.
The $\twoheadrightarrow_r$ relation brings us close to a useful notion of evaluation, but we are not there yet. While $((f \bullet t) \bullet f) \twoheadrightarrow_r t$, it is also the case that $((f \bullet t) \bullet f) \twoheadrightarrow_r (t \bullet f)$ and $((f \bullet t) \bullet f) \twoheadrightarrow_r ((f \bullet t) \bullet f)$. For an evaluator, however, we are only interested in whether a B evaluates to a result and a result is either f or to t; anything else is irrelevant.

We use two definitions to state this desire formally. The first specifies once and for all what we consider a result R for B "programs."

$$
\begin{array}{rcl}
R & = & t \\
 & | & f
\end{array}
$$

Obviously, R is a subset of B ($R \subset B$) because all results are also expressions of our "programming language."

Our second definition specifies evaluation as the $eval_r^{\twoheadrightarrow r}$ relation, which maps each expression to a result.

$$
\begin{array}{rcl}
eval_r^{\twoheadrightarrow r} : B & \longrightarrow & R \\
eval_r^{\twoheadrightarrow r}(B) & = & \begin{cases} f & \text{if } B \twoheadrightarrow_r f \\ t & \text{if } B \twoheadrightarrow_r t \end{cases}
\end{array}
$$

Here, we're using yet another notation to define a relation. This particular notation is suggestive of a **function**, i.e., a relation that maps each element to at most one element. We use the function notation because $eval_r^{\twoheadrightarrow r}$ must be a function if it is going to make sense as an evaluator (for a deterministic programming language).

The name of the function comes with both a subscript and a superscript. Naturally, the former just says that the function is based on the relation r, while the latter tells us that the definition of the evaluation function is based on the relation $\twoheadrightarrow_r$. We decorate the name of the function with both because there are many alternative definitions. For example, the following definition uses the equivalence relation based on r instead of the reduction relation.

$$
eval_r^{=r}(B) = \begin{cases} f & \text{if } B =_r f \\ t & \text{if } B =_r t \end{cases}
$$

The equivalence relation $=_\mathbf{r}$ is of course just the compatible, reflexive, transitive and symmetric closure of $\mathbf{r}$. Defining an evaluation function via $=_\mathbf{r}$ shows that a program's computation really just generalizes the notion of calculation from algebra.

Exercise 1.5. Among the relations $\mathbf{r}$, $\succ_\mathbf{r}$, $\approx_\mathbf{r}$, $\leadsto_\mathbf{r}$, $\rightarrow_\mathbf{r}$, $\twoheadrightarrow_\mathbf{r}$, and $=_\mathbf{r}$ which are functions? For each non-function relation, find an expression and two expressions that it relates to.

Exercise 1.6. Use the above definitions to find the results of $eval_\mathbf{r}^{=\mathbf{r}}(((\mathbf{f} \bullet \mathbf{t}) \bullet \mathbf{t}))$ and $eval_\mathbf{r}^{\twoheadrightarrow\mathbf{r}}(((\mathbf{f} \bullet \mathbf{t}) \bullet \mathbf{f}))$

1·7 **Notation Summary.** The following table summarizes the notions and the notations introduced so far.

name	definition	intuition
$\_$	the base relation on members of an expression grammar	a single "reduction" step with no context
$\rightarrow_\_$	the compatible closure of $\_$ with respect to the expression grammar	a single step within a context
$\twoheadrightarrow_\_$	the reflexive–transitive closure of $\rightarrow_\_$	multiple evaluation steps (zero or more)
$=_\_$	the symmetric–transitive closure of $\twoheadrightarrow_\_$	equates expressions that produce the same result
$eval_\_^-$	a relation projected to a range (results)	complete evaluation based on $\twoheadrightarrow_\_$ or $=_\_$
$eval_\_$	a generic *eval* relation	

2 • Analyzing Syntactic Semantics

Once we have a syntax and a semantics for a programming language, we can ask questions, experiment, and contemplate alternatives. In this part of the book, we look at the most basic questions that programming language theoreticians ask, and we study how to answer them. In the second part of the book, we introduce a tool for experimenting with syntax and semantics, which usually helps formulate conjectures and questions.

Here we use the syntax and semantics introduced in the first chapter to illustrate what kinds of questions to ask and how to answer them rigorously. The first section shows how to formulate questions about a language in mathematical terms. The second section formulates answers as mathematical theorems and proofs, introducing the key proof techniques for the rest of this part of the book.

2·1 From Questions to Mathematical Claims.
The first chapter defines several evaluators, including $eval_{\mathbf{r}}^{\longrightarrow\!\!\!\!\mathbf{r}}$. Viewed from the perspective of a language implementor, this function uses something like a machine whose initial, intermediate, and final states are B expressions and whose instructions are the $\longrightarrow_{\mathbf{r}}$ relation. It launches the program, waits until the machine reaches a final state ($\mathbf{t}$ or $\mathbf{f}$), and reports this final result.

One obvious question is whether this evaluator always produces exactly one result for some fixed program. In mathematical terms, we are asking whether the evaluator is a function. If so, we know that the implementation of the evaluator is broken if we ever observe two distinct results for one and the same program.

Now recall that, like a relation, a function is a set of pairs; each pair combines an "input" with the "output." The difference between a relation and a function is that the latter contains at most one pair for any input. Thus, our first question means to ask whether the following claim holds:

for all B_0, $(B_0, R_0) \in eval_{\mathbf{r}}^{=\mathbf{r}}$ and $(B_0, R_1) \in eval_{\mathbf{r}}^{=\mathbf{r}}$ implies $R_0 = R_1$.

In functional notation, this becomes

for all B_0, $eval_{\mathbf{r}}^{=\mathbf{r}}(B_0) = R_0$ and $eval_{\mathbf{r}}^{=\mathbf{r}}(B_0) = R_1$ implies $R_0 = R_1$.

Chapter 1 does not just define one evaluator; it actually defines *two*. Ideally, the two definitions should introduce the same function. That is, the two evaluators should produce identical results when given the same program. Proving such a claim would allow us to use the two definitions interchangeably and according to our needs. For example, while arguing with a mathematics teacher, we could use $eval_{\mathbf{r}}^{=\mathbf{r}}$ to demonstrate that program execution generalizes seventh grade algebra. Then again, we should probably use $eval_{\mathbf{r}}^{\twoheadrightarrow\mathbf{r}}$ when we discuss the semantics of B with a software engineer charged with the implementation of the B programming language.

Thus our second question concerns the relationship between the equational evaluator, $eval_{\mathbf{r}}^{=\mathbf{r}}$, and the directional evaluator, $eval_{\mathbf{r}}^{\twoheadrightarrow\mathbf{r}}$. Specifically, we should be wondering whether they are the same function:

$$eval_{\mathbf{r}}^{\twoheadrightarrow\mathbf{r}} = eval_{\mathbf{r}}^{=\mathbf{r}}$$

Given our understanding of functions as sets of pairs, the question is whether the two sets contain the same elements:

for all B_0 and R_0, $((B_0, R_0) \in eval_{\mathbf{r}}^{=\mathbf{r}}$ if and only if $(B_0, R_0) \in eval_{\mathbf{r}}^{\twoheadrightarrow\mathbf{r}})$

A rough translation of this statement is

for all B_0 and R_0, $(eval_{\mathbf{r}}^{=\mathbf{r}}(B_0) = R_0$ if and only if $eval_{\mathbf{r}}^{\twoheadrightarrow\mathbf{r}}(B_0) = R_0)$

meaning if $eval_{\mathbf{r}}^{=\mathbf{r}}$ is defined for B_0 and the output is R_0, then $eval_{\mathbf{r}}^{\twoheadrightarrow\mathbf{r}}$ is defined for B_0 and the output is also R_0, and vice versa.

Naturally, the very phrase is "is defined" suggests yet another question, namely, whether the evaluator produces an output for all possible inputs. This statement has a straightforward mathematical formulation as,

for all B, there exists an R such that $(B, R) \in eval_{\mathbf{r}}$

Note how we dropped the superscript from $eval_{\mathbf{r}}$ assuming it does not matter which one we use.

2·2 Answers as Theorems.
Now that we understand the simplest questions we can ask about the syntax and semantics of a programming language, we state the obvious, namely, that answers are theorems about the mathematical model. Our first theorem states that $eval_{\mathbf{r}}^{=\mathbf{r}}$ is a function.

Theorem 2.1: If $eval_{\mathbf{r}}^{=\mathbf{r}}(B_0) = R_1$ and $eval_{\mathbf{r}}^{=\mathbf{r}}(B_0) = R_2$, then $R_1 = R_2$.

In stating and proving the theorem for $eval_{\mathbf{r}}^{=\mathbf{r}}$, we are following history in first establishing **consistency** for the equational calculus. Once we prove that the two definitions specify the same relation, we also know that $eval_{\mathbf{r}}^{\twoheadrightarrow\mathbf{r}}$ is a function, too. Also following convention, we drop the quantification prefixes (for all, there exists) from theorems when obvious, and we use functional notation to mean that the result exists and is a specific value.

Proof for Theorem 2.1: To prove the theorem, we assume the antecedent and prove that the conclusion follows. That is, we assume that $eval_{\mathbf{r}}^{=\mathbf{r}}(B_0) = R_1$ and $eval_{\mathbf{r}}^{=\mathbf{r}}(B_0) = R_2$ for some $B_0, R_1,$ and R_2. Based on these assumptions, we now attempt to prove that $R_1 = R_2$. By the definition of $eval_{\mathbf{r}}^{=\mathbf{r}}$, our assumptions imply that $B_0 =_{\mathbf{r}} R_1$ and $B_0 =_{\mathbf{r}} R_2$. Note the use of $=_{\mathbf{r}}$, as opposed to $=$. Because $=_{\mathbf{r}}$ is an equivalence relation (by definition), $R_1 =_{\mathbf{r}} R_2$. To reach the desired conclusion that $R_1 = R_2$, i.e., that R_1 and R_2 are identical, we must study the nature of this equivalence relation and the nature of calculations. (to be continued)

The last argument of the preceding proof demands that we study the shape of proofs (or proof trees) of $M =_{\mathbf{r}} N$ for $M, N \in B$. Since $=_{\mathbf{r}}$ is the reflexive, symmetric, and transitive closure of the one-step reduction $\rightarrow_{\mathbf{r}}$, a calculation to prove $M =_{\mathbf{r}} N$ consists of a series of such one-step reductions in both directions:

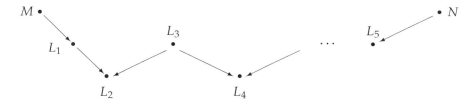

In this picture, each expression $L_i \in B$ and each arrow represents a $\rightarrow_{\mathbf{r}}$ relation between two neighboring terms in the sequence. Formally, every $L_i \longrightarrow L_j$ corresponds to $L_i \rightarrow_{\mathbf{r}} L_j$.

The critical insight from this picture is that it might just be possible to reshape such calculations so that all reduction steps go from M to some L and from N to the same L. In other words, if $M =_{\mathbf{r}} N$ perhaps there is an expression L such that $M \twoheadrightarrow_{\mathbf{r}} L$ and $N \twoheadrightarrow_{\mathbf{r}} L$:

If we can prove that such an L always exists for two equal terms, the proof of consistency is finished.

Proof for Theorem 2.1: (remainder) Recall that we have

$$R_1 =_{\mathbf{r}} R_2$$

By the (as yet unproved) claim, there must be an expression L such that

$$R_1 \longrightarrow_{\mathbf{r}} L \qquad \text{and} \qquad R_2 \longrightarrow_{\mathbf{r}} L$$

But elements of R, which are just $\mathtt{t}$ and $\mathtt{f}$, are clearly not reducible to anything except themselves. So $L = R_1$ and $L = R_2$, which means that $R_1 = R_2$.

By the preceding reasoning, we have reduced the proof of $eval_{\mathbf{r}}^{\overline{}\mathbf{r}}$'s consistency to a claim about the shape of proof trees that establish $M =_{\mathbf{r}} N$ and our ability to re-shape them. This crucial insight is due to Church and Rosser, who used this idea to analyze the consistency of a language called the λ-calculus (which is the topic of the next chapter). Accordingly the lemma is named after them.[1]

Lemma 2.2 [Consistency for $=_{\mathbf{r}}$]: If $M =_{\mathbf{r}} N$, then there exists an expression L such that $M \longrightarrow_{\mathbf{r}} L$ and $N \longrightarrow_{\mathbf{r}} L$.

Proof for Lemma 2.2: Since we are given the equation $M =_{\mathbf{r}} N$, and since the definition of $=_{\mathbf{r}}$ inductively extends $\longrightarrow_{\mathbf{r}}$ to its reflexive, symmetric, transitive closure, we prove the lemma by induction of the structure of the derivation of $M =_{\mathbf{r}} N$, that is, the structure of its proof tree:

- Base case:
  - **Case $M \longrightarrow_{\mathbf{r}} N$**
    Let $L = N$, and the claim holds.

- Inductive cases:
  - **Case $M =_{\mathbf{r}} N$ because $N =_{\mathbf{r}} M$**
    By induction, an L exists for $N =_{\mathbf{r}} M$, and that is the L we want.
  - **Case $M =_{\mathbf{r}} N$ because $M =_{\mathbf{r}} L_0$ and $L_0 =_{\mathbf{r}} N$**
    By induction, there exists an L_1 such that $M \longrightarrow_{\mathbf{r}} L_1$ and $L_0 \longrightarrow_{\mathbf{r}} L_1$. Also by induction, there exists an L_2 such that $N \longrightarrow_{\mathbf{r}} L_2$ and $L_0 \longrightarrow_{\mathbf{r}} L_2$. In pictures we have:

---

[1] If we were plain mathematicians studying the λ-calculus, we would call the following lemma a "theorem." We are, however, computer scientists interested in the consistency of our evaluator and thus just use Church and Rosser's idea as an auxiliary step; we do not see it as an end goal of our work.

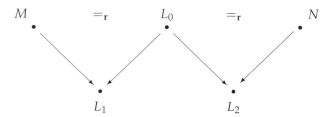

Now suppose that, whenever an expression L_0 reduces to both L_1 and L_2, there exists some expression L_3 such that $L_1 \twoheadrightarrow_\mathbf{r} L_3$ and $L_2 \twoheadrightarrow_\mathbf{r} L_3$. Then the claim we want to prove holds, because $M \twoheadrightarrow_\mathbf{r} L_3$ and $N \twoheadrightarrow_\mathbf{r} L_3$.

Again, we have finished the proof modulo the proof of yet another claim about the reduction system. Specifically, we assumed that if we encounter the situation on the left, it is possible to find a term $L' \in B$ such that we can construct the situation on the right:

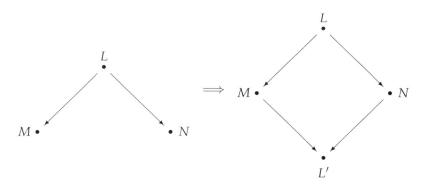

This property is called **diamond property** because the picture demands that "reduction branch" can be completed to the shape of a diamond. When the transitive, reflexive, and compatible closure of a notion of reduction, such as $\mathbf{r}$, satisfies the diamond property, it is called **Church-Rosser**.

> **Lemma 2.3 [Church-Rosser ($\twoheadrightarrow_\mathbf{r}$)]:** If $L \twoheadrightarrow_\mathbf{r} M$ and $L \twoheadrightarrow_\mathbf{r} N$, there exists an expression L' such that $M \twoheadrightarrow_\mathbf{r} L'$ and $N \twoheadrightarrow_\mathbf{r} L'$.

Since $L \twoheadrightarrow_\mathbf{r} M$ consists of a series of $\rightarrow_\mathbf{r}$ proof steps, it is natural to check whether this latter relation also satisfies a diamond property. If it does, it should be possible to compose the small diamonds for $\rightarrow_\mathbf{r}$ to obtain one large diamond for $\twoheadrightarrow_\mathbf{r}$. Although the diamond property does not quite hold for $\rightarrow_\mathbf{r}$, a sufficiently strong property holds.

Lemma 2.4 [Diamond-like ($\rightarrow_r$)]: If $L \rightarrow_r M$ and $L \rightarrow_r N$ for $M \neq N$, then either

- $M \rightarrow_r N$,
- $N \rightarrow_r M$, or
- there exists an L' such that $M \rightarrow_r L'$ and $N \rightarrow_r L'$.

That is, a "reduction branch" of expressions can be completed to a diamond or there is a "triangle" style completion.

Proof for Lemma 2.4:   To prove this lemma, recall that $\rightarrow_r$ is defined inductively as the compatible closure of r. Hence it is natural to assume $L \rightarrow_r M$ and to proceed by structural induction on the structure of its proof:

- Base case:
  - **Case $L\, r\, M$**
    By the definition of r, there are two subcases.
    * **Case $L = (\mathtt{f} \bullet B_0)$ and $M = B_0$**
      The expression L might be reduced in two ways with $\rightarrow_r$ for N: to B_0, or to $(\mathtt{f} \bullet B_0')$ with $B_0 \rightarrow_r B_0'$. Since $N \neq M$, $N = (\mathtt{f} \bullet B_0')$ for some B_0' and $B_0\, r\, B_0'$. In that case, take $L' = B_0'$ because $M = B_0 \rightarrow_r B_0'$ and, by the definition of r, $N \rightarrow_r B_0'$.
    * **Case $L = (\mathtt{t} \bullet B_0)$ and $M = \mathtt{t}$**
      Given that $M \neq N$, $N = (\mathtt{t} \bullet B_0')$. Therefore, we have $N \rightarrow_r M$, the second possible consequence.
- For the inductive cases, assume without loss of generality that $L \not{r} N$; otherwise swap N and M.
  - **Case $L = (B_1 \bullet B_2)$, $M = (B_1' \bullet B_2)$ because $B_1 \rightarrow_r B_1'$**
    We have two sub-cases:
    * $N = (B_1'' \bullet B_2)$, where $B_1 \rightarrow_r B_1''$. Since $B_1 \rightarrow_r B_1'$, and $B_1 \rightarrow_r B_1''$, we can apply induction to this branch of the proof tree. If $B_1'' \rightarrow_r B_1'$, then $M \rightarrow_r N$ and the claim holds; similarly, if $B_1' \rightarrow_r B_1''$, then $N \rightarrow_r M$ and the claim holds. Finally, if $B_1' \rightarrow_r B_1'''$ and $B_1'' \rightarrow_r B_1'''$, then $M \rightarrow_r (B_1''' \bullet B_2)$ and $N \rightarrow_r (B_1''' \bullet B_2)$, and the claim holds with $L' = (B_1''' \bullet B_2)$.
    * $N = (B_1 \bullet B_2')$ with $B_2 \rightarrow_r B_2'$. Since $B_1 \rightarrow_r B_1'$, $N \rightarrow_r (B_1' \bullet B_2')$. Similarly, $M \rightarrow_r (B_1' \bullet B_2')$. Thus, the claim holds with $L' = (B_1' \bullet B_2')$.

   – **Case** $L = (B_1 \bullet B_2)$, $M = (B_1 \bullet B_2')$ **because** $B_2 \to_r B_2'$
    This case is analogous to the previous one.

Now that we know that the one-step reduction satisfies a diamond-like property, we can show that its transitive–reflexive closure satifies the diamond property. That is, we can prove the "big diamond" lemma.

   Proof for Lemma 2.3:   Assume that $L \twoheadrightarrow_r M$ and $L \twoheadrightarrow_r N$. By the inductive definition of the reduction relation $\twoheadrightarrow_r$, $L \to_r^m M$ and $L \to_r^n N$ for some $m, n \in \mathbb{N}$, where $\to_r^m$ means m steps with $\to_r$. Pictorially, we have

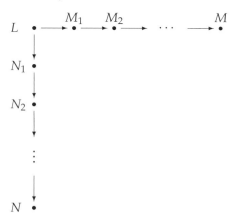

Using the diamond-like property for the one-step reduction, we can now fill in expressions L_{11}, L_{21}, L_{12}, etc. until the entire square is filled out:

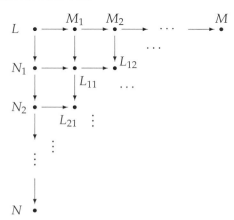

Formally, this proof can also be cast as an induction on the number of reduction steps.

Exercise 2.1. Prove lemma 2.3 formally.

The preceding arguments also show that $M =_r R$ if and only if $M \twoheadrightarrow_r R$. Consequently, the theorem-answer for our second question—whether the two evaluators are equal—falls out as a consequence.

Theorem 2.5: $eval_r^{\twoheadrightarrow r} = eval_r^{=r}$

Proof for Theorem 2.5: We show that each element of $eval_r^{=r}$ is also in $eval_r^{\twoheadrightarrow r}$ and vice versa. Thus, assume that $eval_r^{=r}(B_0) = R_0$. By definition, $B_0 =_r R_0$. From lemma 2.2, $B_0 \twoheadrightarrow_r R_0$ because the latter is not reducible. This, of course, implies $eval_r^{\twoheadrightarrow r}(B_0) = R_0$ according to the definition of this second evaluator.

For the other direction, assume $eval_r^{\twoheadrightarrow r}(B_1) = R_1$, which means $B_1 \twoheadrightarrow_r R_1$ by the definition of the function. In turn, the definition of $=_r$ as symmetric (and equivalence) closure of $\twoheadrightarrow_r$ implies $eval_r^{=r}(B_1) = R_1$.

For the programmer and anyone else who wishes to reason about the evaluation process of B expressions, the theorem says that symmetric reasoning steps do not help in the evaluation of B expressions. The directional $\twoheadrightarrow_r$ relation suffices.[2]

At this point, we know that the evaluators are functions, and that the two evaluators are identical. The only question left is whether the evaluators terminate for every program that they are given.

Theorem 2.6: For all B_0, there is an R_0 such that $eval_r(B_0) = R_0$.

While $eval_r(B_0) = R_0$ does not specify which evaluator is meant, it is clear that the theorem refers to both.

Proof for Theorem 2.6: Consider a single reduction step:

$$B_0 \to_r B_1$$

Because of the definition of $\to_r$ as the compatible closure of r, this means that B_1 contains fewer instances of $\bullet$ than B_0. Since

---

[2]The next few chapters introduce languages for which such apparent backward steps truly shorten calculations on occasion.

B_0 contains a finite number k of • and since it is impossible for an element of B to contain fewer than zero instances of •, a chain of the shape

$$B_0 \rightarrow_\mathbf{r} B_1 \rightarrow_\mathbf{r} \ldots \rightarrow_\mathbf{r} B_n$$

may contain at most $n \leq k$ number of steps.

Thus, the question is whether a non-result expression from B is always reducible. Put differently, we are asking whether there is a B_j for every B_i not in R such that $B_i \rightarrow_\mathbf{r} B_j$. To prove this claim, we proceed by induction on the structure of the expression B_i:

- **Case $B_i = \mathtt{t}$**

  This case contradicts the assumption that B_i is not in R.

- **Case $B_i = \mathtt{f}$**

  As for the first case, B_i is not in R.

- **Case $B_i = B_1 \bullet B_2$**

  If B_1 is in R, the claim is established because $\mathbf{r}$ reduces B_i to either $\mathtt{t}$ or B_2 and either of which serves as B_j.

  Otherwise, by induction, B_1 is reducible to B_1' and, by construction, $B_1 \bullet B_2 \rightarrow_\mathbf{r} B_1' \bullet B_2$, and we take this last expression as B_j.

Using this theorem, it is possible to decide the equality of B expressions. The algorithm simply evaluates both expressions and compares the results. Of course, full-fledged programming languages include arbitrary non-terminating expressions and thus preclude a programmer from deciding the equivalence of expressions in this way.

3 · The λ-Calculus

The B language represents a small sliver of the kind of expression language that every programming language contains. Despite B's simplicity, modeling the language and reasoning about it illustrates many of the basic techniques of a syntactic approach to semantics. The origins of this approach go back much further than B, however.

In the 1920s and 30s, Alonzo Church and some others designed and worked on the λ-**calculus**, with the goal of creating a minimal logical system for studying the foundations of mathematical functions. Even though this original system turned out to be self-contradictory, the syntax for working with functions survived. Programming language researchers discovered it as both an inspiration for language design and the creation of language models.

Roughly speaking, the λ-calculus is a system for expressing function definitions and function applications. The syntax consists of just expressions, which semantically denote functions. Today, this focus on expressions is also found in Scheme, Haskell, and other functional programming languages.

Here we study the λ-calculus from a historical and syntactic perspective: its reduction semantics, its use as a quasi-programming language, and its inspirational power. The chapter thus serves as a bridge between our sample study of B expressions and the study of a full-fledged Scheme-like language in the rest of this part of the book.

3·1 Functions and the λ-Calculus.
The syntax of the λ-calculus provides a simple, regular method for writing down functions for application, and also as the inputs and outputs of other functions. The specification of such functions in the λ-calculus concentrates on the rule for going from an argument to a result, and it ignores the issues of naming the function and its domain and range. For example, while a mathematician specifies the identity function on some set A as

$$f : \begin{cases} A & \longrightarrow & A \\ x & \longmapsto & x \end{cases}$$

in the λ-calculus syntax, we write

$$(\lambda x.x)$$

An informal reading of this function "definition" says, "if the argument is called x, then the output of the function is x," In other words, the function outputs whatever it inputs.

To write down the application of a function f to an argument a, the λ-calculus uses mathematical syntax, modulo the placement of parentheses:

$$(f\ a)$$

For example, the expression

$$((\lambda x.x)\ a)$$

denotes the application of the identity function to a. Another possible argument for the identity function is itself:

$$((\lambda x.x)\ (\lambda x.x))$$

Here is an expression representing a function that takes an argument, ignores it, and returns the identity function:

$$(\lambda y.(\lambda x.x))$$

The intent of

$$(\lambda y.(\lambda x.y))$$

is complex. The first λ informs us that it is a function; the second λ says that the function returns a function, no matter what the argument is. This second function also consumes one argument—like all functions in the λ-calculus— and then returns the argument that the first function originally received.

The λ-calculus supports only single-argument functions, but this last example shows how a function can effectively take two arguments, x and y, by consuming the first argument, then returning another function to get the second argument. This concept is called **currying**.

In conventional mathematics, the application of f to a is equal to

$$\ldots a \ldots a \ldots$$

where the definition of f is

$$f(x) = \ldots x \ldots x \ldots$$

The simplification of λ-calculus expressions works just like that: $((\lambda x.x)\ a)$ is equal to a, which is the result of taking the body (the part after the dot) of $(\lambda x.x)$ and replacing x, dubbed the **formal argument** or **parameter** (the part before the dot), with the actual argument a. Here are several examples:

$$
\begin{array}{lcll}
((\lambda x.x)\ a) & \rightarrow & a & \text{by replacing } x \text{ with } a \text{ in } x \\
((\lambda x.x)\ (\lambda y.y)) & \rightarrow & (\lambda y.y) & \text{by replacing } x \text{ with } (\lambda y.y) \text{ in } x \\
((\lambda y.(\lambda x.y))\ a) & \rightarrow & (\lambda x.a) & \text{by replacing } y \text{ with } a \text{ in } (\lambda x.y)
\end{array}
$$

3·2 λ-Calculus: Syntax and Reductions.

The general grammar for expressions in the λ-calculus is defined by M (with aliases N, L):

$$
\begin{array}{rcl}
M, N, L & = & X \\
& | & (\lambda X.M) \\
& | & (M\ M) \\
X, Y, Z & = & \text{a variable: } x, y, \ldots
\end{array}
$$

The following are example members of M:

$$
x, \quad (x\ y), \quad (\lambda x.x), \quad ((x\ y)\ (z\ w)), \quad (\lambda y.(\lambda z.y)), \quad ((\lambda y.(y\ y))\ (\lambda y.(y\ y)))
$$

The first example, x, has no particular intuitive meaning, since x is left un-defined. Similarly, $(x\ y)$ means "x applied to y", but we cannot say more, since x and y are undefined. In contrast, the example $(\lambda x.x)$ corresponds to the identity function. The difference between it and the first two examples is that x appears **free** in the first two expressions, but **bound** in the last one.

With this terminology we can formulate the general thought that the meaning of expressions with free variables is open to interpretation. Conversely, the meaning of an expression without free variables—which is called a **closed** expression—is explicable. In particular, if M contains one free variable, X, then $(\lambda X.M)$ is supposed to be the notation for a function that maps an argument N to M with all occurrences of X substituted by N.

Of course a naive substitution can mess up the intent underlying the expressions. If M is

$$
(x(\lambda x.x))
$$

the intent is to apply x to the identity function. Evaluating the application of $(\lambda x.M)$ to $(\lambda y.y)$ should therefore equal the application of the identity function to itself. A naive replacement of all occurrences of x (though not the formal argument occurrences) with $(\lambda x.x)$ yields

$$
((\lambda y.y)(\lambda x.(\lambda y.y)))
$$

which is clearly not what we want. What we do want is a substitution of all free variables in a function's body with the argument expression.

It is therefore imperative to understand the concept of "free variable" properly. To this end we define the function $\mathcal{FV}$, which maps a λ-calculus expression to its set of **free variables**. Intuitively, x is a free variable in an expression if it appears outside the context of any $(\lambda x.\_)$. More formally, we define it as follows:

$$
\begin{array}{rcl}
\mathcal{FV}(\,X\,) & = & \{X\} \\
\mathcal{FV}(\,(\lambda X.M)\,) & = & \mathcal{FV}(M) \setminus \{X\} \\
\mathcal{FV}(\,(M_1\ M_2)\,) & = & \mathcal{FV}(M_1)\ \cup\ \mathcal{FV}(M_2)
\end{array}
$$

Here are some examples for $\mathcal{FV}$:

$$
\begin{array}{rcl}
\mathcal{FV}(\,x\,) & = & \{x\} \\
\mathcal{FV}(\,(x\ (y\ x))\,) & = & \{x,y\} \\
\mathcal{FV}(\,(\lambda x.(x\ y))\,) & = & \{y\} \\
\mathcal{FV}(\,(z\ (\lambda z.z))\,) & = & \{z\}
\end{array}
$$

Exercise 3.1. Define the function $\mathcal{BV}$, which determines the set of bound variables in a λ-calculus expression.

The next step in formulating the λ-calculus as a rigorous system is to define the meaning of substituting an expression N for the free variable X in a λ-calculus expression M. Following convention, we use the notation $M[X \leftarrow N]$ to denote this **substitution function**. Its definition requires some care to avoid the above-mentioned problems and another one:

$$
\begin{array}{rcl}
X_1[X_1 \leftarrow M] & = & M \\
X_2[X_1 \leftarrow M] & = & X_2, \quad \text{if } X_1 \neq X_2 \\
(\lambda X_1.M_1)[X_1 \leftarrow M_2] & = & (\lambda X_1.M_1) \\
(\lambda X_1.M_1)[X_2 \leftarrow M_2] & = & (\lambda X_3.M_1[X_1 \leftarrow X_3][X_2 \leftarrow M_2]), \\
& & \quad \text{if } \ X_1 \ \neq \ X_2 \\
& & \qquad\quad X_3 \ \notin \ \mathcal{FV}(\,(\lambda X_1.M_1)\,) \\
& & \qquad\quad X_3 \ \notin \ \mathcal{FV}(\,M_2\,) \\
(M_1\ M_2)[X \leftarrow M_3] & = & (M_1[X \leftarrow M_3]\ M_2[X \leftarrow M_3])
\end{array}
$$

Here are some simple examples:

$$
\begin{array}{rcl}
x[x \leftarrow (\lambda y.y)] & = & (\lambda y.y) \\
z[x \leftarrow (\lambda y.y)] & = & z \\
(\lambda x.x)[x \leftarrow (\lambda y.y)] & = & (\lambda x.x) \\
(\lambda y.(x\ y))[x \leftarrow (\lambda y.y)] & = & (\lambda z.((\lambda y.y)\ z))\ \text{ or }\ (\lambda y.((\lambda y.y)\ y)) \\
(\lambda y.(x\ y))[x \leftarrow (\lambda x.y)] & = & (\lambda z.((\lambda x.y)\ z))
\end{array}
$$

The definition of $\_[\_ \leftarrow \_]$ makes it clear that, despite its name, substitution is *not* a function:

$$(\lambda y.(x\ y))[x \leftarrow (\lambda x.y)] \quad = \quad (\lambda z.((\lambda x.y)\ z))$$

The result depends on what replacement is chosen for the formal argument in the fourth clause of the definition of substitution. Our last example shows why it is so important to define substitution carefully:

$$(\lambda y.(x\ y))[x \leftarrow (\lambda x.y)] \quad = \quad (\lambda z.((\lambda x.y)\ z))$$

Note how the y in the replacement expression is free and remains free in the result of the substitution. A naive replacement of all free x with $(\lambda x.y)$ in $(\lambda y.(x\ y))$ would yield

$$(\lambda y.((\lambda x.y)\ y))$$

but this would clearly violate the original intent of the given expressions. In particular, while y is free in the replacement expression, it is suddenly bound in the naive result.

Exercise 3.2. Explain the intent of $(\lambda x.(\lambda y.(x\ y)))$ and $(\lambda x.y)$. Assume initially that y represents a constant, say, a number.

Finally, to define the general reduction relation **n** for the λ-calculus, we first define three simple notions of reduction, α, β, and η.

$(\lambda X_1.M)$ $\quad$ if $X_2 \notin \mathcal{FV}(M)$	α	$(\lambda X_2.M[X_1 \leftarrow X_2])$
$((\lambda X.M_1)\ M_2)$	β	$M_1[X \leftarrow M_2]$
$(\lambda X.(M\ X))$ $\quad$ if $X \notin \mathcal{FV}(M)$	η	M

- α renames the formal argument of a function. It formalizes that the name of a formal argument is arbitrary, as long as it is used consistently. Thus, for example, $(\lambda x.x)$ and $(\lambda y.y)$ are indistinguishable as functions; both consume an argument and return it.

- β is the major relation, formalizing how the application of a function to an argument works.

- η encodes that, if a function f takes its argument and immediately applies g to the argument, then f is basically like g.

The original and most general notion of reduction for the λ-calculus is the union of these three:

$$\mathbf{n} = \alpha \cup \beta \cup \eta$$

As usual, we define $\to_n$ as the compatible closure of $\mathbf{n}$, $\twoheadrightarrow_n$ as the reflexive–transitive closure of $\to_n$, and $=_n$ as the symmetric closure of $\twoheadrightarrow_n$. Also $\to_n^\alpha$, $\to_n^\beta$, and $\to_n^\eta$ are the compatible closures of α, β, and η, respectively.[1]

Here is one of many possible reductions for $((\lambda x.((\lambda z.z)\ x))\ (\lambda x.x))$, where for each step, the chosen redex is underlined:

$$
\begin{aligned}
((\lambda x.((\lambda z.z)\ x))\ \underline{(\lambda x.x)}) \quad &\to_n^\alpha \quad ((\lambda x.((\lambda z.z)\ x))\ (\lambda y.y)) \\
&\to_n^\eta \quad \underline{((\lambda z.z)\ (\lambda y.y))} \\
&\to_n^\beta \quad (\lambda y.y)
\end{aligned}
$$

And this is a different reduction of the same expression:

$$
\begin{aligned}
(\underline{(\lambda x.((\lambda z.z)\ x))\ (\lambda x.x)}) \quad &\to_n^\beta \quad \underline{((\lambda x.x)\ (\lambda x.x))} \\
&\to_n^\beta \quad (\lambda x.x)
\end{aligned}
$$

While the two reductions and their results differ, it is also apparent that the results are the same in some sense.

Exercise 3.3. Use a reduction to make the two results syntactically equal.

The parentheses in an expression are often redundant, and they can make large expressions difficult to read. Thus, the λ-calculus comes with a couple of conventions for dropping parentheses, plus one for dropping λs:

- application associates to the left, e.g., the quasi-expression $M_1\ M_2\ M_3$ is short for $((M_1\ M_2)\ M_3)$;

- application binds expressions more strongly than abstraction, e.g., read $\lambda X.M_1 M_2$ as $(\lambda X.(M_1\ M_2))$; and

- consecutive lambdas are collapsed into one, e.g., $\lambda XYZ.M$ abbreviates $(\lambda X.(\lambda Y.(\lambda Z.M)))$.

With this, $((\lambda x.((\lambda z.z)\ x))\ (\lambda x.x))$ becomes $(\lambda x.(\lambda z.z)\ x)\ \lambda x.x$, and the first reduction above can be abbreviated as follows:

$$
\begin{aligned}
(\lambda x.(\lambda z.z)\ x)\ \underline{\lambda x.x} \quad &\to_n^\alpha \quad (\lambda x.(\lambda z.z)\ x)\ \lambda y.y \\
&\to_n^\eta \quad \underline{(\lambda z.z)\ \lambda y.y} \\
&\to_n^\beta \quad \lambda y.y
\end{aligned}
$$

---

[1] The compatible closure of α would normally be written $\to_\alpha$, but we use $\to_n^\alpha$ to emphasize that $\to_n = \to_n^\alpha \cup \to_n^\beta \cup \to_n^\eta$.

Exercise 3.4. Reduce the expressions

- $(\lambda x.x)$

- $(\lambda x.(\lambda y.y\ x))\ (\lambda y.y)\ (\lambda x.x\ x)$

- $(\lambda x.(\lambda y.y\ x))\ ((\lambda x.x\ x)\ (\lambda x.x\ x))$

with $\rightarrow_n$ until no more $\rightarrow_n^\beta$ reductions are possible. Show all steps.

Exercise 3.5. Prove the following equivalences:

- $(\lambda x.x) =_n (\lambda y.y)$

- $(\lambda x.(\lambda y.(\lambda z.z\ z)\ y)\ x)(\lambda x.x\ x) =_n (\lambda a.a\ ((\lambda g.g)\ a))\ (\lambda b.b\ b)$

- $\lambda y.(\lambda x.\lambda y.x)\ (y\ y) =_n \lambda a.\lambda b.(a\ a)$

- $(\lambda f.\lambda g.\lambda x.f\ x\ (g\ x))(\lambda x.\lambda y.x)(\lambda x.\lambda y.x) =_n \lambda x.x$

While the λ-calculus is not a programming language and despite its seeming simplicity, it turns out that one can mimic programming in this system. The next few sections show the basic approach, starting with an encoding of booleans as functions. We study this idea for historical purposes and to convey the context in which the λ-calculus was discovered as a basis for a programming language.

3·3 **Encoding Booleans.** In contrast to high school mathematics, programs use functions defined by cases, and programmers consider case distinctions an essential element of programming. As it turns out, encoding "true," "false," and an "if" expression is straightforward in the λ-calculus:

$$
\begin{array}{lcl}
\text{true} & \doteq & \lambda x.\lambda y.x \\
\text{false} & \doteq & \lambda x.\lambda y.y \\
\text{if} & \doteq & \lambda v.\lambda t.\lambda f.v\ t\ f
\end{array}
$$

The $\doteq$ notation indicates that we are defining a shorthand, or "macro," for an expression.

The macros for true, false, and if are useful if they behave in a useful way. For example, we would expect that

$$\text{if true } M\ N =_n M$$

for any M and N. And indeed, this equation holds:

$$
\begin{array}{rcl}
\text{if true } M \ N & = & (\lambda v.\lambda t.\lambda f.v \ t \ f) \ (\lambda x.\lambda y.x) \ M \ N \\
& \to_{\mathbf{n}}^{\beta} & (\lambda t.\lambda f.(\lambda x.\lambda y.x) \ t \ f) \ M \ N \\
& \to_{\mathbf{n}}^{\beta} & (\lambda f.(\lambda x.\lambda y.x) \ M \ f) \ N \\
& \to_{\mathbf{n}}^{\beta} & (\lambda x.\lambda y.x) \ M \ N \\
& \to_{\mathbf{n}}^{\beta} & (\lambda y.M) \ N \\
& \to_{\mathbf{n}}^{\beta} & M
\end{array}
$$

Similarly, if false $M \ N =_{\mathbf{n}} N$:

$$
\begin{array}{rcl}
\text{if false } M \ N & = & (\lambda v.\lambda t.\lambda f.v \ t \ f) \ (\lambda x.\lambda y.y) \ M \ N \\
& \to_{\mathbf{n}}^{\beta} & (\lambda t.\lambda f.(\lambda x.\lambda y.y) \ t \ f) \ M \ N \\
& \to_{\mathbf{n}}^{\beta} & (\lambda f.(\lambda x.\lambda y.y) \ M \ f) \ N \\
& \to_{\mathbf{n}}^{\beta} & (\lambda x.\lambda y.y) \ M \ N \\
& \to_{\mathbf{n}}^{\beta} & (\lambda y.y) \ N \\
& \to_{\mathbf{n}}^{\beta} & N
\end{array}
$$

Actually, it turns out that (if true) $=_{\mathbf{n}}$ true and (if false) $=_{\mathbf{n}}$ false. In other words, our representation of true acts like a conditional that branches on its first argument, and false acts like a conditional that branches on its second argument; the if macro is simply introduced for readability.

Exercise 3.6. Show that (if true) $=_{\mathbf{n}}$ true and (if false) $=_{\mathbf{n}}$ false.

Exercise 3.7. Define macros for binary and and or prefix operators. Show that they satisfy some of the expected equations, e.g., and true $M =_{\mathbf{n}} M$ and or false $M =_{\mathbf{n}} M$.

3·4 Encoding Pairs.

Modern programming languages also come with structures and records. For simplicity, we encode pairs in the λ-calculus, which suffices to demonstrate the power of the system.

To encode pairs, we need three operations: one that combines two values into a single value; one that extracts the first (left) value from a pair; and one that extracts the second (right) value. In other words, we need functions mkpair, fst, and snd that obey the following equations:

$$
\begin{array}{rcl}
\text{fst (mkpair } M \ N) & =_{\mathbf{n}} & M \\
\text{snd (mkpair } M \ N) & =_{\mathbf{n}} & N
\end{array}
$$

The notation $\langle M, N \rangle$ is shorthand for the pair whose first element is M and whose second element is N. One way to find definitions for mkpair, etc. is to consider what a $\langle M, N \rangle$ value might look like.

Since our only values are functions, $\langle M, N \rangle$ must be a function. This function has to contain the expressions M and N, and it has to have some way of returning one or the other to a user of the pair who requests the first or second item. At the same time, the only way to use a function is to apply it. In turn, first and second must call the function with a value that selects one or the other component.

All this suggests that a pair is a function that accepts true or false and returns the first component or the second one in response:

$$\langle M, N \rangle \doteq \lambda s.\text{if } s\ M\ N$$

As already mentioned, the fst function takes a pair, then applies it to true:

$$\text{fst} \doteq \lambda p.p\ \text{true}$$

Similarly, snd applies its pair argument to false. Finally, to define mkpair, we abstract the abbreviation of $\langle M, N \rangle$ over arbitrary M and N.

$\langle M, N \rangle$	$\doteq$	$\lambda s.s\ M\ N$
mkpair	$\doteq$	$\lambda x.\lambda y.\lambda s.s\ x\ y$
fst	$\doteq$	$\lambda p.p\ \text{true}$
snd	$\doteq$	$\lambda p.p\ \text{false}$

Exercise 3.8. Show that mkpair, fst, and snd satisfy the equations at the beginning of this section.

3·5 **Encoding Numbers.** There are many ways to encode the natural numbers 0, 1, 2, ... in the λ-calculus. The earliest encoding is due to Church; the encoded numbers are therefore called **Church numerals**. As always, a natural number n is encoded as a function. Specifically, it is a function of two arguments, f and x, and f is applied to x n times to represent n. Thus, the function for 0 takes an f and x and returns x, meaning f is applied zero times. The function representing 1 applies f to x once, 2 applies f twice, and so on.

0	$\doteq$	$\lambda f.\lambda x.x$
1	$\doteq$	$\lambda f.\lambda x.f\ x$
2	$\doteq$	$\lambda f.\lambda x.f\ (f\ x)$
3	$\doteq$	$\lambda f.\lambda x.f\ (f\ (f\ x))$
	$\cdots$	
n	$\doteq$	$\lambda f.\lambda x.\underbrace{f\ (\ldots(f}_{n}\ x)\ldots)$

Like booleans and pairs, the data type of natural numbers comes with a number of operations: add1, add, iszero, etc. A function such as add1 consumes the representation of a number n and produces the representation of a number:

$$\text{add1} \doteq \lambda n.(\lambda f.\lambda x. \cdots)$$

We also know that the result of add1 n should be

$$\lambda f.\lambda x. \underbrace{f\ (\ldots (f\ x)\ldots)}_{n+1}$$

The key insight is that (nfx) applies f n times to x. Hence, $f(nfx)$ applies f $n+1$ times to x.

$$\boxed{\text{add1} \doteq \lambda n.\lambda f.\lambda x.f\ (n\ f\ x)}$$

To add two numbers n and m, all we have to do is recall what addition is from our childhood. Back then we learned that adding n to m is like taking n "fingers" and then putting up m more fingers, one at a time. That is, n plus m means adding 1 to n, m times. The mentioning of "times" suggests that we exploit the nature of the encoding of m, which applies a function f m times to some x. In particular, m can apply add1 to n m times!

$$\boxed{\text{add} \doteq \lambda n.\lambda m.m\ \text{add1}\ n}$$

The idea of using the number as a function is also useful for defining iszero, a function that takes a number and returns true if the number is 0, false otherwise. We can define iszero with a function that ignores its argument and always returns false; if this function is applied 0 times to true, the result is true; if it is applied $n > 0$ times, the result is false.

$$\boxed{\text{iszero} \doteq \lambda n.n\ (\lambda x.\text{false})\ \text{true}}$$

Besides add1 and iszero, a system for working with natural numbers requires sub1, the function for subtracting 1 from any natural number greater than 0. In contrast to add1 and iszero, sub1 is complicated. Let us start with the outline of the function again:

$$\text{sub1} \doteq \lambda n.(\lambda f.\lambda x. \cdots)$$

The result is a numeral representation that applies f one less time than n:

$$\lambda f.\lambda x. \underbrace{f\ (\ldots (f\ x)\ldots)}_{n-1}$$

Of course, there is no such thing as the inverse of an arbitrary function application or reversing a function application, so we must engineer this "subtraction" in some other way.

In the λ-calculus sub1 consists of two parts that realize one single insight. The latter is that given n, f, and x, we need to use n to iterate the application of f, but skip the first time to subtract 1. Here are the two pieces that are needed to code up this idea:

- The iterated function consumes and produces pairs, where the first element of the pair keeps track of skipping. The initial pair is ⟨true, x⟩, where the true indicates that one application of f needs to be skipped. The initial output is ⟨false, x⟩, and the false disables further skipping. The next iteration receives ⟨false, x⟩ and produces ⟨false, (f x)⟩, etc.

- To get the function to iterate, we need to "lift" f to operate on pairs that start with true or false. We call the lifting operation wrap.

$$
\begin{array}{lcl}
\text{wrap } f & \dot{=} & \lambda p.\langle \text{false, if (fst } p) \text{ (snd } p) \text{ (} f \text{ (snd } p)))\rangle \\
\text{sub1} & \dot{=} & \lambda n.\lambda f.\lambda x.\text{snd } (n \text{ (wrap } f) \langle \text{true, } x\rangle)
\end{array}
$$

Exercise 3.9. Show that add1 1 $=_n$ 2.

Exercise 3.10. Show that iszero 1 $=_n$ false.

Exercise 3.11. Show that sub1 1 $=_n$ 0.

Exercise 3.12. Define mult, the function that multiplies two natural numbers. Recall from elementary school that n times m means $\underbrace{n + \ldots + n}_{m \text{ times}}$.

3·6 **Encodings and Errors.** The encoding for 0 is exactly the same as the encoding for false. Thus, no program can distinguish 0 from false. Programmers must be careful that only true and false appear in boolean contexts, that only Church numerals appear as arguments to add, mult, etc. If not, it is impossible to recognize the mistake within the program and signal an error. Things go wrong in surprising ways.

Analogously, the C programming language uses the same pattern of bits to implement 0, false, and the null pointer. Just like λ-calculus encodings, C programs may use a bit pattern for false where a 0 is expected and nobody may ever notice—even though this should not happen.

Exercise 3.13. The λ-calculus provides no mechanism for signalling an error. What does happen when sub1 is applied to 0? What about (iszero true)?

$3 \cdot 7$ **Recursion.** An exercise in the previous section requests the definition of mult via the iteration built into Church numerals. Given the functions iszero, add, and sub1 from the previous section, an alternative is to implement mult without any knowledge of the way that numbers are encoded, which is the way that programmers normally implement functions.

The natural definition of such a mult is a function that checks whether the first argument is 0, and if not, adds the second argument to the result of using mult on the first argument, decremented by 1.

$$\text{mult} \overset{?}{=} \lambda n.\lambda m.\text{if (iszero } n) \; 0 \; (\text{add } m \; (\text{mult (sub1 } n) \; m))$$

The problem with this definition is that mult refers to itself. It thus can not be a macro, because macros are just abbreviations that are interchangeable with their defined expression. In short, the definition is illegal.

Recursion via Self-Application. If the mult macro cannot refer to itself, the question becomes how a multiplier function could get a handle to itself. The definition of the multiplier function is not available as it is defined and, due to the lack of named functions, we do not even have a handle that refers to the function. Later, however, when we call the multiplier function, we necesarily have a handle to it, and we could supply the function to itself. As we have seen twice before, it is possible in the λ-calculus to apply the identity function to itself; the general case might just work, too.

Thus, instead of referring to itself directly, the multiplier function could use a protocol that forces its future users to supply a multiply function t (itself) as well as arguments to multiply. More precisely, using this strategy, the function we define is no longer a multiplier function, but the *maker* of a multiplier function. It takes some function t and, using t, produces a multiplier function.

$$\boxed{\text{mkmult}_0 \overset{.}{=} \lambda t.\lambda n.\lambda m.\text{if (iszero } n) \; 0 \; (\text{add } m \; (t \; (\text{sub1 } n) \; m))}$$

This mkmult_0 macro is truly an abbreviation; $(\text{mkmult}_0 \; t)$ produces a multiplication function, assuming that t is a multiplication function. Obviously, this is a problem, because it means that mkmult_0 still is not a multiplication function. We tried to parameterize the original mult definition by itself, but in doing so we lost the mult definition.

Although we cannot supply a multiplication function for the call to the mkmult_0 function, we could instead supply the multiplication maker itself. The question is whether this would be useful, or whether we would end up in an infinite regress. As it turns out, supplying a maker to a maker can work.

If we assume that applying a multiplication maker to a multiplication maker produces a multiplier, we can use the same trick in the body of the definition. That is, if t is guaranteed to be the multiplication maker, we can apply t to *itself* in the body of the maker wherever a multiplier is needed. After all, t is a maker, and applying a maker to itself produces a multiplier.

mkmult	$\doteq$	$\lambda t.\lambda n.\lambda m.$if (iszero n) 0 (add m (($t\ t$) (sub1 n) m))
mult	$\doteq$	(mkmult mkmult)

The second line says that if mkmult works, then we can get a mult function by applying mkmult to itself. Note that both lines are abbreviations; all self-references have been eliminated.

Let us try this suspicious function on 0 and m (for some arbitrary m) to make sure that we get 0 back. We expand abbreviations only as necessary, and we assume that abbreviations like iszero and 0 behave in the expected way:

mult 0 m
$=$ (mkmult mkmult) 0 m
$\rightarrow_n$ ($\lambda n.\lambda m.$if (iszero n) 0 (add m ((mkmult mkmult) (sub1 n) m))) 0 m
$\rightarrow_n$ ($\lambda m.$if (iszero 0) 0 (add m ((mkmult mkmult) (sub1 0) m))) m
$\rightarrow_n$ if (iszero 0) 0 (add m ((mkmult mkmult) (sub1 0) m))
$\twoheadrightarrow_n$ if true 0 (add m ((mkmult mkmult) (sub1 0) m))
$\twoheadrightarrow_n$ 0

So far, so good. What if we multiply n and m, for some $n \neq 0$?

mult n m
$=$ (mkmult mkmult) n m
$\twoheadrightarrow_n$ if (iszero n) 0 (add m ((mkmult mkmult) (sub1 n) m))
$\twoheadrightarrow_n$ if false 0 (add m ((mkmult mkmult) (sub1 n) m))
$\twoheadrightarrow_n$ (add m ((mkmult mkmult) (sub1 n) m))

Since mult $=$ (mkmult mkmult), the last step above can also be abbreviated as (add m (mult (sub1 n) m)). Thus,

mult 0 m $\twoheadrightarrow_n$ 0
mult n m $\twoheadrightarrow_n$ (add m (mult (sub1 n) m)) if $n \neq 0$

These equations describe exactly the relationship we want among mult, add, sub1, and 0.

Exercise 3.14. Define a macro mksum such that (mksum mksum) acts like a "sum" function by consuming a number n and adding all the numbers from 0 to n.

Lifting Out Self-Application. The technique of the previous section is empowering because it allows the definition of any recursive function we might want. It is clumsy, though, because we have to define a maker function that applies an initial argument to itself for every recursive call. For protection against abuses of this protocol and for convenience, it is best to pull the self-application pattern out into its own abstraction.

More concretely, we want a function, call it mk, that takes any maker, such as $mkmult_0$, and produces the desired recursive function. For example, $(mk\ mkmult_0)$ should be a multiplier.

$$mk \overset{?}{=} \lambda t.t\ (mk\ t)$$

While this mk definition is ill-formed, it contains the right idea. The mk function is supposed to take a maker, t, and produce a recursive function. It does so by calling the function-expecting maker with $(mk\ t)$—which creates a recursive function. To turn this circular mk definition into a proper abbreviation, we use the self-application technique again.

$$
\begin{array}{rcl}
mkmk & \doteq & \lambda k.\lambda t.t\ ((k\ k)\ t) \\
mk & \doteq & (mkmk\ mkmk)
\end{array}
$$

And indeed, $(mk\ mkmult_0)$ behaves like mult:

$$
\begin{array}{rl}
& (mk\ mkmult_0)\ 0\ m \\
= & ((mkmk\ mkmk)\ mkmult_0)\ 0\ m \\
= & (((\lambda k.\lambda t.t\ ((k\ k)\ t))\ mkmk)\ mkmult_0)\ 0\ m \\
\twoheadrightarrow_n & \text{if (iszero 0) 0 (add } m\ (((mkmk\ mkmk)\ mkmult_0)\ (sub1\ 0)\ m)) \\
\twoheadrightarrow_n & 0
\end{array}
$$

$$
\begin{array}{rl}
& (mk\ mkmult_0)\ n\ m \\
= & ((mkmk\ mkmk)\ mkmult_0)\ n\ m \\
= & (((\lambda k.\lambda t.t\ ((k\ k)\ t))\ mkmk)\ mkmult_0)\ n\ m \\
\twoheadrightarrow_n & \text{if (iszero } n)\ 0\ (\text{add } m\ (((mkmk\ mkmk)\ mkmult_0)\ (sub1\ n)\ m)) \\
\twoheadrightarrow_n & (\text{add } m\ (((mkmk\ mkmk)\ mkmult_0)\ (sub1\ n)\ m)) \\
= & (\text{add } m\ ((mk\ mkmult_0)\ (sub1\ n)\ m))
\end{array}
$$

Fixed Points and the Y Combinator. The mk function should seem mysterious at this point. Somehow, it manages to apply $mkmult_0$ to something that causes the latter to produce a multiplier—even though mkmult$_0$ can only make a multiplier when it is given the multiplier that it is supposed to make!

In other words, mk finds a function f such that

$$\text{mkmult}_0 \, f =_\mathbf{n} f$$

and f acts just like a multiplier. This function f is called a **fixed point** of mkmult$_0$.

As it turns out, mk can find the fixed point of any function. In other words, if applying mk to M produces N, then applying M to N produces N again.

Theorem 3.1: $M \, (\text{mk } M) =_\mathbf{n} (\text{mk } M)$ for any M

Proof for Theorem 3.1: Since $=_\mathbf{n}$ is the symmetric closure of $\twoheadrightarrow_\mathbf{n}$, we prove mk $M \twoheadrightarrow_\mathbf{n} (M \, (\text{mk } M))$ and conclude the equation from there:

$$
\begin{aligned}
\text{mk } M \quad &= \quad (\text{mkmk mkmk}) \, M \\
&= \quad ((\lambda k.\lambda t.t \, ((k \, k) \, t)) \, \text{mkmk}) \, M \\
&\rightarrow_\mathbf{n} \quad (\lambda t.t \, ((\text{mkmk mkmk}) \, t)) \, M \\
&\rightarrow_\mathbf{n} \quad M \, ((\text{mkmk mkmk}) \, M) \\
&= \quad M \, (\text{mk } M)
\end{aligned}
$$

A function that behaves like mk is called a **fixed-point operator**. The mk function is only one of many fixed-point operators in the λ-calculus. The most famous one is called the Y combinator.[2]

$$\text{Y} \doteq \lambda f.(\lambda x.f \, (x \, x)) \, (\lambda x.f \, (x \, x))$$

In general, Y lets us define recursive functions more easily than the manual technique of Section 3.7. For example, we can define sum as

$$\text{sum} \doteq \text{Y} \, (\lambda s.\lambda n.\text{if (iszero } n) \, 0 \, (\text{add } n \, (s \, (\text{sub1 } n))))$$

Since we do not have to repeat a large maker expression, we can skip the intermediate maker abbreviations mksum, and instead apply Y directly to a maker function.

A programmer who sees the above definition of sum pronounces the Y combinator as "define the recursive function;" then adds "s" because s is the formal argument of Y's actual argument; and finally interprets $\lambda n \dots$ as the recursive definition of s.

---

[2]The term Y **combinator** often refers to the whole family of fixed-point operators.

Exercise 3.15. Prove that $M (Y M) =_n (Y M)$ for any M.

Exercise 3.16. Define an encoding for Lisp cons cells, consisting of the following macros:

- null, a constant

- cons, a function that takes two arguments and returns a cons cell

- isnull, a function that returns true if its argument is null, false if it is a cons cell

- car, a function that takes a cons cell and returns its first element

- cdr, a function that takes a cons cell and returns its second element

Show that your encoding satisfies the following equations:

$$
\begin{array}{lll}
(\text{isnull null}) & =_n & \text{true} \\
(\text{isnull (cons } M\ N)) & =_n & \text{false} \\
(\text{car (cons } M\ N)) & =_n & M \\
(\text{cdr (cons } M\ N)) & =_n & N
\end{array}
$$

Your encoding need not assign any particular meaning to expressions such as (car null) or (car cons).

Exercise 3.17. Using the encoding from the previous exercise, define length, which takes a list of booleans and returns the number of cons cells in the list. A list of booleans is either null or (cons $b\ l$), where b is true or false and l is a list of booleans.

3·8 Consistency and Normal Forms.
Any definition of a system of equations poses a "consistency challenge." Consistency means that the equations are meaningful; in particular, it should be impossible to prove equality for any two arbitrary terms.[3]

Let us start with the most obvious non-equation anyone can think of:

$$\text{true} \neq_n \text{false}$$

or written without abbreviations

$$\lambda xy.x \neq_n \lambda xy.y$$

---

[3]An alternative is to map distinct terms into distinct elements of a non-trivial model. Such a model has a carrier with more than one element and comes with a relation that is faithful to the defined equivalence relation. It took λ-calculus theoreticians some 30 years to construct such a model, however, while the theories of conversion and reduction evolved and produced "syntactic" consistency results.

On one hand, it is "obviously" true that these two functions cannot possibly be equal. Both take two arguments; one returns the first and the other returns the second. Furthermore, the only reductions that apply to either λ expression is $\rightarrow_n^\alpha$, which just renames the formal argument. On the other hand, the previous section demonstrated the usefulness of "backwards" calculations (for the Y combinator). So perhaps the λ-calculus harbors other surprises and can prove any two terms equal.

The consistency theorem of the λ-calculus states that two terms are provably equal in the λ-calculus if they are reducible to some common term.

> **Theorem 3.2 [Consistency for $=_n$]:** If $M =_n N$, then there exists an L' such that $M \twoheadrightarrow_n L'$ and $N \twoheadrightarrow_n L'$.

The theorem implies that the equation true $=_n$ false is not provable. Since, as argued above, it is easy to see that true and false are α reducible only to terms that have the same shape but different formal argument names, there is no reduction to a common term.

To establish a natural generalization of this first consequence, we need to contemplate what it means for an expression to be irreducible. Clearly, true and false are in some form of "canonical" shape, yet it is possible to apply an arbitrary number of $\rightarrow_n^\alpha$ reductions to these expressions. This is also true for any expression that contains a λ expression.

Given that the notion of α reduction exists solely for renaming formal arguments, we must focus on reducibility via $\rightarrow_n^\beta$ or $\rightarrow_n^\eta$. Conversely, we say that if neither of those reductions applies, a term is in normal form.

> An expression is in $\beta\eta$ **normal form**
> if it contains neither a β nor a η redex.
>
> M **has a** $\beta\eta$ **normal form** N if
> $M =_n N$ and N is a $\beta\eta$ normal form.

Equipped with this concept, we can now state our inequality example in its most general form. Remember that $=_\alpha$ is the equivalence generated by the compatible closure of α.

> **Theorem 3.3 [$\beta\eta$ normal forms]:** If M and N are $\beta\eta$ normal forms, $M =_n N$ holds if and only if $M =_\alpha N$.

Put differently, if an expression has a $\beta\eta$ normal form, then it has exactly *one* $\beta\eta$ normal form modulo α renamings of its bound variables.

The proof of theorem 3.3 is based on the Consistency Theorem (theorem 3.2). For the latter, its proof hinges on the fact that **n** satisfies the Church-Rosser property, i.e., the diamond property holds for $\twoheadrightarrow_n$.

Lemma 3.4 [Church-Rosser ($\twoheadrightarrow_n$)]: If $L \twoheadrightarrow_r M$, $L \twoheadrightarrow_r N$, there exists an expression L' such that $M \twoheadrightarrow_r L'$ and $N \twoheadrightarrow_r L'$.

For the simple calculus of booleans in chapters 1 and 2, the Church-Rosser property for **r** is a generalization of a diamond property for the single-step relation. For the λ-calculus, however, the one-step relation $\rightarrow_n$ does not obey the diamond property or even a slightly contorted one. The reason is that a $\rightarrow_n^\beta$ step may duplicate reducible expressions:

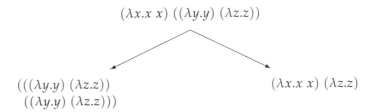

$$(\lambda x.x\ x)\ ((\lambda y.y)\ (\lambda z.z))$$

$$(((\lambda y.y)\ (\lambda z.z))\qquad\qquad\qquad (\lambda x.x\ x)\ (\lambda z.z)$$
$$((\lambda y.y)\ (\lambda z.z)))$$

Unfortunately, there is no expression L such that a single step converts the two bottom expressions into L. As the next chapter shows, the way around this problem is to define the notion of parallel reductions, which reduces independent sub-expression simultaneously, so that both $((\lambda y.y)\ (\lambda z.z))$ subexpressions on the left can be reduced at once. Since the proof of theorem 3.2 is available in many texts on the λ-calculus, it is omitted here; the next chapter contains a proof of a Church-Rosser lemma for a closely related calculus.

3.9 Normal Forms and Reduction Strategies.
At first glance, a $\beta\eta$ normal form is just like the result of a B program. By definition, no work-related reduction rule applies; α reduction simply does not perform any useful work in terms of computations.

In some sense, reductions of λ-calculus expressions to $\beta\eta$ normal form are also more "realistic" than the reductions of B programs to t or f. While the latter system reduces every expression to either t or f, some λ-calculus expressions have a $\beta\eta$ normal form and some do not. For example, Ω has no $\beta\eta$ normal form.

$$\Omega \doteq ((\lambda x.x\ x)\ (\lambda x.x\ x))$$

Of course, every programmer knows that some programs loop forever, so this is not a real surprise. Indeed, it helps confirm that the λ-calculus is just like a programming language.

Exercise 3.18. Prove that $((\lambda x.x\ x)\ (\lambda x.x\ x))$ has no $\beta\eta$ normal form.

Some properties are surprises, though. For example, even if an expression has a $\beta\eta$ normal form, there may be an infinite reduction sequence for the expression that never reaches a $\beta\eta$ normal form:

$$(\lambda y.\lambda z.z)((\lambda x.x\ x)\ (\lambda w.w\ w))$$
$$\rightarrow_\mathbf{n}\quad \lambda z.z \qquad\qquad\qquad\qquad \beta\eta \text{ normal form}$$

$$(\lambda y.\lambda z.z)((\lambda x.x\ x)\ (\lambda w.w\ w))$$
$$\rightarrow_\mathbf{n}\quad (\lambda y.\lambda z.z)((\lambda w.w\ w)\ (\lambda w.w\ w))$$
$$\rightarrow_\mathbf{n}\quad (\lambda y.\lambda z.z)((\lambda w.w\ w)\ (\lambda w.w\ w))$$
$$\rightarrow_\mathbf{n}\quad \cdots \qquad\qquad\qquad\qquad \text{same expression forever}$$

In some sense, this phenomenon is similar to the problem in parallel programming languages where a program evaluator may work on independent parts of the program at the same time and where one of those parts may never yield a result.

Combining this example with theorem 3.3 clarifies that an expression has at most one $\beta\eta$ normal form and that it is unique modulo the renaming of formal arguments. What we do not know is how to find this normal form. Intuitively, the problem with the non-terminating reduction above is that we are evaluating the argument of a function application although it is not needed. No matter what argument this function is applied to, it always produces $(\lambda z.z)$.

This observation suggests a strategy for picking the next redex strategically. Specifically, it suggests we apply the leftmost β or η reduction in an expression to reach a $\beta\eta$ normal form.

$M \rightarrow_\mathbf{\bar{n}} N$	if	$M\ \beta\ N$
$M \rightarrow_\mathbf{\bar{n}} N$	if	$M\ \eta\ N$
$(\lambda X.M) \rightarrow_\mathbf{\bar{n}} (\lambda X.N)$	if	$M \rightarrow_\mathbf{\bar{n}} N$ and $(\lambda X.M)$ is not an η redex
$(M\ N) \rightarrow_\mathbf{\bar{n}} (M'\ N)$	if	$M \rightarrow_\mathbf{\bar{n}} M'$ and $(M\ N)$ is not a β redex
$(M\ N) \rightarrow_\mathbf{\bar{n}} (M\ N')$	if	$N \rightarrow_\mathbf{\bar{n}} N'$, and M is in $\beta\eta$ normal form and $(M\ N)$ is not a β redex

The next theorem captures the essential property of the $\rightarrow_\mathbf{\bar{n}}$ relation.

Theorem 3.5 [$\beta\eta$ Normal-Order Reduction]: M has $\beta\eta$ normal form N if and only if $M \twoheadrightarrow_\mathbf{\bar{n}} N$.

The $\twoheadrightarrow_\mathbf{\bar{n}}$ relation is guaranteed to find a $\beta\eta$ normal form if one exists. Again, the proof of this theorem is available in many texts on the λ-calculus. The next chapter contains a proof of an analogous theorem for a closely related calculus that is also relevant for programming languages.

Together, the notion of normal form and normal-order reduction imply seemingly natural definitions for evaluators. The first just specifies that closed terms are evaluated to normal form:

$$eval_{\bar{\mathbf{n}}}^{=}(M) \stackrel{?}{=} N \text{ if } M =_{\bar{\mathbf{n}}} N \text{ and } N \text{ is a } \beta\eta \text{ normal form}$$

The second uses normal-order reduction:

$$eval_{\bar{\mathbf{n}}}^{\rightarrow}(M) \stackrel{?}{=} N \text{ if } M \twoheadrightarrow_{\bar{\mathbf{n}}} N \text{ and } N \text{ is a } \beta\eta \text{ normal form}$$

These definitions are analogous to those for $eval_{\mathbf{r}}$.

Unfortunately, they are also entirely unrealistic. No practical programming languages uses normal forms as results of computations, and no such language uses normal-order reduction. The primary reason is that reduction to normal-form demands the reduction of redexes under λ expressions. These, however, correspond in realistic languages to first-class procedures or objects with an apply method. When such languages include programs and expressions of this kind, they do not prematurely reduce them to any normal form. Instead, the evaluation stops when the evaluator has reduced the expression to a procedure or an object.

The secondary reason is that normal-order reduction duplicates the evaluation of expression. For example, in the diagram on page 40 the reduction on the left corresponds to $\beta\eta$ normal-order and how it duplicates a β redex. In contrast, the reduction sequence on the right produces the identity function in fewer steps because it reduces the argument to the function before it reduces the application of the function to the argument.

Naturally, people recognized these conflicts between the λ-calculus and existing programming languages. In response, they invented concepts to resolve them. For example, the notions of **head normal form** and **weak head normal form** were introduced to study different notions of termination for the evaluator. The combination of β normal-order reduction to weak head normal form resembles Algol 60's call-by-name parameter passing technique.

Most famously, the **applicative order** reduction strategy was introduced in a failed attempt to model the call-by-value parameter passing technique found in Algol 60 and modern programming languages. The strategy differs from the normal-order strategy in two regards. First, it uses only β reductions. Second, it applies β to a function application only when the argument expression is in normal form with respect to applicative order.

When combined with the idea of weak head normal form and when reductions within λ expressions are eliminated, the applicative reduction order is indeed an approximation of the call-by-value parameter passing technique. Sadly, though, the equations of the λ-calculus are useless then, as are all other reduction strategies, because they suggest relationships between expressions that violate the call-by-value regime of the evaluator.

Thus, we end this chapter with the problem of relating programming languages to equational systems of logic. People studied this problem in the 1950s and 60s, specifically the ideas of connecting abstract (or virtual) machines for notations borrowed from the λ-calculus and the λ-calculus itself. The next chapter explains how this problem was finally resolved.

$3 \cdot 10$ History.
Church [19] invented the lambda calculus in the 1920s and 30s, before Turing came up with his machines. Church and his students explored its theory of conversion, the reduction systems, and the encodings of numbers, booleans, and recursion. Kleene, one of the students, created the sub1 function; Rosser, another one Church's students, made key contributions to the proof of the consistency theorem.

Barendregt [8] provided a comprehensive study of Church's λ-calculus as a logical system, including proof techniques applicable to the calculus. His book does not cover the λ-calculus as a calculus for a programming language.

4 · ISWIM

In the late 1950s and early 1960s, people discovered the connection between programming languages and various aspects of the λ-calculus. The motivations ranged from a desire to specify the meaning of Algol 60 to the goal of understanding the landscape of programming languages from the perspective of well-understood mathematical systems. People thus wanted to learn how to design programming languages systematically.

Landin was a prominent member of this group of researchers. He designed a language dubbed ISWIM[1] that is based on the λ-calculus and explored its applications and implementations via abstract or virtual machines. Loosely speaking, ISWIM is a mostly functional programming language; the Scheme programming language [101] is ISWIM's closest living relative.

While people appreciated the power of ISWIM and took it as a source of inspiration, they also realized that the relationship between ISWIM and the λ-calculus was not straightforward. Plotkin eventually designed a variant of the λ-calculus that had an obvious and natural correspondence to ISWIM. He also showed that this correspondence is a general principle, and he instantiated the principle for two variants of ISWIM: one for call-by-name and another one for call-by-value.

This chapter and the following one present ISWIM, its calculus, and their mutual relationship. Specifically, this chapter presents the syntax and the "calculation" system of ISWIM. This includes the definition of an evaluator and an excursion into the most general system of equalities that it defines. The following chapter shows how a meta-theorem for the λ-calculus naturally defines a high-level abstract machine for ISWIM.

4·1 **ISWIM Expressions.** ISWIM is a family of programming languages that is parameterized over literal constants and primitive operators. Each member of the family generalizes the grammar of the λ-calculus with its own set b of basic constants and with a family o^n of multi-arity functions.

---

[1] ISWIM stands for "if you see what I mean."

$$
\begin{aligned}
M, N, L, K \quad &= \quad X \\
&\mid \quad (\lambda X.M) \\
&\mid \quad (M\ M) \\
&\mid \quad b \\
&\mid \quad (o^n\ M\ \ldots\ M) \\
&\quad\text{constraint: } n = m \text{ for } (o^n\ M_1\ \ldots\ M_m) \\
X, Y, Z \quad &= \quad \text{a variable: } x, y, \ldots \\
b \quad &= \quad \text{a basic constant} \\
o^n \quad &= \quad \text{an } n\text{-ary primitive operation}
\end{aligned}
$$

For concreteness, we use the following running example for b and o^n.

$$
\begin{aligned}
b \quad &= \quad \{\ulcorner n \urcorner \mid n \in \mathbb{Z}\} \\
o^1 \quad &= \quad \{\mathtt{add1}, \mathtt{sub1}, \mathtt{iszero}\} \\
o^2 \quad &= \quad \{+, -, *, \uparrow\}
\end{aligned}
$$

The syntactic object $\ulcorner 1 \urcorner$ is called a **numeral** and represents the integer 1; $+$ represents an addition operator, $\uparrow$ is exponentiation, etc.

The $\mathcal{FV}$ and $\cdot[\cdot \leftarrow \cdot]$ relations naturally extend to the new grammar.

$$
\begin{aligned}
\mathcal{FV}(\, b\,) \quad &= \quad \varnothing \\
\mathcal{FV}(\, X\,) \quad &= \quad \{X\} \\
\mathcal{FV}(\, (\lambda X.M)\,) \quad &= \quad \mathcal{FV}(M) \setminus \{X\} \\
\mathcal{FV}(\, (M_1\ M_2)\,) \quad &= \quad \mathcal{FV}(M_1) \cup \mathcal{FV}(M_2) \\
\mathcal{FV}(\, (o^n\ M_1 \ldots M_n)\,) \quad &= \quad \mathcal{FV}(M_1) \cup \ldots \mathcal{FV}(M_n) \\[2mm]
X_1[X_1 \leftarrow M] \quad &= \quad M \\
X_2[X_1 \leftarrow M] \quad &= \quad X_2 \\
&\qquad \text{where } X_1 \neq X_2 \\
(\lambda X_1.M_1)[X_1 \leftarrow M_2] \quad &= \quad (\lambda X_1.M_1) \\
(\lambda X_1.M_1)[X_2 \leftarrow M_2] \quad &= \quad (\lambda X_3.M_1[X_1 \leftarrow X_3][X_2 \leftarrow M_2]) \\
&\qquad \text{if } \quad X_1 \;\neq\; X_2 \\
&\qquad\qquad\quad X_3 \;\notin\; \mathcal{FV}(\, (\lambda X_1.M_1)\,) \\
&\qquad\qquad\quad X_3 \;\notin\; \mathcal{FV}(M_2) \\
(M_1\ M_2)[X \leftarrow M_3] \quad &= \quad (M_1[X \leftarrow M_3]\ M_2[X \leftarrow M_3]) \\
b[X \leftarrow M] \quad &= \quad b \\
(o^n\ M_1\ \ldots\ M_n)[X \leftarrow M] \quad &= \quad (o^n\ M_1[X \leftarrow M]\ \ldots\ M_n[X \leftarrow M])
\end{aligned}
$$

4·2 **Calculating with ISWIM.** Inspired by Algol 60's call-by-value para-
meter-passing technique, Landin designed ISWIM's function in an
analogous manner. That is, in ISWIM a function application evaluates the
argument before the function takes control. Doing so eliminates the computational overhead of evaluating an argument several times in the function
body or of keeping track whether an argument has been evaluated. It also
eliminates incongruities from the pure λ-calculus such as the expression

$$((\lambda x.\ulcorner 1\urcorner)\ (\texttt{sub1}\ \lambda y.(\lambda x.y)))$$

which applies $\texttt{sub1}$ to something other than a numeral; due to β reduction,
the mis-application is never discovered in the pure λ-calculus.

Because functions in ISWIM accept only evaluated arguments, we must
first agree on the nature of **values**, that is, the terms for which evaluation
immediately knows the result. Put differently, values are the "objects" to
which arbitrary expressions reduce. Thus, the set of values V (aliases U and
W) is naturally defined as a a subset of the set of expressions.

$$
\begin{aligned}
V, U, W \quad = \quad & b \\
| \quad & X \\
| \quad & (\lambda X.M)
\end{aligned}
$$

Basic constants are values, obviously, but so are functions, i.e, λ abstractions,
regardless of the shape of their bodies. Landin thus introduced the notion of
functions as first-class values into the study of programming languages.

An application (expression) is never a value. Indeed, it is the only vehicle
for specifying computations.

Variables are values, too, and that specification deserves an explanation.
Variables in the λ-calculus have one and only one purpose: as a formal argument or **parameter**. To a programmer, a parameter plays the role of a place
holder for a function's actual argument. Since an ISWIM function is assumed
to consume values, variables always stand for values. We therefore identify
them with values by including X in the set of values, for now. Section 4.7
reviews this decision.

Based on the specification of values, we can define the primary notion of
reduction for ISWIM.

$$((\lambda X.M)\ V) \quad \beta_v \quad M[X \leftarrow V]$$

The relation β_v differs from β in that the argument must be a member of V.
In ISWIM, it is not legal to substitute arbitrary terms M for occurrences of
the function parameter in a function's body.

Restricting the argument to be a value forces the reduction of argument expressions to values before the application of a function is evaluated. For example, $((\lambda x.1)\ (\mathtt{sub1}\ \lambda y.y))$ cannot be reduced to 1 because $(\mathtt{sub1}\ \lambda y.y)$ is not a member of V.

In addition to function application, a system for calculating with ISWIM expressions must account for primitive operations. Since ISWIM is a family of programming languages, with a grammar that is parameterized over the set b of literal constants and the set o^n of primitive operators, we need a general notion of reduction for these sets. To this end we introduce the partial δ **function**:

$$\delta : o^n \times \underbrace{b \times \ldots \times b}_{n} \longrightarrow V$$

That is, the δ function maps o^n plus n basic constants to a value. Adding a δ function to a calculus introduces a second notion of reduction.

For our running example of integer constants and operators, we choose the following concrete δ function.

$$
\begin{aligned}
\delta(\mathtt{add1}, \ulcorner m \urcorner) &= \ulcorner m+1 \urcorner \\
\delta(\mathtt{sub1}, \ulcorner m \urcorner) &= \ulcorner m-1 \urcorner \\
\delta(\mathtt{iszero}, \ulcorner 0 \urcorner) &= \lambda xy.x \\
\delta(\mathtt{iszero}, \ulcorner n \urcorner) &= \lambda xy.y \qquad n \neq 0 \\[1em]
\delta(+, \ulcorner m \urcorner, \ulcorner n \urcorner) &= \ulcorner m+n \urcorner \\
\delta(-, \ulcorner m \urcorner, \ulcorner n \urcorner) &= \ulcorner m-n \urcorner \\
\delta(*, \ulcorner m \urcorner, \ulcorner n \urcorner) &= \ulcorner m \cdot n \urcorner \\
\delta(\uparrow, \ulcorner m \urcorner, \ulcorner n \urcorner) &= \ulcorner m^n \urcorner
\end{aligned}
$$

The first two clauses of this δ function specify functions that add 1 to, or subtract it from, an integer. The last four introduce addition, subtraction, multiplication, and exponentiation into ISWIM by interpreting the corresponding symbols via mathematical operations on integers. Finally, the third and fourth clauses are less obvious. Given a numeral, $\mathtt{iszero}$ returns a function of two arguments; if the given numeral is $\ulcorner 0 \urcorner$, this function returns the first argument, otherwise the second one.

To illuminate the purpose of $\mathtt{iszero}$, consider the following, helpful if0 abbreviation.

$$
(\mathsf{if0}\ L\ M\ N) \ \doteq\ (((\mathtt{iszero}\ L)\ (\lambda X.M)\ (\lambda X.N))\ \ulcorner 0 \urcorner)
$$
$$
\text{where } X \notin \mathcal{FV}(M) \cup \mathcal{FV}(N)
$$

The *test* expression L is assumed to evaluate to a numeral. A $\ulcorner 0 \urcorner$ as L causes $(\mathtt{iszero}\ L)$ to produce $\lambda xy.x$, which in turn selects $(\lambda X.M)$, which contains the *then* expression. For all other numerals, the function returned by (iszero L) selects ($\lambda X.N$), which is related to the *else* expression. The chosen abstractions are applied to $\ulcorner 0 \urcorner$, meaning that the seemingly superfluous ($\lambda X. \cdots$) disappears because X does not occur free in either the *then* or the *else* branch of the conditional.

Combining β_v and δ creates **v**, the complete notion of reduction for Landin's ISWIM programming language.

$$\mathbf{v} = \beta_v \cup \delta$$

As usual, $\rightarrow_\mathbf{v}$ is the compatible closure of **v**, $\twoheadrightarrow_\mathbf{v}$ is the reflexive-transitive closure of $\rightarrow_\mathbf{v}$, and $=_\mathbf{v}$ is the symmetric closure of $\twoheadrightarrow_\mathbf{v}$.

Exercise 4.1. Show a reduction of

$$(\lambda w.(-\ (w\ \ulcorner 1 \urcorner)\ \ulcorner 5 \urcorner))\ ((\lambda x.x\ \ulcorner 10 \urcorner)\ \lambda yz.(+\ z\ y))$$

to a value with $\rightarrow_\mathbf{v}$.

Exercise 4.2. Prove with a calculation that

$$(\mathrm{if0}\ \ulcorner 0 \urcorner\ \ulcorner 1 \urcorner\ \ulcorner 2 \urcorner) =_\mathbf{v} \ulcorner 1 \urcorner$$

and

$$(\mathrm{if0}\ \ulcorner -1 \urcorner\ \ulcorner 1 \urcorner\ \ulcorner 2 \urcorner) =_\mathbf{v} \ulcorner 2 \urcorner$$

Now develop an example that demonstrates the need for the ($\lambda X. \cdots$)s in if0.

4·3 Alpha, Eta, and Quotients.

In contrast to the plain λ-calculus, the calculation system for ISWIM expressions includes neither the α notion of reduction nor η. With the former we lose the ability to rename the parameters of functions; with the latter we can no longer simplify "indirect" function applications.

The loss of α does not really affect our ability to determine the result of an ISWIM program, though intermediate results may differ due to choices made during substitution. In calculations using the λ-calculus, we could eliminate such small differences with α reductions. For ISWIM, we simply calculate with sets of α-equivalent terms. That is, $=_\mathbf{v}$ is really defined on such sets, instead of individual terms.

The loss of η is more significant. The elimination of this notion of reduction is needed to establish a logical form of consistency. We postpone the explanation of this statement until we have enough material in this chapter to discuss the role of the ISWIM calculus.[2]

---

[2]An intuitive explanation is that η asserts that every expression denotes a function. While this is true in the λ-calculus, it clearly does not hold for ISWIM, which contains functions plus other forms of data, e.g., numerals.

4.4 **The Y_v Combinator.** For the pure λ-calculus, the Y combinator finds the fixed point of any expression. We can therefore use the Y combinator to define recursive functions:

$$
\begin{aligned}
Y\,f \quad &= \quad (\lambda f.(\lambda x.f\ (x\ x))\ (\lambda x.f\ (x\ x)))\ f \\
&\to_v \quad (\lambda x.f\ (x\ x))\ (\lambda x.f\ (x\ x)) \\
&\to_v \quad f\ ((\lambda x.f\ (x\ x))\ (\lambda x.f\ (x\ x))) \qquad\qquad (\dagger)\\
&\ _v\!\!\leftarrow \quad f\ ((\lambda f.((\lambda x.f\ (x\ x))\ (\lambda x.f\ (x\ x))))f) \\
&\ _v\!\!\leftarrow \quad f\ (Y\ f)
\end{aligned}
$$

Unfortunately, the equation $(f\ (Y\ f)) =_v (Y\ f)$ is irrelevant. The problem is that the argument to f in the step labeled with $\dagger$ is not a value. Therefore, the application of Y to f does not reduce to a value, meaning it isn't a useful mechanism for creating recursive functions in ISWIM.

We can eliminate the problem by changing each application M within Y to $(\lambda x.M\ x)$, because its application is supposed to return a function. This small modification leads to the Y_v combinator.

$$
\boxed{\;Y_v = \;(\lambda f.(\lambda x.((\lambda g.\,(f\ (\lambda x.((g\ g)\ x))))(\lambda g.\,(f\ (\lambda x.((g\ g)\ x))))\ x)))\;}
$$

The Y_v combinator has *all* the desired properties. In particular, it reduces to a function when applied to a function that also returns a function, and it produces the fixed point of such functions.

Theorem 4.1 [Fixed-Point Theorem for Y_v]: If $K = \lambda ZX.L$, then $(K\ (Y_v\ K)) =_v (Y_v\ K)$.

Proof for Theorem 4.1: $K = \lambda ZX.L$ means K is a function-producing function, and $Y_v\ K$ reduces to a value:

$$
Y_v\ K \to_v \lambda x.(\lambda g.(K\ (\lambda x.((g\ g)\ x))))(\lambda g.(K\ (\lambda x.((g\ g)\ x))))\ x
$$

Let us name this value V:

$$
\begin{aligned}
Y_v\ K \to_v V \quad &\to_v \quad \lambda x.((K\ V)\ x) \\
&= \quad \lambda x.(([\lambda ZX.L]\ V)\ x) \\
&\twoheadrightarrow_v \quad \lambda x.L[Z \leftarrow V][X \leftarrow x] \\
&= \quad \lambda X.L[Z \leftarrow V] \\
&\ _v\!\!\leftarrow \quad ((\lambda ZX.L)\ V) \\
&= \quad (K\ V) \\
&\ _v\!\!\leftarrow \quad (K\ (Y_v\ K))
\end{aligned}
$$

The calculation in the proof looks complicated because arguments to procedures must be values before β_v applies. To simplify future calculations, we show that an argument that is provably equal to a value—but is not necessarily a value yet—can already be used as if it were a value.

Theorem 4.2: If $M =_{\mathbf{v}} V$, then for all X, N,

$$((\lambda X.N)\ M) =_{\mathbf{v}} N[X \leftarrow M]\ .$$

Proof for Theorem 4.2: Let us calculate:

$$((\lambda X.N)\ M) =_{\mathbf{v}} ((\lambda X.N)\ V) =_{\mathbf{v}} N[X \leftarrow V]$$

Now we just need to show that

$$N[X \leftarrow V] =_{\mathbf{v}} N[X \leftarrow M]$$

which we do by structural induction on N. Specifically, we show

$$N[X \leftarrow M] =_{\mathbf{v}} N[X \leftarrow L]$$

if $M =_{\mathbf{v}} L$:

- **Case $N = b$, a constant**
  $b[X \leftarrow M] = b =_{\mathbf{v}} b = b[X \leftarrow L]$.

- **Case $N = Y$, a variable**
  If $Y = X$, then $X[X \leftarrow M] = M =_{\mathbf{v}} L = X[X \leftarrow L]$.
  Otherwise, $Y[X \leftarrow M] = Y =_{\mathbf{v}} Y = Y[X \leftarrow L]$.

- **Case $N = (\lambda Y.N')$**
  If $Y = X$, then $N[X \leftarrow M] = N =_{\mathbf{v}} N = N[X \leftarrow L]$.
  Otherwise, by induction, $N'[X \leftarrow M] =_{\mathbf{v}} N'[X \leftarrow L]$:

  $$
  \begin{aligned}
  (\lambda Y.N')[X \leftarrow M] &= &(\lambda Y.N'[X \leftarrow M])\\
  &=_{\mathbf{v}} &(\lambda Y.N'[X \leftarrow L])\\
  &= &(\lambda Y.N')[X \leftarrow L]
  \end{aligned}
  $$

- **Case $N = (N_1\ N_2)$**
  By induction, $N_i[X \leftarrow M] =_{\mathbf{v}} N_i[X \leftarrow L]$ for $i \in \{1, 2\}$:

  $$
  \begin{aligned}
  (N_1\ N_2)[X \leftarrow M] &= &(N_1[X \leftarrow M]\ N_2[X \leftarrow M])\\
  &=_{\mathbf{v}} &(N_1[X \leftarrow L]\ N_2[X \leftarrow L])\\
  &= &(N_1\ N_2)[X \leftarrow L]
  \end{aligned}
  $$

- **Case $N = (o^n\ N_1 \ldots N_n)$**
  Analogous to the previous case.

4·5 **Evaluation.** From the last few sections, we have learned that expressions with free variables just may not have any meaning. It is thus natural to define that a **program** is a closed ISWIM expression. The problem is how to define an evaluator considering that one and the same program may reduce to several distinct values:

$$(\lambda x.x) \ (\lambda y.(\lambda x.x) \ \lceil 0 \rceil)$$

is clearly equivalent to both

$$\lambda y.(\lambda x.x) \ \lceil 0 \rceil$$

and

$$\lambda y.\lceil 0 \rceil$$

Which one is *the* result of the evaluation?

While all of these results hopefully represent one and the same function, it is also clear that there are infinitely many ways to represent a function. We therefore adopt a solution that essentially all practical programming systems implement. When a program reduces to a function value, the *eval*$_\mathbf{v}$ function merely returns the token function, indicating that the value is a function.

We define A, the set of **answers**, to be the set of results for evaluating ISWIM programs. The evaluator maps programs to answers.

$$A = b \cup \{\texttt{function}\}$$

$$\begin{aligned} eval_\mathbf{v} : M &\longrightarrow A \\ eval_\mathbf{v}(M) &= \begin{cases} b & \text{if } M =_\mathbf{v} b \\ \texttt{function} & \text{if } M =_\mathbf{v} \lambda X.N \end{cases} \end{aligned}$$

If $eval_\mathbf{v}(M)$ does not exist, we say that M's evaluation **diverges** or that it gets stuck. For example, Ω diverges; $\texttt{add1}(\lambda x.x)$ is stuck.

Exercise 4.3. Suppose that we try to strengthen the evaluation function as follows:

$$eval_1(M) = \begin{cases} b & \text{if } M =_\mathbf{v} b \\ \texttt{function1} & \text{if } M =_\mathbf{v} \lambda X.N \qquad N \neq \lambda Y.N' \text{ for any } Y, N' \\ \texttt{function+} & \text{if } M =_\mathbf{v} \lambda X.\lambda Y.N \end{cases}$$

Is $eval_1$ a function? If so, prove it. If not, provide a counter-example.

4·6 **Consistency.** The definition of ISWIM's evaluator relies on an equational calculus for ISWIM. Although the calculus is based on intuitive arguments and is almost as easy to use as a system of arithmetic, it is far from obvious whether the evaluator is a function that always returns a unique answer for a program. For a programmer who needs a deterministic, reliable programming language, however, this fact is crucial and needs to be established as rigorously as possible. In other words, we need to prove a consistency theorem for $eval_v$ just like the one we proved for $eval_r$.

We start with the desired theorem for ISWIM and work our way through the same proof plan that we used to establish the consistency of $eval_r$.

Theorem 4.3 [Consistency of Evaluation]: The relation $eval_v$ is a partial function.

Proof for Theorem 4.3: Assume that the ISWIM calculus is consistent, i.e., if $M =_v N$ then there exists an expression L such that $M \longrightarrow\!\!\!\rightarrow_v L$ and $N \longrightarrow\!\!\!\rightarrow_v L$.

Let $eval_v(M) = A_1$ and $eval_v(M) = A_2$ for answers A_1 and A_2. We need to show that $A_1 = A_2$. Based on the definition of ISWIM answers, we distinguish four cases:

- **Case $A_1 \in b$, $A_2 \in b$**

  It follows from the consistency of the calculus that two basic constants are provably equal if and only if they are identical, because neither is reducible.

- **Case $A_1 = $ function, $A_2 \in b$**

  By the definition of $eval_v$, there exists an expression N such that $M =_v \lambda x.N$ and for the constant b, $M =_v b$. By symmetry and transitivity, $A_2 =_v \lambda x.N$. Again by the consistency of the calculus and the irreducibility of constants, $\lambda x.N \longrightarrow\!\!\!\rightarrow_v b$. But by definition of the reduction relation $\longrightarrow\!\!\!\rightarrow_v$, $\lambda x.N \longrightarrow\!\!\!\rightarrow_v K$ implies that $K = \lambda x.K'$. That is, it is impossible that $\lambda x.N$ reduces to b, meaning that the assumptions of this case are contradictory.

- **Case $A_1 \in b$, $A_2 = $ function**

  Analogous to the previous case.

- **Case $A_1 = $ function, $A_2 = $ function**

  Then $A_1 = A_2$.

These are all possible cases, and hence, it is always true that $A_1 = A_2$, so $eval_v$ is a function.

The proof of the key theorem for $eval_v$ is incomplete because we lack a consistency lemma for the calculus of ISWIM. Put differently, thus far we have only reduced the functionality theorem to ISWIM's consistency lemma.

Lemma 4.4 [Consistency ($=_v$)]: If $M =_v N$, then there exists an expression L such that $M \twoheadrightarrow_v L$ and $N \twoheadrightarrow_v L$.

Proof for Lemma 4.4: The proof is essentially a replica of the proof for $=_r$ (lemma 2.2). It assumes a diamond property for the reduction relation $\twoheadrightarrow_v$ also known as Church-Rosser of **v**.

Now we have arrived at the core of the problem; we must show that ISWIM satisfies the Church-Rosser property.

Lemma 4.5 [Church-Rosser (v)]: If $L \twoheadrightarrow_v M$ and $L \twoheadrightarrow_v N$, then there exists an expression K such that $M \twoheadrightarrow_v K$ and $N \twoheadrightarrow_v K$.

For $\twoheadrightarrow_r$, a diamond-like property holds for the single-step relation $\rightarrow_r$, from which the diamond property for the transitive closure easily follows. But, given the example from the previous chapter, it is clear that the diamond property *cannot* hold for $\rightarrow_v$. The β_v reduction can copy redexes in the argument of a function, which prevents the existence of the common contractum in certain diamonds. For an example, consider the expression

$$((\lambda x.(x\ x))\ (\lambda y.((\lambda x.x)\ (\lambda x.x))))$$

which contains the two overlapping and underlined β_v-redexes. By reducing one or the other redex, we get the expressions

$$((\lambda x.(x\ x))\ (\lambda y.(\lambda x.x)))$$

and

$$((\lambda y.((\lambda x.x)\ (\lambda x.x)))\ (\lambda y.((\lambda x.x)\ (\lambda x.x))))$$

The first expression contains one redex, the second one two. All redexes are underlined. By the definition of "diamond property," we should use the one-step reduction on the redex in the first expression and one of the redexes in the second expression to reduce the two expressions to a common expression. As the diagram in figure 4.1 shows, this is impossible. Hence, the one-step relation $\rightarrow_v$ does not satisfy the diamond property.

Since the problem of the one-step relation based on **v** is caused by reductions that duplicate redexes, the problem suggests the solution[3] of introducing a relation $\hookrightarrow_v$ that reduces β_v redexes in parallel. More precisely, $\hookrightarrow_v$ extends the one-step reduction $\rightarrow_v$ by reducing all non-overlapping redexes in parallel. If this extension satisfies the diamond property, then we can prove

---

[3]Although the idea seems natural in hindsight, it was not introduced until the 1950's by W. Tait and Per Martin-Löf, according to Barendregt [8].

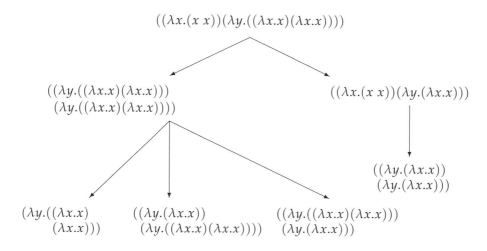

Figure 4.1: One-step relations lack the diamond property

the diamond property for the $\twoheadrightarrow_{\mathbf{v}}$ reduction because the transitive-reflexive closure of $\hookrightarrow_{\mathbf{v}}$ is the same as that of $\rightarrow_{\mathbf{v}}$.

The definition of $\hookrightarrow_{\mathbf{v}}$ is straightforward.

$$
\begin{array}{lll}
M & \hookrightarrow_{\mathbf{v}} & M \\
(o^n\ b_1\ \dots b_n) & \hookrightarrow_{\mathbf{v}} & V & \text{if } \delta(o^n, b_1, \dots, b_n) = V \\
((\lambda X.M)\ U) & \hookrightarrow_{\mathbf{v}} & M'[X \leftarrow V] & \text{if } M \hookrightarrow_{\mathbf{v}} M'\ \&\ U \hookrightarrow_{\mathbf{v}} V \\
(M\ N) & \hookrightarrow_{\mathbf{v}} & (M'\ N') & \text{if } M \hookrightarrow_{\mathbf{v}} M'\ \&\ N \hookrightarrow_{\mathbf{v}} N' \\
(\lambda X.M) & \hookrightarrow_{\mathbf{v}} & (\lambda X.M') & \text{if } M \hookrightarrow_{\mathbf{v}} M' \\
(o^n\ M_1\ \dots\ M_n) & \hookrightarrow_{\mathbf{v}} & (o^n\ M_1'\ \dots\ M_n') & \text{if } M_i \hookrightarrow_{\mathbf{v}} M_i', i \in [1, n]
\end{array}
$$

As with $\mathbf{v}$ we assume that $\hookrightarrow_{\mathbf{v}}$ applies to sets of α equivalent terms.

And indeed, $\hookrightarrow_{\mathbf{v}}$ satisfies the diamond property.

Lemma 4.6 [Diamond Property ($\hookrightarrow_{\mathbf{v}}$)]: If $L \hookrightarrow_{\mathbf{v}} M$ and $L \hookrightarrow_{\mathbf{v}} N$, there exists an expression K such that $M \hookrightarrow_{\mathbf{v}} K$ and $N \hookrightarrow_{\mathbf{v}} K$.

Proof for Lemma 4.6: By induction on the structure of the proof tree of $L \hookrightarrow_{\mathbf{v}} M$.

- **Case** $L = (o^n\ b_1 \dots\ b_n), M = \delta(o^n, b_1, \dots, b_n)$
  Since δ is a function there is no other possible reduction for L; set $K = N = M$.

- **Case** $L = ((\lambda X.M_0)\ U)$, $M = M_0'[X \leftarrow V]$, $M_0 \hookrightarrow_{\mathbf{v}} M_0'$, **and** $U \hookrightarrow_{\mathbf{v}} V$
  There are two possiblities for the reduction path $L \hookrightarrow_{\mathbf{v}} N$. Either the two parts of the application merely reduce separately, or the application is reduced via $\beta_{\mathbf{v}}$:

  - **Case** $L = ((\lambda X.M_0)U)$, $N = ((\lambda X.M_0'')U')$, $U \hookrightarrow_{\mathbf{v}} U'$, **and** $M_0 \hookrightarrow_{\mathbf{v}} M_0''$
    In this case, M_0, M_0', and M_0'' satisfy the antecedent of the inductive hypothesis, as do U, V, and U'. Hence, there are expressions K_0 and W that complete the upper half of these two diamonds. If we also knew that substitution and parallel reduction commute, we could conclude $K = K_0[X \leftarrow W]$, because $((\lambda X.M_0'')\ U') \hookrightarrow_{\mathbf{v}} K_0[X \leftarrow W]$ and $M_0'[X \leftarrow V] \hookrightarrow_{\mathbf{v}} K_0[X \leftarrow W]$.

  - **Case** $L = ((\lambda X.M_0)U)$, $N = M_0''[X \leftarrow V']$, $U \hookrightarrow_{\mathbf{v}} V'$, **and** $M_0 \hookrightarrow_{\mathbf{v}} M_0''$
    As in the first subcase, M_0, M_0', and M_0'' and U, V, and V' determine upper halves of diamonds. By the induction hypothesis, each yields two lower halves of diamonds and related terms K_0 and W. And again, if substitution and parallel reduction commute, setting $K = K_0[X \leftarrow W]$ concludes the subcase.

  To complete this case, we are obliged to prove the commutation property. We postpone this step, formulating the claim as a separate lemma (see 4.7) because other cases also depend on it.

- **Case** $L = (L_1\ L_2)$, $M = (M_1\ M_2)$, **and** $L_i \hookrightarrow_{\mathbf{v}} M_i$
  Analogous to the previous case.

- **Case** $L = (o^n\ L_1 \ldots L_n)$, $M = (o^n\ M_1 \ldots M_n)$, $L_i \hookrightarrow_{\mathbf{v}} M_i$
  There are two cases:

  - **Case** $L_1 = b_1, \ldots L_n = b_n$, $N = \delta(o^n, b_1, \ldots, b_n)$
    Then $M = L$ and $K = N$.

  - **Case** $N = (o^n\ N_1 \ldots N_n)$, $L_i \hookrightarrow_{\mathbf{v}} N_i$
    Using the inductive hypothesis n times, plus an appropriate "glue" step, yields the conclusion.

- **Case** $L = (\lambda X.L_0)$, $M = (\lambda X.M_0)$, **and** $L_0 \hookrightarrow_{\mathbf{v}} M_0$
  The only possibility is $N = (\lambda X.N_0)$ with $L_0 \hookrightarrow_{\mathbf{v}} N_0$. The induction hypothesis applies to L_0, M_0, and N_0 and yields an expression K_0; set $K = (\lambda X.K_0)$.

To finish the preceding proof, we need to show that substitutions in expressions that are related by parallel reduction do not affect the reduction step. We prove a general version, using substitution of arbitrary expressions not just values.

Lemma 4.7 [Substitution Lemma]: If $M \hookrightarrow_{\mathbf{v}} M'$ and $N \hookrightarrow_{\mathbf{v}} N'$, then $M[X \leftarrow N] \hookrightarrow_{\mathbf{v}} M'[X \leftarrow N']$.

Proof for Lemma 4.7: By structural induction on $M \hookrightarrow_{\mathbf{v}} M'$:

- **Case** $M = (o^n \ b_1 \ldots \ b_n)$, $M' = \delta(o^n, b_1, \ldots, b_n)$

  M and M' are closed, meaning both $M[X \leftarrow N] = M$ and $M'[X \leftarrow N] = M'$, and we know already that $M \hookrightarrow_{\mathbf{v}} M'$.

- **Case** $M = ((\lambda X_0.M_0) \ W)$, $M' = M_0'[X_0 \leftarrow V]$, $M_0 \hookrightarrow_{\mathbf{v}} M_0'$, **and** $W \hookrightarrow_{\mathbf{v}} V$

  By induction, both $M_0[X \leftarrow N] \hookrightarrow_{\mathbf{v}} M_0'[X \leftarrow N']$ and $W[X \leftarrow N] \hookrightarrow_{\mathbf{v}} V[X \leftarrow N']$. Thus:

$$
\begin{aligned}
& M[X \leftarrow N] \\
= \ & ((\lambda X_0.M_0[X \leftarrow N]) \ W[X \leftarrow N]) \\
\hookrightarrow_{\mathbf{v}} \ & M_0'[X \leftarrow N'][X_0 \leftarrow V[X \leftarrow N']] \\
= \ & M_0'[X_0 \leftarrow V][X \leftarrow N'] \qquad\qquad (\dagger) \\
=_\alpha \ & M'[X \leftarrow N']
\end{aligned}
$$

  Equation ($\dagger$) is a basic property of the substitution function. We leave this step as an exercise.

- **Case** $M = (M_1 \ M_2)$, $M' = (M_1' \ M_2')$, **and** $M_i \hookrightarrow_{\mathbf{v}} M_i'$

  By induction, $M_i[X \leftarrow N] \hookrightarrow_{\mathbf{v}} M_i'[X \leftarrow N']$ for both $i = 1$ and $i = 2$. Thus,

$$
\begin{aligned}
M[X \leftarrow N] \quad = \quad & (M_1[X \leftarrow N] \ M_2[X \leftarrow N]) \\
\hookrightarrow_{\mathbf{v}} \quad & (M_1'[X \leftarrow N'] \ M_2'[X \leftarrow N']) \\
= \quad & (M_1' \ M_2')[X \leftarrow N'] \\
= \quad & M'[X \leftarrow N']
\end{aligned}
$$

  So the claim holds.

- **Case** $M = (o^n \ M_1 \ldots \ M_n)$, $M' = (o^n \ M_1' \ldots \ M_n')$, **and** $M_i \hookrightarrow_{\mathbf{v}} M_i'$

  Analogous to the previous case.

- **Case** $M = (\lambda X.M_0)$, $M' = (\lambda X.M_0')$, **and** $M_0 \hookrightarrow_{\mathbf{v}} M_0'$

  Analogous to the previous case.

Exercise 4.4. Prove that if $N \hookrightarrow_v N'$, then $M[X \leftarrow N] \hookrightarrow_v M[X \leftarrow N']$.

Exercise 4.5. Prove that if $X \notin \mathcal{FV}(L)$ then

$$K[X \leftarrow L][X' \leftarrow M[X \leftarrow L]] =_\alpha K[X' \leftarrow M][X \leftarrow L]$$

Exercise 4.6. Prove that the transitive-reflexive closure of the parallel reduction $\hookrightarrow_v$ is the same as $\twoheadrightarrow_v$. This fact, along with lemma 4.6, proves lemma 4.5.

4.7 Observational Equivalence.

Let us step back for a moment and contemplate the question of what an equation in the ISWIM calculus means. One take is to say the equation $M =_v N$ means that M and N are equal according to the "axioms" (notions of reductions) and "inference rules" of the ISWIM logic (compatibility, reflexivity, symmetry, and transitivity), and that this is all there is to it. Clearly, such a view is operational but unsatisfying. For example, it does not explain why the ISWIM calculus leaves out η, even though it has played an important role historically.

An alternative take is to say that, besides providing the means for evaluating programs, the calculus also helps programmers figure out when one expression behaves just like another expression. Performing such "mental" calculations is critical in many situations. For example, if M is a procedure and N is supposed to be an equivalent procedure that performs the computations faster than M, then we would like to think that the two expressions are equal in some sense. Taking this view immediately reveals that the ISWIM calculus is insufficient. While $\lambda x.\Omega$ and $\lambda x.(\Omega\ \Omega)$ are obviously equivalent—both diverge—it is impossible to equate them in the ISWIM calculus. Furthermore, this view of a system of equations also suggest that we should accept as many "axioms" as possible; ruling out η looks almost bad now.

The purpose of this section is to introduce the notion of "observational equivalence" as a powerful, all-encompassing equivalence relationship for expressions in a programming language. Logicians speak of **models** and of **truth** in this context.

So, here is the problem. We wish to develop an equivalence relation that equates ISWIM expressions if they behave in the same way. For the special instance of complete programs, we have an obvious solution. Specifically, if both expressions are complete programs and we know that $eval_v(M) = eval_v(N)$, then they are behaviorally equivalent expressions. In general, however, M and N are sub-expressions of some program, i.e., they contain free variables whose meaning is determined by the context. In this case, we

cannot evaluate them independently and determine whether they are interchangeable. Hence, what we really need is a general relation that explains
when expressions are "equivalent in behavior."

To understand the notion of "equivalent in behavior," we must recall that
the user of a program can only *observe*—and is primarily interested—in its
output for specific inputs. In other words, such an observer treats programs
as black boxes. Thus, if a programmer replaces one expression with another
in some program, the user's primary interest is that the observable outputs
do not change. Our first insight is then that a comparison of arbitrary expressions involves how they influence the observable outputs and effects of the
surrounding program.

From the perspective of a library designer, that is, a programmer who
creates reusable code, the problem is that the surrounding program context
is not known. The functions of a library are supposed to be used wherever
they are needed. This then suggests that two expressions are to be considered
"behaviorally equivalent" if a programmer can use them interchangeably in
arbitrary program contexts.

Our first step in refining the idea of "behavioral equivalence" is necessarily the effort to define the notion of "program context" formally. Roughly
speaking, a context is an expression with a **hole**, written $[\,]$, where an expression could appear.

$$
\begin{aligned}
C \quad = \quad & [\,] \\
| \quad & (\lambda X.C) \\
| \quad & (C\ M) \\
| \quad & (M\ C) \\
| \quad & (o^n\ M\ \ldots\ M\ C\ M\ \ldots\ M)
\end{aligned}
$$

$C[M]$ means "fill the hole $[\,]$ in C with M" (without
regard to variables in C and M).

For example, $(\lambda x.[\,])$ is a context; $(\lambda[\,].x)$ is not a context, because expressions cannot occur between λ and the dot. To fill the context means to provide a body for the λ expression, e.g.,

$$(\lambda x.[\,])[y] = (\lambda x.y)$$

Unlike substitution, filling a context hole can capture variables:

$$(\lambda x.[\,])[(x\ \ulcorner 10 \urcorner)] = (\lambda x.(x\ \ulcorner 10 \urcorner))$$

Here the application of a free x to $\ulcorner 10 \urcorner$ is used as the body of the $\lambda x.$ abstraction, and doing so binds the x to the parameter of the λ.

Contexts are a formal tool for capturing the notion "compatible with the syntactic constructions of a language." To explain this idea in detail, consider the following definition.

> $M \rightarrow_{c\mathbf{v}} N$
> for some context C, $M = C[M']$, $N = C[N']$, and $M' \mathbf{v} N'$

It introduces the relation $\rightarrow_{c\mathbf{v}}$, which relates two expressions if two subexpressions in the exact same syntactic position are related via $\mathbf{v}$. The notion of "same syntactic position" is expressed via the use of the same context.

This new relation is identical to the reduction relation generated by $\mathbf{v}$, meaning contexts provide a simple and elegant characterization of what it takes to move from a notion of reduction to a reduction relation (its compatible closure).

Lemma 4.8: $\rightarrow_{c\mathbf{v}} = \rightarrow_{\mathbf{v}}$

Conversely, this lemma is the essential characterization of contexts for a language like the λ-calculus. From now on we assume that the set of contexts is always defined to satisfy this kind of lemma.

Exercise 4.7. Prove lemma 4.8 via structural induction.

Using contexts, we can express an equivalence relation that relates behaviorally indistinguishable expressions. Two expressions M and N are **observationally equivalent**, written $M \simeq_{\mathbf{v}} N$, if and only if they are indistinguishable in all contexts C.

> $M \simeq_{\mathbf{v}} N$ if and only if
> $eval_{\mathbf{v}}(C[M]) = eval_{\mathbf{v}}(C[N])$ for all ISWIM contexts C

Since $eval_{\mathbf{v}}$ is a partial function, the equation $eval_{\mathbf{v}}(C[M]) = eval_{\mathbf{v}}(C[N])$ must be read as $eval_{\mathbf{v}}$ is undefined for both $C[M]$ and $C[N]$ or it is defined for both and the results are identical ($=$).

Intuitively, the following observational equivalences should hold:

$$((\lambda x.(x \ulcorner 10 \urcorner)) \, (\lambda z. \ulcorner 20 \urcorner)) \quad \simeq_{\mathbf{v}} \quad \ulcorner 20 \urcorner \tag{4.1}$$

$$\lambda x.\Omega \quad \simeq_{\mathbf{v}} \quad \lambda x.(\Omega \, \Omega) \tag{4.2}$$

$$(\ulcorner 10 \urcorner \, x) \quad \simeq_{\mathbf{v}} \quad (\ulcorner 20 \urcorner \, y) \tag{4.3}$$

Equation 4.1 should hold because two $\beta_{\mathbf{v}}$ steps reduce the expression on the left to the expression on the right, no matter in which context the expression occurs. Hence, the two expressions behave equivalently everywhere. As argued above, the two expressions in equation 4.2 diverge no matter what the surrounding program context looks like. Finally, equation 4.3 deals with two expressions that get stuck independently of their contexts, implying that an external observer cannot get a result if the results of these expressions are needed for the program evaluation. Of course, neither of these arguments are true proofs; for those, we need to develop more insight into the nature of the observational equivalence relation.

Observational equivalence obviously extends the natural equivalence relation on programs. If programs M and N are observationally equivalent, then they are programs in the empty context, i.e., $eval_{\mathbf{v}}(M) = eval_{\mathbf{v}}(N)$. Naturally, this is the least we should expect from this relation. Furthermore, if two expressions are observationally equivalent, embedding the expressions in contexts should yield observationally equivalent expressions. After all, the added pieces are identical and should not affect the effects of the expressions on the output of a program. In short, observational equivalence is compatible with the syntactic constructions of the syntax of ISWIM.

Theorem 4.9: For any expressions M, N, and L,

1. $M \simeq_{\mathbf{v}} M$;

2. if $L \simeq_{\mathbf{v}} M$ and $M \simeq_{\mathbf{v}} N$, then $L \simeq_{\mathbf{v}} N$;

3. if $L \simeq_{\mathbf{v}} M$, then $M \simeq_{\mathbf{v}} L$; and

4. if $M \simeq_{\mathbf{v}} N$, then $C[M] \simeq_{\mathbf{v}} C[N]$ for all contexts C.

Proof for Theorem 4.9: Points 1 through 3 are simple exercises. As for point 4, assume $M \simeq_{\mathbf{v}} N$ and let C' be an arbitrary context. Then, $C'[C]$ is a context for M and N. By assumption $M \simeq_{\mathbf{v}} N$ and therefore,

$$eval_{\mathbf{v}}(C'[C[M]]) = eval_{\mathbf{v}}(C'[C[N]])$$

which is what we had to prove.

An equivalence relation that is compatible with syntactic operations is called a **congruence relation**. In contrast to $=_{\mathbf{v}}$, $\simeq_{\mathbf{v}}$ is not generated as a compatible closure from some small relation. Any compatible equivalence relation is, however, a congruence relation. Checking this last fact is easy and left as an exercise.

Observational equivalence is the largest congruence relation on expressions that extends the evaluation function $eval_{\mathbf{v}}$ viewed as an equivalence.

Theorem 4.10: Let **R** be a congruence relation such that $M \, \mathbf{R} \, N$ for expression M and N implies $eval_\mathbf{v}(M) = eval_\mathbf{v}(N)$. If $M \, \mathbf{R} \, N$, then $M \simeq_\mathbf{v} N$.

Proof for Theorem 4.10:   We assume $M \not\simeq_\mathbf{v} N$ and show $M \, \not\!\mathbf{R} \, N$. By assumption there exists a separating context C. That is,

$$eval_\mathbf{v}(C[M]) \neq eval_\mathbf{v}(C[N])$$

Therefore, $C[M] \, \not\!\mathbf{R} \, C[N]$. Since **R** is supposed to be a congruence relation, we cannot have $M \, \mathbf{R} \, N$, because that would lead to a contradiction.

The proposition shows that observational equivalence is the most basic, the most fundamental congruence relation on expressions. All other relations only approximate the accuracy with which observational equivalence identifies expressions. Another consequence of this proposition is that ISWIM is sound with respect to observational equivalence. Unfortunately, it is also incomplete; the calculus cannot *prove* all observational equivalence relations.

Theorem 4.11 [Soundness, Incompleteness]: If we can show $M =_\mathbf{v} N$, then $M \simeq_\mathbf{v} N$. But $M \simeq_\mathbf{v} N$ does not imply that we can prove $M =_\mathbf{v} N$.

Proof for Theorem 4.11:   As pointed out, $=_\mathbf{v}$ as the compatible closure of **v** is a congruence relation. Moreover, $eval_\mathbf{v}$ is defined based on $=_\mathbf{v}$ such that if $M =_\mathbf{v} N$, then $eval_\mathbf{v}(M) = eval_\mathbf{v}(N)$.

For the inverse direction, we refer to our counter-example and sketch the proof that it is one. Consider the expressions $(\Omega \, \Omega)$ and Ω. Both terms diverge and are therefore observationally equivalent; but both reduce to themselves only, and therefore cannot be provably $=_\mathbf{v}$. (to be continued in the next chapter)

To complete the proof of the Incompleteness Theorem, we still lack some tools for reasoning about equality in the calculus. The next chapter develops those tools for ISWIM and completes the proof of the theorem.

The Soundness Theorem clarifies that the addition of η would render the ISWIM calculus unsound. For example, η would identify the expressions $\lambda x.(\Omega \, x)$ and Ω. The observational equivalence relation separates the two expressions, however, with the following context:

$$D = (\lambda x.\ulcorner 10 \urcorner)[\,]$$

While

$$eval_\mathbf{v}(D[\lambda x.(\Omega\ x)]) = \ulcorner 10 \urcorner$$

we see that $eval_\mathbf{v}(D[\Omega])$ is undefined. In short,

$$\lambda x.(\Omega\ x) \not\simeq_\mathbf{v} \Omega$$

This last equation is of course what we would expect for a language that employs call-by-value. An infinite loop under a λ is only triggered if the function is called; until then, it should remain harmless. Removing the λ triggers the infinite loop and has therefore a visible effect.

In addition, the Soundness Theorem explains why the inclusion of variables in the set of values is acceptable. Doing so is sound and includes a collection of natural equations, such as

$$(\lambda x.M)z =_\mathbf{v} M[x \leftarrow z]$$

Put differently, it allows programmers to reason easily about certain expressions with free variables in a sound manner.

Exercise 4.8. Restrict η so that the above pair of expressions is no longer related via the refined notion of reduction. Is it possible to add the revised relation to $\mathbf{v}$ while preserving soundness?

Exercise 4.9. Consider the following evaluation function $eval_0$, plus its associated observational equivalence relation $\simeq_0$:

$$eval_0(M) = \text{value} \quad \text{if} \quad M =_\mathbf{v} V \quad \text{for some } V$$

$$M \simeq_0 N \qquad\qquad \text{if} \quad eval_0(C[M]) = eval_0(C[N]) \quad \text{for all } C$$

Does $M \simeq_0 N$ imply anything about $M \simeq_\mathbf{v} N$? How about the opposite direction? Sketch a rationale for the answers.

4·8 **History.** Landin was one of several people who started using the λ-calculus to explain programming language concepts, and then he turned it into a language by itself. In a series of papers, he showed how to evaluate such programs recursively and with abstract machines; he explained how to model Algol 60's semantics via a translation into his programming language; and finally, he argued that ISWIM could serve as a basis for understanding the entire landscape of programming languages [68].

According to Landin, the structure and interpretation of ISWIM shows that all programming languages share a common core and are separated by domain-specific libraries. The common core contains just a few mechanisms: names, procedures, applications, mutation, exception mechanisms, and other forms of non-local control. Domain-specific libraries support numerical computations, string-processing, or manipulations of lists, just like FORTRAN, SNOBOL, LISP, and other early programming languages.

Furthermore, Landin's work points out, to programmers and implementors alike, that it is possible to think of a programming language as an advanced form of arithmetic and algebra. Since all of us are used to calculating with numbers and booleans, we should be able to calculate with programs, too; programming languages merely support more complex forms of data than those. Landin's work leaves open when a calculus works for a programming language and when it does not, though his papers clearly demonstrate that the equations of the λ-calculus do not work properly for ISWIM.

In 1968, Morris [79] studied programming in the λ-calculus and introduced the notion of observational equivalence as the most general relation for reasoning about program transformations. He did not address the relationship between the calculus and its use as a programming language.

Plotkin completed this aspect of Landin's work in the 1970s [83]. His paper introduced two variants of the functional core of ISWIM, with recursively defined evaluators and calculi, and he proved a general series of theorems about the relationship of these three pieces.

In particular, Plotkin's first variant of ISWIM uses the call-by-name regime for passing arguments to a function, and the other one relies on call-by-value. For each language, his paper develops a variant of the λ-calculus: λ_n and λ_v. Each calculus relates to the corresponding variant of ISWIM in the same uniform manner:

1. the evaluator defined via the calculus is equal to the recursive one;

2. the calculus satisfies a soundness theorem with respect to the observational equivalence induced by the evaluator function; and

3. the calculus has standard reductions, which uniformly apply the basic notion of reduction in leftmost-outermost manner.

The latter topic is the subject of the next chapter.

Exercise 4.10. Design a variant of ISWIM and that uses call-by-name to pass parameters, i.e., passing arguments before evaluating them. The variant should have the same syntax as the ISWIM in this chapter. Prove the soundness of the call-by-name evaluator. Where and how does it differ from the one given in this chapter?

5 • An Abstract Syntax Machine

The definition of the ISWIM evaluator is elegant but difficult to implement. In order to determine the result of a program, a programmer can liberally apply the rules of the equational system in any order, in any direction, and at any place in the program. This flexibility is not a good basis for implementing the evaluator as a (meta-)program, however. We know from the Consistency Theorem that a program *has* a value when it *reduces* to one, so it is already clear that an algorithm can use the reduction relation instead of the equality relation.

Still, even a restriction to the reduction relation leaves too many choices. The real solution is to find a uniform strategy that deterministically picks a single redex from all possible redexes and that promises to get to the value of a program if it has one. Not surprisingly, proof theoreticians are interested in such a standard strategy, too, because it helps constructs proofs of equality if there is one, and because it helps with meta-proofs that some equalities are not provable (within the calculus).

In this chapter, we develop this so-called Curry-Feys standardization strategy and prove an appropriate theorem. The constructive content of the theorem is the basis for the formulation of a **syntactic machine** for ISWIM. Like a computer, a syntactic machine has states and deterministic instructions that take the machine from one state into another. Unlike a computer, a syntactic computer uses programs as states and reductions as instructions. In the following chapter, we turn this high-level abstract syntax machine into a register machine, suitable for an actual, fast implementation. The last two sections of this chapter show how to use the abstract syntax machine to reason about the evaluation process and the induced notion of observational equivalence.

5·1 Standard Reductions. Consider the following program:

$$(((\lambda xy.y)\ (\lambda x.((\lambda z.z\ z\ z)\ (\lambda z.z\ z\ z))))\ \ulcorner 7 \urcorner)$$

Both underlined sub-expressions are redexes. According to the Consistency Theorem it suffices to reduce these two redexes in order to obtain the value of this program. The question is which redex we should reduce first.[1]

---

[1]One could also try to reduce redexes in parallel. We focus on sequential strategies instead, which reduce one reducible sub-expression at a time.

By reducing the larger redex, the evaluation process makes progress:

$$((\lambda y.y)\ \ulcorner 7 \urcorner)$$

This expression is one reduction step away from the result, $\ulcorner 7 \urcorner$. If the evaluator were to choose the inner redex, however, and if it were to continue in this way, it would not find the result of the program:

$$((\lambda xy.y)\ (\lambda x.((\lambda z.z\ z\ z)\ (\lambda z.z\ z\ z)))\ \ulcorner 7 \urcorner)$$
$$\rightarrow_v\ \ ((\lambda xy.y)\ (\lambda x.((\lambda z.z\ z\ z)\ (\lambda z.z\ z\ z)\ (\lambda z.z\ z\ z))))\ \ulcorner 7 \urcorner)$$
$$\rightarrow_v\ \ \ldots$$

The problem with the second strategy is obvious: it does not find the result of the program because it reduces sub-expressions inside of λ-abstractions, and it leaves the outer applications of the program intact. This observation also hints at a simple solution. A good evaluation strategy based on reductions should only pick redexes that are outside of abstractions. We make this more precise with a pair of rules:

1. If the expression is an application whose immediate sub-expressions are values, and if the expression is a redex, then it is the next redex to be reduced. Otherwise, the program *cannot* have a value.

2. If the expression is an application but does not consist only of values, then pick one of the non-values and search for a potential redex in it.

The second rule is ambiguous because it permits distinct sub-expressions of a program to be candidates for further reduction. Since a deterministic strategy should pick a unique sub-expression as a candidate for further reduction, we *arbitrarily* choose to search for redexes in such an application from left to right, because it unifies the evaluation of primitive applications and of abbreviations such as if0:

2′. If the program is an application but does not consist only of values, then pick the leftmost non-value and search for a redex in it.

By following the above algorithm, we divide a program into an application consisting of values and the context of the application. The shape of such a context is determined by the two rules. It is either a hole or an application, and the sub-context is to the right of values. Since these contexts play a special role in our subsequent investigations, we provide a formal definition for this set of **evaluation contexts** E.

$$
\begin{aligned}
E\ =\ \ &[\,] \\
|\ \ &(V\ E) \\
|\ \ &(E\ M) \\
|\ \ &(o^n\ V \ldots V\ E\ M \ldots M)
\end{aligned}
$$

To verify that our informal strategy picks a unique sub-expression from a program as a potential redex, we show that every program is either a value or a unique evaluation context filled with an application consisting of values.

Lemma 5.1 [Unique Evaluation Contexts]: For all M, either $M = V$, or there exists a unique evaluation context E such that $M = E[(V_1\ V_2)]$ or $M = E[(o^n\ V_1 \dots V_n)]$

Proof for Lemma 5.1: By induction on the structure of M. The theorem holds for the case when M is a variable or a basic constant, because those are values. Similarly, when $M = (\lambda X.N)$, it holds, because λ-expressions are values.

Otherwise, M is an operator application or function application. Assume that $M = (o^n\ N_1 \dots N_n)$. If all $N_i \in V$, we are done. Otherwise, there is a leftmost argument expression N_i (where $1 \leq i \leq n$) that is not a value. By induction, N_i can be partitioned into a unique evaluation context E' and some application L. Then $E = (o^n\ N_1 \dots N_{i-1}\ E'\ N_{i+1} \dots N_n)$ is an evaluation context, and $M = E[L]$. The context is unique since i is the minimal index such that $N_1, \dots N_{i-1} \in V$ and E' is unique by induction.

The proof for the remaining case of function application proceeds in an analogous manner.

It follows from theorem 5.1 that if $M = E[L]$ where L is an application consisting of values, then L is uniquely determined. If L is moreover a β_v or a δ redex, it is *the* redex that, according to our above rules, must be reduced. Reducing it produces a new program, which can be decomposed again. In short, to get an answer for a program, proceed as follows: if it is a value, there is nothing to do; otherwise decompose the program into an evaluation context and a redex, reduce the redex, and start over. We formalize this idea with the **standard reduction relation** $\longmapsto_\mathbf{v}$.

$$E[M] \longmapsto_\mathbf{v} E[M']\quad\text{if } M\ \mathbf{v}\ M'$$

We pronounce $M \longmapsto_\mathbf{v} N$ as "M standard-reduces to N." As usual, the double-arrow version, $\longmapsto\!\!\!\!\twoheadrightarrow_\mathbf{v}$, denotes the transitive-reflexive closure of the relation ($\longmapsto_\mathbf{v}$).

By theorem 5.1, the standard reduction relation is a partial function. Composing standard reduction steps creates a function that relates programs to values, which suggests an alternative definition for an evaluator.

$$eval_\mathbf{v}^\mathsf{s}(M) = \begin{cases} b & \text{if } M \longmapsto\!\!\!\!\twoheadrightarrow_\mathbf{v} b \\ \texttt{function} & \text{if } M \longmapsto\!\!\!\!\twoheadrightarrow_\mathbf{v} \lambda X.N, \text{ for some } N \end{cases}$$

Exercise 5.1. Show the reduction of

$$(+ ((\lambda x.(\lambda y.y)\ x)\ (-\ \ulcorner 2 \urcorner \ulcorner 1 \urcorner))\ \ulcorner 8 \urcorner)$$

to a value with $\longmapsto_{\mathbf{v}}$. For each step, identify the evaluation context.

We claim that this new evaluator function is the same as the original one.

> **Theorem 5.2**: $eval_{\mathbf{v}} = eval_{\mathbf{v}}^{s}$.

> **Proof for Theorem 5.2**: The proof distinguishes two cases, proving both directions in each case.

> First, assume $eval_{\mathbf{v}}(M) = b$ and prove that $eval_{\mathbf{v}}^{s}(M) = b$. By Church-Rosser and the fact that constants are irreducible with respect to $\mathbf{v}$,
> $$M \twoheadrightarrow_{\mathbf{v}} b$$

> If we could prove that this implies
> $$M \longmapsto\!\!\!\twoheadrightarrow_{\mathbf{v}} b$$

> which is a natural conjecture in this context, we would be able to conclude that $eval_{\mathbf{v}}^{s}(M) = b$.

> For the other direction, assume $eval_{\mathbf{v}}^{s}(M) = b$. It follows that $M \longmapsto\!\!\!\twoheadrightarrow_{\mathbf{v}} b$. Hence by an easy argument, $M =_{\mathbf{v}} b$, which of course implies that $eval_{\mathbf{v}}(M) = b$.

> Second, assume $eval_{\mathbf{v}}(M) = \texttt{function}$ and prove $eval_{\mathbf{v}}^{s}(M) = \texttt{function}$. By definition, there exist some X and N such that $M \twoheadrightarrow_{\mathbf{v}} \lambda X.N$. As above, we conjecture that $M \longmapsto\!\!\!\twoheadrightarrow_{\mathbf{v}} \lambda X.N$. We may conclude from here that $eval_{\mathbf{v}}^{s}(M) = \texttt{function}$. We leave the inverse direction for this case as an exercise.

The preceding theorem is incomplete. It relies on the seemingly obvious conjecture that
$$M \twoheadrightarrow_{\mathbf{v}} V \text{ if and only if } M \longmapsto\!\!\!\twoheadrightarrow_{\mathbf{v}} V$$

A moment's reflection, however, shows that the left-to-right implication cannot possibly hold. Since a $\twoheadrightarrow_{\mathbf{v}}$ reduction might reduce expressions within a λ-abstraction, we may have a $\twoheadrightarrow_{\mathbf{v}}$ reduction sequence such as

$$(\lambda x.x)(\lambda x.((\lambda x.x)\ulcorner 5 \urcorner)) \twoheadrightarrow_{\mathbf{v}} \lambda x.5$$

which cannot be simulated with $\longmapsto\!\!\!\twoheadrightarrow_{\mathbf{v}}$ sequences. What we can hope for is that a standard reduction series goes from M to a value V if there is a $\twoheadrightarrow_{\mathbf{v}}$ reduction series from M to some value U that is like V. For basic values though, we should expect the claim to hold.

Lemma 5.3: $M \twoheadrightarrow_\mathbf{v} U$ if and only if for some value V, $M \longmapsto\!\!\!\twoheadrightarrow_\mathbf{v} V$ and $V \twoheadrightarrow_\mathbf{v} U$.

In particular, $M \twoheadrightarrow_\mathbf{v} b$ if and only if $M \longmapsto\!\!\!\twoheadrightarrow_\mathbf{v} b$.

Using the precise statement of lemma 5.3, we can fix the proof of theorem 5.2. We defer the proof of the lemma until the next section.

Exercise 5.2. Suppose that we try to strengthen the evaluation function as follows:

$$eval_1^s(M) = \begin{cases} b & \text{if } M \longmapsto\!\!\!\twoheadrightarrow_\mathbf{v} b \\ \texttt{function1} & \text{if } M \longmapsto\!\!\!\twoheadrightarrow_\mathbf{v} \lambda X.N, \text{ if } N \neq \lambda Y.K \text{ for any } Y, K \\ \texttt{function+} & \text{if } M \longmapsto\!\!\!\twoheadrightarrow_\mathbf{v} \lambda X.\lambda Y.N \end{cases}$$

Is $eval_1^s$ a function? If so, prove it. If not, provide a counter-example.

5·2 The Standard Reduction Theorem.

The proof of lemma 5.3 requires a complex argument. The difficult part of the proof is clearly the left-to-right direction; the right-to-left direction is implied by the fact that $\longmapsto_\mathbf{v}$ and $\longmapsto\!\!\!\twoheadrightarrow_\mathbf{v}$ are subsets of $\rightarrow_\mathbf{v}$ and $\twoheadrightarrow_\mathbf{v}$, respectively.

A naive proof attempt for the left-to-right direction could proceed by induction on the number of one-step reductions from M to U. Assume the reduction sequence looks like this:

$$M = M_0 \rightarrow_\mathbf{v} M_1 \rightarrow_\mathbf{v} \ldots \rightarrow_\mathbf{v} M_m = U$$

For $m = 0$ the claim vacuously holds, but when $m > 0$ the claim is impossible to prove by the simple-minded induction. While the inductive hypothesis says that for $M_1 \twoheadrightarrow_\mathbf{v} U$ there exists a value V such that $M_1 \longmapsto\!\!\!\twoheadrightarrow_\mathbf{v} V$, it is obvious that for many pairs M_0, M_1 it is *not* the case that $M_0 \longmapsto\!\!\!\twoheadrightarrow_\mathbf{v} M_1$. For example, the reduction step from M_0 to M_1 could be inside of a λ-abstraction that is a part of the final answer.

The common mathematical solution to this proof problem is to generalize the inductive hypothesis. Instead of proving that programs reduce to values if and only if they reduce to values via the transitive closure of the standard reduction *function*, we prove that there is a canonical sequence of reduction steps for every ordinary sequence of reductions steps.

From the informal claim it is clear that a statement of the general claim requires a formal definition of "canonicity" for reduction sequences, known as **standard reduction sequence**s, $\mathcal{R}$. A standard reduction sequence generalizes the idea of a sequence of expressions that are related via the standard reduction function. In standard reduction sequences, an expression can relate to its successor if a sub-expression in a λ-abstraction standard reduces to another expression. Finally, a standard reduction sequence also permits incomplete reductions. That is, a sequence may skip the reduction of a surrounding standard redex; if it does, though, it does so for the rest of the sequence.

- $b \subset \mathcal{R}$

- $X \subset \mathcal{R}$

- If $M_1 \diamond \ldots \diamond M_m \in \mathcal{R}$, then
  $(\lambda X.M_1) \diamond \ldots \diamond (\lambda X.M_m) \in \mathcal{R}$

- If $M_1 \diamond \ldots \diamond M_m \in \mathcal{R}$ and $N_1 \diamond \ldots \diamond N_n \in \mathcal{R}$, then
  $(M_1\ N_1) \diamond \ldots \diamond (M_m\ N_1) \diamond (M_m\ N_2) \diamond \ldots \diamond (M_m\ N_n) \in \mathcal{R}$

- If $M_{i,1} \diamond \ldots \diamond M_{i,n_i} \in \mathcal{R}$ for $1 \leq i \leq m$ and $n_i \geq 1$, then

$$(o^m\ M_{1,1}\ M_{2,1} \ldots M_{m,1}) \diamond$$
$$(o^m\ M_{1,2}\ M_{2,1} \ldots M_{m,1}) \diamond$$
$$\ldots$$
$$(o^m\ M_{1,n_1}\ M_{2,1} \ldots M_{m,1}) \diamond$$
$$(o^m\ M_{1,n_1}\ M_{2,2} \ldots M_{m,1}) \diamond$$
$$\ldots$$
$$(o^m\ M_{1,n_1}\ M_{2,n_2} \ldots M_{m,n_m}) \in \mathcal{R}$$

- If $M_1 \diamond \ldots \diamond M_m \in \mathcal{R}$ and $M_0 \longmapsto_{\mathbf{v}} M_1$, then
  $M_0 \diamond M_1 \diamond \ldots \diamond M_m \in \mathcal{R}$

We can now formulate a theorem whose proof uses a reasonably simple induction argument. The general idea for the theorem and its proof is due to Curry and Feys, who proved it for Church's pure λ-calculus. The theorem for ISWIM and the proof idea are due to Plotkin.

Theorem 5.4 [Curry-Feys Standardization]: $M \twoheadrightarrow_{\mathbf{v}} N$ if and only if there is $L_1 \diamond \ldots \diamond L_n \in \mathcal{R}$ such that $M = L_1$ and $N = L_n$.

Proof for Theorem 5.4: From right to left, the claim is a consequence of the fact that if K precedes L in a standard reduction sequence, then, by definition, K reduces to L.

To prove the left-to-right direction, assume $M \twoheadrightarrow_{\mathbf{v}} N$. By the definition of $\twoheadrightarrow_{\mathbf{v}}$, this means that there exist expressions $M_1, \ldots M_m$ such that

$$M \rightarrow_{\mathbf{v}} M_1 \rightarrow_{\mathbf{v}} \ldots M_m \rightarrow_{\mathbf{v}} N$$

The critical idea is to exploit that parallel reduction extends the one-step relation:

$$M \hookrightarrow_{\mathbf{v}} M_1 \hookrightarrow_{\mathbf{v}} \ldots M_m \hookrightarrow_{\mathbf{v}} N$$

and that such a sequence of parallel reduction steps can be transformed into a standard reduction sequence. The algorithm for doing so is the subject of lemma 5.5 below.

The proof of the main lemma relies on a size function $| \cdot |$ for derivations of parallel reductions. The size of such derivations is approximately the number of $\mathbf{v}$-redexes that an ordinary reduction between expressions would have had to reduce.

$$
\begin{array}{rcl}
\#(X, M) & = & \text{the number of free } X \text{ in } M \\[4pt]
| M \hookrightarrow_{\mathbf{v}} M | & = & 0 \\
| (o^n \, b_1 \ldots \, b_n) \hookrightarrow_{\mathbf{v}} \delta(o^n, b_1, \ldots, b_n) | & = & 1 \\
| (\lambda X.M)U \hookrightarrow_{\mathbf{v}} M'[X \leftarrow V] | & = & s_1 + \#(X, M') \times s_2 + 1 \\
& & \text{where } s_1 = | M \hookrightarrow_{\mathbf{v}} M' | \\
& & \text{and } s_2 = | U \hookrightarrow_{\mathbf{v}} V | \\
| (M \, N) \hookrightarrow_{\mathbf{v}} (M' \, N') | & = & s_1 + s_2 \\
& & \text{where } s_1 = | M \hookrightarrow_{\mathbf{v}} M' | \\
& & \text{and } s_2 = | N \hookrightarrow_{\mathbf{v}} N' | \\
| (o^m \, M_1 \ldots M_m) \hookrightarrow_{\mathbf{v}} (o^m \, M'_1 \ldots M'_m) | & = & \Sigma_{i=1}^{m} s_i \\
& & \text{where } s_i = | M_i \hookrightarrow_{\mathbf{v}} M'_i | \\
| (\lambda X.M) \hookrightarrow_{\mathbf{v}} (\lambda X.M') | & = & | M \hookrightarrow_{\mathbf{v}} M' |
\end{array}
$$

Lemma 5.5: If $M \hookrightarrow_{\mathbf{v}} N$ and $N \diamond N_2 \diamond \ldots \diamond N_n \in \mathcal{R}$, then there is a $L_1 \diamond \ldots \diamond L_p \in \mathcal{R}$ such that $M = L_1$ and $L_p = N_n$.

Proof for Lemma 5.5: By triple lexicographic induction on the length n of the given standard reduction sequence, the size of the derivation $M \hookrightarrow_{\mathbf{v}} N$, and the structure of M. It proceeds by case analysis on the last step in the derivation of $M \hookrightarrow_{\mathbf{v}} N$:

- **Case** $M = N$
  This case is trivial.

- **Case** $M = (o^m \, b_1 \ldots \, b_m), N = \delta(o^m, b_1, \ldots, b_m)$
  A δ-step that transforms the outermost application is also a standard reduction step. By combining this with the standard reduction sequence from N to N_n yields the required standard reduction sequence from M to N_n.

- **Case** $M = ((\lambda X.K)\, U)$, $N = L[X \leftarrow V]$, $K \hookrightarrow_{\mathbf{v}} L$, $U \hookrightarrow_{\mathbf{v}} V$

  M is also a $\beta_{\mathbf{v}}$-redex, which as in the previous case, implies that a $\beta_{\mathbf{v}}$-step from M to $K[X \leftarrow U]$ is a standard reduction step. By the assumptions and lemma 4.7, the latter expression also parallel reduces to $L[X \leftarrow V]$. Indeed, we can prove a stronger version of this lemma, which shows that the size of this derivation is strictly smaller than the size of the derivation of $((\lambda X.K)\, U) \hookrightarrow_{\mathbf{v}} L[X \leftarrow V]$; see lemma 5.8 below. Thus, the induction hypothesis applies and there must be a standard reduction sequence $L_2 \diamond \ldots \diamond L_p$ such that $K[X \leftarrow U] = L_2$ and $L_p = N_n$. Since $M \longmapsto_{\mathbf{v}} K[X \leftarrow U]$, the expression sequence $M \diamond L_2 \diamond \ldots L_p$ is the required standard reduction sequence.

- **Case** $M = (M'\, M'')$, $N = (N'\, N'')$, $M' \hookrightarrow_{\mathbf{v}} N'$, $M'' \hookrightarrow_{\mathbf{v}} N''$

  Because the standard reduction sequence $N \diamond N_2 \diamond \ldots \diamond N_n$ could be formed in two different ways, we must consider two subcases:

  - **Case** $N \longmapsto_{\mathbf{v}} N_2$

    This case relies on lemma 5.6 below, which shows that if $M \hookrightarrow_{\mathbf{v}} N$ and $N \longmapsto_{\mathbf{v}} N_2$ then there exists an expression K such that $M \longmapsto_{\mathbf{v}} K$ and $K \hookrightarrow_{\mathbf{v}} N_2$. Now, $K \hookrightarrow_{\mathbf{v}} N_2$ and $N_2 \diamond N_3 \diamond \ldots \diamond N_n$ is a standard reduction sequence that is shorter than the original one. Hence, by induction hypothesis there exists a standard reduction sequence $L_2 \diamond \ldots \diamond L_p$ such that $K = L_2$ and $L_p = N_n$. Moreover, $M \longmapsto_{\mathbf{v}} K$, and hence $M \diamond L_2 \diamond \ldots \diamond L_p$ is the desired standard reduction sequence.

  - **Case otherwise**

    $N' \diamond \ldots \diamond N'_k$ and $N'' \diamond \ldots \diamond N''_j$ are standard reduction sequences such that $N \diamond N_2 \diamond \ldots \diamond N_n$ is identical to

    $$(N'\, N'') \diamond \ldots \diamond (N'_k\, N'') \diamond (N'_k\, N''_2) \diamond \ldots (N'_k\, N''_j)$$

    By the assumptions of the case and the induction hypothesis, which applies twice because M' and M'' are proper parts of M, there exist two standard reduction sequences $L'_1 \diamond \ldots \diamond L'_{l_1}$ and $L''_1 \diamond \ldots \diamond L''_{l_2}$ such that $M' = L'_1$ and $L'_{l_1} = N'_k$ and $M'' = L''_1$ and $L''_{l_2} = N''_j$. Clearly, these two sequences form a single reduction sequence $L_1 \diamond \ldots \diamond L_p$ such that $L_1 = (L'_1\, L''_1) = (M'\, M'')$ and

$L_p = (L'_{l_1} \, L''_{l_2}) = (N'_k \, N''_j) = N_n$, which is precisely what the lemma demands.

- **Case** $M = (o^m \, M_1 \ldots M_m)$, $N = (o^m \, N'_1 \ldots N'_m)$, $M_i \hookrightarrow_\mathbf{v} N_i$

  Again, the standard reduction sequence starting at N could be the result of two different formation rules. The proofs in both subcases though are completely analogous to the two subcases in the previous case so that there is no need for further elaboration.

- **Case** $M = (\lambda X.K)$, $N = (\lambda X.L)$, $K \hookrightarrow_\mathbf{v} L$

  By the definition of standard reduction sequences, all of the expressions N_i are λ-abstractions, say, $N_i = \lambda X.N'_i$. Hence, $K \hookrightarrow_\mathbf{v} L$ and $L \diamond N'_2 \diamond \ldots \diamond N'_n$ is a standard reduction sequence. Since K is a proper sub-expression of M, the induction hypothesis applies and there must be a standard reduction sequence $L'_1 \diamond \ldots \diamond L'_p$ such that $K = L'_1$ and $L'_p = N'_n$. By taking $L_i = \lambda X.L'_i$, we get the desired standard reduction sequence.

These are all possible cases and we have thus finished the proof.

Lemma 5.6: If $M \hookrightarrow_\mathbf{v} N$ and $N \longmapsto_\mathbf{v} L$, then there exists an expression N^* such that $M \longmapsto_\mathbf{v} N^*$ and $N^* \hookrightarrow_\mathbf{v} L$.

Proof for Lemma 5.6: By double lexicographic induction on the size of the derivation of $M \hookrightarrow_\mathbf{v} N$ and the structure of M. It proceeds by case analysis on the last step of in the derivation of $M \hookrightarrow_\mathbf{v} N$:

- **Case** $M = N$

  In this case, the conclusion vacuously holds.

- **Case** $M = (o^m \, b_1 \, \ldots \, b_m)$, $N = \delta(o^m, b_1, \ldots, b_m)$

  Since the result of a δ-step is a value, it is impossible that N standard reduces to some other expression.

- **Case** $M = ((\lambda X.K) \, U)$, $N = L[X \leftarrow V]$, $K \hookrightarrow_\mathbf{v} L$, $U \hookrightarrow_\mathbf{v} V$

  M is also a $\beta_\mathbf{v}$-redex, and therefore $M \longmapsto_\mathbf{v} K[X \leftarrow U]$. Next, by lemma 4.7

  $$K[X \leftarrow U] \hookrightarrow_\mathbf{v} L[X \leftarrow V]$$

  In lemma 5.8, we also show that this derivation is smaller than the derivation of $M \hookrightarrow_\mathbf{v} N$. By induction hypothesis, there must be an expression N^* such that $K[X \leftarrow U] \longmapsto_{\mathbf{v}}$ $N^* \hookrightarrow_{\mathbf{v}} L[X \leftarrow V]$. Hence we can prove the desired conclusion as follows:

$$M \longmapsto_{\mathbf{v}} K[X \leftarrow U] \longmapsto_{\mathbf{v}} N^* \hookrightarrow_{\mathbf{v}} L[X \leftarrow V]$$

- **Case** $M = (M'\ M'')$, $N = (N'\ N'')$, $M' \hookrightarrow_{\mathbf{v}} N'$, $M'' \hookrightarrow_{\mathbf{v}} N''$
  Here we distinguish three subcases according to the standard reduction step from N to L:

  - **Case** $N = ((\lambda X.K')\ N'')$ where $N'' \in V$
    That is, N is a $\beta_{\mathbf{v}}$-redex and L is its contractum. By the assumed parallel reductions and lemma 5.7 below, there exist $(\lambda X.K)$ and N^{**} such that

    $$M' \longmapsto\!\!\!\!\twoheadrightarrow_{\mathbf{v}} (\lambda X.K) \hookrightarrow_{\mathbf{v}} (\lambda X.K')$$

    and $M'' \longmapsto\!\!\!\!\twoheadrightarrow_{\mathbf{v}} N^{**} \hookrightarrow_{\mathbf{v}} N''$. Hence,

    $$
    \begin{aligned}
    (M'\ M'') \quad &\longmapsto\!\!\!\!\twoheadrightarrow_{\mathbf{v}} \quad ((\lambda X.K)\ M'') \\
    &\longmapsto\!\!\!\!\twoheadrightarrow_{\mathbf{v}} \quad ((\lambda X.K)\ N^{**}) \\
    &\longmapsto_{\mathbf{v}} \quad K[X \leftarrow N^{**}] \\
    &\hookrightarrow_{\mathbf{v}} \quad K'[X \leftarrow N'']
    \end{aligned}
    $$

    which is precisely what the lemma claims.

  - **Case** $N = (E[K]\ N'')$
    Then, $L = (E[K']\ N'')$ where $(K, K') \in \mathbf{v}$ and

    $$M' \hookrightarrow_{\mathbf{v}} E[K] \longmapsto_{\mathbf{v}} E[K']$$

    By the induction hypothesis, which applies because M' is a proper sub-expression of M, this means that there exists an expression N_1^* such that

    $$M' \longmapsto\!\!\!\!\twoheadrightarrow_{\mathbf{v}} N_1^* \hookrightarrow_{\mathbf{v}} E[K']$$

    which implies that

    $$(M'\ M'') \longmapsto\!\!\!\!\twoheadrightarrow_{\mathbf{v}} (N_1^*\ M'') \hookrightarrow_{\mathbf{v}} (E[K']\ N'')$$

    In other words, $N^* = (N_1^*\ M'')$.

  - **Case** $N = (N'\ E[K])$ and $N' \in V$
    In this case, $L = (N'\ E[K'])$ where $(K, K') \in \mathbf{v}$ and

    $$M'' \hookrightarrow_{\mathbf{v}} E[K] \longmapsto_{\mathbf{v}} E[K']$$

The induction hypothesis again implies the existence of an expression N_2^* such that

$$M'' \longmapsto\!\!\!\twoheadrightarrow_\mathbf{v} N_2^* \hookrightarrow_\mathbf{v} E[K']$$

Since M' may not be a value, we apply the following lemma to get a value N_1^* such that

$$M' \longmapsto\!\!\!\twoheadrightarrow_\mathbf{v} N_1^* \hookrightarrow_\mathbf{v} N'$$

Putting it all together, we get

$$
\begin{aligned}
(M'\ M'') &\longmapsto\!\!\!\twoheadrightarrow_\mathbf{v} & (N_1^*\ M'') \\
&\longmapsto\!\!\!\twoheadrightarrow_\mathbf{v} & (N_1^*\ N_2^*) \\
&\longmapsto\!\!\!\twoheadrightarrow_\mathbf{v} & (N_1^*\ N_2^*) \\
&\hookrightarrow_\mathbf{v} & (N'\ E[K'])
\end{aligned}
$$

And thus, $N^* = (N_1^*\ N_2^*)$ in this last subcase.

- **Case** $M = (o^m\ M_1 \dots M_m)$, $N = (o^m\ N_1' \dots N_m')$, $M_i \hookrightarrow_\mathbf{v} N_i$
  The proof is analoguous to the preceding one, though instead of a $\beta_\mathbf{v}$ step the first subcase is a δ-step. That is, all N_i' are basic constants and N standard reduces to a value. Since lemma 5.7 shows that an expression that parallel reduces to a basic constant also standard reduces to it, the rest of the argument is straightforward.

- **Case** $M = (\lambda X.K)$, $N = (\lambda X.L)$, $K \hookrightarrow_\mathbf{v} L$
  This case is again impossible because the standard reduction function is undefined on values.

Lemma 5.7: Let M be an application.

1. If $M \hookrightarrow_\mathbf{v} (\lambda X.N)$ then there exists an expression $(\lambda X.L)$ such that $M \longmapsto\!\!\!\twoheadrightarrow_\mathbf{v} (\lambda X.L) \hookrightarrow_\mathbf{v} (\lambda X.N)$.

2. If $M \hookrightarrow_\mathbf{v} N$ where $N = x$ or $N = b$ then $M \longmapsto\!\!\!\twoheadrightarrow_\mathbf{v} N$.

Proof for Lemma 5.7: Both implications follow from an induction argument on the size of the derivation for the parallel reduction in the antecedent.

1. Only a parallel δ or a parallel $\beta_\mathbf{v}$ reduction can transform an application into a λ-abstraction. Clearly, δ reductions

are also standard reductions and therefore the result is immediate in that case. Parallel β_v redexes are standard redexes. Thus, $M = ((\lambda Y.M')\ U)$, which parallel reduces to $(\lambda X.N) = N'[Y \leftarrow V]$ because $M' \hookrightarrow_v N'$ and $U \hookrightarrow_v V$ by lemma 4.7. Hence,

$$((\lambda Y.M')\ U) \longmapsto_v M'[Y \leftarrow U] \hookrightarrow_v N'[Y \leftarrow V] = (\lambda X.N)$$

By lemma 5.8, we also know that the latter derivation is shorter than the original parallel reduction step and therefore, by inductive hypothesis, there exists a λ expression $(\lambda X.L)$ such that

$$((\lambda Y.M')\ U) \longmapsto_v M'[Y \leftarrow U] \longmapsto_v (\lambda X.L) \hookrightarrow_v (\lambda X.N)$$

2. Again, the only two parallel reductions that can transform a redex in the shape of an application into a constant or variable are δ and the β_v (parallel) reductions. Thus the argument proceeds as for the first part.

This covers all cases and wraps up the proof.

Lemma 5.8: If $M \hookrightarrow_v N$ has size s_M and $U \hookrightarrow_v V$ has size s_U then (i) $M[X \leftarrow U] \hookrightarrow_v N[X \leftarrow V]$ and (ii)

$$|\ M[X \leftarrow U] \hookrightarrow_v N[X \leftarrow V]\ | \leq s_M + \#(X, N) \times s_U$$

Remark 1: This lemma strengthens lemma 4.7. For completeness, we repeat the original proof and add annotations that validate the claim.

Remark 2: The lemma implies that the size of the derivation of $((\lambda X.M)\ U) \hookrightarrow_v N[X \leftarrow V]$ is strictly larger than the size of $M[X \leftarrow U] \hookrightarrow_v N[X \leftarrow V]$.

Proof for Lemma 5.8: The proof is an induction on M and proceeds by case analysis on the last step in the derivation of $M \hookrightarrow_v N$:

- **Case $M = N$**
  In this special case, the claim says that if $U \hookrightarrow_v V$ then $M[X \leftarrow U] \hookrightarrow_v M[X \leftarrow V]$. *As to the claim about size: the assumption implies that $s_M = 0$, and therefore it must be true that $s \leq \#(X, M) \times s_U$.* The derivation of this specialized claim is an induction on the structure of M:

– **Case** $M = b$
$M[X \leftarrow U] = b \hookrightarrow_{\mathbf{v}} b = M[X \leftarrow V]$;
Size: $s = 0$.

– **Case** $M = X$
$M[X \leftarrow U] = U \hookrightarrow_{\mathbf{v}} V = M[X \leftarrow V]$;
Size: $s = s_U = \#(X, M) \times s_U$.

– **Case** $M = Y \neq X$
$M[X \leftarrow U] = y \hookrightarrow_{\mathbf{v}} y = M[X \leftarrow V]$;
Size: $s = 0$.

– **Case** $M = (\lambda Y.K)$
By induction hypothesis for K:

$$
\begin{aligned}
M[X \leftarrow U] \quad &= \quad (\lambda Y.K[X \leftarrow U)] \\
&\hookrightarrow_{\mathbf{v}} \quad (\lambda Y.K[X \leftarrow V]) \\
&= \quad M[X \leftarrow V]
\end{aligned}
$$

Size: $s = \#(X, K) \times s_U = \#(X, M) \times s_U$.

– **Case** $M = (K\ L)$
By induction hypothesis for K, L:

$$
\begin{aligned}
M[X \leftarrow U] \quad &= \quad (K[X \leftarrow U]\ L[X \leftarrow U]) \\
&\hookrightarrow_{\mathbf{v}} \quad (K[X \leftarrow V]\ L[X \leftarrow V]) \\
&= \quad M[X \leftarrow V]
\end{aligned}
$$

Size: $s = \#(X, K) \times s_U + \#(X, L) \times s_U = \#(X, M) \times s_U$.

• **Case** $M = (o^m\ b_1 \dots b_m), N = \delta(o^m, b_1, \dots, b_m)$
M and N are closed, so $M[X \leftarrow U] = M$, $N[X \leftarrow V] = N$,
and the result follows directly from the assumption.
Size: $s = 0$.

• **Case** $M = ((\lambda Y.K)\ W), N = L[y \leftarrow W'], K \hookrightarrow_{\mathbf{v}} L$, **and**
$W \hookrightarrow_{\mathbf{v}} W'$

A simple calculation shows that the claim holds:

$$
\begin{aligned}
M[X \leftarrow U] \quad &= \quad ((\lambda Y.K[X \leftarrow U])\ W[X \leftarrow U]) \\
&\hookrightarrow_{\mathbf{v}} \quad L[X \leftarrow V][Y \leftarrow W'[X \leftarrow V]] \\
&= \quad L[Y \leftarrow W'][X \leftarrow V] \qquad (\dagger) \\
&= \quad N[X \leftarrow V]
\end{aligned}
$$

Equation ($\dagger$) follows from a simple induction on the structure of L, which we leave as an exercise.

The size of the derivation is calculated as follows. Let us assume the following conventions about sizes:

$$s_K : \quad K \hookrightarrow_v L$$
$$s_K' : \quad K[X \leftarrow U] \hookrightarrow_v L[X \leftarrow V]$$
$$s_W : \quad W \hookrightarrow_v W'$$
$$s_W' : \quad W[X \leftarrow U] \hookrightarrow_v W'[X \leftarrow V]$$

By induction hypothesis,

$$s_K' \quad \leq \quad s_K + \#(X, L) \times s_U$$
$$s_W' \quad \leq \quad s_W + \#(X, W') \times s_U$$

Hence, the size for the entire derivation is

$$
\begin{aligned}
s \quad &= \quad s_K' + \#(Y, L) \times s_W' + 1 \\
&\leq \quad s_K + \#(X, L) \times s_U + \\
&\qquad \#(Y, L) \times (s_W + \#(X, W') \times s_U) + 1 \\
&= \quad s_K + \#(Y, L) \times s_W + 1 + (\#(Y, L) \times \#(X, W') + \\
&\qquad \#(X, L)) \times s_U \\
&= \quad s_M + \#(X, N) \times s_U
\end{aligned}
$$

- **Case** $M = (M_1 \ M_2)$, $N = (N_1 \ N_2)$, $M_i \hookrightarrow_v N_i$
  By the induction hypothesis, $M_i[X \leftarrow U] \hookrightarrow_v N_i[X \leftarrow V]$ for both $i = 1$ and $i = 2$. Thus,

$$
\begin{aligned}
M[X \leftarrow U] \quad &= \quad (M_1[X \leftarrow U] \ M_2[X \leftarrow U)] \\
&\hookrightarrow_v \quad (N_1[X \leftarrow V] \ N_2[X \leftarrow V)] \\
&= \quad (N_1 \ N_2)[X \leftarrow V] \\
&= \quad N[X \leftarrow V]
\end{aligned}
$$

For the size argument, we begin again with conventions:

$$s_i : \quad M_i \hookrightarrow_v N_i$$
$$s_i' : \quad M_i[X \leftarrow U] \hookrightarrow_v N_i[X \leftarrow V]$$

Thus, by induction hypothesis,

$$s_i' \leq s_i + \#(X, N_i) \times s_U$$

The rest follows from a simple calculation:

$$
\begin{aligned}
s &= s_1' + s_2' \\
&\leq s_1 + \#(X, N_1) \times s_U + s_2 + \#(X, N_2) \times s_U \\
&= s_1 + s_2 + (\#(X, N_1) + \#(X, N_2)) \times s_U \\
&= s_M + \#(X, N) \times s_U
\end{aligned}
$$

- **Case** $M = (o^m \, M_1 \ldots M_m)$, $N = (o^m \, N_1' \ldots N_m')$, $M_i \hookrightarrow_{\mathbf{v}} N_i$
  Analogous to the previous case.
- **Case** $M = (\lambda X.K)$, $N = (\lambda X.L)$, $K \hookrightarrow_{\mathbf{v}} L$
  Analogous to the previous case.

The first reward of working through the proof of the Standard Reduction Theorem is a proof of lemma 5.3, the missing piece of the correctness proof for the abstract syntax machine.

Lemma 5.3, Restated: $M \twoheadrightarrow_{\mathbf{v}} U$ if and only if $M \longmapsto\!\!\!\twoheadrightarrow_{\mathbf{v}} V$ for some value V and $V \twoheadrightarrow_{\mathbf{v}} U$.

In particular, if $U \in b$ then $M \twoheadrightarrow_{\mathbf{v}} U$ if and only if $M \longmapsto\!\!\!\twoheadrightarrow_{\mathbf{v}} U$.

Proof for Lemma 5.3:   To prove the left to right direction, assume that

$$ M \twoheadrightarrow_{\mathbf{v}} U $$

and that M is not a value. It follows from theorem 5.5 that there exists a standard reduction sequence $L_1 \diamond \ldots \diamond L_p$ such that $M = L_1$ and $L_p = U$. By induction on the length of the sequence, there exists an index i such that L_i is the first value in the sequence and

$$ M = L_1 \longmapsto\!\!\!\twoheadrightarrow_{\mathbf{v}} L_i $$

Set $V = L_i$; trivially, $L_i \twoheadrightarrow_{\mathbf{v}} U$. Moreover, constants can occur only at the end of a standard reduction sequence of values if the standard reduction sequence is a singleton. Hence, the second part of the lemma concerning basic constants obviously holds.

In summary, we have shown that the specification of the evaluation function based on the equational system is equivalent to an evaluator based on the standard reduction function. Since the latter is a truly algorithmic specification, we can now implement the evaluator without complex searches.

5·3 **Reasoning about Observational Equivalence.** The end of the preceding chapter introduces the notion of observational equivalence. This relation is the largest congruence relation that is consistent with $=_\mathbf{v}$, so it equates an expression M with a value V if the former reduces to the latter. Finally, theorem 4.11 shows that reasoning with the ISWIM calculus is sound but incomplete with respect to observational equivalence, except that we did not completely finish the proof of this theorem. The second reward of the Standard Reduction Theorem is a proof of the observational equivalence

$$(\Omega\ \Omega) \simeq_\mathbf{v} \Omega$$

which in turn finishes the Incompleteness theorem.

Our key tool for this proof is the notion of an active expression. An expression in a program becomes active during the evaluation process if it has to be evaluated in order to make progress toward the final answer. The standard reduction relation naturally captures this idea. In order to formulate this idea as a provable lemma we start with the definition of the **kind** of an expression.

> Two expressions are **of the same kind**
> if and only if
> both are values or both are applications.

Lemma 5.9 [Activity]: If $eval_\mathbf{v}(C[M])$ is defined for a closed expression M and context C, then

(i) either $eval_\mathbf{v}(C[M'])$ is defined for all closed expressions M' that are of the same kind as M; or

(ii) for all closed expressions M' that are of the same kind as M, there is some evaluation context E such that

(a) if M is an application, then

$$C[M'] \longmapsto\!\!\!\rightarrow_\mathbf{v} E[M']$$

(b) if M is a λ-abstraction, then for some U,

$$C[M'] \longmapsto\!\!\!\rightarrow_\mathbf{v} E[(M'\ U)]$$

(c) if M is a constant, then for some primitive o^n, some values $V_1, \ldots, V_m$, and expressions $N_1, \ldots, N_p$,

$$C[M'] \longmapsto\!\!\!\rightarrow_\mathbf{v} E[(o^n\ V_1\ \ldots\ V_m\ M'\ N_1 \ldots\ N_p)]$$

Proof for Lemma 5.9: Intuitively, the proof proceeds by induction on the number of standard reduction steps in the reduction:

$$C[M] \longmapsto\!\!\!\twoheadrightarrow_{\mathbf{v}} V$$

However, because M may be duplicated during $\beta_{\mathbf{v}}$-reductions, the induction hypothesis needs to be strengthened. The stronger claim is the subject of the following lemma.

An appropriate generalization of the Activity Lemma requires the notion of a multi-hole context, which naturally generalizes the concept of a context.

$$
\begin{aligned}
\overline{C} \quad = \quad & [\,]_n \\
| \quad & M \\
| \quad & (\lambda x.\overline{C}) \\
| \quad & (\overline{C}\ \overline{C}) \\
| \quad & (o^n\ \overline{C} \ldots \overline{C})
\end{aligned}
$$

If $\overline{C}$ is a multi-hole context with m holes, it is well-formed if each hole $[\,]$ has a distinct label $i \in [1, m]$.

If $\overline{C}$ is a multi-hole context with m holes, then $\overline{C}[M_1, \ldots, M_n]$ for $n \leq m$ means the expression generated by replacing each $[\,]_i$ in $\overline{C}$ with M_i.

The stronger version of lemma 5.9 re-states the claim for m expressions and contexts with m holes.

Lemma 5.10: If $eval_{\mathbf{v}}(\overline{C}[M_1, \ldots, M_m])$ is defined for closed expressions $M_1, \ldots, M_m$ and a context $\overline{C}$ with m holes, then

(i) either $eval_{\mathbf{v}}(\overline{C}[M_1', \ldots, M_m'])$ is defined for all closed expressions $M_1', \ldots, M_m'$ that are of the same kind as $M_1, \ldots, M_m$, respectively; or

(ii) for all closed expressions $M_1', \ldots, M_m'$ that are of the same kind as $M_1, \ldots, M_m$, respectively, there is some evaluation context E such that for some $i \in [1, m]$,

(a) if M_i is an application, then

$$\overline{C}[M_1', \ldots, M_m'] \longmapsto\!\!\!\twoheadrightarrow_{\mathbf{v}} E[M_i']$$

(b) if M_i is a λ-abstraction, then for some value U,

$$\overline{C}[M_1', \ldots, M_m'] \longmapsto\!\!\!\!\rightarrow_{\mathbf{v}} E[(M_i'\ U)]$$

(c) if M_i is a constant, then for some primitive o^n, some values $V_1, \ldots, V_m$, and expressions $N_1, \ldots, N_p$,

$$\overline{C}[M_1', \ldots, M_m'] \longmapsto\!\!\!\!\rightarrow_{\mathbf{v}} E[(o^n\ V_1\ \ldots\ V_m\ M_i'\ N_1\ \ldots\ N_p)]$$

Proof for Lemma 5.10: The proof is an induction on the number of steps in the standard reduction sequence for the original program.

If $\overline{C}[M_1, \ldots, M_m]$ is a value, part (i) of the conclusion clearly applies. So, assume that

$$\overline{C}[M_1, \ldots, M_m] \longmapsto_{\mathbf{v}} K \longmapsto\!\!\!\!\rightarrow_{\mathbf{v}} V$$

for some expression K and value V. By theorem 5.1, either the program can be partitioned into an evaluation context E' and a $\beta_{\mathbf{v}}$ redex $(N\ L)$ such that

$$E'[(N\ L)] = \overline{C}[M_1, \ldots, M_m]$$

or an evaluation context E' and a δ redex $(o^n\ b_1'\ \ldots\ b_n')$ such that

$$E'[(o^n\ b_1'\ \ldots\ b_n')] = \overline{C}[M_1, \ldots, M_m]$$

We deal with the first case; the proof of the second case proceeds in an analogous manner.

1. Some expression M_i contains the redex $(N\ L)$ (or is equal to it). Since $(N\ L)$ is an application and E' an evaluation context, this is only possible if M_i is an application. If this is the case, the first clause of part (ii) of the lemma's conclusion holds: for any expressions $M_1', \ldots, M_m'$ of the correct kind,

$$E = \overline{C}[M_1', \ldots, M_{i-1}', [\,]_i, \ldots, M_m']$$

is an evaluation context. The key to this claim is that the expressions $M_1', \ldots, M_m'$ are of the same kind as the expressions $M_1, \ldots, M_m$, respectively. If

$$E' = E_1[(M_j\ E_2)]$$

where M_j, $1 \le j \le m$, is a value, and E_1 and E_2 are evaluation contexts, then if M_j' were an application, E would not be an evaluation context.

2. None of the expressions $M_1, \ldots, M_m$ contains the redex, but the redex contains some of them. Let us split the case:

(a) Some λ-abstraction M_i is N. Now the second clause of part (ii) holds: for all closed expressions $M_1', \ldots, M_m'$,

$$E = \overline{C}[M_1', \ldots, M_{i-1}', [\,]_i, \ldots, M_m']$$

and U differs from L only in occurrences of holes of $\overline{C}$. Again, as in the preceding case, E is an evaluation context because the expressions $M_1', \ldots, M_m'$ are of the right kind. Similarly, if $L = M_j$, for some j, $1 \le j \le m$, then if M_j' were not a value, U would not be a value.

(b) The value N is a λ-abstraction, $\lambda X.N'$, that may contain some of the expressions $M_1, \ldots, M_m$:

$$\begin{aligned}
\overline{C}[M_1, \ldots, M_m] \quad &= \quad E'[((\lambda X.N')\, L)] \\
&\longmapsto_{\mathbf{v}} \quad E'[N'[x \leftarrow L]]
\end{aligned}$$

As in the first subcase, since the expressions $M_1', \ldots, M_m'$ are of the same kind,

$$\begin{aligned}
\overline{C}[M_1', \ldots, M_m'] \quad &= \quad E''[((\lambda X.N'')\, L')] \\
&\longmapsto_{\mathbf{v}} \quad E''[N''[x \leftarrow L']]
\end{aligned}$$

for some evaluation context E'', expression N'', and value L' that differ accordingly from E', N', and L respectively. Since the expressions $M_1, \ldots, M_m$ are closed, there is some context $\overline{C}'$ of q holes and a sequence of indices $1 \le j_1, \ldots, j_q \le m$ such that

$$E'[N'[x \leftarrow L]] = \overline{C}'[M_{j_1}, \ldots, M_{j_q}]$$

and

$$E''[N''[x \leftarrow L']] = \overline{C}'[M_{j_1}', \ldots, M_{j_q}']$$

The intermediate program satisfies the antecedent of our claim; the reduction

$$\overline{C}'[M_{j_1}, \ldots, M_{j_q}] \longmapsto\!\!\!\longrightarrow_{\mathbf{v}} V$$

is shorter than the original one; and therefore the induction hypothesis applies.

Equipped with the Activity Lemma, we are ready to finish theorem 4.11 with the following lemma, which shows the observational equivalence of two expressions that are not provably equal in the ISWIM calculus ($=_\mathbf{v}$).

Lemma 5.11: $\Omega \simeq_\mathbf{v} (\Omega\,\Omega)$

Proof for Lemma 5.11: Assume for some C that $eval_\mathbf{v}(C[\Omega])$ is defined. By the Activity Lemma, it could be the case that for all closed expressions M there is some evaluation context such that

$$C[M] \longmapsto\!\!\!\!\longrightarrow_\mathbf{v} E[M]$$

But this contradicts the assumption that $C[\Omega]$ is defined because $E[\Omega]$ is a diverging program. Hence, $eval_\mathbf{v}(C[M])$ is defined for all closed expressions M and in particular for $M = (\Omega\,\Omega)$.

Conversely, assume that $eval_\mathbf{v}(C[(\Omega\,\Omega)])$ is defined, then by an argument along the same lines, $eval_\mathbf{v}(C[\Omega])$ is defined.

Clearly, if one of the programs returns an abstraction, then so does the other, and both return the same basic constant. In short, for all C,

$$eval_\mathbf{v}(C[(\Omega\,\Omega)]) = eval_\mathbf{v}(C[\Omega])$$

which proves that $\Omega \simeq_\mathbf{v} (\Omega\,\Omega)$.

5·4 Uniform Evaluation.

Using the Standard Reduction Theorem, we can also prove the implicitly made claim that an ISWIM program (1) reduces to a value and therefore $eval_\mathbf{v}$ is defined; (2) reduces to a stuck program; or (3) reduces forever. Indeed, the standard reduction relation equips us with the means to specify stuck states. A program is stuck if the maximal standard reduction sequence starting with a program is of finite length and does not end in a value, i.e.,

$$M_1 \longmapsto_\mathbf{v} M_2 \longmapsto_\mathbf{v} \ldots \longmapsto_\mathbf{v} M_m$$

such that $\longmapsto_\mathbf{v}$ is undefined for some application M_m. Such an irreducible application must contain an application of two values or of a primitive operator to a sequence of values such that neither the $\beta_\mathbf{v}$ nor the δ reduction applies:

$$M_m \;=\; E[(b\,V)]$$

or

$$M_m \;=\; E[(o^n\,V_1 \ldots V_n)] \qquad \text{where some } V_i \text{ is a } \lambda\text{-abstraction}$$
$$\text{or } \delta(o^n, V_1, \ldots, V_n) \text{ is undefined.}$$

Adopting a machine-oriented view, programs for which $\longmapsto_v$ is undefined are called **stuck states**. Stuck states play an important role in the analysis of programming languages. A precise understanding of the stuck states of any given programming language is therefore crucial. We start with a formal definition of ISWIM stuck states.

An application M is **stuck** if

1. $M = (o^m\ b_1 \ldots b_m)$ and $\delta(o^m, b_1, \ldots, b_m)$ is undefined; or

2. $M = (o^m\ V_1 \ldots V_{i-1}\ (\lambda X.N)\ V_{i+1} \ldots V_m)$; or

3. $M = (b\ V)$.

A program M is **stuck** if $M = E[N]$ for some evaluation context E and a stuck application N.

Now we can state and prove the theorem about the uniform evaluation of ISWIM programs, claimed at the beginning of this section.

Theorem 5.12 [Uniform Evaluation]: If M is a closed expression, then either

1. $M \longmapsto\!\!\!\!\twoheadrightarrow_v V$ for some value V;

2. $M \longmapsto\!\!\!\!\twoheadrightarrow_v N$ for some stuck program N; or

3. for all N such that $M \longmapsto\!\!\!\!\twoheadrightarrow_v N$, there exists an expression L such that $N \longmapsto_v L$.

Proof for Theorem 5.12: Unless M is at the beginning of an infinite sequence of $\longmapsto_v$ reduction steps (case 3), we may assume there exists an N such that $M \longmapsto\!\!\!\!\twoheadrightarrow_v N$ and $\longmapsto_v$ is undefined for N. That is,

$$M = M_1 \longmapsto_v M_2 \longmapsto_v M_3 \longmapsto_v \ldots \longmapsto_v M_m = N$$

By the Unique Evaluation Context Lemma N is either a value (case 1) or there is an evaluation context E, possibly a primitive o^n, and values $U, V, V_1, \ldots, V_n$ such that

$$N = E[(U\ V)] \text{ or } N = E[(o^n\ V_1\ \ldots\ V_n)]$$

If the applications in the hole are redexes, we have a contradiction to our assumption that N is irreducible. Hence, U is not a λ-abstraction but instead a basic constant. Similarly, some V_i

must not be a basic constant or $\delta(o^n, V_1, \ldots, V_n)$ is not defined. Hence, N is a stuck program (case 3).

In conclusion, programs either diverge, reduce to a value, or get to a stuck state.

While logicians usually look for the most elegant proof of a theorem, computer scientists are happy with any proof. The proof of the Uniform Evaluation Theorem, however, is an exception. It is possible to prove it with a technique that applies to a number of different situations relevant to computer scientists.

The alternative proof starts with a description of the "good" expression.

> An expression satisfies the **VSR property** if
>
> 1. it a value, or
>
> 2. it is a stuck expression, or
>
> 3. it contains a standard redex.

The key insight is that the standard reduction of a good expression produces a good expression and that all such expressions are able to make progress via standard reduction, unless they are values or stuck.

Lemma 5.13 [Preservation]: If M satisfies the *VSR* property and if for some N, $M \longmapsto_{\mathbf{v}} N$, then N satisfies the *VSR* property.

Lemma 5.14 [Progress]: All expressions M that satisfy *VSR* are either values, stuck expressions or there exists an N such that $M \longmapsto_{\mathbf{v}} N$.

From these lemmas, the proof of uniform evaluation follows immediately.

Proof for Theorem 5.12: By progress, M satisfies the *VSR* property. Hence, unless it is a value or a stuck expression, there exists an N such that $M \longmapsto_{\mathbf{v}} N$. By preservation, N also satisfies *VSR*. Thus, unless M is at the beginning of an infinite sequence of $\longmapsto_{\mathbf{v}}$ steps, it reduces to a value or to a stuck state.

Chapter 8 defines a language with a uniform treatment of stuck states.

Exercise 5.3. Prove lemma 5.14. Hint: Use the Unique Evaluation Context Lemma.

Exercise 5.4. Prove lemma 5.13.

5·5 **History.** As discussed in the history section of the preceding chapter, the development and investigation of ISWIM's calculus is due to Plotkin [83]. For the Standard Reduction Theorem, Plotkin's work heavily relies on Curry and Feys's comprehensive study of Combinatory Logic [24]. The presentation here takes Felleisen and Friedman's [34] formulation of the standard reduction function in terms of evaluation contexts, a small insight from their effort to scale Plotkin's programs to languages with effects. The Activity Lemma is a first step to reason about observational equivalence and comes from Plotkin's work [84] on the full abstraction problem, i.e., the search for a mathematical model of a sequential programming language whose theory of equality coincides with observational equivalence.

Exercise 5.5. Design a standard reduction function and an evaluator based on standard reduction for the call-by-name variant of ISWIM developed in exercise 4.10. Remember to re-use the fundamental notion of reduction from exercise 4.10, but change whatever else requires changing. Where do the call-by-value and the call-by-name standard reduction functions differ? Prove the equivalence between the evaluator based on the equational ISWIM calculus and the one based on standard reduction.

6 • Abstract Register Machines

Depending on the context, the efficiency of an evaluator may not matter. For example, if the goal is simply to define $eval_v^s$ formally, then efficiency is of no interest, and the standard reduction relation is a good compromise between a general calculus and a machine. If we want to explain how to *implement* a programming language, however, then we may want to formulate an abstract machine that is easily and efficiently translatable into a program in an existing programming language.

In this chapter, we derive a series of more and more efficient machines, starting from the syntactic machine based on the standard reduction function. We begin with the observation that this machine must dissect the program into an evaluation context and a "machine instruction" for every single step. From there we proceed to separate the "instructions" from the evaluation context; to make the representation for the evaluation context efficient for its primary uses; and to finally eliminate the overhead of substitutions via environments. For each stage, we show how to prove the correctness of the new machine design by defining an evaluator based on the machine and proving its equivalence to the preceding evaluators.

6·1 The CC Machine.
Every evaluation cycle in the syntactic machine based of the preceding chapter performs three steps. First, it tests whether the program is a value; if so, the machine stops. Second, and otherwise, the machine partitions the program into an evaluation context, E, and an application, $(U\ V)$ or $(o^n\ V_1 \ldots V_n)$. Third and finally, if the application is a β_v or δ redex, the machine constructs the contractum M and fills the evaluation context E with the contractum M. The result of such a step is the next machine state, and the evaluation cycle starts over from here.

An obvious inefficiency in this machine is the repeated partitioning of a program into an evaluation context and a redex. Clearly, the evaluation context of the $n + 1$st step is closely related to the one for the nth step. For example, consider the evaluation of

$$(\text{add1}\ ((\lambda x.((\lambda y.((\lambda z.x)\ \ulcorner 3 \urcorner))\ \ulcorner 2 \urcorner))\ \ulcorner 1 \urcorner))$$

which is a fairly typical example:

$$(\text{add1}\ \underline{((\lambda x.((\lambda y.((\lambda z.x)\ \ulcorner 3 \urcorner))\ \ulcorner 2 \urcorner))\ \ulcorner 1 \urcorner)})$$

$$\longmapsto_v \quad (\text{add1 } \underline{((\lambda y.((\lambda z.\ulcorner 1\urcorner)\ \ulcorner 3\urcorner))\ \ulcorner 2\urcorner)})$$
$$\longmapsto_v \quad (\text{add1 } \underline{((\lambda z.\ulcorner 1\urcorner)\ \ulcorner 3\urcorner)})$$
$$\longmapsto_v \quad (\text{add1 } \underline{\ulcorner 1\urcorner})$$
$$\longmapsto_v \quad \ulcorner 2\urcorner.$$

The redexes in each intermediate state are underlined, the evaluation context is the part of the term that is plain; it is (add1 []) for the first three states, but the machine has to recompute this fact for every stage.

To eliminate the repeated context recognition, we can separate program states into the "current subterm of interest" and the "current evaluation context." Putting the former into the hole of the latter yields the complete program. Following tradition, we refer to the term of interest as the **control string** M and the evaluation context simply as the **context** E. These two elements are paired together to form the machine's states: $\langle M, E \rangle$. The machine is called the **CC machine**.

In addition to the reduction tasks of the syntactic machine, the CC machine is responsible for finding the redex. Initially, the entire program is the control string, and the initial evaluation context is the empty context. The machine's search instructions implement rules 1 and 2' from the beginning of the previous chapter. That is, if the control string is not an application that consists of values, the leftmost non-value becomes the control string, and the rest becomes a part of the evaluation context.

For example, if the control string is $((K\ L)\ M)$ and the evaluation context is E, then the machine must search for the redex in $(K\ L)$, and it must remember the shape of the rest of the program. Consequently the next state of the machine must have $(K\ L)$ as the control string component and must refine the current context E to a context of the shape $E[([]\ M)]$. In other words, the CC machine must have a state transition of the form

$$\langle (M\ N), E \rangle \longmapsto_v \langle M, E[([]\ N)] \rangle \quad \text{if} \quad M \notin V$$

Search rules for other shapes of applications are needed, too.

After the control string becomes a redex, the CC machine must simulate the actions of the syntactic machine on a redex. Thus it must have the following two instructions:

$$\langle (o^m\ b_1 \ldots b_m), E \rangle \quad \longmapsto_v \quad \langle V, E \rangle \text{ where } V = \delta(o^m, b_1, \ldots, b_m) \qquad [\text{ccffi}]$$
$$\langle ((\lambda X.M)V), E \rangle \quad \longmapsto_v \quad \langle M[X \leftarrow V], E \rangle \qquad\qquad\qquad\qquad [\text{ccfi}_v]$$

The result of such a transition can be a state that pairs a value with an evaluation context. In the syntactic machine, this corresponds to a step of the form $E[L] \longmapsto_v E[V]$. The syntactic machine would then divide $E[V]$ into a new redex L' and a new evaluation context E' that is distinct from E. But the syntactic machine clearly does not pick random pieces from the evaluation context to form the next redex. If $E = E^*[((\lambda X.M) [])]$, then $E' = E^*$ and $L' = ((\lambda X.M) V)$. That is, the new redex is formed from the innermost application in E, and E' is the rest of E.

Thus, for a faithful and efficient simulation of the syntactic machine, the CC machine needs a set of instructions that exploit the information surrounding the hole of the context when the control string is a value. In the running example, the CC machine would have to make a transition like this:

$$\langle V, E^*[((\lambda X.M) [])]\rangle \longmapsto \langle ((\lambda X.M) V), E^*\rangle$$

At this point, the control string is an application again, and the search process starts over.

Putting it all together, the evaluation process on a CC machine consists of shifting pieces of the control string into the evaluation context such that the control string becomes a redex. Once the control string has turned into a redex, an ordinary contraction occurs. If the result is a value, the machine must shift pieces of the evaluation context back to the control string.

Our analysis covers all the cases now, and it is time to define the transition function for the CC machine ($\longmapsto_{cc}$) and the induced evaluator.

$$eval_{cc}(M) = \begin{cases} b & \text{if } \langle M, []\rangle \longmapsto\!\!\!\!\twoheadrightarrow_{cc} \langle b, []\rangle \\ \text{function} & \text{if } \langle M, []\rangle \longmapsto\!\!\!\!\twoheadrightarrow_{cc} \langle \lambda X.N, []\rangle \end{cases}$$

$\longmapsto_{cc}$		
$\langle (M\ N), E\rangle$ $\quad$ if $M \notin V$	$\langle M, E[([]\ N)]\rangle$	[cc1]
$\langle (V\ M), E\rangle$ $\quad$ if $M \notin V$	$\langle M, E[(V\ [])]\rangle$	[cc2]
$\langle (o^n\ V_1 \ldots V_i\ M\ N \ldots), E\rangle$ $\quad$ if $M \notin V$	$\langle M, E[(o^n\ V_1 \ldots V_i\ []\ N \ldots)]\rangle$	[cc3]
$\langle ((\lambda X.M)\ V), E\rangle$	$\langle M[X \leftarrow V], E\rangle$	[ccfi$_v$]
$\langle (o^m\ b_1 \ldots b_m), E\rangle$	$\langle \delta(o^m, b_1, \ldots, b_m), E\rangle$	[ccffi]
$\langle V, E[(U\ [])]\rangle$	$\langle (U\ V), E\rangle$	[cc4]
$\langle V, E[([]\ N)]\rangle$	$\langle (V\ N), E\rangle$	[cc5]
$\langle V, E[(o^n\ V_1 \ldots V_i\ []\ N \ldots)]\rangle$	$\langle (o^n\ V_1 \ldots V_i\ V\ N \ldots), E\rangle$	[cc6]

The relation $\longmapsto\!\!\!\!\twoheadrightarrow_{cc}$ denotes the transitive-reflexive closure of $\longmapsto_{cc}$.

By the derivation of the CC machine, it is almost obvious that it faithfully implements the syntactic machine. Since evaluation on both machines is defined as a partial function from programs to answers, a formal justification for this claim must show that the two functions are identical.

Theorem 6.1: $eval_{cc} = eval_v^s$.

Proof for Theorem 6.1: We need to show that if $eval_{cc}(M) = A$ then $eval_v^s(M) = A$ and vice versa. By the definition of the two evaluation functions, this requires a proof that

$$M \longmapsto\!\!\!\rightarrow_v V \quad \text{if and only if} \quad \langle M, [\,] \rangle \longmapsto\!\!\!\rightarrow_{cc} \langle V, [\,] \rangle$$

When the machine reaches a stuck state or is in an infinite execution sequence, the evaluator is undefined.

A natural approach to the proof of this claim is an induction of the length of the given transition sequence. Since intermediate states have non-empty evaluation contexts, however, we need a stronger induction hypothesis than the theorem statement:

for all E, M, and V:
$E[M] \longmapsto\!\!\!\rightarrow_v V$ if and only if $\langle M, E \rangle \longmapsto\!\!\!\rightarrow_{cc} \langle V, [\,] \rangle$

This hypothesis clearly implies the general theorem. Thus, the rest of the proof is a proof of this intermediate claim. The proof for each direction is an induction on the length of the given reduction sequence.

To prove the left-to-right direction, assume $E[M] \longmapsto\!\!\!\rightarrow_v V$. If the reduction sequence is empty, the conclusion is immediate, so assume there is at least one step:

$$E[M] \longmapsto_v E'[N] \longmapsto\!\!\!\rightarrow_v V$$

where $L\mathbf{v}N$ for some application expression L where $E'[L] = E[M]$. By the inductive hypothesis, $\langle N, E' \rangle \longmapsto\!\!\!\rightarrow_{cc} \langle V, [\,] \rangle$. To conclude the proof, we must show that

$$\langle M, E \rangle \longmapsto\!\!\!\rightarrow_{cc} \langle N, E' \rangle$$

If L is inside M (or the same), then E' must be an extension of E (or the same). Otherwise, M must be a value, because it is inside the redex and also in an evaluation position. Thus, depending on the shape of M and E, there are four possibilities:

- **Case** $M = E''[L]$

  Then, $E' = E[E'']$ meaning the composition of the evaluation contexts E and E'' produces the one for the contractum. We factor out the proof that $\langle M, E \rangle \longmapsto\!\!\!\rightarrow_{cc} \langle L, E[E''] \rangle$ immediately follows (see lemma 6.2 below). Because $L\mathbf{v}N$, a [ccffi] or [ccfi$_v$] transition completes the argument:

  $$\langle L, E[E''] \rangle \longmapsto\!\!\!\rightarrow_{cc} \langle N, E[E''] \rangle$$

- **Case** $E = E'[((\lambda X.N')\,[])], M \in V$

  A first step puts the redex into the control position, which enables a [ccfi$_v$] reduction:

  $$\begin{aligned}
  \langle M, E'[((\lambda X.N')\,[])] \rangle &\longmapsto_{cc} &\langle ((\lambda X.N')\,M), E' \rangle \\
  &\longmapsto_{cc} &\langle N'[X \leftarrow M], E' \rangle
  \end{aligned}$$

  Since the assumptions imply that $N = N'[X \leftarrow M]$, this proves the conclusion.

- **Case** $E = E''[([]\,K)], M \in V$

  We split the case according to the nature of K:

  1. If $K \in V$ then $L = (M\,K)$, which implies the conclusion.
  2. If $K \notin V$ then there exists an evaluation context E''' such that $K = E'''[L]$. Hence, $E' = E''[(M\,E''')]$ and

     $$\begin{aligned}
     \langle M, E''[([]\,K)] \rangle &\longmapsto_{cc} &\langle (M\,K), E'' \rangle \\
     &\longmapsto_{cc} &\langle K, E''[(M\,[])] \rangle \\
     &\longmapsto\!\!\!\rightarrow_{cc} &\langle L, E''[(M\,E''')] \rangle \\
     & &\quad\text{by lemma 6.2} \\
     &\longmapsto\!\!\!\rightarrow_{cc} &\langle N, E''[(M\,E''')] \rangle \\
     &= &\langle N, E' \rangle
     \end{aligned}$$

- **Case** $E = E'[(o^n\,b_1 \ldots []\,\ldots\,b_n)], M \in b$

  Appropriate adaptations of the proofs of the second and third case prove the conclusion.

For the right-to-left direction, assume $\langle M, E \rangle \longmapsto\!\!\!\rightarrow_{cc} \langle V, [] \rangle$. The proof is a again an induction on the number of transition steps. If there are none, then $\langle M, E \rangle = \langle V, [] \rangle$, that is, $M \in V$ and $E = []$, which implies the claim. Otherwise, there is a first transition step:

$$\langle M, E \rangle \longmapsto_{cc} \langle N, E' \rangle \longmapsto\!\!\!\rightarrow_{cc} \langle V, [] \rangle$$

By inductive hypothesis, $E'[N] \longmapsto\!\!\!\to_{\mathbf{v}} V$. The rest of the proof depends on the chosen CC transition from the initial state to $\langle N, E' \rangle$. If the first transition was one of [cc1], ..., [cc6], then $E[M] = E'[N]$, and the conclusion follows. If it is a [ccfi$_{\mathbf{v}}$] or a [ccffi] transition, then $E[M] \longmapsto_{\mathbf{v}} E'[N]$, so $E[M] \longmapsto_{\mathbf{v}} E'[N] \longmapsto\!\!\!\to_{\mathbf{v}} V$.

To complete the preceding proof, we need a lemma about reductions in nested evaluation contexts.

Lemma 6.2: If $M = E'[L]$ and $L \mathbf{v} L'$ for some L', then

$$\langle M, E \rangle \longmapsto\!\!\!\to_{\mathsf{cc}} \langle L, E[E'] \rangle$$

Proof for Lemma 6.2: The proof is an induction on the structure of E'. If $E' = [\,]$ then the conclusion is immediate. Otherwise, E' has one of the following three shapes:

$$E' = (E'' \ N)$$
$$E' = (V \ E'')$$
$$E' = (o^m \ V_1 \ \ldots V_n \ E'' \ N \ldots)$$

In each case, the machine can move the pieces surrounding E'' to the context component, e.g.,

$$\langle (E''[L] \ N), E \rangle \longmapsto_{\mathsf{cc}} \langle E''[L], E[([\,] \ N)] \rangle$$

Since E'' is a component of E', the conclusion follows from the inductive hypothesis.

Exercise 6.1. Show the reduction of

$$\langle \, (\, (\, ((\lambda f.\lambda x.f \ x) \ \lambda y.(+ \ y \ y)) \ \ulcorner 1 \urcorner) \, , [\,] \rangle$$

to $\langle V, [\,] \rangle$ with $\longmapsto_{\mathsf{cc}}$.

Exercise 6.2. Implement the CC machine in a "real world" programming language in a faithful manner, especially with regard to evaluation contexts. What inefficiencies are observable?

$6 \cdot 2$ **The SCC Machine.** The CC machine faithfully immitates the syntactic machine by performing all of the work on the control string. Consider the following example:

$$((\lambda x.x) \ ((\lambda x.x) \ \ulcorner 5 \urcorner))$$

consisting of an application of two applications, which evaluates as follows:

$$\langle((\lambda x.x)\,((\lambda x.x)\,\ulcorner 5\urcorner)),[\,]\rangle \quad \longmapsto_{cc} \quad \langle((\lambda x.x)\,\ulcorner 5\urcorner),((\lambda x.x)\,[\,])\rangle$$
$$\longmapsto_{cc} \quad \langle\ulcorner 5\urcorner,((\lambda x.x)\,[\,])\rangle$$

At this point, the CC machine is forced to construct an application such that one of the application rules can put the second application in the control string register:

$$\cdots \quad \longmapsto_{cc} \quad \langle((\lambda x.x)\,\ulcorner 5\urcorner),[\,]\rangle$$
$$\longmapsto_{cc} \quad \langle\ulcorner 5\urcorner,[\,]\rangle$$

The next-to-last step is needed because the CC machine exploits only information in the control string position for a $[ccfi_v]$ step. One way to simplify the CC machine is to enrich the rules concerning values in the control string position with information about the structure of the context.

A similar simplification is possible when the value returned belongs into the function position. A simple variation of the first example shows how the machine again moves information into the control string even though the next step is clearly a re-combination:

$$\langle(((\lambda x.x)\,(\lambda x.x))\,((\lambda x.x)\,\ulcorner 5\urcorner)),[\,]\rangle$$
$$\longmapsto_{cc} \quad \langle((\lambda x.x)\,(\lambda x.x)),([\,]\,((\lambda x.x)\,\ulcorner 5\urcorner))\rangle$$
$$\longmapsto_{cc} \quad \langle(\lambda x.x),([\,]\,((\lambda x.x)\,\ulcorner 5\urcorner))\rangle$$

Now the machine constructs an application only to move on to the evaluation of the argument expression:

$$\longmapsto_{cc} \quad \langle((\lambda x.x)\,((\lambda x.x)\,\ulcorner 5\urcorner)),[\,]\rangle$$
$$\longmapsto_{cc} \quad \langle((\lambda x.x)\,\ulcorner 5\urcorner),((\lambda x.x)\,[\,])\rangle$$
$$\cdots$$

Instead of constructing the application, the machine could always put the argument into the control register and put the value for the function position into the evaluation context. If the argument is a value, the modified machine can perform a reduction. If not, the current CC machine would have reached this state, too.

Once we have a machine that combines the recognition of a value with the reduction of a redex, when possible, we can also omit the specialized treatment of applications. The current CC machine has three distinct transitions for dealing with applications and three more for dealing with primitive applications. Side-conditions ensure that only one transition applies to any given application. These separate rules are only necessary because the machine performs all the work on the control string and uses the control stack only as a simple memory. Together with the previously suggested simplifications, we can eliminate the side-conditions, the reduction rules, and the rule [cc2], which exists only to move arguments from evaluation contexts into the control string position.

The simplified CC machine has fewer transitions and no side-conditions. Given a state, finding the applicable transition rule is easy. If the control string is an application, shift a fixed portion to the evaluation context and concentrate on one sub-expression. If it is a value, check the innermost application of the evaluation context. If the hole is in the last position of the application, perform a reduction, otherwise swap information between the control string register and the evaluation context register.

$$eval_{\text{scc}}(M) = \begin{cases} b & \text{if } \langle M, [\,] \rangle \longmapsto\!\!\!\!\twoheadrightarrow_{\text{scc}} \langle b, [\,] \rangle \\ \texttt{function} & \text{if } \langle M, [\,] \rangle \longmapsto\!\!\!\!\twoheadrightarrow_{\text{scc}} \langle \lambda X.N, [\,] \rangle \end{cases}$$

$\longmapsto_{\text{scc}}$		
$\langle (M\ N), E \rangle$	$\langle M, E[([\,]\ N)] \rangle$	[scc1]
$\langle (o^m\ M\ N \ldots), E \rangle$	$\langle M, E[(o^m\ [\,]\ N \ldots)] \rangle$	[scc2]
$\langle V, E[((\lambda X.M)\ [\,])] \rangle$	$\langle M[X \leftarrow V], E \rangle$	[scc3]
$\langle V, E[([\,]\ N)] \rangle$	$\langle N, E[(V\ [\,])] \rangle$	[scc4]
$\langle b_m, E[(o^m\ b_1 \ldots b_{m-1}\ [\,])] \rangle$	$\langle \delta(o^m, b_1, \ldots, b_m), E \rangle$	[scc5]
$\langle V, E[(o^n\ V_1 \ldots V_i\ [\,]\ N\ L \ldots)] \rangle$	$\langle N, E[(o^n\ V_1 \ldots V_i\ V[\,]\ L \ldots)] \rangle$	[scc6]

The CC machine and the simplified version define the same evaluator.

Theorem 6.3: $eval_{\text{scc}} = eval_{\text{cc}}$.

Proof for Theorem 6.3: The proof of this theorem is analoguous to the proof of theorem 6.1. That is, unfolding the definition of the two evaluation functions leads to the proof obligation that

$$\langle M, [\,] \rangle \longmapsto\!\!\!\!\twoheadrightarrow_{\text{cc}} \langle V, [\,] \rangle \qquad \text{if and only if} \qquad \langle M, [\,] \rangle \longmapsto\!\!\!\!\twoheadrightarrow_{\text{scc}} \langle V, [\,] \rangle$$

The correct stregthening of this claim to an inductive hypothesis extends it to arbitrary intermediate states:

$$\langle M, E \rangle \longmapsto\!\!\!\!\twoheadrightarrow_{\text{cc}} \langle V, [\,] \rangle \qquad \text{if and only if} \qquad \langle M, E \rangle \longmapsto\!\!\!\!\twoheadrightarrow_{\text{scc}} \langle V, [\,] \rangle$$

The key idea for the proof of the intermediate claim is that for any given program, the CC machine and the SCC machine quickly synchronize at some state provided the initial state leads to a result. More precisely, given $\langle M, E \rangle$ such that $E[M] = E'[L]$ and L is a **v**-redex, there exists a state $\langle N, E'' \rangle$ such that

$$\langle M, E \rangle \longmapsto^+_{cc} \langle N, E'' \rangle \qquad \text{and} \qquad \langle M, E \rangle \longmapsto^+_{scc} \langle N, E'' \rangle$$

By definition, M is either a value or an expression that contains a redex. Moreover, if M is a value, the evaluation context must contain an innermost application: $E = E'[(o \ V_1 \ldots \ V_m \ [] \ N_1 \ldots \ N_n)]$, $E = E'[(V \ [])]$, or $E = E'[([] \ N)]$. Hence, the initial state $\langle M, E \rangle$ falls into one of the following four possibilities:

- **Case** $M = E'[L]$
  The CC machine evaluates the initial state as follows:

$$\langle E'[L], E \rangle \longmapsto\!\!\!\to_{cc} \langle L, E[E'] \rangle \longmapsto_{cc} \langle N, E[E'] \rangle$$

  The SCC machine eventually reaches the same state as the CC machine; the intermediate states though depend on the shape of the redex L. If $L = ((\lambda X.L') \ L'')$, then the SCC machine reaches $\langle L'', E[E'[((\lambda X.L') \ [])]] \rangle$ as the next to last state; otherwise, the next to last state of the SCC transition is $\langle b, E[E'[(o^n \ b_1 \ldots \ b_i \ [])]] \rangle$ where $L = (o^n \ b_1 \ldots b_i \ b)$.

- **Case** $M \in V, E = E'[((\lambda X.L') \ [])]$
  In this case, the CC machine creates a redex in the control component and reduces it:

$$\langle M, E'[((\lambda X.L') \ [])] \rangle \quad \begin{aligned} &\longmapsto_{cc} \quad \langle ((\lambda X.L') \ M), E' \rangle \\ &\longmapsto_{cc} \quad \langle L'[X \leftarrow M], E' \rangle \end{aligned}$$

  The SCC machine avoids the first step and immediately goes into the same state.

- **Case** $M \in V, E = E'[([] \ N)]$
  If $N \in V$, the proof of this case proceeds along the lines of the second case. Otherwise,

$$\langle M, E'[([] \ N)] \rangle \longmapsto_{cc} \langle (M \ N), E' \rangle, \longmapsto_{cc} \langle N, E'[(M \ [])] \rangle$$

  Again, the SCC machine skips the intermediate state.

- **Case** $M \in V, E = E'[(o^p \ V_1 \ldots V_m \ [] \ N_1 \ldots N_n)]$
  The transition sequences depend on the shape of the sequence $N_1, \ldots N_n$. There are three possible cases:

1. If the sequence $N_1, \ldots N_n$ is empty, $M, V_1, \ldots V_m$ must be basic constants and $\delta(o^p, V_1, \ldots V_m, V) = U$ for some value U. It follows that

$$\langle M, E'[(o^p\ V_1 \ldots V_n\ [])]\rangle$$
$$\longmapsto_{cc}\ \langle (o^p\ V_1 \ldots V_n\ M), E'\rangle$$
$$\longmapsto_{cc}\ \langle U, E'\rangle$$

As in the previous case, the SCC machine reaches the final state by skiping the intermediate state.

2. If $N_1, \ldots N_n$ is not empty but $N_1, \ldots N_n \in V$, then

$$\langle M, E'[(o^p\ V_1 \ldots V_m\ []\ N_1 \ldots N_n)]\rangle$$
$$\longmapsto_{cc}\ \langle (o^p\ V_1 \ldots V_m\ M\ N_1 \ldots N_n), E'\rangle$$
$$\longmapsto_{cc}\ \langle U, E'\rangle$$

Now, the SCC machine needs to perform a number of additional steps, which serve to verify that the additional arguments are values:

$$\langle M, E'[(o^p\ V_1 \ldots V_m\ []\ N_1 \ldots N_n)]\rangle$$
$$\longmapsto_{scc}\ \langle N_1, E'[(o\ V_1 \ldots V_m\ M\ []\ N_2 \ldots N_n)]\rangle$$
$$\longmapsto\!\!\!\!\longrightarrow_{scc}\ \cdots$$
$$\longmapsto\!\!\!\!\longrightarrow_{scc}\ \langle N_n, E'[(o^p\ V_1 \ldots\ N_{n-1}\ [])]\rangle$$
$$\longmapsto_{scc}\ \langle U, E'\rangle$$

3. If $N_1, \ldots N_n$ is not empty and $N_i \notin V$, then both machines reach the intermediate state

$$\langle N_i, E'[(o^p\ V_1 \ldots\ V_n N_1 \ldots\ N_{i-1}\ []\ N_{i+1} \ldots)]\rangle$$

after an appropriate number of steps.

The rest of the proof is a straightforward induction on the number of transition steps. The proof for the opposite direction proceeds in the same fashion.

Exercise 6.3. Show the reduction of

$$\langle\,(\,(\,((\lambda f.\lambda x.f\ x)\ \lambda y.(+\ y\ y))\ \ulcorner 1 \urcorner\,),[\,]\,\rangle$$

to $\langle V, [\,]\rangle$ with $\longmapsto_{scc}$.

Exercise 6.4. Implement the SCC machine in a faithful manner, especially with regard to evaluation contexts.

6·3 **The CK Machine.** Each step of an evaluation on the CC or SCC machine refers to the innermost application of the evaluation context, that is, the application that directly contains the hole. Consequently, the transitions always access the evaluation context from the inside and in a last-in, first-out fashion. Transition steps depend on the precise shape of the first element but not on the rest of the data structure chosen to represent contexts.

The observation suggests that the evaluation context register should be a list of applications with a hole, so that the innermost part is easily accessed or added at the front of the list:

$$\begin{aligned}
\kappa &= \kappa_s \ldots \kappa_s \\
\kappa_s &= (V\,[\,]) \mid ([\,]\ N) \mid (o^n\ V \ldots V\,[\,]\ N \ldots N)
\end{aligned}$$

For readability and for ease of implementation, we tag each case of this construction. For efficiency, we also invert the list of values in a primitive application. And finally, we do not use a sequence of frames but an explicitly linked structure, which can be directly implemented.

$$\begin{aligned}
\kappa \quad=\quad & \texttt{mt} \\
\mid\ & \langle \texttt{fn}, V, \kappa \rangle \\
\mid\ & \langle \texttt{ar}, N, \kappa \rangle \\
\mid\ & \langle \texttt{op}, \langle V, \ldots, V, o^n \rangle, \langle N, \ldots, N \rangle, \kappa \rangle
\end{aligned}$$

This data structure is called a **continuation**; κ (the Greek letter *kappa*) is frequently used to range over continuations. Hence the machine is called CK machine; its transition function ($\longmapsto_{ck}$) maps an expression-continuation pair to a new expression-continuation pair.

$$eval_{ck}(M) = \begin{cases} b & \text{if } \langle M, \texttt{mt} \rangle \longmapsto_{ck} \langle b, \texttt{mt} \rangle \\ \texttt{function} & \text{if } \langle M, \texttt{mt} \rangle \longmapsto_{ck} \langle \lambda X.N, \texttt{mt} \rangle \end{cases}$$

$\longmapsto_{ck}$		
$\langle (M\ N), \kappa \rangle$	$\langle M, \langle \texttt{ar}, N, \kappa \rangle \rangle$	[ck1]
$\langle (o^n\ M\ N \ldots), \kappa \rangle$	$\langle M, \langle \texttt{op}, \langle o^n \rangle, \langle N, \ldots \rangle, \kappa \rangle \rangle$	[ck2]
$\langle V, \langle \texttt{fn}, (\lambda X.M), \kappa \rangle \rangle$	$\langle M[X \leftarrow V], \kappa \rangle$	[ck3]
$\langle V, \langle \texttt{ar}, N, \kappa \rangle \rangle$	$\langle N, \langle \texttt{fn}, V, \kappa \rangle \rangle$	[ck4]
$\langle b_m, \langle \texttt{op}, \langle b_{m-1}, \ldots, b_1, o^n \rangle, \langle \rangle, \kappa \rangle \rangle$	$\langle \delta(o^m, b_1, \ldots, b_m), \kappa \rangle$	[ck5]
$\left\langle \begin{array}{c} V, \langle \texttt{op}, \langle U, \ldots, o^n \rangle, \\ \langle N, L, \ldots \rangle, \\ \kappa \rangle \end{array} \right\rangle$	$\left\langle \begin{array}{c} N, \langle \texttt{op}, \langle V, U, \ldots, o^n \rangle, \\ \langle L, \ldots \rangle, \\ \kappa \rangle \end{array} \right\rangle$	[ck6]

The difference between the SCC ad CK machine is one of data structure representation. Hence, all we need is a way to find a corresponding CK state for each SCC state, and vice versa. Such a theorem is easy to state now.

Theorem 6.4: $eval_{ck} = eval_{scc}$.

The key to this proof is to determine a function that maps states in the CK machine to corresponding states in the SCC machine and another function that maps states in the SCC machine to the CK machine.

E	κ
$[\,]$	mt
$E'[([\,]\ N)]$	$\langle \text{ar}, N, \kappa' \rangle$
$E'[(V\ [\,])]$	$\langle \text{fn}, V, \kappa' \rangle$
$E'[(o^n\ V_1 \ldots\ V_i\ [\,]\ N_1 \ldots\ N_k)]$	$\langle \text{op}, \langle V_i, \ldots V_1, o^n \rangle, \langle N_1, \ldots, N_k \rangle, \kappa' \rangle$
where E' corresponds to κ' and vice versa	

Formulating the functions is a straightforward exercise from here.

Proof for Theorem 6.4: Based on the translations between states in the two machines, we can check that

1. if $\langle M, E \rangle \longmapsto_{scc} \langle N, E' \rangle$, then $\langle M, \kappa \rangle \longmapsto_{ck} \langle N, \kappa' \rangle$
2. if $\langle M, \kappa \rangle \longmapsto_{ck} \langle N, \kappa' \rangle$, then $\langle M, E \rangle \longmapsto_{scc} \langle N, E' \rangle$

if E and E' correspond to κ and κ' and vice versa. A simple induction on the length of the transition sequences implies the theorem.

Exercise 6.5. Show the reduction of

$$\langle (\,(\,(\,(\lambda f.\lambda x.f\ x)\ \lambda y.(+\ y\ y))\ \ulcorner 1 \urcorner)\,, \text{mt} \rangle$$

to $\langle V, \text{mt} \rangle$ with $\longmapsto_{ck}$.

Exercise 6.6. Implement the CK machine in a faithful manner, especially with regard to substitutions.

6·4 **The CEK Machine.** For the machines considered so far, the reduction of a β_v-redex requires the substitution of a value for all free occurrences of a variable in an expression. A naive implementation of substitution would be expensive. Furthermore, in the (normal) case that substitution procedures a non-value expression, the machine immediately traverses the result of the substitution again.

This last insight suggests that we delay the work of substitution until it is actually needed. In other words, we keep the substitution around until the machine encounters the variable that is to be replaced and perform the substitution just in time. One way to represent delayed substitutions is to replace expressions with a pair whose first component M is an expression, possibly with free variables, and whose second component is a substitution that covers at least all free variables of M. The pair is called a **closure**; the representation of the substitution is an **environment**. Of course, environments cannot associate variables with plain expressions, because this would re-introduce plain expressions into the machine. An environment must associate variables with closures, too. Thus, the definitions for environments and closures are mututally recursive.

Before we can formulate a machine that uses environments and closures, though, we need to decide how to represent the former. The most natural choice is a finite mapping from variables to closures. Of course, a finite mapping has two views: as a finite set and as a function. In either case, it is possible to compute the domain of an environment, $\mathrm{dom}(\cdot)$, and a "functional" update, $\mathcal{E}[X \leftarrow c]$.

$$
\begin{aligned}
c &= \{\langle M, \mathcal{E}\rangle \mid \mathcal{FV}(M) \subseteq \mathrm{dom}(\mathcal{E})\} \\
v &= \{\langle V, \mathcal{E}\rangle \mid \langle V, \mathcal{E}\rangle \in c\} \\
\mathcal{E} &= \{\langle X_1, c_1\rangle, \dots, \langle X_n, c_n\rangle\}
\end{aligned}
$$

a finite function: for all $i \neq j$, $X_i \neq X_j$

$$
\begin{aligned}
\mathrm{dom}(\{\langle X_1, c_1\rangle, \dots, \langle X_n, c_n\rangle\}) &= \{X_1, \dots, X_n\} \\
\mathrm{rng}(\{\langle X_1, c_1\rangle, \dots, \langle X_n, c_n\rangle\}) &= \{c_1, \dots, c_n\}
\end{aligned}
$$

$$
\mathcal{E}[X \leftarrow c](Y) = \begin{cases} c & \text{if } X = Y \\ \mathcal{E}(Y) & \text{if } X \neq Y \end{cases}
$$

A moment's reflection reminds us that expressions also occur within the continuations in the states of the (S)CC machine. For consistency, we must replace those too with closures.

$$
\begin{aligned}
\overline{\kappa} \quad = \quad & \mathtt{mt} \\
\mid \quad & \langle \mathtt{fn}, v, \overline{\kappa}\rangle \\
\mid \quad & \langle \mathtt{ar}, c, \overline{\kappa}\rangle \\
\mid \quad & \langle \mathtt{op}, \langle v, \dots, v, o^n\rangle, \langle c, \dots, c\rangle, \overline{\kappa}\rangle
\end{aligned}
$$

Based on these defininitions, we can reformulate the CK machine into a machine that works on control strings with environments and modified continuations: the CEK machine. Its transitions are similar to those of the CK machine, except that the delaying of substitutions forces the introduction of a rule for looking up the value of a variable.

$$eval_{\mathsf{cek}}(M) = \left\{ \begin{array}{ll} b & \text{if } \langle\langle M,\varnothing\rangle,\mathtt{mt}\rangle \longmapsto_{\mathsf{cek}} \langle\langle b,\mathcal{E}\rangle,\mathtt{mt}\rangle \\ \mathtt{function} & \text{if } \langle\langle M,\varnothing\rangle,\mathtt{mt}\rangle \longmapsto_{\mathsf{cek}} \langle\langle \lambda X.N,\mathcal{E}\rangle,\mathtt{mt}\rangle \end{array} \right.$$

$\longmapsto_{\mathsf{cek}}$

$\langle\langle (M\ N),\mathcal{E}\rangle,\bar{\kappa}\rangle$	$\langle\langle M,\mathcal{E}\rangle,\langle\mathtt{ar},\langle N,\mathcal{E}\rangle,\bar{\kappa}\rangle\rangle$	[cek1]
$\langle\langle (o^n\ M\ N\ldots),\mathcal{E}\rangle,\bar{\kappa}\rangle$	$\left\langle \begin{array}{l} \langle M,\mathcal{E}\rangle, \\ \langle\mathtt{op},\langle o^n\rangle,\langle\langle N,\mathcal{E}\rangle,\ldots\rangle,\bar{\kappa}\rangle \end{array} \right\rangle$	[cek2]
$\langle\langle V,\mathcal{E}\rangle,\langle\mathtt{fn},\langle(\lambda X_1.M),\mathcal{E}'\rangle,\bar{\kappa}\rangle\rangle$ if $V \notin X$	$\langle\langle M,\mathcal{E}'[X_1 \leftarrow \langle V,\mathcal{E}\rangle]\rangle,\bar{\kappa}\rangle$	[cek3]
$\langle\langle V,\mathcal{E}\rangle,\langle\mathtt{ar},\langle N,\mathcal{E}'\rangle,\bar{\kappa}\rangle\rangle$ if $V \notin X$	$\langle\langle N,\mathcal{E}'\rangle,\langle\mathtt{fn},\langle V,\mathcal{E}\rangle,\bar{\kappa}\rangle\rangle$	[cek4]
$\left\langle \begin{array}{l} \langle b_m,\mathcal{E}\rangle, \\ \langle\mathtt{op},\langle c_{m-1},\ldots,c_1,o^n\rangle, \\ \qquad\langle\rangle,\bar{\kappa}\rangle \end{array} \right\rangle$ where $c_i = \langle b_i,\mathcal{E}_i\rangle$	$\langle\langle\delta(o^m,b_1,\ldots,b_m),\varnothing\rangle,\bar{\kappa}\rangle$	[cek5]
$\left\langle \begin{array}{l} \langle V,\mathcal{E}\rangle, \\ \langle\mathtt{op},\langle c,\ldots,o^n\rangle, \\ \qquad\langle\langle N,\mathcal{E}_N\rangle,c_L,\ldots\rangle,\bar{\kappa}\rangle \end{array} \right\rangle$ if $V \notin X$	$\left\langle \begin{array}{l} \langle N,\mathcal{E}_N\rangle, \\ \langle\mathtt{op},\langle\langle V,\mathcal{E}\rangle,c,\ldots,o^n\rangle, \\ \qquad\langle c_L,\ldots\rangle,\bar{\kappa}\rangle \end{array} \right\rangle$	[cek6]
$\langle\langle X,\mathcal{E}\rangle,\bar{\kappa}\rangle$	$\langle v,\bar{\kappa}\rangle$ where $v = \mathcal{E}(X)$	[cek7]

The CEK machine perfectly simulates the CK machine.

Theorem 6.5: $eval_{\mathsf{cek}} = eval_{\mathsf{ck}}$.

As in the preceding sections, the key to this proof is to find a correspondence between closures and expressions, in particular, that a closure's environment represents a number of delayed substitutions:

$$\mathcal{U}(\langle M,\{\langle X_1,c_1\rangle,\ldots\langle X_n,c_n\rangle\}\rangle) = M[X_1 \leftarrow \mathcal{U}(c_1)]\ldots[X_n \leftarrow \mathcal{U}(c_n)]$$

Plotkin dubbed this translation from closures to closed expressions an "unload" function.

Since closures also occur inside of CEK continuation codes, the translation of CEK states into CK states also requires a traversal of CEK continuation codes that replaces these closures with closed expressions:

$$
\mathcal{T}_{\mathsf{cek}\to\mathsf{ck}}(\overline{\kappa}) = \begin{cases} [\,], & \text{if } \overline{\kappa} = \mathtt{mt} \\ \langle \mathtt{ar}, \mathcal{U}(c), \mathcal{T}_{\mathsf{cek}\to\mathsf{ck}}(\overline{\kappa}') \rangle, & \text{if } \overline{\kappa} = \langle \mathtt{ar}, c, \overline{\kappa}' \rangle \\ \langle \mathtt{fn}, \mathcal{U}(c), \mathcal{T}_{\mathsf{cek}\to\mathsf{ck}}(\overline{\kappa}') \rangle, & \text{if } \overline{\kappa} = \langle \mathtt{fn}, c, \overline{\kappa}' \rangle \\ \langle \mathtt{op}, \langle \mathcal{U}(c'), \ldots o^n \rangle, \langle \mathcal{U}(c), \ldots \rangle, \mathcal{T}_{\mathsf{cek}\to\mathsf{ck}}(\overline{\kappa}') \rangle, \\ \qquad \text{if } \overline{\kappa} = \langle \mathtt{op}, \langle c', \ldots o^n \rangle, \langle c, \ldots \rangle, \overline{\kappa}' \rangle \end{cases}
$$

Unfortunately, it is impossible to define inverses of the $\mathcal{U}$ and $\mathcal{T}_{\mathsf{cek}\to\mathsf{ck}}$ functions. Given a closed expression, there are usually many closures that map to this expression via $\mathcal{U}$. As a result, the simple proof method for verifying equivalence theorems for evaluators fails here, and we need a slightly more sophisticated argument.

Proof for Theorem 6.5: Given the translation from CEK states, we can check that for any intermediate state $\langle c, \overline{\kappa} \rangle$ in an execution sequence of CEK states, there is a state $\langle c', \overline{\kappa}' \rangle$ such that

$$
\langle c, \overline{\kappa} \rangle \longmapsto\!\!\!\!\rightarrow_{\mathsf{cek}} \langle c', \overline{\kappa}' \rangle
$$

and

$$
\langle \mathcal{U}(c), \mathcal{T}_{\mathsf{cek}\to\mathsf{ck}}(\overline{\kappa}) \rangle \longmapsto_{\mathsf{ck}} \langle \mathcal{U}(c', \mathcal{T}_{\mathsf{cek}\to\mathsf{ck}}(\overline{\kappa}')) \rangle
$$

The "stuttering" is due to the variable lookup rule [cek7] in the CEK transition function. Hence, by induction,

$$
\langle \langle M, \varnothing \rangle, \mathtt{mt} \rangle \longmapsto\!\!\!\!\rightarrow_{\mathsf{cek}} \langle \langle V, \mathcal{E} \rangle, \mathtt{mt} \rangle
$$

implies

$$
\langle M, \mathtt{mt} \rangle \longmapsto\!\!\!\!\rightarrow_{\mathsf{ck}} \langle \mathcal{U}(\langle V, \mathcal{E} \rangle), \mathtt{mt} \rangle
$$

which proves the left-to-right direction.

As mentioned, the right-to-left direction requires a stronger induction hypothesis than the left-to-right direction. In addition to the initial state of the transition sequence of the CK machine, we need to know the initial state of the CEK machine:

For every CK state $\langle M_1, \kappa_1 \rangle$ and CEK state $\langle \langle M_1', \mathcal{E} \rangle, \overline{\kappa}_1' \rangle$ such that $M_1 = \mathcal{U}(\langle M_1', \mathcal{E} \rangle)$ and $\kappa_1 = \mathcal{T}_{\mathsf{cek}\to\mathsf{ck}}(\overline{\kappa}_1')$, if

$$
\langle M_1, \kappa_1 \rangle \longmapsto\!\!\!\!\rightarrow_{\mathsf{ck}} \langle V, \mathtt{mt} \rangle
$$

then for some closure c with $\mathcal{U}(c) = V$,

$$
\langle \langle M_1', \mathcal{E} \rangle, \overline{\kappa}_1' \rangle \longmapsto\!\!\!\!\rightarrow_{\mathsf{cek}} \langle c, \mathtt{mt} \rangle
$$

The theorem follows from specializing the two initial states to $\langle M, \mathtt{mt} \rangle$ and $\langle \langle M, \varnothing \rangle, \mathtt{mt} \rangle$.

The proof of the strengthened claim is by induction on the length of the transition sequence in the CK machine. It proceeds by case analysis of the initial state of the CK machine:

- **Case** $M_1 = (L\ N)$

  The CK machine performs a [ck1] instruction:

  $$\langle (L\ N), \kappa_1 \rangle \longmapsto_{\mathsf{ck}} \langle L, \langle \mathtt{ar}, N, \kappa_1 \rangle \rangle$$

  By assumption of the claim, $\langle M_1', \mathcal{E} \rangle = \langle (L'\ N'), \mathcal{E} \rangle$ such that $L = \mathcal{U}(\langle L', \mathcal{E} \rangle)$ and $N = \mathcal{U}(\langle N', \mathcal{E} \rangle)$ because $\mathcal{U}$ preserves an expression's kind and shape in the translation process. Hence,

  $$\langle \langle (L'\ N'), \mathcal{E} \rangle, \overline{\kappa}_1' \rangle \longmapsto_{\mathsf{ck}} \langle \langle L', \mathcal{E} \rangle, \langle \mathtt{ar}, \langle N', \mathcal{E} \rangle, \overline{\kappa}_1' \rangle \rangle$$

  Clearly, $\mathcal{T}_{\mathsf{cek} \to \mathsf{ck}}(\langle \mathtt{ar}, \langle N', \mathcal{E} \rangle, \overline{\kappa}_1' \rangle) = \langle \mathtt{ar}, N, \kappa_1 \rangle$. Thus the inductive hypothesis applies and proves the claim here.

- **Case** $M_1 \in V, \kappa_1 = \langle \mathtt{fn}, (\lambda X.N), \kappa_2 \rangle$

  Here the CK transition sequence begins as follows:

  $$\langle M_1, \langle \mathtt{fn}, (\lambda X.N), \kappa_2 \rangle \rangle \longmapsto_{\mathsf{ck}} \langle N[X \leftarrow M_1], \kappa_2 \rangle$$

  Given the definition of $\mathcal{U}$, there are two kinds of CEK states that can map to the given CK state:

  - **Case** $M_1' \notin X$

    In this case, the CEK step directly corresponds to the CK step:

    $$\langle \langle M_1', \mathcal{E} \rangle, \langle \mathtt{fn}, \langle (\lambda X.N), \mathcal{E}' \rangle, \overline{\kappa}_2 \rangle \rangle$$
    $$\longmapsto_{\mathsf{cek}} \quad \langle \langle N, \mathcal{E}'[X \leftarrow \langle M_1', \mathcal{E} \rangle] \rangle, \overline{\kappa}_2 \rangle$$

  - **Case** $M_1' \in X, \mathcal{U}(\mathcal{E}(M_1')) = M_1$

    If the value is a variable, the CEK machine first looks up the value of the variable in the environment before it performs an appropriate transition:

    $$\langle \langle M_1', \mathcal{E} \rangle, \langle \mathtt{fn}, \langle (\lambda X.N'), \mathcal{E}' \rangle, \overline{\kappa}_2 \rangle \rangle$$
    $$\longmapsto_{\mathsf{cek}} \quad \langle \mathcal{E}(M_1'), \langle \mathtt{fn}, \langle (\lambda X.N), \mathcal{E}' \rangle, \overline{\kappa}_2 \rangle \rangle$$
    $$\longmapsto_{\mathsf{cek}} \quad \langle \langle N, \mathcal{E}'[X \leftarrow \mathcal{E}(M_1')] \rangle, \overline{\kappa}_2 \rangle$$

In both cases, the assumptions imply that $\mathcal{U}(\langle M_1', \mathcal{E}\rangle) = M_1$. Hence, to finish the case, we must show that

$$\mathcal{U}(\langle N', \mathcal{E}'[X \leftarrow c]\rangle) = N[X \leftarrow \mathcal{U}(c)]$$

where $cl = \langle M_1', \mathcal{E}\rangle$. From the definition of $\mathcal{U}$, if $\mathcal{E} = \{\langle X_1, c_1\rangle, \ldots, \langle X_1, c_1\rangle\}$,

$$\begin{aligned}
&\mathcal{U}(\langle \lambda X.N', \mathcal{E}'\rangle)\\
={}& \lambda X.N'[X_1 \leftarrow \mathcal{U}(c_1)] \ldots [X_n \leftarrow \mathcal{U}(c_n)]\\
={}& \lambda X.N
\end{aligned}$$

which implies

$$N'[X_1 \leftarrow \mathcal{U}(c_1)] \ldots [X_n \leftarrow \mathcal{U}(c_n)] = N.$$

By the Substitution Lemma (lemma 4.7),

$$\begin{aligned}
&N[X \leftarrow \mathcal{U}(c)]\\
={}& N'[X_1 \leftarrow \mathcal{U}(c_1)] \ldots [X_n \leftarrow \mathcal{U}(c_n)][X \leftarrow \mathcal{U}(c)]\\
={}& \mathcal{U}(\langle N', \mathcal{E}[X \leftarrow c]\rangle)
\end{aligned}$$

The rest follows again by induction on the length of the CK transition sequence.

The proof of the other cases are analoguous to the last one.

Exercise 6.7. Show the reduction of

$$\langle \langle (((\lambda f.\lambda x.f\ x)\ \lambda y.(+\ y\ y))\ \ulcorner 1 \urcorner), \varnothing \rangle, \mathtt{mt} \rangle$$

to $\langle \langle V, \mathcal{E}\rangle, \mathtt{mt}\rangle$ with $\longmapsto_{\mathsf{cek}}$.

Exercise 6.8. Implement the CEK machine. Use functions or linked lists for environments.

6·5 History.

Landin's SECD machine is the original and widely cited abstract machine for ISWIM [68]. Like all machines, the SECD machine defines an evaluator. The proof of equivalence between the SECD-evaluator and the evaluator inspired by standard reduction relation is a consequence of Plotkin's work [83]. Unfortunately, the correspondence theorem between ISWIM's SECD machine and the λ-calculus does not scale (smoothly) when imperative effects are added to the language.

This last observation motivated Felleisen and Friedman to introduce the CEK machine [34], inspired by Reynolds's work [93] on definitional interpreters. Felleisen also added a systematic derivation of machines from calculi and vice versa in his dissertation [32].

Exercise 6.9. Design a CC, SCC, CK, and CEK machine for the call-by-name variant of ISWIM from exercises 4.10 and 5.5. Implement the CEK machine for call-by-name ISWIM and compare it with the machine for call-by-value ISWIM.

7 • Tail Calls and More Space Savings

Different specifications of evaluators serve different purposes. The calculus helps us reason about the equivalence of expressions in addition to the evaluation of programs. With the standard reduction relation, we get a goal-driven mechanism for evaluation and we get a first meta-theorem for reasoning about observational equivalence without the equational calculus. From the preceding chapter, we know that the standard reduction relation also serves as a good starting point for the derivation of reasonably efficient abstract machines. The focus, thus far, has always been on the correctness of the evaluator, i.e., on its equivalence with the first evaluator.

In this chapter, we show how to use our machines for reasoning about something entirely different: the space consumption of a program evaluation. Space consumption is a close cousin to the efficiency of data structures (e.g., stacks) and meta operations (e.g., substitutions) in that it addresses another aspect of resource consumption. For example, consider Ω, which is a simple program that loops forever. All of our machines—from the standard reduction machine to the CEK machine—evaluate Ω with a constant amount of space. Contrast this situation with Java where the simple program

```
class Main {
  public static void main(String argv[]) {
    main(argv);
  }
}
```

exhausts the "stack space" of the Java Virtual Machine in a short time.

The chapter starts with a brief historical detour, namely, a look at Landin's original **SECD machine** and its space problems. In the remaining sections we consider the consumption of stack space and environment space in turn, which naturally introduces the notions of "tail call optimization" and "safe for space."

7·1 SECD Machine.

Landin's SECD machine, like all of our abstract machines, rewrites machine states into machine states based on notions of reduction. Unlike our machines, the SECD machine implements function calls in a manner that is analogous to a hardware engineer's understanding, not one derived from a mathematical notion of evaluation.

A state in the SECD machine is a tuple of four components:

S   a stack for tracking values $\hat{V}$ locally
E   an environment, associating variables X with values $\hat{V}$
C   a control string for directing the execution
D   a "dump" representing a saved state: $\langle \hat{S}, \hat{\mathcal{E}}, \hat{C}, \hat{D} \rangle$

In terms of conventional language implementations, the S part corresponds to the procedure-local stack, and the D part is the rest of the stack.

$$
\begin{aligned}
\hat{S} \ &= \ \epsilon \\
&| \ \ \hat{V} \, S \\
\hat{\mathcal{E}} \ &= \ \{\langle X_1, \hat{V}_1 \rangle, \ldots, \langle X_n, \hat{V}_n \rangle\} \\
&\quad \text{a finite function: for all } i \neq j, X_i \neq X_j \\
\hat{C} \ &= \ \epsilon \\
&| \ \ \text{ap} \ \hat{C} \\
&| \ \ \text{prim}_{o^n} \ \hat{C} \\
&| \ \ M \, \hat{C} \\
\hat{D} \ &= \ \epsilon \\
&| \ \ \langle \hat{S}, \hat{\mathcal{E}}, \hat{C}, \hat{D} \rangle \\
\hat{V} \ &= \ b \\
&| \ \ \langle \lambda X.M, \hat{\mathcal{E}} \rangle
\end{aligned}
$$

Based on these definitions, here is Landin's original machine for evaluating ISWIM programs.

$$
eval_{\text{secd}}(M) = \begin{cases} b & \text{if } \langle \epsilon, \varnothing, M, \epsilon \rangle \longmapsto_{\text{secd}} \langle b, \hat{\mathcal{E}}, \epsilon, \epsilon \rangle \\ \text{function} & \text{if } \langle \epsilon, \varnothing, M, \epsilon \rangle \longmapsto_{\text{secd}} \langle \langle \lambda X.N, \hat{\mathcal{E}}' \rangle, \hat{\mathcal{E}}, \epsilon, \epsilon \rangle \end{cases}
$$

	$\longmapsto_{\text{secd}}$	
$\langle \hat{S}, \hat{\mathcal{E}}, b \, \hat{C}, \hat{D} \rangle$	$\langle b \, \hat{S}, \hat{\mathcal{E}}, \hat{C}, \hat{D} \rangle$	[secd1]
$\langle \hat{S}, \hat{\mathcal{E}}, X \, \hat{C}, \hat{D} \rangle$	$\langle \hat{V} \, \hat{S}, \hat{\mathcal{E}}, \hat{C}, \hat{D} \rangle$	[secd2]
	where $\hat{V} = \hat{\mathcal{E}}(X)$	
$\langle \hat{S}, \hat{\mathcal{E}}, (o^p \, M_1 \ldots M_n) \, \hat{C}, \hat{D} \rangle$	$\langle \hat{S}, \hat{\mathcal{E}}, M_1 \ldots M_n \, \text{prim}_{o^p} \, \hat{C}, \hat{D} \rangle$	[secdPA]
$\langle b_n \ldots b_1 \, \hat{S}, \hat{\mathcal{E}}, \text{prim}_{o^n} \, \hat{C}, \hat{D} \rangle$	$\langle \delta(o^n, b_1, \ldots, b_n) \, \hat{S}, \hat{\mathcal{E}}, \hat{C}, \hat{D} \rangle \rangle$	[secd3]
$\langle \hat{S}, \hat{\mathcal{E}}, (M \, N) \, \hat{C}, \hat{D} \rangle$	$\langle \hat{S}, \hat{\mathcal{E}}, M \, N \, \text{ap} \, \hat{C}, \hat{D} \rangle$	[secdLA]
$\langle \hat{S}, \hat{\mathcal{E}}, (\lambda X.M) \, \hat{C}, \hat{D} \rangle$	$\langle \langle \lambda X.M, \hat{\mathcal{E}} \rangle \, \hat{S}, \hat{\mathcal{E}}, \hat{C}, \hat{D} \rangle$	[secd4]
$\langle \hat{V} \, \langle \lambda X.M, \hat{\mathcal{E}}' \rangle \, \hat{S}, \hat{\mathcal{E}}, \text{ap} \, C, D \rangle$	$\langle \epsilon, \hat{\mathcal{E}}'[X \leftarrow \hat{V}], M, \langle \hat{S}, \hat{\mathcal{E}}, C, D \rangle \rangle$	[secd5]
$\langle \hat{V} \, \hat{S}, \hat{\mathcal{E}}, \varnothing, \langle \hat{S}', \hat{\mathcal{E}}', C', D \rangle \rangle$	$\langle \hat{V} \, \hat{S}', \hat{\mathcal{E}}', C', D \rangle$	[secd6]

The SECD and CEK machines produce the same result for any expression that has a result.

Theorem 7.1: $eval_{\text{secd}} = eval_{\text{cek}}$

Proof for Theorem 7.1:   Plotkin [83] proved that $eval_{\text{secd}} = eval_{\text{v}}$. From the preceding chapter we know that $eval_{\text{v}} = eval_{\text{cek}}$.

Exercise 7.1. From a modern perspective, the SECD machine "compiles" applications "on the fly" into control strings. An alternative presentation starts with a compilation from ISWIM expressions to "byte codes," i.e., control strings without any applications left:

$$\hat{C} = \epsilon \quad | \quad \text{ap} \, \hat{C} \quad | \quad \text{prim}_{o^n} \, \hat{C} \quad | \quad b \, \hat{C} \quad | \quad X \, \hat{C} \quad | \quad \langle X, \hat{C} \rangle \, \hat{C}$$

Design a compiler $[\![\cdot]\!]_{\text{secd}}$ from ISWIM expressions to byte codes and revise the SCED machine to work on just those:

$$eval^c_{\text{secd}}(M) = \begin{cases} b & \text{if } \langle \epsilon, \emptyset, [\![M]\!]_{\text{secd}}, \epsilon \rangle \longmapsto_{\text{secd}} \langle b, \hat{\mathcal{E}}, \epsilon, \epsilon \rangle \\ \text{function} & \text{if } \langle \epsilon, \emptyset, [\![M]\!]_{\text{secd}}, \epsilon \rangle \longmapsto_{\text{secd}} \langle \langle \lambda X.\hat{C}, \hat{\mathcal{E}}' \rangle, \hat{\mathcal{E}}, \epsilon, \epsilon \rangle \end{cases}$$

7·2 **Space for Evaluation Contexts.** For our purposes, the more interesting fact is that the CEK and SECD machines produce the same result in different ways. In particular, a programmer might *notice* the difference when using a real machine with *finite resources*.

The difference between SECD and CEK is in how context is accumulated and saved while sub-expressions are evaluated.

- In the SECD machine, the stack provides a working area for assembling application arguments. Function calls introduce a new frame on top of the dump, packaging the current stack, the current environment, and the current control string.

  This form of context accumulation was due to the conventional view of function call execution in the late 1950s and early 1960s. It has remained the corner stone of all implementations derived from the languages dominant during this era.

- In the CEK machine, the continuation is modified when a function or an argument expression is evaluated, regardless of whether they are complex expressions. The argument stack is thus subsumed by the continuation. Function application, however, always shrinks the continuation rather than expanding it.

This view of context accumulation dates to the mid 1970s and Steele and Sussman's work on implementing the Scheme programming language. Due to its origin in Scheme, this form of evaluation context management dominates in the functional programming language community, even though Steele and Sussman borrowed it from ACTORS, a theoretical model of *object-oriented programming*.[1]

Due to this difference, the SECD and CEK machines behave differently on recursive programs. Consider the evaluation of Ω, for example. Both machines loop forever on this expression—just as they should, considering that they correctly implement $eval_v$. The nature of the infinite loops differ, however. In particular, the states of the CEK machine never grow beyond a certain size while evaluating the program:

$$\langle\langle((\lambda x.x\ x)(\lambda x.x\ x)),\varnothing\rangle,\mathrm{mt}\rangle$$
$$\longmapsto_{\mathsf{cek}}\ \langle\langle(\lambda x.x\ x),\varnothing\rangle,\langle\mathrm{ar},\langle(\lambda x.x\ x),\varnothing\rangle,\mathrm{mt}\rangle\rangle$$
$$\longmapsto_{\mathsf{cek}}\ \langle\langle(\lambda x.x\ x),\varnothing\rangle,\langle\mathrm{fn},\langle(\lambda x.x\ x),\varnothing\rangle,\mathrm{mt}\rangle\rangle$$
$$\longmapsto_{\mathsf{cek}}\ \langle\langle(x\ x),\{\langle x,c\rangle\}\rangle,\mathrm{mt}\rangle \hspace{2cm} (\dagger)$$
$$\longmapsto_{\mathsf{cek}}\ \langle\langle x,\{\langle x,c\rangle\}\rangle,\langle\mathrm{ar},\langle x,\{\langle x,c\rangle\}\rangle,\mathrm{mt}\rangle\rangle$$
$$\longmapsto_{\mathsf{cek}}\ \langle\langle(\lambda x.x\ x),\varnothing\rangle,\langle\mathrm{ar},\langle x,\{\langle x,c\rangle\}\rangle,\mathrm{mt}\rangle\rangle$$
$$\longmapsto_{\mathsf{cek}}\ \langle\langle x,\{\langle x,c\rangle\}\rangle,\langle\mathrm{fn},\langle(\lambda x.x\ x),\varnothing\rangle,\mathrm{mt}\rangle\rangle$$
$$\longmapsto_{\mathsf{cek}}\ \langle\langle(\lambda x.x\ x),\varnothing\rangle,\langle\mathrm{fn},\langle(\lambda x.x\ x),\varnothing\rangle,\mathrm{mt}\rangle\rangle$$
$$\longmapsto_{\mathsf{cek}}\ \langle\langle(x\ x),\{\langle x,c\rangle\}\rangle,\mathrm{mt}\rangle \hspace{2cm} (\ddagger)$$
$$\dots$$

where $c = \langle(\lambda x.x\ x),\varnothing\rangle$. Notice how the last state ($\ddagger$) is identical to the one five steps earlier ($\dagger$).

In contrast, the state of the SECD machine grows in size repeatedly:

$$\langle\epsilon,\varnothing,((\lambda x.x\ x)\ (\lambda x.x\ x)),\epsilon\rangle$$
$$\longmapsto_{\mathsf{secd}}\ \langle\epsilon,\varnothing,(\lambda x.x\ x)(\lambda x.x\ x)\mathrm{ap},\epsilon\rangle$$
$$\longmapsto_{\mathsf{secd}}\ \langle\langle\lambda x.(x\ x),\varnothing\rangle,\varnothing,\lambda x.(x\ x)\ \mathrm{ap},\epsilon\rangle$$
$$\longmapsto_{\mathsf{secd}}\ \langle\langle\lambda x.(x\ x),\varnothing\rangle\ \langle\lambda x.(x\ x),\varnothing\rangle,\varnothing,\mathrm{ap},\epsilon\rangle$$
$$\longmapsto_{\mathsf{secd}}\ \langle\epsilon,\{\langle x,\hat{V}\rangle\},(x\ x),\langle\epsilon,\varnothing,\epsilon,\epsilon\rangle\rangle \hspace{1cm} (\S)$$
$$\longmapsto_{\mathsf{secd}}\ \langle\epsilon,\{\langle x,\hat{V}\rangle\},x\ x\ \mathrm{ap},\langle\epsilon,\varnothing,\epsilon,\epsilon\rangle\rangle$$
$$\longmapsto_{\mathsf{secd}}\ \langle\hat{V},\{\langle x,\hat{V}\rangle\},x\ \mathrm{ap},\langle\epsilon,\varnothing,\epsilon,\epsilon\rangle\rangle$$
$$\longmapsto_{\mathsf{secd}}\ \langle\hat{V}\ \hat{V},\{\langle x,\hat{V}\rangle\},\mathrm{ap},\langle\epsilon,\varnothing,\epsilon,\epsilon\rangle\rangle$$
$$\longmapsto_{\mathsf{secd}}\ \langle\epsilon,\{\langle x,\hat{V}\rangle\},(x\ x),\langle\epsilon,\{\langle x,\hat{V}\rangle\},\epsilon,\langle\epsilon,\varnothing,\epsilon,\epsilon\rangle\rangle\rangle \hspace{0.3cm} (\P)$$

where $\hat{V} = \langle\lambda x.(x\ x),\varnothing\rangle$. Here the last state ($\P$) has the same stack, environment, and control string as the one five steps earlier ($\S$) but a larger dump.

---

[1] Personal communication with Guy Steele, April 2004.

Indeed, if we continue the evaluation for another five steps, this situation repeats itself:

$$\longmapsto_{\text{secd}} \quad \langle \epsilon, \{\langle x, \hat{V}\rangle\}, (x\ x), \underline{\langle \epsilon, \{\langle x, \hat{V}\rangle\}, \epsilon, \langle \epsilon, \{\langle x, \hat{V}\rangle\}, \epsilon, \langle \epsilon, \varnothing, \epsilon, \epsilon \rangle\rangle\rangle}\rangle$$

In general, the SECD machine generates the following series of dumps:

$$\hat{D}_0 = \langle \epsilon, \varnothing, \epsilon, \epsilon \rangle$$
$$\hat{D}_{i+1} = \langle \epsilon, \{\langle x, \hat{V}\rangle\}, \epsilon, \hat{D}_i \rangle$$

Theoretically, there is no limit to this growth; practically, a faithful implementation of the SECD machine eventually exhausts the available space.

More generally, the notion of saving control context on argument evaluations, rather than on function calls, corresponds to the notion of **tail call optimization**[2] (TCO) in interpreters and compilers. TCO demands that the execution of tail calls must not consume any space for saving control contexts. At this point, the only language that has accepted TCO as part of its standard is the Scheme programming language [101]. Thus, the following program runs forever in Scheme, without running out of stack space:

```
(define (f x) (f x))
(f 'ignored)
```

because the function call (f 'ignored) is in tail-position within f.

Of course, the relevance of TCO extends beyond infinite loops to any (mutually) recursive (collection of) function(s). In a programming language that respects TCO, a programmer may match the organization of functions and methods to that of the data. In a language that does not, a programmer is forced to rework the organization to use for, while, and other loops. While such a re-organization may not require much extra work for linear data collections, it is unnatural and difficult to use for non-linear data.

Exercise 7.2. Which of the following expressions loop with a bounded size in the CEK machine?

- $Y_V\ (\lambda f.\lambda x.f\ x)\ \ulcorner 0 \urcorner$

- $Y_V\ (\lambda f.\lambda x.\text{if0}\ x\ (f\ \ulcorner 10 \urcorner)\ (f\ (-\ x\ \ulcorner 1 \urcorner)))\ \ulcorner 0 \urcorner$

- $Y_V\ (\lambda f.\lambda x.\text{if0}\ x\ (f\ \ulcorner 10 \urcorner)\ (-\ (f\ x)\ \ulcorner 1 \urcorner))\ \ulcorner 0 \urcorner$

---

[2]This approach to evaluation is not really an "optimization" in the sense of an optional performance improvement, but the original term "tail recursion elimination" is even worse.

Exercise 7.3. Which of the following expressions execute in the CEK machine with a bounded size that is independent of n, for a non-negative n?

- Y_V $(\lambda f.\lambda x.\text{if0 } x \text{ false } (\text{not } (f (- x 1))))$ $\ulcorner n \urcorner$

- Y_V $(\lambda f.\lambda z.\lambda x.\text{if0 } x \text{ } z \text{ } (f (\text{not } z) (- x 1)))$ false $\ulcorner n \urcorner$

Exercise 7.4. Revise Landin's SECD machine so that it implements tail-calls properly.

7.3 Space for Environments.
Now we know that the CEK machine behaves quantitatively better than the SECD machine. The question is whether it is good enough.

Remember that the CEK machine is derived from the standard reduction machine. While we know that the two define the same evaluator, we might now ask how $\longmapsto_{\text{cek}}$ compares to $\longmapsto_v$ as far as asymptotic space is concerned. Surprisingly, the latter consumes less space than the former. Consider the function

$$F \doteq (\lambda f.(\lambda x.((f f) (\lambda x.x))))$$

and what happens on the standard reduction machine when it used in a program:

$$
\begin{aligned}
((F\,F)\ \ulcorner 0 \urcorner) \quad &\longmapsto_v \quad ((\lambda x.((F\,F)\ (\lambda x.x)))\ \ulcorner 0 \urcorner) \\
&\longmapsto_v \quad ((F\,F)\ (\lambda.xx)) \\
&\longmapsto_v \quad ((\lambda x.((F\,F)\ (\lambda x.x)))\ (\lambda.xx)) \quad (\dagger) \\
&\longmapsto_v \quad ((F\,F)\ (\lambda.xx)) \\
&\longmapsto_v \quad \dots
\end{aligned}
$$

Clearly, the largest expression in this infinite sequence of machine states is never larger than the contractum of the fourth step ($\dagger$).

In contrast, running the same program on the CEK machine creates an infinite sequence of ever-growing states:

$$
\begin{aligned}
&\langle \langle ((F\,F)\ \ulcorner 0 \urcorner), \varnothing \rangle, \text{mt} \rangle \\
\longmapsto_{\text{cek}} \quad &\langle \langle ((f\,f)\ (\lambda x.x)), \mathcal{E}_0 \rangle, \text{mt} \rangle \\
&\text{where } \mathcal{E}_0 = \{ \langle x, \langle \ulcorner 0 \urcorner, \varnothing \rangle \rangle \} \cup \{ \langle f, \langle F, \varnothing \rangle \rangle \} \\
\longmapsto_{\text{cek}} \quad &\langle \langle ((f\,f)\ (\lambda x.x)), \mathcal{E}_1 \rangle, \text{mt} \rangle \\
&\text{where } \mathcal{E}_1 = \{ \langle x, \langle (\lambda x.x), \mathcal{E}_0 \rangle \rangle \} \cup \{ \langle f, \langle F, \varnothing \rangle \rangle \} \\
\longmapsto_{\text{cek}} \quad &\dots
\end{aligned}
$$

Although the last CEK state of this sequence looks deceptively similar to the intermediate one, the definition of $\mathcal{E}_1$ shows that it contains $\mathcal{E}_0$, i.e., $\mathcal{E}_1$ is larger than $\mathcal{E}_0$. In general, the environments belong to the following series:

$$\begin{aligned} \mathcal{E}_0 &= \{\langle x, \langle \ulcorner 0 \urcorner, \varnothing \rangle \rangle, \langle f, \langle \mathsf{F}, \varnothing \rangle \rangle\} \\ \mathcal{E}_{i+1} &= \{\langle x, \langle (\lambda x.x), \mathcal{E}_i \rangle \rangle, \langle f, \langle \mathsf{F}, \varnothing \rangle \rangle\} \end{aligned}$$

which means that the machine states keep growing, too.

The problem of the CEK machine is obviously due to the way closures such as

$$\langle (\lambda x.x), \mathcal{E}_i \rangle$$

retain bindings via $\mathcal{E}_i$ that are actually unnecessary. After all, $(\lambda x.x)$ has no free variables, and therefore $\varnothing$ is a perfectly fine environment for this λ expression. In other words, when we decided to delay substitutions and encode them as environments, we overlooked that such "delayed substitutions" would accumulate, regardless of whether they were necessary in the first place. Immediately applying a vacuous substitution such as $\mathcal{E}_i$ to $(\lambda x.x)$, however, would not affect the expression at all. Hence, the states of the standard reduction machine do not grow as the above program is evaluated.

If the substitution is actually needed, reductions via $\longmapsto_v$ grow, too. For example, replacing F in the example with

$$\mathsf{G} \doteq (\lambda f.(\lambda x.((f\ f)\ (\lambda y.x))))$$

produces an infinite series of growing states on both the standard reduction machine as well as the CEK machine. The reason is that x is free in $(\lambda y.x)$, so the immediate substitution for x in $(\lambda y.x)$ changes the expression.

To repair the CEK machine and obtain the same space consumption as the standard reduction machine, we can change closure formation to discard unnecessary substitutions from an environment. Given an expression M and an environment $\mathcal{E}$, the closure should be $\langle M, \mathcal{E}|\mathcal{FV}(M) \rangle$ where $\mathcal{E}|\mathcal{FV}(M)$ is $\mathcal{E}$ with its domain restricted to $\mathcal{FV}(M)$. For example, closing $(\lambda x.x)$ with $\mathcal{E}_0$ creates the closure $\langle (\lambda x.x), \varnothing \rangle$ in this world. A machine with the same space consumption as the standard reduction machine is called **safe for space**.

Exercise 7.5. Formulate a CEK machine that prunes environments when it creates closures. Implement the revised CEK machine in a "real world" programming language in a faithful manner.

Exercise 7.6. Formulate a CEK machine that prunes environments only when it creates closures for basic constants and functions. Compare this machine with the one from the preceding exercise. Is it possible for an ISWIM program to consume less space on this machine than on the one from exercise 7.5?

Exercise 7.7. Revise the SECD machine from exercise 7.4 so that it is safe for space.

7·4 History.
Landin invented the SECD machine in an attempt to provide an evaluation mechanism for ISWIM [68]. While people recognized the lack of tail-call optimizations in the SECD machine, they failed to understand the "space safety" issue. Chase [17] observed space problems when implementing and optimizing an ISWIM-like language through a CEK-like interpreter. Later, Appel described the optimizing compiler for SML and included a rigorous description of Chase's notions; he also coined the phrase "safe for space" [6]. In the mid 90s, Clinger's [21] formalized both tail-call safety as well as space safety with space complexity classes.

8 • Control: Errors, Exceptions, and Continuations

The evaluation of an ISWIM program might get stuck. One typical example is the application of a division primitive to 0; another one is the use of a numeral in function position. For programs whose evaluation gets stuck, the ISWIM interpreter produces no result; the function is undefined. Put differently, the evaluator identifies programs that run forever with programs that run into a stuck state. Identifying such vastly different behaviors is unproductive for programmers and users alike.

We could fix this problem with the addition of an error clause to the definition of the evaluator:

$$eval(M) = \begin{cases} b & \text{if } M \longmapsto_{\mathbf{v}} b \\ \texttt{function} & \text{if } M \longmapsto_{\mathbf{v}} \lambda X.N \\ \texttt{err} & \text{if } M \longmapsto_{\mathbf{v}} N \text{ and } N \text{ is stuck} \end{cases}$$

A superior solution is to equip the programming language with an error-signaling mechanism. Providing this form of linguistic expressiveness allows the language designer to turn partial primitives into total primitives that may signal an error at run-time, and it allows programmers to define error-signaling functions, which, in turn, makes error messages precise and helpful for debugging.

It is a short step from adding error signaling to providing a full-fledged exception mechanisms. With such constructs, it is possible to raise an exception when an error is encountered, but the program may also be equipped with remedial actions. Such **exception-handling** constructs are highly desirable in practice, and they are provided by many programming languages.

Finally, some programming languages support a general control construct with which programmers can implement all forms of special-purpose mechanisms for composing actions in a non-functional manner. Scheme [101], for example, comes with a construct for reifying the current evaluation context and another one for installing this reified context later.

The core of this chapter consists of four sections, one per control mechanism plus one comparing ISWIM with its first extension on a semantic basis. Each section on a control mechanism introduces the basic mechanism and comes with several semantic models of the construct.

$8 \cdot 1$ **Error ISWIM.** Since a program can encounter many different types of error situations, we add an entire set of errors to ISWIM. Each such error plays the role of a syntactic construct. We call the resulting language **Error ISWIM**.

$$
\begin{aligned}
M &= \ldots & \text{same as plain ISWIM} \\
&\mid \quad \text{err}_l \\
l &\in \text{Labels} & \text{an unspecified set of labels}
\end{aligned}
$$

We assume that the set is non-empty but make no other restrictions for now.

As mentioned, the err_l construct plays two roles. First, stuck expressions are now reducible to some specific err_l. Second, a programmer-defined function may contain an err_l expression so that it can signal an error for bad inputs. Once an err_l expression becomes "active," it must stop the rest of the computation. Thus we need two kinds of reductions: one introduces err_l for stuck states, and another takes care of "active" err_l sub-expressions.

Let us look at the error-signaling for stuck expressions first. We know from section 5.4 that there are three kinds of stuck expressions: applications of primitive operations to constants for which δ is undefined; applications of primitives to λ expressions; and applications of basic constants to values.

We consider each case in turn. First, an error message for an application of a primitive operation to a bad batch of constants depends on the operation and the constants. We simply assume that the δ function returns an appropriate err_l element for bad inputs to a primitive operation:

$$
\delta : o^n \times \underbrace{b \times \ldots \times b}_{n} \longrightarrow V \cup \text{err}_l
$$

In other words, δ in Error ISWIM is a total function that either returns a value or signals a run-time error for all properly formed combinations of primitive operations and basic constants. Here is a sample extension of ISWIM with arithmetic primitives.

$$
\begin{aligned}
\delta(/, \ulcorner m \urcorner, \ulcorner n \urcorner) &= \ulcorner m/n \urcorner & \text{if } n \neq \ulcorner 0 \urcorner \\
\delta(/, \ulcorner m \urcorner, \ulcorner 0 \urcorner) &= \text{err}_0
\end{aligned}
$$

If we were to add vector operations to ISWIM, referencing into a vector would be another partial operation.

Second, an application of a primitive operation to a value other than a constant must also reduce to an error. For example, applying the addition primitive to any abstraction signals an error with the misused primitive operation as a label:

$$
(+ \ (\lambda xy.x) \ 0) \to \text{err}_+
$$

Although the addition of information about V would improve the quality of the error message, doing so poses a (minor) problem for a language designer-modeler; see exercise 8.8 below.

Finally, consider the application of some basic constant b to an arbitrary value V. Here we use an error labeled with b, suggesting its abuse:

$$(b\ V) \rightarrow \text{err}_b$$

Again, the error messages omits any mention of V.

It is time to formulate these ideas as notions of reductions for a calculus of Error ISWIM.

$$
\begin{array}{lll}
(o^m\ b_1 \ldots b_m) & \delta_{\text{err}} & \text{err}_l \\
\quad \text{if } \delta(o^m, b_1, \ldots b_m) = \text{err}_l \\
(o^m\ b_1 \ldots b_{i-1}\ (\lambda X.N)\ V_{i+1} \ldots V_m) & \delta_{\text{err}} & \text{err}_{\langle m,i \rangle} \\
(b\ V) & \delta_{\text{err}} & \text{err}_b
\end{array}
$$

An application M is **faulty** if $M\ \delta_{\text{err}}\ \text{err}_l$ for some err_l.

This definition overloads δ as both the interpretation function for primitive operations and as notion of reduction for successful applications of primitives. In this manner, the δ notion of reduction remains the same as for ISWIM, while the separate reduction δ_{err} captures the erroneous cases.

At this point, we know how errors are introduced into programs. Stuck states generate them, and programmers may use them in their functions wherever they like. The question now is what happens when an error becomes the "active" sub-expression. Clearly, the error should eliminate any computation that would have been executed if the evaluation of the sub-expression had not signaled an error. A precise formulation of this idea requires a case-by-case consideration of all forms of computation:

1. Take application as an example. If a function is applied to err_l, the appliction must be terminated. We can express this requirement with the following informal notion of reduction:

$$((\lambda X.M)\ \text{err}_l) \rightarrow \text{err}_l$$

2. Similarly, when err_l occurs in function position, there is no function to be applied so the application also reduces to err_l:

$$(\text{err}_l\ N) \rightarrow \text{err}_l$$

3. Of course, if an error shows up in the middle of primitive application, a reduction must eliminate it:

$$(o^n \ V_1 \ldots V_{i-1} \ \text{err}_l \ N_{i+1} \ \ldots N_n) \rightarrow \text{err}_l$$

The rules clarify that err_l is *not* an ordinary value; otherwise applications like $((\lambda x.\ulcorner 5 \urcorner) \ \text{err}_l)$ would reduce to $\ulcorner 5 \urcorner$.

We also need to consider the situation when err_l occurs as the body of a procedure. Since a procedure like $(\lambda x.\text{err}_l)$ may never be invoked, the err_l should not propagate through the abstraction. The hidden err_l should only become visible when the λ-abstraction is applied to a value. In other words, $(\lambda x.\text{err}_l)$ remains an irreducible value.

One natural summary of these rules is a notion of reduction that eliminates any evaluation context surrounding err_l.

$$\boxed{E[\text{err}_l] \ \textbf{error} \ \text{err}_l}$$

It is natural because the evaluation context surrounding a redex represents the rest of the computation, and the purpose of err_l is to eliminate the rest of the computation.

In conclusion, our ideas imply that the basic notion of reduction for Error ISWIM is an extension of $\textbf{v}$ with δ_{err} and **error**.

$$\boxed{\textbf{e} = \beta_\textbf{v} \cup \delta \cup \delta_{\text{err}} \cup \textbf{error}}$$

From this, the definition for the language evaluator follows easily.

$$\boxed{\begin{aligned} A_\textbf{e} &= b \cup \{\texttt{function}\} \cup \{\text{err}_l \mid l \in \text{Labels}\} \\[1ex] eval_\textbf{e} : M &\longrightarrow A_\textbf{e} \\ eval_\textbf{e}(M) &= \begin{cases} b & \text{if } M =_\textbf{e} b \\ \texttt{function} & \text{if } M =_\textbf{e} \lambda X.N \\ \text{err}_l & \text{if } M =_\textbf{e} \text{err}_l \end{cases} \end{aligned}}$$

Exercise 8.1. Show two different series of $\rightarrow_\textbf{e}$ reductions of

$$(+ \ (- \ 4 \ \text{err}_a) \ \text{err}_b)$$

to err_l with $\rightarrow_\textbf{e}$. Indicate the **e** redex for each step. Is the resulting l unique?

Consistency for Error ISWIM. As always, we need to check that the evaluator for Error ISWIM is a function. That is, our goal is to establish a consistency theorem for Error ISWIM.

Theorem 8.1 [Consistency for Error ISWIM]: The relation $eval_e$ is a partial function.

The proof of this theorem has the same structure as the proof of theorem 4.3, the corresponding theorem for $eval_v$. The theorem follows from a consistency lemma, which proves that provably equal results reduce to some common expression. The proof of the consistency lemma once again relies a Church-Rosser property for the underlying notion of reduction. The Church-Rosser property obviously holds for δ and β_v extended to the new syntax; an adaptation of the proof for ISWIM to Error ISWIM is straightforward. Furthermore, the relations that introduce and move err_l in Error ISWIM calculations also satisfy a Church-Rosser property. Thus it is fortunate that, under mild conditions, combinations of such relations are also Church-Rosser.

We first deal with the extension of the ISWIM calculus to the new syntax. We define **w** as the extension of **v** to the full set of Error ISWIM expressions.

$$\mathbf{w} = \delta \cup \beta_v$$

Lemma 8.2 [Church-Rosser (w)]: If $L \twoheadrightarrow_{\mathbf{w}} M$ and $L \twoheadrightarrow_{\mathbf{w}} N$, there exists an expression K such that $M \twoheadrightarrow_{\mathbf{w}} K$ and $N \twoheadrightarrow_{\mathbf{w}} K$.

The proof is essentially the same as for $\twoheadrightarrow_{\mathbf{v}}$.

Next we turn to the analysis of the two new notions of reduction. We define **f** as the rest of **e**:

$$\mathbf{f} = \mathbf{error} \cup \delta_{err}$$

Unlike **v** or **w**, this notion of reduction never duplicates expressions or creates new opportunities to reduce sub-expressions. We might therefore expect that the one-step relation satisfies the diamond property, but, unfortunately, this claim does not hold. Consider the reduction from $E[err_l]$ to err_l. If $E[err_l]$ also reduces to $E'[err_l]$ for some evaluation context E', then $E'[err_l]$ directly reduces to err_l. Hence it is not the one-step reduction $\rightarrow_{\mathbf{f}}$ but its reflexive closure $\rightarrow_{\mathbf{f}}^0$ that satisfies the diamond property.

Lemma 8.3 [Church-Rosser (f)]: If $L \twoheadrightarrow_{\mathbf{f}} M$ and $L \twoheadrightarrow_{\mathbf{f}} N$ then there exists an expression K such that $M \twoheadrightarrow_{\mathbf{f}} K$ and $N \twoheadrightarrow_{\mathbf{f}} K$.

Proof for Lemma 8.3:   We first prove the claim for a subset of the relation: If $L \rightarrow_{\mathbf{f}}^0 M$ and $L \rightarrow_{\mathbf{f}}^0 N$ then there exists an expression K such that $M \rightarrow_{\mathbf{f}}^0 K$ and $N \rightarrow_{\mathbf{f}}^0 K$. The lemma clearly follows from this claim. The proof proceeds by case analysis of the reduction from L to M:

- **Case L is faulty; $M = \text{err}_l$**

  Clearly, if L is faulty and $L \to_{\mathbf{f}}^0 N$ then N is faulty. Hence, $K = \text{err}_l$ is the desired fourth expression.

- **Case $L = E[\text{err}_l]; M = \text{err}_l$**

  It is easy to check that any **f**-reduction applied to $E[\text{err}_l]$ yields an expression of the shape $E'[\text{err}_l]$ for some evaluation context E', which implies that the reduction **error** applies to N.

- **Case $L = M$**

  Set $K = N$.

- **Case $L = C[L']$, $M = C[\text{err}_l]$, $L' \mathbf{f} \text{err}_l$**

  If $N = C'[L']$ for some context C', $K = C'[\text{err}_l]$ because $C[L'] \to_{\mathbf{f}}^0 C'[L']$ implies that for all N', $C[N'] \to_{\mathbf{f}}^0 C'[N']$. Otherwise $N = C'[\text{err}_l]$ by the definition of compatibility, in which case $K = M = N$.

Exercise 8.2. Prove that if L is faulty and $L \to_{\mathbf{f}} N$, then N is faulty and reduces to the same error element.

Exercise 8.3. Prove that If $L = E[\text{err}_l]$ and $L \to_{\mathbf{f}} M$, then there exists an evaluation context E' such that $M = E'[\text{err}_l]$.

After establishing that each of the notions of reduction **w** and **f** satisfy the Church-Rosser property, we need to show that these results can be combined. Intuitively, the combination of **w** and **f** should be Church-Rosser, because the two notions of reduction do not interfere with each other. That is, if two reductions apply to a term, the redexes do not overlap and the reduction of one redex may destroy but not otherwise affect the other redex. Technically speaking, the two one-step reductions commute. For an explanation of this proof strategy and its origins, see Barendregt's comprehensive study of λ-calculus and especially chapter 3.

If we can show that the one-step relations based on **w** and **f** commute, the commutation for their transitive closures clearly follows. The one-step relations do not commute, however. Consider the expression

$$((\lambda f.(f\ (f\ \ulcorner 0 \urcorner))) (\lambda x.(\underline{\text{add1}\ (\lambda x.x)})))$$

Reducing the underlined δ_{err}-redex first yields

$$((\lambda f.(f\ (f\ \ulcorner 0 \urcorner))) (\lambda x.\text{err}_{\text{add1}})) \to_{\mathbf{e}} ((\lambda x.\text{err}_{\text{add1}})\ ((\lambda x.\text{err}_{\text{add1}})\ \ulcorner 0 \urcorner))$$

but reducing the β_v-redex first requires *two* δ_{err}-reductions to reach confluence:

$$((\lambda x.(\text{add1 } (\lambda x.x)))\, ((\lambda x.(\text{add1 } (\lambda x.x)))\, \lceil 0 \rceil))$$
$$\rightarrow_e\ ((\lambda x.\text{err}_{\text{add1}})\, ((\lambda x.(\text{add1 } (\lambda x.x)))\, \lceil 0 \rceil))$$
$$\rightarrow_e\ ((\lambda x.\text{err}_{\text{add1}})\, ((\lambda x.\text{err}_{\text{add1}})\, \lceil 0 \rceil))$$

Fortunately, it is still possible to extend a commutativity result for the one-
step relations to the full reductions when only one direction needs multiple
steps. The proof of the following lemma illustrates the idea.

Lemma 8.4: The reductions $\twoheadrightarrow_w$ and $\twoheadrightarrow_f$ commute.

Proof for Lemma 8.4:   The first step of the proof shows that for
all L, M, and N such that $L \rightarrow_w M$ and $L \rightarrow_f N$, there exists a
K such that $M \twoheadrightarrow_f K$ and $N \rightarrow_w^0 K$. The proof is an induction on
the structure of $L \rightarrow_w M$:

- **Case** $L = ((\lambda X.L')\, V)$, $M = L'[X \leftarrow V]$

  Only two subcases are possible because a value cannot reduce to err_l:

  - **Case** $N = ((\lambda X.L'')\, V)$, $L' \rightarrow_f L''$
    If we can show that $M[X \leftarrow V] \rightarrow_f M'[X \leftarrow V]$ for
    $M \rightarrow_f M'$, then we can take $K = L''[X \leftarrow V]$.
  - **Case** $N = ((\lambda X.L')\, V')$, $V \rightarrow_f V'$
    If we can show that $M[X \leftarrow V] \twoheadrightarrow_f M[X \leftarrow V']$ for
    $V \rightarrow_f V'$, then we can take $K = L'[X \leftarrow V']$.

- **Case** $L\, \delta\, M$

  Then, by definition of δ and δ_{err}, $L \rightarrow_f N$ is impossible.

- **Case** $L = C[L']$, $M = C[M']$, $L'\, \mathbf{w}\, M'$

  If $C[L'] \rightarrow_f C[L'']$, the claim follows from the inductive hypothesis. Otherwise, $C[L'] \rightarrow_f C'[L']$ and $K = C'[M']$ is the
  correct choice.

The lemma follows by a simple induction on the length of the two
reduction sequences.

Based on the preceding lemma and the two diamond lemmas, we can now
prove that the reduction generated by **e** satisfies the crucial diamond lemma.

Lemma 8.5 [Church-Rosser (e)]: If $L \twoheadrightarrow_e M$ and $L \twoheadrightarrow_e N$, then
there exists an expression K such that $M \twoheadrightarrow_e K$ and $N \twoheadrightarrow_e K$.

Proof for Lemma 8.5: For the cases where $L = M$ or $L = N$, the lemma obviously holds. Thus assume $L \neq M$ and $L \neq N$. The proof is an induction on the product of the reduction steps from L to M and L to N. Pick an $M_1 \neq L$ and an $N_1 \neq L$ such that the reduction steps from L to M_1 and N_1 are either **f** or **w** steps. Four cases are possible; each case follows from either lemma 8.4 or the Church-Rosser lemma for the individual notions of reduction.

Exercise 8.4. Spell out the four cases in the proof of lemma 8.5 and finish the proof.

Exercise 8.5. Complete the proof of consistency, i.e., show that if $M =_e N$ then M and N reduce to a common Error ISWIM expression.

Standard Reduction for Error ISWIM. A calculus-based specification of an evaluator does not lend itself immediately to a good implementation. What we really need is a strategy-based specification that picks a unique redex from a program and rewrites the program until it turns into an answer. For ISWIM, the correct strategy selects the leftmost-outermost redex, reduces it, and continues the evaluation with the resulting program. Technically, recall that the deterministic ISWIM evaluator partitions the program into an evaluation context E and a **v**-redex M. If N is the contractum of M, the next state in the evaluation sequence is $E[N]$: $E[M] \longmapsto_v E[N]$. The strategy works because for every program that is not a value, there is a unique partitioning of the program into an evaluation context and a **v**-redex.

Unique partitioning fails for Error ISWIM. To see why, note that the expression $(+ \ulcorner 1 \urcorner (+ \ulcorner 2 \urcorner \mathrm{err}_a))$ has two distinct partitioning into an evaluation context and an **e** redex:

1. $(+ \ulcorner 1 \urcorner [\,])$ and $(+ \ulcorner 2 \urcorner \mathrm{err}_a)$, because the latter **e** reduces to err_a;

2. $[\,]$ and $(+ \ulcorner 1 \urcorner (+ \ulcorner 2 \urcorner \mathrm{err}_a))$, because the latter also **e** reduces to err_a.

Thus, there are two ways to match $E[M]$ and $E[N]$ with M **e** N.

Consequently, we cannot define $\longmapsto_e$ as the closure of **e** over E. To avoid non-determinism, we define $\longmapsto_e$ to propagate errors directly and close only over the remaining notions of reduction, β_v, δ, and δ_{err}.

$$\tilde{e} = \beta_v \cup \delta \cup \delta_{\mathrm{err}}$$

$$
\begin{aligned}
E[M] &\longmapsto_e E[N] \quad \text{if} \quad M \,\tilde{e}\, N \\
E[\mathrm{err}_l] &\longmapsto_e \mathrm{err}_l
\end{aligned}
$$

As usual, this definition induces an evaluator specification.

$$eval_e^s(M) = \begin{cases} b & \text{if } M \longmapsto_e b \\ \text{function} & \text{if } M \longmapsto_e \lambda X.N \\ \text{err}_l & \text{if } M \longmapsto_e \text{err}_l \end{cases}$$

Given the adapted definition of a standard reduction relation, we can state and prove a unique partitioning theorem.

> **Lemma 8.6 [Unique Evaluation Contexts for Error ISWIM]:**
> Every closed Error ISWIM expression M is either a value, or there exists a unique evaluation context E such that $M = E[(V\ U)]$, $M = E[(o^m\ V_1 \dots V_m)]$, or $M = E[\text{err}_l]$ (for some l).

> **Proof for Lemma 8.6:** The proof is similar to that of lemma 5.1.

It is useful to introduce a separate definition for $\longmapsto_e$ redex shapes.

$$\begin{aligned} M_{re} \quad = \quad & (V\ V) \\ | \quad & (o^m\ V \dots V) \\ | \quad & \text{err}_l \end{aligned}$$

While the Unique Evaluation Lemma for Error ISWIM validates that the new specification of the evaluator, $eval_e^s$, is a partial function, we really want to know that the new evaluator function is equal to the old one and can be used in its place. This is also true, though we do not prove it here.

> **Theorem 8.7:** $eval_e^s = eval_e$

Exercise 8.6. Adapt the proof of theorem 5.5 to prove theorem 8.7.

Exercise 8.7. If there is a single error element err_0, a feasible alternative for propagating err_0 through applications is the following notion of reduction:

$$\begin{aligned} E_a \quad = \quad & [] \\ | \quad & (M\ E_a) \\ | \quad & (E_a\ M) \\ | \quad & (o^m\ M \dots M\ E_a\ M \dots M) \end{aligned}$$

$$\begin{aligned} E[M] \quad &\longmapsto_{e'} \quad E[N] \quad \text{if} \quad M\ \tilde{e}\ N \\ E_a[\text{err}_0] \quad &\longmapsto_{e'} \quad \text{err}_0 \end{aligned}$$

Demonstrate that $\longmapsto_{e'}$ is a not function. Is $eval_{e'}^s$, defined in terms of $\longmapsto_{e'}$, a function? Is $eval_{e'}^s$ a function when there are at least two error elements?

Exercise 8.8. What would go wrong if we added the notion of reduction

$$(b\ V) \rightarrow \text{err}_b\ V$$

to the calculus of Error ISWIM? Is it possible to add the reduction

$$E[(b\ V)] \longmapsto \text{err}_b\ V$$

to the standard reduction machine? What does this suggest about the usefulness of calculi versus standard reduction machines for specifying programming language constructs?

8·2 Relating ISWIM and Error ISWIM.

The extension of a programming language almost immediately raises the question whether programs of the original language are executed correctly on the new evaluator. More specifically, given the same set of constants, primitives, and δ notion of reduction, we wish to know whether ISWIM programs are evaluated to the same answer by both the ISWIM and the Error ISWIM evaluator.

Theorem 8.8: For any M in ISWIM,

1. $eval_{\mathbf{v}}(M) = A$ implies that $eval_{\mathbf{e}}(M) = A$;
2. $eval_{\mathbf{e}}(M) = A$ and $A \neq \text{err}_l$ implies that $eval_{\mathbf{v}}(M) = A$;
3. $eval_{\mathbf{e}}(M) = \text{err}_l$ implies that $eval_{\mathbf{v}}$ is undefined for M; and
4. if $eval_{\mathbf{e}}$ is undefined for M, then $eval_{\mathbf{v}}$ is undefined for M.

Proof for Theorem 8.8: For the proof of the first claim assume $M =_{\mathbf{v}} V$. Since $\mathbf{v}$ interpreted on the extended language (see $\mathbf{w}$ above) is a strict subset of $\mathbf{e}$, it is clearly true that $M =_{\mathbf{e}} V$.

For the proof of the second claim, recall that by theorem 8.7, $eval_{\mathbf{e}} = eval_{\mathbf{e}}^s$. Hence, assume $M \longmapsto\!\!\!\rightarrow_{\mathbf{e}} V$. Since error elements are not values, none of the standard reduction steps from M to V can be a step based on δ_{err} or **error**.

We prove this statement by induction on the length of the standard reduction sequence from M to V. The base case is obvious, the induction step follows:

- **Case** $M \longmapsto_{\mathbf{e}} M_1 \longmapsto\!\!\!\rightarrow_{\mathbf{e}} V$
  We know that $M = E[M']$ for some unique evaluation context E and an $\mathbf{e}$-redex M'. If $M'\ \delta_{\text{err}}\ \text{err}_l$ or $M' = \text{err}_l$, $M \longmapsto_{\mathbf{e}} \text{err}_l$. Hence, $M \longmapsto_{\mathbf{v}} M_1$ and, by induction, the claim holds.

The third claim follows from the observation that if for some
ISWIM program M such that $M \longmapsto\!\!\!\to_e N$, then $M \longmapsto\!\!\!\to_v N$ and
N is in ISWIM as long as we reduce standard reduction β_v or δ
redexes. Hence, if $M \longmapsto\!\!\!\to_e \mathsf{err}_l$, then

$$M \longmapsto\!\!\!\to_v E[N] \longmapsto\!\!\!\to_e E[\mathsf{err}_l] \longmapsto_e \mathsf{err}_l$$

for some evaluation context E and faulty application N. Hence,
$eval_v$ is undefined for M.

Finally, a minor adaptation of this observation proves the fourth
claim. Specifically, if for all N such that $M \longmapsto\!\!\!\to_e N$ we also have
$N \longmapsto\!\!\!\to_e L$, then all transitions are according to δ or β_v, and thus
$eval_v$ is also undefined for M.

In addition to the relationship between evaluators, language extensions
also raise the question whether equational (and other) reasoning about expressions of the base language remains valid in the context of the extended
language. While this is obviously true at the level of calculi:

$$=_v \subseteq =_e$$

we must also pose this question at the level of "truth," i.e., observational
equivalence. Technically speaking, we are asking whether an observational
equivalence about two ISWIM expressions is still an observational equivalence in Error ISWIM. Not surprisingly, the answer is "no." Because the occurrence of any stuck expression in a ISWIM program M means the evaluator is undefined for M, stuck expressions are observationally equivalent.
Indeed, they are also equivalent with expressions that trigger infinite loops
when evaluated.

In order to express the relationship between the two observational equivalence relations, we begin with the obvious, namely, that Error ISWIM contexts are exactly those of ISWIM except that they may contain error elements.
The definition of observational equivalence for Error ISWIM looks just like
the one for ISWIM, but the expressions and contexts are drawn from the
extended language.

$M \simeq_e N$ if and only if
$\quad eval_e(C[M]) = eval_e(C[N])$ for all Error ISWIM contexts C

The following theorem formalizes the discussed relationship between the
observational equivalence relations of ISWIM and Error ISWIM.

Theorem 8.9: For and M and N,

1. $M \simeq_{\mathbf{e}} N$ implies $M \simeq_{\mathbf{v}} N$; but
2. $M \simeq_{\mathbf{v}} N$ does not imply $M \simeq_{\mathbf{e}} N$.

Proof for Theorem 8.9: The first part follows from a contrapositive argument. Any ISWIM context that observationally separates two ISWIM expressions is also an Error ISWIM context.

For the second part, it is an easy exercise to show that

$$(\lambda fx.((f\ x)\ \Omega)) \simeq_{\mathbf{v}} (\lambda fx.\Omega)$$

In Error ISWIM the two expressions are distinguishable with

$$C = ([\ ]\ (\lambda x.\mathbf{err}_l)\ (\lambda x.x))\ .$$

Whereas $eval_{\mathbf{e}}(C[(\lambda fx.((f\ x)\ \Omega))]) = \mathbf{err}_l$, $eval_{\mathbf{e}}$ is undefined for $(C[(\lambda fx.\Omega)])$.

The proof of the theorem reveals why Error ISWIM can distinguish more ISWIM expressions than ISWIM itself. Some expressions that used to be observationally equivalent to divergence are now equal to errors. This is true no matter how many error elements are available in Error ISWIM, even if there is just one. This also means that the only way such expressions can be distinguished is via programs that eventually return errors.

Theorem 8.10: If M and N are such that $M \simeq_{\mathbf{v}} N$ and $M\not\simeq_{\mathbf{e}}N$, then there exists a context C over Error ISWIM such that $C[M]$ and $C[N]$ are programs and one of the following conditions hold:

1. There exist errors $\mathbf{err}_l$ and $\mathbf{err}_k$ with $\mathbf{err}_l \neq \mathbf{err}_k$ and

$$eval_{\mathbf{e}}(C[M]) = \mathbf{err}_l \text{ and } eval_{\mathbf{e}}(C[N]) = \mathbf{err}_k$$

2. There exists an error $\mathbf{err}_l$ and

$$eval_{\mathbf{e}}(C[M]) = \mathbf{err}_l \text{ and } eval_{\mathbf{e}}(C[N]) \text{ diverges}$$

3. There exists an error $\mathbf{err}_k$ and

$$eval_{\mathbf{e}}(C[M]) \text{ diverges and } eval_{\mathbf{e}}(C[N]) = \mathbf{err}_k$$

Proving this theorem illustrates how to reason about observational equivalence in general and in the presence of errors.

Proof for Theorem 8.10: Let M and N be such that $M \simeq_v N$ and $M \not\approx_e N$. Assume without loss of generality that M and N can be distinguished by observing answers distinct from errors. That is, for basic constants b_M and b_N and Error ISWIM context C such that $C[M]$ and $C[N]$ are programs,

$$eval_e(C[M]) = b_1, eval_e(C[N]) = b_2, \text{ and } b_1 \neq b_2 .$$

Since C is an Error ISWIM context, it may contain several error elements. These error elements clearly cannot play any role in the evaluation, however, because once a program is an evaluation context filled with some err_l, the answer must be err_l. Thus, let C' be like C except that all occurrences of error elements are replaced by Ω. By the following lemma,

$$eval_e(C[M]) = eval_e(C'[M]) = b_1$$

and

$$eval_e(C[N]) = eval_e(C'[N]) = b_2,$$

which means that some ISWIM context can already observe differences between M and N: $M \not\simeq_v N$. This contradiction to the assumptions of the theorem proves that the context C cannot exist.

We have left to prove that if a program has a proper answer, occurrences of error elements in the program can be ignored. The corresponding lemma is a version of the Activity Lemma (lemma 5.9) for Error ISWIM.

Lemma 8.11: Let C be an m-hole context over Error ISWIM. If $eval_e(C[err_{l_1}, \ldots err_{l_m}]) = a$ and $a \notin err_l$, $eval_e(C[\Omega, \ldots \Omega]) = a$.

Proof for Lemma 8.11: By assumption,

$$C[err_{l_1}, \ldots err_{l_m}] \longmapsto\!\!\!\!\twoheadrightarrow_e V$$

for some value $V \notin err_l$. We prove by induction on the length of the reduction sequence that $C[\Omega, \ldots \Omega]$ reduces to a value. The base case clearly holds, so assume that for some program M,

$$C[err_{l_1}, \ldots err_{l_m}] \longmapsto_e M \longmapsto\!\!\!\!\twoheadrightarrow_e V$$

By the definition of standard reduction, there must be some evaluation context E and standard redex M_{re} such that

$$C[err_{l_1}, \ldots err_{l_m}] = E[M_{re}]$$

The standard redex M_{re} cannot be an error element and it cannot be a δ_{err} redex; both would contradict the assumption. But M_{re} reduces to some N such that for some n-ary context C',

$$M = C'[\text{err}_{l'_1}, \ldots \text{err}_{l'_n}]$$

where $l'_1, \ldots l'_n$ is a (possibly repetitive) permutation of $l_1, \ldots l_m$. This clearly means that

$$C[\Omega, \ldots \Omega] \longmapsto_{\mathbf{e}} C'[\Omega, \ldots \Omega]$$

and, by inductive hypothesis,

$$C'[\Omega, \ldots \Omega] \longmapsto_{\mathbf{e}} V'$$

for some value V'. Moreover, if V was a basic constant, then $V' = V$ and if V was a λ-abstraction then so is V'. Hence,

$$eval_{\mathbf{e}}(C[\Omega, \ldots \Omega]) = a$$

Investigations into the relationship of programming languages and their extensions are suggestive of the relative expressive power. Theorem 8.9, for example, shows that Error ISWIM can express programming ideas that ISWIM cannot. As a result, Error ISWIM distinguishes ISWIM expressions that ISWIM equates. For more detail on this line of research, we refer the reader to Felleisen's work on the expressive power of programming languages [33].

Exercise 8.9. Suppose that we weaken the evaluator as follows:

1. the set of answers: $A_{\mathbf{e}} = b \cup \{\texttt{function}\} \cup \{\texttt{err}\}$

2. the evaluator: $eval_{\hat{\mathbf{e}}} : \text{Error ISWIM} \longrightarrow A_{\mathbf{e}}$

$$eval_{\hat{\mathbf{e}}}(M) = \begin{cases} b & \text{if } M =_{\mathbf{e}} b \\ \texttt{function} & \text{if } M =_{\mathbf{e}} \lambda X.N \\ \texttt{err} & \text{if } M =_{\mathbf{e}} \text{err}_l \end{cases}$$

3. the observational equivalence relation

$M \simeq_{\hat{\mathbf{e}}} N$ if and only if
$eval_{\hat{\mathbf{e}}}(C[M]) = eval_{\hat{\mathbf{e}}}(C[N])$ for all Error ISWIM contexts C

Is $\simeq_{\hat{e}}$ also weakened, in the sense that $M \simeq_{\hat{e}} N$ does not imply $M \simeq_{e} N$?

Exercise 8.10. Use the proof of theorem 8.9 to show that Error ISWIM can reveal the order in which a binary procedure invokes its functional parameters. Hint: Separate the cases where the set of errors contains only one element (err_0) and the case where it contains at least two distinct elements.

Exercise 8.11. Use theorem 8.1 to prove that for any ISWIM expressions M and N, $M =_{v} N$ implies $M =_{e} N$. Conclude that for all M and N, $M =_{e} N$ implies $M \simeq_{v} N$. (Use the Church-Rosser theorem for ISWIM, theorem 4.4.) Also prove that $M =_{e} N$ implies $M \simeq_{e} N$.

8·3 **Handler ISWIM.** Some programming languages do not signal errors but raise **exceptions** when things go wrong. In contrast to errors, which stop an evaluation, exceptions merely suspend the ordinary flow of program control. A program may catch exceptions with **exception handlers**, recovering from undesirable situations through alternative computations.

A typical syntax for raising exceptions is

$$(\texttt{throw } b)$$

The constant b is the exception proper; it is used to communicate information from the place where the exception is raised to the handler that takes care of it. An exception handler is installed as follows:

$$(\texttt{catch } M_1 \texttt{ with } \lambda X.M_2)$$

The expression M_1 is the protected **body** and the λ expression is the **handler**. The evaluation of such a `catch` expression starts with the body. If the body returns a value, this value becomes the answer of the `catch` expression. If the evaluation of the body raises an exception, the handler is used to determine a result. Specifically, the λ expression is applied to the constant that comes with the exception.

Historically, Lisp provided exception handlers that used the keywords `catch` and `throw`. Later, ML introduced the analog of λ expressions as handlers so that programs could easily deal with exception-based transfer of control. We use a mix of notation to acknowledge the influences of both and introduce **Handler ISWIM** as an extension of plain ISWIM with `throw` and `catch` forms.

M	$=$	$\dots$	same as plain ISWIM
	$\|$	$(\texttt{throw } b)$	
	$\|$	$(\texttt{catch } M \texttt{ with } \lambda X.M)$	

The syntax for the `catch` expression is unusual when compared to all the other expressions we have introduced so far. It has two sub-expressions but one of them has a rather special form: M and $\lambda X.M$. In general, this kind of specialization requires only one special consideration, namely, a proper adaptation of substitution.

$$
\begin{aligned}
& (\texttt{catch } M \texttt{ with } (\lambda X_1.M_1))[X_2 \leftarrow M_2] \\
= \ & (\texttt{catch } M[X_2 \leftarrow M_2] \texttt{ with } (\lambda X_1.M_1)[X_2 \leftarrow M_2])
\end{aligned}
$$

In other words, we get to specify the syntactic structure of the handler, but by viewing it as a plain λ expression, we also get to re-use our substitution (meta)function.

Exception handlers are useful in many situations. For example, the evaluation of a deeply nested arithmetic expression may signal that a division-by-zero occurred or an overflow happened. At the same time, a symbolic constant `infinity` might be an appropriate result if this happens. In such a case, it suffices to surround the entire arithmetic expression with a `catch` expression and let the handler take care of any exceptions. Similarly, if there are two methods for computing a result, but the first and faster one may signal an exception, a program may start with the first method and switch to the second one when an exception occurs. In this case, the exception handler is used to implement a control construct for backtracking.

To illustrate, we consider a procedure that multiplies the elements of a list of numbers. A plain ISWIM version of the procedure traverses the list and multiplies the elements one by one:

$$
\begin{aligned}
\Pi \doteq \mathsf{Y}_{\mathsf{V}} \ (\lambda \pi.\lambda l. \\
(\mathsf{if0} \quad & (\mathsf{isnull} \ l) \\
& \ulcorner 1 \urcorner \\
& (* \ (\mathsf{car} \ l) \ (\pi \ (\mathsf{cdr} \ l)))))
\end{aligned}
$$

In Handler ISWIM, the procedure can check for an occurrence of $\ulcorner 0 \urcorner$ in the list and can exit the potentially deep recursion immediately, because the result is $\ulcorner 0 \urcorner$. Exiting can be implemented by raising an exception that is handled by a surrounding handler:

$$
\begin{aligned}
\Pi^0 \ &\doteq \ \lambda l.(\texttt{catch } (\Pi' \ l) \texttt{ with } \lambda x.x) \\
\text{where} \\
\Pi' \ &\doteq \ \mathsf{Y}_{\mathsf{V}}(\lambda \pi. \ \lambda l. \quad (\mathsf{if0} \quad (\mathsf{isnull} \ l) \qquad\qquad\qquad \ulcorner 1 \urcorner \\
& \qquad\qquad\qquad\qquad (\mathsf{if0} \quad (\mathsf{car} \ l) \qquad\qquad\quad (\texttt{throw } \ulcorner 0 \urcorner) \\
& \qquad\qquad\qquad\qquad\qquad\quad (* \ (\mathsf{car} \ l) \ (\pi \ (\mathsf{cdr} \ l)))))
\end{aligned}
$$

This example is particularly instructive. It shows how signaling an exception indicates that the proper result is found, short-cutting the rest of the computation.

Now that we have an understanding of the syntax of exceptions and handlers combined with an intuition for their pragmatics, we can turn to the semantics of the language. A calculus for Handler ISWIM must clearly incorporate the equations for the applications of functions and primitives. Furthermore, it is clear that $(\texttt{throw } b)$ expressions should behave just like $\texttt{err}_b$ expressions:

$$E[(\texttt{throw } b)] \rightarrow (\texttt{throw } b)$$

though we must be careful with an adaptation of this notation from Error ISWIM. There the evaluation context E represents some pending computation. At the same time, evaluation contexts are also those contexts that, according to the Standard Reduction Theorem for Error ISWIM, specify all possible remainders of a computation.

In Handler ISWIM, evaluation contexts must play a different role. On one hand, an evaluation context is what a $\texttt{throw}$ expression eliminates. On the other hand, the context

$$(\texttt{catch } [\,] \texttt{ with } \lambda x.M)$$

represents a pending "exception handling" computation. If any expression plugged into the hole of this context raises an exception, this exception should *not* eliminate the rest of the context. Hence, the set of evaluation contexts in Handler ISWIM is the set E from Error ISWIM, but it does not represent the set of all possible pending computations. We therefore use F for this set, not E.

$$F = [\,] \mid (V\ F) \mid (F\ M) \mid (o^m\ V\ \dots\ V\ F\ M\ \dots\ M)$$

As for $\texttt{catch}$ expressions, the notions of reduction are now straightforward. If the protected body reduces to a value, this value is the result of the entire $\texttt{catch}$ expression:

$$(\texttt{catch } U \texttt{ with } \lambda X.M) \rightarrow U$$

Otherwise, if it raises an exception, nothing is propagated; instead, the handler is applied to the basic constant associated with the error:

$$(\texttt{catch } (\texttt{throw } b) \texttt{ with } \lambda X.M) \rightarrow ((\lambda X.M)\ b)$$

The following definition formally introduces these three notions of reduction
with names.

$$
\begin{array}{lll}
F[(\texttt{throw}\ b)] & \textbf{throw} & (\texttt{throw}\ b) \\
(\texttt{catch}\ V\ \texttt{with}\ \lambda X.M) & \textbf{return} & V \\
(\texttt{catch}\ (\texttt{throw}\ b)\ \texttt{with}\ \lambda X.M) & \textbf{catch} & ((\lambda X.M)\ b)
\end{array}
$$

Of course, these rules leave open how a throw expression may appear
when a primitive operation is undefined for its arguments or when other
errors occur. For the former, let us assume that we have Error ISWIM's to-
tal δ function, producing some $\texttt{err}_l$ if the given primitive application is not
defined.

$$
\begin{array}{lll}
(o^m\ b_1 \ldots b_m) & \delta_{\texttt{err}} & (\texttt{throw}\ b) \\
\quad \text{if}\ \delta(o^m, b_1, \ldots b_m) = \texttt{err}_b & & \\
(o^m\ b_1 \ldots b_{i-1}\ (\lambda X.N)\ V_{i+1}\ \ldots\ V_m) & \delta_{\texttt{err}} & (\texttt{throw}\ \ulcorner i \urcorner) \\
(b\ V) & \delta_{\texttt{err}} & (\texttt{throw}\ b)
\end{array}
$$

As in Error ISWIM, this definition overloads δ, using it as an interpretation
for primitive applications as well as a notion of reduction. In case δ returns
$\texttt{err}_b$ for some primitive application, the $\delta_{\texttt{err}}$ notion of reduction for Handler
ISWIM reduces the application to $(\texttt{throw}\ b)$.

From all of this, it follows that the notion of reduction for Handler ISWIM
combines a notational adaptation of **v** from ISWIM to the syntax of Handler
ISWIM with $\delta_{\texttt{err}}$, **throw**, **return**, and **catch**.

$$
\mathbf{h} = \beta_{\mathsf{v}} \cup \delta \cup \delta_{\texttt{err}} \cup \textbf{throw} \cup \textbf{return} \cup \textbf{catch}
$$

The calculus itself is generated via the reflexive-transitive-symmetric and
compatible closure, respectively. It induces the evaluator as usual.

$$
\begin{array}{ll}
eval_{\mathbf{h}} : M \longrightarrow A_{\mathbf{e}} & \\[4pt]
eval_{\mathbf{h}}(M) = \left\{
\begin{array}{ll}
b & \text{if}\ M =_{\mathbf{h}} b \\
\texttt{function} & \text{if}\ M =_{\mathbf{h}} \lambda X.N \\
\texttt{err}_b & \text{if}\ M =_{\mathbf{h}} (\texttt{throw}\ b)
\end{array}
\right.
\end{array}
$$

The set of answers includes all basic constants, the symbol function, and
error elements indexed with basic constants.

Consistency for Handler ISWIM. The evaluator for Handler ISWIM is a
function, just like all previous evaluators.

Theorem 8.12 [Consistency with Handlers]: The relation $eval_h$ is a partial function.

Proof for Theorem 8.12: The relations **catch** and **return** obviously satisfy the diamond property and Church-Rosser. It is also straightforward to show that the proof of Church-Rosser for the notion of reduction

$$\mathbf{e} = \beta_v \cup \delta \cup \delta_{err} \cup \mathbf{throw}$$

extends to the full Handler ISWIM syntax. If the reduction based on **e** commutes with the one based on **catch** and **return**, we have Church-Rosser for **h** and thus consistency.

To prove the commutativity of **catch** and **return** with the old reductions, we must inspect two cases for arbitrary contexts C over Handler ISWIM:

- **Case** $C[(\text{catch } (\text{throw } b) \text{ with } \lambda X.M)] \to C[((\lambda X.M) b)]$
  Then, a reduction step according to one of δ, β_v, δ_{err}, or **throw** either modifies the context C or the handler:

  - **Case** $C[(\text{catch } (\text{throw } b) \text{ with } \lambda X.M)]$
    $\to C'[(\text{catch } (\text{throw } b) \text{ with } \lambda X.M)]$
    $C[((\lambda X.M) b)]$ and $C'[(\text{catch } (\text{throw } b) \text{ with } \lambda X.M)]$
    both reduce to $C'[((\lambda X.M) b)]$.
  - **Case** $C[(\text{catch } (\text{throw } b) \text{ with } \lambda X.M)]$
    $\to C[(\text{catch } (\text{throw } b) \text{ with } \lambda X.M')]$
    In this case, the common contractum is $C[((\lambda X.M') b)]$.

  In both cases, the reductions to the common contractum always require one step, which shows that the one-step reduction relations and hence their transitive closures commute.

- **Case** $C[(\text{catch } U \text{ with } \lambda X.M)] \to C[U]$
  In this case, a reduction can affect C, U, and V, which requires an analysis of three subcases. Otherwise the proof of this case proceeds as the first one.

Standard Reduction for Handler ISWIM.

The usual definition of a deterministic evaluation function for a language just makes the basic notion of reduction compatible with the constructions of evaluation contexts. While this is also true for Handler ISWIM, we must carefully inspect what evaluation contexts are and what they are not.

As discussed, the set F of contexts, which is used to define **throw**, is not comprehensive enough because we must be able to reduce redexes in protected bodies. For example,

$$(\texttt{catch } ((\lambda x.x) \ \ulcorner 0 \urcorner) \text{ with } \lambda x.x)$$

should reduce to

$$(\texttt{catch } \ulcorner 0 \urcorner \text{ with } \lambda x.x)$$

even though $(\texttt{catch } [\ ] \text{ with } \lambda X.M)$ is not a member of F.

Naturally, the solution is to define a new kind of evaluation context, E, appropriate for Handler ISWIM. An E context represents the entire rest of the computation, including all the pending $\texttt{catch}$ expressions, with respect to the expression in its hole.

$$
\begin{array}{rcll}
E & = & \ldots & \text{same as plain ISWIM} \\
  & | & (\texttt{catch } E \text{ with } \lambda X.M) &
\end{array}
$$

As with Error ISWIM, we must define the standard reduction relation so that it avoids ambiguities due to multiple matching **throw** reductions. Instead of one special rule, two are needed; one for an uncaught exception, and one within a $\texttt{catch}$ expression.

The complete definition of the standard reduction function for Handler ISWIM follows.[1]

$$\tilde{\textbf{h}} = \beta_{\text{v}} \cup \delta \cup \delta_{\text{err}} \cup \textbf{return} \cup \textbf{catch}$$

$$
\begin{array}{lcl}
E[M] & \longmapsto_{\textbf{h}} & E[N] \\
\quad \text{if } M \, \tilde{\textbf{h}} \, N & & \\
E\left[\begin{array}{l} (\texttt{catch } F[(\texttt{throw } b)] \\ \quad \text{with } \lambda X.M) \end{array}\right] & \longmapsto_{\textbf{h}} & E\left[\begin{array}{l} (\texttt{catch } (\texttt{throw } b) \\ \quad \text{with } \lambda X.M) \end{array}\right] \\
\quad \text{if } F \neq [] & & \\
F[(\texttt{throw } b)] & \longmapsto_{\textbf{h}} & (\texttt{throw } b) \\
\quad \text{if } F \neq [] & &
\end{array}
$$

Note how the first two standard reduction steps take place in E contexts, while the last one uses F only. Since the standard reduction relation is not compatible with the syntactic constructions of Handler ISWIM, this last clause of the definition exists for the purpose of raising an exception that is not signaled during the evaluation of a protected body. It is a special case; see exercise 8.13 on how to eliminate this special case.

---

[1]The side-conditions $F \neq []$ are not strictly needed. Even without them, $eval_{\textbf{h}}^{\text{s}}$ remains a function, though a proof of this fact is needlessly complicated.

The definition of the standard reduction evaluator is straightforward.

$$eval_{\mathbf{h}}^{\mathsf{s}}(M) = \begin{cases} b & \text{if } M \longmapsto\!\!\!\!\twoheadrightarrow_{\mathbf{h}} b \\ \texttt{function} & \text{if } M \longmapsto\!\!\!\!\twoheadrightarrow_{\mathbf{h}} \lambda X.N \\ \texttt{err}_b & \text{if } M \longmapsto\!\!\!\!\twoheadrightarrow_{\mathbf{h}} (\texttt{throw } b) \end{cases}$$

A correctness proof of this new specification of the evaluator consists of the usual steps, though stating the unique partitioning property of the system requires more cases than before.

Lemma 8.13 [Unique Evaluation Contexts]: For every closed Handler ISWIM expression M, one of the following is true:

- M is a value or for some b, $M = (\texttt{throw } b)$.
- There exist a unique standard context E and a standard re-dex M_{rh} such that $M = E[M_{\mathsf{rh}}]$ where

$$\begin{aligned} M_{\mathsf{rh}} \quad = \quad & (V \; V) \\ | \quad & (o^m \; V \ldots V) \\ | \quad & (\texttt{catch } V \texttt{ with } \lambda X.M) \\ | \quad & (\texttt{catch } (\texttt{throw } b) \texttt{ with } \lambda X.M) \end{aligned}$$

- There exist a unique standard context E and non-empty F such that $M = E[(\texttt{catch } F[(\texttt{throw } b)] \texttt{ with } \lambda X.M)]$.
- There exists a non-empty F such that $M = F[(\texttt{throw } b)]$.

Second, we must show that the evaluator based on the standard reduction function is equal to the evaluator based on the calculus.

Theorem 8.14: $eval_{\mathbf{h}}^{\mathsf{s}} = eval_{\mathbf{h}}$

We leave the proof of this theorem to an exercise.

Exercise 8.12. Adapt the proof of ISWIM's Standard Reduction Theorem to Handler ISWIM.

Machines for Exceptions. As we saw in previous chapters, a syntactic machine, such as the standard reduction function, is a good compromise for understanding and analyzing the mechanical behavior of programs. It is more algorithmic than a calculus, yet it requires no auxiliary data structures such as stacks, activation records, etc. For a good implementation, though, it is still too abstract and too inefficient. For that, we need machines that eliminate the obvious inefficiencies from the standard reduction machine and that use appropriate data representations.

Although the derivation of concrete machines is in principle a straightforward task, Handler ISWIM's introduction of handlers adds a new dimension to the design space and thus poses a new challenge. We therefore study the derivation of the CC machine and then briefly sketch improvements that accommodate exception handlers in an efficient manner.

The Handler CC Machine. The standard reduction machine for Handler ISWIM (page 134) extends the one for ISWIM. The basic difference is that, in contrast to the ISWIM machine, the Handler ISWIM machine distinguishes two notions of "rest of computation:" its F contexts represent the rest of the computation up to the (currently) closest catch expression; its E contexts denotes the rest of the entire computation relative to some standard redex.

$$
eval_{cc+h}(M) = \begin{cases} b & \text{if } \langle M, [\,] \rangle \longmapsto\!\!\!\twoheadrightarrow_{cc} \langle b, [\,] \rangle \\ \text{function} & \text{if } \langle M, [\,] \rangle \longmapsto\!\!\!\twoheadrightarrow_{cc} \langle \lambda X.N, [\,] \rangle \\ \text{err}_b & \text{if } \langle M, [\,] \rangle \longmapsto\!\!\!\twoheadrightarrow_{cc} \langle (\text{throw } b), [\,] \rangle \end{cases}
$$

	$\longmapsto_{cc}$	
$\langle M, E \rangle$ if $M\,\delta_{\text{err}}(\text{throw } b)$	$\langle (\text{throw } b), E \rangle$	[cc7]
$\langle (\text{throw } b), F \rangle$ if $F \neq [\,]$	$\langle (\text{throw } b), [\,] \rangle$	[cc8]
$\langle (\text{catch } M \text{ with } \lambda X.N), E \rangle$	$\left\langle M, \atop E[(\text{catch } [\,] \text{ with } \lambda X.N)] \right\rangle$	[cc9]
$\left\langle V, \atop E[(\text{catch } [\,] \text{ with } \lambda X.N)] \right\rangle$	$\langle V, E \rangle$	[cc10]
$\left\langle (\text{throw } b), \atop E[(\text{catch } F \text{ with } \lambda X.N)] \right\rangle$ if $F \neq [\,]$	$\left\langle (\text{throw } b), \atop E[(\text{catch } [\,] \text{ with } \lambda X.N)] \right\rangle$	[cc11]
$\left\langle (\text{throw } b), \atop E[(\text{catch } [\,] \text{ with } \lambda X.N)] \right\rangle$	$\left\langle ((\lambda X.N)\, b), \atop E \right\rangle$	[cc12]

A naive adaptation of the design strategy for machines suggests a mere separation of E contexts from control strings. Doing so avoids the repeated partitioning task. Machine states for the revised CC machine are thus pairs consisting of closed expressions and E contexts. As usual, the instructions shift information from the control string to the context until a standard redex is found; these instructions include one new rule for moving handlers from catch expressions to contexts for the evaluation of protected bodies ([cc9]).

Once the redex is found and if this redex is a δ- or a β_v-redex, the CC machine for Handler ISWIM proceeds as before. If the redex is a δ_{err}-redex, the machine places an appropriate throw expression in its control register ([cc7]). Finally, if the control string is an throw expression, then the machine erases the portion of the surrounding context up to the closest handler, if it exists ([cc11]), or the entire context otherwise ([cc8]). The remaining two rules specify how values are returned from catch expressions ([cc10]) or how exceptions are handled ([cc12]).

This machine-based Handler ISWIM evaluator is equivalent to the one induced by the standard reduction for the same language.

Theorem 8.15: $eval_{cc+h} = eval_h^s$

It suffices to check that the six new CC instructions faithfully implement the five instructions that differentiate the Handler ISWIM standard reduction machine from the one for ISWIM.

Exercise 8.13. Eliminate [cc8] by wrapping the initial program with a handler.

Exercise 8.14. Prove theorem 8.15. Argue why the suggested proof strategy works. Then prove how the two instruction sets implement each other.

Exercise 8.15. Implement the CC machine for Handler ISWIM in some programming language in a faithful manner. What inefficiencies are observable?

The CHC Machine. One major bottleneck of the naive CC machine for Handler ISWIM is obvious. Although the machine maintains the E context as a separate data structure, the transition implementing **throw** must find the innermost handler with respect to the hole of the context. To do so, it partitions the E context to determine the F context between the hole and innermost catch expression. This traversal of the E context repeats the search for the redex. If the machine separated out this innermost F context, the **throw** instruction would simply replace its evaluation context with an empty one.

One way of separating the innermost F context from the rest of the E context is to represent all of E as a stack of F contexts. Each element is the F context between two currently active catch expressions, that is, handlers whose catch expressions surrounds the hole. To handle exceptions correctly, the F contexts must be paired with their surrounding handlers. Here is an appropriate data structure:

$$
\begin{aligned}
H &= \epsilon \\
&\mid \langle \lambda X.M, F \rangle \, H
\end{aligned}
$$

Put differently, the optimized machine has three registers: C for the control string; H for the stack of handlers paired with F contexts; and the current control context (F). We therefore call it the **CHC machine**.

Given this insight, reformulating the machine instructions can focus on two scenarios:

$$\langle(\texttt{catch } M \texttt{ with } \lambda X.N), H, F\rangle \rightarrow \langle M, \langle \lambda X.N, F\rangle H, [\,]\rangle$$

That is, when the new machine encounters a `catch` expression, it pushes the current F context and the new handler on the stack. And:

$$\langle V, \langle \lambda X.N, F\rangle H, [\,]\rangle \rightarrow \langle V, H, F\rangle$$

When the body of a `catch` expression is reduced to a value, the CHC machine pops that stack, throwing away the current handler and reinstalling the surrounding F context.

$$eval_{\text{chc}}(M) = \begin{cases} b & \text{if } \langle M, \epsilon, [\,]\rangle \longmapsto\!\!\!\twoheadrightarrow_{\text{chc}} \langle b, \epsilon, [\,]\rangle \\ \texttt{function} & \text{if } \langle M, \epsilon, [\,]\rangle \longmapsto\!\!\!\twoheadrightarrow_{\text{chc}} \langle \lambda X.N, \epsilon, [\,]\rangle \\ \texttt{err}_b & \text{if } \langle M, \epsilon, [\,]\rangle \longmapsto\!\!\!\twoheadrightarrow_{\text{chc}} \langle(\texttt{throw } b), \epsilon, [\,]\rangle \end{cases}$$

$\longmapsto_{\text{chc}}$		
$\langle(MN), H, F\rangle$ if $M \notin V$	$\langle M, H, F[([\,]\ N)]\rangle$	[chc1]
$\langle(VM), H, F\rangle$ if $M \notin V$	$\langle M, H, F[(V\ [\,])]\rangle$	[chc2]
$\langle(o^n\ V_1 \ldots V_i\ M\ N \ldots), H, F\rangle$ if $M \notin V$	$\langle M, H, \\ F[(o^n\ V_1 \ldots V_i\ [\,]\ N \ldots)]\rangle$	[chc3]
$\langle((\lambda X.M)\ V), H, F\rangle$	$\langle M[X \leftarrow V], H, F\rangle$	[chcfi$_v$]
$\langle(o^m\ b_1 \ldots\ b_m), H, F\rangle$	$\langle \delta(o^m, b_1, \ldots b_m), H, F\rangle$	[chcffi]
$\langle V, H, F[(U\ [\,])]\rangle$	$\langle(U\ V), H, F\rangle$	[chc4]
$\langle V, H, F[([\,]\ N)]\rangle$	$\langle(V\ N), H, F\rangle$	[chc5]
$\langle V, H, \\ F[(o^n\ V_1 \ldots V_i\ [\,]\ N \ldots)]\rangle$	$\langle(o^n\ V_1 \ldots V_i\ V\ N \ldots), H, \\ F\rangle$	[chc6]
$\langle M, H, F\rangle$ if $M\ \delta_{\text{err}}\ (\texttt{throw } b)$	$\langle(\texttt{throw } b), H, F\rangle$	[chc7]
$\langle(\texttt{throw } b), \epsilon, F\rangle$ if $F \neq [\,]$	$\langle(\texttt{throw } b), \epsilon, [\,]\rangle$	[chc8]
$\langle(\texttt{catch } M \texttt{ with } \lambda X.N), H, F\rangle$	$\langle M, \langle \lambda X.N, F\rangle H, [\,]\rangle$	[chc9]
$\langle V, \langle U, F\rangle H, [\,]\rangle$	$\langle V, H, F\rangle$	[chc10]
$\langle(\texttt{throw } b), H, F\rangle$ if $H \neq \epsilon, F \neq [\,]$	$\langle(\texttt{throw } b), H, [\,]\rangle$	[chc11]
$\langle(\texttt{throw } b), \langle U, F\rangle H, [\,]\rangle$	$\langle(U\ b), H, F\rangle$	[chc12]

The first eight instruction of the CHC machine are just reformulated instructions from the CC machine for ISWIM. Because ISWIM expressions do not involve `catch` expressions, these instructions do not use the H register. For the same reason, they use only F contexts. The rule [chc9] shows when the content of the F register is pushed on the H register.

A comparison of rule [chc8] with rule [chc12] shows again that the elimination of an E context without a `catch` expression (surrounding the hole) is a special case of throwing an exception to the closest handler. Indeed, the connection is now so obvious that we could merge rules [chc8] and [chc12] without affecting the correctness theorem.

Theorem 8.16: $eval_{chc} = eval_{cc+h}$

The correctness proof demands a relationship between the states of the CC machine for Handler ISWIM and those of its CHC machine. The idea for the conversions is the above-mentioned representation invariant that the E context of a CC machine state is turned into a stack of handlers paired with F contexts. Conversely, given such a stack, we can create an E context by wrapping the hole with the F contexts mingled with the handlers.

Exercise 8.16. Prove theorem 8.16. Use the suggested strategy.

Exercise 8.17. Implement the CHC machine for Handler ISWIM in some programming language in a faithful manner, especially with regard to evaluation contexts.

Exercise 8.18. Show that it is indeed possible to merge rules [chc8] and [chc12] without affecting theorem 8.16.

Exercise 8.19. Consider the following merger of rules [chc11] and [chc12]:

$$\langle(\texttt{throw}\ b), \langle U, F\rangle\ H, F'\rangle \longmapsto_{chc} \langle(U\ b), H, F\rangle$$

Does this simplification of the CHC instruction set preserve correctness?

Exercise 8.20. Derive CK and CEK machines from the CHC machine.

Exercise 8.21. Design an alternative to the CHC machine that reserves a new register for the current error handler. Prove its equivalence with the above CHC machine.

$8 \cdot 4$ Continuation ISWIM and Total Control. Handler ISWIM introduces a simple form of flow control for programs. Some programming languages provide total access to the flow of control. This section pro-

vides a brief introduction to this form of control construct, starting with a reformulation of Handler ISWIM's calculus.

Although Handler ISWIM's basic notion of reduction for `catch` and `throw` naturally grow out of our study of Error ISWIM, reformulating **catch** as

$$(\texttt{catch}\ F[(\texttt{throw}\ b)]\ \texttt{with}\ \lambda X.M) \quad \textbf{catch}' \quad (\lambda X.M)\ b$$

provides direct intuition into the inter-workings of exceptions and handlers. Specifically, this rule says that the raising of an exception is equivalent to the application of the closest exception handler to the exception value.

What this revised rule also shows is that the context of the exception, F, is lost forever. There is no way to resume this computation with a replacement value that might just work. To make this precise, imagine a program that should not fail, even if some function call signals a division-by-zero error. Instead, when such an exception is signaled, the computation should be resumed with a very large number. For example, the control program for a physical device may benefit from such a computation strategy because it is better to approximate solutions in some cases than to fail.

One way to accommodate such **resumable exceptions** is to raise not only an exception with a `throw` expression but to also grab the surrounding F context up to the surrounding exception handler:

$$(\texttt{catch}\ F[(\texttt{throw}\ b)]\ \texttt{with}\ \lambda XC.M) \quad \textbf{cntrl} \quad (\lambda XC.M)\ b\ (\lambda Y.F[Y])$$

That is, the exception handler consumes two arguments now: the exception value (some basic constant) and a function that reifies the F context of the exception raising expression. In the programming language literature, $\lambda x.F[x]$ is known as a **continuation**.[2]

In such a programming language, it is indeed possible to resume a computation that raises an exception. Say division-by-zero is signaled via `throw` $\ulcorner 0 \urcorner$ and no other form raises this error and e is the expression that demands the above-mentioned protection from division-by-zero errors. Then the following expression is what we need:

$$(\texttt{catch}\ e\ \texttt{with}\ (\lambda xc.\text{if0}\ x\ (c\ \texttt{inf})\ (\texttt{throw}\ x)))$$

It sets up a handler that immediately inspects the exception value x. Assuming the inspection discovers that the exception value is $\ulcorner 0 \urcorner$, the exception context is applied to `inf`, some very large number; otherwise, the exception is re-raised.

---

[2]Technically, it is a **functional continuation** or **composable continuation**. People occasionally add the word "object" to distinguish reified continuations from those that exist in abstract machines.

Suppose the expression e eventually signals an exception. Then the computation proceeds as follows:

$$
\begin{aligned}
& (\text{catch } e \text{ with } (\lambda xc.\text{if0 } x \ (c \text{ inf}) \ (\text{throw } x))) \\
= \ & (\text{catch } F[(/ \ \ulcorner 1 \urcorner \ \ulcorner 0 \urcorner)] \text{ with } (\lambda xc.\text{if0 } x \ (c \text{ inf}) \ (\text{throw } x))) \\
= \ & (\text{catch } F[(\text{throw } \ulcorner 0 \urcorner)] \text{ with } (\lambda xc.\text{if0 } x \ (c \text{ inf}) \ (\text{throw } x))) \\
= \ & (\lambda xc.\text{if0 } x \ (c \text{ inf}) \ (\text{throw } x)) \ \ulcorner 0 \urcorner \ (\lambda y.F[y]) \\
= \ & (\text{if0 } \ulcorner 0 \urcorner \ ((\lambda y.F[y]) \text{ inf}) \ (\text{throw } \ulcorner 0 \urcorner)) \\
= \ & F[\text{inf}]
\end{aligned}
$$

In other words, the computation of e is resumed exactly where the division-by-zero error is discovered. The handler, however, is no longer available. Hence, if $F[\text{inf}]$ signals the exception again, the evaluation is stopped.

Exercise 8.22. Design a recursive function D that consumes a function f and some value v. The function D applies f to v and resumes this computation for all exceptions with inf until it produces a value. In particular, if $(f \ v)$ repeatedly raises an exception, the call to D never terminates.

Let us formulate the syntax and semantics of Control ISWIM, a programming language that gives programs complete power over the control flow.

$$
\begin{aligned}
M \ \ = \ \ & \ldots & \text{same as plain ISWIM} \\
| \ \ & (\text{throw } b) \\
| \ \ & (\text{catch } M \text{ with } \lambda X.\lambda Y.M)
\end{aligned}
$$

Like Handler ISWIM, Control ISWIM extends ISWIM with a catch and a throw expression. Indeed, the only difference is that, in Control ISWIM, the former requires a handler of two arguments instead of one; otherwise, the syntax of Control ISWIM is just that of Handler ISWIM. And just like for Handler ISWIM, we deal with the handler sub-expressions also as if it were a plain λ expression, especially as far as substitution is concerned.

$$
\begin{aligned}
& (\text{catch } M \text{ with } (\lambda X_1.\lambda Y.M_1))[X_2 \leftarrow M_2] \\
= \ & (\text{catch } M[X_2 \leftarrow M_2] \text{ with } (\lambda X_1.\lambda Y.M_1)[X_2 \leftarrow M_2])
\end{aligned}
$$

The calculus for Control ISWIM is a seemingly simple variation of the one for Handler ISWIM. We start with its definition of F contexts.

$$
F = [] \ | \ (V \ F) \ | \ (F \ M) \ | \ (o^m \ V \ \ldots \ V \ F \ M \ \ldots \ M)
$$

Here is the set of new notions of reduction. Of course, the only one that truly differs is **cntrl**. All others look just as before, except that they apply to the new syntax of Control ISWIM.

$$\mathbf{c} = \beta_v \cup \delta \cup \delta_{\mathrm{err}} \cup \mathbf{throw} \cup \mathbf{return} \cup \mathbf{cntrl}$$

$$
\begin{array}{rcl}
F[(\texttt{throw}\ b)] & \mathbf{throw} & (\texttt{throw}\ b) \\
(\texttt{catch}\ F[(\texttt{throw}\ b)]\ \texttt{with}\ \lambda XZ.M) & \mathbf{cntrl} & (\lambda XZ.M)\ b\ (\lambda Y.F[Y]) \\
\text{if}\ Y \notin \mathcal{FV}(F[\ulcorner 5 \urcorner]) & & \\
(\texttt{catch}\ V\ \texttt{with}\ \lambda X.M) & \mathbf{return} & V \\
(o^m\ b_1 \ldots b_m) & \delta_{\mathrm{err}} & (\texttt{throw}\ b) \\
\text{if}\ \delta(o^m, b_1, \ldots b_m) = \mathrm{err}_b & & \\
(o^m\ b_1 \ldots b_{i-1}\ (\lambda X.N)\ V_{i+1}\ \ldots\ V_m) & \delta_{\mathrm{err}} & (\texttt{throw}\ \ulcorner i \urcorner) \\
(b\ V) & \delta_{\mathrm{err}} & (\texttt{throw}\ b)
\end{array}
$$

As usual, $\rightarrow_\mathbf{c}$ is the compatible closure of $\mathbf{c}$; $\twoheadrightarrow_\mathbf{c}$ is the transitive-reflexive closure of $\rightarrow_\mathbf{c}$; and $=_\mathbf{c}$ is its reflexive-transitive-symmetric closure.

The evaluation function for Control ISWIM has the same range as the one for Handler ISWIM, and it is of course defined in an analogous manner.

$$
\begin{array}{rcl}
eval_\mathbf{c} : M & \longrightarrow & A_\mathbf{e} \\[4pt]
eval_\mathbf{c}(M) & = & \left\{
\begin{array}{ll}
b & \text{if}\ M =_\mathbf{c} b \\
\text{function} & \text{if}\ M =_\mathbf{c} \lambda X.N \\
\mathrm{err}_b & \text{if}\ M =_\mathbf{c} (\texttt{throw}\ b)
\end{array}
\right.
\end{array}
$$

Theorem 8.17 [Consistency for Control ISWIM]: The relation $eval_\mathbf{c}$ is a partial function.

Exercise 8.23. Prove theorem 8.17.

Standard Reduction for Control ISWIM. Following our usual program, we next adapt the standard reduction theorem of Handler ISWIM to Control ISWIM. Doing so requires an adaptation of two definitions: the one for the set of contexts in which standard reduction steps take place and the standard reduction function.

Both adaptations are straightforward. As far as contexts are concerned, there is only change required. Since the syntax of catch expressions in Control ISWIM demands a handler function of two parameters, the contexts for evaluating protected bodies must do so, too.

$$
\begin{array}{rcl}
E & = & \ldots \qquad\qquad\qquad\qquad\qquad \text{same as plain ISWIM} \\
& | & (\texttt{catch}\ E\ \texttt{with}\ \lambda X.\lambda Y.M)
\end{array}
$$

The standard reduction function needs to grab the current continuation and immediately supply it to the exception handler when an exception is signaled. Otherwise, Control ISWIM's standard reduction function is just like Handler ISWIM's.

$$\tilde{c} = \beta_v \cup \delta \cup \delta_{err} \cup \mathbf{return}$$

$$
\begin{array}{lcl}
E[M] & \longmapsto_c & E[N] \\
\quad \text{if } M \,\tilde{c}\, N & & \\
E\left[\begin{array}{l} (\texttt{catch } F[(\texttt{throw } b)] \\ \quad \texttt{with } \lambda X\, Y.M) \end{array}\right] & \longmapsto_c & E[(\lambda XY.M)\, b\, (\lambda Z.F[Z])] \\
F[(\texttt{throw } b)] & \longmapsto_c & (\texttt{throw } b) \\
\quad \text{if } F \neq [\,] & &
\end{array}
$$

The definition of the standard reduction function for Control ISWIM now looks just like the one for Handler ISWIM, except for the standard reduction function that it uses.

$$
eval_c^s(M) = \begin{cases} b & \text{if } M \longmapsto\!\!\!\!\!\rightarrow_c b \\ \texttt{function} & \text{if } M \longmapsto\!\!\!\!\!\rightarrow_c \lambda X.N \\ err_b & \text{if } M \longmapsto\!\!\!\!\!\rightarrow_c (\texttt{throw } b) \end{cases}
$$

It is now time to re-state the two correctness theorems, starting with the unique evaluation lemma.

Lemma 8.18 [Unique Evaluation Contexts]: For every closed Control ISWIM expression M, one of the following is true:

- M is a value or for some b, $M = (\texttt{throw } b)$.
- There exist a unique standard context E and a standard redex M_{rh} such that $M = E[M_{rh}]$ where

$$
\begin{array}{lcl}
M_{rh} & = & (V\, V) \\
& | & (o^m\, V \ldots V) \\
& | & (\texttt{catch } V \texttt{ with } \lambda X\, Y.M)
\end{array}
$$

- There exist a unique standard context E and context F such that $M = E[(\texttt{catch } F[(\texttt{throw } b)] \texttt{ with } \lambda X\, Y.M)]$.
- There exists a non-empty F such that $M = F[(\texttt{throw } b)]$.

Note the subtle but important differences between this theorem and the corresponding theorem for Handler ISWIM(theorem 8.13, page 135). In particular, it is no longer possible to partition an expression into a throw expression and a E context. Instead, the throw expression is always associated with a surrounding catch expression or the top-level of the expression.

The final theorem states that the correctness of the standard reduction machine for Control ISWIM.

Theorem 8.19: $eval_c^s = eval_c$

Exercise 8.24. Prove theorem 8.19.

Exercise 8.25. Implement the standard reduction machine for the Control ISWIM programming language in some favorite programming language in a faithful manner.

Exercise 8.26. Derive CC, CK, and CEK machines from the standard reduction machine for Control ISWIM.

8·5 **History.** Landin equipped his ISWIM language with a "jump operator," a construct for grabbing a continuation and combining it with a function into a closure. He used this jump operator for his ISWIM-based models of Algol 60. Independently, Sussman and Steele [104] added continuation operators to their Scheme programming language, with a syntax like the one for Lisp's catch and throw, though with a semantics closely related to the continuation operators of this chapter.

With her 1985 dissertation, Talcott [105] initiated a theoretical investigation of control constructs. Felleisen and his colleagues [32, 36, 37] developed a calculus for an ISWIM-style language with control operators, thus extending Plotkin's research program on the relationship between programming languages and their calculi. With Wright, Felleisen studied an exception-handling mechanism like the one in this chapter [118]. This chapter's extension of the exception handling mechanism to first-class functional continuations and control delimiters is due to Sitaram [100], though its addition to a practical programming language did not come about until 2007 [42].

9 • State: Imperative Assignment

Many functional programming languages come with imperative constructs, e.g., assignment statements. Adding such linguistic mechanisms allows programmers to establish channels of communication between functions that are otherwise unrelated. Without imperative assignment, such forms of communication could only be realized with complex programming patterns that may involve changes to the entire program.

For this reason, higher-order functional programming languages have included assignment statements for variables or constructs for manipulating mutable data from almost the very beginning. Landin, for example, used assignments in ISWIM to model Algol 60's assignment statement, including Algol's **own variables**, now known as **static variables**. Steele and Sussman added set! to the Scheme language and wrote several seminal technical reports on the nature of state. Milner's ML language has supported first-class reference cells as early as the 1980s.

The introduction of assignments into a language should severely constrain the order in which expressions are to be evaluated.[1] After all, depending on the order of expression evaluation, a fragment such as

```
(define (f a1 a2) x)
(define x 0)
(f (set! x (+ x 1)) (set! x (* 2 x)))
```

could produce 2 or 1.[2]

Because of this new complexity, this chapter's organization differs from the one for the previous chapters. After a brief introduction to the basic assignment mechanism of State ISWIM, the chapter presents a machine-based evaluator for the language. Inspired by this machine, the next section introduces a full-fledged language calculus for State ISWIM. The rest of the chapter develops an appropriate machine for the language.

---

[1] ... unless programmers are willing to accept evaluators that are not functions but relations.

[2] For example the Scheme Report [101] would require the program to produce either 1 or 2, because it demands an evaluation that corresponds to *some* sequential evaluation of the expressions in an application. Some traditional imperative languages use an even looser standard than Scheme, allowing the evaluator to return 0 for this program, too. For a detailed look at this issue, see part II.

9·1 Programming in State ISWIM.

9·1 **Programming in State ISWIM.** As always, we start the introduction of a new programming language with the abstract syntax. State ISWIM's syntax is that of ISWIM, with just one expression form added: (set X M). The shape of this new expression form is borrowed from the Scheme programming language; X is often called the **left-hand side** while M is dubbed **right-hand side**. The purpose of the new form is to evaluate the right-hand side to some value V and to associate X with V for future references. Of course, the evaluation of another set expression changes the value for X again.

$$
\begin{array}{rll}
M, N, L, K & = & \dots \qquad\qquad \text{same as plain ISWIM} \\
& | & (\text{set } X \ M)
\end{array}
$$

The variables on the left-hand side of set expressions in a program are collectively called its **assignable variables**.

Let us look at some examples, starting with

$$((\lambda x.((\lambda y.x) (\text{set } x (+ x \ \ulcorner 1 \urcorner)))) \ \ulcorner 12 \urcorner)$$

The outermost application, $((\lambda x.M) \ \ulcorner 12 \urcorner)$, causes an association of $\ulcorner 12 \urcorner$ with x for the evaluation of the function body M. If this application were in plain ISWIM, we would express the association via a substitution of $\ulcorner 12 \urcorner$ for x. Because x occurs as the left-hand side of some set expression in M, such a substitution makes no sense in State ISWIM. We therefore just keep track of the value of x on the side:

$$
\begin{array}{rll}
& ((\lambda x.((\lambda y.x) (\text{set } x (+ x \ \ulcorner 1 \urcorner)))) \ \ulcorner 12 \urcorner) & \\
\rightarrow & ((\lambda y.x) (\text{set } x (+ x \ \ulcorner 1 \urcorner))) & \text{with} \quad x = \ulcorner 12 \urcorner
\end{array}
$$

According to the informal description of set, it is now time to evaluate the right-hand side of the set expression. Given that x stands for $\ulcorner 12 \urcorner$ at the moment, we start by replacing x with its value:

$$
\begin{array}{rll}
\dots & ((\lambda y.x) (\text{set } x (+ x \ \ulcorner 1 \urcorner))) & \text{with} \quad x = \ulcorner 12 \urcorner \\
\rightarrow & ((\lambda y.x) (\text{set } x (+ \ \ulcorner 12 \urcorner \ \ulcorner 1 \urcorner))) & \text{with} \quad x = \ulcorner 12 \urcorner \\
\rightarrow & ((\lambda y.x) (\text{set } x \ \ulcorner 13 \urcorner)) & \text{with} \quad x = \ulcorner 12 \urcorner
\end{array}
$$

At this point, we need to note that x is associated with $\ulcorner 13 \urcorner$:

$$
\begin{array}{rll}
\dots & ((\lambda y.x) (\text{set } x \ \ulcorner 13 \urcorner)) & \text{with} \quad x = \ulcorner 12 \urcorner \\
\rightarrow & ((\lambda y.x) \ ???) & \text{with} \quad x = \ulcorner 13 \urcorner, y = ???
\end{array}
$$

For the time being, we associate y with ??? because the informal description of State ISWIM does not inform us what the result of a set expression is.

The rest is straightforward:

$$\begin{aligned} \ldots \quad & x \qquad \text{with} \quad x = \ulcorner 13 \urcorner, y =??? \\ \rightarrow \quad & \ulcorner 13 \urcorner \end{aligned}$$

There is only x left to evaluate. Our side condition says that it stands for $\ulcorner 13 \urcorner$, and this is therefore our result.

While this first example gives us an idea of how to think about set expressions, it also points out that the informal specification of the language extension is incomplete. It fails to specify to what a set expression evaluates. For the purposes of this chapter, we choose to use the old value of the left-hand side as the result of a set expression. Using this value avoids yet another syntactic extension of ISWIM.[3]

To make examples easier to read, we introduce two macros.

$$\begin{array}{ll} \text{let } X_1 = M_1 \ldots X_n = M_n \text{ in } N & \doteq \quad ((\lambda X_1 \ldots X_n.N) \; M_1 \ldots M_n) \\[2mm] (\text{seq } M_1 \ldots M_n) & \doteq \quad ((\lambda X_1 \ldots X_n.X_n) M_1 \ldots M_n) \end{array}$$

The let macro introduces block-level variable definitions; the seq macro sequences the evaluation of some expressions, discarding the result of all but the last. Both abbreviations are useful in an imperative context; the first sets up mutable variables and the second allows sequences of set expressions.

Exercise 9.1. Consider this partial expression:

$$\text{let } x = V \; y = U \text{ in } (\text{seq } M \; \cdots)$$

Add an expression M that swaps the values that x and y represent. Sketch the evaluation of the complete expression, like we did above.

For a second example, let us look at Algol 60's notion of own variables, which are assignable variables that are visible in just one function. More concretely, suppose we need a function that doubles its input but also counts how often it is called. Here is just such a function definition, using let and seq expressions:

$$\begin{aligned} CP \doteq \quad & \text{let } c = \ulcorner 0 \urcorner \\ & \text{in} \\ & \qquad \lambda x. \\ & \qquad\quad (\text{seq} \\ & \qquad\qquad (\text{set } c \; (+ \; c \; \ulcorner 1 \urcorner)) \\ & \qquad\qquad (* \; \ulcorner 2 \urcorner \; x)) \end{aligned}$$

---

[3]In most imperative languages, set expressions return a special value, such as void or unit, whose only purpose is to indicate the completion of the expression evaluation.

Unlike function definitions in plain ISWIM, this one is a let expression, i.e., a function application. The result, though, is a function whose body sequences two expressions: the first one increases the variable set up in the outer let expression; the second one doubles the given argument. Given that c has the initial value $\lceil 0 \rceil$, the function CP counts how often it is called; furthermore, it also performs the specified computation. The function's counting is useless, however, precisely because the own variable c is only visible in the body of the function. No matter how often the function is called, c cannot affect the result of the computation in any manner. Its value remains hidden.

Our final example shows how an own variable can be shared among several functions. Specifically, we show how a function can count how many times it is called *and* make this information available to the rest of the world:

$$
\begin{aligned}
PP \doteq \quad & \text{let } c = \lceil 0 \rceil \\
& \text{in} \\
& \quad \langle \lambda x. \\
& \qquad (\text{seq} \\
& \qquad\quad (\text{set } c \ (+ \ c \ \lceil 1 \rceil)) \\
& \qquad\quad (* \ \lceil 2 \rceil \ x)), \\
& \qquad \lambda y.c \rangle
\end{aligned}
$$

Like CP, PP also uses a let to set up a counter variable. Instead of a function, though, the let expression produces a pair of functions. The first function is like the preceding one, counting how often it is called and doubling its argument. The second one throws away its argument and returns the value of the counter c. In other words, no matter from where the first function is called, it communicates to the second function that it is called one more time through a secret, hidden channel. If the rest of the program needs to know how often the doubling function was used, a call to the second function with any input value reveals the current value of the counter.

In summary, State ISWIM comes with a set expression that acts just like an assignment statement. Furthermore, the combination of assignments with higher-order functions supports idioms of programming that traditional imperative languages can only provide as built-in features. Indeed, State ISWIM can simulate stateful object-oriented programming.

9·2 **An Evaluator for State ISWIM.** When a language provides assignment statements, the nature of variables no longer resembles that of mathematical variables. In contrast to a mathematical variable, which represents some fixed (but unknown) value, an assignable variable denotes a varying association between names and values. Hence, it is clear that assignable variables play a special role, and we thus start our development with a firm definition of this concept.

$$
\begin{aligned}
\mathcal{AV}(\,X\,) &= \varnothing \\
\mathcal{AV}(\,(\lambda X.M)\,) &= \mathcal{AV}(M) \setminus \{\,X\,\} \\
\mathcal{AV}(\,(M_1\ M_2)\,) &= \mathcal{AV}(M_1) \cup \mathcal{AV}(M_2) \\
\mathcal{AV}(\,(\mathsf{set}\ X\ M)\,) &= \mathcal{AV}(M) \cup \{\,X\,\} \\
\mathcal{AV}(\,b\,) &= \varnothing \\
\mathcal{AV}(\,(o^n\ M_1\ \ldots M_n)\,) &= \cup_{i=1}^{i=n} \mathcal{AV}(M_i)
\end{aligned}
$$

We must also revise the definition of the $\mathcal{FV}$ function:

$$
\mathcal{FV}(\,(\mathsf{set}\ X\ M)\,) = \mathcal{FV}(M) \cup \{\,X\,\}
$$

This extension confirms that set expressions do *not* introduce new binding positions into the language.

Next we move on to the development of a machine for State ISWIM, based on our intuition of how machines work and how assignment works in a higher-order world. From the example in the preceding section, we get one critical clue about such a machine:

> *We cannot use substitution when applying a function to an argument if the function's parameter is assignable. Instead, we must keep around a table that tracks the association between the variable and its current value.*

This insight suggests three new machine instructions:

1. When the value of a variable is needed, it is in the table.

2. A set expression changes the table.

3. The application of a function with an assignable parameter must add an entry to the table.

Although these three instructions appear to have obvious translations into symbolic relations, their formulation in English hides a critical detail. Let us illustrate this point with an example:

$$
((\lambda x.(\mathsf{seq}\ (\mathsf{set}\ x\ \ulcorner 5 \urcorner)\ ((\lambda x.(\mathsf{seq}\ (\mathsf{set}\ x\ (+\ x\ x))\ x))\ \ulcorner 9 \urcorner)))\ \ulcorner 0 \urcorner)
$$

With let, the expression becomes easier to read than with λ:

$$
\begin{aligned}
&\mathsf{let}\ x\ =\ \ulcorner 0 \urcorner \\
&\mathsf{in} \\
&\quad (\mathsf{seq}\ (\mathsf{set}\ x\ \ulcorner 5 \urcorner) \\
&\qquad \mathsf{let}\ x\ =\ \ulcorner 9 \urcorner \\
&\quad\quad \mathsf{in} \\
&\qquad\quad (\mathsf{seq}\ (\mathsf{set}\ x\ (+\ x\ x)) \\
&\qquad\qquad x))
\end{aligned}
$$

but do verify that the two expressions are equivalent! An informal under-
standing of this expression is straightforward. It initializes a first x with $\ulcorner 0 \urcorner$
and a second x with $\ulcorner 9 \urcorner$. The body of the outer let expression sets the outer x
to $\ulcorner 5 \urcorner$ because the x in this set expression is bound to the outer binding occurrence. Similarly, the body of the inner let sets the inner x to $\ulcorner 18 \urcorner$ because
this reference to x is to the inner binding occurrence. The overall result is
obtained by looking up the value of this x in the table and is therefore $\ulcorner 18 \urcorner$.

The problem is that a naive rendering of the new machine instructions
might just not maintain the table properly. Suppose we formulate the third
new machine instruction as follows:

$$((\lambda X.M)\ V) \text{ with } \ldots \rightarrow M \text{ with } X = V \ldots \text{ if } X \in \mathcal{AV}(\ M\ )$$

Applying this to the example expression twice gives us a table with *two* en-
tries for x:

$$((\lambda x.(\text{seq (set } x\ \ulcorner 5 \urcorner)\ ((\lambda x.(\text{seq (set } x\ (+\ x\ x))\ x))\ \ulcorner 9 \urcorner)))\ \ulcorner 0 \urcorner)$$
$$\text{with } \ldots$$
$$\rightarrow \quad (\text{seq (set } x\ \ulcorner 5 \urcorner)\ ((\lambda x.(\text{seq (set } x\ (+\ x\ x))\ x))\ \ulcorner 9 \urcorner))$$
$$\text{with } x = \ulcorner 0 \urcorner, \ldots$$
$$\rightarrow \quad ((\lambda x.(\text{seq (set } x\ (+\ x\ x))\ x))\ \ulcorner 9 \urcorner)$$
$$\text{with } x = \ulcorner 5 \urcorner, \ldots$$
$$\rightarrow \quad (\text{seq (set } x\ (+\ x\ x))\ x)$$
$$\text{with } x = \ulcorner 5 \urcorner, x = \ulcorner 9 \urcorner, \ldots$$

This is in some sense to be expected from an expression with two occurrences
of x. While the convention of always using the most recently added occurrence of the variable works out for this expression, it does not in general.
Instead, variables of the same name in the table leads to a confusion, and a
formal system must avoid such confusion.

Our solution to this problem is to rename the parameters of a function
as it is applied so that no variable is ever stuck into the table twice. Doing
so just exploits the α-equivalence relation of ISWIM and our variable convention of using whatever name is best suited to the situation. Furthermore,
it guarantees that these "tables" are finite functions that map variables to
values. Following convention, we call them **store**s.

$$\Sigma \;\; = \;\; \{\langle X_1, V_1 \rangle, \ldots, \langle X_n, V_n \rangle\}$$
$$\text{finite function: for all } i \neq j, X_i \neq X_j$$

Stores, like environments, are finite functions and come with dom and
rng operations that map these functions to finite sets. In contrast to the environments from previous chapters, stores map variables to *syntactic values*,

however, not closures. Stores—also like finite tables—come with a natural extension operation that adds one new binding or replaces an old one.

$$
\text{For } \Sigma = \{\langle X_1, V_1 \rangle, \ldots, \langle X_n, V_n \rangle\},
$$

$$
\Sigma[X \leftarrow V] = \begin{cases} \{\langle X_1, V_1 \rangle, \ldots \langle X_i, V \rangle \ldots \langle X_n, V_n \rangle\} \\ \quad \text{if for some } i, X_i = X \\ \{\langle X_1, V_1 \rangle, \ldots \langle X_i, V_i \rangle \ldots \langle X_n, V_n \rangle, \langle X, V \rangle\} \\ \quad \text{if for all } i, X_i \neq X \end{cases}
$$

Besides tables, we also need a revised notion of evaluation context.

$$
\begin{aligned} E &= \ldots &\text{same as plain ISWIM} \\ &\mid \quad (\text{set } X\ E) \end{aligned}
$$

This additional clause reminds us that State ISWIM extends ISWIM with set expressions and that their evaluation starts with the right-hand side.

Equipped with these definitions, we can now specify a machine that uses pairs of expressions and stores as machine states and that rewrites such states. We call it the **CS machine,** following the tradition of calling the expression in a machine a control string.

$$
\begin{aligned} eval_{cs} : M &\longrightarrow A \\ eval_{cs}(M) &= \begin{cases} b & \text{if } \langle M, \varnothing \rangle \longmapsto_{cs} \langle b, \Sigma \rangle \\ \text{function} & \text{if } \langle M, \varnothing \rangle \longmapsto_{cs} \langle \lambda X.N, \Sigma \rangle \end{cases} \end{aligned}
$$

$\longmapsto_{cs}$		
$\langle E[((\lambda X.M)\ V)], \Sigma \rangle$ $\quad$ if $X \notin \mathcal{AV}(M)$	$\langle E[M[X \leftarrow V]], \Sigma \rangle$	$[\text{csfi}_v]$
$\langle E[((\lambda X.M)\ V)], \Sigma \rangle$ $\quad$ if $X \in \mathcal{AV}(M)$ $\quad\quad Y \notin \text{dom}(\Sigma) \cup \mathcal{FV}(E[M])$	$\langle E[M[X \leftarrow Y]], \Sigma[Y \leftarrow V] \rangle$	$[\text{csfi}_s]$
$\langle E[X], \Sigma[X \leftarrow V] \rangle$	$\langle E[V], \Sigma[X \leftarrow V] \rangle$	$[\text{cs!}]$
$\langle E[(\text{set } X\ V)], \Sigma[X \leftarrow U] \rangle$	$\langle E[U], \Sigma[X \leftarrow V] \rangle$	$[\text{cs} =]$
$\langle E[(o^n\ V_1 \ldots V_n)], \Sigma \rangle$	$\langle E[\delta(o^n, V_1, \ldots V_n)], \Sigma \rangle$	$[\text{csffi}]$

The first instruction implements the familiar β_v notion of reduction; the last one is δ combined with a store. Neither of these two rules touches the store. The remaining rules use the store:

[csfi$_s$] When a function parameter is assignable in the function body, the CS machine rewrites the control string by substituting a *new* variable for the parameter into the function body. It also adds the *new* variable to the current store and maps it to the argument value. Here, "new" means a variable that does not occur free in the control string or in the store's domain. One result of this rewrite is that such "new" variables occur free in the control string. Of course, their values are available in the store.

[cs!] When the control string needs the value of a free variable X, the CS machine uses the store to look up the value V of the variable, and it replaces this one free occurrence of X with V. After all, the value of other occurrences of X is needed at other points and, by the time it is needed, a set expression may have changed it.

[cs =] A (set X V) expression transforms a store that maps X to some U into one that associates X with V. The instruction then uses U as the return value for the complete set expression.

The design of a formal evaluator also demands close attention to all definitions. Until now, we have simply used V to refer to values, but ISWIM and its calculus use a "permissive" definition for V that just does not apply to State ISWIM and its CS machine. Specifically, in ISWIM the set of values includes variables. While the machine is always run on closed expressions, i.e., expressions without free variables, including variables in the set of values is useful for program calculations. For State ISWIM, variables-as-values would introduce problems. In this world, a machine state such as

$$\langle(((\lambda x.(\text{seq }(\text{set } x \ \cdots) \ \cdots))) \ y, \Sigma\rangle$$

can be rewritten in two different ways. On one hand, [cs!] would replace y with its value from Σ; on the other hand, [csfi$_s$] would put y into the store.

In order to define a deterministic evaluator, we need to resolve this problem. We choose to introduce a restrictive notion of values for the CS machine.

$$
\begin{aligned}
V \quad &= \quad b \\
&| \quad (\lambda X.M)
\end{aligned}
$$

Put differently, because free variables serve as addresses into the store of the CS machine, they are *not* values. Consequently, when a variable from the store domain is used as an argument to a function, the machine extracts the value from the store before applying the function. And that is precisely the behavior we want for a call-by-value language, as opposed to a call-by-reference language.

Now it is clear from the description of the machine instructions that each of them is a function rewriting one CS state into another one. Hence, the evaluator based on the CS machine is a function, too, just as desired.

Theorem 9.1 [Consistency of State ISWIM (Part I)]: The relation $eval_{cs}$ is a partial function.

Exercise 9.2. Prove that the stores $\Sigma = \{(x_1, V_1), \ldots, (x_n, V_n)\}$ in all states reachable from $\langle P, \varnothing \rangle$ satisfy the following condition:

$$\cup_{i=1}^{i=n} \mathcal{FV}(V_i) \subseteq \{x_1, \ldots, x_n\}$$

Furthermore, a similar condition holds for the control string M:

$$\mathcal{FV}(M) \subseteq \{x_1, \ldots, x_n\}$$

That is, the CS machine assigns meaning to all free variables in its states.

Exercise 9.3. Prove theorem 9.1. Hint: Show that at most one machine instruction applies to any given machine state.

Exercise 9.4. Explain why the CS machine evaluates the expressions in an application from left to right. Argue why left-to-right evaluation is critical for the usefulness of the seq abbreviation.

Exercise 9.5. Show that the execution of the following program never terminates:

$$
\begin{aligned}
&\mathsf{let}\ f = \ulcorner 0 \urcorner \\
&\mathsf{in} \\
&\qquad (\mathsf{seq} \\
&\qquad\quad (\mathsf{set}\ f\ (\lambda x.(f\ x))) \\
&\qquad\quad (f\ \ulcorner 0 \urcorner))
\end{aligned}
$$

Examples like this have inspired many people to investigate an imperative variant of the Y combinator:

$$
\begin{aligned}
\mathsf{Y}_! \ \dot{=} \ &\lambda f. \\
&\mathsf{let}\ g = \ulcorner 0 \urcorner \\
&\quad \mathsf{in} \\
&\qquad (\mathsf{seq} \\
&\qquad\quad (\mathsf{set}\ g\ (f\ (\lambda x.(g\ x)))) \\
&\qquad\quad g)
\end{aligned}
$$

Show that the evaluation of $((\mathsf{Y}_!\ (\lambda h.(\lambda x.(h\ x))))\ V)$ fails to terminate for all V. Then use $\mathsf{Y}_!$ to define the factorial function and apply it to $\ulcorner 2 \urcorner$.

$9 \cdot 3$ **The State ISWIM Calculus.** When Plotkin studied the relationship between ISWIM and the λ-calculus, the former came with a evaluator and a machine but not a calculus. The λ_v-calculus is the theoretically well-founded response to this missing piece, and the λ_n-calculus demonstrates that the relationship between languages and calculi is uniform.

The existence of the CS machine raises the question whether there is also a calculus for State ISWIM, i.e., an equational logic in which we can reason about imperative programs. A brief analysis of the machine suggests a natural path for such a development. The only non-syntactic component of the CS machine is the store. Thus, if we can "internalize" the store of the machine's state into the syntax of the programming language, we should be able to derive notions of reduction from the machine's instructions.

At first glance, a store is just a series of variable definitions. Such constructs are common in all programming languages, so it should not be difficult to create one for stores. The only question is what scope to use for such variable declarations. To understand the scoping of the store, let us look at some sample states, starting with the first example in section 9.1:

$$\langle ((\lambda y.x) \, (\mathsf{set} \, x \, (+ \, x \, \ulcorner 1 \urcorner))), \{ \, (x, \ulcorner 12 \urcorner) \, \} \rangle$$

Here the store maps x to $\ulcorner 12 \urcorner$, and a plain let expression (or its expansion) can represent this store:

$$\mathsf{let} \, x = \ulcorner 12 \urcorner \, \mathsf{in} \, ((\lambda y.x) \, (\mathsf{set} \, x \, (+ \, x \, \ulcorner 1 \urcorner)))$$

In contrast, the program from exercise 9.5 creates a cyclic store:

$$\left\langle \begin{array}{l} \mathsf{let} \, f = \ulcorner 0 \urcorner \\ \mathsf{in} \, (\mathsf{seq} \\ \quad (\mathsf{set} \, f \\ \quad\quad (\lambda x.(f \, x))) \\ \quad (f \, \ulcorner 0 \urcorner)) \end{array} , \varnothing \right\rangle \longmapsto_{\mathsf{cs}} \left\langle \begin{array}{l} (\mathsf{seq} \\ \quad (\mathsf{set} \, f \\ \quad\quad (\lambda x.(f \, x))) \\ \quad (f \, \ulcorner 0 \urcorner)) \end{array} , \{ \, (f, \ulcorner 0 \urcorner) \, \} \right\rangle$$

$$\longmapsto_{\mathsf{cs}} \langle \, (f \, \ulcorner 0 \urcorner) \, , \{ \, (f, (\lambda x.(f \, x))) \, \} \rangle$$

Specifically, the evaluation reaches a state whose store maps the variable f to a λ expression that contains a reference to f. Of course this form of self-reference is nothing but a recursion, which we can represent via the Y combinator.

In general, programs in State ISWIM are capable of setting up any kind of mutual recursion. For example, this program fragment

$$\mathsf{let} f = \ulcorner 0 \urcorner \; g = \ulcorner 1 \urcorner$$
$$\mathsf{in}$$
$$(\mathsf{seq}$$
$$\quad (\mathsf{set} \; f \; (\lambda x.(g \; x))) \; (\mathsf{set} \; g \; (\lambda x.(f \; x)))$$
$$\quad \cdots)$$

creates a store on the CS machine that makes f refer to g and g refer to f:

$$\{ \; (f,(\lambda x.(g \; x))), \; (g,(\lambda x.(f \; x))), \; \}$$

Hence, a declaration construct for representing the store must establish a general, mutually recursive scope for all its definitions.

Exercise 9.6. Validate that the evaluation of the last example proceeds as advertised.

This analysis suggests a construct for introducing mutually recursive definitions. For convenience, we reuse the syntax of stores in this revised definition of State ISWIM.

$$
\begin{array}{rll}
M & = & \ldots \qquad\qquad\qquad\qquad\qquad\qquad \text{same as plain ISWIM} \\
  & | & (\mathsf{set} \; X \; M) \\
  & | & (\mathsf{letrec} \; \Sigma \; M) \\[1em]
\Sigma & = & \{\langle X_1, V_1 \rangle, \ldots, \langle X_n, V_n \rangle\} \\
  & & \text{finite function: for all } i \neq j, X_i \neq X_j \\[1em]
V & = & b \\
  & | & (\lambda X.M)
\end{array}
$$

A `letrec` expression pairs variables with λ expressions and basic constants but not with other variables. As in the Scheme programming language, the intention is that `letrec` binds the variables to their respective variables in a mutually recursive manner and then evaluates the body of the expression.

The introduction of a new binding constructs into a calculus demands a precise specification of scope, substitution, and α-equivalence. For the first, we extend the definition of the free-variables function to State ISWIM's extended syntax in the most natural manner.

$$
\begin{array}{rcl}
\mathcal{FV}(\, (\mathsf{set} \; X \; M) \,) & = & \mathcal{FV}(M) \cup \{ \, X \, \} \\
\mathcal{FV}(\, (\mathsf{letrec} \; \{\langle X_1, V_1 \rangle, \ldots, \langle X_n, V_n \rangle\} \; M) \,) & = & \\
& & (\cup_{i=1}^{i=n} \mathcal{FV}(V_i) \cup \mathcal{FV}(M)) \setminus \{X_1, \ldots, X_n\}
\end{array}
$$

The subtraction of *all* locally defined variables from the free variables of the sub-expressions clarifies how all new variables are bound everywhere.

For completeness, we also adapt the definition of the "assignable variables" function to the extended syntax.

$$\mathcal{AV}(\; (\texttt{letrec}\; \{\langle X_1, V_1\rangle, \ldots, \langle X_n, V_n\rangle\}M)\;) = (\cup_{i=1}^{i=n}\mathcal{AV}(V_i) \cup \mathcal{AV}(M)) \setminus \{X_1, \ldots, X_n\}$$

In contrast, the substitution function (see page 46) demands a complex extension, especially concerning `set` expressions.

$$
\begin{aligned}
&(\texttt{set}\; X\; M)[Y \leftarrow N] = (\texttt{set}\; X\; M[Y \leftarrow N]) \quad \text{if } X \neq Y\\
&(\texttt{set}\; X\; M)[X \leftarrow Y] = (\texttt{set}\; Y\; M[X \leftarrow Y])
\end{aligned}
$$

$$
(\texttt{letrec}\; \left\{ \begin{array}{l} \langle X_1, V_1\rangle,\\ \ldots,\\ \langle X_n, V_n\rangle \end{array} \right\}\; M)[X \leftarrow N] = (\texttt{letrec}\; \left\{ \begin{array}{l} \langle X_1, V_1\rangle,\\ \ldots,\\ \langle X_n, V_n\rangle \end{array} \right\}\; M)
$$
$$\text{if for some } i,\, X_i = X$$

$$
(\texttt{letrec}\; \left\{ \begin{array}{l} \langle X_1, V_1\rangle,\\ \ldots,\\ \langle X_n, V_n\rangle \end{array} \right\}\; M)[X \leftarrow N] =
$$
$$
(\texttt{letrec}\; \left\{ \begin{array}{l} \langle Y_1, V_1[X_1 \leftarrow Y_1] \ldots [X_n \leftarrow Y_n][X \leftarrow N]\rangle,\\ \ldots,\\ \langle Y_n, V_n[X_1 \leftarrow Y_1] \ldots [X_n \leftarrow Y_n][X \leftarrow N]\rangle \end{array} \right\}\; M[X_1 \leftarrow Y_1] \ldots [X_n \leftarrow Y_n][X \leftarrow N])
$$
$$
\begin{aligned}
&\text{if} \quad \text{for all } i,\, X_i \neq X\\
&\qquad Y_1, \ldots, Y_n \;\notin\; \mathcal{FV}(\; (\texttt{letrec}\; \{\langle X_1, V_1\rangle, \ldots, \langle X_n, V_n\rangle\}\; M)\;)\\
&\qquad Y_1, \ldots, Y_n \;\notin\; \mathcal{FV}(\; N\;)
\end{aligned}
$$

Since the definition of substitution relies on variable renaming for binding constructs, we need a version of the function that substitutes variables for assignable variables. In general, we assume that assignable variables are only subject to substitution if the new expression is a variable.

Last but not least, we can now extend α-equivalence to the State ISWIM language with `letrec`. In a multi-variable declaration construct, each variable can be renamed one at a time, and this is true for `letrec`, too.

$$
(\texttt{letrec}\; \{\langle X_1, V_1\rangle, \ldots, \langle X_i, V_i\rangle, \ldots, \langle X_n, V_n\rangle\}\; M) \quad \alpha_{\texttt{letrec}} \quad (\texttt{letrec}\; \{\langle X_1, V_1[X_i \leftarrow Y]\rangle, \ldots, \langle Y, V_i[X_i \leftarrow Y]\rangle, \ldots, \langle X_n, V_n[X_i \leftarrow Y]\rangle\}\; M[X_i \leftarrow Y])
$$
$$\text{if } Y \notin \cup_{i=1}^{i=n}\mathcal{FV}(V_i) \cup \mathcal{FV}(M)$$

With the extended syntax and the adapted meta-functions in place, we can now try to design the basic notions of reductions. Let us take [csfi$_s$] as the starting point. Its purpose is to allocate storage for a function parameter if it is an assignable variable. Given that letrec represents the store, here is a natural rendering for this machine instruction as a notion of reduction.

$$((\lambda X.M)\ V)\quad \textbf{alloc}\quad (\texttt{letrec}\ \{\langle X, V\rangle\}\ M)$$
$$\text{if}\ X \in \mathcal{AV}(M)$$

The rule uses X to allocate storage in a mini-store, a letrec expression that surrounds the body of the function.

Of course, this function body could be a value—either another function or a basic constant—and then the letrec may just block it from reaching a surrounding application. To wit,

$$((\lambda y.y)((\lambda x.(\lambda z.(\texttt{seq}\ (\texttt{set}\ x\ (+\ x\ \ulcorner 1\urcorner))x)))\ \ulcorner 0\urcorner))$$
$$\rightarrow\quad ((\lambda y.y)(\texttt{letrec}\ \{\langle x, \ulcorner 0\urcorner\rangle\}(\lambda z.(\texttt{seq}\ (\texttt{set}\ x\ (+\ x\ \ulcorner 1\urcorner))\ x))))$$

Here $(\lambda y.y)$ should consume $(\lambda z.(\texttt{seq}\ (\texttt{set}\ x\ (+\ x\ \ulcorner 1\urcorner))\ x))$ in a context where x is bound to $\ulcorner 0\urcorner$ in the store. The insight is to lift the letrec expression through evaluation contexts like this

$$E[(\texttt{letrec}\ \Sigma\ M)]\quad \rightarrow\quad (\texttt{letrec}\ \Sigma\ E[M])$$

Of course, doing this is only possible if the free variables of E are not bound by Σ; otherwise lifting letrec expressions changes the store. We therefore formulate the notion of reduction such that it performs a renaming substitution for the letrec expression as we lift it out of evaluation contexts.

$$E[(\texttt{letrec}\quad\quad \textbf{lift}\quad (\texttt{letrec}$$
$$\left\{\begin{array}{l}\langle X_1, V_1\rangle,\\ \ldots,\\ \langle X_n, V_n\rangle\end{array}\right\}\quad\quad \left\{\begin{array}{l}\langle Y_1, V_1[X_1 \leftarrow Y_1]\ldots[X_n \leftarrow Y_n]\rangle,\\ \ldots,\\ \langle Y_n, V_n[X_1 \leftarrow Y_1]\ldots[X_n \leftarrow Y_n]\rangle\end{array}\right\}$$
$$M)]\quad\quad\quad\quad E[M[X_1 \leftarrow Y_1]\ldots[X_n \leftarrow Y_n]])$$
$$\text{if}\ Y_1,\ldots,Y_n \notin \mathcal{FV}(E[(\texttt{letrec}\ \{\langle X_1, V_1\rangle,\ldots,\langle X_n, V_n\rangle\}\ M)])$$

The **lift** reduction clearly demands a clarification of what evaluation contexts are in this version of State ISWIM; after all, we added a new construct. A letrec expression consists of a number of values and an expression, its body, which definitely must be evaluated. Hence, it is to be expected that

$$(\texttt{letrec}\ \Sigma\ E)$$

is an evaluation context, but admitting these contexts into the set of evaluation contexts would make the **lift** relation unsound:

$$\frac{(\texttt{letrec } \{\langle x, \ulcorner 0 \urcorner \rangle\}}{\frac{(\texttt{letrec } \{\langle y, \lambda z.x \rangle\}}{M))}} \quad \rightarrow \quad \frac{(\texttt{letrec } \{\langle y, \lambda z.x \rangle\}}{\frac{(\texttt{letrec } \{\langle x, \ulcorner 0 \urcorner \rangle\}}{M))}}$$

The expression on the left is closed if M is closed. Lifting the inner `letrec`
through the underlined evaluation context, however, creates an expression
with a free x.

Since changing the scope of expressions is unsound, we stick to the set of
evaluation contexts from section 9.2 on the CS machine.

$$\boxed{E = [\,] \mid (V\ E) \mid (E\ M) \mid (o^n\ V \ldots V\ E\ M \ldots M) \mid (\texttt{set}\ X\ E)}$$

This decision leaves open how the body of a `letrec` expression is actually
evaluated or, more precisely, how the body of nested `letrec` expressions
are evaluated. In order to understand this point, we need to examine the
remaining two CS machine instructions: one for evaluating `set` expressions
and one for dereferencing (assignable) variables.

As it turns out, both are easy to reformulate for the calculus.

$$\boxed{\begin{array}{lcl} (\texttt{letrec } \Sigma[X \leftarrow V]\ E[X]) & \textbf{deref} & (\texttt{letrec } \Sigma[X \leftarrow V]\ E[V]) \\ (\texttt{letrec } \Sigma[X \leftarrow U]\ E[(\texttt{set } X\ V)]) & \textbf{assign} & (\texttt{letrec } \Sigma[X \leftarrow V]\ E[U]) \end{array}}$$

The difference is that these relations work with a *local* `letrec` expression
instead of a global store. Of course, the very mention of "local" raises the
question of what happens when, say, a variable reference is separated from
its declaration by some intervening `letrec`. Here is an example that makes
this objection precise:

$$(\texttt{letrec } \{\langle x, \ulcorner 0 \urcorner \rangle\}\ (\texttt{letrec } \{\langle y, \ulcorner 1 \urcorner \rangle\}\ \underline{x}))$$

In this case, the underlined reference to x occurs in an evaluation context
with respect to the *inner* but not the *outer* `letrec` expression. As a result, it
is impossible to dereference x and to continue the evaluation of the program.

Our solution to this last problem is to introduce a notion of reduction that
merges the bindings of neighboring `letrec` expressions:

$$(\texttt{letrec } \Sigma\ (\texttt{letrec } \Sigma'\ M)) \quad \textbf{merge} \quad (\texttt{letrec } \Sigma \oplus \Sigma'\ M),$$

Just like **lift**, **merge** works only when the inner binding does not interfere
with the outer ones. The actual definition therefore incorporates the same
kind of renaming that the definition of **lift** uses.

$$\begin{array}{l} (\texttt{letrec } \Sigma \\ \quad (\texttt{letrec} \\ \qquad \left\{ \begin{array}{l} \langle X_1, V_1 \rangle, \\ \ldots, \\ \langle X_n, V_n \rangle \end{array} \right\} \\ \quad M)) \\[1em] \text{if } Y_1, \ldots, Y_n \notin \left\{ \begin{array}{l} \cup \{ \mathcal{FV}(U_i) \mid U_i \in \mathrm{rng}(\Sigma) \} \\ \cup \\ \mathcal{FV}((\texttt{letrec } \{ \langle X_1, V_1 \rangle, \ldots, \langle X_n, V_n \rangle \} M)) \\ \cup \\ \mathrm{dom}(\Sigma) \end{array} \right. \end{array}$$

$$\textbf{merge} \quad \begin{array}{l} (\texttt{letrec } \Sigma \\ \qquad \oplus \\ \qquad \left\{ \begin{array}{l} \langle Y_1, V_1[X_1 \leftarrow Y_1] \ldots [X_n \leftarrow Y_n] \rangle, \\ \ldots, \\ \langle Y_n, V_n[X_1 \leftarrow Y_1] \ldots [X_n \leftarrow Y_n] \rangle \end{array} \right\} \\ \qquad M[X_1 \leftarrow Y_1] \ldots [X_n \leftarrow Y_n]) \end{array}$$

The new variables for the inner letrec definitions are chosen so that they do not accidentally capture free variables in the surrounding letrec definitions; so that they do not clash with the variables from that definition; and so that they do not interfere with variables that are already free in the inner letrec expression.

Defining the function that combines letrec bindings is straightforward.

$$\begin{array}{rl} \text{For } \Sigma = \{ \langle X_1, V_1 \rangle, \ldots, \langle X_n, V_n \rangle \}, \\ \Sigma \oplus \Sigma' &= \{ \langle X_1, V_1 \rangle, \ldots, \langle X_n, V_n \rangle, \langle X_1', V_1' \rangle, \ldots, \langle X_m', V_m' \rangle \} \\ \text{if } \Sigma' &= \{ \langle X_1', V_1' \rangle, \ldots, \langle X_m', V_m' \rangle \} \end{array}$$

While the function applies to any two sets of bindings, we know from its use in the definition of **merge** that it is guaranteed to create a finite function and thus a valid set of bindings.

Exercise 9.7. Make up examples that justify the variable renaming of the **merge** notion of reduction.

We are ready to collect our notions of reduction for State ISWIM.

$$s = \beta_\mathsf{v} \cup \delta \cup \textbf{alloc} \cup \textbf{deref} \cup \textbf{assign} \cup \textbf{lift} \cup \textbf{merge}$$

The complete notions of reduction includes *delta* and β_v, extended to the new syntax. The latter must also be suitably restricted.

$$((\lambda X.M)V) \quad \beta_\mathsf{v} \quad M[X \leftarrow V] \quad \text{if } X \notin \mathcal{AV}(M)$$

To obtain the full system of equations ($=_\mathsf{s}$), form the compatible, reflexive, symmetric, and transitive closure as usual.

Considering the complexity of State ISWIM's notion of reduction—a relation made from seven separate relations—an example is in order now:

$$((\lambda x.$$
$$(+\ulcorner 3\urcorner$$
$$(\texttt{letrec}\ \{\langle y,\ulcorner 1\urcorner\rangle\}$$
$$(\ (\lambda z.(+\ z\ y))$$
$$(\texttt{set}\ x\ (+\ x\ulcorner 1\urcorner))))))$$
$$\ulcorner 0\urcorner)$$

It is reduced as follows, using each notion of reduction at least once:

alloc $(\texttt{letrec}\ \{\langle x,\ulcorner 0\urcorner\rangle\}$
                   $(+\ulcorner 3\urcorner$
                   $(\texttt{letrec}\ \{\langle y,\ulcorner 1\urcorner\rangle\}$
                   $((\lambda z.(+\ z\ y))\ (\texttt{set}\ x\ (+\ x\ulcorner 1\urcorner))))))$

lift $(\texttt{letrec}\ \{\langle x,\ulcorner 0\urcorner\rangle\}$
                   $(\texttt{letrec}\ \{\langle y,\ulcorner 1\urcorner\rangle\}$
                   $(+\ulcorner 3\urcorner$
                   $((\lambda z.(+\ z\ y))\ (\texttt{set}\ x\ (+\ x\ulcorner 1\urcorner))))))$

merge $(\texttt{letrec}\ \{\langle x,\ulcorner 0\urcorner\rangle, \langle y,\ulcorner 1\urcorner\rangle\}$
                   $(+\ulcorner 3\urcorner$
                   $((\lambda z.(+\ z\ y))\ (\texttt{set}\ x\ (+\ x\ulcorner 1\urcorner)))))$

deref; δ $(\texttt{letrec}\ \{\langle x,\ulcorner 0\urcorner\rangle, \langle y,\ulcorner 1\urcorner\rangle\}$
                   $(+\ulcorner 3\urcorner$
                   $((\lambda z.(+\ z\ y))\ (\texttt{set}\ x\ulcorner 1\urcorner))))$

assign $(\texttt{letrec}\ \{\langle x,\ulcorner 1\urcorner\rangle, \langle y,\ulcorner 1\urcorner\rangle\}$
                   $(+\ulcorner 3\urcorner$
                   $((\lambda z.(+\ z\ y))\ \ulcorner 0\urcorner)))$

β_v $(\texttt{letrec}\ \{\langle x,\ulcorner 1\urcorner\rangle, \langle y,\ulcorner 1\urcorner\rangle\}$
                   $(+\ulcorner 3\urcorner\ (+\ulcorner 0\urcorner\ y)))$

This particular reduction sequence is mostly canonical, except that the first
two steps could be swapped.

With a final **deref** followed by two uses of δ, the result is a `letrec` expression with a basic constant as a body:

deref; δ $(\texttt{letrec } \{\langle x, \ulcorner 1 \urcorner \rangle, \langle y, \ulcorner 1 \urcorner \rangle\}$
                                  $\ulcorner 4 \urcorner)$

This example points out that the reduction of a program may not end with a value. Instead, we may obtain values wrapped in `letrec` expressions

$$(\texttt{letrec } \Sigma \, V)$$

which we have to translate to final answers from A. If V is a basic constant, the store has become irrelevant. Otherwise it is a λ expression, and the answer in that case is `function`.

$$
\begin{aligned}
&eval_s : M \quad \longrightarrow \quad A \\
&eval_s(M) \quad = \\
&\qquad \begin{cases} b & \text{if } M =_s b \text{ or } M =_s (\texttt{letrec } \Sigma \, b) \\ \texttt{function} & \text{if } M =_s \lambda X.N \text{ or } M =_s (\texttt{letrec } \Sigma \, \lambda X.N) \end{cases}
\end{aligned}
$$

Consistency. Since we already have an evaluator for State ISWIM, it is tempting to claim that $eval_{cs} = eval_s$. Unfortunately, the claim itself is simplistic and proving it directly is difficult, if not impossible. First, the definition of $eval_{cs}$ is based on the CS machine, which interprets only the `letrec`-free subset of State ISWIM. Second, while it is straightforward to add this construct to the machine, proving the equivalence between the machine-based evaluator and the calculus-based one is only simple in the left-to-right direction. We continue to follow the conventional strategy, beginning with a consistency theorem and a standard reduction theorem.

> **Theorem 9.2 [Consistency of State ISWIM (Part II)]**: The relation $eval_s$ is a partial function.

Exercise 9.8. Prove the second consistency theorem for State ISWIM.

The Standard Reduction Theorem. For a proof that $eval_{cs}$ and $eval_s$ define the same evaluator for State ISWIM with `letrec`, we need to develop a standardization theorem and its algorithms. That is, we need to define a syntactic machine and prove two points. First, an evaluator based on this syntactic machine is equivalent to $eval_s$. Second, it is also equivalent—in a sense to be determined—with $eval_{cs}$.

In the context of plain ISWIM, the standard reduction relation is defined in a very simple manner:

$$E[M] \longmapsto_v E[N] \quad \text{if } M \mathbf{\ v\ } N$$

For State ISWIM a standard reduction relation is not quite that simple to define because of letrec expressions. First, the outermost expression might just be a letrec. Second, after applying **lift** to an evaluation context at the root of the program, a letrec expression can become the outermost expression.

We overcome the definition with the introduction of standard evaluation contexts for State ISWIM.

$$E_s = E \mid (\texttt{letrec } \Sigma \, E)$$

The definition is not self-referential but simply acknowledges that a plain evaluation context might optionally be surrounded by a letrec expression.

The standard reduction relation reduces leftmost-outermost redexes in E_s contexts, just like the standard reduction relations of previous chapters.

$$E_s[M] \longmapsto_s E_s[N] \quad \text{if } M \text{ s } N$$

Unfortunately, this definition does not introduce a step function that can also serve as an instruction for a syntactic machine. Consider this expression:

$$E_1[E_2[(\texttt{letrec } \Sigma \, M)]]$$

As long as $E_1 \neq []$ and $E_2 \neq []$, there are (at least) two ways of partitioning this expression into a E_s context and a **lift** redex:

1. $E_1[E_2[(\texttt{letrec } \Sigma \, M)]] \longmapsto_s E_1[(\texttt{letrec } \Sigma \, E_2[M])]$

2. $E_1[E_2[(\texttt{letrec } \Sigma \, M)]] \longmapsto_s (\texttt{letrec } \Sigma \, E_1[E_2[M]])$

Although the relation $\longmapsto_s$ is not a function, it doesn't introduce any inconsistencies into the evaluation process. Choosing a non-maximal evaluation context for a use of **lift** merely delays the full lift of a letrec expression to the top. The standard reduction relation thus induces a definition for an evaluator function as usual.

$$eval_s^s(M) = \begin{cases} b & \text{if} \quad M \longmapsto\!\!\!\to_s b \\ & \text{or} \quad M \longmapsto\!\!\!\to_s (\texttt{letrec } \Sigma \, b) \\ \texttt{function} & \text{if} \quad M \longmapsto\!\!\!\to_s \lambda X.N \\ & \text{or} \quad M \longmapsto\!\!\!\to_s (\texttt{letrec } \Sigma \, \lambda X.N) \end{cases}$$

The evaluator is correct, i.e., equivalent to the one based on the equational calculus for State ISWIM.

Theorem 9.3: $eval_s = eval_s^s$.

Exercise 9.9. Develop the notion of a standard reduction sequence for State ISWIM, based on our standard reduction relation. Then prove a standard reduction lemma and use it to prove theorem 9.3.

Thus far, we do not have a syntactic machine. Our informal definition for a abstract syntax machine (with or without registers) is that at any one point only one instruction applies to the current state. The formulation of $\longmapsto_s$, however, allows distinct instances of **lift** to apply to one and the same machine state. We overcome this minor problem with the more stringent strategy of always picking the largest possible evaluation context.

$$eval_{s2}(M) = \begin{cases} b & \text{if} \quad M \longmapsto_{s2} b \\ & \text{or} \quad M \longmapsto_{s2} (\texttt{letrec } \Sigma \ b) \\ \texttt{function} & \text{if} \quad M \longmapsto_{s2} \lambda X.N \\ & \text{or} \quad M \longmapsto_{s2} (\texttt{letrec } \Sigma \ \lambda X.N) \end{cases}$$

$\longmapsto_{s2}$		
$E_s[((\lambda X.M) \ V)]$ $\quad$ if $X \notin \mathcal{AV}(M)$	$E_s[M[X \leftarrow V]]$	[s2fi$_v$]
$E_s[(o^n \ V_1 \dots V_n)]$	$E_s[\delta(o^n, V_1, \dots V_n)]$	[s2ffi]
$E_s[((\lambda X.M) \ V)]$ $\quad$ if $X \in \mathcal{AV}(M)$	$E_s[(\texttt{letrec } \{\langle X, V \rangle\} \ M)]$	[s2fi$_s$]
$E[(\texttt{letrec } \Sigma \ M)]$ $\quad$ if $E \neq []$	$(\texttt{letrec } \Sigma \ E[M])$	[s2liftE]
$(\texttt{letrec } \Sigma \ E[(\texttt{letrec } \Sigma' \ M)])$ $\quad$ where $\quad \Sigma^* = \Sigma'[X_1' \leftarrow Y_1] \dots [X_n' \leftarrow Y_n]$ $\quad$ and $\quad M^* = M[X_1' \leftarrow Y_1] \dots [X_n' \leftarrow Y_n]$ $\quad$ if $\quad \text{dom}(\Sigma') = \{X_1', \dots, X_n'\}$ $\quad$ and $\quad \text{dom}(\Sigma) \cap \{Y_1, \dots, Y_n\} = \emptyset$	$(\texttt{letrec } \Sigma \oplus \Sigma^* \ E[M^*])$	[s2liftR]
$(\texttt{letrec } \Sigma[X \leftarrow V] \ E[X])$	$(\texttt{letrec } \Sigma[X \leftarrow V] \ E[V])$	[s2derefR]
$(\texttt{letrec } \Sigma[X \leftarrow V]$ $\quad E[(\texttt{set } X \ U)])$	$(\texttt{letrec } \Sigma[X \leftarrow U]$ $\quad E[V])$	[s2assignR]

The complex-looking side-condition for rule [s2liftR] says that the variables declared in the nested **letrec** must be renamed so that they do not conflict with the names in the outermost **letrec**. Since the latter are only variables free in E, there is no need to add $\mathcal{FV}(E)$ as a part of the last condition.

Exercise 9.10. Prove that $eval_s^s = eval_{s2}$.

Ideally, we would like to conclude that the exercise implies the equivalence between $eval_s$ and $eval_{cs}$. We cannot state the theorem in the usual form, though, because the two evaluators do not even agree on their input language. Thus, in order to connect the two evaluators, we first extend the language of CS machine instructions with a transition for `letrec` expressions.

$$
\begin{array}{|rl|r|}
\hline
\multicolumn{2}{|c|}{\longmapsto_{cs}} & \\
\hline
\langle E[(\texttt{letrec } \Sigma' \ M)], \Sigma \rangle \mid \langle E[M^*], \Sigma \oplus \Sigma^* \rangle & & [\text{csR}] \\
\text{where} \quad \Sigma^* = \Sigma'[X'_1 \leftarrow Y_1] \ldots [X'_n \leftarrow Y_n] & & \\
\text{and} \quad M^* = M[X'_1 \leftarrow Y_1] \ldots [X'_n \leftarrow Y_n] & & \\
\text{if} \quad \text{dom}(\Sigma') = \{X'_1, \ldots, X'_n\} & & \\
\text{and} \quad \text{dom}(\Sigma) \cap \{Y_1, \ldots, Y_n\} = \varnothing & & \\
\hline
\end{array}
$$

Exercise 9.11. Explain the condition on the [csR] instruction for the CS machine. Compare it with the condition on the [s2lift] rule for $eval_{s2}$.

With this instruction added to the CS machine, the evaluator can now cope with the full syntax of State ISWIM. By putting together exercise 9.10 and theorem 9.3, it is finally possible to express in what sense the CS machine and the calculus for State ISWIM agree.

Theorem 9.4: $eval_{s2} = eval_{cs}$.

Proof for Theorem 9.4: For all closed State ISWIM expressions M, prove

$$
\begin{aligned}
&(\texttt{letrec } \{\} \ M) \longmapsto\!\!\!\!\twoheadrightarrow_{s2} (\texttt{letrec } \Sigma \ V) \\
&\text{if and only if} \\
&(\texttt{letrec } \{\} \ M) \longmapsto\!\!\!\!\twoheadrightarrow_{cs} (\texttt{letrec } \Sigma \ V)
\end{aligned}
$$

The additional `letrec` expressions facilitates a direct proof, yet it does not affect the reduction sequences.

Exercise 9.12. Demonstrate that `letrec` expressions can be considered an abbreviation in State ISWIM:

$$
(\texttt{letrec } \{\langle X_1, V_1 \rangle, \ldots, \langle X_n, V_n \rangle\} \ M) \ \dot{=} \ \begin{aligned}[t] &\texttt{let } \{\langle X_1, \ulcorner 42 \urcorner \rangle, \ldots, \langle X_n, \ulcorner 42 \urcorner \rangle\} \\ &\texttt{in } (\texttt{seq } (\texttt{set } X_1 \ V_1) \\ &\qquad\qquad \cdots \\ &\qquad\quad (\texttt{set } X_n \ V_n) \\ &\qquad\quad M) \end{aligned}
$$

Re-prove the consistency and the standard reduction theorem using `letrec` as just an abbreviation.

9.4 **The CESK Machine.** Like the abstract syntax machine for ISWIM, the CS machine is quite abstract. For every transition that implements a notion of reduction, the machine has to partition the control string into an evaluation context and a redex, and it may have to perform a substitution. In short, the CS machine lacks the registers of the CEK machine.

Not surprisingly, we can get all of our old refinements back by equipping each CEK state with a store and by adapting the transitions appropriately. Before we do so, however, let us remove the [csfi$_v$] instruction from the CS machine (see page 151). Its purpose is to implement β_v accurately, but it should be obvious that sticking the argument value into the store and looking it up later has the same result. In addition, we introduce a separate notion of **location**, i.e., a slot in the store where the machine can place values. The meta-variable σ ranges over locations.

$\longmapsto_{cs}$		
$\langle E, \Sigma \rangle$ if $\sigma \notin \mathrm{dom}(\Sigma)$	$\langle E[M[X \leftarrow \sigma]], \Sigma[\sigma \leftarrow V] \rangle$	[csfi$_s$]
$\langle E[\sigma], \Sigma[\sigma \leftarrow V] \rangle$	$\langle E[V], \Sigma[\sigma \leftarrow V] \rangle$	[cs!]

The elimination of [csfi$_v$] simplifies the [csfi$_s$] instruction as well. It is no longer necessary to check whether the parameter of a function is an assignable variable, and it suffices to pick a location that is not in the domain of the store.

Exercise 9.13. Complete the simplified CS machine. Make a detailed argument for the correctness of this simplification.

Now we can introduce the ingredients necessary for transforming the CEK machine into a CESK machine.[4]

$$
\begin{aligned}
\sigma \;&\in\; \text{Locations} \\
\overline{\mathcal{E}} \;&=\; \{ \langle X_1, \sigma_1 \rangle, \ldots, \langle X_n, \sigma_n \rangle \} \\
&\quad\;\; \text{if for all } i \neq j, X_i \neq X_j \\
c \;&=\; \langle V, \overline{\mathcal{E}} \rangle \\
\overline{\Sigma} \;&=\; \{ \langle \sigma_1, c_1 \rangle, \ldots, \langle \sigma_n, c_n \rangle \} \\
&\quad\;\; \text{if for all } i \neq j, \sigma_i \neq \sigma_j \\
\overline{\kappa} \;&=\; \mathtt{mt} \\
&\;\mid\; \langle \mathtt{fn}, v, \overline{\kappa} \rangle \\
&\;\mid\; \langle \mathtt{ar}, c, \overline{\kappa} \rangle \\
&\;\mid\; \langle \mathtt{op}, \langle v, \ldots, v, o^n \rangle, \langle c, \ldots, c \rangle, \overline{\kappa} \rangle \\
&\;\mid\; \langle \mathtt{set}, \sigma, \overline{\kappa} \rangle
\end{aligned}
$$

---

[4]CESK machine is the historical name; logically, CEKS is the correct choice.

In this setting, environments are finite mappings from variables to locations. Naturally, we also reformulate closures to use these new kind of environments. A store is a finite mapping from locations to closures. Looking up the value of a variable X takes two steps: first we look up its location in the current environment $\overline{\mathcal{E}}$, and then we retrieve its value from the current store $\overline{\Sigma}$. We denote this process with $\overline{\Sigma}(\overline{\mathcal{E}}(X))$, exploiting the nature of environments and stores as functions. Finally, continuations are adapted to use the new kinds of environments. In addition, we introduce a new kind of continuation frame for remembering to assign a value to a location.

At this point we can equip the CEK machine with a Store register and turn it into the CESK machine.

$$eval_{\mathsf{cesk}}(M) = \begin{cases} b \\ \quad \text{if } \langle\langle M,\varnothing\rangle,\varnothing,\mathtt{mt}\rangle \longmapsto\!\!\!\!\twoheadrightarrow_{\mathsf{cesk}} \langle\langle b,\overline{\mathcal{E}}\rangle,\overline{\Sigma},\mathtt{mt}\rangle \\ \mathsf{function} \\ \quad \text{if } \langle\langle M,\varnothing\rangle,\varnothing,\mathtt{mt}\rangle \longmapsto\!\!\!\!\twoheadrightarrow_{\mathsf{cesk}} \langle\langle \lambda X.N,\overline{\mathcal{E}}\rangle,\overline{\Sigma},\mathtt{mt}\rangle \end{cases}$$

$\longmapsto_{\mathsf{cesk}}$		
$\langle\langle(M\ N),\overline{\mathcal{E}}\rangle,\overline{\Sigma},\overline{\kappa}\rangle$	$\langle\langle M,\overline{\mathcal{E}}\rangle,\overline{\Sigma},\langle\mathtt{ar},\langle N,\overline{\mathcal{E}}\rangle,\overline{\kappa}\rangle\rangle$	[cesk1]
$\langle\langle(o^n\ M\ N\dots),\overline{\mathcal{E}}\rangle,\overline{\Sigma},\overline{\kappa}\rangle$	$\left\langle\begin{array}{l}\langle M,\overline{\mathcal{E}}\rangle,\overline{\Sigma}, \\ \langle\mathtt{op},\langle o^n\rangle,\langle\langle N,\overline{\mathcal{E}}\rangle,\dots\rangle,\overline{\kappa}\rangle\end{array}\right\rangle$	[cesk2]
$\left\langle\begin{array}{l}\langle V,\overline{\mathcal{E}}\rangle,\overline{\Sigma}, \\ \langle\mathtt{fn},\langle(\lambda X.M),\overline{\mathcal{E}}'\rangle,\overline{\kappa}\rangle\end{array}\right\rangle$ if $V\notin X, \sigma\notin\mathrm{dom}(\overline{\Sigma})$	$\left\langle\begin{array}{l}\langle M,\overline{\mathcal{E}}'[X\leftarrow\sigma]\rangle, \\ \overline{\Sigma}[\sigma\leftarrow\langle V,\overline{\mathcal{E}}\rangle],\overline{\kappa}\end{array}\right\rangle$	[cesk3]*
$\langle\langle V,\overline{\mathcal{E}}\rangle,\overline{\Sigma},\langle\mathtt{ar},\langle N,\overline{\mathcal{E}}'\rangle,\overline{\kappa}\rangle\rangle$ if $V\notin X$	$\langle\langle N,\overline{\mathcal{E}}'\rangle,\overline{\Sigma},\langle\mathtt{fn},\langle V,\overline{\mathcal{E}}\rangle,\overline{\kappa}\rangle\rangle$	[cesk4]
$\left\langle\begin{array}{l}\langle b_m,\overline{\mathcal{E}}\rangle,\overline{\Sigma}, \\ \langle\mathtt{op},\langle c_{m-1},\dots,c_1,o^n\rangle, \\ \quad\langle\rangle,\overline{\kappa}\rangle\end{array}\right\rangle$ where $c_i=\langle b_i,\overline{\mathcal{E}}_i\rangle$	$\langle\langle\delta(o^m,b_1,\dots,b_m),\varnothing\rangle,\overline{\Sigma},\overline{\kappa}\rangle$	[cesk5]
$\left\langle\begin{array}{l}\langle V,\overline{\mathcal{E}}\rangle,\overline{\Sigma}, \\ \langle\mathtt{op},\langle c,\dots,o^n\rangle, \\ \quad\langle\langle N,\overline{\mathcal{E}}_N\rangle,c_L,\dots\rangle,\overline{\kappa}\rangle\end{array}\right\rangle$ if $V\notin X$	$\left\langle\begin{array}{l}\langle N,\overline{\mathcal{E}}_N\rangle,\overline{\Sigma}, \\ \langle\mathtt{op},\langle\langle V,\overline{\mathcal{E}}\rangle,c,\dots,o^n\rangle, \\ \quad\langle c_L,\dots\rangle,\overline{\kappa}\rangle\end{array}\right\rangle$	[cesk6]
$\langle\langle X,\overline{\mathcal{E}}\rangle,\overline{\Sigma},\overline{\kappa}\rangle$	$\langle\overline{\Sigma}(\overline{\mathcal{E}}(X)),\overline{\Sigma},\overline{\kappa}\rangle$	[cesk7]*
$\langle\langle(\mathtt{set}\ X\ M),\overline{\mathcal{E}}\rangle,\overline{\Sigma},\overline{\kappa}\rangle$	$\langle\langle M,\overline{\mathcal{E}}\rangle,\overline{\Sigma},\langle\mathtt{set},\overline{\mathcal{E}}(X),\overline{\kappa}\rangle\rangle$	[cesk8]*
$\langle\langle V,\overline{\mathcal{E}}'\rangle,\overline{\Sigma},\langle\mathtt{set},\sigma,\overline{\kappa}\rangle\rangle$ if $V\notin X$	$\langle\overline{\Sigma}(\sigma),\overline{\Sigma}[\sigma\leftarrow\langle V,\overline{\mathcal{E}}'\rangle],\overline{\kappa}\rangle$	[cesk9]*

Most of the instructions do not manipulate the store at all. The interesting instructions are those labeled with asterisks ($*$):

[cesk3] **and** [ceks7] The instructions for applying a λ expression to a value and for looking up the value of a variable have changed in accordance to the preceding discussion.

[cesk8] When the CESK machine has identified a set redex, it shifts the right-hand side to the control string register, looks up the location σ of the variable, and uses it to create a continuation of the shape $\langle \text{set}, \sigma, \overline{\kappa} \rangle$.

[cesk9] Once it has obtained a value for the right-hand side, the machine places this value into the specified location and simultaneously re-trieves the value from this location. The latter becomes the result of the set expression.

Exercise 9.14. Add an instruction for the evaluation of letrec expressions to the CESK machine.

Exercise 9.15. Derive CSC, SCSC, and CSK machines from the simplified CS machine of exercise 9.13. Use those machines to prove the evaluator based on the simplified CS machine equivalent to $eval_{\text{cesk}}$.

Exercise 9.16. Implement the CESK machine in a real-world programming language. Use linked lists to implement environments and stores.

$9 \cdot 5$ **Space and Garbage Collection.** The introduction of a store creates a new space problem: garbage. Every time a function is applied, the machine allocates a previously unused location and expands the store, placing the argument value into this location. Clearly, if a store provides only a finite number of locations, many programs sooner or later exhaust the available storage space—even though many of these locations cannot possibly affect the execution of the program anymore. If a machine can prove[5] that some location doesn't affect the rest of the execution, the location is called **garbage**, and machines may reclaim it via **garbage collection**.

Let us start with an example, specifically the definition of a factorial and its application to some numeral $\ulcorner n \urcorner$:

---

[5] In principle, *all* such locations are garbage but the literature on garbage collection uses the narrower definition that focuses on provability as opposed to truth. See the history section.

$$(\texttt{letrec} \; \{ \; \langle !, \lambda x.\text{if0} \; x \; \ulcorner 1 \urcorner \; (* \; x \; (! \; (- \; x \; \ulcorner 1 \urcorner)))\rangle \; \}$$
$$(! \; \ulcorner n \urcorner))$$

$$\twoheadrightarrow_s \quad (\texttt{letrec} \; \left\{ \begin{array}{l} \langle x_n, \ulcorner n \urcorner \rangle, \\ \langle !, \lambda x.\text{if0} \; x \; \ulcorner 1 \urcorner \; (* \; x \; (! \; (- \; x \; \ulcorner 1 \urcorner)))\rangle \end{array} \right\}$$
$$(* \; \ulcorner n \urcorner \; (! \; \ulcorner n-1 \urcorner)))$$

$$\twoheadrightarrow_s \quad (\texttt{letrec} \; \left\{ \begin{array}{l} \langle x_{n-1}, \ulcorner n-1 \urcorner \rangle, \\ \langle x_n, \ulcorner n \urcorner \rangle, \\ \langle !, \lambda x.\text{if0} \; x \; \ulcorner 1 \urcorner \; (* \; x \; (! \; (- \; x \; \ulcorner 1 \urcorner)))\rangle \end{array} \right\}$$
$$(* \; \ulcorner n \urcorner \; (* \; \ulcorner n-1 \urcorner \; (! \; \ulcorner n-1 \urcorner))))$$

$\dots$

$$\twoheadrightarrow_s \quad (\texttt{letrec} \; \left\{ \begin{array}{l} \langle x_{n-i}, \ulcorner n-i \urcorner \rangle, \\ \dots \\ \langle x_{n-1}, \ulcorner n-1 \urcorner \rangle, \\ \langle x_n, \ulcorner n \urcorner \rangle, \\ \langle !, \lambda x.\text{if0} \; x \; \ulcorner 1 \urcorner \; (* \; x \; (! \; (- \; x \; \ulcorner 1 \urcorner)))\rangle \end{array} \right\}$$
$$(* \; \ulcorner n \urcorner \; (* \; \ulcorner n-1 \urcorner \; \dots \; (* \; \ulcorner n-i \urcorner \; (! \; \ulcorner n-1-i \urcorner)) \dots)))$$

The reduction sequence in the State ISWIM calculus shows how each application of the ! function introduces one more definition into the surrounding letrec expressions. At the same time, there are no references to these additional variables from the body of the letrec expression nor from the body of the ! function. In other words, it is impossible that these variables can play any useful role during the rest of the reduction process.

Garbage Collection: Specification. Variable definitions such as those for $x_n, x_{n-1}, \dots$ are examples of garbage. They exist in local letrec definitions, yet they cannot affect the computation. Hence, removing these definitions is not only acceptable but beneficial in a world that allows only a fixed number of variable definitions or—as they are known at the level of the CESK machine—storage locations.

Our observation suggests a quite simple notion of reduction for garbage collection in the State ISWIM calculus.

$$\boxed{\begin{array}{l} (\texttt{letrec} \; \Sigma \oplus \Sigma' \; M) \; \textbf{gc} \; (\texttt{letrec} \; \Sigma \; M) \\ \quad \text{if } \text{dom}(\Sigma') \cap ((\cup_{V \in \text{rng}(\Sigma)} \mathcal{FV}(V)) \cup \mathcal{FV}(M)) = \varnothing \end{array}}$$

The rule assumes a partitioning of the definitions in a letrec expression into two halves. If one half of the partition has no reference to the second, and if this second half is also not referenced in the body of the letrec expression, the second half is garbage and can be removed.

Note how the rule does not assume anything about the second half of the store. In particular, this second half of the definitions may contain self-referential definitions or mutually referential definitions; neither form matters. For example, in this `letrec` expression

$$(\texttt{letrec} \; \{ \; \langle u, \lambda w.(u \; \ulcorner 42 \urcorner) \rangle$$

$$\langle x, \lambda w.x \rangle$$
$$\langle y, \lambda w.z \rangle$$
$$\langle z, \lambda w.y \rangle \qquad \}$$
$$u)$$

the first half of the definitions consists of one binding (u) and the second consists of three: $x, y,$ and z. Of those in the second, x refers to itself, y refers to z, and the latter refers to the former. Still, the body consists of just a reference to u, and it is therefore legitimate to remove the second half of the `letrec` definitions:

$$(\texttt{letrec} \; \{ \; \langle u, \lambda w.(u \; \ulcorner 42 \urcorner) \rangle \}$$
$$u)$$

While it is possible to use the **deref** reduction on this result, the definition for u cannot be eliminated immediately afterward, because the context of the expression may apply the function.

The garbage collection rule introduces a form of non-determinism into the reduction system. First, the **gc** relation overlaps with every other relation if the expression contains garbage in any of its `letrec` expressions. Second, the **gc** reduction does not have to remove all garbage at once. For example, it is legitimate for the above expression to remove just the definition of x; to dereference the body of the `letrec`; and to collect the rest of the garbage at the end. At the same time, once all garbage is removed from an expression, the reduction system still reaches a "canonical" state.

In summary, the garbage collection rule acts like garbage collectors in modern programming languages. It is useful at "random" points during the execution. It eliminates all forms of `letrec` definitions, including definitions with direct and indirect cycles. It is not a model of an implementation, however, because the rule assumes that a partitioning is feasible without creating it. Put differently, it is a non-algorithmic *specification* of garbage collection, not an *implementation*.

Still, it is possible to refine this specification of the garbage collection process and to use it to prove the correctness of one particular implementation.

We start with a translation of **gc** into the world of the CS machine.

$$\begin{array}{|c|c|}
\hline
 & \longmapsto_{\text{cs}} \\
\hline
\langle M, \Sigma \oplus \Sigma' \rangle & \langle M, \Sigma \rangle \quad [\text{csgc}] \\
\quad \text{if } \text{dom}(\Sigma') \cap ((\cup_{V \in \text{rng}(\Sigma)} \mathcal{FV}(V)) \cup \mathcal{FV}(M)) = \varnothing & \\
\hline
\end{array}$$

Not surprisingly, this machine instruction looks like the original **gc** relation. After all, the CS machine just separates the top-level letrec expression from its body.

Exercise 9.17. Prove that **gc** satisfies the Church-Rosser property and commutes with s. Conclude that evaluation with garbage collection is still a function.

Exercise 9.18. Argue that the evaluator based on the extended State ISWIM calculus is still equivalent to the CS-machine evaluator with [csgc].

The next step is to refine the garbage collection instruction for the CESK machine. Since this machine uses closures (CE) for the control string register plus store (S) and continuation (K) registers, it is no longer just a question of finding free variables in a control string. Instead, the domain of the associated environment dictates which variables may appear free in the syntax. Furthermore, such closures appear in both the continuation and the store, meaning we must search for free variables there, too. Last but not least, the CESK machine no longer deals with variables and variable declarations but locations and stores.

What we need is not a "free variable" function, but a function that looks for potentially useful locations. The literature calls these locations "live" and we therefore use $\mathcal{LL}$, for **live locations**, as the function name.

$$\begin{aligned}
\mathcal{LL}(\langle M, \overline{\mathcal{E}} \rangle) &= \mathcal{LL}(\overline{\mathcal{E}}) \\[6pt]
\mathcal{LL}(\overline{\mathcal{E}}) &= \text{rng}(\overline{\mathcal{E}}) \\[6pt]
\mathcal{LL}(\{\langle \sigma_1, c_1 \rangle, \ldots, \langle \sigma_n, c_n \rangle\}) &= \cup_{i=1}^{i=n} \mathcal{LL}(c_i) \\[6pt]
\mathcal{LL}(\text{mt}) &= \varnothing \\
\mathcal{LL}(\langle \text{fn}, \langle V, \overline{\mathcal{E}} \rangle, \overline{\kappa} \rangle) &= \mathcal{LL}(\overline{\mathcal{E}}) \cup \mathcal{LL}(\overline{\kappa}) \\
\mathcal{LL}(\langle \text{ar}, \langle N, \overline{\mathcal{E}} \rangle, \overline{\kappa} \rangle) &= \mathcal{LL}(\overline{\mathcal{E}}) \cup \mathcal{LL}(\overline{\kappa}) \\
\mathcal{LL}(\langle \text{op}, \langle c_1, \ldots, o^n \rangle, \langle \ldots, c_n \rangle, \overline{\kappa} \rangle) &= \cup_{i=1}^{i=n} \mathcal{LL}(c_i) \cup \mathcal{LL}(\overline{\kappa}) \\
\mathcal{LL}(\langle \text{set}, \sigma, \overline{\kappa} \rangle) &= \{\sigma\} \cup \mathcal{LL}(\overline{\kappa})
\end{aligned}$$

The definition introduces an entire family of $\mathcal{LL}$ functions. The first clause searches closures for live locations, a set that is computed by the function in the second clause. It specifies that for any given environment, its entire range is the set of potentially useful locations. The third and fourth clause concern the collection of live locations from stores and continuations, respectively. In both cases, the $\mathcal{LL}$ functions search for environments and extract the useful locations from there. The case for a $\langle set, \sigma, \overline{\kappa} \rangle$ continuation is the only one when the $\mathcal{LL}$ function finds a potentially useful location directly.

With $\mathcal{LL}$ in place, the instruction for collecting garbage in the CESK machine is just like the one for the CS machine, except that the search for free variables in the control string is replaced by the search for live locations.

$$
\begin{array}{|c|c|c|}
\hline
\langle c, \overline{\Sigma} \oplus \overline{\Sigma}', \overline{\kappa} \rangle & \longmapsto_{\text{cesk}} & \\
\quad \text{if } \text{dom}(\overline{\Sigma}') \cap \left(\begin{array}{c} \left(\bigcup_{cl \in \text{rng}(\overline{\Sigma})} \mathcal{LL}(cl) \right) \\ \cup \, \mathcal{LL}(c) \cup \mathcal{LL}(\overline{\kappa}) \end{array} \right) = \varnothing & \langle c, \overline{\Sigma}, \overline{\kappa} \rangle & [\text{ceskgc}] \\
\hline
\end{array}
$$

It is straightforward to see how this instruction refines the [csgc] instruction, yet it remains at the level of a specification that assumes some partitioning.

Exercise 9.19. Prove that the [ceskgc] instruction implements [csgc].

Implementation. The standard algorithm for finding the minimal set of live locations "colors" the store's locations "black," "gray," or "white." A black location is live, and the closure at this location references only black and gray locations. In contrast, a gray location is live, but the closure at that location might reference a white one. Finally, a white location contains a potentially useless value. At the end of the coloring process, no slots are gray, and all white slots are garbage. Here is a step-wise description:

- Color all locations white.

- Color a location gray if it is reachable from the current environment.

- For every environment $\overline{\mathcal{E}}$ referenced by the current continuation, color all locations referenced by $\overline{\mathcal{E}}$ gray.

- Repeat the following steps until there are no gray-colored locations:

    - Choose a gray location, σ.
    - If the closure at σ is $\langle c, \overline{\mathcal{E}} \rangle$, color all locations referenced by $\overline{\mathcal{E}}$ gray.
    - Color σ black.

We can formulate this coloring process as a "sub-machine" on a triple: the set of gray locations, the set of black locations, and the store.

$$\langle \mathcal{G}, \mathcal{B}, \overline{\Sigma}\rangle \quad \longmapsto_{gc} \quad \langle ((\mathcal{G} \cup \mathcal{LL}(\overline{\Sigma}(\sigma_0))) \backslash (\mathcal{B} \cup \{\sigma_0\})), \mathcal{B} \cup \{\sigma_0\}, \overline{\Sigma}\rangle$$
$$\text{if } \sigma_0 \in \mathcal{G}$$

Each step picks a random location from the set of gray locations. For this location, it determines the locations of reachable locations with the $\mathcal{LL}$ function. That is, it computes the locations to which the closure in the chosen location refers. From those locations, the instruction subtracts the chosen location and all black-colored locations.

Another way to understand this "sub-machine" is to think of it as a graph traversal algorithm. The store determines the adjaceny relation of the graph. The gray locations are the as yet-to-inspected locations; the black ones are those that have been inspected.

Now it is straightforward to provide an implementation of the instruction for garbage collection in the CESK machine.

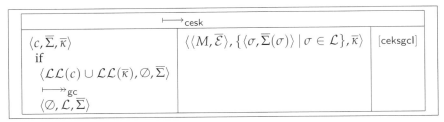

The instruction starts the "sub-machine" with the locations reachable from the control string closure and an empty set of black locations. When the coloring process is complete, it restricts the store to those locations that are colored black. The remaining locations have been identified as garbage.

Exercise 9.20. Prove that for all initial states $\langle \mathcal{G}, \overline{\Sigma}, \varnothing\rangle$ with $\mathcal{G} \subseteq \text{dom}(\overline{\Sigma})$ the "sub-machine" for garbage collection terminates with a final state of the shape $\langle \varnothing, \mathcal{L}, \overline{\Sigma}\rangle$ for some set of locations $\mathcal{L}$.

Exercise 9.21. Prove that the [ceskgcl] instruction implements [ceskgc] provided that the latter is used to remove the largest $\overline{\Sigma}'$ such that the side condition of the instruction is satisfied.

Exercise 9.22. Implement the CESK machine. Every other step taken by the machine should be a [ceskgcl] step that collects as many slots as possible. Of course, real-world language implementations collect garbage only when needed.

9·6 History.

History. The State ISWIM language corresponds to the functional subset of Scheme enriched with `set!` and restricted `letrec` expressions. Its calculus is due to work by Felleisen with Friedman and Hieb [32, 35, 37]. Their abstract machines are again inspired by the definitional interpreters of Reynolds [93].

Felleisen and Hieb also suggested the specification of garbage collection for the State ISWIM calculus. Morrisett, Felleisen, and Harper [80] worked out a precise semantic (model-based) definition of garbage and garbage collection as well as the details of the (proof-oriented) specification and implementation rules.

Demers and Donahue [28] created the first logical system for reasoning about higher-order functional language with reference cells. Their logic combines judgments on the purity of expressions with those on the effects of expressions plus some equational axioms.

Mason and Talcott [72, 73] presented an alternative approach to reasoning about stateful programs like those of State ISWIM. The approach relies on collecting useful observational equivalences and using those as if they were axioms of an equational logic. Mason's dissertation contains a different kind of correctness proof for the implementation of a garbage collection correctness theorem.

10 • Simply Typed ISWIM

According to ISWIM's grammar, the expression

$$(+ \ulcorner 1 \urcorner \ -)$$

is not well-formed, and therefore the evaluator does not have to deal with such an expression. In contrast,

$$(+ \ulcorner 1 \urcorner \ (\lambda x. \ulcorner 9 \urcorner))$$

is well-formed but it, too, is obviously a "bad" expression. Technically, it is a stuck expression, for which the ISWIM evaluator is undefined and for which the Error ISWIM evaluator signals a run-time error. For a variant of ISWIM with string constants, the evaluator may also signal a run-time error when it encounters expressions such $(* \ulcorner 2 \urcorner$ "hello world").[1] Yet another run-time error comes from constants showing up in the function position of applications, e.g., $(\ulcorner 5 \urcorner \ (\lambda x.x))$.

It is the task of **type systems** and **type checkers** to disallow the evaluation of expressions that may get stuck or signal run-time errors. Roughly speaking, a type system consists of a language of *claims* and a *claim checker*. The type language is a notation for formulating simple claims about programs, also known as **types**. A claim checker confirms that the types follow from first principles. Put differently, a type system is a mechanism for stating and establishing (simple) theorems about a program. Such a proof system is sound if it validates only claims that are true according to the evaluator. When a type system cannot validate a type claim about some expression, we speak of a **type error**.

In this chapter, we introduce **Simply Typed ISWIM**, an explicitly typed variant of ISWIM. We then show how to use a reduction semantics to analyze the type system. Technically, we state and prove theorems about the relationship between the type system of Simply Typed ISWIM and two variants and their evaluators. It is *not* the purpose of this chapter to study the design and range of type systems; while the design of a type system is related to the design of an evaluator, the two are quite different kinds of engineering tasks.

---

[1] Some scripting languages allow such multiplications for pragmatic reasons. The type systems of this chapter naturally accommodates such expressions, if desired.

10·1

Simply Typed ISWIM. The purpose of a type system is to classify programs into one of two categories: "good" and "bad." Running the evaluator on a "good" program should not cause any bad effects; a "bad" program simply is not going to be evaluated. We consider stuck expressions in plain ISWIM or run-time errors in Error ISWIM as bad effects and leave it at that.

While expressions such as $(+\ \ulcorner 1 \urcorner\ (\lambda x.\ulcorner 9 \urcorner))$ and $(\ulcorner 5 \urcorner\ (\lambda x.x))$ are obviously stuck expressions, a program may not contain any immediately stuck expressions but still cause the evaluator to get stuck later. For example,

$$(((\lambda x.x)\ \ulcorner 5 \urcorner)\ (\lambda x.x))$$

is such a program. After a single reduction, it consists of an application with a basic constant in the function position of an application:

$$(\ulcorner 5 \urcorner\ (\lambda x.x))$$

Of course, the stuck expression does not have to show up after a single step. It may take arbitrarily long before it does, but the purpose of a type system is to discover this problem *without running the program first*. After all, a program may go into an infinite loop and, if it does, the type system would not produce any answer at all if it tried to run the program.

Put differently, we want a type system to classify programs based on their (abstract) syntax. One easy refinement is to think of types as classifying the values of a programming language and of type checkers as classifying what kind of values an expression may produce. For a numeric ISWIM, like the one mentioned in chapter 4, we might then introduce a classification system with two categories

$$
\begin{aligned}
T\ \ =\ \ &\texttt{num}\\
|\ \ &\texttt{function}
\end{aligned}
$$

because such a language contains two kinds of values: numbers (`num`) and λ expressions or functions (`function`).

The type checker would then ensure, for example, that the addition operation is always applied to numbers. Conversely, it would reject

$$(+\ \ulcorner 1 \urcorner\ (\lambda x.\ulcorner 9 \urcorner))$$

More generally, the type checker classifies the values that each expression produces during evaluation. Consider this expression:

$$(+\ \ulcorner 1 \urcorner\ ((\lambda y.\ulcorner 13 \urcorner)\ \ulcorner 42 \urcorner))$$

It is a primitive application that applies $+$ to a numeral ($\ulcorner 1 \urcorner$) and an expression $((\lambda y.\ulcorner 13 \urcorner)\ \ulcorner 42 \urcorner)$. Assuming the type checker can classify the latter as num, i.e., an expression that always produces numbers, it can classify the entire expression as a num-producing one.

Given that programs are constructed according to algebraic or structural rules of composition, it is natural to want a type checker that composes its results in an equally structural or algebraic manner. That is, for each expression, the type checker should classify the sub-expressions and should then be able to determine for the entire expression whether its results are always of the num or function kind. For example, an application consists of two sub-expressions. Unless the first one is classified as a function-producing expression, the type checker cannot bless the application as a good one. Take a look at this expression:

$$(\, (\mathsf{if0} \; M \; (\lambda x.\ulcorner 8 \urcorner) \; (\lambda xy.y) \,) \; \ulcorner 7 \urcorner)$$

Both arms of the if0 expression are of type function, so the application expression that uses the result of the if0 expression could be well-typed. Now suppose though that the expression is just a part of a program:

$$(+ \; \ulcorner 1 \urcorner \; (\, (\mathsf{if0} \; M \; (\lambda x.\ulcorner 8 \urcorner) \; (\lambda xy.y) \,) \; \ulcorner 7 \urcorner))$$

The result of the application expression is either a number or an identity function, depending on whether M produces $\ulcorner 0 \urcorner$ or not. Thus, the addition expression could potentially get stuck, and a type checker should not classify this program as "good."

Obviously, the type function does not encode enough information about the kind of function that this (or any) expression produces. Some functions expect numbers; some others expect other functions. Some functions produce numbers; some others produce other functions. The type for a function needs to expose this information.

Mathematics suggests a natural solution. There, a function description consists of two pieces: its domain and range, plus what the function computes. Following this idea, a type system should include types of the form

$$(\mathsf{num} \to \mathsf{num}), (\mathsf{num} \to (\mathsf{num} \to \mathsf{num})), \text{ and } ((\mathsf{num} \to \mathsf{num}) \to \mathsf{num}).$$

The left-hand side of the arrow specifies the domain of a function, that is, the type of value that a function consumes. The right-hand side classifies the type of value that a function returns. Hence, the first type is for a function that takes a number and produces a number; the second one is for a function from numbers to functions from numbers to numbers; and the last one is assigned to functions that consume functions from numbers to numbers and produce a number.

One obvious question at this point is how the type checker determines the domain or the range of a function. For Simply Typed ISWIM, the domain comes from the programmer. More concretely, Simply Typed ISWIM is a language with the following (abstract) syntax for λ expressions:

$$(\lambda X{:}T.M)$$

where T is a type that constrains the domain type for the procedure. As for the range type, remember that the type checker classifies expressions, and it must classify the function body, too. Thus, if the type checker classifies the body as S, we just assume that the programmer wishes to use the type

$$(T \rightarrow S)$$

for the λ expression.

Types and Expressions. Now that we have a basic idea of types and type checking, it is time to introduce the notation for types and the syntax of the simply typed variant of ISWIM.

Like in chapter 4, we introduce an entire family of languages, parameterized over the constants and operations used.

$$
\begin{aligned}
M \;\; = \;\; & X \\
| \;\; & (\lambda X{:}T.M) \\
| \;\; & (M\ M) \\
| \;\; & b \\
| \;\; & (o^n\ M\ \ldots\ M)
\end{aligned}
$$

The meta-variable T ranges over the types for Simply Typed ISWIM.

$$
\begin{aligned}
T, S \;\; &= \;\; B \\
&| \;\; (T \rightarrow T) \\
B \;\; &= \;\; \text{some basic types}
\end{aligned}
$$

Since Simply Typed ISWIM is a family of languages, the notation for types contains one parameter: B. This set represents the types for the various constants in the language. For our running example of numeric ISWIM, B would contain a single type.

$$B \;\; = \;\; \text{num}$$

For a language that supports both numbers and booleans, we would classify those as two distinct sets of constants with two distinct types.

Type Checking, Part 1. The purpose of type checking is to classify each expression via a type. A classification must imply that the expression produces a value of this kind, and in particular, that the expression does not raise any exception or gets stuck during evaluation.

The simplest expression is a constant. To assign a type to a constant, we must know the intent of the language designer. For now, we assume that each member of the Simply Typed ISWIM family comes with a function

$$\mathcal{B} : b \longrightarrow T$$

which performs this task. Similarly, we assume that there are functions that provide a type for each primitive operation in the language:

$$\Delta^n : o^n \underbrace{T \dots T}_{n} \longrightarrow T$$

For our running example of numeric ISWIM, $\mathcal{B}$ maps all basic constants to num, and Δ requires num arguments for all operations.

$$
\begin{array}{lll}
\mathcal{B}(b) & = & \text{num} \\[6pt]
\Delta^1(\text{add1}, \text{num}) & = & \text{num} \\
\Delta^1(\text{sub1}, \text{num}) & = & \text{num} \\
\Delta^1(\text{iszero}, \text{num}) & = & (\text{num} \rightarrow (\text{num} \rightarrow \text{num})) \\[6pt]
\Delta^2(+, \text{num}, \text{num}) & = & \text{num} \\
\Delta^2(-, \text{num}, \text{num}) & = & \text{num} \\
\Delta^2(*, \text{num}, \text{num}) & = & \text{num} \\
\Delta^2(\uparrow, \text{num}, \text{num}) & = & \text{num}
\end{array}
$$

Note that Δ^n maps $n + 1$ arguments to a type.

Equipped with $\mathcal{B}$, we can specify the type checker for constants:

a constant b is classified as type B if $\mathcal{B}(b) = B$.

Here is the conventional way of expressing this verbose rule with mathematical symbols:

$$\vdash b : B \qquad \text{if } \mathcal{B}(b) = B$$

Read the notation $\vdash M : T$ aloud as "the expression M is classified as type T," and it becomes straightforward to go back and forth between the mathematical specifications and the informal ones.

The Δ function helps us assign types to the applications of primitives:

$$(o^n \, M_1 \dots M_n)$$

Recall that type checkers are to classify all sub-expressions of an expression first and then compute a type for the entire expression from these classifications. Assuming that the type checker can classify M_1 as B_1 and so on, the primitive application should have the type

$$\Delta^n(o^n, B_1, \ldots, B_n)$$

In other words, the type checker uses Δ on the primitive operation and the types of its arguments to compute the type of the expression. Again, we introduce a mathematical notation for this kind of specification to avoid verbose informal sentences:

$$\frac{\vdash M_1 : B_1 \ \ldots \ \ \ \vdash M_n : B_n}{\vdash (o^n \ M_1 \ \ldots \ M_n) : T} \qquad \text{if } \Delta(o^n, B_1, \ldots, B_n) = T$$

Read the rule aloud starting with "assuming;" followed by the type classifications above the horizontal line, know as the **antecedent(s)**; followed by "we have that;" and finish with the type classification below the line, usually called **consequence**.

Now that we have rules for basic constants and primitive operations, we need rules for expressions of the form X, $(\lambda X{:}T.M)$, and $(M \ M)$. And this raises the question what the type of a variable should be. For the evaluation of expressions in the calculus, we did not need to retrieve the *value* of a variable; the reduction rules replace (bound) variables with values. As we derived the CEK machine, though, we encountered a similar problem. Instead of replacing variables with values, we equipped the machine with an environment for keeping track of the values of variables.

For the type checker, we use **type environments** to associate variables with their types.

$$\Gamma = \{X_1{:}T_1, \ldots, X_n{:}T_n\}$$
a finite function: for all $i \neq j, X_i \neq X_j$

As usual, we use the function notation $\Gamma(X)$ to look up the type for a variable X in a type environment Γ.

Given that Simply Typed ISWIM comes with variables, its type checker determines the type of an expression using both the expression M and a type environment Γ that assigns types to all free variables in the expression M. We use the notation

$$\Gamma \vdash M : T$$

for saying that the type checker maps M and Γ to type T and pronounce this **type judgment** as "the expression M is classified as type T in the type environment Γ." For the rules concerning basic constants and primitive operations, the environment is simply passed along to check the types of subexpressions:

$$\Gamma \vdash b : B \qquad \text{if } \mathcal{B}(b) = B$$

$$\frac{\Gamma \vdash M_1 : B_1 \ \ldots \ \ \Gamma \vdash M_n : B_n}{\Gamma \vdash (o^n \ M_1 \ldots M_n) : T} \qquad \text{if } \Delta^n(o^n, B_1, \ldots, B_n) = T$$

When the type checker encounters a variable X, it consults the type environment to determine its type:

a variable X is classified as type T in context Γ if $\Gamma(X) = T$.

The mathematical notation for this rule is:

$$\Gamma \vdash X : T \qquad \text{if } \Gamma(X) = T$$

Variables flow into the environment when the type checker deals with a λ expression:

$$\lambda x{:}\text{num}.(+ \ x \ \ulcorner 3 \urcorner)$$

This expression is a function and must therefore have a type of the form $(T \rightarrow S)$. Given that the programmer has declared x to have the type num, it is obvious that $T = \text{num}$. The remaining questions are what the return type is and how to type check the body of the function:

$$(+ \ x \ \ulcorner 3 \urcorner)$$

It contains one free variable, x, but the body does not contain any type information about it. What we do know from the "function header" is that x stands for values of type num, and we can express this idea with an extension of the type environment for the entire expression: $\Gamma[x \leftarrow \text{num}]$. Thus, if we check the body in this revised environment, we should get an appropriate type for the function body. In our example, we get num. Furthermore, since the value of the body *is* the result of a call to this function, its type is the result type:

assuming M is classified as type S in $\Gamma[X \leftarrow T]$,
$\lambda x{:}T.M$ is classified as $(T \rightarrow S)$ in context Γ.

Translating this into a mathematical rule is straightforward:

$$\frac{\Gamma[X \leftarrow T] \vdash M : S}{\Gamma \vdash (\lambda x{:}T.M) : (T \rightarrow S)}$$

Remember that the horizontal line is read as "assuming" followed by the type judgments above the line, and ending in "we have that" followed by the judgment below the line.

An application expression $(M\ N)$ must evaluate M to a function to avoid getting stuck. Hence, a type checker must succeed in classifying M as $(T \rightarrow S)$; otherwise the expression may not evaluate in a regular manner. Furthermore, the type of N must equal T, the argument type expected by the function to which M evaluates. When the λ bound variable is then replaced during a β_v reduction, the value belongs to the expected set of values. In short, we get this rule for applications:

$$\frac{\Gamma \vdash M : (T \rightarrow S) \quad \Gamma \vdash N : T}{\Gamma \vdash (M\ N) : S}$$

Because application is the last kind of expression in Simply Typed ISWIM, we know how the type checker should handle all kinds of programs.

Considering the novelty of these typing rules, let us work through an example. To do so, we use instances of the rules to type expressions and glue them together into a tree at the end. Say we wish to classify the following function:

$$(\lambda f{:}(\mathtt{num} \rightarrow \mathtt{num}).(f\ \ulcorner 0 \urcorner))$$

The only rule that applies here is the one for λ expression, and here is its approximate instantiation:

$$\frac{\{f{:}(\mathtt{num} \rightarrow \mathtt{num})\} \vdash (f\ \ulcorner 0 \urcorner) : \boxed{?}}{\varnothing \vdash (\lambda f{:}(\mathtt{num} \rightarrow \mathtt{num}).(f\ \ulcorner 0 \urcorner)) : ((\mathtt{num} \rightarrow \mathtt{num}) \rightarrow \boxed{?})}$$

Unless we look ahead, we cannot know the result type of a function, and the instance of the type checking rule reflects this lack of knowledge with a question mark. The next step is to type check the application $(f\ \ulcorner 0 \urcorner)$ which proceeds according to this rule instance:

$$\frac{\{f{:}(\mathtt{num} \rightarrow \mathtt{num})\} \vdash f : (\mathtt{num} \rightarrow \mathtt{num}) \quad \{f{:}(\mathtt{num} \rightarrow \mathtt{num})\} \vdash \ulcorner 0 \urcorner : \mathtt{num}}{\{f{:}(\mathtt{num} \rightarrow \mathtt{num})\} \vdash (f\ \ulcorner 0 \urcorner) : \mathtt{num}}$$

Of course the judgments above the line are just instances of the rules for variables and constants:

1. $\{f{:}(\mathtt{num} \rightarrow \mathtt{num})\} \vdash f : (\mathtt{num} \rightarrow \mathtt{num})$

2. $\{f{:}(\mathtt{num} \rightarrow \mathtt{num})\} \vdash \ulcorner 0 \urcorner : \mathtt{num}$

Together they explain why $(f \ulcorner 0\urcorner)$ is classified as num, and they thus eliminate the question mark from the above instance of the rule for λ expressions.

It is customary to glue together these instances of rules into a single "tree" of antecedents and consequences:

$$\frac{\dfrac{\{f{:}(\text{num} \rightarrow \text{num})\} \vdash f : (\text{num} \rightarrow \text{num}) \quad \{f{:}(\text{num} \rightarrow \text{num})\} \vdash \ulcorner 0\urcorner : \text{num}}{\{f{:}(\text{num} \rightarrow \text{num})\} \vdash (f \ulcorner 0\urcorner) : \text{num}}}{\varnothing \vdash (\lambda f{:}(\text{num} \rightarrow \text{num}).(f \ulcorner 0\urcorner)) : ((\text{num} \rightarrow \text{num}) \rightarrow \text{num})}$$

The leaves of such trees are always instances of the rules for constants or variables. The branches in the tree are due to the rules for primitive and proper application, which have several assumptions above the line. Here is another example:

$$\frac{\Pi_1 \qquad \dfrac{\dfrac{\{y{:}\text{num}\} \vdash y : \text{num}}{\{y{:}\text{num}\} \vdash (\texttt{add1} \ y) : \text{num}}}{\varnothing \vdash (\lambda y{:}\text{num}.(\texttt{add1} \ y)) : (\text{num} \rightarrow \text{num})}}{\varnothing \vdash ((\lambda f{:}(\text{num} \rightarrow \text{num}).(f \ulcorner 0\urcorner)) \ (\lambda y{:}\text{num}.(\texttt{add1} \ y))) : \text{num}}$$

The symbol Π_1 represents the tree from above, justifying the type for the function expression in the application. The separate sub-tree on the right validates the type for the argument, which turns out to be a function, too.

Exercise 10.1. Replace T_1, T_2, and T_3 with specific types in

$$\varnothing \vdash (\lambda x{:}T_1.\lambda y{:}T_2.(y \ x)) \ \ulcorner 10\urcorner \ (\lambda z{:}\text{num}.(\texttt{iszero} \ z)) : T_3$$

and construct a tree to justify the choices. Are the choices unique?

Type Checking, Part 2. The preceding subsection developed the basic ideas of type checking. Roughly speaking, type checking is a process of recursively traversing the program and classifying each and every sub-expression of the program with a type. We have expressed this idea with five rules that specify how the type checker performs the classification.

Here are all the rules collected in one place.

$$\boxed{\Gamma \vdash b : B \quad \text{if } \mathcal{B}(b) = B} \qquad\qquad \boxed{\Gamma \vdash X : T \quad \text{if } \Gamma(X) = T}$$

$$\boxed{\frac{\Gamma[X \leftarrow T] \vdash M : S}{\Gamma \vdash (\lambda x{:}T.M) : (T \rightarrow S)}} \qquad\qquad \boxed{\frac{\Gamma \vdash M : (T \rightarrow S) \quad \Gamma \vdash N : T}{\Gamma \vdash (M \ N) : S}}$$

$$\boxed{\frac{\Gamma \vdash M_1 : B_1 \ \ldots \quad \Gamma \vdash M_n : B_n}{\Gamma \vdash (o^n \ M_1 \ldots M_n) : T} \quad \text{if } \Delta^n(o^n, B_1, \ldots, B_n) = T}$$

The conclusion of each of these five rules matches exactly one syntactic construct in Simply Typed ISWIM.

One challenge is to design a type checker that actually satisfies these rules. Like an evaluator or a compiler from a programming language to the language of a machine, a type checker is just a program that consumes (representations of) programs. Specifically, it consumes expressions and produces a type, all according to the type system.

The type checker for Simply Typed ISWIM is indeed a straightforward recursive function.

$$
\begin{aligned}
\Gamma[\![X]\!] &= \Gamma(X) \\
\Gamma[\![\lambda X{:}T.M]\!] &= (T \to \Gamma[X \leftarrow T][\![M]\!]) \\
\Gamma[\![(M\ N)]\!] &= S \\
\quad \text{if } \Gamma[\![M]\!] = (T \to S) \text{ and } \Gamma[\![N]\!] = T \\
\Gamma[\![b]\!] &= \mathcal{B}(b) \\
\Gamma[\![(o^n\ M_1 \ldots M_n)]\!] &= \Delta(o^n, \Gamma[\![M_1]\!], \ldots, \Gamma[\![M_n]\!])
\end{aligned}
$$

We use the infix notation $\cdot[\![\cdot]\!]$ for this two-argument function. The first argument (to the left of the brackets) is the type environment; the second argument (between the brackets) is the expression to be checked. The result is the type of the expression, if any, in the given type environment.

Naturally, the organization of the type checker matches that of Simply Typed ISWIM's grammar. The five clauses correspond to the clauses of the grammar. On the right-hand side of each clause, we see that the type checker classifies each sub-expression and uses the results to compute type for the overall expressions from these intermediate results.

As is, the type checker is actually a partial function that does not have a result for all possible inputs, even if we assume that the given type environment has types for all free variables of the given term. Consider

$$
\varnothing[\![(+\ \ulcorner 1 \urcorner\ (\lambda x.\ulcorner 9 \urcorner))]\!]
$$

For these two arguments, the type checker is undefined, as a simple calculation shows. Of course, the given expression is our very first example of a stuck expression in this chapter, and it motivated the idea of type checking. The fact that $\cdot[\![\cdot]\!]$ is undefined for this expression just shows that we should not run this program on the evaluator. It also does not violate our specifications for the type checker; it is actually impossible to form a tree of judgments for this expression, i.e., there is no type T such that

$$
\varnothing \vdash (+\ \ulcorner 1 \urcorner\ (\lambda x.\ulcorner 9 \urcorner)) : T
$$

can be justified with our type checking rules.

With this insight in hand, let us take a second look at the type checker. The right-hand sides of its five clauses are closely related to the rules, making it nearly obvious that the type checker implements its specifications.

> **Theorem 10.1:** For all Γ and M such that $\mathcal{FV}(M) \subseteq \text{dom}(\Gamma)$, $\Gamma[\![M]\!]$ is defined and $\Gamma[\![M]\!] = T$ if and only if the type judgment $\Gamma \vdash M : T$ can be validated as the consequence of a tree of rules.

> **Proof for Theorem 10.1:** For each direction, use the assumption to prove the desired conclusion via structural induction on the expression. Use the grammar to guide the case analysis.

The theorem statement implicitly specifies type errors in a formal manner. A program suffers from a type error if the type checker is undefined in the empty type environment.

Working through the proof of theorem 10.1 clarifies why the type checker is undefined. There are two problem cases: function application and primitive application. The function expression in an application may not have a function type, or the type of the argument may not match the domain type of the function type. In some primitive application, the type of some argument of may not equal some element of B.

Exercise 10.2. Implement the type checker machine in some programming language. Signal an error if the type checker cannot classify one of the subexpressions.

Semantics. The grammar of Simply Typed ISWIM differs from the grammar of ISWIM in just one point: the type declarations for function parameters. Since these parameters exist solely for the purpose of type checking, we may ignore them for all other purposes, in particular for the evaluation of programs (closed expressions).

Here then is the abstract syntax for Simply Typed ISWIM.

$$
\begin{aligned}
E &= [\,] \mid (V\ E) \mid (E\ M) \mid (o^n\ V \ldots V\ E\ M \ldots M) \\
V &= \lambda X{:}T.M \mid b
\end{aligned}
$$

$$
eval_{\mathbf{v}}^{s}(M) = \begin{cases} b & \text{if } M \longmapsto\!\!\!\to_{\mathbf{v}} b \\ \texttt{function} & \text{if } M \longmapsto\!\!\!\to_{\mathbf{v}} \lambda X{:}T.N \end{cases}
$$

$\longmapsto_{\mathbf{v}}$		
$E[((\lambda X{:}T.M)\ V)]$	$E[M[X \leftarrow V]]$	[STfi$_{\mathbf{v}}$]
$E[(o^n\ V_1\ \ldots\ V_n)]$	$E[\delta(o^n, V_1, \ldots, V_n)]$	[STffi]

$10 \cdot 2$ **Typed Programs Don't Go Wrong.** Our agreement is that the purpose of our type system is to classify as "bad" all programs whose evaluation may end up getting stuck. Conversely, the type checker assigns a program or expression a type only if its evaluation does not get stuck. With a syntactic machine, it is actually straightforward to formulate this claim not just as a slogan but as a mathematical theorem and to prove this theorem in a near-mechanical manner.

Of course, Simply Typed ISWIM is not just a language but a family of programming languages. The choice of constants, primitive operations, and above all δ determines what kind of member language we are working in. As for typing, however, the choices for $\mathcal{B}$ and Δ determine whether a program or an expression is classified as "good." Thus, unless we choose these type assignments carefully and make sure that they agree with δ, we may be working with a type system whose predictions about the program execution are useless.

To make life simple for our first soundness theorem, we demand that for every primitive application $(o^n \, b_1 \, \ldots \, b_n)$, δ and Δ are consistent with each other.

Assumption 1 (Soundness of Primitives)

$\delta(o^n, b_1, \ldots, b_n) = V$ implies $\mathcal{B}(b_1) = B_1, \ldots \, \mathcal{B}(b_n) = B_n,$
$\Delta(o^n, B_1, \ldots, B_n) = T,$
and $\vdash V : T$

$\Delta(o^n, B_1, \ldots, B_n) = T,$
$\mathcal{B}(b_1) = B_1, \ldots \, \mathcal{B}(b_n) = B_n$ implies $\exists V \, \delta(o^n, b_1, \ldots b_n) = V$

With this assumption in place, we can state the central theorem about our type system and its relationship to the syntactic machine.

Theorem 10.2 [Soundness (Simply Typed ISWIM)]: For all M and T, if $\varnothing \vdash M : T$ then

- $M \longmapsto\!\!\!\twoheadrightarrow_{\mathbf{v}} V$ and $\varnothing \vdash V : T$, or
- $M \longmapsto\!\!\!\twoheadrightarrow_{\mathbf{v}} M'$ implies that $M' \longmapsto_{\mathbf{v}} M''$ for some M''.

The theorem's content is an important message to the working software engineer. It says that the evaluation of a typed program is guaranteed to produce a value or to run forever. If it produces a value, the value has the same type as the program. In short, the type system succeeds in filtering out all those programs whose evaluation may get stuck, and it properly predicts the type of any result.

The proof of theorem 10.2 proceeds just like the second proof of the Uniform Evaluation Theorem (theorem 5.12, page 85) from chapter 5. In other words, we prove two lemmas: a preservation lemma, showing that all terms in a reduction sequence have the same type as the first expression, and a progress lemma, showing that all typed expressions are either values or are a redex for the standard reduction function.

Lemma 10.3 [Preservation]: If $\varnothing \vdash M : T$ and $M \longmapsto_{\mathbf{v}} N$, then $\varnothing \vdash N : T$.

Proof for Lemma 10.3: Let us assume $\varnothing \vdash M : T$ and $M \longmapsto_{\mathbf{v}} N$ and let us consider how M can reduce to N:

- **Case** $M = E[((\lambda X{:}S'.K)\ V)]$

  In this case, $N = E[K[X \leftarrow V]]$. Because M is well-typed, we know that all sub-expressions are typed, based on the design of our type system. The rule for typing applications implies that $\varnothing \vdash (\lambda X{:}S'.K) : (S' \to S)$ for some S, S', and $\varnothing \vdash V : S'$. Since X has type S' in K and V has type S', too, we should also expect that $K[X \leftarrow V]$ is well-typed and that it has type S. From here, it is easy to conclude that $E[K[X \leftarrow V]]$ has type T, the same type as M.

- **Case** $M = E[(o^n\ b_1\ \ldots\ b_n)]$

  Here $N = E[\delta(o^n, b_1, \ldots, b_n)]$. As in the first case, $\varnothing \vdash M : T$ means that $(o^n\ b_1\ \ldots\ b_n)$ is well-typed. Considering that there is only one typing rule that could have been used to type this primitive application, we know that $\mathcal{B}(b_i) = B_i$ and that for some S, $\Delta(o^n, B_1, \ldots, B_n) = S$. Now we use assumption 1 to conclude that $\delta(o^n, b_1, \ldots, b_n) = V$ and that $\varnothing \vdash V : S$. And as in the first case, we can again conclude that $E[V]$ has type T.

These are the only two cases, and we have thus finished the proof.

The preceding proof relies on several steps that, while seemingly obvious, demand a rigorous justification, especially if we were to apply this proof technique to more subtle type systems than that of Simply Typed ISWIM. Before we state those steps as auxiliary lemmas, however, we state and prove the second main lemma.

Lemma 10.4 [Progress]: If $\varnothing \vdash M : T$, then either $M \in V$ or $M \longmapsto_{\mathbf{v}} N$ for some N.

Proof for Lemma 10.4: Suppose $\varnothing \vdash M : T$. From the Unique Evaluation Context Lemma for ISWIM, which clearly holds for Simply Typed ISWIM, we know that M is either a value or one of the following two cases holds:

- **Case** $M = E[(V\ U)]$

  By an argument just like in the proof of lemma 10.3, $(V\ U)$ must have a type. Since only one typing rule applies, V must be a function, meaning some expression $\lambda X{:}T.K$. This implies that the application is a β_v redex, i.e., $N = E[K[X \leftarrow U]]$.

- **Case** $M = E[(o^n\ V_1\ \dots\ V_n)]$

  Again, $(o^n\ V_1\ \dots\ V_n)$ is well-typed, meaning there exists $B_1, \dots, B_n$ such that $\varnothing \vdash V_1 : B_1, \dots, \varnothing \vdash V_n : B_n$ and $\Delta(o^n, B_1, \dots, B_n) = S$ for some type S. Since λ expressions are not classified as primitive types, we may conclude that $V_1, \dots, V_n \in b$. By assumption 1 again, we get that there exists a V such that $\delta(o^n, V_1, \dots, V_n) = V$. Set $N = E[V]$.

In short, M is either a value, or it is standard-reducible.

Like the Preservation Lemma, the Progress Lemma relies on a number of auxiliary lemmas. Indeed, the two are relying on the very same lemmas, except that the Progress Lemma also needs one concerning the shape of values.

Lemma 10.5: If $\varnothing \vdash V : (T \to S)$, then $V = \lambda X{:}T.M$. Also, if $\varnothing \vdash V : B$, then $V \in b$.

Our second auxiliary lemma shows that if a program has a type, all subexpressions have a type, too.

Lemma 10.6: A proof tree for $\varnothing \vdash C[M] : T$ contains a proof tree for $\Gamma \vdash M : T'$ for some Γ and T'.

The third lemma confirms that the replacement of an expression in the hole of a program context with an expression of the same type does not affect the typing of the overall expression.

Lemma 10.7: If a proof tree for $\varnothing \vdash C[M] : T$ contains a proof tree for $\Gamma \vdash M : T'$, then $\Gamma \vdash N : T'$ implies $\varnothing \vdash C[N] : T$.

Because the typing rules work with type environments while the evaluation rules use substitution, we need a lemma that relates the types of an expression before and after substitution.

Lemma 10.8: If $\Gamma[X \leftarrow T'] \vdash M : T$ and $\Gamma \vdash V : T'$, then $\Gamma \vdash M[X \leftarrow V] : T$.

As stated, the lemma is a bit stronger than actually needed in the proof of lemma 10.4.

Exercise 10.3. Prove lemmas 10.5 through 10.8.

Exercise 10.4. Prove theorem 10.2 with the help of the Progress and Preservation Lemmas.

Logic, Models, and Soundness. The Soundness Theorem clarifies in which sense a type system is a mechanism for stating and establishing theorems about a program, a statement we made in the introduction.

In logical terms, the evaluator and its abstract machine make up a **model**, a mathematical structure that represents the reality which we wish to observe and about which we wish to make predictions, i.e., state theorems.

The type language is a **proof system** or, more concisely, a **logic**, a system of stating and systematically verifying claims. With the type language, programmers express claims about the evaluation of a program on this machine. For example, when a programmer writes down

$$(\lambda f{:}(\texttt{num} \rightarrow \texttt{num}).M)$$

the type checker verifies that this function is applied only to functions from numbers to numbers throughout the entire program evaluation. Similarly, if the type checker derives that

$$\Gamma \vdash (\lambda f{:}(\texttt{num} \rightarrow \texttt{num}).M) : ((\texttt{num} \rightarrow \texttt{num}) \rightarrow \texttt{num}) \, ,$$

it proves the claim that the function always produces a number, no matter what f is. In general, an expression **provably** has a type if the type judgment $\Gamma \vdash M :$ is the conclusion of some tree of rules.

Our Soundness Theorem connects the logic of type checking with the model of execution. It shows that all provable types from the type system are **true** types, that is, no matter which program we execute, the machine never evaluates any expression to a value that does not belong to the predicted type of value. Logicians refer to this as the soundness of a logic, and programming language researchers stuck to this name.

Soundness is critical for the working software engineer. It guarantees many small claims about programs and thus eliminates a large number of small, but annoying problems from consideration. This, of course, reduces the workload for engineers during testing, debugging and maintenance, especially when compared to work in programming languages with unsound type systems.

Exercise 10.5. In logic, the complement of soundness is **completeness**. A complete type system filters out exactly those programs that get stuck during evaluation and no others. Put differently, all run-time errors are turned into type errors and all programs with type errors signal run-time errors. Is the type system of Simply Typed ISWIM complete? Consider the expression

$$((\text{if0} \ulcorner 0\urcorner (\lambda x{:}\text{num}.\ulcorner 0\urcorner) (\lambda x{:}(\text{num} \rightarrow \text{num}).x)) \ulcorner 42\urcorner) .$$

Does it type check? Does its evaluation get stuck?

10·3 **Types and Recursion.** Unfortunately, the introduction of a type system nearly cripples ISWIM. It not only eliminates "bad" programs; it also throws out many "good" functions or requires the language designers to build them in as primitive functions.

In a nutshell, the problem is that no Simply Typed ISWIM program can go into an infinite loop, given a reasonable restriction on δ. With infinite loops eliminated, a lot of useful recursive functions disappear, too. Put into the most concise form, we can restate the Soundness Theorem for Simply Typed ISWIM with just one clause.[2]

> **Theorem 10.9 [Normalization]:** For all M and T, if $\varnothing \vdash M : T$ then $eval_{\mathbf{v}}(M)$ is defined, i.e., there exists a value V such that $M \longmapsto\!\!\!\!\twoheadrightarrow_{\mathbf{v}} V$ and $\varnothing \vdash V : T$.

As stated, the claim is not a theorem yet. Suppose Simply Typed ISWIM came with a primitive operation ∞ that is interpreted as follows:

$$\delta(\infty, \ulcorner 0\urcorner) = \lambda x{:}\text{num}.((\infty \ulcorner 0\urcorner) x) .$$

This variant clearly contains diverging programs:

$$
\begin{aligned}
((\infty \ulcorner 0\urcorner) \ulcorner 1\urcorner) \quad &\longmapsto_{\mathbf{v}} \quad ((\lambda x{:}\text{num}.((\infty \ulcorner 0\urcorner) x)) \ulcorner 1\urcorner) \\
&\longmapsto_{\mathbf{v}} \quad ((\infty \ulcorner 0\urcorner) \ulcorner 1\urcorner) \\
&\longmapsto_{\mathbf{v}} \quad \cdots
\end{aligned}
$$

because this reduction sequence does not end.

---

[2]In the context of the simply typed λ-calculus, the theorem is called a *weak normalization* theorem because it proves that all standard reduction sequences (for all expressions) are finite. A *strong normalization* theorem proves that *all* reduction sequences are finite.

With one small and reasonable constraint on δ, though, it is easy to prove the Normalization Theorem.

Assumption 2 (Recursion-free Primitives)

$\delta(o^n, b_1, \ldots, b_n) = (\lambda X{:}T.M)$ implies M contains no primitive.

Exercise 10.6. Consider an extension of the numeric variant of Simply Typed ISWIM with a primitive operation y that has the following interpretation:

$$\delta(\mathsf{y}, \ulcorner n \urcorner) = \lambda v{:}((\mathtt{num} \to \mathtt{num}) \to (\mathtt{num} \to \mathtt{num})).(v\ (\lambda x{:}\mathtt{num}.(\mathsf{y}\ \ulcorner n \urcorner)\ v\ x))\ .$$

Demonstrate that it is possible to define recursive functions via y.

We prove the Normalization Theorem at the end of this section. Before we do so, however, we equip Simply Typed ISWIM with the power to define all desirable recursive functions in a typed world (in which case the Normalization Theorem does not apply).

Recursion for Simply Typed ISWIM. There are several distinct methods for adding recursion to Simply Typed ISWIM. One simple alternative is to give each function a name; a function may then refer to itself in its definition, which is the essence of recursion. A more pragmatic alternative is to introduce a construct, such as `letrec` from chapter 9, for defining several potentially mutually recursive functions at once. The historical solution is to add the Y combinator itself to the language.

Here we present the historical solution, starting with the extended syntax.

$$
\begin{array}{rcll}
M & = & \ldots & \text{same as Simply Typed ISWIM} \\
  & | & (\mathtt{fix}\ M) &
\end{array}
$$

Our extended language, dubbed Recursive ST ISWIM, adds one new expression form to the syntax of Simply Typed ISWIM. The new form does not involve any variables, and it is therefore trivial to adapt the $\mathcal{FV}$ function.

With the extension of a typed programming language, we must also add typing rules and notions of reduction for the new constructs. The typing rule for $(\mathtt{fix}\ M)$ looks complex but merely explicates the implicit fixed point reasoning behind the Y combinator.

$$\frac{\Gamma \vdash M : (T \to T)}{\Gamma \vdash (\mathtt{fix}\ M) : T}$$

One way to understand this typing rule is to say that $(\texttt{fix } M)$ evaluates its sub-expression M to a function from T to T and that it uses this function to produce a value of type T. Its absolutely simplest instance in numeric Recursive ST ISWIM is

$$(\texttt{fix } (\lambda x\texttt{:num}.x))$$

which uses a function on numbers to produce a number.

To ensure that $(\texttt{fix } M)$ produces a fixed point of M, we formulate a notion of reduction that just says so.

$$\boxed{\begin{array}{c} (\texttt{fix } (\lambda X\texttt{:}T.M)) \quad \textbf{y} \quad M[X \leftarrow (\texttt{fix } (\lambda X\texttt{:}T.M))] \\[2ex] \textbf{v} \quad = \quad \dots \quad \text{same as Simply Typed ISWIM} \\ \cup \quad \textbf{y} \end{array}}$$

Let us examine the simple example of mksum, a function that, without types, we would have written in the λ-calculus to compute the sum from $\ulcorner 0 \urcorner$ to $\ulcorner n \urcorner$:

$$\text{mksum} = (\lambda s\texttt{:(num} \rightarrow \texttt{num}).(\lambda n\texttt{:num}.(\texttt{ifz } n\ n\ (+\ n\ (s\ (-\ n\ \ulcorner 1 \urcorner)))))))$$

It is easy to check that $(\texttt{fix mksum})$ has a type:

$$\cfrac{\cfrac{\dots}{\varnothing \vdash \text{mksum} : ((\texttt{num} \rightarrow \texttt{num}) \rightarrow (\texttt{num} \rightarrow \texttt{num}))}}{\varnothing \vdash (\texttt{fix mksum}) : (\texttt{num} \rightarrow \texttt{num})}$$

An application of this expression to $\ulcorner 1 \urcorner$ also proceeds along expected lines, as a simple calculation shows.

Exercise 10.7. Show that $(\texttt{fix mksum}) \ulcorner 1 \urcorner =_{\textbf{v}} \ulcorner 1 \urcorner$.

We now have all the ingredients for a Recursive ST ISWIM evaluator.

$$\boxed{\begin{array}{l} E \quad = \quad \dots \qquad \text{same as Simply Typed ISWIM} \\ \quad | \quad (\texttt{fix } E) \\[2ex] eval_{\textbf{v}}^{\texttt{s}}(M) = \left\{ \begin{array}{ll} b & \text{if } M \longmapsto\!\!\!\!\rightarrow_{\textbf{v}} b \\ \texttt{function} & \text{if } M \longmapsto\!\!\!\!\rightarrow_{\textbf{v}} \lambda X\texttt{:}T.N \end{array} \right. \\[4ex] \begin{array}{|l|l|l|} \hline \multicolumn{2}{c}{\longmapsto_{\textbf{v}}} & \\ \hline E[((\lambda X\texttt{:}T.M)\ V)] & E[M[X \leftarrow V]] & [\text{RTfi}_\textbf{v}] \\ E[(o^n\ V_1\ \dots\ V_n)] & E[\delta(o^n, V_1, \dots, V_n)] & [\text{RTffi}] \\ E[(\texttt{fix } \lambda X\texttt{:}T.M)] & E[M[X \leftarrow (\texttt{fix } \lambda X\texttt{:}T.M)]] & [\text{RTfix}] \\ \hline \end{array} \end{array}}$$

The proof that this reduction function is the standard reduction system for the extended **v** is straightforward.

The type system for Recursive ST ISWIM is sound for this evaluator.

> **Theorem 10.10 [Soundness (Recursive ST ISWIM)]:** For all M and T, if $\varnothing \vdash M : T$, then
>
> - $M \longmapsto\!\!\!\twoheadrightarrow_{\mathbf{v}} V$ and $\varnothing \vdash V : T$, or
> - $M \longmapsto\!\!\!\twoheadrightarrow_{\mathbf{v}} M'$ implies that $M' \longmapsto\!\!\!\twoheadrightarrow_{\mathbf{v}} M''$ for some M''.

It is easy to see how the preservation-and-progress strategy can be adapted to the extended language. If $(\texttt{fix } \lambda X{:}T.M)$ has type T, then X can be replaced with $(\texttt{fix } \lambda X{:}T.M)$ in M without changing its type (see lemma 10.8).

Exercise 10.8. Complete the type tree for mksum.

Exercise 10.9. Demonstrate that

$$(\lambda X{:}T.M) \, (\texttt{fix } (\lambda X{:}T.M)) =_{\mathbf{v}} (\texttt{fix } (\lambda X{:}T.M))$$

assuming there is some value V such that $(\texttt{fix } (\lambda X{:}T.M)) =_{\mathbf{v}} V$.

Exercise 10.10. Prove that $\varnothing \vdash (\texttt{fix } \lambda x{:}T.x) : T$. Is it really possible that fix can manufacture a value of any type T out of thin air? What if $T = \texttt{num}$?

Proof of the Normalization Theorem. The proof of the normalization theorem differs from all the other proofs in this part of the book. Skip this subsection for a first reading of this chapter.[3]

We start with a restatement of the Normalization Theorem that fits our purpose best.

> **Theorem 10.11 [Normalization]:** For all M and T, if $\varnothing \vdash M : T$ then there exists a value V such that $M \longmapsto\!\!\!\twoheadrightarrow_{\mathbf{v}} V$.

Remember that the theorem depends on assumption 2.

Even ignoring the complications of a recursion-generating δ function, simple induction does not suffice to prove that all typed expressions terminate. Consider any $\beta_{\mathbf{v}}$ reduction with a function whose parameter occurs many times in the function's body:

$$(\lambda x{:}T. \cdots x \cdots x \cdots)(\lambda y{:}S. \cdots) \longmapsto_{\mathbf{v}} \cdots (\lambda y{:}S. \cdots) \cdots (\lambda y{:}S. \cdots) \cdots$$

The result of such a step is not merely a part of the input, so structural induction does not apply. Typical size metrics also do not apply, since the

---

[3]The proof idea is due to W. Tait.

step expands the size of the expression, and even the total number of function expressions goes up with the step.

The reason that reduction must eventually terminate, though, is that a step like the one above uses up a function with a bigger type than any function that it duplicates. Thus, an expression's type is the key to proving the normalization theorem by induction. With that insight, we define the **termination predicate**, $\mathcal{T}$.

$$
\begin{array}{ll}
\mathcal{T}(M, B) & \text{if } \emptyset \vdash M : B \text{ and } M \longmapsto_{\mathbf{v}} V \text{ for some } V \\
\mathcal{T}(M, (T_1 \rightarrow T_2)) & \text{if } \emptyset \vdash M : (T_1 \rightarrow T_2) \text{ and } M \longmapsto_{\mathbf{v}} V \text{ for some } V \\
& \text{plus } \mathcal{T}(N, T_1) \text{ implies } \mathcal{T}((M\ N), T_2)
\end{array}
$$

As desired, $\mathcal{T}$ captures the idea that a typed expression reduces to some value, but the clause for functions also says that, no matter what argument they are applied to, the application satisfies $\mathcal{T}$ at the range type if the argument also satisfies $\mathcal{T}$ at the domain type.

Before we proceed to the main lemma, we prove that $\mathcal{T}$ is preserved across reduction sequences. Indeed, it is preserved in both directions.

Lemma 10.12: If $M \longmapsto_{\mathbf{v}} N$, $\mathcal{T}(M, T)$ if and only if $\mathcal{T}(N, T)$.

Proof for Lemma 10.12: We use induction on T:

- **Case $T = B$**

  If either M or N terminates, then clearly both terminate with the same b. Furthermore, M and N have the same type by the Preservation Lemma, meaning the claim holds.

- **Case $T = (T_1 \rightarrow T_2)$ for some T_1 and T_2**

  Assume $\mathcal{T}(M, T)$, so that $M \longmapsto_{\mathbf{v}} V$ for some V. Clearly, $N \longmapsto_{\mathbf{v}} V$ by the definition of the standard reduction function. This proves the first half of the desired conclusion

  For the second half, assume that for any K with $\mathcal{T}(K, T_1)$, we have $\mathcal{T}((M\ K), T_2)$. Since $M \longmapsto_{\mathbf{v}} N$, $(M\ K) \longmapsto_{\mathbf{v}} (N\ K)$ and, by induction, $\mathcal{T}((N\ K), T_2)$.

  To prove the other direction, assume $\mathcal{T}(N, T)$ and use a similar argument to get $\mathcal{T}(M, T)$.

Equipped with this critical property of $\mathcal{T}$, we can now state a lemma that generalizes the desired theorem and that can serve as a useful hypothesis for a structurally inductive proof.

Lemma 10.13: For all $\Gamma = \{\langle X_1, T_1 \rangle, \ldots, \langle X_n, T_n \rangle\}$, if $\Gamma \vdash M : T$ and if, for some $V_1, \ldots, V_n$, $\mathcal{T}(V_1, T_1), \ldots, \mathcal{T}(V_n, T_n)$, then

$$\mathcal{T}(M[X_1 \leftarrow V_1] \ldots [X_n \leftarrow V_n], T)$$

Note how the lemma implies the Normalization Theorem. If Γ is empty, $\mathcal{T}(M, T)$ and therefore for some V, $M \longmapsto\!\!\!\longrightarrow_{\mathbf{v}} V$.

Proof for Lemma 10.13: We proceed by induction on the structure of $\Gamma \vdash M : T$ and consider all five cases:

- **Case $\Gamma \vdash X : T$**
  $X = X_i$ for some $i \in [1, n]$. Therefore,

  $$X[X_1 \leftarrow V_1] \ldots [X_n \leftarrow V_n] = V_i$$

  and by assumption, $\mathcal{T}(V_i, T)$, meaning the claim holds.

- **Case $\Gamma \vdash b : T$ for some $T \in B$**
  $b[X_1 \leftarrow V_1] \ldots [X_n \leftarrow V_n] = b$ and the claim holds.

- **Case $\Gamma \vdash (\lambda X{:}S_1.N) : (S_1 \rightarrow S_2)$**
  Clearly $M' \doteq M[X_1 \leftarrow V_1] \ldots [X_n \leftarrow V_n]$ terminates, because M is a value, and the substitution does not change it. This proves the first part of the claim for a λ expression.
  To prove the rest of the claim, choose an arbitrary N' such that $\mathcal{T}(N', S_1)$. We must show that $\mathcal{T}((M' \ N'), S_2)$. By the definition of $\mathcal{T}$, $N' \longmapsto\!\!\!\longrightarrow_{\mathbf{v}} V$ for some V. Since M' is a value, we can see that

  $$\begin{aligned} (M' \ N') \quad &\longmapsto\!\!\!\longrightarrow_{\mathbf{v}} \quad (M' \ V) \\ &\longmapsto\!\!\!\longrightarrow_{\mathbf{v}} \quad N[X_1 \leftarrow V_1] \ldots [X_n \leftarrow V_n][X \leftarrow V] \end{aligned}$$

That N' reduces to V also implies $\mathcal{T}(V, S_1)$ by a simple multi-step extension of lemma 10.12. By the typing rule for λ expressions, $\Gamma[X \leftarrow S_1] \vdash N : S_2$, meaning

$$\{\langle X_1, T_1 \rangle, \ldots, \langle X_n, T_n \rangle, \langle X, S_1 \rangle\} \vdash N : S_2$$

and

$$\mathcal{T}(V_1, T_1), \ldots, \mathcal{T}(V_n, T_n), \mathcal{T}(V, S_2)$$

so that by the induction hypothesis, we may conclude

$$\mathcal{T}(N[X_1 \leftarrow V_1] \ldots [X_n \leftarrow V_n][X \leftarrow V], S_2)$$

Again by a multi-step-extended lemma 10.12 (in the reverse direction), we now get $\mathcal{T}((M' \ N'), S_2)$, the desired second half of our claim.

- **Case** $\Gamma \vdash (M_1 \ M_2) : T$

  By the typing rule for applications and by induction,

  $$\mathcal{T}(M_1[X_1 \leftarrow V_1] \ldots [X_n \leftarrow V_n], (S \rightarrow T))$$

  and

  $$\mathcal{T}(M_2[X_1 \leftarrow V_1] \ldots [X_n \leftarrow V_n], S)$$

  for some S. By the definition of $\mathcal{T}$ for function types,

  $$\mathcal{T}\left(\begin{pmatrix} & M_1[X_1 \leftarrow V_1] \ldots [X_n \leftarrow V_n] \\ & M_2[X_1 \leftarrow V_1] \ldots [X_n \leftarrow V_n] \end{pmatrix} , T \right)$$

  We can lift the substitutions out to get the conclusion:

  $$\mathcal{T}(\ (M_1 \ M_2)[X_1 \leftarrow V_1] \ldots [X_n \leftarrow V_n], T)$$

- **Case** $\Gamma \vdash (o^m \ M_1 \ldots \ M_m) : T$

  By the typing rule for primitive applications and induction,

  $$\mathcal{T}(M_1[X_1 \leftarrow V_1] \ldots [X_n \leftarrow V_n], B_1),$$
  $$\ldots$$
  $$\mathcal{T}(M_n[X_1 \leftarrow V_1] \ldots [X_n \leftarrow V_n], B_n)$$

  Thus, M eventually reduces to $(o^n \ b_1 \ldots \ b_m)$ by lemma 10.5. According to assumption 1, $\delta(o^n, b_1, \ldots, b_n) = V$ for some V such that $\varnothing \vdash V : T$.

  Unfortunately, we are stuck now because V has nothing to do with the original expression and therefore the induction hypothesis is useless. What we do know is that according to assumption 2, V contains no primitive operations. Thus, if we had a lemma like the one we are proving now for *expressions that do not contain primitive operations*, we could conclude $\mathcal{T}(V, T)$ and, with a multi-step extension of lemma 10.12,

  $$\mathcal{T}((o^m \ M_1 \ldots \ M_m)[X_1 \leftarrow V_1] \ldots [X_n \leftarrow V_n], T)$$

The following lemma validates the same claim as the preceding one for expressions without primitive operations.

Lemma 10.14: For all $\Gamma = \{\langle X_1, T_1 \rangle, \ldots, \langle X_n, T_n \rangle\}$, if

- M contains no primitive applications,

- $\Gamma \vdash M : T$, and
- for some $V_1, \ldots, V_n, \mathcal{T}(V_1, T_1), \ldots, \mathcal{T}(V_n, T_n)$,

then $\mathcal{T}(M[X_1 \leftarrow V_1] \ldots [X_n \leftarrow V_n], T)$.

Proof for Lemma 10.14: The proof proceeds just like the one for the previous lemma (10.13). The first four cases are identical. Because of the additional condition that M not contain any primitive operations, the last case is impossible, meaning the proof suffices for this lemma.

The proof of this lemma completes the proof of the Normalization Theorem.

10·4 Typed Programs Go to Specific Stuck States.

The exclusion of primitive-operation errors from Simply Typed ISWIM creates an entirely unrealistic language model. All full-fledged, real-world programming languages come with division for numbers, array indexing, functions for extracting the head and the tail of a list, and so on. We must therefore ask what such operations should do when confronted with bad arguments, because we also know that practical type systems do not rule out that, for example, $\ulcorner 0 \urcorner$ flows into the second argument position of a division operation.

Formally, we would like to relax assumption 1 so that δ is no longer total for all properly typed primitive applications.

Assumption 1′ (Soundness of Partial Primitives)

$$\delta(o^n, b_1, \ldots, b_n) = V \quad \text{implies} \quad \begin{aligned} &\mathcal{B}(b_1) = B_1, \ldots \mathcal{B}(b_n) = B_n, \\ &\Delta(o^n, B_1, \ldots, B_n) = T, \\ &\text{and } \vdash V : T \end{aligned}$$

For example, it is now possible to include division into the programming language. In this world, we have that $(/ \ulcorner n \urcorner \ulcorner 0 \urcorner)$ is well-typed

$$\frac{\Gamma \vdash \ulcorner n \urcorner : \mathrm{num} \qquad \Gamma \vdash \ulcorner 0 \urcorner : \mathrm{num}}{\Gamma \vdash (/ \ulcorner n \urcorner \ulcorner 0 \urcorner) : \mathrm{num}}$$

but also

$$\delta(/, \ulcorner n \urcorner, \ulcorner 0 \urcorner) \text{ is undefined}$$

Assumption 1 eliminated this contradiction from Simply Typed ISWIM; assumption 1′ admits it into this variant of Simply Typed ISWIM, dubbed Partial ST ISWIM. The word "partial" here refers to the partiality of δ.

In short, the Partial ST ISWIM family of programming languages has the same parameterized syntax and type system as Simply Typed ISWIM. The only difference between the two is formulated in assumption $1'$, which lacks the second clause of assumption 1.

Given that this second clause of assumption 1 is invoked exactly once in the proof of the Soundness Theorem for Simply Typed ISWIM, it is relatively easy to reformulate this theorem for the new language.

> **Theorem 10.15 [Soundness (Partial ST ISWIM)]:** For all M and T, if $\varnothing \vdash M : T$, if $\varnothing \vdash M : T$ then
>
> - $M \longmapsto\!\!\!\rightarrow_\mathbf{v} V$ and $\varnothing \vdash V : T$,
> - $M \longmapsto\!\!\!\rightarrow_\mathbf{v} M'$ implies that $M' \longmapsto\!\!\!\rightarrow_\mathbf{v} M''$ for some M'', or
> - $M \longmapsto\!\!\!\rightarrow_\mathbf{v} E[(o^n\ b_1\ \dots\ b_n)]$, $\varnothing \vdash E[(o^n b_1\ \dots\ b_n)] : T$, and $\delta(o^n, b_1, \dots, b_n)$ is undefined.

This reformulated theorem admits the possibility that the evaluation of well-typed programs might get stuck. More precisely, the reduction sequence starting with a well-typed program may end with an expression whose standard redex is a well-typed primitive application for which δ is undefined. Thus, if a programming language manual lists all those places where δ is undefined, a programmer knows exactly where to start the search for errors when an evaluation gets stuck. No function application can cause the error; only those primitive applications in a program may go wrong that use a primitive that is partial according to the manual.

Exercise 10.11. Adapt the proof of theorem 10.2 to verify theorem 10.15.

Exercise 10.12. Does the Normalization Theorem hold for Partial ST ISWIM? If so, prove it. If not, provide a counter-example, add $(\text{fix } M)$ and make Partial ST ISWIM recursive, too.

Exercise 10.13. Chapter 8 shows how to make the δ function always total, via the addition of errors (also known as exceptions) to ISWIM. Design a sound type system for Error ISWIM and prove it correct.

10·5 History.
The simple type system from this section is the creation of Alonzo Church [18], who wanted to repair a problem with the untyped λ-calculus. Milner [77] pointed out the advantages of sound type systems in the context of programming languages; he also coined the slogan "well-typed programs don't go wrong." The proof technique of this chapter was generalized and imported into the world of programming languages by Wright and Felleisen [118], who corrected Milner's phrase

to "well-typed programs go to specific stuck states." Curry and Feys originally developed the proof technique of subject reduction for the λ-calculus and combinatory logic [24]; Harper assigned it the commonly-used phrase "progress and preservation" technique.[4]

---

[4]Personal discussion of the Wright-Felleisen technical report (Rice University, 1991) between the first author and Bob Harper at the 1991 *Conference on the Principles of Programming Languages* in Orlando, FL.

Part II

PLT Redex

Contents, Part II

11 • The Basics

PLT Redex supports semantics engineering with a domain-specific notation and a suite of tools embedded into PLT Scheme. Using the domain-specific notation, a semantics engineer formulates concise and precise models of programming languages: their syntax and semantics. The tools assist with the exploration of the models: testing, debugging, checking for subject-reduction properties, typesetting, and other life-cycle activities.

A basic Redex model consists of two pieces: a regular-tree grammar and a collection of reduction rules. The former describes those S-expressions that serve as the representation of subject-language expressions and contexts. The latter are pattern-based formulations of reductions, possibly in context, familiar from part I of the book. Redex tools are PLT Scheme functions on Redex languages, reductions, and S-expressions. Some tools open separate windows to display their results; others respond with plain values.

This chapter presents the basic elements of Redex, starting with a section that collects the minimal PLT Scheme knowledge for its proper use. Every first-time user of Redex should read this first section, even those readers who are familiar with Scheme. The remainder of the chapter uses the illustrative example of boolean expressions from part I(1) to introduce Redex features: the specification of syntax and reduction rules and the use of `traces`, a tool for inspecting concrete reduction graphs.

Note: The tutorial assumes that readers study the first three chapters in a sequential order. The remaining chapters are independent of each other. The appendix of this chapter is a concise usage manual for DrScheme. We urge readers who are new to DrScheme to work through this appendix before tackling part II.

11·1 PLT Redex and PLT Scheme.
An effective use of Redex demands some basic knowledge of functional programming in PLT Scheme. Fortunately, learning the necessary bits and pieces is easy.

Here are the most important things a semantics engineer must know:

1. Every Redex program is a module in the `scheme` language of DrScheme that imports the `redex` module:

   ```
   #lang scheme
   (require redex)
   ```

To follow along with the rest of this section, open DrScheme, set the language to **Module**, and enter the above two lines.

2. `(define x` *expression*`)` is a **variable definition** that binds the variable x to the value of `expression`.

3. `(define (f x)` *expression*`)` is a **function definition** that binds the variable f to a function of one parameter, x, and the right-hand side `expression`. Naturally, `(define (g x y)` *expression*`)` introduces a function g of two arguments.

4. `(f 19/3)` is a **function application** of f to the number $6\frac{1}{3}$. Similarly, `(g 1 2)` applies the function g to two arguments.

5. `+`, `expt`, `<`, `list`, etc are **primitive operations**. Just like user-defined functions, they are applied in prefix style.

6. `define-struct` introduces a new structure definition. Its shape is

   `(define-struct name (`*field* `...))`

   and it introduces a "maker" function to construct new instances of the structure: `make-`*name*, a predicate to recognize values of this structure: *name*`?`, and one selector for each field: *name*`-`*field*. The "maker" accepts one argument for each field value, and the predicate and selectors each accept a single argument. Redex programmers do not generally need to make new structures, but Redex itself provides several structure definitions and its tools produce their values.

We introduce other PLT Scheme constructs and functions as needed.

A semantics engineer works with a fully parenthesized syntax of the subject language. To define a language's syntax, it suffices to enter a language definition. It determines the subset of those **S-expression**s that are useful for the subject language, e.g., as programs, expressions, variables, literal constants, or contexts. Roughly speaking, an S-expression is either a number, e.g., 42; a boolean: `#t` or `#f` for true and false; a symbol, e.g., `'hello`; or a list of S-expressions, constructed with `cons` and `null`, e.g., `(cons 'f (cons 2 null))` or, equivalently with the `list` primitive, e.g., `(list 'f 2)`.

The construction of S-expressions for Redex is greatly simplified with a Quine-style quasiquotation system: `term` constructs Redex S-expressions and `unquote` (abbreviated with a comma) computes values to be inserted. For now, assume that `term` traverses an S-expression that contains symbols without the `'` prefix and adds the missing quotation mark; it also converts sequences of S-expressions enclosed in (and) into lists. When this traversal encounters an unquote expression, it computes the value of its sub-expression and incorporates it into the S-expression. For example,

```
(term (lambda (x) x))
```

is turned into

```
(list 'lambda (list 'x) 'x)
```

Also, assuming the program contains (define my-var 361/9), both

```
(term (f (unquote (sqrt my-var)))))
```

and

```
(term (f ,(sqrt my-var)))
```

become

```
(list 'f 6⅓)
```

The first example uses the unquote keyword; the second employs its abbreviation as a comma. When unquote is abbreviated with comma, its surrounding parentheses are omitted.

PLT Scheme supports the entire unicode character set, not just ASCII, so we can also write the first example above as

```
(term (λ (x) x))
```

and, as expected, it is equivalent to

```
(list 'λ (list 'x) 'x)
```

Two symbols are only equivalent, however, when their printed representations match up, character for character. Thus the symbols 'lambda and 'λ are treated as distinct symbols.

Exercise 11.1. What does (term (+ ,(first (term (,(+ 12 34)))) 5)) produce? Check the prediction with a Redex module in DrScheme.

11·2 Specifying Abstract Syntax.
The first notational feature of Redex is define-language, which serves to specify the abstract syntax of a programming language (as fully parenthesized notation).

```
(define-language bool-any-lang
  [B true
     false
     (∨ B B)]
  [C (∨ C B)
     (∨ B C)
     hole])
```

Immediately following `define-language` is `bool-any-lang`, the name of the language. The rest of the definition is a sequence of grammar productions. Technically, these productions specify a regular-tree grammar, which determines the set of S-expressions that may serve as syntax for the subject language. Each production defines the meaning of a non-terminal; in this example, we get two such definitions: B (for boolean expressions) and C (for contexts). Each non-terminal is followed by a series of alternative clauses. For example, the B non-terminal generates (∨ B B) for the conjunction of two boolean formulas and the two booleans `true` and `false`.

Given these preliminaries, the following quoted S-expressions are legitimate B expressions.

```
(define B1 (term true))
(define B2 (term false))
(define B3 (term (∨ true false)))
(define B4 (term (∨ ,B1 ,B2)))
(define B5 (term (∨ false ,B4)))
```

The first three are obvious. The fourth one uses `unquote` and thus generates the equivalent of the third example. Finally, the fifth example produces:

```
(term (∨ false (∨ true false)))
```

We use PLT Scheme's variable definition facility to assign names to concrete expression representations from B. This way we can reuse the same example in different contexts. Doing so also tends to improve the readability of Redex programs, especially when mnemonic names are chosen.

Constructing instances of C proceeds in a similar manner.

```
(define C1 (term hole))
(define C2 (term (∨ (∨ false false) hole)))
(define C3 (term (∨ hole true)))
```

As we know from part I, "filling the hole" is the most useful operation on contexts. The operation is highly useful for the specification of reduction relations, and Redex therefore employs an intuitive notation, e.g.,

```
(in-hole C true)
```

which says that C is to be filled with `true`.

Finally, we need one more piece of information about Redex's grammar specifications. Given a grammar, Redex classifies each of the symbols that appear in the grammar in one of three different ways: literals, non-terminals, and core features of Redex. In this grammar, B and C are classified as non-terminals, since they appear at the beginning of non-terminal clauses in the grammar. The literals in this grammar are true, false, and ∨, and Redex identifies them as such simply because they are not in either of the other two categories. In contrast, hole is a Redex keyword. Unlike the use of false, hole does not denote the literal occurrence of the text h-o-l-e in a B expression, but turns the set C into a collection of contexts, not ordinary expressions.

Once Redex has processed a syntax specification, it is possible to use the redex-match tool in conjunction with the grammar. The purpose of redex-match is to match a pattern with an expression. It accepts a language, a pattern, and an expression. If the pattern fails to match the expression, the tool produces #f; in case of success, it produces a list of substitutions. For example, we may ask whether (term (∨ false true)) is a (member of) B.

```
> (redex-match bool-any-lang
               B
               (term (∨ false true)))
(list
 (make-match
  (list (make-bind 'B (list '∨ 'false 'true)))))
```

The box shows a sample interaction with a read-eval-print loop. In this case, redex-match succeeds and produces a single match structure, which contains a list of bindings. A binding associates a pattern variable with expressions from the model. Here the only pattern variable, 'B, is mapped to the S-expression (list '∨ 'false 'true), as expected.

A pattern may match an expression in several different ways. Consider the example of matching a filled context with an expression.

```
> (redex-match bool-any-lang
               (in-hole C (∨ true B))
               (term (∨ true (∨ true false))))
(list
 (make-match
  (list
   (make-bind 'B (list '∨ 'true 'false))
   (make-bind 'C (make-hole))))
 (make-match
  (list
   (make-bind 'B 'false)
   (make-bind 'C (list '∨ 'true (make-hole)))))))
```

The pattern now contains two variables: C, the context, and B, an arbitrary (sub-)expression, and this use of redex-match produces a list of two matches. The first match sets B to just false and C to (term (∨ true hole)); the second one sets B to the entire expression and C to just hole.

Exercise 11.2. Formulate a grammar of simple addition expressions A. The syntax should contain 0, 1, and 2 plus the addition of arbitrary expressions. Equip the language with contexts, i.e., addition expressions with a hole.

11·3 **Specifying Reduction Relations.** Once we have defined the syntax of a language, we can proceed to the specification of reduction systems for this syntax. Redex's reduction-relation form accepts the name of a language and a series of rules that define a reduction relation in the sense of part I. Each rule begins with an arrow (-->) followed by a Redex pattern and expression. The pattern on the left-hand side describes redexes and their contexts; the right-hand side expression determines the result of a use of such a rule on a specific expression. The latter acts much like term PLT Scheme expressions, but without the explicit term wrapper. Each rule may be given a name, via an optional third piece of a rule description.

Here is the specification of a reduction relation for our running example.

```
(define bool-any-red
  (reduction-relation
   bool-any-lang
   (--> (in-hole C (∨ true B))
        (in-hole C true)
        ∨-true)
   (--> (in-hole C (∨ false B))
        (in-hole C B)
        ∨-false)))
```

The sample code clarifies that the result of reduction-relation is a value, to which we assign the name bool-any-red in this case. The first rule of bool-any-red, called ∨-true, uses this left-hand side:

```
(in-hole C (∨ true B))
```

a pattern with the rather obvious meaning of

> splitting an S-expression into a context C filled with a ∨ expression whose sub-expressions are true and an arbitrary B.

Thus, for example, the pattern matches the B expression

```
(term (∨ (∨ true (∨ false true)) false))
```

by setting the pattern variable C to (∨ hole false) and the pattern variable B to (∨ false true). In contrast, the pattern does not match the expression (term (∨ false true)).

Naturally, this matching is performed by redex-match. Thus, when we ask redex-match to determine the feasible matches for a pattern such as (in-hole C (∨ true B)), we expect an encoding of our expected result.

```
> (redex-match bool-any-lang
               (in-hole C (∨ true B))
               (term (∨ (∨ true (∨ false true)) false)))
(list
 (make-match
  (list
   (make-bind 'B (list '∨ 'false 'true))
   (make-bind 'C (list '∨ (make-hole) 'false)))))
```

On the right-hand side of ∨-true in bool-any-red, we find

```
(in-hole C true)
```

It is also highly suggestive, demanding the construction of an expression from C—as determined by the left-hand side pattern of the same rule—filled with true. For the example above, when C is (∨ hole false), the right hand side creates (∨ true false) for the given expression.

The second rule of bool-any-red also specifies the simplification of a ∨ expression in the hole of a C context. In this case, the first argument to the ∨ expression is false, and the second argument is an arbitrary B. The result of this rule is B, placed back into the hole of context C.

In short, the bool-any-red system describes the reduction relation for the B language from chapters 1 and 2 in part I of the book. What this simple example illustrates is the conciseness of Redex specifications. Not counting the syntax for definitions, a Redex specification for a programming language and its reduction system are as long as a paper-and-pencil description, and the two barely differ. As a matter of fact, a programmer who is familiar with unicode can make the two kinds of specifications look nearly identical.

Exercise 11.3. Formulate a reduction system for modulo 3 arithmetic on the syntax of exercise 11.2. Start with the following rules; add others as needed:

1. (+ 0 A) should reduce to A, and

2. (+ A 0) should reduce to A, too.

$11{\cdot}4$ **Tracing.** Once we have defined a reduction system, the next natural step is to experiment with it. At a minimum, experimentation means "playing with examples," e.g., determining whether some expression exhibits the desired behavior.

For this purpose, Redex provides a tool called `traces`. This PLT Scheme function consumes a Redex-specified language, a reduction relation, and an expression. Here is a typical use of `traces`.

```
(traces bool-any-red
        (term (∨ (∨ true false) (∨ true true))))
```

With this function call, we are asking to see how the expression

```
(term (∨ (∨ true false) (∨ true true)))
```

reduces, using the `bool-any-red` reduction relation. The `traces` tool opens a window and draws a directed graph of all reduction sequences starting from the given expression according to the specified reduction system. A directed arrow in the graph means that the expression from which the arrow originates is reduced to the expression where the arrow ends. If the corresponding rule has a name, the arrow is labeled with this name, which helps with studying complex reduction graphs.

For our running example, the `traces` tool displays the following graph.

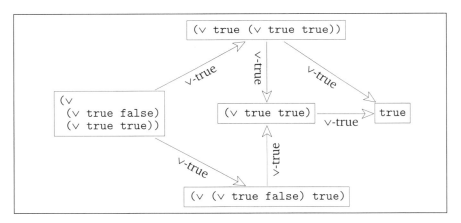

The graph confirms that the `bool-any-red` reduction system generates several reduction sequences from a non-atomic expression to its result. That is, for any such expression, any or both of the two reduction relations may apply. Still, the expression reduces to `true` along all paths in the graph, suggesting that the evaluator based on the reduction system may be deterministic.

Because graphs cannot always be automatically arranged in a readable manner, the nodes may be dragged to appropriate positions and the font size is adjustable. Furthermore, the `traces` window supports exporting its content as a PostScript file so that these graphs can easily be included in papers.

The following module combines the example fragments presented so far in a complete, running Redex program. Recall that the first line indicates that this is a PLT Scheme module in the `scheme` language, and that the second line imports the Redex library.

```scheme
#lang scheme

(require redex)

(define-language bool-lang
  [B true
     false
     (∨ B B)]
  [C (∨ C B)
     (∨ B C)
     hole])

(define bool-red
  (reduction-relation
   bool-lang
   (--> (in-hole C (∨ false B))
        (in-hole C false)
        ∨-false)
   (--> (in-hole C (∨ true B))
        (in-hole C B)
        ∨-true)))

(traces bool-red
        (term (∨ (∨ true false) (∨ true true))))
```

Exercise 11.4. Use `traces` to create reductions graphs of the language formulated in exercises 11.2 and 11.3.

11·5 Variation on a Theme.
The first four sections of this chapter develop the full-fledged reduction systems for the boolean expression example from part I(1). While this development illustrates the gen-

erality of Redex, semantics engineers are usually much more interested in abstract syntactic machines than unrestricted reductions. That is, they tend to prefer a function like the standard reduction function in part I(6) or like the transition function for the CS machine in part I(10).

Fortunately, specifying such a reduction for the boolean expression example is a straightforward variation. All it requires is a small change to the grammar for contexts C. Instead of allowing holes to appear anywhere in a boolean expression, a standard reduction relation needs holes only in a leftmost-outermost position.

```
(define-language bool-standard-lang
  [B true
     false
     (∨ B B)]
  [E (∨ E B)
     hole])

(define bool-standard-red
  (reduction-relation
   bool-standard-lang
   (--> (in-hole E (∨ true B))
        (in-hole E true)
        ∨-true)
   (--> (in-hole E (∨ false B))
        (in-hole E B)
        ∨-false)))
```

The best way to illustrate the difference between bool-any-lang and its reduction system bool-any-red and the above revision is to use traces for the exact same sample expression.

```
(traces bool-standard-red
        (term (∨ (∨ true false) (∨ true true))))
```

In contrast to the first graph, this one reduces the given expression with a single path to its result: true. At least for this sample expression, our experimentation confirms that this second Redex model reduces according to the desired leftmost-outermost or standard reduction strategy.

Exercise 11.5. Try to formulate a specification of evaluation contexts for the language formulated in exercises 11.2 and 11.3 and explored in exercise 11.4. Use `traces` to check your attempts.

12 · Variables and Meta-functions

It is easy to model the boolean language in Redex. For a language such as ISWIM, though, a model requires Redex constructs for the definition of meta-functions, e.g., $\mathcal{FV}$ and δ. Section 1 of this chapter introduces a few additional features of define-language; section 2 focuses on the specification and use of meta-functions in Redex, which are critical for our running example, a model of ISWIM from part I(4) and its standard reduction relation (part I(5)).

12·1 More on Redex Grammars. To get started, here is the Redex grammar of the ISWIM language and its evaluation contexts.

```
(define-language iswim
  ((M N L K) X (λ X M) (M M) b (o2 M M) (o1 M))
  (o o1 o2)
  (o1 add1 sub1 iszero)
  (o2 + - * ↑)
  (b number)
  ((V U W) b X (λ X M))
  (E hole (V E) (E M) (o V ... E M ...))
  ((X Y Z) variable-not-otherwise-mentioned))
```

This grammar is written more compactly than the one in the first chapter of this part. Each production occupies just one single line. Of course, the amount of whitespace used in PLT Scheme is insignificant, as long as there is at least some whitespace. So, for example, the o non-terminal (the second one, standing for "primitive **o**perations") has two productions, o1 and o2. This grammar specifications also uses several additional features:

Multiple non-terminals The first line, the sixth, and the last one list multiple non-terminals. Specifically, the non-terminals M, N, L, and K all denote ISWIM expressions (namely variables, λ expressions, applications, basic constants, and primitive operations) because they appear together in a list where a single non-terminal would ordinarily appear. Similarly, V, U, and W are defined together, as are X, Y, and Z.

Number This language exploits Redex's embedding in PLT Scheme via the built-in number non-terminal (used as the definition of b), that matches any PLT Scheme number.

Variable-not-otherwise-mentioned The definition of ISWIM variables admits any name except for λ, add1, sub1, iszero, +, -, *, and $\uparrow$. That is, the Redex keyword variable-not-otherwise-mentioned means "use as variable any symbol not mentioned as a literal in the grammar of this language."

Ellipses Finally, Redex treats A ... as a possibly empty sequence of instances of A. Like all other pieces of notation, this works both in grammars as well as patterns in the reduction rules. Thus,

```
(o M ...)
```

is a pattern that matches any list that begins with a primitive operation and continues with some number of ISWIM expressions.

Furthermore, Redex permits the specification of ambiguous patterns involving ellipses. Specifically, consider the last production of the E non-terminal:

```
(o V ... E M ...)
```

It contains two ellipses, specifying that o followed by some sequence of values of unspecified length, an evaluation context, and another sequence of expressions is a legal evaluation context E. Hence, the evaluation context can match any position inside a primitive application expression, as long as the expressions to its left are values. For example, (term (+ 1 2)) matches E in two different ways.

```
> (redex-match iswim (in-hole E number) (term (+ 1 2)))
(list
 (make-match
  (list
   (make-bind 'E (list '+ 1 (make-hole)))
   (make-bind 'number 2)))
 (make-match
  (list
   (make-bind 'E (list '+ (make-hole) 2))
   (make-bind 'number 1))))
```

As we know from part I(5), this ambiguity is resolved in the specification of the standard reduction relation. Nevertheless, Redex does not require a resolution, and allowing these kinds of ambiguities makes its pattern language a good match for reduction systems like those in part I.

Exercise 12.1. Formulate the grammar of Error ISWIM (part I(8)) in Redex.

Exercise 12.2. Formulate the grammar of State ISWIM (part I(9)) in Redex.

12·2 Meta-functions.
In addition to specifying grammars and reduction rules, semantics engineers can and must write meta-functions, which are mathematical functions on the entities within the model. Some examples from part I are $\mathcal{FV}$, the function that collects the free variables of a λ-calculus expression; $\cdot[\cdot \leftarrow \cdot]$, a capture-avoiding substitution function; and the evaluator functions.

In Redex, such mathematical meta-functions are formulated with the same pattern and expression notation as in a reduction relation. Their definition is introduced via `define-metafunction`. Here is an illustrative example, the δ function for our Redex model of ISWIM; compare it with the definition of δ in part I(4).

```
(define-metafunction iswim
  [(δ (iszero 0)) (λ x (λ y x))]
  [(δ (iszero b)) (λ x (λ y y))]
  [(δ (add1 b)) ,(add1 (term b))]
  [(δ (sub1 b)) ,(sub1 (term b))]
  [(δ (+ b_1 b_2)) ,(+ (term b_1) (term b_2))]
  [(δ (- b_1 b_2)) ,(- (term b_1) (term b_2))]
  [(δ (* b_1 b_2)) ,(* (term b_1) (term b_2))]
  [(δ (↑ b_1 b_2)) ,(expt (term b_1) (term b_2))])
```

Each such definition begins with a language from which non-terminals are drawn. Following that is a series of clauses, which define the meta-function in a casewise manner. Each case is bracketed with [and] and consists of a pattern and an expression, much like the Redex specification of a reduction relation. In contrast to a reduction relation, the application of a meta-function picks the first matching pattern (from the top) to determine a result; all other matching clauses are ignored.

For the δ meta-function, the first clause specifies that δ returns the expression $(\lambda\ x\ (\lambda\ y\ x))$ if it receives an argument of the form (iszero 0).

```
> (term (δ (iszero 0)))
(list 'λ 'x (list 'λ 'y 'x))
```

The application of a meta-function looks just like the application of any PLT Scheme function, except it must happen within `term`.

The second clause of δ determines what happens when `iszero` receives a non-zero number. Since the clauses in a meta-function are matched in order, we know that this clause can only match when the first clause fails, and thus this second clause applies only when b is not 0.

```
> (term (δ (iszero 2)))
(list 'λ 'x (list 'λ 'y 'y))
```

Finally, the last four clauses use a new feature in Redex's pattern matcher, namely, the ability to decorate non-terminals, i.e., pattern variables, with numbers.[1] The patterns b_1 and b_2 each match the b non-terminal independently and bind b_1 and b_2 on the right-hand side to their respective matches.

These clauses of δ also exploit Redex's embedding into PLT Scheme to determine the result. Just as with `term` expressions, the appearance of the comma (,) on the right-hand side of a clause of a meta-function is treated as an escape to PLT Scheme code. In this case, the δ function uses PLT Scheme's primitive operators to compute the appropriate algebraic operation. Each use of the `term` operator returns to the subject language to pick up the binding for b_1 or b_2, which we know from the grammar must have matched the number pattern and thus must be PLT Scheme numbers.

```
> (term (δ (+ 1 2)))
3
```

Compare the clause for + to the corresponding clause in the definition in part I(4):

$$\delta(+, \ulcorner m \urcorner, \ulcorner n \urcorner) \quad = \quad \ulcorner m + n \urcorner$$

This definition defers to our understanding of mathematics for ISWIM's plus operation, which is just a symbol without meaning until we agree to interpret it via δ. Hence, both definitions turn the addition operator on the left-hand side of the equation into a mathematical function on the on the right side that happens to be referred to with the same symbol. In both cases, the meaning of the one on the right is assumed to be a more primitive notion that

---

[1]The notation is borrowed from LaTeX and alludes to subscripting.

embodies the true knowledge of addition. Beware that PLT Scheme's notion of numbers only approximates the one from mathematics, even though its approximation is better than that of most programming languages.

Formulating a Redex model of ISWIM also demands a capture-avoiding substitution function. Spelling out this substitution function is a complex undertaking, and defining it in an economical manner requires the introduction of several Redex features.

```
(define-metafunction iswim

  ;; 1. X_1 bound, so don't continue in λ body
  [(subst (λ X_1 any_1) X_1 any_2)
   (λ X_1 any_1)]

  ;; 2. do capture avoiding substitution
  ;;    by generating a fresh name
  [(subst (λ X_1 any_1) X_2 any_2)
   (λ X_3
     (subst (subst-var any_1 X_1 X_3) X_2 any_2))
   (where X_3 ,(variable-not-in (term (X_2 any_1 any_2))
                                (term X_1)))]
  ;; 3. replace X_1 with any_1
  [(subst X_1 X_1 any_1) any_1]

  ;; the last two cases just recur on
  ;; the tree structure of the term
  [(subst (any_2 ...) X_1 any_1)
   ((subst any_2 X_1 any_1) ...)]
  [(subst any_2 X_1 any_1) any_2])
```

The first new feature shows up in the pattern of the first clause, which duplicates X_1. Whenever a variable is duplicated in a Redex pattern, the pattern is constrained to match only when the corresponding pieces are identical. In this case, it means that the first case applies when the variable bound by the λ expression is the same as the variable being substituted.

Our second addition is any, a pattern that matches an arbitrary expression, even if that expression does not match any of the non-terminals given in the grammar. This feature helps to collapse the last few cases of the mathematical substitution function into one clause of subst. As a result, this Redex meta-function is trivial to reuse in extensions or variants of ISWIM as long as these extensions do not introduce binding constructs other than λ.

In the first few clauses of subst, the any pattern is used to match the subject expression as well as its body if it is a λ-expressions. The most interesting use of any, though, shows up in the last two clauses:

1. The penultimate clause matches any subject language expession of the form (any ...). In other words, it matches any expression that has the shape of a list. When such a pattern is found, the subst meta-function recurs on all the pieces.

2. The last clause matches any subject language term that has not been matched by one of the other clauses. It simply returns this piece.

Combined, the two clauses empower subst to perform substitutions in primitive applications, even though the function does not explicitly contain any cases for such expressions. The penultimate clause matches because such expressions are made up from lists; the recursion on the primitive operator then uses the last clause to replace it.

```
> (term (subst (+ x (- y z)) z 5))
(list '+ 'x (list '- 'y 5))
```

There are three additional noteworthy points concerning subst. First, subst employs a where clause, which binds (sequences of) variables to subject expressions. That is, the right-hand side of a where clause is automatically wrapped in term. Hence, the use of unquote (comma) escapes to PLT Scheme. In this particular case, subst introduces the variable X_3 to stand for a fresh ISWIM variable.

Second, to choose fresh variables Redex meta-functions may employ the variable-not-in function, which consumes an expression and a variable. It produces the latter, if it does not occur as a symbol in the given expression or deterministically derives a variant otherwise. Thus, the PLT Scheme expression

```
(where X_3 ,(variable-not-in (term (X_2 any_1 any_2))
                             (term X_1)))
```

demands (whatever) X_1 (represents), if it does not occur in the λ-bound variable of the given expression, the body of that λ expression, or the value that is substituted in. The preferred result is the original parameter of the λ expression. Because the variable-not-in function is deterministic, it always returns the same output given a particular input. This ensures that applying a reduction-relation to the same expression multiple times always produces precisely the same results, and not just some α-equivalent results.

Third, this substitution function is tuned for efficiency. A naive formulation of the mathematical substitution function as a Redex meta-function recursively calls subst twice when given a λ expression. In the worst case, such a function consumes an exponential amount of time. We reduce this running time to a quadratic one with the definition of the auxiliary metafunction subst-var.

```
(define-metafunction iswim
  [(subst-var (any_1 ...) variable_1 variable_2)
   ((subst-var any_1 variable_1 variable_2) ...)]
  [(subst-var variable_1 variable_1 variable_2) variable_2]
  [(subst-var any_1 variable_1 variable_2) any_1])
```

This meta-function is not capture avoiding. It just blindly replaces any occurrences of its second argument within the first one by the third. The definition uses the same technique as the last two cases of the subst function and thus applies to all S-expressions. Of course, this definition works only because the function assumes that the third argument simply does not occur in the first.

With these meta-functions, we can now formulate a Redex definition for ISWIM's standard reduction relation. The definition consists of only two rules, just like its mathematical counterpart.

```
(define iswim-red
  (reduction-relation
   iswim
   (--> (in-hole E ((λ X M) V))
        (in-hole E (subst M X V))
        βv)
   (--> (in-hole E (o b ...))
        (in-hole E (δ (o b ...)))
        δ)))
```

Each rule uses one of the meta-functions. When the application of a metafunction appears on the right-hand side of a rule, Redex dispatches to the meta-function, exactly like in a term expressions. No special notation is required to identify meta-functions.

Now that we have built a complete Redex model of ISWIM, we can trace the reductions of sample ISWIM programs. Consider this expression:

$$((\lambda\ y\ (y\ y))\ (\lambda\ x\ (x\ x)))$$

As we know from part I(3), its standard reduction sequence does not terminate, because the expression reduces to itself. Redex's `traces` function indicates this loop in a reduction sequence with the display of a cyclic graph.

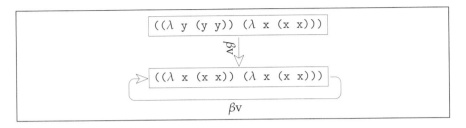

Since `traces` considers two terms identical only if the bound variables have the same names, the original term has to be reduced once before the function discovers the cycle.

Exercise 12.3. Formulate the $\mathcal{FV}$ function for ISWIM (part I(4)) in Redex.

Exercise 12.4. In the context of exercise 12.1, formulate the $\mathcal{AV}$ function for State ISWIM as a Redex meta-function.

Exercise 12.5. Revise the `subst` function from this chapter so that it works for the Error ISWIM model from exercise 12.2.

12·3 Reductions via `with` Clauses.
Even though we can now formulate the Redex model for ISWIM in a reasonably economical manner, the specification of the standard reduction does not truly mirror the mathematical one. In particular, it somewhat obscures the relationship between notions of reductions and standard reduction steps, which comes out so clearly in the mathematical formulation.

Here is the specification of the standard reduction function from part I(5).

$$E[M] \longmapsto_{\mathbf{v}} E[M'] \quad \text{if } M \mathbf{v} M'$$

In contrast to our Redex formulation of standard reduction, this mathematical definition shows that standard reduction is the syntactically compatible closure of **v** with respect to evaluation contexts. At the same time, the **v** notion of reduction is formulated in the most concise fashion possible, without any clutter.

Since lifting a notion of reduction is a common operation, Redex supports it with a simple generalization of the `reduction-relation` construct. In particular, clauses in `reduction-relation` do not have to specify the `-->` relation. They may specify an arbitrary relation instead, which can then be "lifted" to `-->` via `with` clauses:

```
(reduction-relation
  language clauses ...
  with
  [(new-rel new-from new-to)
   (old-rel old-from old-to)] ...)
```

Specifically, each clause following `with` defines `new-rel` in terms of `old-rel`. The two patterns `new-from` and `new-to` specify how expressions relate according to `new-rel` if the variables `old-from` and `old-to` are related according to some already defined relation `old-rel` (defined above `with`). Still, from the outside only the `-->` relation is visible and used in tools, e.g., traces.

Given the ability to add `with` clauses to `reduction-relation`, it is indeed possible to define a Redex model of ISWIM that faithfully mimics the mathematical one.

```
(define iswim-standard
  (reduction-relation
   iswim
   (v ((λ X M) V) (subst M X V) βv)
   (v (o b ...) (δ (o b ...)) δ)
   with
   [(--> (in-hole E M) (in-hole E N)) (v M N)]))
```

This illustrative example of `with` first introduces the two pieces of **v**: β_v and δ. Then, the `with` clause shows how the standard reduction relation is the compatible closure of **v** with respect to evaluation contexts.

Exercise 12.6. Formulate a general reduction relation for ISWIM using a `with` clause. Use `traces` to demonstrate that programs may be reduced to values along several different paths in a reduction graph.

13 • Layered Development

Most software engineers develop their products in an iterative fashion. They start with a kernel and add layers of features around this kernel in a spiral fashion until the customers or the users are satisfied. This iterative approach mimics the scientific method of developing models and improving them as additional information from experiments becomes available.

A semantics engineer should develop models of programming languages in the same fashion. The models should consist of an easily understood, well-explored, and relevant kernel language to which the engineer should add linguistic constructs to study their interaction with the kernel.[1]

Reduction semantics allows this form of scientific approach more than any other kind of semantics. In part I, we have seen several extensions of ISWIM with additional constructs, e.g., exceptions, exception handlers, control transfer, and mutation. Most of these extensions specify an enlarged grammar and a set of additional reduction rules, while the core grammar and the core reductions are just interpreted over the extended language.

In support of this approach, Redex provides constructs for extending the grammar and the reduction rules of an existing model:

1. with `define-extended-language`, a semantics engineer adds grammatical productions to the grammar of the model; and

2. the `extend-reduction-relation` feature helps extend reductions.

This chapter introduces these constructs and illustrates their meaning with Error ISWIM from part I(8.1).

13·1 Extending Languages.
Let us briefly recall the Error ISWIM language from part I(8), which extends ISWIM with exceptions for signaling errors. From a grammatical perspective—with which we are concerned in this section—it introduces both syntactic elements for writing down exceptions and primitive operations that signal them.

---

[1]Really good language development work should then transfer these features from the model to an existing language and should explore their pragmatics via modifications of reasonably large code bases.

The following box shows the grammar specification of Error ISWIM as an extension to ISWIM.

$$
\begin{array}{rll}
M & = & \ldots \qquad \text{same as plain ISWIM} \\
& | & \text{err}_b \\
o^2 & = & \ldots \qquad \text{same as arithmetic ISWIM} \\
& | & /
\end{array}
$$

The notation for this grammar employs a concise mathematical style, using nothing but "..." to remind the reader of ISWIM's core grammar. In order to make the example concrete, the grammar also instantiates Error ISWIM to an extension of arithmetic ISWIM with the introduction of numeric division.

A Redex programmer uses literally the same style.

```
(define-extended-language e-iswim
  iswim
  (M ....
     (err b))
  (o2 ....
     /))
```

Let us examine the new elements of this Redex definition step by step. Each define-extended-language definition consists of the name for the new language, the base language, and grammar productions:

```
(define-extended-language new-language old-language
  new-nonterminal-definitions ...)
```

These additional productions either supplement or replace the original ones. If a production replaces a non-terminal from the base language, all of the other productions in the base and the extended language refer to this new one. In addition, a four-period ellipsis (....) can be used to indicate that some production extends a production from the original grammar.

In this light, interpreting the Redex definition for e-iswim is straightforward. Both the definitions for M and for o2 use the four-period ellipsis, so they include all of the clauses from the original definitions for M and o2 as well as the specified additions. The remaining productions from ISWIM are effectively copied. Put differently, the above is short for the following alternative definition of Error ISWIM's syntax.

```
(define-language e-iswim-full
  ((M N L K) X (λ X M) (M M) b (o2 M M) (o1 M) (err b))
  (o o1 o2)
  (o1 add1 sub1 iszero)
  (o2 + - * ↑ /)
  (b number)
  ((V U W) b X (λ X M))
  (E hole (V E) (E M) (o V ... E M ...))
  ((X Y Z) variable-not-otherwise-mentioned))
```

Writing out the "expanded" version of the grammar also clarifies that a Redex grammar extension re-interprets all of the original clauses in the new context. In particular, for the running example, the set V of values now also includes λ expressions that have division expressions in their body, even though the old definition of V does not. We can confirm this re-interpretation with an interactive exploration.

```
> (redex-match e-iswim               > (redex-match iswim
              V                                    V
              (term                                (term
                (λ x                                 (λ x
                  (/ 1 x))))                           (/ 1 x))))
(list                                #f
 (make-match
  (list
   (make-bind
    'V
    (list
     'λ
     'x
     (list '/ 1 'x))))))
```

The redex-match on the left shows that (λ x (/ 1 x)) is indeed an element of V in the e-iswim language. In contrast, the very same expression is rejected as an element of V with respect to the iswim language.

Similarly, the "expanded" version illustrates a subtle point concerning variable-not-otherwise-mentioned. Because err is mentioned as a literal in the grammar for Error ISWIM, it can no longer serve as a variable. Put differently, even though we call Error ISWIM an extension of ISWIM, the relationship between the two languages is quite subtle in Redex.

```
> (redex-match          > (redex-match
   e-iswim                  iswim
   M (term (λ err err)))    M (term (λ err err)))
#f                       (list
                          (make-match
                          (list
                          (make-bind
                          'M
                          (list
                          'λ
                          'err
                          'err)))))
```

The above interaction contrasts how redex-match rejects an iswim program from e-iswim.

In summary, Redex supports extending language grammars in an economical and intuitive manner. An extended grammar inherits all those productions for non-terminals that are not mentioned; it truly extends those that include . . . .; and it basically represents a conservative extension in the mathematical sense of superset.[2]

Exercise 13.1. Formulate the syntax of Handler ISWIM as both a Redex grammar that extends ISWIM and one that extends Error ISWIM.

Exercise 13.2. Formulate the syntax of State ISWIM as a Redex grammar that extends ISWIM. Compare with the full grammar from exercise 12.1.

13·2 Extending Reduction Relations.

Once a language's grammar has been suitably extended, it is time to extend the evaluator, too. If the evaluator is based on a calculus, we must add notions of reduction and possibly revise the set of general contexts. If it is using a standard reduction relation—the most common scenario—we add clauses; in this case, we must also ensure that the set of evaluation contexts is properly revised for the extended language.

In analogy to define-extended-language, Redex provides the linguistic form extend-reduction-relation for extending a reduction. The form accepts an existing reduction relation, a language, and contextual clauses for the relation:

---

[2]A mathematical model is about *abstract* syntax, which means that literals and variables belong to separate categories. To make Redex convenient, it uses a form of syntax that is almost but not really abstract.

```
(extend-reduction-relation reduction-relation
                           language
                           new-clauses ...)
```

If the clauses have new names, they are added to the relation. If any of the clauses have names that match the names of clauses in the original relation, the new clauses replace the ones from the original relation. Furthermore, just as define-extended-language interprets grammar productions from the base language within the larger context, extend-reduction-relation re-interprets the original clauses of the reduction for the extended language.

Let us apply this new knowledge to Error ISWIM. This language semantically extends ISWIM in two different ways. First, it introduces reductions for signaling exceptions, i.e., for aborting the rest of a computation and pushing an exception to the top of the program. Second, the language demands that δ, the interpretation function for primitive operations, is total—even for primitive operations that represent partial functions.

The instance of Error ISWIM in this chapter includes only one such operator: /. All other operators are total functions and are already available in plain ISWIM. Thus our first modeling task is to define a δ function that interprets division *and* ISWIM's primitive operations.

```
(define-metafunction e-iswim
  [($\delta$/ (/ b 0)) (err 0)]
  [($\delta$/ (/ b_1 b_2)) ,(/ (term b_1) (term b_2))]
  [($\delta$/ (o V ...)) ($\delta$ (o V ...))])
```

With δ/ in place, we turn to the second task, namely, the definition of the extended reduction relation. While this definition is not the one from part I(8), it is close and has an intuitive meaning. Given that ISWIM comes with two rules, the rule set for Error ISWIM inherits the β_v rule and replaces the δ rule so that δ/ is used instead of plain δ.[3] Finally, the last three rules turn faulty applications into exceptions and propagate exceptions through evaluation contexts.

One noteworthy detail concerns the rule labeled δerr1. It is the first reduction rule to exploit Redex's embedding into PLT Scheme. Specifically, Redex interprets (term (b ...)) as a list (of numbers), because b matches numbers and there is a single set of parenthesis. The length of this list, plus 1, is the position of the λ expression in the argument list to the primitive

---

[3]Recall that in part I(8), we left the old δ reduction alone and supplemented it with a notion of reduction for those cases when the δ function signals an error. In principle, Redex could mimic this mathematical trick, but doing so would complicate its overall architecture and make its use less intuitive in many other cases.

operation. The computation turns this position into an appropriate label for
the exception.

```
(define e-iswim-red-first-try
  (extend-reduction-relation
   iswim-red
   e-iswim
   (--> (in-hole E (o b ...))
        (in-hole E (δ/ (o b ...)))
        δ)
   (--> (in-hole E (o b ... (λ X M) V ...))
        (in-hole E (err ,(add1 (length (term (b ...))))))
        δerr1)
   (--> (in-hole E (b V))
        (in-hole E (err b))
        δerr2)
   (--> (in-hole E (err b))
        (err b)
        err)))
```

Since extend-reduction-relation re-interprets the rules from the original reduction relation in terms of the new grammar, β_v works properly, even
when neither the evaluation context nor the body of the λ expression are
plain ISWIM expressions. Again traces illustrates this point best.

```
(traces e-iswim-red-first-try
        (term
         (/ ((λ x (/ 1 x)) 7)
            2)))
```

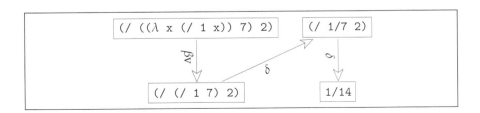

Tracing an expression that does signal an exception yields a surprise.

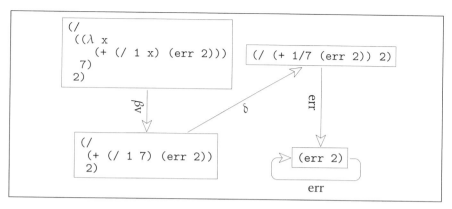

The last node in the above graph is connected to itself because the notion of reduction for pushing exceptions through evaluation contexts does not exclude empty contexts. In part I(8), we recognize this problem in two ways. First, for Error ISWIM we define the evaluator so that it produces a result if the program reduces either to a value or to an exception. The fact that the exception reduces to itself again is simply ignored. Second, while this elegant and lazy approach to mathematics works fine for Error ISWIM, it is awkward for the specification of true standard reduction relations and for such complex languages as Handler ISWIM, which is why we apply appropriate side conditions for those. For this reason, Redex provides additional mechanism for restricting and expressing reductions, and we explore those next.

Exercise 13.3. Confirm that tracing ISWIM expressions in the reduction system of Error ISWIM works just like before.

Exercise 13.4. Formulate the reduction relation of Handler ISWIM as a Redex extension of ISWIM's reduction system. Is it possible to formulate the reductions as an extension of Error ISWIM's specification?

Exercise 13.5. Formulate the reduction relation of Control ISWIM as a Redex extension of ISWIM's reduction system. Is it possible to formulate it as an extension of Handler ISWIM's reduction system?

Exercise 13.6. Formulate a Redex model of the reduction system for Simply Typed ISWIM from part I(10). Recall that the reduction system ignores the type annotations in λ expressions. Then extend the model so that it allows the creation of recursive functions.

$13 \cdot 3$ **Side Conditions.** Our work with Redex has revealed the small, but surprising insight that Error ISWIM's evaluator is defined even if the standard reduction sequence starting from some program is infinitely long. Put differently, the evaluator accepts the reducible expression (err b) as an answer. While there is nothing wrong with using a reducible expression as an answer[4] and while Redex's traces tool can cope with this kind of reduction sequence, it is better to use finite instead of infinite standard reduction sequences, for both mathematical and practical reasons.

In the case of Error ISWIM, the problem is easy to fix with a side condition on the err rule that restricts E to be non-empty.

```
(define e-iswim-red
  (extend-reduction-relation
   iswim-red
   e-iswim
   (--> (in-hole E (o b ...))
        (in-hole E (δ/ (o b ...)))
        δ)
   (--> (in-hole E (o b ... (λ X M) V ...))
        (in-hole E (err ,(add1 (length (term (b ...))))))
        δerr1)
   (--> (in-hole E (b V))
        (in-hole E (err b))
        δerr2)
   (--> (in-hole E (err b))
        (err b)
        err
        (side-condition
         (not (equal? (term hole) (term E)))))))
```

Take a close look at the last reduction rule (err). It still specifies that exceptions eliminate surrounding evaluation contexts, but it also comes with a side-condition clause. This side condition expresses in Redex notation that E is not to be empty for this rule to apply. Again, just like in the δerr1 rule, the actual computation is performed in PLT Scheme. That is, term extracts the evaluation context E, and the result is then compared to the empty context with the equal? predicate.

If we trace an expression from Error ISWIM with this revised reduction system, we no longer see cyclic references from an exception node to itself.

---

[4]Indeed, Plotkin's introduction of λ calculi for call-by-name and call-by-value ISWIM rests on this innovative idea.

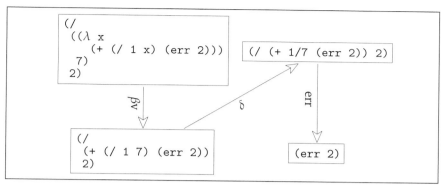

Lastly, let us reformulate the Redex version of the standard reduction relation for Error ISWIM so that it looks like the mathematical version.

$$\tilde{\mathbf{e}} = \beta_v \cup \delta \cup \delta_{err}$$

$$E[M] \longmapsto_e E[N] \quad \text{if} \quad M \, \tilde{\mathbf{e}} \, N$$
$$E[err_l] \longmapsto_e err_l$$

Just as for ISWIM, the standard reduction relation is the compatibility closure of the notion of reduction with respect to evaluation contexts combined with a relation that needs direct access to the evaluation context.

While Redex does not support the simultaneous combination of a relation and its closure with respect to some context, the use of `with` clauses allows semantics engineers to mimic the style of the above mathematical definition quite closely.

```
(define e-iswim-red2
  (reduction-relation
   e-iswim
   (ē ((λ X M) V) (subst M X V) βv)
   (ē (o b ...) (δ/ (o b ...)) δ)
   (ē (o b ... (λ X M) V ...)
      (err ,(add1 (length (term (b ...)))))
      δerr1)
   (ē (b V) (err b) δerr2)
   (--> (in-hole E (err b))
        (err b)
        (side-condition
         (not (equal? (term E) (term hole)))))
   with
   [(--> (in-hole E a) (in-hole E b)) (ē a b)]))
```

The `e-iswim-red2` relation is defined in two stages. The first stage introduces ē and one clause for the externally visible `-->` relation. In the `with`
clauses, ē is closed with respect to evaluation contexts in order to introduce
the rest of the `-->` relation.

Exercise 13.7. Formulate the standard reduction relation of Handler ISWIM
in Redex. Use `with` clauses to mimic the mathematical definition in part I(8).

Exercise 13.8. Formulate the standard reduction relation of Control ISWIM
in Redex. Use `with` clauses to mimic the mathematical definition in part I(8).

14 · Testing

Working software engineers rely on good test suites. Tests written *before* developing software can help with the design process. In addition, (regression) test suites enable engineers to refactor and to maintain code with confidence.

Semantics engineers need support for unit testing for more or less the same reasons. To this end, Redex provides several tools with a focus on testing the outcome of reducing individual programs. Unlike a proof, of course, tests do not establish a theorem. Instead, they help discover flaws in models and conjectures, and the flaws can be eliminated before making significant investments in proofs.

In this chapter, we introduce Redex's testing tools. The last section illustrates their use with an example concerning the CK machine from part I(6).

14·1 Test Cases, Test Suites.
A Redex test case is formulated with test-->>, which accepts a reduction relation, an expression, and an expected final result.

```
> (test-->> iswim-red
            (term ((λ x (+ x x)) 2))
            (term 4))
```

Redex reduces the expression to a canonical form, if any, and compares the actual result with the expected one. A successful test case runs silently. An unsuccessful test case signals a failure.

```
> (test-->> iswim-red
            (term ((λ x (- x x)) 2))
            (term 4))
FAILED
expected: 4
  actual: 0
```

Specifically, it displays "FAILED" followed by the source location of the failure (if available), the expected result, and the actual result.

For test cases concerning meta-functions, Redex offers the test-equal tool. It accepts two expressions, evaluates them, and compares them for equality. A typical test case uses the meta-function in the first expression, with the second one being a plain result. The following test case checks that δ correctly adds 1 and 2.

```
> (test-equal (term (δ (+ 1 2))) (term 3))
```

Like test-->>, test-equal displays FAILED when it determines that the results of its two expressions differ. It shows the first value as the actual result, and it shows the second value as the expected result.

```
> (test-equal (term (δ (iszero 0))) (term (λ x (λ y y))))
FAILED
  actual: (λ x (λ y x))
expected: (λ x (λ y y))
```

Finally, the test-results tool gathers basic statistics about preceding tests. It prints out how many tests failed (if any) and the total number of tests that were evaluated since test-results was called last or since the beginning of a DrScheme evaluation.

```
> (test-results)
2 tests failed (out of 4 total).
```

To define test suites, package up several test cases in a function followed by a call to test-results.

```
(define (test-suite)
  (test-->> iswim-red
            (term ((λ x (- x x)) 2))
            (term 4))
  (test-->> iswim-red
            (term ((λ x (+ x x)) 2))
            (term 4))
  (test-results))
```

Exercise 14.1. Develop a test suite for the model of Error ISWIM.

Exercise 14.2. Develop a test suite for Handler ISWIM (exercise 13.7).

14·2 Abstracting over Test Cases. Given that Redex tools are just PLT Scheme functions and reduction relations are first-class values,

it is possible to abstract over test cases and test suites. Doing so is especially useful when a model comes with more than one reduction system.

Thus far, we have worked with an ISWIM model that comes with a standard reduction relation. If we were interested in the relation of the standard reduction relation to the original calculus, we could introduce an appropriate reduction relation via a straightforward extension.

```
(define-extended-language iswim-calculus
  iswim
  (C hole (M C) (C M) (o M ... C M ...) (λ X C)))

(define iswim->
  (reduction-relation
   iswim-calculus
   (--> (in-hole C ((λ X M) V))
        (in-hole C (subst M X V)) βv)
   (--> (in-hole C (o b ...))
        (in-hole C (δ (o b ...))) δ)))
```

Now that ISWIM comes with two reduction relations—both `iswim-red` and `iswim->`—it makes sense to abstract the test suite over the reduction relation and to run it on both.

```
(define (abstract-test-suite rr label)
  (printf "testing ~a\n" label)
  (test-->> rr
            (term ((λ x (+ x x)) 2))
            (term 4))
  (test-->> rr
            (term ((λ x (- x x)) 2))
            (term 0))
  (test-results))
```

Naturally, we would like to see the same number of successes and failures for both runs. As a matter of fact, a test suite for comparing the standard reduction relation with the plain reduction relation should really compare the results for the given test cases, and as long as they are numbers, they should be the identical.

Exercise 14.3. Add additional test cases to `abstract-test-suite`.

14·3 Testing Properties.
Comparing results of different reduction relations is an instance of checking properties of irreducible forms. Redex comes with two functions for testing of properties: `test-predicate` and `apply-reduction-relation*`.

The former, `apply-reduction-relation*`, reduces an expression according to some given reduction relation. Its result is a list of *all* irreducible expressions, if any. Of course, the function diverges if any of the reduction sequences does not end in an irreducible expression.

```
> (apply-reduction-relation* iswim-red
                             (term ((λ x (- x 1)) 2)))
(list 1)
```

In this example, the `apply-reduction-relation*` function reduces the application of (λ x (- x 1)) to 2 using the ISWIM standard reduction relation. This application reduces to 1, and thus `apply-reduction-relation*` produces a list with a single element, 1.

With `apply-reduction-relation*` we can now define a function that consumes an expression and reduces it to an irreducible form with both the ISWIM reduction relation and its standard reduction relation.

```
(define (same-answer? exp)
  (define calculus-answers
    (apply-reduction-relation* iswim-> exp))
  (define stdred-answers
    (apply-reduction-relation* iswim-red exp))
  (and (equal? (length calculus-answers) 1)
       (equal? (length stdred-answers) 1)
       (equal? (first calculus-answers)
               (first stdred-answers))))
```

Note how the comparison expression of `same-answer?` checks three properties: the length of the two result lists and whether the two `first` items from these lists are equal.

In order to hook up `same-answer?` with the unit testing framework, we use `test-predicate` with the predicate and a term.

```
(define (stdred-test-suite)
  (test-predicate same-answer? (term ((λ x (- x x)) 2)))
  (test-predicate same-answer? (term ((λ x (+ x x)) 2)))
  (test-results))
```

This test suite compares the results of the two reduction relations for two expressions.

Exercise 14.4. Turn the test suite of exercise 14.3 into a test suite that compares the results of ISWIM's reduction relation and standard reduction relation.

Exercise 14.5. Define a predicate for testing the conjecture that all programs (closed ISWIM expressions) reduce to closed irreducible expressions (if any). Then use the predicate to develop a small test suite.

14·4 The CK Machine.
Redex is not just about modeling reduction relations; it can also express abstract machines, as long as they are formulated like those of part I(6) or the CS machine of part I(9).

To understand how machine models work in Redex, we consider the CK machine. Since the CK machine reduces expressions (Control strings) combined with continuations (κ), its state space extends ISWIM's grammar with the latter. Hence we formulate it via define-extended-language.

```
(define-extended-language iswim-mach
  iswim
  (κ mt (fn V κ) (ar N κ) (op (V ... o) (N ...) κ)))
```

As in part I(6), κ is either empty, a function waiting to be applied, a suspended argument evaluation, or a partially evaluated primitive operation.

The reduction relation for the CK machine is a transliteration of the transition function given in part I(6.4).

```
(define ck
  (reduction-relation
   iswim-mach
   (--> ((M N) κ) (M (ar N κ)))
   (--> ((o M N ...) κ) (M (op (o) (N ...) κ)))
   (--> (V (fn (λ X M) κ)) ((subst M X V) κ))
   (--> (V (ar N κ)) (N (fn V κ)))
   (--> (b_m (op (b_1 ... o) () κ)) ((δ (o b_m b_1 ...)) κ))
   (--> (V (op (U ... o) (N M ...) κ))
        (N (op (V U ... o) (M ...) κ)))))
```

Note how neither the state-space grammar nor the transition function requires any new features of Redex. Our abstract machines are just ordinary instances of reduction semantics.

Once we have a Redex model of the CK machine, it is natural to ask if the machine produces the "same" answers as the standard reduction. Before we can formulate a function like same-answer?, though, we must clarify what it means for an ISWIM value to be the same as the answer of an evaluation on the CK machine. A machine reduction does not end in values but in final machine states. We do know, however, that final states always have the shape (V mt) for some value V and the empty continuation mt. One way to relate these states to values then is to project out the value with a meta-function.

```
(define-metafunction iswim-mach
  [(φ (V mt)) V])
```

An equivalent alternative is to use first from PLT Scheme, exploiting the pun between S-expressions and expression representations.

Equipped with φ, we can define a predicate for comparing the outcomes of expressions run on the abstract syntax machine and the CK machine.

```
(define (same-ck-stdred? exp)
  (define stdred-answers
    (apply-reduction-relation* iswim-red exp))
  (define machine-answers
    (apply-reduction-relation* ck (term (,exp mt))))
  (and (equal? (length stdred-answers) 1)
       (equal? (length machine-answers) 1)
       (equal? (first stdred-answers)
               (term (φ ,(first machine-answers))))))
```

The function same-ck-stdred? returns true when both the application of the standard reduction relation and the machine-reduction relation produce a single result and when the translation of the first and only machine answer into plain syntax is equal to the single answer at the end of the standard reduction sequence.

Here is a test case using the same-ck-stdred? function.

```
> (test-predicate same-ck-stdred? (term ((λ x (- x 1)) 2)))
FAILED
  #<procedure:same-ck-stdred?> does not hold for
  ((λ x (- x 1)) 2)
```

Surprisingly, it fails. To debug the model, we turn to traces. We focus on the CK machine side of the problem because we know from early tests that the standard reduction relation reduces this sample expression properly.

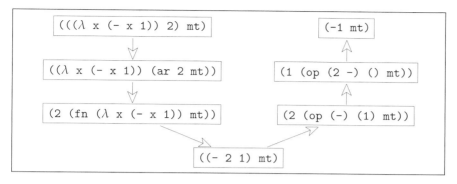

The state in the middle of the reduction graph is clearly reasonable. After applying the procedure and performing the substitution we are left with the expression (- 2 1) in the empty continuation. Thus, one of the steps on the right side of the diagram should reveal the error. The next two steps are collecting the arguments to the subtraction operator into an op continuation and also seem proper. The problem, then, shows up in the last step, where the δ function is applied to 1 and 2, in the wrong order.

In short, our debugging session with traces reveals an error in the CK-machine rule concerning δ reductions. Comparing the Redex specification with the specification in part I(6.4), the mismatch is obvious. While the former applies δ to just the constants, the latter reverses the sequence of constants first. Redex does not have any direct support for reversing a sequence. Once again, we can exploit the embedding into PLT Scheme to accomplish the reversal. Specifically, we construct (term (b_m b_m-1 ... o)) and then use the reverse primitive to put the arguments in the proper order.

```
(define ck-fix
  (reduction-relation
   iswim-mach
   (--> ((M N) κ) (M (ar N κ)))
   (--> ((o M N ...) κ) (M (op (o) (N ...) κ)))
   (--> (V (fn (λ X M) κ)) ((subst M X V) κ))
   (--> (V (ar N κ)) (N (fn V κ)))
   (--> (b_m (op (b_m-1 ... o) () κ))
        ((δ ,(reverse (term (b_m b_m-1 ... o)))) κ))
   (--> (V (op (U ... o) (N M ...) κ))
        (N (op (V U ... o) (M ...) κ))))))
```

With this revision of the CK reductions, the test case above passes, and all other terminating expression pass the same test, too.

Exercise 14.6. Formulate a Redex model of the CC machine. Then develop a predicate that checks whether the CC machine and the abstract syntax machine produce the same answers. Alternative, develop a predicate that checks the equivalence of the CK and the CC machine.

Exercise 14.7. Formulate a Redex model and a test suite for the CS machine from part I(9.2).

15 · Debugging

When users report an error in a software system, developers first formulate a test case that replicates the erroneous behavior. After that, they use various tools to discover what the error actually is. The latter step is called "debugging," because the removal of an error often coincides with its discovery.

Since Redex programs tend to be relatively small, its support for debugging is entirely graphical. In particular, the `traces` tool can paint the expressions in a reduction graph, based on an optionally specified predicate. Clearly, this capability is especially useful for testing and then debugging claims for which we intend to use a subject-reduction proof strategy. From part I, we know that this condition applies when working with type systems. In this case, the predicate is the type checker, and `traces` can highlight all those reachable expressions for which typing fails.

This chapter introduces visual debugging with `traces`. In the first section, we show how to use `traces` to find a reduction rule that creates illegal syntax with respect to the given language. The remainder of the chapter is dedicated to debugging a complete Redex model of Simply Typed ISWIM, which for illustrative purposes has been seeded with a simple error.

15·1 Visual Debugging, Take 1.
Reasonably large Redex models often deal with complex grammars and reduction systems. Initial drafts often suffer from mistakes in the reduction system that introduce illegal syntax, i.e., expressions that according to the grammar of the subject language are ill-formed. Worse, due to any patterns in reduction rules and meta-functions, such mistakes may escape discovery for a while and, when discovered, are not easy to spot. Although Redex does not automatically check whether a reduction rule relates expressions of the appropriate categories, it is easy to formulate an appropriate predicate and to use it for debugging purposes.

In this section, we present a solution to exercises 11.2 and 11.3 that is seeded with just such a mistake. Recall that the exercises request a model for a language of modulo-3 arithmetic. The syntax of the language is to include 0, 1, and 2 plus addition expressions; the reductions are to reduce all expressions in this subject language to a literal constant. Here is the grammar, which is clearly straightforward.

```
(define-language mod-lang
  (A 0 1 2 (+ A A))
  (C hole (+ C A) (+ A C)))
```

The following reduction relation is mostly correct, but it contains an obvious mistake. Take a quick look and find it before reading on.

```
(define mod3
  (reduction-relation mod-lang
    (--> (in-hole C (+ 0 A)) (in-hole C A) 0left)
    (--> (in-hole C (+ A 0)) (in-hole C A) 0right)
    (--> (in-hole C (+ 1 1)) (in-hole C 2) 1-1)
    (--> (in-hole C (+ 1 2)) (in-hole C 0) 1-2)
    (--> (in-hole C (+ 2 1)) (in-hole C 3) 2-1)
    (--> (in-hole C (+ 2 2)) (in-hole C 1) 2-2)))
```

Our penultimate rule contains 3 on the right-hand side. This implies that no instance of this pattern can possibly belong to the set A (from language mod-lang).

Naturally, this kind of mistake does not escape anyone's attention for long, and any test suite discovers it.

```
> (test-->> mod3 (term (+ (+ 0 (+ 1 2)) 2)) (term 2))

> (test-->> mod3 (term (+ (+ 1 1) (+ 1 1))) (term 1))

> (test-->> mod3 (term (+ 0 (+ 0 (+ 0 1)))) (term 1))

> (test-->> mod3 (term (+ (+ (+ (+ 0 1) 0) 1) 0)) (term 2))

> (test-->> mod3 (term (+ (+ 1 1) (+ 2 1))) (term 2))
FAILED
expected: 2
  actual: (+ (+ 1 1) 3)
  actual: (+ 2 3)

> (test-results)
1 test failed (out of 5 total).
```

In this case, the last test case fails and signals that the reduction system ends in an expression that contains 3.

At this point, we could just inspect the reduction rules for an occurrence of 3. Usually though, an inspection doesn't reveal the mistake that easily, because the reduction rules may reduce expressions even if some pieces aren't legal syntax. For such cases, it is necessary to inspect the actual reduction graph for the test case expression that revealed the bug. Since these graphs are potentially large, the traces tool supports an automated inspection mode.

In PLT Scheme, functions may specify optional keyword parameters with optional default values. The traces tool supports a #:pred keyword argument, which, if present, must be a predicate on expressions. This predicate is then applied to each expression that appears in the traces window. When the predicate returns #f, the corresponding expression in the window is colored with a pink background; otherwise it stays white.[1] The default value for the #:pred parameter of traces is a predicate that always returns #t.

To find the mistake in mod3, we want to supply a predicate that produces #t if the expression is a legal mod-lang expression.

```
(traces mod3 (term (+ (+ 1 1) (+ 2 1)))
        #:pred (redex-match mod-lang A))
```

Note how this use of redex-match uses only two arguments: a language and a pattern. Instead of returning a match, it returns a predicate that accepts term expressions and determines whether they match the pattern with respect to the specified grammar. Here is an equivalent definition:

```
(define (legal-mod-lang? e) (redex-match mod-lang A e))
```

This formulation is less efficient, however, than the above with the two-argument form of redex-match, because the pattern argument is compiled.

Here is the graph that the above use of traces produces.

---

[1] Since PLT Scheme treats all values different from #f as true, Redex permits predicates to return specific colors, which are then used to paint expressions. Furthermore, if the predicate accepts two arguments, Redex supplies graph connectivity information to the predicate, which we have found useful for advanced subject reduction proofs. See the manual for details.

Of the four expressions in this graph, two are colored white, two appear pink. In both cases, the (+ 2 1) sub-expression is reduced to 3. Furthermore, in both cases, the arrow going into the pink box is labeled with 2-1, the name of the penultimate reduction rule. We have thus identified the flawed rule in mod-red and are now in a position to fix it.

Exercise 15.1. In addition to traces, Redex also provides the stepper tool. This tool accepts the same arguments as traces but it displays its result in a manner that is well-suited for reduction sequences of complex expressions.

Formulate a call-by-value Y combinator in ISWIM, and use traces and stepper to explore the reduction sequence for the following ISWIM program:

```
((Y (λ x .
   (ifz x
        ⌈0⌉
        (+ x (tri (- x ⌈1⌉))))))
 ⌈3⌉)
```

15·2 Type Checking, Take 1.
By now, it is straightforward to create a Redex model of Simply Typed ISWIM that specifies its grammar and reduction system; see exercise 13.6. As a matter of fact, if an ISWIM model is available, it is worthwhile extending it, because the only change to the grammar is the addition of types to the parameters in λ expressions.

```
(define-extended-language t-iswim iswim
  (M X (λ X T M) (M M) b (o2 M M) (o1 M))
  (V b X (λ X T M))
  ((T S) (-> T T) num)
  (Γ ((X T) ...)))
```

Since λ expressions show up in two places—the definition of M and the definition of V—the extended grammar overrides two productions, not just one. In addition, it adds a definition of types (T and S) and a definition of environments, Γ. While part I(10) represents type environments as finite functions, we choose a concrete representation for our Redex model: lists of pairs containing a variable and a type.

As specified in part I(10), the reduction relation for Simply Typed ISWIM is like the one for ISWIM, except that it reduces λ expressions with typed parameters, and it ignores the types during reductions.

```
(define t-iswim-red
  (reduction-relation
   t-iswim
   (--> (in-hole E ((λ X T M) V))
        (in-hole E (t-subst V X M))
        βv)
   (--> (in-hole E (o b ...))
        (in-hole E (δ (o b ...)))
        δ)))
```

The t-subst meta-function is just like subst in section 12.2, but it traverses λ expressions with typed parameters. Its definition is left as an exercise.

Once we have added types to ISWIM, we need a type checker; and for a Redex model, we want an algorithmic type checker. In part I(10), the algorithmic type checker is a *partial* function from type environments and expressions to types. While the domain-range description suggests a meta-function approach in Redex, we must still decide how to deal with the type checker's partiality.

When it comes to meta-functions, we actually have two choices for dealing with partiality. The first is to turn the partial mathematical function into a total meta-function, returning a distinct PLT Scheme value—for example, #f—when the mathematical function is undefined for some type. The alternative is to exploit the exception that a partial meta-function raises when it receives an input that is outside of the domain described through its clauses. In this section, we use the first approach; in the last section of this chapter, we demonstrate how to deal with the PLT Scheme exceptions that meta-functions may raise.

Recall that Simply Typed ISWIM is a family of languages that is parameterized over a set of literal constants and primitive operators. Our mathematical model therefore assumes the existence of functions B and Δ for assigning types to constants and operators. Thus, we start with a formulation of these functions in Redex.

```
;; B : b -> 'num or #f
;; returns the type of literal constants
(define-metafunction t-iswim
  [(B number) num]
  [(B any) #f])
```

```
;; Δ : (o T ...) -> T or #f
;; returns the result type for the operator
(define-metafunction t-iswim
  [(Δ (iszero num)) (-> num (-> num num))]
  [(Δ (add1 num)) num]
  [(Δ (sub1 num)) num]
  [(Δ (+ num num)) num]
  [(Δ (- num num)) num]
  [(Δ (* num num)) num]
  [(Δ (/ num num)) num]
  [(Δ (↑ num num)) num]
  [(Δ any) #f])
```

These definitions match those in part I(10.1) except for their last lines, which produce the result #f for any non-matching input. That is, B maps all numbers to the type num, and Δ accepts the primitive operators and the types of their arguments and returns the types of their results. To this end, the meta-function uses the special Redex pattern number, which matches an arbitrary number; in contrast, num is not special to Redex, so it is treated as the literal (that denotes the type of numbers).

Equipped with these basics, we can define the meta-function for type-checking Simply Typed ISWIM expressions in type environments.

```
;; TC : Γ M -> T or #f
;; type checks a term M in the environment Γ
(define-metafunction t-iswim
  [(TC Γ b)
   (B b)]
  [(TC Γ X)
   (TCvar Γ X)]
  [(TC ((Y S) ...) (λ X T M))
   (TCλ T (TC ((Y S) ... (X T)) M))]
  [(TC Γ (M N))
   (TCapp (TC Γ M) (TC Γ N))]
  [(TC Γ (o M ...))
   (TCo (o (TC Γ M) ...))])
```

Like the mathematical type-checking function, TC is defined by five cases, one for each syntactic form in ISWIM. In most cases, TC recursively computes the types of the sub-expressions and then calls an auxiliary meta-function to implement the case-specific type-checking rule for that case.

• The TCvar function exploits the concrete representation of environments to specify how to type check variable references. Specifically, the first case decomposes the environment into three pieces. The first and third are just sequences of bindings, and the second piece must be a single binding whose name matches the second argument (Y) to TCvar.

```
;; TCvar : Γ X -> T or #f
(define-metafunction t-iswim
  [(TCvar ((X T_1) ... (Y T_2) (Z T_3) ...) Y)
   T_2
   (side-condition (not (member (term Y) (term (Z ...)))))]
  [(TCvar Γ X) #f])
```

One subtle aspect of this definition is the side-condition on the first case, which ensures that the chosen binding is the right-most one. Consider type-checking this expression

(λ x num (λ x (-> num num) x))

When the type-checker encounters the gray-shaded occurrence of x, it is bound to the nearest enclosing x binding of type (-> num num). Because TC's clause for λ expressions adds this binding to the right end of the type environment, TCvar must retrieve it from there.

If this side-condition were not present, the TCvar meta-function would signal an exception:

```
TCvar:
  clause 0 matched (TCvar ((x num) (x (-> num num))) x)
  2 different ways
```

This error message indicates that the first clause in the function matched the input expression in multiple different ways, with different bindings for the pattern variables. Since meta-functions are expected to be functions, Redex checks for this condition and signals an error whenever a meta-function, as written, could produce multiple responses to a single input (via multiple matches in a single clause).

Note: An equivalent and conventional way to define TCvar uses three cases and skips the use of the potentially ambiguous double ellipses.

```
;; TCvar : Γ X -> T or #f
(define-metafunction t-iswim
  [(TCvar ((Y S) ... (X T)) X) T]
  [(TCvar ((Y S) ... (X T)) Z) (TCvar ((Y S) ...) Z)]
  [(TCvar () Z) #f])
```

Instead, this alternative definition of TCvar exploits the clause ordering of meta-functions so that in the second one, the variables X and Z are guaranteed to differ. The case when they are identical is covered by the first clause.

• The TCλ function's first argument is the type of a λ expression's parameter, and its second argument is the result of type-checking the body of the same λ expression. Thus, the second argument might be #f if the body failed to type-check.

```
;; TCλ : T (or/c T #f) -> T or #f
;; type checks a lambda expression, given the type
;; of the parameter and the type of the body
(define-metafunction t-iswim
  [(TCλ T S) (-> T S)]
  [(TCλ T #f) #f])
```

Accordingly, TCλ returns a function type only when the second argument is a proper type, and propagates #f otherwise.

• The TCapp function's first case checks to see if the function position's type is an arrow type and if the argument's type matches the domain of the function. If so, TCapp returns the range type.

```
;; TCapp : (or/c T #f) (or/c T #f) -> T or #f
(define-metafunction t-iswim
  [(TCapp (-> S T) S) T]
  [(TCapp any_1 any_2) #f])
```

The second case uses Redex's any pattern to cover all of the remaining cases: when either argument to TCapp fails to be a type; when the first argument is not a function type; and when the first one is a function type, but the second one fails to match the argument type of the first argument. In any of these situations, the entire program fails to type-check, so TCapp returns #f. Note that erasing the numeric labels in the pattern for the second case, i.e., using (TCApp any any) in lieu of (TCApp any_1 any_2), would restrict this pattern to match two identical arguments, as with any other duplicated pattern variable.

• The final auxiliary function deals with primitive operations.

```
;; TCo : o (or/c T #f) ... -> T or #f
(define-metafunction t-iswim
  [(TCo (o T ...)) (Δ (o T ...))]
  [(TCo (o any ...)) #f])
```

The second case again uses the `any` pattern to cover the case of a type error in the argument to a primitive operation.

Exercise 15.2. Modify the definition of `subst` in section 12.2 so that it deals with λ expressions with typed parameters.

15.3 Visual Debugging, Take 2.
Try to spot the bug before reading on. This model of Simply Typed ISWIM is quite small, less than 100 lines of code. Most conventional programmers would barely acknowledge that it needs test cases, because such trivial jobs are easy to get right.

So let us set up and run some test cases that explore the type checker.

```
> (test-equal
   (term (TC () ((λ x (-> num num) x) 5)))
   (term #f))

> (test-equal
   (term (TC () (+ x y)))
   (term #f))

> (test-equal
   (term (TC () (+ 1 2)))
   (term num))

> (test-equal
   (term (TC () (((λ x num (λ y num x)) 4) 2)))
   (term num))

> (test-results)
All 4 tests passed.
```

The first example demonstrates that the type checker finds a mismatch between a function's type and an argument's type in an application. The second example shows how the type checker deals with free variables. Note in both cases, the expected result is (term #f). For the last two examples, the type checker correctly says that the type of the given expression is (term num).

Now that we know that the type checker recognizes badly typed expressions, let us run some more successful test cases for programs.

```
> (test-equal
    (term (TC () ((λ x num 2) 4)))
    (term num))

> (test-equal
    (term (TC () (((λ x num (λ y num x)) 2) 3)))
    (term num))

> (test-equal
    (term (TC () (+ ((λ x num x) 1) 2)))
    (term num))

> (test-results)
All 3 tests passed.
```

Following our convention, programs are closed and have type (term num).
Of course, it is also natural to run examples once the type checker has con-
firmed their status as programs.

```
> (test-->> t-iswim-red
            (term ((λ x num 2) 4)) 2)
FAILED
expected: 2
  actual: 4

> (test-->> t-iswim-red
            (term (((λ x num (λ y num x)) 2) 3)) 2)
FAILED
expected: 2
  actual: (2 3)

> (test-->> t-iswim-red
            (term (+ ((λ x num x) 1) 2)) 3)

> (test-results)
2 tests failed (out of 3 total).
```

Of these three cases, the first two fail and the last one succeeds.
   At this point, we must switch from testing to debugging. The challenge
that we are facing here is that programs get stuck even though they type
check. Put differently, the model does not seem to satisfy the acclaimed relationship between the type checker and the reduction semantics. Given that

the proof of the type soundness shows that every expression in a reduction sequence type checks, we would like to see just that with Redex.

To do so, we supply a #:pred argument to traces. Here we use the type checker as a predicate, which means that well-typed expressions are colored white and expressions without types turn pink. We try the successful test case first.

```
(traces t-iswim-red
        (term (+ ((λ x num x) 1) 2))
        #:pred
        (λ (x) (term (TC () ,x))))
```

Since it type checks, the leftmost box in the screenshot below has a white background. The first reduction step applies the λ expression, producing (+ 1 2), which also type checks. Finally we have 3 and it type checks as (term num). As expected, tracing this expression does not uncover the error.

Let us move to the second example, which in the given model, produces the wrong result.

```
(traces t-iswim-red
        (term (((λ x num (λ y num x)) 2) 3))
        #:pred
        (λ (x) (term (TC () ,x))))
```

Clearly, the first expression is well-typed, and the TC function agrees. But the expression (2 3) is obviously a stuck expression, and TC recognizes this problem, not classifying the expression with any type. As a result, the second expression appears on a pink background.

This trace suggests that the bug must be in the βv rule. Looking at the rule, we see it calls t-subst with the wrong order of arguments. Hence, t-subst replaces all free occurrences of the function parameter in the argument with the body of the function.

Exercise 15.3. Why does the last test case not reveal the problem with βv?

Exercise 15.4. Introduce an error into the type checker and try to use `traces` to find the bug.

Exercise 15.5. We claim that the CS machine for State ISWIM (see exercise 14.7) does not introduce free variables into the control string unless they also occur in the domain of the store. Use `traces` to illustrate this claim for several examples.

15·4 Type Checking, Take 2.

This optional section demonstrates a different approach for turning partial functions from the mathematical model into Redex functions. Specifically, we transliterate the type checker in a one-to-one fashion from part I(10) into Redex.

```
;; TC : Γ M -> T
;; exception: exn:fail:redex if no type exists
;; type checks a term M in the environment Γ
(define-metafunction t-iswim
  [(TC Γ b) (B b)]
  [(TC Γ X) (TCvar Γ X)]
  [(TC ((Y S) ...) (λ X T M))
   (-> T (TC ((Y S) ... (X T)) M))]
  [(TC Γ (M N)) (TCapp (TC Γ M) (TC Γ N))]
  [(TC Γ (o M ...)) (Δ (o (TC Γ M) ...))])

;; TCvar : Γ X -> T
(define-metafunction t-iswim
  [(TCvar ((Y T_1) ... (X T_2) (Z T_3) ...) X)
   T_2
   (side-condition (not (member (term X) (term (Z ...)))))])

;; TCapp : T T -> T
(define-metafunction t-iswim
  [(TCapp (-> S T) S) T])
```

Both B and Δ are defined as before, minus the catch-all clauses.

As a result, none of the functions produces `#f` anymore, and none of the auxiliary functions must account for `#f` as a potential input. Instead, when Redex finds that none of the available patterns matches, it raises a PLT Scheme exception with an error message that informs Redex users which meta-function application failed.

The exception raised by Redex is an instance of an exn:fail:redex structure. Hence, the header of the TC meta-function mentions not only its signature and its purpose, but also the exceptions that it may raise; see the underlined comment in the above code display. The construct with-handlers
evaluates expressions within the dynamic extent of exception handlers. Using it, we can turn the type checker into a predicate for traces.

```
(define (simply-typed? x)
  (with-handlers ((exn:fail:redex? (lambda (x) #f)))
    (term (TC () ,x))))
```

The first line sets up exn:fail:redex? as the predicate for the handler
(lambda (x) #f). Hence, if the evaluation of (term (TC () ,x)) signals
an exception for which exn:fail:redex? produces true, the handler is applied to this exception and returns #f.

With this setup, we can run traces like before.

```
(traces t-iswim-red
        (term (+ ((λ x num x) 1) 2))
        #:pred
        simply-typed?)
```

The result is just like in the preceding section.

16 · Case Study 1
Order of Evaluation

Many programming languages with imperative constructs avoid specifying the order in which the arguments of a function call are evaluated. In doing so, language designers give language implementors the freedom to write compilers that rearrange the order in which argument expressions are evaluated. Such compilers produce code for function applications that is faster than code based on a fixed order of evaluation. Unfortunately, programmers cannot easily reason about the behavior of their programs, unless they strictly avoid expressions with imperative effects, i.e., **side-effects**.

Standard Scheme—as described in its R^6RS report [101]—is such a language with an indeterminate **order of argument evaluation**, i.e., the order of evaluation for the sub-expressions of a function application is undetermined.[1] In acknowledgment of the difficulties of reasoning about programs in such a world, the report insists that the evaluation of these sub-expressions be consistent with *some* fixed ordering, though possibly a different one each time the application is evaluated.

In this chapter, we develop a model of a variant of ISWIM with an R^6RS-compliant order of argument evaluation. We start with a primitive model and refine it several times, using the `traces` tool for guidance.

16·1 Adding Mutation.
Studying the under-specification of the order of argument evaluation demands the use of a language with effects. In principle, we could use Error ISWIM or its extensions or State ISWIM. These languages offer a variety of effects that complicate reasoning about programs when the order of argument evaluation is indeterminate. A model, however, should not use a large set of linguistic constructs but the smallest one needed to make the point. We therefore start with a small extension of ISWIM that provides a single mutable variable.

```
(define-extended-language iswim!
  iswim
  (P (V M))
  (M .... (get) (set M))
  (E .... (set E)))
```

---

[1] The evaluation order of programs in PLT Scheme is always left to right.

The `iswim!` language adds two expression forms to ISWIM, enabling programs to assign a value to a variable and to retrieve it. Technically, the extension consists of two distinct pieces. First, it introduces the category of programs P as a pair of a value and an expression. The left part holds the current value of the mutable variable, the right one is the control string. Second, `iswim!` extends the M non-terminal with `get` and `set` expressions for retrieving and modifying the assignable variable, respectively.

The `iswim!` extension of the ISWIM programming language does not modify any other syntactic categories. In particular, it inherits the specification of evaluation contexts E. As exercise 9.4 in part I(9) explains, our choice determines a left-to-right order of argument evaluation.

Of course, before we can confirm this claim with some examples, we need a reduction semantics, which we specify with four rules.

```
(define red!
  (reduction-relation
   iswim!
   (--> (V_s (in-hole E ((λ X M) V)))
        (V_s (in-hole E (subst M X V)))
        βv)
   (--> (V_s (in-hole E (o b ...)))
        (V_s (in-hole E (δ (o b ...)))))
        δ)
   (--> (V_s (in-hole E (get)))
        (V_s (in-hole E V_s))
        get)
   (--> (V_s (in-hole E (set V_n)))
        (V_n (in-hole E V_n))
        set)))
```

The first two are the same as the original ISWIM rules, but adapted so that they reduce the right part of a program P. The last two reduce `get` and `set` expressions, respectively. A `get` expression is replaced with the current content of the cell and a `set` expression updates the content of the cell with its argument, which it also returns.

Here is a our main example for the chapter and a reduction sequence created with `traces`.

```
(define main-example
  (term (0 (+ (set (+ (get) 1))
              (set (- (get) 1))))))
```

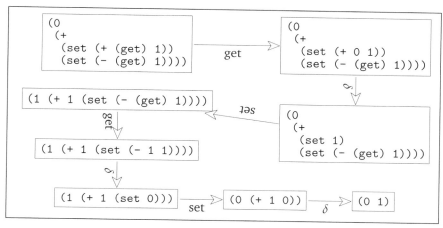

As claimed, the evaluation of the arguments to + proceeds from left to right in iswim!. That is, the program first increments the value of the cell to 1 and then decrements it again to 0, yielding the final configuration of (0 1).

In the remainder of this chapter, we focus on models of an unspecified order of argument evaluation for primitive applications.

16·2 Evaluation Everywhere.

As a warm-up exercise, we start with a model of the order of argument evaluation for the C programming language. Like the R⁶RS document, the C standard description does not specify the order of argument evaluation, but in contrast to R⁶RS, C's order of argument evaluation is completely unspecified. Of course, the fewer constraints a document contains the easier it is to model.

In order to evaluate the sub-expressions of primitive applications in an arbitrary order, we simply need to change the set of evaluation contexts.

```
(define-extended-language C-lang
  iswim!
  (E hole (V E) (E M) (o M ... E M ...) (set E)))
```

These evaluation contexts specify that, in contrast to iswim, reductions can take place anywhere in an application. Indeed, the reduction process can switch focus from one argument expression to another in arbitrary ways.

Otherwise it suffices to re-interpret the rules using the new grammar.

```
(define C-red
  (extend-reduction-relation red! C-lang))
```

Let us take a look at the result of applying traces to main-example now.

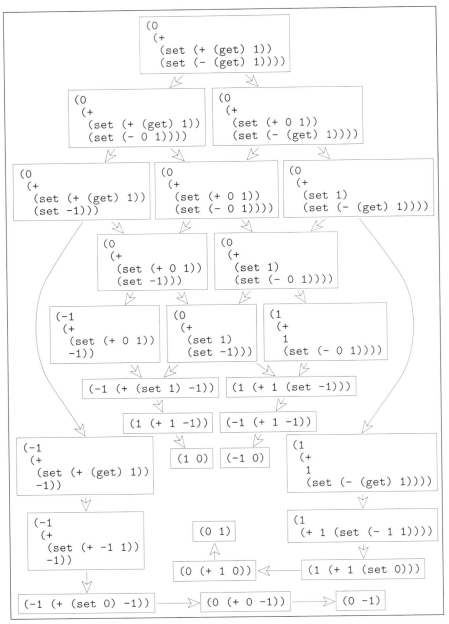

An inspection of the graph shows that the arguments are evaluated in an interleaving manner. Of the four final results near the bottom of the graph, two cases store a final variable value of 0; in the other two cases, we have -1 and 1 in the cell. Tracing through the graph, we can see that the two non-zero final outcomes in the middle correspond to an evaluation that reduces the two get expressions before either of the set expressions is evaluated. Since the two get expressions are in different arguments to the + primitive, these reduction sequences correspond to concurrent or interleaving evaluations that switch back and forth between the two arguments.

Exercise 16.1. Use test--`>>` to develop a test suite for iswim! equipped with C-red. Note that the form accepts not just a single expected result but a sequence of results. See the documentation for details.

$16 \cdot 3$ R^6RS: A First Attempt. R^6RS Scheme disallows interleaving evaluations of primitive applications. The only legitimate outcomes are those of the two outermost paths in the above graph. The right-hand path corresponds to the choice of evaluating the left argument of the outermost + expression first; along the left-hand path, the right argument of the same + expression is reduced first. Thus, our goal is to construct a reduction system that preserves the outermost paths, but not the inner ones.

One way to fix an order of evaluation is to add a new form of primitive application, one that explicitly marks the expression to be reduced to a value next. Then reductions may insert a marker into a primitive application when none is present, and the evaluation contexts would allow reductions only when a marker is present. Another way is to express the random choice in the existing language. The viability of this second strategy clearly depends on the expressive power [33] of the subject language. When it is a viable strategy—as it is here—it is preferable to the first one because it avoids the many proof-technical[2] problems of artificial constructs.

We implement the stay-with-the-language strategy with a two-pronged approach. On the one hand, we do not allow reductions to take place within arbitrary primitive applications; on the other hand, we introduce reductions that transform primitive applications so that the restricted reductions may reduce a primitive application into a form where the δ rule may fire.

Let us start with the grammar of evaluation contexts. The following sch language restricts the set of evaluation contexts of iswim! so that reductions in primitive applications apply only when there is exactly one expression that is not already a value.

---

[2]Constructs introduced to express intermediate states must satisfy invariants that do not necessarily hold if they are a part of the regular language syntax. Hence, it is often necessary to establish these invariants via separate lemmas and to carry them through proofs separately.

```
(define-extended-language sch
  iswim!
  (E hole (V E) (E M) (o V ... E V ...) (set E)))
```

The reduction that balances this restriction transforms a primitive application expression into one with only a single reducible expression by lifting out a randomly chosen argument into a λ application.

```
(define sch1-red
  (extend-reduction-relation
   red!
   sch
   (--> (in-hole E (o M_1 ... M_2 M_3 ...))
        (in-hole E ((λ X (o M_1 ... X M_3 ...))
                    M_2))
        lift
        (fresh X))))
```

The key to this new reduction is a Redex pattern that matches an arbitrary primitive application in multiple, different ways. More precisely, the pattern (o M_1 ... M_2 M_3 ...) matches once for each argument, binding the chosen argument to M2. Consider matching the pattern with the expression (+ (* 1 2) (↑ 3 4)).

```
> (redex-match sch
               (o M_1 ... M_2 M_3 ...)
               (term (+ (* 1 2) (↑ 3 4))))
(list
 (make-match
  (list
   (make-bind 'M_1 (list (list '* 1 2)))
   (make-bind 'M_2 (list '↑ 3 4))
   (make-bind 'M_3 empty)
   (make-bind 'o '+)))
 (make-match
  (list
   (make-bind 'M_1 empty)
   (make-bind 'M_2 (list '* 1 2))
   (make-bind 'M_3 (list (list '↑ 3 4)))
   (make-bind 'o '+))))
```

What we get is a list of two matches: one where M_2 matches (↑ 3 4) and another one where it matches (* 1 2). In both cases, M_1 ... and M_3 ... match all of the expressions to the left and right of M_2, respectively.

Turning to main-example, we can see that it too matches in two different ways, because there are two arguments to the outer addition expression.

```
> (redex-match sch
              (o M_1 ... M_2 M_3 ...)
              (term (+ (set (+ (get) 1))
                       (set (- (get) 1)))))
(list
 (make-match
  (list
   (make-bind
    'M_1
    (list (list 'set (list '+ (list 'get) 1))))
   (make-bind
    'M_2
    (list 'set (list '- (list 'get) 1)))
   (make-bind 'M_3 empty)
   (make-bind 'o '+)))
 (make-match
  (list
   (make-bind 'M_1 empty)
   (make-bind
    'M_2
    (list 'set (list '+ (list 'get) 1)))
   (make-bind
    'M_3
    (list (list 'set (list '- (list 'get) 1))))
   (make-bind 'o '+))))
```

The first match binds M_2 to the second argument to the outermost addition expression, namely (set (- (get) 1)), and the second result binds M_2 to the first argument (set (+ (get) 1)).

It is now easy to understand how the lift reduction rule in sch1-red works. The pattern (o M_1 ... M_2 M_3 ...) matches as many times as there are arguments, binding the "pivot" argument to M2. For each match, the reduction relation creates an application of λ expression and argument M2, meaning the reduction sequence branches. Overall, the reduction gradually turns the primitive application into one that has only one reducible expression.

For example, if we applied `lift` to (+ (↑ 1 2) (* 1 2)), we would get ((λ x (+ x (↑ 3 4))) (* 1 2)) and ((λ x (+ (* 1 2) x)) (↑ 3 4)). Of course, this reduction works only because we generate a fresh occurrence of X rather than just always using X.

To understand how our example expression reduces with the new reduction relation, we use `traces` to explore its reduction graph.

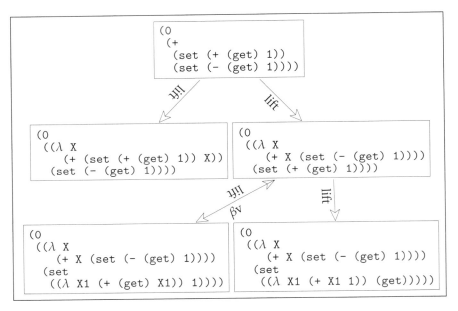

The first two steps look promising; each lifts out one of the arguments to the outermost + expression. A look at the bottom left expression, however, reveals that the reduction system fails us. The expression is connected to the one in the top middle by an arrow with two arrowheads, which indicates that the system reduces these expressions to each other.

A second look shows that the step from the middle row to the bottom right transforms (+ (get) 1) to ((λ x1 (+ (get) x1)) 1). The step in the other direction is a plain β_v reduction. In other words, the `lift` relation moves a value out of a primitive application, and doing so is completely useless. It merely pollutes reduction sequences with cycles when there should not be any. After all, the goal is to characterize an abstract machine that reduces programs to values, and cycles do not belong into such a machine.

16·4 R⁶RS: A Second Attempt. Now that we have identified the problem with the proposed `lift` reduction, it is fairly straight-

forward to fix it. Specifically, we need to restrain the `lift` relation so that it does not apply when the targeted expression is already a value.

We start with the formulation of the set NV of non-values.[3]

```
(define-extended-language sch/nv
  sch
  (NV (side-condition M_1 (not (V? (term M_1))))))

(define V? (redex-match sch V))
```

The introduction of NV uses a new feature of redex grammars. Instead of a production proper, the clause specifies a pattern (M_1) and restricts it via a PLT Scheme predicate. Technically, we are using a `side-condition` on patterns. Such a condition consists of two parts: the first one is a pattern, the second one is a PLT Scheme expression that involves pattern variables. Redex uses such productions by first matching the pattern with some expression and then evaluating the PLT Scheme expression on the match. If the latter produces #t, the complete `side-condition` pattern itself matches.

In this case, the NV non-terminal is an `iswim!` expression that does not satisfy the V? predicate. The latter is defined via a two-argument `redex-match`, enforcing that the expression does not also belong to the set V of values. Using the newly defined non-terminal NV, we can reformulate the reduction for lifting expressions.

```
(define sch2-red
  (extend-reduction-relation
   red!
   sch/nv
   (--> (in-hole E (o M_1 ... NV M_3 ...))
        (in-hole E ((λ X (o M_1 ... X M_3 ...))
                    NV))
        lift
        (fresh X))))
```

This new formulation ensures that whatever the relation lifts is not a value.

Once again, we test this model by running `traces` on `main-example`. As in the preceding section, the following reduction graph starts correctly, but quickly reveals a flaw in the reduction sequence.

---

[3]Compare with Moggi's computational λ-calculus [78].

```
(0
 (+
  (set (+ (get) 1))
  (set (- (get) 1))))
```

```
(0
 ((λ X
   (+ (set (+ (get) 1)) X))
  (set (- (get) 1))))
```

```
(0
 ((λ X
   (+ X (set (- (get) 1))))
  (set (+ (get) 1))))
```

```
(0
 ((λ X (+ X (set (- (get) 1))))
  (set ((λ X1 (+ X1 1)) (get)))))
```

The step leading to the bottommost expression transforms the expression (-
(get) 1) into ((λ x1 (- x1 1)) (get)). This lifts out an expression even
though it is already the only expression that needs to be evaluated.

16·5 R⁶RS: Finally.

To rectify such useless lifts, we need to restrict
our attention to primitive application expressions that contain
at least two non-values. Using the technique of multiple ellipses, we can
formulate such a pattern with little extra effort.

```
(define sch3-red
  (extend-reduction-relation
   red!
   sch/nv
   (--> (in-hole E (o M_1 ... NV_1 M_2 ... NV_2 M_3 ...))
        (in-hole E ((λ X (o M_1 ... X M_2 ... NV_2 M_3 ...))
                    NV_1))
        left-lift
        (fresh X))

   (--> (in-hole E (o M_1 ... NV_1 M_2 ... NV_2 M_3 ...))
        (in-hole E ((λ X (o M_1 ... NV_1 M_2 ... X M_3 ...))
                    NV_2))
        right-lift
        (fresh X))))
```

All that is needed is a second occurrence of NV and enough ellipsis patterns
to accommodate other expressions. We then use this pattern for two rules:
one of them lifts the left non-value and the other one lifts the right one.

A reduction graph for `main-example` follows.

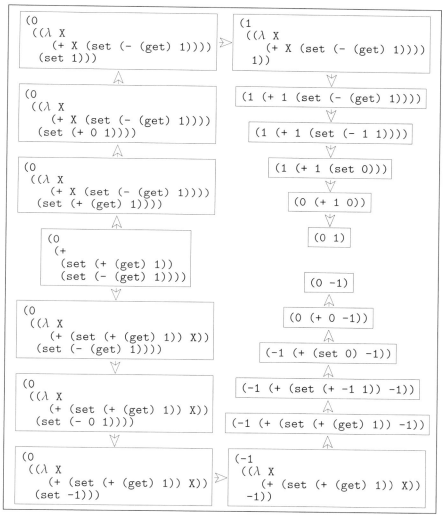

It shows, sch3-red is a "perfect" model of the R^{6}RS constraint on the order of argument evaluation. The graph contains a single branch, meaning the evaluator chooses an order for the outermost primitive application and the rest of the evaluation is completely determined. Of course, the existence of a single choice point also implies that there are exactly two feasible outcomes: one with a result of 1 and another one with a result of -1. The assignable variable stands for 0 in both cases.

It is also possible for expressions to evaluate to the same value under all possible reduction paths while differing entirely on the store. Consider this program:

```
(0 (+ (set 1) (set 2)))
```

It terminates with either 1 or 2 in the mutable cell, depending on the order of argument evaluation. In either case, the result of the expression is 3.

Both examples illustrate the lack of confluence in the model. It is exactly the kind of under-specification that the authors of the R^{6}RS standard desired. Scaling this strategy to general function applications is now an exercise.

17 · Case Study 2
Continuations as Values

At this point, we have covered enough of Redex to tackle all kinds of language models, in particular all the flavors of ISWIM from part I: functional ISWIM; ISWIM with exceptions and handlers; ISWIM with full-fledged continuations; and ISWIM with assignment statements. The material also suffices for many similar languages that can be found in the research literature. One piece of the literature, namely, modeling first-class continuation objects, requires some additional machinery.

One classical representation of reified continuations are λ expressions that encapsulate some control context. This kind of representation is easy to deal with. A different kind of representation—and one commonly found in the literature on control—uses evaluation contexts directly as values. Doing so exploits assumptions about context decompositions that a formal framework such as Redex simply cannot use.

In this chapter, we use two models to explore ISWIM equipped with the `call-with-current-continuation` function [20], also known as `call/cc`. The first model uses a λ-based representation; the second one maps continuations to evaluation contexts and introduces the necessary Redex mechanism for doing so.

17·1 Continuations as Functions. Following the tradition in the literature, we create our continuation-oriented model of flow of control as an extension of plain ISWIM.

```
(define-extended-language c-iswim
  iswim
  (M ....
     (call/cc M)
     (abort M))
  (E ....
     (call/cc E)))
```

The definition of `c-iswim` extends `iswim` with two constructs: `abort`, for terminating a computation and switching to another one, and `call/cc`, for grabbing the current rest of the computation—the so-called **continuation**— and turning it into a first-class value—dubbed **continuation object** or, if no confusion is possible, just continuation. In addition, the grammar extends the productions for evaluation contexts so that the sub-expression `call/cc` is evaluated; the lack of a similar evaluation context for `abort` implies that this construct does not evaluate its sub-expression.

The reduction system of ISWIM requires two extensions to cope with the two syntactic additions.

```
(define c-iswim-red
  (extend-reduction-relation
   iswim-red
   c-iswim
   (--> (in-hole E (call/cc V))
        (in-hole E (V (λ X (abort (in-hole E X)))))
        (fresh X)
        call/cc)
   (--> (in-hole E (abort M))
        M
        throw)))
```

The first rule handles an application of `call/cc`. Its contractum shows how `call/cc` grabs the evaluation context and constructs a λ expression from it. When this function is applied to some argument U, the `abort` expression discards the then-current evaluation context and causes the evaluation of `E[U]`, i.e., the encapsulated context filled with U. In short, `call/cc` and `abort` collaborate so that programs may switch back and forth between different evaluation contexts or continuations.

Note how the `call/cc` rule demands with (`fresh X`) that the parameter of the new function does not interfere with any free variables on the left-hand side of the rule. Technically, the constraint is equivalent to

```
(where X ,(variable-not-in (term (in-hole E V)) 'X))
```

Indeed, `variable-not-in` chooses 'X as a variable if it is available, or it deterministically creates a derivative of the symbol so that results and graphs become repeatable. Of course, in a paper-and-pencil model, we could and would loosen this constraint to

```
(where X ,(variable-not-in (term E) 'X))
```

i.e., we would only demand that X does not occur in E. Even though evaluation contexts for program reductions are already closed—because reductions do not create free variables—adding this `fresh` constraint ensures that we can continue to use the reduction system for open expressions, too.

While this chapter cannot possibly begin to explain the pragmatics of continuations, let us consider an example that uses a continuation to abort a doomed use of a primitive operation:

```
(+
  1
  (call/cc
    (λ k
      (+ (λ y y) (k 12)))))
```

The inner, underlined + expression has a λ expression as its first argument, meaning that if it ever were to become the focus of evaluation, the evaluation would get stuck. However, the following reduction graph shows that the application of the continuation erases this primitive application before anything bad can happen.

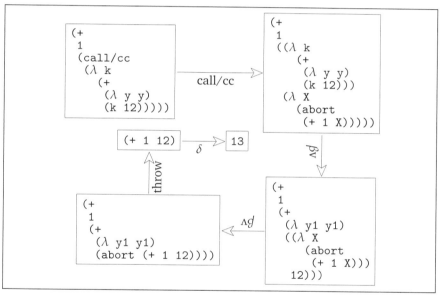

This can be seen most clearly in the expression in the middle of the second row. At this point, the abort expression has one sub-expression: the original context of the call/cc operation filled with 12, the argument to k. The next step erases the context of the abort expression and replaces it with its sub-expression, which then reduces to 13.

17·2 Continuations as Evaluation Contexts.

Instead of reifying continuations as "abortive" functions, it is also possible to treat contexts themselves as values that are introduced by call/cc and eliminated via application. Doing so, however, requires an extension to Redex, and to demonstrate why, we first study an ill-fated attempt. Following that, we introduce a new Redex construct to get the model of the first attempt to work.

Attempt 1. Consider the following extension of ISWIM. Like the one in the preceding section, it adds `call/cc` expressions and evaluation contexts for `call/cc` expressions to the grammar.

```
(define-extended-language ☠-iswim
  iswim
  (M ....
     (call/cc M)
     (cont E))
  (V ....
     (cont E))
  (E ....
     (call/cc E)))
```

Unlike the first model, this one uses evaluation contexts as expressions and values. These contexts are wrapped with the constructor `cont` to distinguish them from those contexts used to pick out redexes. Note how the model does not include `abort` expressions, because the termination action of a continuation application is built into the reduction rule for context applications.[1]

As in the preceding section, there are two reduction rules, one for grabbing and one for throwing a continuation.

```
(define ☠-iswim-red
  (extend-reduction-relation
   iswim-red
   ☠-iswim
   (--> (in-hole E (call/cc V))
        (in-hole E (V (cont E)))
        call/cc)
   (--> (in-hole E_1 ((cont E_2) V))
        (in-hole E_2 V)
        throw)))
```

The first rule simply grabs the evaluation context, turns it into a value with `cont`, and applies the argument of `call/cc` to this reified continuation. The second one transforms the application of an evaluation context-turned-value

---

[1]It is now impossible to macro-express [33] `abort` but this is of no concern here.

to some other value V into the evaluation context filled with V; the surround-ing context is discarded during this process.

Although this reduction system looks rather elegant, it suffers from a fa-tal flaw; if we use it on any expression involving `call/cc`, Redex reports an error. Roughly speaking, the problem is that any expression derived from the non-terminal V may now contain a hole. This possibility, in turn, causes Redex to consider sub-expressions of values as candidates for a context de-composition, even though sub-expressions of values clearly should not be reduced for an standard reduction semantics.

The problem manifests itself with an error message from Redex that a single expression can have a hole in two different places. For example, when the following `c-iswim` expression is supplied to `appy-reduction-relation*`

```
(+ 42 ((λ k (k 1)) (cont (+ 42 hole))))
```

Redex signals the error

```
matcher.ss: found two holes
```

This is Redex's way of saying that it failed to decompose the expression into a context with a single hole and a redex.

Let us look at how Redex uses the productions for E when it attempts to decompose a program into a context and a redex. Given that E is a non-terminal, Redex considers all derivations possible according to the grammar. Here is the problematic derivation:

```
        E
--> (E V)
--> (hole V)
--> (hole (cont E))
--> (hole (cont hole))
```

It implies that when Redex matches E against some expression, it must con-sider matching it with the pattern `(hole (cont hole))`. That pattern, how-ever, contains two holes, and Redex therefore signals an error.

In summary, this example reveals a fundamental assumption behind Re-dex's design. Redex is built to apply notions of reduction in context, but only in contexts with a single hole. Put differently, Redex cannot reduce two re-dexes in two distinct positions simultaneously; in particular, it is impossible to use Redex for modeling parallel reductions such as those used for the proof of the Church-Rosser lemma in part I(4). In this section, the restriction has a positive consequence in that it prevents us from introducing ambiguities into the grammar and the reduction system of a popular model of continuations.

Attempt 2.   To support the design principle and the notion of contexts-as-values at the same time, Redex provides `hide-hole`. A pattern of the form `(hide-hole P)` matches the same expressions as the pattern P does, but `hide-hole` tells Redex not to consider P as the source of a hole during expression decomposition.

Since we know that the evaluation contexts used inside `cont` should not be considered places where evaluation should take place, we can exploit `hide-hole` to inform Redex of this choice for a revision of our model.

```
(define-extended-language ☺-iswim
  iswim
  (M ....
     (call/cc M)
     (cont (hide-hole E)))
  (V ....
     (cont (hide-hole E)))
  (E ....
     (call/cc E)))
```

Using this new definition of M and V, the reduction rules in 💀-iswim-red behave properly. The trace below shows how this revised reduction system is used to reduce the example from section 17.1.

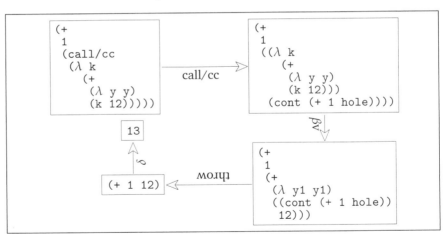

As before, the example reduces to 13. Our continuations-as-contexts model requires one less step, though, than the continuations-as-functions model. The `abort` step in the latter is added to the reduction of applications of continuations in the former.

18 · Typesetting

The delivery of a major software product requires more than just running the software. Software engineers package up the components into one bundle, install them on all intended target platforms, check each installation, upload the product to servers, and perform many other such tasks. Of course, good software engineering teams automate this step with programmed scripts, just like they automate as many other parts of the process as possible.

A semantics engineer delivers a product, too. The product bundle includes the model, its test cases, and documentation. Documentation usually implies a paper, at least in the form of a technical report.[1] Redex provides comprehensive support for typesetting models, grammars, reduction-relations, and meta-functions. To get a typeset model to look just right, a semantics engineer may need to script Redex's typesetting machinery, which requires a solid understanding of how Redex is connected to its host language, PLT Scheme.

In this chapter, we demonstrate Redex's typesetting support. We begin with the parts that are completely automated. Starting with the third section, we describe the data structures that are used to represent models for typesetting, and we demonstrate how to manipulate the representation to improve typesetting results where necessary. For a complete understanding of these last few sections, a reader may need to consult the PLT Scheme documentation.

18·1 The Defaults.
Getting started with Redex's typesetting tools is straightforward. Indeed, if the model does not contain any escapes to PLT Scheme code, Redex can typeset it without any configuration at all.

Redex provides three functions for typesetting pieces of models:

1. `render-language`,

2. `render-reduction-relation`, and

3. `render-metafunction`.

---

[1] A semantics engineer might also deliver a presentation. For that purpose, the authors use PLT Slideshow (see documentation), which can work directly with the `pict`s that Redex generates when typesetting models.

Each function accepts one or two arguments. The first argument is the appropriate piece of a model: a language, a reduction-relation, or a metafunction. The second, optional argument is a file name and, if it is present, the typeset piece of the model is saved as PostScript in the named file. More precisely, these functions produce an Encapsulated PostScript file, which is suitable for inclusion into larger documents.

When no file name is supplied, then instead of generating a PostScript file, the functions produce a pict value. A pict encapsulates an arbitrary drawing procedure with bounding-box information. DrScheme can render picts values directly, and PLT Scheme scripts can use them as first-class values. For now, there is no need to understand picts in any detail. We use them here so that we can demonstrate how a semantics engineer interactively uses typesetting functions for rendering a model.

Rendering the iswim grammar produces an image that uses the standard notation for writing down grammars. In particular, the rendered form uses "::=" in grammar productions to separate non-terminals from their definitions, and it uses a vertical bar to separate alternatives.[2]

```
> (render-language iswim)
```
$M, N, L, K ::= X \mid (\lambda X M) \mid (M M) \mid b \mid (o2\ M M) \mid (o1\ M)$
$o ::= o1 \mid o2$
$o1 ::= add1 \mid sub1 \mid iszero$
$o2 ::= + \mid - \mid * \mid \uparrow$
$b ::= number$
$V, U, W ::= b \mid X \mid (\lambda X M)$
$E ::= [] \mid (V E) \mid (E M) \mid (o\ V\ ...\ E M\ ...)$
$X, Y, Z ::= variable\text{-}not\text{-}otherwise\text{-}mentioned$

---

[2]The boxes in this section simulate DrScheme's interactive behavior by using Redex to create encapsulated PostScript. To get a sense of how it would look in DrScheme, here is a screenshot.

Welcome to <u>DrScheme</u>, version 4.1.4 [3m].
Language: Module; memory limit: 512 megabytes.
```
> (render-language iswim)
```
$M, N, L, K ::= X \mid (\lambda X M) \mid (M M) \mid b \mid (o2\ M M) \mid (o1\ M)$
$o ::= o1 \mid o2$
$o1 ::= add1 \mid sub1 \mid iszero$
$o2 ::= + \mid - \mid * \mid \uparrow$
$b ::= number$
$V, U, W ::= b \mid X \mid (\lambda X M)$
$E ::= [] \mid (V E) \mid (E M) \mid (o\ V\ ...\ E M\ ...)$
$X, Y, Z ::= variable\text{-}not\text{-}otherwise\text{-}mentioned$

Like languages, reduction relations are typeset using conventional mathematics notation. In particular, a context is filled with the redex and contractum, respectively, and reduction relations are rendered with a plain arrow. The default style breaks rules into two lines, placing the arrow and optional label on the right-hand side of the first line.

```
> (render-reduction-relation iswim-red)
```
$$E[((\lambda\, X\, M)\, V)] \longrightarrow (\beta v)$$
$$E[\textsc{subst}[\![M, X, V]\!]\ ]$$

$$E[(o\, b\, ...)] \longrightarrow \qquad (\delta)$$
$$E[\delta[\![(o\, b\, ...)]\!]\ ]$$

Note how uses of meta-functions employ a SMALL CAPS font and embed the arguments between blackboard-bold brackets, so that meta-function uses stand out as separate entities.

Finally, the definitions of meta-functions are typeset in the "by clauses" manner used in mathematics books and in some functional and logical programming languages.

```
> (render-metafunction δ)
```
$$\delta[\![(\text{iszero } 0)]\!] = (\lambda\, x\, (\lambda\, y\, x))$$
$$\delta[\![(\text{iszero } b)]\!] = (\lambda\, x\, (\lambda\, y\, y))$$
$$\delta[\![(\text{add1 } b)]\!] = (\texttt{add1 } b)$$
$$\delta[\![(\text{sub1 } b)]\!] = (\texttt{sub1 } b)$$
$$\delta[\![(+ \, b_1\, b_2)]\!] = (\texttt{+ } b_1\ b_2)$$
$$\delta[\![(- \, b_1\, b_2)]\!] = (\texttt{- } b_1\ b_2)$$
$$\delta[\![(* \, b_1\, b_2)]\!] = (\texttt{* } b_1\ b_2)$$
$$\delta[\![(\uparrow \, b_1\, b_2)]\!] = (\texttt{expt } b_1\ b_2)$$

The ordering of clauses matches the one from the Redex model. As with uses of meta-functions, the formal parameters—actually patterns—are again embedded in blackboard-bold brackets.

While the ISWIM language and its reduction relation look reasonable by default, the typesetting of the δ meta-function has portions that are highlighted with a pink background and use a fixed-width font. This highlighting informs readers that the model's definition escapes to PLT Scheme code, which indicates that Redex has no rules for typesetting these portions in a mathematical style. Later, in section 18.5, we explain how to replace those pink fragments with mathematical expressions.

18·2 **Simple Specializations.** Some adjustments to Redex's typesetting are straightforward and do not require the use of much PLT Scheme. Most importantly, Redex uses the line breaks of the model's code to insert line breaks in the typeset output. Often, a semantics engineer can create a properly formatted figure with just a few tweaks to the source grammars, reduction relations, and meta-functions.

A source program's text is usually written with a fixed-width font, while a typeset model uses variable-width fonts, so the layout of a typeset model cannot exactly match the source. To manage this difference, Redex positions the beginning of each line relative to other lines in a way that matches the source. Thus, on the right-hand side of the following example, b_2 and b_3 are lined up in the output, because b_3 starts in the same column as b_2 in the original source.

```
> (render-reduction-relation      > (render-reduction-relation
   (reduction-relation               (reduction-relation
    iswim                             iswim
    (--> (* b_1 (+ b_2 b_3))          (--> (* b_1
         (+ (* b_1 b_2)                     (+ b_2
            (* b_1 b_3)))))               b_3))
(* b₁ (+ b₂ b₃)) ⟶                    (+ (* b_1
(+ (* b₁ b₂)                                b_2)
   (* b₁ b₃))                            (* b_1
                                           b_3)))))
                                   (* b₁        ⟶
                                      (+ b₂
                                        b₃))
                                   (+ (* b₁
                                       b₂)
                                     (* b₁
                                       b₃))
```

After the beginning of each line is positioned, Redex typesets the rest of the line independently. In the example, the closing parenthesis following each of b_2 and b_3 line up only because the subscript "2" and "3" have the same width. If the subscripts were twee and drie, the closing parentheses would not line up in the output, since "b_{twee}" and "b_{drie}" have different widths with variable-width fonts.

Eliding Nonterminals. Our Redex grammar of ISWIM specifies both the language and the sets of grammatical elements needed to specify a reduction semantics. Even though the specification of a single grammar makes the model concise and easy to work with, a single grammar is often inappropriate in a paper. At least in a typical setting, the two pieces should be presented in two distinct steps. Similarly, it is often understood that X, Y, and Z stand for variables, so that there is no need for displaying their definitions in a grammar. Generally speaking, it is common that a semantics engineer wishes to elide certain non-terminals in some PostScript figures.

For this reason, the `render-language` function accepts an optional argument that specifies the set of non-terminals to include in the rendering of a grammar. In the following example, a call to `language-nts` returns the list of non-terminals in the ISWIM grammar as symbols. The PLT Scheme function `remove*` is used to elide the non-terminals for variables, values, and evaluation contexts from the list, because those are needed only for the semantics.

```
> (render-language
    iswim
    #:nts
    (remove* '(X Y Z V U W E) (language-nts iswim)))
```
$$M, N, L, K ::= X \mid (\lambda\, X\, M) \mid (M\, M) \mid b \mid (o2\, M\, M) \mid (o1\, M)$$
$$o ::= o1 \mid o2$$
$$o1 ::= \mathsf{add1} \mid \mathsf{sub1} \mid \mathsf{iszero}$$
$$o2 ::= + \mid - \mid * \mid \uparrow$$
$$b ::= number$$

Conversely, the next sample interaction displays just the parts of the `iswim` language grammar that are introduced to specify the reduction relations. In other words, it creates an image for the value and evaluation context pieces, which are listed directly with `#:nts`.

```
> (render-language iswim #:nts '(U V W E))
```
$$V, U, W ::= b \mid X \mid (\lambda\, X\, M)$$
$$E ::= [] \mid (V\, E) \mid (E\, M) \mid (o\, V \ldots E\, M \ldots)$$

Reduction Relations Styles. Reduction relations can be typeset in a number of different styles. By default, the left-hand side and the right-hand side of a rule are placed on top of each other, with the arrow at the end of the first line. Redex also supports a style where the arrows are along the left-hand side column, and vertical space is reduced between rules as much as possible. Specify this style by supplying `'compact-vertical` after the `#:style` keyword.

```
> (render-reduction-relation iswim-red
                             #:style 'compact-vertical)
```
$$E[((\lambda\, X\, M)\, V)] \qquad (\beta\mathsf{v})$$
$$\longrightarrow E[\textsc{subst}[\![M, X, V]\!]\,]$$

$$E[(o\; b\; ...)] \qquad\qquad (\delta)$$
$$\longrightarrow E[\delta[\![(o\; b\; ...)]\!]\,]$$

Another option is to use Redex's 'horizontal style for rendering reduction relations, which fits the entire ISWIM relation on two lines.

```
> (render-reduction-relation iswim-red
                             #:style 'horizontal)
```
$$E[((\lambda\, X\, M)\, V)] \longrightarrow E[\textsc{subst}[\![M, X, V]\!]\,]\; (\beta\mathsf{v})$$

$$E[(o\; b\; ...)] \longrightarrow E[\delta[\![(o\; b\; ...)]\!]\,]\qquad (\delta)$$

Redex supports a few other styles for typesetting reduction relations. See `render-reduction-relation` in the documentation.

Font Substitutions. Redex provides six parameters that control the fonts and font sizes used with the typesetting functions: `label-style`, `literal-style`, `metafunction-style`, `non-terminal-style`, `default-style`, and `non-terminal-subscript-style`. The full definition of the style datatype is fairly complex, but one possibility is to simply create a font object—specifying size, weight, italics, underline, etc.—and install that as a style. See the documentation for details on parameters, font parameters, and fonts.

Beyond font customizations, Redex supports other simple tweaks to the layout, including changing the formatting of the arrows in the reduction relation, using ordinary quote marks instead of curly quote marks for strings, and various spacing parameters, e.g., the separation between reduction rules.

18·3 The `lw` Structure.

The task of rendering Redex models as `pict`s is fundamentally a language-processing problem. The Redex typesetting functions parse the model's elements,[3] create a parse tree, analyze it, and finally traverse it again to generate `pict`s. For the cases when the generated `pict` is not automatically typeset as desired, Redex allows PLT Scheme scripts to manipulate the parse tree before it is used to generate a `pict`.

---

[3]Of course, the PLT Scheme reader performs much of the parsing work for Redex.

Thus, a semantics engineer who wishes to script the `pict` rendering process must understand the parse trees behind the process. In principle, a parse tree is just an instance of `lw` structures:

```
(define-struct lw
  (e line line-span column column-span unq? metafunction?))
```

Here is a typed view [107] of the same `define-struct` declaration:

```
(define-type-alias ParseTree
  (U Symbol String (Listof (U 'spring lw)) Pict))
(define-struct: lw ([e : ParseTree]
                    [line : Integer]
                    [line-span : Integer]
                    [column : Integer]
                    [column-span : Integer]
                    [unq? : Boolean]
                    [metafunction? : Boolean]))
```

As always with parse trees, every expression in, say, a Redex grammar is mapped to an instance of `lw`. If some given expression has sub-expressions, their representations are stored in the e field of the `lw` structure.

The rest of the section is an introduction to the nature of `lw` structures and their creation process. The remaining sections explains hooks that Redex provides for rewriting `lw` parse trees globally.

Each instance of `lw` has seven fields:

- **e**: This field contains the actual content of the corresponding piece of the program text and is one of the following values:

  - a symbol, if the original program text is an identifier;
  - a string that contains the characters representing any other kind of expression (numbers, booleans, etc);
  - a list of `lw` structures, possibly including `'spring` (see below);
  - or a `pict`.

  Naturally, Redex never creates a parse tree with a `pict` in an e field directly, but scripts may insert them.

- **line** & **line-span**: These two fields contain the starting line number and the number of extra lines that the corresponding text spans.

- **column** & **column-span**: These two fields contain numbers indicating the start column and the column span of the corresponding source text. If the text spans multiple lines, the column span is the span for the last—not necessarily the widest—of the lines (starting from column 0).

- **unq?**: This field indicates if the corresponding expression is unquoted, i.e., ordinary PLT Scheme code.

- **metafunction?**: This field indicates whether the corresponding piece of program text represents the use of a meta-function.

The syntactic form `to-lw` parses Redex expressions into `lw` parse trees. Once we have a parse tree, we can use `render-lw` to generate a `pict` from it; this latter form accepts a language and an `lw` structure, and it produces a `pict`. The remaining subsections explain how these two tools collaborate.

Atomic Expressions. Consider the case of non-terminal X in `iswim`.

```
> (to-lw X)                     | > (render-lw iswim (to-lw X))
(make-lw 'X 1 0 7 1 #f #f)      | X
```

In this case, the e field of the parse tree is the identifier, which is represented as a symbol. It does not span any extra lines, but it spans the seventh column. Because the text is neither unquoted nor a meta-function call, the last two arguments are #f. When the parse tree is typeset, the *X* is rendered in italics.

A terminal is typeset in a sans-serif font by default.

```
> (to-lw x)                     | > (render-lw iswim (to-lw x))
(make-lw 'x 1 0 7 1 #f #f)      | x
```

Finally, the parse tree of a number uses a string representation in the e field. Other than that, it is treated just like a symbol.

```
> (to-lw 2)                     | > (render-lw iswim (to-lw 2))
(make-lw "2" 1 0 7 1 #f #f)     | 2
```

Nested Expressions. Not surprisingly, the parse tree of a function application, say (f x), uses a list of `lw` structures.

```
> (to-lw (f x))                 | > (render-lw
(make-lw                        |     iswim
 (list                          |     (to-lw (f x)))
  (make-lw "(" 1 0 7 1 #f #f)   | (f x)
  (make-lw 'f 1 0 8 1 #f #f)    |
  (make-lw 'x 1 0 10 1 #f #f)   |
  (make-lw ")" 1 0 11 1 #f #f)) |
 1 0 7 5 #f #f)                 |
```

There is no `lw` structure that corresponds to the blank space between the `f`
and the `x`. Instead, column information records spacing. When Redex renders this `lw` structure, it leaves a space in the output that corresponds to the
empty column 9. Furthermore, the list of `lw` structures includes not only the
sub-expressions, but also explicit elements for the surrounding parentheses.

```
> (to-lw [f x])                          > (render-lw
(make-lw                                     iswim
 (list                                       (to-lw [f x]))
  (make-lw "[" 1 0 7 1 #f #f)             [f x]
  (make-lw 'f 1 0 8 1 #f #f)
  (make-lw 'x 1 0 10 1 #f #f)
  (make-lw "]" 1 0 11 1 #f #f))
 1 0 7 5 #f #f)
```

The `to-lw` form records source line and column information. In the above
example, `f` and `x` are on the same line but different columns. In the next
example, `f` and `x` are on different lines, but in the same column. Note how
the `lw` structure records this line and column information properly.

```
> (to-lw (f                              > (render-lw
         x))                                 iswim
(make-lw                                     (to-lw (f
 (list                                               x)))
  (make-lw "(" 1 0 7 1 #f #f)             (f
  (make-lw 'f 1 0 8 1 #f #f)               x)
  (make-lw 'x 2 0 8 1 #f #f)
  (make-lw ")" 2 0 9 1 #f #f))
 1 1 7 3 #f #f)
```

Also compare the line and column fields in the outermost `lw` structure of the
two examples. In the first of the two examples, the line span is 0 because the
entire expression is on a single line; the column span is 5 and consists of five
characters: two parentheses, the characters `#\f` and `#\x`, and a space in the
middle. In contrast, the second example's line span is 1, and it covers only 3
columns.

In addition, the second example illustrates how Redex lays out multiple
lines. The left edge of the `x` in the `pict` is lined up with the left edge of the `f`,
because the column number of the `x` in the original source is the same as the
column number of the `f`.

Recall, though, that Redex's layout algorithm adjusts only the beginning of the lines. In particular, when two words line up in the program's source due to its fixed-width font, they do not necessarily line up in the output.

```
> (to-lw (sit stand              > (render-lw
         wax wane))                iswim
(make-lw                           (to-lw (sit stand
 (list                                    wax wane)))
  (make-lw "(" 1 0 7 1 #f #f)   (sit stand
  (make-lw 'sit 1 0 8 3 #f #f)    wax wane)
  (make-lw 'stand 1 0 12 5 #f #f)
  (make-lw 'wax 2 0 8 3 #f #f)
  (make-lw 'wane 2 0 12 4 #f #f)
  (make-lw ")" 2 0 16 1 #f #f))
 1 1 7 10 #f #f)
```

To describe the layout process, we must distinguish **logical space** from **physical space**. The former is the layout of the original source text as measured for a specific Redex expression through the columns and lines of its `lw` structure. The latter is the amount of space that a block actually takes up when it is typeset. Redex's layout algorithm works in terms of logical space.

Logical space is usually derived from the layout of code in a fixed-width font, but it is not required to correspond to characters. Consider the following example.

```
> (render-lw
   iswim
   (make-lw
    (list
     (make-lw "(" 1 0 9 1 #f #f)
     (make-lw 'big-f 1 0 10 1 #f #f)
     (make-lw 'x 1 0 12 1 #f #f)
     (make-lw 'y 2 0 12 1 #f #f)
     (make-lw ")" 2 0 13 1 #f #f))
    1 1 9 5 #f #f))
(big-f x
       y)
```

Even though `big-f` takes up four keyboard characters, the `lw` structures measures it like a single character in logical space. Hence, Redex's typesetter lines up x with y.

Placing Parentheses. Unfortunately, PLT Scheme's underlying source tracking mechanism does not track the locations of closing parentheses, which
means that Redex occasionally must guess where the parentheses are. In
the example below, Redex does not detect that the right parenthesis of (f
x) is on the line below the expression; instead it produces a parse tree that
indicates the parenthesis immediately follows the x.

```
> (to-lw (f                        > (render-lw
         x                             iswim
         ))                            (to-lw (f
(make-lw                                      x
 (list                                        )))
  (make-lw "(" 1 0 7 1 #f #f)      (f
  (make-lw 'f 1 0 8 1 #f #f)        x)
  (make-lw 'x 2 0 8 1 #f #f)
  (make-lw ")" 2 0 9 1 #f #f))
 1 1 7 3 #f #f)
```

When Redex guesses during parsing, it uses the standard formatting conventions for PLT Scheme, which dictate that parentheses appear in fairly regular
places. For example, it is customary to put the right parenthesis on the same
line as the expression that it closes, rather than the line below.

Uses of Meta-functions. The use of a meta-function, such as δ, is parsed
into an instance of lw whose last field is #t instead of #f.

```
> (to-lw (δ (add1 2)))             > (render-lw
(make-lw                              iswim
 (list                                (to-lw (δ (add1 2))))
  (make-lw "(" 1 0 7 1 #f #f)      δ⟦(add1 2)⟧
  (make-lw 'δ 1 0 8 1 #f #t)
  (make-lw
   (list
    (make-lw "(" 1 0 10 1 #f #f)
    (make-lw 'add1 1 0 11 4 #f #f)
    (make-lw "2" 1 0 16 1 #f #f)
    (make-lw ")" 1 0 17 1 #f #f))
   1 0 10 8 #f #f)
  (make-lw ")" 1 0 18 1 #f #f))
 1 0 7 12 #f #f)
```

Creating a pict from such a parse tree inserts blackboard-bold brackets around the argument to δ. If the meta-function is applied to more than one S-expression, render-lw inserts commas between the arguments.

```
> (to-lw (TC Γ (λ X num X)))          > (render-lw
(make-lw                                  t-iswim
 (list                                    (to-lw
  (make-lw "(" 1 0 7 1 #f #f)              (TC Γ (λ X num X))))
  (make-lw 'TC 1 0 8 2 #f #t)          TC⟦Γ, (λ X num X)⟧
  (make-lw 'Γ 1 0 11 1 #f #f)
  (make-lw
   (list
    (make-lw "(" 1 0 13 1 #f #f)
    (make-lw 'λ 1 0 14 1 #f #f)
    (make-lw 'X 1 0 16 1 #f #f)
    (make-lw 'num 1 0 18 3 #f #f)
    (make-lw 'X 1 0 22 1 #f #f)
    (make-lw ")" 1 0 23 1 #f #f))
   1 0 13 11 #f #f)
  (make-lw ")" 1 0 24 1 #f #f))
 1 0 7 18 #f #f)
```

Unquote and Pink Backgrounds. Redex tracks escapes to PLT Scheme via special marks in lw structures. Consider the following simplistic example.

```
> (to-lw (f ,a))                      > (render-lw
(make-lw                                  iswim
 (list                                    (to-lw (f ,a)))
  (make-lw "(" 1 0 7 1 #f #f)          (f a)
  (make-lw 'f 1 0 8 1 #f #f)
  (make-lw
   (list
    (make-lw "" 1 0 10 0 #f #f)
    'spring
    (make-lw 'a 1 0 11 1 #t #f))
   1 0 10 2 #f #f)
  (make-lw ")" 1 0 12 1 #f #f))
 1 0 7 6 #f #f)
```

The parse tree on the left shows that the source expressions are nested in some manner. The outer instance of lw contains a left parenthesis, an f, a nested expression, and a right parenthesis. The representation of the nested expression contains an empty string, 'spring, and 'a.

From this example, we see that the unquote sub-expression is treated as a nested sub-expression when Redex creates the parse tree. It is not treated as an ordinary sub-expression, however. First, no parentheses are recorded for the escaping expression. Second, the representation starts with an empty string followed by 'spring, both of which are used for layout purposes. Specifically, the empty string is an anchor in case subsequent lines need to align with the position of the comma in the original text. The 'spring ensures that Redex adds no white space to the pict when the lw structure is rendered. Finally, the structure for 'a has a #t in the second to last field, signaling that the expression is an escape to Scheme. As such, it is rendered with a pink background.

Escaping to PLT Scheme is especially useful when the computation depends on pieces of the left-hand side. The next example illustrates the structure of parse trees that involve complex escaping expressions. Notice the nested term expression in the escaping expression; Redex treats such sub-expressions term as escapes from PLT Scheme back to the object language.

```
> (to-lw ,(add1 (term b)))         > (render-lw
(make-lw                               iswim
 (list                                 (to-lw
  (make-lw "" 1 0 7 0 #f #f)            ,(add1 (term b)))))
  'spring                          (add1 b)
  (make-lw
   (list
    (make-lw "(" 1 0 8 1 #t #f)
    (make-lw 'add1 1 0 9 4 #t #f)
    (make-lw
     (list
      (make-lw "" 1 0 14 0 #t #f)
      'spring
      (make-lw 'b 1 0 20 1 #f #f))
     1 0 14 7 #t #f)
    (make-lw ")" 1 0 21 1 #t #f))
   1 0 8 14 #t #f))
 1 0 7 15 #f #f)
```

Accordingly, the corresponding lw structure is marked as a non-escaping parse tree, and render-lw renders the background of the object-language expression in white, surrounded by the pink of the PLT Scheme expression.

The example also demonstrates that `to-lw` treats `term` much like it treats `unquote`. Specifically, `term` itself does not appear anywhere in the parse tree. Instead, the constructor is stripped away and is represented with a `lw` structure that contains a list whose first two elements are an empty string and `'spring`, respectively.

$18 \cdot 4$ **Rewriting Calls to Meta-functions.** The preceding sections clarify that Redex needs help with two particular aspects of the typesetting process: calls to meta-functions and escapes to PLT Scheme code. In both cases, installing a special-purpose rewriting function can improve the rendered output. Redex uses such rewriting functions to re-shuffle all parse trees for meta-function calls and escapes to PLT Scheme. In this section, we illustrate the general process for meta-function calls. The next section demonstrates how to deal with code in the host language.

Let us jump right into a concrete example. In part I, we use the notation $M\{X{:=}V\}$ to express the substitution of all free occurrences of X in M with V. An ideal rendering of, say, the ISWIM reduction relation should use this notation. Redex supports such global changes with a syntactic form:

```
(with-compound-rewriter name-expr proc-expr
  render-expr)
```

Its purpose is to evaluate the *render-expr* expression while all calls to the meta-function named by *name-expr* are re-parsed via calls to the PLT Scheme function produced by *proc-expr*. Put differently, during the evaluation of the *render-expr* expression, Redex uses *proc-expr*'s result to transform meta-function calls whenever `render-lw` is invoked, either directly or as part of the typesetting done with one of the higher-level functions described earlier in this chapter.

The following sample interaction demonstrates how Redex typesets calls to the meta-function `subst` while it renders `iswim`'s `reduction-relation`.

```
> (with-compound-rewriter 'subst subst-rw
    (render-reduction-relation
     iswim-red #:style 'horizontal))
```

$$E[((\lambda\, X\, M)\, V)] \longrightarrow E[M\{X{:=}V\}] \quad (\beta v)$$

$$E[(o\, b\, ...)] \longrightarrow E[\delta[\![(o\, b\, ...)]\!]\,] \quad (\delta)$$

Compare the output with the default typesetting on page 279.

Naturally, the interesting part of this example is `subst-rw`, whose purpose is to rewrite the parse tree of calls to `subst`. In general, a rewriting function accepts a list of `lw` structures; the structures correspond to the `e` field of the `lw` structure that encloses the meta-function call. The rewriting function should return a list of `lw` structures, strings, or `pict`s. If strings or `pict`s are included in the result list, Redex automatically wraps them with new `lw` structures that fill up the available logical space.

Here is the definition of `subst-rw`.

```
;; subst-rw : (Listof lw) -> (Listof (U String lw))
(define (subst-rw lws)
  (list ""
        (list-ref lws 2)
        "{"
        (list-ref lws 3)
        ":="
        (list-ref lws 4)
        "}"))
```

The `subst-rw` function accepts uses of the `subst` meta-function that are represented as `lw`-based parse trees; its result is an improved parse tree. To this end, `subst-rw` constructs a list containing the three arguments to `subst` with appropriate delimiters added. The three calls to `list-ref` extract the individual arguments to `subst`, leaving behind the parentheses and the name of the meta-function.

Since shuffling parse trees is not straightforward, we recommend that Redex programmers experiment with examples. In this case, it is best to look at the parse tree of a call to `subst` and its default rendering as a `pict`.

```
> (to-lw (subst M X V))
(make-lw
 (list
  (make-lw "(" 1 0 7 1 #f #f)
  (make-lw 'subst 1 0 8 5 #f #t)
  (make-lw 'M 1 0 14 1 #f #f)
  (make-lw 'X 1 0 16 1 #f #f)
  (make-lw 'V 1 0 18 1 #f #f)
  (make-lw ")" 1 0 19 1 #f #f))
 1 0 7 13 #f #f)
```

```
> (render-lw
   iswim
   (to-lw (subst M X V)))
SUBST⟦M, X, V⟧
```

This experiment shows that a call to a meta-function generates a `lw` structure and that its e field contains the actual call syntax. It is the content of this e field that `with-compound-writer` supplies to its rewriting function.

One remaining puzzle concerns the empty string as the first element in the result list of `subst-rw`. Without this empty string, Redex would insert a gap between the "[" and the "*M*" in the final output. The gap corresponds to the place where the meta-function name SUBST used to be. Since the strings in the subst-rw function's result are expanded to fill the available space, however, that gap is filled with something that takes all of the available logical space but no physical space. Once again, we recommend experimentation with actual code to understand this detail.

18·5 Rewriting PLT Scheme Code.
Escapes to Scheme should almost never appear in print with a pink background, though for draft papers it is perfectly acceptable. In support of typesetting such escaping expressions, Redex provides with-unquote-rewriter, which is a syntactic form that works much like with-compound-rewriter.

Using with-unquote-rewriter requires more knowledge of PLT Scheme than the use of any other Redex tool. The form accepts a function, which is called to rewrite the parse tree for each pink region, and an expression. As for with-compound-rewriter, Redex installs the unquote rewriter for the entire dynamic extent of a rendering expression.

The following example shows a use of with-unquote-rewriter. Its purpose is to replace the use of PLT Scheme operations in the definition of δ with mathematical notation. From the default rendering (page 279), we know that all but the first two clauses of δ escape to PLT Scheme to compute the result.

```
> (with-unquote-rewriter rewrite-uq
                         (render-metafunction δ))
```
$\delta[\![(\text{iszero } 0)]\!] = (\lambda \, x \, (\lambda \, y \, x))$
$\delta[\![(\text{iszero } b)]\!] = (\lambda \, x \, (\lambda \, y \, y))$
$\delta[\![(\text{add1 } b)]\!] = b{+}1$
$\delta[\![(\text{sub1 } b)]\!] = b{-}1$
$\delta[\![(+ \, b_1 \, b_2)]\!] = b_1{+}b_2$
$\delta[\![(- \, b_1 \, b_2)]\!] = b_1{-}b_2$
$\delta[\![(* \, b_1 \, b_2)]\!] = b_1 b_2$
$\delta[\![(\uparrow \, b_1 \, b_2)]\!] = b_1 {}^\wedge b_2$

Once we install rewrite-uq during the rendering process, however, we get normal algebraic expressions for these clauses. In particular, note how multiplication is expressed via juxtaposition.

Like with-compound-rewriter, with-unquote-rewriter applies its rewriting function to a parse tree. Unlike the former, it provides a single lw structure every time it finds one that has its unq? field set to #t. The desired result is, of course, a lw structure whose unq? field is #f.

The remainder of this section is dedicated to a study of one concrete example: the function `rewrite-uq` used in the above sample interaction.

```
;; rewrite-uq : lw -> lw
;; copy the given instance, rewrite e via rewrite-lst
(define (rewrite-uq a-lw)
  (struct-copy lw
               a-lw
               [e (rewrite-lst (lw-e a-lw))]
               [unq? #f]))

;; rewrite-lst : (Listof lw) -> (Listof lw)
;; rewrite the parse tree of an escaping expression
(define (rewrite-lst eles)
  (define hd (lw-e (list-ref eles 1)))
  (define a1 (list-ref (lw-e (list-ref eles 2)) 2))
  (define rst
    (if (<= (length eles) 4)
        '()
        (list 'spring
              (list-ref (lw-e (list-ref eles 3)) 2))))
  (case hd
    [(add1) (list a1 (just-after "+1" a1))]
    [(sub1) (list a1 (just-after "-1" a1))]
    [(+)    (cons a1 (cons (just-after "+" a1) rst))]
    [(-)    (cons a1 (cons (just-after "-" a1) rst))]
    [(expt) (cons a1 (cons (just-after "^" a1) rst))]
    [(*)    (cons a1 rst)]))
```

The first step when rewriting the `lw` structure is to make a copy that looks just like the original, except for the e and unq? fields. We accomplish this with PLT Scheme's `struct-copy` form, which accepts the name of the structure (in this case, `lw`), an instance of the structure (a-lw), and bindings for those fields where the copy is supposed to differ from the original (e and unq?); it constructs a new instance of the structure from these specifications via a shallow copy.

As the definition of `rewrite-uq` shows, the `rewrite-lst` function accepts the content of the e field from escaping expressions. Experiments with `to-lw` reveal that the e field is always a list of `lw` structures. The experiment on page 289 concerning `(to-lw ,(add1 (term b)))` is a particularly good one. It is taken from the third clause of the δ meta-function. The result illustrates how the parse tree—just below the symbol `'spring`—of an escaping expression contains a list of `lw` structures. Note how all `lw` structures in these parse trees carry a `unq?` field with value #t, except for the one that represents b. Indeed, b's parse tree represents the `term` part of the original input, and it therefore introduces an extra layer of a `lw` structure.

Equipped with this understanding, we can now return to the definition of `rewrite-1st`. Pause to look closely at the definition before reading further, because the definition introduces several new PLT Scheme constructs. The function definition starts with three local definitions:

1. `hd` is the head token of the parse tree, e.g., `'add1` or `'+`, and it represents the name of the PLT Scheme function;

2. `a1` is the first argument to the PLT Scheme function;

3. `rst` is a rendering of the optional second argument to the PLT Scheme function as a list of two parse trees.

For a complete appreciation of the various indexes to `list-ref`, study the above parse tree and determine which pieces these expressions extract.

The rest of the function definition uses a `case` expression, which dispatches on the function symbol. For a one-argument PLT Scheme function such as `add1`, the result is constructed with

```
(list a1 (just-after "+1" a1))
```

The Redex function `just-after` produces a new `lw` structure whose e field is the same as its first argument and whose other fields are taken from its second argument. For a two-argument function such as `'+`, the result incorporates `rst`:

```
(cons a1 (cons (just-after "+" a1) rst))
```

Redex assembles `rewrite-1st`'s result and integrates it into the surrounding parse tree for each call. For example, for `(add1 (term b))`, `rewrite-1st` rewrites it into a use of an infix + expression.

While this first attempt at rewriting δ produces a quite mathematical looking `pict`, a purist would still complain, because the rendering uses a caret operator for exponentiation. Conventionally, exponentiation uses a superscript-like notation, not an infix operator. That is, given the expression `(expt (term b1) (term b2))` in the penultimate clause of δ, the corresponding pict should contain $b_1^{b_2}$. To accomplish this, our rewriting function must create a `pict` instance directly while rewriting the input.

Redex owes this flexibility to PLT Scheme's `pict` data structure and its `slideshow/pict` library. First, recall that an `lw` structure may contain a `pict` in its e field. If so, Redex's typesetting tools use this `pict` when they render the parse tree. Second, it is easy to create arbitrary picts from existing parse trees, though doing so requires some knowledge of the pict library.

Here we demonstrate the power of this library with one simple example: the creation of an exponent pict. Consider the following function definition.

```
;; exponent : -> pict
;; create a pict for the exponent of b_1 to the b_2
(define (exponent)
  (define b
    (text "b" (non-terminal-style)))
  (define one
    (text "1" (non-terminal-subscript-style)))
  (define b2
    (hbl-append
     (text "b" (non-terminal-style))
     (text "2" (non-terminal-subscript-style))))
  (define lifted-b2
    (drop-below-ascent (scale b2 .7) −6))
  (hbl-append b (lbl-superimpose lifted-b2 one)))
```

The exponent function constructs a pict of the desired mathematical nota-tion via text, hbl-append, and drop-below-ascent. As mentioned in sec-tion 18.2, the non-terminal-style and non-terminal-subscript-style parameters both return font specifications. The text function accepts a string and a font specification and returns a pict of the given string using the given font. Then, the hbl-append function places these two side-by-side in a horizontal manner that aligns text baselines. The drop-below-ascent func-tion moves b_2 "up into the air" relative to its baseline and scale is used to make the exponent slightly smaller. Finally, lbl-superimpose superimposes two picts, lining them up on their left in the horizontal direction and on their baseline in the vertical direction.

To use the exponent function, we modify the rewrite-uq function and obtain rewrite-uq/exponent. This new function employs exponent in the clauses concerning exponentiation.

```
[(expt) (list (just-after (exponent) a1))]
```

As a result, when Redex finally puts all the pieces together, exponentiation is rendered in a mathematical manner.

Finally, we use with-unquote-rewriter to typeset the δ function that uses the traditional exponentiation notation and obtain the desired result.

```
> (with-unquote-rewriter rewrite-uq/exponent
                          (render-metafunction δ))
```

$\delta[\![(\text{iszero } 0)]\!] \; = \; (\lambda\, x\, (\lambda\, y\, x))$

$\delta[\![(\text{iszero } b)]\!] \; = \; (\lambda\, x\, (\lambda\, y\, y))$

$\delta[\![(\text{add1 } b)]\!] \; = \; b+1$

$\delta[\![(\text{sub1 } b)]\!] \; = \; b-1$

$\delta[\![(+\, b_1\, b_2)]\!] \; = \; b_1+b_2$

$\delta[\![(-\, b_1\, b_2)]\!] \; = \; b_1-b_2$

$\delta[\![(*\, b_1\, b_2)]\!] \; = \; b_1 b_2$

$\delta[\![(\uparrow\, b_1\, b_2)]\!] \; = \; b_1^{b_2}$

A · Appendix: A Tour of DrScheme

Good software engineers know their tool suite inside out. One critical tool is the programming language, another one is the integrated development environment (IDE) that supports it. Redex is a lightweight tool for semantics engineers; DrScheme is its complementary IDE.

This appendix introduces DrScheme for Redex programmers. Based on the traditional Scheme mode of work, DrScheme is sensitive to parenthetical languages and interactive. It also comes with an extensive help system.

A·1 **Getting Started.** Point a browser to `http://www.plt-scheme.org/`, download DrScheme, and start it up.

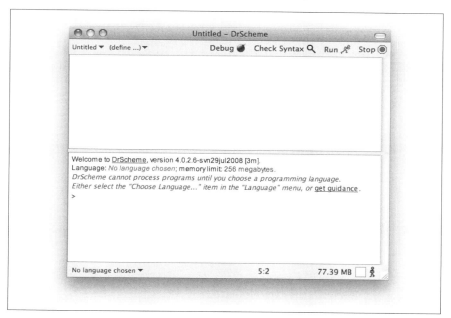

PLT Scheme is not just one language, it is a family of programming languages. Similarly, DrScheme is not just a programming environment for a language, it supports all of PLT Scheme's languages. Thus, when it starts up for the very first time, DrScheme demands that users specify a language.

Since Redex programs are really just PLT Scheme modules that import additional notation, the first step is to set DrScheme's language to **Module**. To do so, use the **Choose Language...** menu item in the **Language** menu.

DrScheme takes its inspiration from Emacs with an added emphasis on graphical user interface actions for novices. When DrScheme is launched, it opens a new window with four panes: a small pane at the top with buttons for important and intuitive functions; a large pane for editing a program, called the **definitions window**; another large pane for interactive explorations of the definitions, called the **interactions window**; and a small status pane at the bottom.

When the language is switched to **Module**, DrScheme automatically inserts one line into the definitions window:

```
#lang scheme
```

Every module starts with a line like this. In this case, the line says that the language of the module is scheme, our name for the core of PLT Scheme. Adding a single line creates a "hello world" program:

```
#lang scheme
"hello world"
```

To see why, click the **Run** button and watch how DrScheme evaluates this program, one expression at a time, printing the values of each expression in the interactions window.

Here is another "hello world" program, written in an extension of scheme that integrates PLT Scheme's extensive and portable GUI libraries:

```
#lang scheme/gui
(send (new frame% [label "Hello!"] [width 200]) show #t)
```

Click **Run** and watch how this expression does not produce a (visible) value but opens a new window, which is under the control of the program.

Of course, the definitions window got its name from the fact that it is the place where functions are defined:

```
#lang scheme

(define (salutation name)
  (string-append "Hello " name))

(define (closing name)
  (string-append "Good bye, " name))
```

When clicking **Run** for this program, DrScheme appears to do almost nothing. What does change is that the blinking line—which indicates keyboard focus—is now located in the interactions window instead of the definitions window. We say that the focus has shifted from the development to the exploration phase.

The interactions window is for exploring the definitions of a program. The interactions window implements a so-called **read-eval-print-loop**, also known as the REPL. After running a program, the REPL is initialized with all of the definitions from the program and the (explicitly or implicitly) imported libraries. The REPL then displays a prompt, >, and waits for users to hit Return after typing a complete S-expression. At that point, the expression is evaluated in the context of the program definitions and the library.

For example, in the context of the last program, the following interactions are possible:

```
> (salutation "Wen")
"Hello Wen"
> (closing "Wen")
"Good bye, Wen"
> (+ (string-length (salutation "Hsing-Huei"))
     (string-length (closing "Helga")))
31
```

The first two interactions use program-defined functions. The last one involves the library functions + and string-length, which are imported by #lang scheme.

In general, the REPL is also a good place for exploring library functions— determining whether they exist and how they work. Often, it suffices to guess the name of a library function and try to use it:

```
> (expt 2 3)
8
```

Another possibility is to type in a word, highlight it, and hit F1. These steps open the default web browser to display the result of searching for the word in PLT Scheme's extensive help system.

All of the boxes in part II that begin with > are interactions recorded at DrScheme's REPL. They show exactly how Redex programmers would interact with DrScheme in the context of their models.

Proficient typists quickly tire of taking their hands off the keyboard to use the mouse. DrScheme therefore supports keyboard shortcuts, such as F5 or Control-t (Command-t under Mac OS X) for running a program or] to close any opening parenthesis, bracket, or brace. The next two sections present tricks and tips for editing programs and running them. The last section is about PLT Scheme programming.

A·2

Editing: Tips & Tricks. Editing in DrScheme is like editing in most other editors. The point where text gets inserted is marked by a vertical blinking line. The arrow keys and the mouse enable navigation within a pane; scroll bars allow access to "hidden" text. Naturally, selection and copy-and-paste actions are available via mouse movements, but also via key strokes.

In addition, DrScheme supports a number of editing actions specifically for programming in PLT Scheme, Redex, and other languages. Because PLT Scheme programs use parentheses as lightweight delimiters, DrScheme has an easy mode for *entering* parentheses as well as for navigating among them. To begin with, entering the (character and the) character is rarely necessary. DrScheme converts [keystrokes to (based on the context in the editor, following the standard conventions of PLT Scheme. Symmetrically, when a programmmer enters a],), or } character, DrScheme searches backwards for the first unclosed delimiter, [, (, or {, and it inserts the match instead of the typed character.[1]

For example, if a programmer enters the literal keystrokes on the left

```
[let [[x [* 9 9]]              (let ([x (* 9 9)]
      [y [* x x]]]                   [y (* x x)])
   [* x x]]                      (* x x))
```

DrScheme creates the program on the right.

Once the parentheses are in place in a program, they are handy signposts for navigating code. In particular, as a programmer navigates adjacent to a parenthesis, DrScheme highlights the associated S-expression with a gray region. Furthermore, DrScheme provides a suite of key bindings for moving back and forth between matching parentheses or through nested layers: `Alt` plus the right or the left arrow key moves back or forth one S-expression, respectively; `Alt` plus the down and the up arrow key moves into or out of nested layers of S-expressions. Naturally, holding down the shift key while navigating creates or extends a selection. Thus, entering `Alt-Shift-Right` followed by `Delete` erases the expression in front of the insertion point.

When the text in the definitions window is larger than the pane, navigation with keystrokes or via the scroll bar becomes cumbersome. In recognition of this problem, DrScheme provides direct access to top-level and nested definitions via the **(define ...)** pop-up menu. It is located in the top-left corner of the DrScheme window. A click on the menu causes DrScheme to list all of the definitions in the file, initially sorted by the file position combined with the relative indentation; the option to sort these names is highly recommended for large programs.

---

[1]Automatic delimiter conversions can be disabled through the **Preferences** dialog.

Beyond textual navigation, DrScheme supports the **contour window**, as opened through the **Show Program Contour** item in the **View** menu. The contour window displays a bird's eye view of the definitions window, showing one pixel per non-blank character in the definitions window. If a programmer uses the **Insert Large Letters...** item from the **Insert** menu to add chapter titles to a program, these words show up as normal sized words in the contour window, greatly facilitating visual navigation. A simple click in the contour window moves the focus in the definition window.

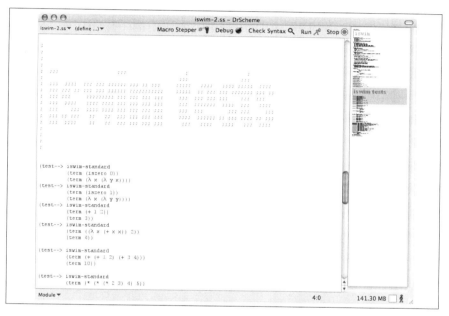

The **Check Syntax** button (or F6) causes DrScheme to analyze the syntactic and lexical structure of the program in the definitions window. By partially compiling the program, DrScheme recovers lexical information that it uses to color the program's elements and to draw **lexcial-scope arrows**.

To display lexical-scope arrows after clicking **Check Syntax**, move the mouse over the binding occurrence of an identifier. In response, DrScheme draws an arrow to each bound occurrence. Moving over a bound occurrence draws an arrow its binding occurrence. A right-click (or `Control`-click under Mac OS X) with the mouse produces a context-sensitive menu, which includes options for α-**renaming**, for jumping back and forth between occurrences, and for jumping to the definition of an imported identifier. If DrScheme paints an identifier with a tan background when the mouse is over the identifier, then the context-sensitive menu also provides a direct link to documentation for the identifier.

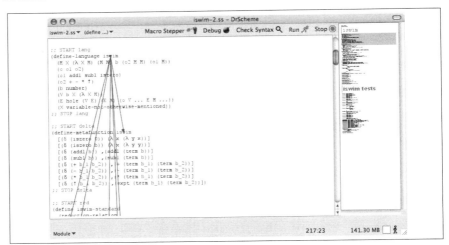

By convention, semantics engineering often uses mathematical symbols and Greek letters for reduction relations and meta-functions. To support such conventions, DrScheme provides a TeX-inspired method for inputting **unicode characters**. Specifically, typing a TeX macro call for a mathematical symbol or Greek letter followed by `Alt-\` (`Control-\` under Mac OS X) replaces the macro call with the corresponding unicode character. For example, `\beta` followed by `Alt-\` produces β. Here are a few more examples.

TeX macro	Char	TeX macro	Char	TeX macro	Char
\alpha	α	\Rightarrow	$\Rightarrow$	\smiley	☺
\delta	δ	\in	$\in$	\frownie	☹
\Omega	Ω	\leq	$\leq$	\skull	☠

Of course, `\lambda` produces λ, but because λ is so common, it is also available via a single keystroke: `Control-\` (`Command-\` under Mac OS X).[2]

Note to Emacs Users on Windows   Under Windows, the menu shortcut key is `Control`, so many menu shortcuts conflict with standard Emacs bindings. For example, `Control-a` in Emacs sends the cursor to the beginning of the line, but the Windows standard binding selects all of the text. To use Emacs-style bindings, un-check the **Enable keybindings in menus** preference in the **General** section of the **Editing** tab in DrScheme's preferences dialog.

---

[2]Note that in plain PLT Scheme code, λ is bound to the same construct as `lambda`.

A·3 **Running Programs: Tips & Tricks.** As we have already seen, DrScheme runs programs by evaluating the content of the definitions window. While this functionality is common for many integrated development environments, DrScheme also supports additional functionality associated with program execution.

To start, recall that running a program is a lightweight action and easily initiated with F5 or Control-t (Command-t under Mac OS X). Doing so actually has two consequences. First, if DrScheme's interactions window is not visible (see **View** menu), it is opened so that the programmer can interact with the program. Second, the expressions and definitions in the editor are evaluated, with the latter being added to the REPL's context. At that point, it is natural for programmers to want to switch back and forth between the two windows; Control-F6 (Alt-Tab under Mac OS X) accomplishes just that, but of course, using the mouse for this purpose works, too. Also, try using Esc-p in the interactions window after evaluating several expressions there.

For a semantics engineer, DrScheme's **printing style** is the most important parameter of the execution environment. The default printing style for the module language is the standard Scheme printer, which, for example, prints (list 1 2 3) as (1 2 3). DrScheme provides two alternatives:

1. **constructor style**, where (list 1 2 3) prints as (list 1 2 3), and

2. **quasiquote style**, where (list 1 2 3) prints as '(1 2 3).

In each case, the output style of the printer mimics the style used to write down the printed value as a program expression. The constructor style is used throughout the tutorial in the examples, and it is the recommended style for Redex programmers. The quasiquote style is more compact than constructor style, however, and is thus easier to read in some situations.

When a program aborts its execution with a run-time error, i.e., a signal that the invariant for some computational primitive is violated, the error comes with **debugging information**, including a stack trace. DrScheme indicates that information is available via two icons, just before the error message: 🔖 and ❌. Clicking the first opens a window showing the stack trace; clicking the second takes DrScheme's keyboard focus to the source code for the top of the stack trace and highlights the respective piece of the program.

Finally, when the execution of a program enters an infinite loop or just consumes too much time, programmers can ask DrScheme to terminate the execution. Clicking the **Stop** button once sends a "break" signal to the program (in the form of a asynchronous exception) to request that it terminate. If the program ignores the request, clicking the **Stop** button a second time lets the programmer force the program to terminate. To directly force a program to terminate, use `Control-k` (`Command-k` under Mac OS X). When DrScheme forces a program to terminate, it cleans up all of the resources that the program is using: GUI windows, network connections, open files, and subsidiary threads (if any).

A·4 Modules, Libraries, and Documentation. PLT Scheme provides a large standard library with support for object-oriented programming, contract programming, concurrent programming, network programming, and hundreds of user-contributed libraries.

Importing a library (or any other module) is straightforward:

```
#lang scheme
(require scheme/html redex "iswim.ss")
. . .
```

This `require` specification imports PLT Scheme's HTML library, the Redex language, and a file (in the local directory) called `"iswim.ss"` that is presumably a Redex model of ISWIM. Because Redex is not only a language but a library, it is possible to write models that script browsers, connect to a network, or perform other external tasks—all by importing and using appropriate libraries.

Exporting from a file, say `"iswim.ss"`, is just as easy:

```
#lang scheme
(provide iswim red subst δ)
. . .
```

The `provide` specification says that the module exports four bindings: `iswim`, the grammar specification; `red`, the reduction relation; `subst`, the capture-avoiding substitution function; and δ, the meta-function for interpreting primitive applications. Through these exports, the model of ISWIM can be used as a building block in another model.

Most of the Redex programs in this tutorial are self-contained, but a few rely on built-in PLT Scheme constructs and functions:

1. `equal?` compares any two PLT Scheme values for extensional equality;

2. `length` computes the length of a list;

3. `member` determines whether some given value is in some list, using `equal?` as the comparison function;

4. `list-ref` consumes a list l and a natural number n and extracts the nth element from l;

5. `remove*` removes every element of one list from another list.

The most widely used syntactic constructs are define, define-struct, and term (like quasiquote) whose meaning is explained in the first chapter of part II. Additional useful constructs are

1. struct-copy, which copies structures modulo those fields for which a separate value is specified (see chapter 8 in part II);

2. case, a special-purpose conditional that dispatches to a clause based on the value of a symbol;

   Example:

   ```
   (case 'a
     [(b) 1]
     [(c) 2]
     [(a) 0]
     [(d a f) 3]
     [(e) 4]
     [else 10])
   ```

   This expression produces 0, even though the symbol 'a is matched in two clauses. That is, the expression searches for the first clause whose header contains the (print representation) of the dispatch-symbol and evaluates the expression in that clause; if no match is found, the else clause is chosen.

3. cond, the all-purpose, multi-pronged conditional of PLT Scheme;

   Example:[3]

   ```
   (cond
     [(member 'a '(b)) 1]
     [(member 'a '(c)) 2]
     [(member 'a '(a)) 0]
     [(member 'a '(d a f)) 3]
     [(member 'a '(e)) 0]
     [else 10])
   ```

   Given a cond expression, PLT Scheme evaluates the conditions—the left parts of each clauses—one at a time. For the first one that evaluates to true, the right-hand expression is evaluated, and its result becomes the result of the entire cond expression. If all conditions evaluate to #f, the expression associated with the else clause is chosen.

---

[3] This example illustrates how the above case example is compiled.

Naturally, PLT Scheme also comes with `if` expressions for two-pronged deci-
sions and several other flavors of conditional expression forms.

Above all else, keep in mind that everything in the PLT Scheme distri-
bution comes with **documentation**. To access this documentation, hit `F1`
in DrScheme. If the insertion point is in the middle of a word, DrScheme
searches for that word in the documentation and displays the search results
in a web browser. If the insertion point is located on whitespace, DrScheme
just opens the front page of the documentation system, which lists all of the
available manuals.

Every page in the documentation system features a search box. Make
good use of it! Furthermore, technical terms, functions, and forms are hy-
perlinked in this documentation, so it is easy to explore a topic.

For user-contributed libraries, visit

```
http://planet.plt-scheme.org/
```

which lists many useful libraries for both Redex and PLT Scheme programming. Using such a user-contributed library is just as easy as using one of the
standard libraries. The relevant `require` specifications start with `planet` and
are always listed with the library on the web site. When DrScheme encounters a reference to such library for the first time, the library is downloaded,
cached, compiled, and then imported; after that, the library behaves just like
a standard library.

Part III

Applications

Contents, Part III

19 · Modular ACL2
Carl Eastlund, Northeastern University

ACL2 is an automated theorem prover and programming language, an applicative subset of Common Lisp. ACL2 lacks modern
constructs for programming in the large, so we have developed
Modular ACL2, which allows programmers to divide programs
and proofs into manageable, composable, and reusable pieces.

In this chapter we present Modular ACL2, a module system for
ACL2. We use PLT Redex to model the process of compiling programs in Modular ACL2 to equivalent, module-free programs in
ACL2. The model has two parts: a per-module translation for
logical reasoning and a whole-program translation for execution.
PLT Redex allows us to prototype and modify the transformations
quickly as well as inspect intermediate stages of the translation.

19·1 **ACL2 and Programming in the Large.** ACL2 is an applicative,
first-order subset of Common Lisp [102] equipped with a theorem prover [60]. Programmers can write programs and declare conjectures
about them in a first-order equational logic. The theorem prover's task is to
verify that conjectures yield a true (non-`nil`) value. To reason about functions, it must first prove them terminating for all possible inputs.

Figure 19.1 demonstrates an example ACL2 program called SQR-ALL.
The program defines two functions, `sqr` and `sqr-all`. The first function
produces the square of its single input n. The second traverses its input
ns as a list, producing a new list containing the square (via `sqr`) of each
element. To admit these function definitions, ACL2 must prove that they
always terminate. Once admitted, users may run the functions and use their
definitions as logical rules in later proof attempts.

Following the functions, SQR-ALL declares two conjectures, `sqr-type`
and `sqr-all-type`. The former claims that `sqr` is closed on the set of integers; the latter claims that `sqr-all` is closed on the set of lists of integers.
To admit these conjectures, ACL2 must prove that they are true (reduce to a

```
(defun sqr (n) (* n n))

(defun sqr-all (ns)
  (cond ((endp ns) nil)
        ((consp ns) (cons (sqr (car ns))
                          (sqr-all (cdr ns))))))

(defthm sqr-type
  (implies (integerp n)
           (integerp (sqr n))))

(defthm sqr-all-type
  (implies (integer-listp ns)
           (integer-listp (sqr-all ns))))

(sqr-all (list 1 2 3))
```

Figure 19.1: The ACL2 program SQR-ALL

value other than `nil`) for all possible assignments to free variables (n and ns respectively). Once admitted, ACL2 may use the conjectures as rules in later proof attempts.

The program concludes by invoking `sqr-all` on `(list 1 2 3)`.

Figure 19.2 shows the subset of ACL2 syntax that we use in our model. We assume two sets of variable names: *var* for local variables and *fvar* for global names. For simplicity, we restrict programs to a sequence of definitions followed by a sequence of expressions.

Our simplified set of definitions includes functions (`defun`), conjectures (`defthm`), stubs (`defstub`), and axioms (`defaxiom`). A stub is a function with no actual implementation, used only for abstract reasoning. An axiom is a logical rule that need not be proved; the theorem prover accepts it unconditionally. Expressions may be constants, variables, conditionals, let-bindings, or function application.

ACL2 development follows a common cycle of think (about a proof), write (the proof as ACL2 code), submit (the proof to ACL2), fail (to admit the proof), and repeat (until successful). One variant of this cycle is described as "the Method" in the ACL2 literature. Clearly, rejected programs are a common occurrence. However, many failures arise from interference between separate parts of a program, rather than syntactic or logical errors in any in-

$$program ::= (def \ldots expr \ldots)$$
$$def ::= (\texttt{defun}\, fvar\, (var \ldots)\, expr)$$
$$\mid (\texttt{defthm}\, fvar\, expr)$$
$$\mid (\texttt{defstub}\, fvar\, (var \ldots)\, \texttt{t})$$
$$\mid (\texttt{defaxiom}\, fvar\, expr)$$
$$expr ::= const \mid var$$
$$\mid (\texttt{cond}\, (expr\, expr) \ldots)$$
$$\mid (\texttt{let}\, ((var\, expr) \ldots)\, expr)$$
$$\mid (fvar\, expr \ldots)$$
$$sig ::= (fvar\, (var \ldots)\, \texttt{t})$$
$$const ::= \texttt{t} \mid \texttt{nil} \mid number$$

Figure 19.2: A subset of ACL2 syntax

dividual part. ACL2 offers tools to alleviate these problems, but the language does not provide a unified, structured solution.

ACL2's global namespace makes name clashes a difficult problem to overcome. The program SQR-ALL might be admitted on its own but fail if used in a program with another definition of sqr, even if no individual file references both definitions of sqr. This problem occurs frequently in the released ACL2 books, many of which may not be included in the same program because of shared internal function names.

Packages, which are named partitions of the global namespace, help programmers separate names in their programs. Programmers may choose the package used by any part of their program; all names default to that package and do not coincide with names from any other package. Packages are not guaranteed to be unique, however, and a duplicated combination of package and function name may always cause a clash. Interaction across package boundaries can be cumbersome and error-prone, as any external function or symbol name not imported at the creation of a new package must carry its source package name at every reference.

The ACL2 theorem prover may reject a valid conjecture if its internal heuristics lead a proof attempt to a dead end. This is often the result of having too many logical rules to choose from and reasoning at the wrong level of abstraction. For instance, in proving sqr-all-type, ACL2 repeats the work of sqr-type by examining sqr and reasoning about *, rather than using the existing rule. This works for small examples, but bypassing high-level rules to reason about functions at a low level can cause larger proof attempts to fail.

Programmers can control the set of logical rules available to the theorem prover either locally within a single proof attempt or from a given point on globally in a program. Both are useful techniques; however, ACL2 does not provide a structured way to determine where theorems should or should not be enabled. Disabled rules may be reenabled later, so disabling a rule does not provide a hard abstraction boundary between parts of a proof.

ACL2 can group definitions into collections to help with name clashes and excess rules. A collection may be a file called a book or a form of definition called an encapsulation block. Definitions in the scope of either are run normally but may be declared local. Upon completion, any local definitions are removed entirely or optionally replaced by a stub. Any names or logical rules thus removed cannot interfere with subsequent parts of the program. This can be used to verify intermediate lemmas without polluting the global theory, or to define abstract functions but hide their definition. Unfortunately, programs built on such abstract functions cannot be executed. Books and encapsulation blocks provide only a one-way boundary: they keep local definitions from getting out, but cannot prevent external names and rules from getting in.

The rest of this chapter describes our new language, Modular ACL2, developed to alleviate the above problems, as well as its implementation as a PLT Redex model. Section 19.2 describes the language, and section 19.3 presents an overview of our two-part model. Section 19.4 discusses the part of our model concerned with local reasoning about modules. Section 19.5 explains the other half of our model, concerned with the execution of whole programs. Section 19.6 evaluates the current design, addressing alternate options and implementation concerns. Section 19.7 details our development process, including previous formulations of Modular ACL2 and the impact of PLT Redex.

19·2 Design of Modular ACL2.
Our goal is to create a coherent linguistic construct for modular programming in ACL2. To that end we have designed the Modular ACL2 language using PLT Redex models. Programs in Modular ACL2 consist of *interfaces* and *modules*. Modules are program fragments with their own namespaces and logical theories; interfaces determine how the program and proof fragments from different modules interact.

In the current design of Modular ACL2, modules and interfaces are defined at the top level. Interfaces contain a set of function signatures and logical statements about them. Modules may be *primitive* or *compound*. Primitive modules import and export definitions via interfaces and contain internal definitions. Compound modules link other modules together, filling in the exports of one module as the implementation for the matching imports of another module. From the logical perspective, a module may be viewed

```
(interface INT-IFC
  (function int-fn (n) t)
  (theorem int-fn-type
    (implies (integerp n)
             (integerp (int-fn n)))))

(interface LIST-IFC
  (function list-fn (ns) t)
  (theorem list-fn-type
    (implies (integer-listp ns)
             (integer-listp (list-fn ns)))))

(module SQR-MOD
  (defun sqr (n) (* n n))
  (export INT-IFC (sqr as int-fn)))

(module MAP-MOD
  (import INT-IFC)
  (defun map-int-fn (ns)
    (cond ((endp ns) nil)
          ((consp ns) (cons (int-fn (car ns))
                            (map-int-fn (cdr ns))))))
  (export LIST-IFC (map-int-fn as list-fn)))

(compound SQR-ALL-MOD = MAP-MOD (SQR-MOD : INT-IFC))

(invoke LIST-IFC (list-fn (list 1 2 3)))
```

Figure 19.3: The Modular ACL2 program SQR-ALL

$$P ::= (I \dots M \dots C \dots E)$$
$$I ::= (\texttt{interface } Ivar \; Fun \dots Thm \dots)$$
$$M ::= (\texttt{module } Mvar \; Imp \dots def \dots Exp \dots)$$
$$C ::= (\texttt{compound } Mvar = Mvar \; (Mvar : Ivar))$$
$$E ::= (\texttt{invoke } Ivar \; expr)$$
$$Fun ::= (\texttt{function } fvar \; (var \dots) \; \texttt{t})$$
$$Thm ::= (\texttt{theorem } fvar \; expr)$$
$$Imp ::= (\texttt{import } Ivar)$$
$$Exp ::= (\texttt{export } Ivar \; (fvar \; \texttt{as } fvar) \dots)$$

Figure 19.4: The grammar of Modular ACL2

as an implication, with the theorems of its imported interfaces as hypotheses and the theorems of its exported interfaces as conclusions. Linking a compound module discharges some of the hypotheses.

Figure 19.3 demonstrates a sample Modular ACL2 program representing one possible translation of SQR-ALL. The program consists of two interfaces, three modules, and an entry point. The original functions are split into separate modules. The function sqr is in the module SQR-MOD, which exports it as int-fn via interface INT-IFC. The theorem int-fn-type in the interface requires int-fn to be closed on the integers; when applied to sqr, it essentially restates the original conjecture sqr-type.

The other function, sqr-all, is split across multiple modules. The module MAP-MOD contains a generalized implementation which maps an arbitrary integer function (int-fn imported from INT-IFC) over a list. This function is exported as list-fn via LIST-IFC, which requires it to be closed on integer lists, as in sqr-all-type. The last module SQR-ALL-MOD links MAP-MOD to SQR-MOD, essentially reconstituting sqr-all by attaching the imported int-fn in MAP-MOD to sqr in SQR-MOD.

The program's entry point invokes the function list-fn exported by SQR-ALL-MOD on (list 1 2 3).

The modular version of SQR-ALL splits the program into several reusable pieces and protects each piece from interfering with the others. For instance, SQR-MOD does not have imports and does not export the name sqr, so the internal function cannot clash with another sqr. Also, the imported interface INT-IFC in MAP-MOD serves as an abstraction barrier. Any attempt to reason about int-fn when verifying map-int-fn must be in terms of the guarantees in INT-IFC; there is no concrete implementation to "confuse" the prover.

See figure 19.4 for the full grammar of Modular ACL2, based on the ACL2 syntax from figure 19.2. Modular ACL2 assumes two additional sets of variable names: *Mvar* for modules and *Ivar* for interfaces. To simplify the model,

get-def-names	:	*(def . . .)* → *(fvar . . .)*	Extracts defined names.
join-imports	:	*(imp . . .)* → *(imp . . .)*	Removes duplicate imports.
prefix	:	*Var, Var* → *Var*	Adds a prefix to a variable.
prefix-names	:	*Var, (Var . . .)* → *(Var . . .)*	Prefixes multiple variables.
rename-[term]*	:	*(fvar . . .), (fvar . . .),* [term] → [term]	Renames identifiers in a given kind of term.

Figure 19.5: Signatures of metafunctions used in the model

we restrict each compound module to link only two modules across a single interface; and we also require a program to define all interfaces first, followed by primitive modules, and then compound modules. Each program ends with an entry point expression, which may invoke functions from a specified interface provided by the module immediately preceding it.

19·3 Modeling Modular ACL2.
Our model defines the meaning of Modular ACL2 in terms of ACL2. We have two separate interpretations of programs: one for logical reasoning and one for execution. The logical form of a program consists of a set of conjectures about individual modules. They represent the claim that each module satisfies its exported interfaces for any valid implementation of its imported interfaces. Programmers can use this form to verify each module of a program in isolation.

The executable form is a concrete implementation of the full program, including a fully linked form of the final module and an entry point expression that invokes the module. Programmers can execute this form of the program, relying on the properties of modules verified in the logical form without having to reprove them each time they are linked.

In our presentation of the PLT Redex model, some common functionality is defined in separate metafunctions, summarized in figure 19.5. The figure describes the general form of term(s) supplied to and produced by the metafunctions. Note that prefix and prefix-names operate on any kind of variable (written *Var*); specific applications use specific kinds of variables (e.g., *fvar*).

The various rename- functions perform a series of substitutions on function and theorem names, replacing all occurrences (bound and binding) of names from the first list with the corresponding name from the second list. The rules shown here use rename-var*, rename-expr*, rename-def*, and rename-export* for terms belonging to *fvar, expr, def,* and *Exp*, respectively.

We make several assumptions about variable names in Modular ACL2 programs so our translations can create new names that are both unique

$$(I \dots M_{pre} \dots M\, M_{post} \dots C \dots E) \longrightarrow (I \dots M) \qquad\qquad \text{[choose module]}$$

$$
\begin{aligned}
(I_{pre} \dots I\, I_{post} \dots &\qquad \longrightarrow (I_{pre} \dots I\, I_{post} \dots \qquad\qquad\qquad \text{[import interface]}\\
(\texttt{module}\ Mvar &\qquad\quad (\texttt{module}\ Mvar\\
Imp\ \dots &\qquad\quad\quad Imp\ \dots\\
(\texttt{import}\ Ivar) &\qquad\quad\quad (\texttt{defstub}\ fvar_{fun}\ (var \dots)\ \texttt{t}) \dots\\
def \dots &\qquad\quad\quad (\texttt{defaxiom}\ fvar_{thm}\ expr) \dots\\
Exp\ \dots)) &\qquad\quad\quad def \dots\\
&\qquad\quad\quad Exp\ \dots))
\end{aligned}
$$

where $I = (\texttt{interface}\ Ivar\ (\texttt{function}\ fvar_{fun}\ (var \dots)\ \texttt{t}) \dots (\texttt{theorem}\ fvar_{thm}\ expr) \dots)$

$$
\begin{aligned}
(I_{pre} \dots I\, I_{post} \dots &\qquad \longrightarrow (I_{pre} \dots I\, I_{post} \dots \qquad\qquad\qquad \text{[export interface]}\\
(\texttt{module}\ Mvar &\qquad\quad (\texttt{module}\ Mvar\\
def \dots &\qquad\quad\quad def \dots\\
(\texttt{export}\ Ivar\ (fvar_{int}\ \texttt{as}\ fvar_{ext}) \dots) &\qquad\quad\quad (\texttt{defthm}\ \mathsf{prefix}[\![Ivar, fvar]\!]\\
Exp\ \dots)) &\qquad\qquad\qquad \mathsf{rename\text{-}expr}^*[\![(fvar_{ext} \dots), (fvar_{int} \dots), expr]\!]\ )\\
&\qquad\quad\quad \dots\\
&\qquad\quad\quad Exp\ \dots))
\end{aligned}
$$

where $I = (\texttt{interface}\ Ivar\ Fun \dots (\texttt{theorem}\ fvar\ expr) \dots)$

$$(I \dots (\texttt{module}\ Mvar\ def \dots)) \longrightarrow (def \dots) \qquad\qquad \text{[finish]}$$

Figure 19.6: Rules for computing the logical meaning of modules

and readable. First, module and interface names must all be unique, as must function and theorem names in a given module. Second, wherever new names are needed, we concatenate the name of the source module or interface with the name of the definition, e.g. PREFIX.name. For these names to be available, the initial program must not contain such "dotted" names, and modules must only import or export a given interface once.

19.4 Logical Meaning of Modules.
The first half of our model establishes the logical meaning of Modular ACL2 programs. Specifically, we translate each primitive module into the conjecture that its exported functions satisfy their properties as well, if its imported functions satisfy the theorems in their respective interfaces. If ACL2 admits the correctness of this conjecture for abstract imports, then the module may be safely linked with concrete implementations and executed. The correctness of compound modules follows from the correctness of their primitive constituents.

We define the logical meaning of each module in three parts: a set of assumptions about its imports, a copy of its definitions, and a set of guarantees about its exports. We construct these parts by a translation from the original module into ACL2. The translation is formulated as a reduction relation with intermediate steps so that we can inspect the process.

Figure 19.6 shows the reduction relation. The reduction rules choose a module, gradually replace its interface imports and exports with definitions, and extract the definitions at the end. The first rule chooses a primitive module nondeterministically and drops the remaining modules and the program entry point.

The second rule replaces a single import in a module with the contents of the imported interface, converted to stubs and axioms. This gives the module a self-contained, abstract definition of the imports. The new definitions use their original names, which were already reserved in the module's namespace by the import declaration.

The third rule replaces an export declaration in a module with the theorems of the exported interface as conjectures. The rule updates their bodies to refer to the module's implementation of the interface's functions, and it assigns the theorems names in the module's namespace. These names are provably unique because of our name conventions, as described above.

The fourth rule completes the translation to ACL2 by producing the definitions inside the module once it contains no import or export declarations. Note that the resulting ACL2 program may introduce unverified or unsound axioms from imported interfaces. Each module should be verified in a separate ACL2 session so that no other proofs may rely on these assumptions.

Figure 19.7 shows steps in the transformation from SQR-ALL's modules to their logical meaning in ACL2. We omit the first step, in which the module nondeterministically chooses either SQR-MOD or MAP-MOD; the two reduction paths begin with the program's interfaces, followed by the respective chosen module. The top three boxes depict the transformation of SQR-MOD; the bottom four correspond to MAP-MOD.

The first step for SQR-MOD replaces the exported interface INT-IFC with its theorems. The "export interface" rule inserts int-fn-type as a conjecture with a new name and replaces the reference to the exported function int-fn with its implementation, sqr. In the second step there are no more interfaces to import or export; the "finish" rule produces the definitions of a module.

The MAP-MOD module has both an imported interface and an exported interface. In its first step, the "import interface" rule replaces the import of INT-IFC with a stub for int-fn and an axiom for int-fn-type, representing the minimum logical properties guaranteed by any implementation of INT-IFC. The "export interface" rule takes effect in the second step, this time filling in a conjecture about map-int-fn based on list-fn-type from LIST-IFC. The "finish" rule produces the final list of definitions.

The model does not construct a logical form for SQR-ALL-MOD. As section 19.5 shows, its correctness follows from the verification of SQR-MOD and MAP-MOD and its logical form is redundant.

```
((interface INT-IFC
   (function int-fn (n) t)
   (theorem int-fn-type
     (implies (integerp n)
              (integerp (int-fn n)))))
 (interface LIST-IFC
   (function list-fn (ns) t)
   (theorem list-fn-type
     (implies (integer-listp ns)
              (integer-listp (list-fn ns)))))
 (module SQR-MOD
   (defun sqr (n) (* n n))
   (export INT-IFC (sqr as int-fn))))
```

```
((interface INT-IFC
   (function int-fn (n) t)
   (theorem int-fn-type
     (implies (integerp n)
              (integerp (int-fn n)))))
 (interface LIST-IFC
   (function list-fn (ns) t)
   (theorem list-fn-type
     (implies (integer-listp ns)
              (integer-listp (list-fn ns)))))
 (module SQR-MOD
   (defun sqr (n) (* n n))
   (defthm INT-IFC.int-fn-type
     (implies (integerp n)
              (integerp (sqr n))))))
```

export interface →

```
((defun sqr (n) (* n n))
 (defthm INT-IFC.int-fn-type
   (implies (integerp n)
            (integerp (sqr n)))))
```

finish

```
((interface INT-IFC
   (function int-fn (n) t)
   (theorem int-fn-type
     (implies (integerp n)
              (integerp (int-fn n)))))
 (interface LIST-IFC
   (function list-fn (ns) t)
   (theorem list-fn-type
     (implies (integer-listp ns)
              (integer-listp (list-fn ns)))))
 (module MAP-MOD
   (import INT-IFC)
   (defun map-int-fn (ns)
     (cond
       ((endp ns) nil)
       ((consp ns)
        (cons
          (int-fn (car ns))
          (map-int-fn (cdr ns))))))
   (export LIST-IFC (map-int-fn as list-fn))))
```

import interface →

```
((interface INT-IFC
   (function int-fn (n) t)
   (theorem int-fn-type
     (implies (integerp n)
              (integerp (int-fn n)))))
 (interface LIST-IFC
   (function list-fn (ns) t)
   (theorem list-fn-type
     (implies (integer-listp ns)
              (integer-listp (list-fn ns)))))
 (module MAP-MOD
   (defstub int-fn (n) t)
   (defaxiom int-fn-type
     (implies (integerp n)
              (integerp (int-fn n))))
   (defun map-int-fn (ns)
     (cond
       ((endp ns) nil)
       ((consp ns)
        (cons
          (int-fn (car ns))
          (map-int-fn (cdr ns))))))
   (export LIST-IFC (map-int-fn as list-fn))))
```

```
((interface INT-IFC
   (function int-fn (n) t)
   (theorem int-fn-type
     (implies (integerp n)
              (integerp (int-fn n)))))
 (interface LIST-IFC
   (function list-fn (ns) t)
   (theorem list-fn-type
     (implies (integer-listp ns)
              (integer-listp (list-fn ns)))))
 (module MAP-MOD
   (defstub int-fn (n) t)
   (defaxiom int-fn-type
     (implies (integerp n)
              (integerp (int-fn n))))
   (defun map-int-fn (ns)
     (cond
       ((endp ns) nil)
       ((consp ns)
        (cons
          (int-fn (car ns))
          (map-int-fn (cdr ns))))))
   (defthm LIST-IFC.list-fn-type
     (implies (integer-listp ns)
              (integer-listp
                (map-int-fn ns))))))
```

export interface ←

```
((defstub int-fn (n) t)
 (defaxiom int-fn-type
   (implies (integerp n)
            (integerp (int-fn n))))
 (defun map-int-fn (ns)
   (cond
     ((endp ns) nil)
     ((consp ns)
      (cons
        (int-fn (car ns))
        (map-int-fn (cdr ns))))))
 (defthm LIST-IFC.list-fn-type
   (implies (integer-listp ns)
            (integer-listp (map-int-fn ns)))))
```

finish →

Figure 19.7: Transforming SQR-ALL to its logical form

$(I_{pre} \ldots I I_{post} \ldots \qquad\qquad \longrightarrow (I_{pre} \ldots I I_{post} \ldots \qquad\qquad\qquad\qquad\qquad$ [link (export first)]
$\quad M_{pre} \ldots M_{one} \qquad\qquad\qquad\qquad M_{pre} \ldots M_{one} M_{mid} \ldots M_{two} M_{post} \ldots$
$\qquad\qquad\qquad\qquad\qquad\qquad\quad$ (module $Mvar_{name}$
$\quad M_{mid} \ldots M_{two} \qquad\qquad\qquad\qquad$ join-imports$⟦(Imp_{pre} \ldots Imp_{post} \ldots Imp_{exp} \ldots)⟧$
$\qquad\qquad\qquad\qquad\qquad\qquad\quad$ rename-def*$⟦old\text{-}fvars_{exp}, new\text{-}fvars_{exp}, def_{exp}⟧$
$\quad M_{post} \ldots \qquad\qquad\qquad\qquad\qquad \ldots$
$\quad$ (compound $Mvar_{name} = \qquad\qquad$ rename-def*$⟦old\text{-}fvars_{imp}, new\text{-}fvars_{imp},$
$\qquad Mvar_{imp} (Mvar_{exp} : Ivar)) \qquad\qquad\qquad$ rename-def*$⟦(fvar_{fun} \ldots), new\text{-}fvars_{fun},$
$\quad C_{post} \ldots \qquad\qquad\qquad\qquad\qquad\qquad\qquad\qquad\qquad def_{imp}⟧ ⟧$
$\quad E_{entry}) \qquad\qquad\qquad\qquad\qquad\qquad \ldots$
$\qquad\qquad\qquad\qquad\qquad\qquad\quad$ rename-export*$⟦old\text{-}fvars_{imp}, new\text{-}fvars_{imp},$
$\qquad\qquad\qquad\qquad\qquad\qquad\qquad\qquad\quad$ rename-export*$⟦(fvar_{fun} \ldots), new\text{-}fvars_{fun},$
$\qquad\qquad\qquad\qquad\qquad\qquad\qquad\qquad\qquad\qquad\qquad Exp_{imp}⟧ ⟧$
$\qquad\qquad\qquad\qquad\qquad\qquad \ldots)$
$\qquad\qquad\qquad\qquad\qquad\quad C_{post} \ldots$
$\qquad\qquad\qquad\qquad\qquad\quad E_{entry})$
where $I = ($interface $Ivar Fun \ldots Thm \ldots)$,
$\qquad M_{one} = ($module $Mvar_{exp} \qquad\qquad\qquad\qquad\qquad\qquad ,$
$\qquad\qquad\qquad Imp_{exp} \ldots def_{exp} \ldots$
$\qquad\qquad\qquad Exp \ldots ($export $Ivar (fvar_{impl}$ as $fvar_{fun}) \ldots) Exp \ldots)$
$\qquad M_{two} = ($module $Mvar_{imp} \qquad\qquad\qquad , old\text{-}fvars_{exp} =$ get-def-names$⟦def_{exp}, \ldots⟧$,
$\qquad\qquad\qquad Imp_{pre} \ldots ($import $Ivar) Imp_{post} \ldots$
$\qquad\qquad\qquad def_{imp} \ldots Exp_{imp} \ldots)$
$\qquad old\text{-}fvars_{imp} =$ get-def-names$⟦def_{imp}, \ldots⟧$,
$\qquad new\text{-}fvars_{exp} =$ prefix-names$⟦Mvar_{exp}, old\text{-}fvars_{exp}⟧$,
$\qquad new\text{-}fvars_{imp} =$ prefix-names$⟦Mvar_{imp}, old\text{-}fvars_{imp}⟧$,
$\qquad new\text{-}fvars_{fun} = ($rename-var*$⟦old\text{-}fvars_{exp}, new\text{-}fvars_{exp}, fvar_{impl}⟧ \ldots)$

Figure 19.8: A rule for computing the executable semantics of a program

19·5 Executable Semantics of Programs.

The second half of our model defines the executable semantics of Modular ACL2 programs by translation to an executable ACL2 program. We iteratively link each compound module, constructing a new, equivalent primitive module from its primitive constituents. When the last module has been linked, we link the program entry point to the module's concrete functions. Those functions and the entry point become the ACL2 program. We show a representative reduction rule in figure 19.8; the three others are variations of the same process.

The reduction rule in the figure links a single compound module, producing an equivalent primitive module. It matches the interface for linking, the exporting module, the importing module, and the compound module.

The rule constructs the resulting primitive module by concatenation and substitution of the parts of the constituent modules. It extracts the internally defined names of each module with get-def-names, constructs unique names for them with prefix-names for use in the new module, and uses rename-var* to construct the updated names for functions implementing the given interface. The new primitive module contains the union of the original modules' unresolved imports, the internal definitions of each original module, and the exports of the importing module, all with the new function and theorem names substituted for the old.

The full reduction relation for the executable semantics consists of three other rules. Two are permutations of the first. The last rule links the program entry point to the final module; the process is similar to the rule shown here.

Figure 19.9 shows the transformation from SQR-ALL to an executable ACL2 program. This takes place in two steps. First, the model produces an implementation for the compound module SQR-ALL-MOD by linking MAP-MOD to SQR-MOD across the interface INT-IFC. The result includes the internal functions of both constituent modules, each given a new, unique name. The reference to int-fn in map-int-fn is replaced with a reference to its concrete implementation, SQR-MOD.sqr, in MAP-MOD.map-int-fn. Like MAP-MOD, the new module exports LIST-IFC.

The second step links SQR-ALL-MOD, the last module in the program, to the program's entry point. The final ACL2 program contains the function definitions from SQR-ALL-MOD followed by the converted entry point, which refers directly to MAP-MOD.map-int-fn.

Note that the middle form of SQR-ALL contains SQR-ALL-MOD as a primitive module that can be translated to a logical form and verified. The resulting program, shown in figure 19.10, is nearly identical to the logical form of SQR-MOD. Both conjecture that (a form of) map-int-fn from MAP-MOD satisfies list-fn-type from LIST-IFC. The only difference is that SQR-MOD refers to the stub int-fn where SQR-ALL-MOD refers to SQR-MOD.sqr, both of which satisfy int-fn-type from INT-IFC. The correctness of SQR-ALL-MOD follows straightforwardly from the more general result verified for SQR-MOD. Thus it is not necessary to verify the compound module separately.

19·6 Summary and Evaluation.

We have demonstrated a PLT Redex model for Modular ACL2, a language for developing ACL2 programs and proofs in composable, reusable components. Components contain arbitrary combinations of functions and conjectures. Aside from those exposed via interfaces, elements of one module may not interfere with another. Because primitive modules are translated to verifiable ACL2 conjectures separately, a proof attempt for one module will not interfere with another; since compound modules are linked for execution using unique renaming of internal definitions, internal names from one module will not clash with another.

The language of the model greatly simplifies the real notation. For instance, ACL2 includes numerous elements not included in our grammar, in-

```
((interface INT-IFC
   (function int-fn (n) t)
   (theorem int-fn-type (implies (integerp n) (integerp (int-fn n)))))
 (interface LIST-IFC
   (function list-fn (ns) t)
   (theorem list-fn-type
     (implies (integer-listp ns) (integer-listp (list-fn ns)))))
 (module SQR-MOD (defun sqr (n) (* n n)) (export INT-IFC (sqr as int-fn)))
 (module MAP-MOD
   (import INT-IFC)
   (defun map-int-fn (ns)
     (cond
       ((endp ns) nil)
       ((consp ns) (cons (int-fn (car ns)) (map-int-fn (cdr ns))))))
   (export LIST-IFC (map-int-fn as list-fn)))
 (compound SQR-ALL-MOD = MAP-MOD (SQR-MOD : INT-IFC))
 (invoke LIST-IFC (list-fn (list 1 2 3))))
```

```
((interface INT-IFC
   (function int-fn (n) t)
   (theorem int-fn-type (implies (integerp n) (integerp (int-fn n)))))
 (interface LIST-IFC
   (function list-fn (ns) t)
   (theorem list-fn-type
     (implies (integer-listp ns) (integer-listp (list-fn ns)))))
 (module SQR-MOD (defun sqr (n) (* n n)) (export INT-IFC (sqr as int-fn)))
 (module MAP-MOD
   (import INT-IFC)
   (defun map-int-fn (ns)
     (cond
       ((endp ns) nil)
       ((consp ns) (cons (int-fn (car ns)) (map-int-fn (cdr ns))))))
   (export LIST-IFC (map-int-fn as list-fn)))
 (module SQR-ALL-MOD
   (defun SQR-MOD.sqr (n) (* n n))
   (defun MAP-MOD.map-int-fn (ns)
     (cond
       ((endp ns) nil)
       ((consp ns)
       (cons (SQR-MOD.sqr (car ns)) (MAP-MOD.map-int-fn (cdr ns))))))
   (export LIST-IFC (MAP-MOD.map-int-fn as list-fn)))
 (invoke LIST-IFC (list-fn (list 1 2 3))))
```

```
((defun SQR-MOD.sqr (n) (* n n))
 (defun MAP-MOD.map-int-fn (ns)
   (cond
     ((endp ns) nil)
     ((consp ns) (cons (SQR-MOD.sqr (car ns)) (MAP-MOD.map-int-fn (cdr ns))))))
 (MAP-MOD.map-int-fn (list 1 2 3)))
```

Figure 19.9: Transforming SQR-ALL to its executable form

```
((defun SQR-MOD.sqr (n) (* n n))
 (defun MAP-MOD.map-int-fn (ns)
   (cond
     ((endp ns) nil)
     ((consp ns) (cons (SQR-MOD.sqr (car ns)) (MAP-MOD.map-int-fn (cdr ns))))))
 (defthm LIST-IFC.list-fn-type
   (implies (integer-listp ns) (integer-listp (MAP-MOD.map-int-fn ns)))))
```

Figure 19.10: The logical form of linked compound module SQR-ALL-MOD

cluding hints and other annotations for the theorem prover, packages, books, macros, and so on. Some of these features, including most of the basic tools for programming and theorem proving, can be added with straightforward extensions. Others pose more of a problem. User-defined macros complicate the renaming step of our model; Modular ACL2 can only support them by duplicating the macro expansion process.

ACL2's existing mechanisms for separating program components, such as packages, books, encapsulation blocks, and local definitions, are largely subsumed by Modular ACL2's module system. For compatibility with existing ACL2 programs, we may investigate a mechanism for converting a book to a module and vice versa. We have not yet explored how modules would interact with the other mechanisms in the same program.

Programs need not be restricted in order nor entry points. A Modular ACL2 program can interleave interface definitions, module definitions, and top-level expressions. This restriction simplifies the model but does not alter its expressiveness; any program can be reordered to fit the current grammar.

Compound modules in our language link two other modules across a single interface. They can be expanded to link together an arbitrary number of modules. This feature is a convenience, but can be expressed in our model by decomposing any compound module into a sequence of smaller compound modules that link incrementally.

Our naming conventions allow our model to create readable, unique names for new definitions. A full implementation must enforce the restrictions on names or find a more permissive mechanism for combining components. An implementation that hands off ACL2 code to the standard ACL2 implementation must generate unique names that are at least readable enough that ACL2's output can be correlated back to the original source code.

For the logical meaning of Modular ACL2, only a module's exported theorems are renamed. An implementation could remove the naming restrictions by analyzing the full module to generate unique names, or by requiring programmers to explicitly declare names for exported theorems as well.

The executable semantics of Modular ACL2 renames every definition, possibly several times. However, the executable behavior of ACL2 can be simulated in other languages such as Lisp or Scheme, as has been done in PLT Scheme with DrACuLa [111]. These languages can implement modules and linking without renaming, for instance by implementing modules as closures and passing imported functions as values.

The current design of Modular ACL2 borrows many elements from PLT Scheme's unit system [40, 82] and is similar to early module systems [115, 116, 117]. Module implementations and specifications are separate entities. Like units, each component has a number of inputs and outputs described by named specifications. We maintain the principle of external connections [39]: modules do not refer to an implementation for their imports; instead, components may be combined by linking any import and export that share a specification. Unlike units, our system does not allow cyclic links, which might introduce new recursions and interfere with ACL2 termination proofs.

Our module system does not have some of the features demonstrated by the ML module system [71]. We do not support a type system for Modular ACL2, nor do we have a subsumption relation on interfaces. Modular ACL2 also does not have sharing constraints or any other way to declare a relationship between two interfaces. This is an important feature which we will explore as we expand our implementation.

Separate compilation is an important consideration for a module system. The executable form of Modular ACL2 does not support separate compilation directly in ACL2, as the code changes each time it is linked. Implementations in other languages, however, can support separate compilation; for instance, PLT Scheme's unit system supports separate compilation and all of the module features of Modular ACL2's executable semantics.

The logical form supports separate verification. As shown in sections 19.4 and 19.5, once a module's proof obligations are discharged it may be linked safely, without further proofs. Modular ACL2 modules can be verified by ACL2 but not certified as books, because books may not contain `defaxiom`. We hope to find a logical form for modules that can be certified; for now, we verify modules at the top level.

19.7 Developing with PLT Redex.
Our model of Modular ACL2 has gone through many stages, guided in large part by the PLT Redex facilities. Along the way we have developed techniques for making the most of these tools.

Our guiding principle for developing Modular ACL2 is simplicity of design. This pays off in a few ways with PLT Redex. Maintaining a simple language and relying on the power of the `reduction-relation` macro to express the complexity of a model can actually yield a simpler set of rules than tailoring a grammar to the operational details of a model. Our first prototype of Modular ACL2 had a distinguished position for components being linked, to save a search through the program at every step. As a result, there were more rules for reordering the program to maintain the invariant than for linking. The current model has fewer than half as many rules, many much simpler than the originals.

Incremental design preserves the simplicity of a model and facilitates exploration of the design space. We endeavor to start with the smallest possible set of features and restrictions on our model, adding only those that are necessary.

One interesting point is that for our model, Redex's determinism is a complicating restriction. Our early implementation imported and exported modules (for the logical side) and linked compound modules (for the executable side) in arbitrary order. All of the examples we inspected were confluent, indicating that each program has unique logical and executable forms. We eventually constrained the order of operations (and, to aid our implementation, the order of components in a program) for the sake of efficiency, but we did so with confidence that our choice of order did not affect the outcome.

With a rapidly changing model, we find a thorough test suite indispensible. We maintain tests for our ACL2 and Modular ACL2 grammars and both reduction relations. Our model has undergone multiple complete revisions, yet our tests have reliably caught the vast majority of our bugs as soon as we introduced them. PLT Redex provides `test-match` for testing terms and grammars, `apply-reduction-relation` and `apply-reduction-relation*` for testing reduction relations, and a library for integrating with the Scheme-Unit testing framework [114].

Acknowledgments. We thank Rex Page of Oklahoma University for the inspiration to explore modularity mechanisms for ACL2, and Dale Vaillancourt of Northeastern University for the first implementation of Modular ACL2. We also thank Pete Manolios, Peter Dillinger, and the rest of the ACL2 community for insights into the soundness, implementation, and possible applications of Modular ACL2.

20 · Modeling Scheme Macros
Martin Gasbichler, Zühlke Engineering AG

This chapter presents a model for the core of hygienic macro expansion. The model employs a non-standard identifier representation using de-Bruijn levels that keep track of binding places as required by hygiene. Another interesting point of the model is that the pervasive use of explicit substitutions allows for a clear designation of the progress of the parsing and expansion process. The combination of the macro expander with a parser from s-expressions to abstract syntax demonstrates the modelling of two interleaved processes. The chapter also uses explicit substitutions for modelling the evaluation of programs, which is a more standard use-case for explicit substitutions. Due to the complexities of macro expansion, we found Redex an indispensable tool for testing and debugging. In addition, Redex eases communicating about and sharing the model among researchers.

This chapter defines a formal semantics for hygienic macros in a language with s-expression-based syntax. The semantics includes a parser and the core of a macro expander. The core macro expander can call transformers such as Scheme's `syntax-rules` (similar to rewriting rules) or the procedural `syntax-case` facility, although the definition of these transformers is outside the scope of this chapter. The definition of the system uses explicit substitutions [1], which are substitutions embedded into the term structure instead of being meta-level operations. Bove and Arbilla were the first to use explicit substitutions to model macros [12], and this chapter builds on their work.

Besides explicit substitutions, the semantics in this chapter are unusual because they start from concrete syntax. Usually, reduction systems for programming languages are defined on a set of terms corresponding to a representation of the abstract syntax. The concrete syntax of the language does not matter. In addition, authors often assume Barendregt's variable convention [8]. The convention implies that bound variables are always distinct from free variables. These two simplifications cannot be used if the language supports macros because macro expansion interleaves with parsing while creating the abstract syntax tree, and (hygienic) macro expansion needs to preserve the correct binding relations, *especially* for variables whose names are not unique.

To specify a semantics for macro expansion, the starting point is the concrete syntax of the language. The first step of the semantics specifies the relation between concrete and abstract syntax by a set of reductions. These reductions parse the concrete syntax, accumulate macro definitions, expand macro applications, and finally produce abstract syntax. The representation of a variable in the abstract syntax is not simply the name of the variable but contains additional information, called a *level*, that is reminiscent of de-Bruijn indices and records the binding place of the variable. This identifier representation is the key ingredient for the modeling of the hygienic macro expansion. The semantics of evaluation of the language differs from an ordinary call-by-value semantics in exactly this point; that is, it relates abstract syntax terms defined over identifiers with levels.

Explicit substitutions, concrete syntax, and de-Bruijn indices are thus specialties of this chapter. They demonstrate that semantics based on reduction relations are applicable to a wide range of domains because they allow the specification of relations between arbitrary term structures.

This chapter is organized as follows: section 20.1 introduces hygienic macros, section 20.2 presents the $\lambda_v^{n,\langle\!\langle\,\rangle\!\rangle}$ calculus, which serves as target language for the macro expander. Section 20.3 presents an initial parser, and section 20.4 the core macro expander. Finally, section 20.5 provides a brief outlook on the definition of transformers as given in the author's dissertation [45]. The type-setting of all the rules in this chapter has been done automatically by a program that takes as its input the PLT Redex rules.

20·1 Hygienic Macros.
A macro is a user-defined source-to-source transformation performed by the compiler. A hygienic macro system prevents the user from writing macros that inadvertently capture variables from the input or that insert variables that are inadvertently captured by surrounding code. In macro systems with local binding constructs for keywords, hygiene also prevents these syntactic binding constructs from inadvertent capture of keywords. Hygiene is important for macros because it gives the macro writer complete freedom over the choice of variable names and ensures that none of the macros can interfere with the bindings in a program. Hygiene is therefore essential for using macros in large programs because it hides the use of names internal to the macro.

The literature characterizes hygienic macros by stating requirements the macros must fulfill. The first definition goes back to Kohlbecker et al. [62]:

Hygiene Condition for Macro Expansion Generated identifiers that become binding instances in the completely expanded program must only bind identifiers that are generated at the same transcription step.

Here the term "transcription step" is defined as the one-step expansion of a macro.

Kohlbecker's definition does not cover the relationship between identifiers inserted by the macro and binding instances in the original input. Clinger and Rees [22] improve this by formulating the following:

Hygiene Condition

1. No high-level macro can insert a binding that captures references other than those inserted by the macro.

2. No high-level macro can insert a reference that is captured by bindings other than those inserted by the macro.

Clinger and Rees also define a condition for local macros that Dybvig et al. [31] summarize as:

Local macros are *referentially transparent* in the sense that free identifiers appearing in the output of a local macro are scoped where the macro definition appears.

The following examples illustrate the hygienic macro facility in Scheme. The define-syntax construct defines a new, global binding for a macro:

- (define-syntax *keyword transformer*)   syntax

In R^{5}RS, the only *transformer* form is a syntax-rules expression, which enables the programmer to write macros in a high-level language similar to rewriting systems. Existing Scheme implementations often provide additional facilities that can be used in place of the *transformer* form.

A syntax-rules expression consists of a list of literals and a list of rules:

- (syntax-rules (*literal* ...)   ((*pattern template*) ...))

Here, *pattern* is an s-expression that is matched against the macro call. For the first pattern that matches the call, the corresponding *template* form replaces the call with all variables in the pattern replaced by the corresponding input forms. A pattern is a variable if it is an identifier and if it is not one of the *literal* identifiers. If a pattern is not a variable, it has to match the input exactly. As an example, consider the following slightly simplified implementation of the cond macro from R^{5}RS:

```
(define-syntax cond
  (syntax-rules (else)
    ((cond ((else expr))) expr)
    ((cond ((test rhs))) (if test rhs))
    ((cond ((test rhs) clause ...))
     (if test rhs (cond (clause ...))))))
```

This macro lists `else` as a literal identifier. Therefore, in the pattern of the
first rule, the identifier `else` has to appear in the input as well, whereas `expr`
is a pattern variable. In the second rule, `test` and `rhs` are both variables and
if the pattern matches, the macro expander replaces them by the corresponding input forms in the template (`if test rhs`). This final rule contains an
ellipsis pattern: `clause ...` matches an arbitrary number of input forms.

For the demonstration of hygiene, consider the implementation of the `or`
syntax from R^{5}RS:

```
(define-syntax or
  (syntax-rules ()
    ((or) #f)
    ((or e1 e2 ...) (let ((temp e1))
                      (if temp temp (or e2 ...))))))
```

The macro consists of two rules: The first rule explains `or` with no arguments
and rewrites to `#f`. The template of the second rule binds the value of the
first argument to a temporary variable, tests its boolean value, returns if
it was not false, and rewrites `or` with the remaining arguments otherwise.
The use of a temporary variable is necessary to prevent duplicate evaluation
of the expression `e1`. Hygiene ensures that the variable the macro is binding
cannot capture free occurrences of the same identifier within the input forms,
in this case `e2` .... That is, in the program

```
(define temp 23)
(or (= 1 2) temp)
```

the identifier `temp` always refers to the global variable and the program evaluates to 23. Without hygiene, the second argument of `or` would be substituted literally into the template, yielding an expression that evaluates to
`#f`:[1]

```
(define temp 23)
(let ((temp (= 1 2)))
  (if temp temp (let ((temp temp))
                  (if temp
                      temp
                      #f))))
```

---

[1] For better readability, we do not expand `let` forms in the examples.

Thus the key to hygienic expansion is to represent identifiers in the macro output not simply by their original names but to use a vehicle that ensures that the binding place remains intact in the macro output. The traditional vehicle is to uniquely rename all identifiers. However, renaming has a number of drawbacks: it needs to generate fresh identifiers, which is not purely functional; it requires a careful implementation that is hard to debug; and it is not descriptive. We thus do not rely on renaming; instead we use an identifier with levels. The level is a natural number and indicates the number of binders between the occurrence of the variable and the abstraction that binds the variable. This representation of identifiers is reminiscent of the de Bruijn notation [27]. Unlike the de-Bruijn notation, identifiers in Λ^n still carry a name along with the level. Keeping this name both improves readability and, more importantly, enables hygienic macro expansion. Keeping the name is important because the identifier may be used with `quote` after macro expansion, making the binding information potentially irrelevant. Using this representation, the hygienic expansion of the example above is:

```
(define⁰ temp 23)
(let⁰ ((temp (=⁰ 1 2)))
   (if¹ temp⁰
       temp⁰
       (let¹ ((temp temp¹))
           (if² temp⁰
               temp⁰
               #f))))
```

Here hygiene is maintained: the level 1 of the identifier reference `temp`^{1} indicates that the binding place is the original global binding, thus no capture has occured. Hygiene analogously applies to macros that insert or bind keywords. Hence the keywords `define`, `if`, and `let` receive a level as well.

It is the task of the parser and the macro expander to derive and maintain the level of the identifiers. Sections 20.3 and 20.4 describe this process. Evaluation of a variant of the λ-calculus that uses de-Bruijn levels is the topic of section 20.2.

Besides preventing macros from capturing free variables, hygiene also ensures that the variables used by the macros are not captured. As an example, the `receive` macro provides a nicer interface to Scheme's multiple return values facility [103]:

```
(define-syntax receive
  (syntax-rules ()
    ((receive formals expression body ...)
     (call-with-values (lambda () expression)
                       (lambda formals body ...)))))
```

In the expression

```
(let ((call-with-values 23))
   (receive (a b c) (values 1 2 3)
      (+ a b c)))
```

the macro `receive` inserts a reference to the variable `call-with-values` within the body of a `let` that binds this variable. However, hygiene ensures that the inserted reference to `call-with-values` still refers to the top-level binding from R^5RS. The hygienic expansion of the expression looks as follows:

```
(let⁰ ((call-with-values 23))
   (call-with-values¹
      (lambda¹ () (values² 1 2 3))
      (lambda¹ (a b c) (+² a⁰ b⁰ c⁰)))))
```

Level numbers are not the complete story for implementing hygiene, however. The following example demonstrates that it is necessary to distinguish the output of each transcription step (in addition to the binding level) to meet Kohlbecker's Hygiene Condition for Macro Expansion:

```
(define-syntax gen-ys
   (syntax-rules ()
      ((gen-ys (id1 id2 id3 ...) ())
       (cmp id1 id2))
      ((gen-ys (id ...) (rest1 rest2 ...))
       (gen-ys (y id ...) (rest2 ...)))))

(define-syntax cmp
   (syntax-rules ()
      ((cmp a b)   (lambda (a) b))))
```

The macro `gen-ys` maintains two lists of identifiers. In the first, it accumulates "generated" identifiers, and the second list contains an arbitrary form for each identifier to be generated. Once the second list is empty, `gen-ys` expands to a macro application of `cmp` with the first two generated identifiers as arguments. Hygiene requires the macro application `(gen-ys () (1 2))` to expand to `(lambda (y) y¹)`, where the inner `y` is free because different transcription steps introduced the two `y`s. Levels alone, however, do not preserve enough information to distinguish identifiers from different transcription steps during the expansion. Consequently, it is necessary to annotate during macro expansion the generated identifiers with information about the transcription step. To that end, we adapt the technique of *marking* from `syntax-case` [31]. Identifiers that appear in the output of a macro receive a mark that indicates the transcription step. Two identifiers are then bound by the same abstraction only if their levels and their marks are equal. In the example above, the generated cmp form is (cmp $^{\{1\}}y$ $^{\{2\}}y$), where 1 and 2 are two different marks that correspond to the two different expansions of gen-ys. These marks allow the parser to produce the expected output (lambda (y) y^1), where the first y does not bind the second.

To further investigate marking, we introduce a binding form for macros that binds the macro identifier in a local scope. This form is called let-syntax and its syntax is analogous to let with the difference that the right-hand side of each binding is a syntax-rules form. The body of such a local macro may insert locally bound variables. For example, the following expression:

```
(let ((a 1))
  (let-syntax ((m (syntax-rules () ((m) a))))
    (let ((a 2))
      (m))))
```

expands to

```
(let ((a 1))
  (let ((a 2))
    a^1)))
```

because the outer binding for a is bound at the place the macro m is bound.

Building on let-syntax, we can now define a macro that generates the definition of another macro:

```
(define-syntax gen-macro
  (syntax-rules ()
    ((genm x)
     (let-syntax
         ((inner (syntax-rules ()
                   ((inner a) (lambda (a) x)))))
       (inner x)))))
(gen-macro y)
```

If a macro expands into the definition of another macro, the generated identifiers of the generated macro are marked twice: once as the output of the macro that expands into the macro definition and then again at every application of the generated macro. Of course, the process of macros generating other macro definitions can be continued ad infinitum. Hence, to support repeated marking of identifiers, we record not a single mark but a set of marks with every identifier. Each mark in the set refers to a macro application that generated the identifier. Two identifiers are then bound by the same abstraction only if their levels and their sets of marks are equal.

We extend the representation of identifiers to include a set of marks. However, marks are only necessary during expansion for deciding capture— in the output of the expander, only the level matters.

Finally, macro expansion needs to treat the `quote` form specially. The operand of `quote` is an s-expression and quote transforms the s-expression into a value whose external representation is the input s-expression. For example (quote 52) evaluates to 52 (the number fifty-two) since the s-expression 52 (the digit "5" followed by the digit "2") is the external representation of the number fifty-two. `Quote` comes in handy for writing literal expressions for lists. For example the expression (quote (1 a)) evaluates to the list of the number one and the symbol with name a.

If `quote` appears in the template of a macro, forms that look like code suddenly become data:

```
(define-syntax foo
  (syntax-rules ()
    ((foo (a (b) c)) (quote b))))
(foo (lambda (x) (+ x x)))
```

evaluates to the symbol x. Ever stranger things can happen if `quote` is passed as an argument to a macro:

```
(define-syntax swap
  (syntax-rules ()
    ((swap a b) (b a))))
(swap x quote)
```

which evaluates to the symbol x, even though the template of `swap` looks as if it would produce a procedure application. This example demonstrates that there are macro definitions for which it is impossible to derive binding information in the output of the macro by analyzing only the macro definition. In general, binding information becomes available only as macro expansion proceeds, so that parsing and macro expansion are interleaved.

20·2 The $\lambda_v^{n,(\!(\,)\!)}$ Calculus.
This section presents a variant of the classical call-by-value λ-calculus based on the language Λ^n that uses identifiers with de-Bruijn levels. The calculus uses explicit substitutions to describe the replacement of the bound variable in a β-redex as originally described by Abadi et. al. [1]. The hygienic macro expander uses Λ^n as its target language and its indexed variables are the key ingredient to preserve hygiene without relying on renaming.

Figure 20.1 contains the abstract syntax for Λ^n. Expressions encompass identifiers with levels, written as x^n, constants and λ-abstractions as values,

$$
\begin{aligned}
e &::= x^n \mid v \mid (@\ ee) \mid e⟦t⟧ \\
v &::= a \mid (\lambda\, x.e) \\
t &::= \langle x^n, v \rangle
\end{aligned}
$$

Figure 20.1: Abstract syntax of Λ^n

and applications, written $(@\ ee)$.[2] Furthermore, explicit substitutions extend the set of expressions—we call them "evaluation substitutions"—to distinguish them from other explicit substitutions that will be introduced later. They are written as $e⟦t⟧$ where t is a pair $\langle x^n, v \rangle$. Such a pair corresponds to the substitution of a variable x^n by the value v, where the value v must be closed.

> **Remark**: Since the evaluation of an unbound variable is an error, we only substitute closed values.

Names are superfluous in Λ^n because the level of a variable already represents the binding information. Hence we identify terms that are equal modulo the names of the bound variables. However, we do not consider terms where the names and the levels do not correspond, for example, $\lambda x.y^0$ or $\lambda x.\lambda y.x^0 y^0$. The author's dissertation [45] contains a formal definition of a predicate for well-formed expressions.

The elimination of the evaluation substitution is the subject of the $\rightarrow_{⟦⟧}$ notion of reduction defined in figure 20.2. Rule (SEvalSubstId) applies an evaluation substitution to an identifier that matches the identifier, and rule (SEvalSubstLam) pushes the evaluation substitution to the body but increments the level of the identifier by one as it moves one binder farther away from its own binder.[3]

The contexts for $\rightarrow_{⟦⟧}$ are defined as:

$$
\begin{aligned}
C_{⟦⟧} &::= C'_{⟦⟧} \mid (@\ C_{⟦⟧} e) \mid (@\ e C_{⟦⟧}) \mid (\lambda\, x.\ C_{⟦⟧}) \\
C'_{⟦⟧} &::= [\ ] \mid C'_{⟦⟧}⟦t⟧
\end{aligned}
$$

They give rise to a one-step reduction $\rightarrow_{⟦⟧}$ for the elimination of evaluation substitutions: $e \rightarrow_{⟦⟧} e'$, iff for some context $C_{⟦⟧}$, $e \equiv C_{⟦⟧}[e_1]$, $e' \equiv C_{⟦⟧}[e_2]$,

---

[2] To draw the distinction between abstract and concrete syntax, the abstract syntax uses @ to mark procedure applications.

[3] Here and from now on, we often omit the description of rules that have an obvious behavior, such as pushing substitutions unchanged into an application or dropping them for constants or terms where they do not apply.

$$\to_{\llparenthesis\rrparenthesis} \subseteq e\llparenthesis t\rrparenthesis \times e$$

$$x^n \llparenthesis \langle x^n, v\rangle \rrparenthesis \to_{\llparenthesis\rrparenthesis} v \qquad\qquad \text{(SEvalSubstId)}$$

$$y^m \llparenthesis \langle x^n, v\rangle \rrparenthesis \to_{\llparenthesis\rrparenthesis} y^m \text{ iff } y^m \neq x^n \qquad \text{(SEvalSubstIdOther)}$$

$$a\llparenthesis t\rrparenthesis \to_{\llparenthesis\rrparenthesis} a \qquad\qquad \text{(SEvalSubstConst)}$$

$$(@\ e_1\ e_2)\llparenthesis t\rrparenthesis \to_{\llparenthesis\rrparenthesis} (@\ e_1\llparenthesis t\rrparenthesis\ e_2\llparenthesis t\rrparenthesis) \qquad \text{(SEvalSubstApp)}$$

$$(\lambda y.e)\llparenthesis \langle x^n, v\rangle \rrparenthesis \to_{\llparenthesis\rrparenthesis} (\lambda y.e\llparenthesis \langle x^{n+1}, v\rangle \rrparenthesis) \qquad \text{(SEvalSubstLam)}$$

Figure 20.2: Elimination of $\llparenthesis\rrparenthesis$

$e_1 \to_{\llparenthesis\rrparenthesis} e_2$. From this, we can derive an equational theory: $e_1 =_{\llparenthesis\rrparenthesis} e_2$ if $e_1 \to^*_{\llparenthesis\rrparenthesis} e_2$.

A second set of contexts C^n are used later to specify evaluation. These contexts do not place the hole under λ-abstractions or under evaluation substitutions:

$$C^n \qquad ::= [\ ]\mid (@\ C^n\ e) \mid (@\ e\ C^n)$$

Both restrictions are necessary to ensure well-formedness of reduced terms. Like the limitation of evaluation substitutions to substitute only closed values, this is a profound deviation from other calculi with explicit substitutions [1]. Additional operators to manipulate the levels of identifiers are required to permit such restrictions.

The basic notion of reduction introduces an expression with an evaluation substitution (with $FV^n(e)$ being defined in [45]):

$$(@\ (\lambda x.e)\ v) \to_{\beta^n_v} e\llparenthesis \langle x^0, v\rangle \rrparenthesis \text{ iff } FV^n(v) = \varnothing \qquad (\beta^n_v)$$

Unlike the classical λ_v-calculus, we assume the argument to be closed as our evaluation substitutions may only substitute closed values.

Together with δ (an unspecified reduction for evaluating functional constants), β^n_v forms the notion of reduction $\to^n_v$:

$$\to^n_v = \delta \cup \beta^n_v$$

The *one-step reduction* $\to^n_v$ is the compatible closure of $\to^n_v$:

$$e \to^n_v e' \text{ if } e \equiv C^n[e_1], e' \equiv C^n[e_2], e_1 \to e_2$$

Definition 20.1 ($\lambda_v^{n,\langle\!\langle\,\rangle\!\rangle}$) *Let* $\to_v^{n,\langle\!\langle\,\rangle\!\rangle} = \to_v^n \cup \to_{\langle\!\langle\,\rangle\!\rangle}$ *and* $\to_v^{n,\langle\!\langle\,\rangle\!\rangle}$ *its reflexive,* *transitive closure.* $=_v^{n,\langle\!\langle\,\rangle\!\rangle}$ *is the smallest equivalence relation generated by* $\to_v^{n,\langle\!\langle\,\rangle\!\rangle}$. *If* $e_1 =_v^{n,\langle\!\langle\,\rangle\!\rangle} e_2$, *we write* $\lambda_v^{n,\langle\!\langle\,\rangle\!\rangle} \vdash e_1 = e_2$.

$\square$

The $\lambda_v^{n,\langle\!\langle\,\rangle\!\rangle}$ calculus is a conservative extension of (a variant of) the λ_v calculus. The proof can be found in the author's dissertation [45] and follows the strategy of Abadi et al. [1] and Rose [95], which in turn use Hardin's interpretation method.

20·3 Parsing Scheme without Macros.

The previous section added identifiers with levels to the classical lambda calculus to include a tool for tracking the binding place of a variable without using renaming techniques. However, the identifiers in usual programming languages are merely symbols. It is the job of the compiler to relate the variables to their binding places using the rules of lexical scoping. To mimic this in Λ^n, we define an s-expression-based source language with ordinary symbol-based variables and define a parsing reduction to translate it to Λ^n. This parsing reduction works interleaved with an expansion reduction, introduced in the next section: Among the syntactic forms which the parsing reduction recognizes are—besides identifiers, applications, and abstractions—also macro applications. The parser transforms the latter into an intermediate form which thereafter the expansion reduction takes as its input and expands to source terms augmented with binding information. Then the parsing reduction steps in again and produces Λ^n-terms and possibly more macro applications to be expanded by the expansion reduction and so forth. The next section describes this interleaving along with the expansion reduction while this section focuses on the parsing reduction only.

As for most s-expression-based languages, the parser is straightforward: either the s-expression is an atom or the first element of a parenthesized expression determines the syntactic role of the expression. The parser then recursively descends into the sub-expressions. To map identifiers from the source code to identifiers with levels, the parser generates explicit substitutions that replace symbols by identifiers with levels. The parser pushes these substitutions inwards and maintains the level of the identifier. Whenever the explicit substitution enters a λ-abstraction, the parser must increment the level of the identifier. This usage of explicit substitutions differs completely from the technique in the previous section where the semantics uses explicit substitutions to relate the evaluation in the calculus to actual implementations. The primary motivation for using explicit substitutions in the parser is the possibility to obtain a concise description of hygienic macro expansion.

$$se \qquad ::= a \mid \texttt{x} \mid (se \ \ldots)$$

Figure 20.3: Concrete syntax based on s-expressions

The macro expander uses its own set of explicit substitutions. And, because parsing and macro expansion must be interleaved, the parser uses explicit substitutions as well.

The source language terms are s-expressions, which consist of constants, symbols, and parenthesized forms. Figure 20.3 contains the definition of this language. The concrete syntax does not define the structure of the syntactic forms such as applications or abstractions; it is merely the input to the parser.

The parser transforms an s-expression into a term of Λ^n by descending into sub-expressions. Just before such a descent, the input of the parser is a mixture of concrete and abstract syntax: the parser has already parsed the context and generated the abstract syntax for it but the sub-expressions are still concrete syntax. For example, for the s-expression (lambda x (x x)), the parser creates in its first step the term $(\lambda x.(\texttt{x x}))$, which is an abstract-syntax λ-abstraction with a concrete syntax body. In the next step, the parser will descend into the body and turn it into an abstract-syntax procedure application. Figure 20.4 describes this mixture of abstract and concrete syntax called *mixture syntax*. The mixture syntax uses the term $^{ks}x^n$ to represent an identifier. The macro expander uses the additional index ks to track the marks of identifiers. This index will be used below in Section 20.4. For now, the set of marks can be safely ignored and we will often omit it. Translating the result of the parser to Λ^n works by dropping the index ks from all identifiers.

To keep track of the binding place of identifiers, the parser also adds *parsing substitutions* to the mixture. A parsing substitution r applied to a mixture term c is written as $c(\!\lvert r \rvert\!)$ and again a mixture term. That is, parsing substitutions are the explicit substitutions that replace symbols by identifiers with labels as sketched in the introduction of this section. A parsing substitution replaces a source-code identifier (a symbol) by a labeled identifier, written as $^{ks}x^n/\texttt{x}$. The parser uses the set *Specials* containing two special identifiers λ and $\star$ that cannot be present in the source code. The parser uses the λ to keep track of uses of the lambda keyword. The $\star$ identifier assigns unbound variables the correct level for global identifiers as it matches any symbol. The parser achieves this tracking by initially applying the two parsing substitutions $(\!\lvert \lambda^0/\texttt{lambda} \rvert\!)(\!\lvert \star^0/\star \rvert\!)$ to its input term.

$$r \qquad ::= {}^{ks}x^n / \mathrm{x}$$
$$c \qquad ::= se \mid a \mid {}^{ks}x^n \mid (\lambda \, x.c) \mid (@ \, c \, c \ldots) \mid c(\!|r|\!)$$
$$lse \qquad ::= se \mid lse(\!|r|\!)$$

Figure 20.4: Mixture of abstract and concrete syntax

$$
\begin{array}{lll}
\hspace{2.2cm} \longmapsto_{\text{Parse}} & & \text{DEP-A} \\
\text{std.red. of} \quad \longrightarrow_{\text{Parse}} & & \text{DEP-B} \\
\hspace{1.5cm} \text{uses} \quad \longmapsto_{\text{El}} & & \text{DEP-C} \\
\hspace{2.2cm} \text{std.red. of} \quad \longrightarrow_{\text{El}} & & \text{DEP-D} \\
\hspace{4.4cm} = \hspace{1cm} \longrightarrow_{(\!|)} & & \text{DEP-E}
\end{array}
$$

Figure 20.5: Dependency of reductions

To make the evolving presentation more precise, we tag the subset of mixture terms consisting of s-expressions subject to parsing substitutions as *lexical s-expressions* and let the variable *lse* range over lexical s-expressions. Lexical s-expressions represent the unparsed (and later also the unexpanded) source terms carrying binding information.

With the concrete syntax and the mixture syntax in place, the definition of the parser is possible. Figure 20.5 displays the dependencies of the reductions that make up the parser. We define the parser as the standard parsing reduction $\longmapsto_{\text{Parse}}$ (see DEP-A in figure 20.4) of a parsing reduction $\longrightarrow_{\text{Parse}}$ (see DEP-B in the figure). The parsing reduction $\longrightarrow_{\text{Parse}}$ turns concrete syntax into mixture syntax until it reaches the base expressions and the generated mixture syntax consists of abstract-syntax forms only. For every λ-abstraction, the parser generates a parsing substitution that replaces the symbol—representing the bound variable—by an identifier whose level refers to the λ-abstraction. For this parsing substitution to take effect, the parser needs to *eliminate* it, which means that the parser pushes the substitutions into the generated mixture syntax until the substitution meets a symbol and turns it into an identifier. The parser calls the standard elimination reduction $\longmapsto_{\text{El}}$ to perform this task (see DEP-C). In fact, $\longrightarrow_{\text{El}}$, the reduction relation upon which $\longmapsto_{\text{El}}$ is built (see DEP-D), not only eliminates parsing reductions but also other explicit substitutions that the macro expander and the macro transfromer later introduce and that serve similar purposes as the parsing substitutions and hence require an analogous elimination. To avoid redefining the parser and the expander during the introduction of the other substitutions, the parser and the expander use the reduction $\rightarrow_{El}$ for the elimination of all explicit substitutions. The reduction $\rightarrow_{El}$ is defined as the union of the individual elimination reductions. For now, it eliminates only parsing substitutions using $\rightarrow_{(\!|\!)}$ (see DEP-E):

$$\rightarrow_{El} = \rightarrow_{(\!|\!)}$$

Later we will redefine $\rightarrow_{El}$ to contain the other substitutions as well.

Next, to define $\mapsto_{El}$ it is also necessary to specify where and when the elimination takes place. Elimination should not happen if the term subject to the substitution is a compound s-expression as this s-expression has not been parsed and its syntactic role is therefore not known. As an example, consider the term $(\texttt{lambda x x})(\!|\lambda^0/\texttt{lambda}|\!)(\!|x^2/\texttt{x}|\!)$. If elimination would push the inner substitution to the s-expression, the result would be $(\lambda^0 \text{ x x})(\!|x^2/\texttt{x}|\!)$: the substitution replaces the symbol $\texttt{lambda}$ by the special identifier λ^0 but does not affect the two symbols x. If we ignore for a moment that this term is not a mixture term (because $(\lambda^0 \text{ x x})$ is an s-expression containing an identifier), we may continue with elimination. That is, we will again eliminate a parsing substitution applied to a compound s-expression. This yields the term $(\lambda^0 \ x^2 \ x^2)$. However the level of the identifier x^2 in the body is wrong, as x is a local variable with level 0 in the body of a λ-abstraction. However, the fact that $(\lambda^0 \ x^2 \ x^2)$ is a λ-abstraction is only known after parsing. We could let the parser fix the level of the identifiers in the body as it turns the s-expression into an abstract-syntax term, but it is also possible to avoid the generation of the spurious identifiers in the first place by not eliminating parsing substitutions applied to compound s-expressions. Instead, the parsing substitutions stick at compound s-expressions until the parser turns the s-expression into abstract syntax. Then, however, all accumulated substitutions have to be eliminated. The innermost substitution arrived first at the term and hence it is natural to eliminate it first. The context EL selects this innermost substitution from a cascade of parsing substitutions:

$$EL \qquad ::= EL(\!|r|\!) \mid [\ ]$$

Using this context, we define the standard elimination reduction (see DEP-C in figure 20.5):

$$c \mapsto_{El} c' \text{ iff } c = EL[c_1], c' = EL[c_2] \text{ for some context } EL \wedge c_1 \rightarrow_{El} c_2$$

and let $\mapsto_{El}^*$ denote the reflexive, transitive closure of $\mapsto_{El}$. As we add new elimination reductions to $\rightarrow_{El}$, we will also extend EL accordingly to ensure that it still selects the innermost substitution.

Next, we define the parsing reduction $\rightarrow_{\text{Parse}}$ and afterwards $\rightarrow_{(\!()\!)}$ for the elimination of parsing substitutions (see DEP-B and DEP-E).

The parsing reduction from figure 20.6 translates from concrete syntax to the abstract syntax from section 20.2. The description of the parsing reduction uses *parsing contexts* defined as[4]:

$$P \qquad ::= P(\!(r)\!) \mid [\,]$$

The role of the parsing contexts is unconventional: while a context usually serves to identify a redex within a term, a parsing context identifies an s-expression inside a stack of parsing substitutions. Parsing contexts thus enable the parser to "peek" under the outer parsing substitutions and identifiy the structure of compound s-expressions. This is necessary as we do not eliminate parsing substitutions applied to compound s-expressions but the parser still needs to determine the syntactic kind of the term. To continue the example from above, the term $(\texttt{lambda x x})(\!(\lambda^0/\texttt{lambda})\!)(\!(x^2/\texttt{x})\!)$ can be written as $P[(\texttt{lambda x x})]$, where P is the parsing context $[\,](\!(\lambda^0/\texttt{lambda})\!)(\!(x^2/\texttt{x})\!)$. The encoding $P[(\texttt{lambda x x})]$ makes it obvious that the term is an s-expression consisting of three other s-expressions. The parsing context P contains information on the meaning of the symbols $\texttt{lambda}$ and $\texttt{x}$ and thus allows the parser to determine the syntactic kind of the term. As a result of peeking, the parser generates abstract syntax forms, which are surrounded by parsing substitutions. The elimination of the parsing substitution will then push the substitutions inward. This also means that elimination works on abstract syntax terms and therefore its semantics is well defined. This is in contrast to traditional renaming approaches which mostly work on unstructured source terms.

The parsing reduction works as follows: The rule (ElSubstSym) eliminates a parsing substitution, if possible. To that end, it uses the $\mapsto^*_{\text{El}}$ reduction (see DEP-C). The parser does not contain a rule for symbols, as the elimination of parsing substitutions turns them into identifiers. (Remember that the parsing substitution $(\!(\star^n/\star)\!)$ matches any symbol.) Also, the concrete syntax and the abstract syntax use the same representation for constants, so the parser does not have to handle them and the remaining rules cover compound s-expressions surrounded by parentheses.

The first element of a compound s-expression determines its syntactic role. If it is another compound s-expression, the outer s-expression must be a procedure application. The rule (NestedAppSimple) covers this case. Otherwise, the first element has to be an identifier, which is represented by

---

[4]The context P is identical to the context EL, but the two serve different purposes and hence receive separate definitions.

$$\to_{\text{Parse}} \subseteq \mathit{lse} \times c$$

$$c \to_{\text{Parse}} c' \text{ iff } c \neq c \mapsto^*_{\text{El}} \text{ where } c \mapsto^*_{\text{El}} c' \qquad \text{(ElSubstSym)}$$

$$P\big[\big(\,(se_{1_1}\ se_{1_2}\ \ldots)\,se_2\ \ldots\big)\big] \to_{\text{Parse}} \big(@\ P\big[(se_{1_1}\ se_{1_2}\ \ldots)\big]\ P[se_2]\ldots\big) \qquad \text{(NestedAppSimple)}$$

$$P\big[(\text{x y } se)\big] \to_{\text{Parse}} P\big[(\lambda\text{y}.se(\!|\text{y}^0/\text{y}|\!))\big] \text{ iff } P[\text{x}] \mapsto^*_{\text{El}} \lambda^n \qquad \text{(LambdaIdSimple)}$$

$$P\big[(\text{x } se_2\ \ldots)\big] \to_{\text{Parse}} P\big[(@\ \text{x } se_2\ldots)\big] \text{ iff } \text{x} \notin \mathit{Specials} \text{ where } P[\text{x}] \mapsto^*_{\text{El}} {}^{ks}x^n \qquad \text{(IdAppSimple)}$$

Figure 20.6: Parsing reduction without macros

---

a symbol in the concrete syntax. The rules (LambdaIdSimple) and (IdApp-Simple) use the elimination for explicit substitutions $\mapsto_{\text{El}}$ to turn the symbol into an identifier and recognize the correct syntax of the compound expression. In the rule (IdAppSimple) this identifier is a variable, hence the whole expression is a procedure application. Note that this rule turns a symbol, written x, into an identifier, written ${}^{ks}x^n$, where x is the name of the identifier. If the identifier at the head is the special identifier λ^n, it corresponds to the syntactic keyword lambda. The rule (LambdaIdSimple) treats this case. Here, the parser needs to generate a fresh parsing substitution to replace the symbol from the parameter position by an identifier with level 0.

To perform the second task of the parser—the elimination of parsing substitutions—a definition of the reduction $\to_{(\!|)}$ is necessary (see DEP-E in figure 20.5). The elimination reduction $\to_{\text{El}}$ is based on $\to_{(\!|)}$ and we have just seen that the rule (ElSubstSym) uses this reduction to eliminate parsing substitutions applied to terms, and the rules (LambdaIdSimple) and (IdApp-Simple) use it to turn the symbol in the head of a compound s-expression into an identifier. Figure 20.7 contains the rules of the $\to_{(\!|)}$ reduction. The parsing reduction has generated mixed terms for λ-abstractions and applications and thereby generated parsing substitutions. Now the elimination of parsing substitutions converts the representation of variables from symbols to identifiers and pushes the parsing substitutions into the mixed terms. The most interesting rules of the elimination reduction behave as follows:

- Rule (ParseSubstStar) applies the substitution for unbound variables. It uses the level associated with the special identifier $\star$ to create an identifier from the symbol.

- Rule (ParseSubstSym) applies the parsing substitution to turn a symbol into an identifier.

$$\rightarrow_{(\!(\!)\!)} \subseteq c(\!|r|\!) \times c$$

$$x(\!|\star^n/\star|\!) \rightarrow_{(\!(\!)\!)} x^n \qquad\qquad \text{(ParseSubstStar)}$$

$$x(\!|id/x|\!) \rightarrow_{(\!(\!)\!)} id \qquad\qquad \text{(ParseSubstSym)}$$

$$a(\!|r|\!) \rightarrow_{(\!(\!)\!)} a \qquad\qquad \text{(ParseSubstConst)}$$

$$^{ks}x^n(\!|r|\!) \rightarrow_{(\!(\!)\!)} {}^{ks}x^n \qquad\qquad \text{(ParseSubstId)}$$

$$x(\!|id/y|\!) \rightarrow_{(\!(\!)\!)} x \text{ iff } x \neq y \wedge y \neq \star \qquad\qquad \text{(ParseSubstSymOther)}$$

$$(\lambda z.lse)(\!|w^n/y|\!) \rightarrow_{(\!(\!)\!)} (\lambda z.lse(\!|w^{n+1}/y|\!)) \qquad\qquad \text{(ParseSubstLamId)}$$

$$(@\ lse_1\ lse_2 \ldots)(\!|r|\!) \rightarrow_{(\!(\!)\!)} (@\ lse_1(\!|r|\!)\ lse_2(\!|r|\!) \ldots) \qquad\qquad \text{(ParseSubstApp)}$$

Figure 20.7: Reduction $\rightarrow_{(\!(\!)\!)}$ without macros

- Dropping the substitution also happens in rule (ParseSubstId) if the substitution is applied to an identifier and in (ParseSubstSymOther) if the substitution is applied to a non-matching symbol.

- Rule (ParseSubstLamId) moves an explicit substitution into the body of an abstraction. This means that the identifier of the substitution is one level farther away from its binding place; consequently the rule increments the level index of the identifier. Note that this preserves lexical scoping because the parser already generates a substitution binding the parameter of the abstraction when it generates the abstract syntax term for the abstraction in rule (LambdaIdSimple).

- For applications, rule (ParseSubstApp) simply needs to propagate the substitution to the operator and the operands.

For the parsing reduction, we define expansion/parsing contexts EP to uniquely identify the left-most outer-most source term that the parser needs to replace by abstract syntax next:

$$EP \qquad ::= (@\ e\ldots EPc\ldots) \mid (\lambda\ x.EP) \mid [\ ]$$

The expansion/parsing contexts give rise to a standard parsing reduction: $c_1 \mapsto_{\text{Parse}} c_2$, if for some expansion/parsing context EP, $c_1 \equiv EP[lse], c_2 \equiv EP[c], lse \rightarrow_{\text{Parse}} c$. The standard parsing reduction is referenced as DEP-A in figure 20.5. Now all reductions from this figure are in place.

We define $\longmapsto^{*}_{\text{Parse}}$ as the reflexive, transitive closure of $\longmapsto_{\text{Parse}}$ and derive a function *parse*:

$$parse : se \rightarrow e$$
$$parse(se) = e \text{ iff } se (\![\lambda^0/\texttt{lambda}]\!) (\![\star^0/\star]\!) \longmapsto^{*}_{\text{Parse}} e$$

The *parse* function maps an input s-expression *se* to a parsed expression *e*. The function annotates the input s-expression by two initial explicit substitutions for parsing: $(\![\lambda^0/\texttt{lambda}]\!)$ binds the keyword `lambda` to the special symbol λ, and $(\![\star^0/\star]\!)$ creates an explicit substitution that is used by the parser to assign the correct level to free identifiers.

We conclude this section with an example of the parsing reduction. Assume *parse* is applied to the term (`lambda x (x y)`). Then the reduction proceeds as follows:

$$(\texttt{lambda x (x y)}) (\![\lambda^0/\texttt{lambda}]\!) (\![\star^0/\star]\!) \rightarrow$$
$$((\text{LambdaIdSimple}))$$

$$(\lambda x. (\texttt{x y}) (\![x^0/\texttt{x}]\!)) (\![\lambda^0/\texttt{lambda}]\!) (\![\star^0/\star]\!) \rightarrow$$
$$((\text{ElSubstSym}),(\text{ParseSubstLamId}),(\text{ParseSubstLamId}))$$

$$(\lambda x. (\texttt{x y}) (\![x^0/\texttt{x}]\!) (\![\lambda^1/\texttt{lambda}]\!) (\![\star^1/\star]\!)) \rightarrow$$
$$((\text{IdAppSimple}))$$

$$(\lambda x. ((@\texttt{x y}) (\![x^0/\texttt{x}]\!) (\![\lambda^1/\texttt{lambda}]\!) (\![\star^1/\star]\!))) \rightarrow$$
$$((\text{ElSubstSym}),(\text{ParseSubstApp}),(\text{ParseSubstApp}))$$

$$(\lambda x. (@(\texttt{x}(\![x^0/\texttt{x}]\!) (\![\lambda^1/\texttt{lambda}]\!) (\![\star^1/\star]\!)) (\texttt{y}(\![x^0/\texttt{x}]\!) (\![\lambda^1/\texttt{lambda}]\!) (\![\star^1/\star]\!)))) \rightarrow$$
$$((\text{ElSubstSym}),(\text{ParseSubstSym}),(\text{ParseSubstId}))$$

$$(\lambda x. (@x^0 (\texttt{y}(\![x^0/\texttt{x}]\!) (\![\lambda^1/\texttt{lambda}]\!) (\![\star^1/\star]\!)))) \rightarrow$$
$$((\text{ElSubstSym}),(\text{ParseSubstSymOther}),(\text{ParseSubstStar}))$$

$$(\lambda x. (@x^0 y^1))$$

The equation labels indicate the rule that applies; it lists multiple rules if the parsing reduction involves the elimination of parsing substitutions. In the result, x^0 is a local variable bound by the surrounding λ whereas y^1 is unbound. The level of the initial parsing substitution $(\![\star^0/\star]\!)$ has been incremented as the substitution enters the scope of the λ, hence y receives the correct level 1.

20·4 The Core Macro Expander.

Having a basic parser for Λ^n we can now turn to the central point of this chapter: a formal description of hygienic macro expansion.

We introduce the language Λ_M, an extension of Λ^n that encompasses macro expansion. The model consists of two parts:

- The core macro expander collects macro definitions and moves them into the scope of λ-abstractions while maintaining hygiene.

- For the macro expansion proper, specifications for each kind of macro transformer extend the core macro expander. Such a specification must provide rules to parse the definition of the transformer, elimination rules for the abstract-syntax representation of the transformer, and, of course, an extension of the core macro expander that handles macro applications where the keyword is bound to a transformer of the respective kind.

This chapter only defines the core macro expander. The author's dissertation [45] contains the specification for the `syntax-rules` transformer from R^{5}RS and a procedural macro expander. It also contains an augmented parser that handles macro applications.

Adding macros to the language requires a binding construct for macros and a syntactic form for macro applications. An identifier that is bound to a macro is commonly called a *keyword*. In the Scheme language, three different binding constructs for keywords exist: `define-syntax` introduces a global, recursive definition for a keyword, `let-syntax` binds a keyword within a local scope and `letrec-syntax` binds a keyword locally and recursively. As the latter construct can be used to simulate the others, we choose to focus on it. However, to keep the presentation reasonably compact, we do not handle (mutually recursive) binding of several keywords.

In our restricted version of `letrec-syntax`, the first argument is the identifier that is bound as the keyword, followed by a transformer and the body. The transformer may be a `syntax-rules` clause from R^{5}RS or some other form. The binding of keywords follows the rules of lexical binding, and variable bindings and keyword bindings may shadow each other. The abstract syntax does not distinguish between variables and keywords but uses the same representation as before. In the new mixture syntax, the level of an identifier represents the number of λ-abstractions *and* `letrec-syntax` binders between the occurrence of the identifier and the corresponding binding place. This chapter does not contain a parser for `letrec-syntax` but operates on its abstract syntax form *letrec-syn* directly. Hence it suffices to know that the parser first records the source code of the transformer, then propagates the parsing substitutions to it, and finally parses the transformer. Consequently, the mixture syntax contains two variants of the *letrec-syn* form, one where the transformer is a lexical s-expression and one where the transformer has been parsed:

$$c \qquad ::= \dots \mid (\textit{letrec-syn } x \textit{ lse lse}) \mid (\textit{letrec-syn } x \textit{ tf lse})$$

Following Scheme and Lisp tradition, we do not introduce a special concrete syntax for macro applications but let parenthesized expressions with the first form being a keyword represent a macro application. The mixture syntax represents macro applications through the term $\langle {}^{ks}x^n lse \rangle$.

The macro expander collects the keyword bound by `letrec-syntax` and uses the identifiers during the expansion of the `letrec-syntax` body. In addition, the expander ensures that the identifiers the macro inserts refer to the same binding place as in the macro definition. This is vital to maintain hygiene. To that end, the expander attaches a mapping from keywords to transformers, called the *set of transformer bindings*, to the terms to be expanded. Whenever expansion enters the scope of a lexical or syntactic binding construct, it applies a shift operator $\uparrow$ to the set of transformer bindings. The shift operator increments the level of all free identifiers within the definitions by one.

Macro expansion also removes *letrec-syn* forms as it records its definition in the set of transformer bindings. Removing *letrec-syn* means removing a binding construct. Therefore the levels of the variables in the body of the removed *letrec-syn* need to be decremented by one. An unshift operator performs this task.

Both the shift and the unshift operator receive a level argument to protect local variables. The level of the operators describes the minimum level of identifiers that are affected by the operators. Whenever the operator enters the scope of a binding construct, the level of the operator is incremented by one to protect the variables bound by the binding construct. The shift operator extends the set of terms: the term $c\uparrow^n$ increments within the term c the levels of all identifiers whose level is greater or equal to n by one. For example, in the term $(@x^0(\lambda y.(@y^0 z^1)))$ the variable y^0 is bound locally but the variables x^0 and z^1 are free. If the macro expander wants to increase the levels of all free variables by one, it applies the shift operator to the term: $(@x^0(\lambda y.(@y^0 z^1)))\uparrow^0$. The expander initially sets the level of the operator to zero as then the operator affects all free variables according to the definition of the shift operator. As the shift operator moves into the outer application, it increases the level of the variable x^0: $(@x^1(\lambda y.(@y^0 z^1)))\uparrow^0$. The level of the operator in turn increases by one as it moves into the λ abstraction: $(@x^1(\lambda y.(@y^0 z^1)\uparrow^1))$. Now the operator does not affect the (local) variable y^0 as its level is lower than the level of the operator. It does however increase the level of z: $(@x^1(\lambda y.(@y^0 z^2)))$.

Besides the level, section 20.1 motivated the need for marking identifiers at each transcription step. To generate these marks, the expander provides the transformer with a fresh mark at each macro application. The transformer propagates the mark to the inserted identifiers. The mark then describes the macro application that introduced (or generated) the identifier. Subsequent transformers, which receive the marked identifiers in their argument, use the mark in addition to the level to distinguish identifiers. As marks, we use natural numbers. With this representation, the expander only needs to maintain a counter, the *current mark*, which it initializes with 0 and which it increments at every transcription step to acquire a fresh mark.

An identifier with name x, level n that has been marked by the marks $k_1, \ldots, k_m$ is written as ${}^{\{k_1,\ldots,k_m\}}x^n$. A mark k attached to an identifier means that the identifier has been introduced at the kth transcription step during the macro expansion process. If the current mark is k', it also means that the introducing transcription step happened k'-k transcription steps ago.

The core macro expander also provides a means for the transformer to perform the marking. A mark operation extends the set of terms just like the parsing substitutions and the shift operator. The mark operation receives as its arguments the term to be marked and the mark to use. We write $c_\sigma{}^k$ for marking a term c with mark k. The core macro expander leaves the introduction of marks to the actual transformers. It does, however, eliminate the marks; consequently, this section includes rules to perform the elimination, which works by pushing the marks inside the terms until they reach an identifier and extend its set of marks.

Once terms have been completely parsed, the marks no longer matter. They are only a means to allow the transformer to avoid capture of an identifier. The transformer still uses the level of the identifier to indicate the binder. Hence, the identifier representation within Λ_n does not change: we can simply drop the marks after macro expansion.

Parsing substitutions, the shift operator, and the mark operator serve similar tasks: they record binding information of identifiers. The subsequent text refers to them in similar contexts. Hence, we introduce the term *expansion substitution* to denote the union of the three. The elimination reduction $\rightarrow_{\text{El}}$ and its context EL from section 20.3 will be extended to eliminate these expansion substitutions. However, the unshift operator is not an expansion substitution, as it only performs post-processing on the output of the macro expander.

Figure 20.8 contains the mixture syntax used during expansion. It is an extension of the mixture syntax used by the parser as defined in figure 20.4. During expansion of a term c, the expander associates a definition set d and a current mark k with the term. This is written as $d, k \vdash c$. A definition set d is either empty (ϵ) or a mapping from keywords to transformers (tf), or a definition set subject to a shift operator. A *normalized definition set* $\underline{d}$ lacks the shift operator and contains only normalized transformers ($\underline{tf}$). The set of terms now includes macro applications, written $\langle\, {}^{ks}x^n\ lse \rangle$, and the two

$$\underline{d} \qquad ::= \epsilon \mid (^{ks}x^n \mapsto \underline{tf} :: \underline{d})$$
$$d \qquad ::= \epsilon \mid (^{ks}x^n \mapsto \underline{tf} :: d) \mid d \uparrow$$
$$lse \qquad ::= \dots \mid lse\uparrow^n \mid lse_{\sigma}{}^k$$
$$c \qquad ::= \dots \mid \langle\, ^{ks}x^n\ lse \rangle \mid (letrec\text{-}syn\ x\ lselse) \mid (letrec\text{-}syn\ x\ tflse) \mid d, k \vdash c \mid c\uparrow^n \mid c_{\sigma}{}^k \mid e\downarrow^n$$

Figure 20.8: Mixture syntax for expansion

variants of *letrec-syn*, as explained above. In addition, it includes the shift operator, written $\uparrow^n$; the mark operator, written σ^k; and the unshift operator, written as $\downarrow^n$, where n indicates the level of the operator that protects local variables from unshifting. Lexical s-expressions now also contain the shift operator and the mark operator, hence the new definition for *lse*.

The goal of this section is the definition of a reduction $\mapsto_{\text{ParseExpandUnshift}}$ that combines parsing, expansion, and elimination of the unshift operator as post-processing. Figure 20.9 shows that this reduction is the union of the standard reduction for expansion (see DEP-B), the elimination of the unshift operator (see DEP-N and DEP-O), and the parsing reduction known from the previous section (see DEP-P). The expansion reduction (see DEP-C) uses in its rules three other standard reductions: first $\mapsto_{\text{Def-El-Tf}}$ (see DEP-D), which normalizes definitions using the reduction $\rightarrow_{\text{Def}}$ and a transformer-specific reduction $\mapsto_{\text{El-Tf}}$, second $\mapsto_{\text{El}}$ (see DEP-H), which eliminates the shift operator; the mark operator and parsing substitutions; and the third $\mapsto_{\text{PT}}$, which parses transformers. The reductions $\mapsto_{\text{El-Tf}}$ and $\mapsto_{\text{PT}}$ deal with transformers and are thus outside the scope of this chapter, but the other reductions are explained in this section.

Figure 20.10 contains the rules for macro expansion proper. The expander collects macro definitions and propagates them through the terms. However, the figure does not include a rule that describes macro application, as the treatment of macro applications depends on the transformer used to define the macro. Consequently, none of the rules increment the current mark or introduce a mark operator, as this happens after a macro application only.

These rules take place within expansion/parsing contexts *EP* from the previous section, extended by a rule for the $\downarrow$ operator:

$$EP \qquad ::= [\ ] \mid (@\ e \dots EPc \dots) \mid (\lambda x.EP) \mid EP\downarrow^n$$

- Rule (ExpandNormDef) uses $\mapsto_{\text{Def-El-Tf}}$, which normalizes definitions (see DEP-D). This reduction is the union of the reduction $\mapsto_{\text{Def}}$ from

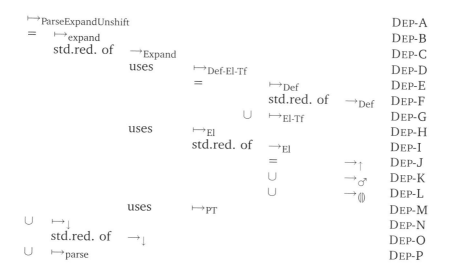

Figure 20.9: Dependency of reductions

figure 20.11 and the normalization of transformers $\longmapsto_{\text{El-Tf}}$, which is part of the specification of a transformer. All other rules require normalized definitions.

- The rule (ExpandElim) generalizes the rule (ElSubstSym) from the parser (figure 20.6) from parsing substitutions to all expansion substitutions.

- The rule (ExpandParseTransformer) parses the transformer argument of a *letrec-syn* once all expansion substitutions have been moved to the transformer. The rule uses the reduction $\longmapsto_{\text{PT}}$ to perform the actual parsing (see DEP-M). This reduction is part of the specification of a transformer; the end of the figure only lists the domain of the reduction.

- Rule (ExpandLetSyn) describes expansion of a *letrec-syn* form. It incorporates the new binding of the keyword x in the definitions and shifts the identifiers in the old definitions. Then the rule associates the resulting definitions with the body *lse* and applies the unshift operator to the result.

$$\rightarrow_{\text{Expand}} \subseteq d, k \vdash c \times c$$

$$d, k \vdash c \rightarrow_{\text{Expand}} \underline{d}_1, k \vdash c \text{ iff } d \notin \underline{d} \text{ where } d \mapsto^*_{\text{Def-El-Tf}} \underline{d}_1 \qquad \text{(ExpandNormDef)}$$

$$\underline{d}, k \vdash c \rightarrow_{\text{Expand}} \underline{d}, k \vdash c' \text{ iff } c' \neq c \text{ where } c \mapsto^*_{\text{El}} c' \qquad \text{(ExpandElim)}$$

$$\underline{d}, k \vdash {}^{ks}x^n \rightarrow_{\text{Expand}} {}^{ks}x^n \qquad \text{(ExpandId)}$$

$$\underline{d}, k \vdash a \rightarrow_{\text{Expand}} a \qquad \text{(ExpandConst)}$$

$$\underline{d}, k \vdash (\lambda x.c) \rightarrow_{\text{Expand}} (\lambda x.(\underline{d} \uparrow), k \vdash c) \qquad \text{(ExpandLam)}$$

$$\underline{d}, k \vdash (@ \, c \ldots) \rightarrow_{\text{Expand}} (@ \, (\underline{d}, k \vdash c) \ldots) \qquad \text{(ExpandApp)}$$

$$\underline{d}, k \vdash (\textit{letrec-syn } x \, \textit{lse}_{tf} \, \textit{lse}) \rightarrow_{\text{Expand}} \underline{d}, k \vdash (\textit{letrec-syn } x \, tf \, \textit{lse}) \qquad \text{(ExpandParseTransformer)}$$

$$\text{where } \textit{lse}_{tf} \mapsto^*_{\text{PT}} tf$$

$$\underline{d}, k \vdash (\textit{letrec-syn } x \, tf \, \textit{lse}) \rightarrow_{\text{Expand}} (((x^0 \mapsto tf) :: (\underline{d} \uparrow)), k \vdash \textit{lse}{\downarrow}^1) \qquad \text{(ExpandLetSyn)}$$

$$\rightarrow_{\text{PT}} \subseteq \textit{lse} \rightarrow tf$$

Figure 20.10: Reduction rules for the core macro expander

Each specification of a transformer contains rules of the form

$$\underline{d}, k \vdash \langle {}^{ks}x^n \textit{lse} \rangle \rightarrow_{\text{Expand}} \underline{d}, k + 1 \vdash \textit{lse}'$$

that handle macro applications by transforming a macro application $\langle {}^{ks}x^n \textit{lse} \rangle$ into a lexical s-expression, where $\underline{d}$ contains the definition of the accordant transformer. These rules use the mark k to mark the generated identifiers of the transformer and increment k by one afterwards.

Figure 20.11 shows the reduction of definitions required for rule (ExpandNormDef) (see DEP-F). The first rule (DefShiftEpsilon) trivially explains shifting of an empty set of transformer bindings. The next rule (DefShiftDefs) promotes the shift operator to the transformer of the first definition and to the rest of the definitions. The initial level of the shift operator for the transformer is 0 as the level of all (free) variables needs to be incremented. In addition to shifting the transformer, the level of the keyword has to be incremented, too: the keywords present in the transformer and also the keywords that have already been bound move one level farther away from their binding place with every *letrec-syn*.

The reduction $\mapsto_{\text{Def}}$ is the extension of $\rightarrow_{\text{Def}}$ to contexts D, which are defined as

$$\rightarrow_{\text{Def}} \subseteq d\uparrow \times d$$

$$(\epsilon \uparrow) \rightarrow_{\text{Def}} \epsilon \qquad\qquad\qquad \text{(DefShiftEpsilon)}$$

$$(((x^n \mapsto tf) :: \underline{d}) \uparrow) \rightarrow_{\text{Def}} ((x^{n+1} \mapsto (tf\uparrow^0)) :: (\underline{d} \uparrow)) \qquad \text{(DefShiftDefs)}$$

Figure 20.11: Reduction for definitions

$$D \qquad ::= [\ ] \mid (^{ks}x^n \mapsto \underline{tf} :: D) \mid D\uparrow$$

$\mapsto^*_{\text{Def}}$ denotes the reflexive, transitive closure of $\mapsto_{\text{Def}}$, defined as:

$$d \mapsto_{\text{Def}} d' \text{ iff } d = D[d_1], d' = D[d_2], d_1 \rightarrow_{\text{Def}} d_2$$

Furthermore, normalization of transformers within the set of transformer bindings is necessary for two reasons:

1. Rule (ExpandLetSyn) stores a non-normalized transformer in the set of transformer bindings.[5]

2. Rule (DefShiftDefs) propagates the shift operator to transformers.

We assume a reduction $\rightarrow_{\text{El-Tf}} \subseteq tf \times tf$ to perform this normalization. Here, we place this reduction in contexts DTF, defined as:

$$DTF \qquad ::= (^{ks}x^n \mapsto EL :: d) \mid (\underline{d}{:}DTF) \mid DTF\uparrow$$

The context DTF uses the context elimination context EL to place the reduction at the innermost expansion substitution. Using DTF we can now define the standard reduction $\mapsto_{\text{El-Tf}}$ of the reduction $\mapsto_{\text{El-Tf}}$:

$$d \mapsto_{\text{El-Tf}} d' \text{ iff } d = DTF[tf_1], d' = DTF[tf_2], tf_1 \rightarrow_{\text{El-Tf}} tf_2$$

The context D places the hole only after normalized definitions, while the context DTF places the hole in the first non-normalized transformer. Hence, even their combination divides the set of transformer bindings uniquely into a context and a redex, and we can combine the reduction relations $\mapsto_{\text{Def}}$ and $\mapsto_{\text{El-Tf}}$ to define $\rightarrow_{\text{Def-El-Tf}}$:

$$\mapsto_{\text{Def-El-Tf}} = \mapsto_{\text{Def}} \cup \mapsto_{\text{El-Tf}}$$

---

[5]Alternatively, we could normalize the transformers before storing them in the set of transformer bindings. However, doing so would demand mingling the unrelated reductions for expansion and normalization of transformers.

$$\to_\uparrow \subseteq c{\uparrow}^n \times c$$

$$(a{\uparrow}^n) \to_\uparrow a \qquad\qquad\qquad\qquad\text{(ShiftConst)}$$

$$(x^n{\uparrow}^m) \to_\uparrow x^{n+1} \text{ iff } n \geq m \qquad\qquad\text{(ShiftId)}$$

$$(x^n{\uparrow}^m) \to_\uparrow x^n \text{ iff } n < m \qquad\qquad\text{(ShiftLocalId)}$$

$$((\lambda x.lse){\uparrow}^n) \to_\uparrow (\lambda x.(lse{\uparrow}^{n+1})) \qquad\qquad\text{(ShiftLam)}$$

$$((letrec\text{-}syn \; x \; lse_{tf} \; lse){\uparrow}^n) \to_\uparrow (letrec\text{-}syn \; x \; (lse_{tf}{\uparrow}^{n+1}) \; (lse{\uparrow}^{n+1})) \qquad\text{(ShiftLetSyn)}$$

$$((@ \; lse_1 \; lse_2 \ldots){\uparrow}^n) \to_\uparrow (@ \; (lse_1{\uparrow}^n) \; (lse_2{\uparrow}^n) \ldots) \qquad\qquad\text{(ShiftApp)}$$

Figure 20.12: Elimination of the $\uparrow$ operator

In addition to $\mapsto_{\text{Def-El-Tf}}$, the macro expander in figure 20.10 also depends on the reduction $\mapsto_{\text{El}}$ (see DEP-H). This reduction eliminates expansion substitutions. So far, expansion substitutions encompass parsing substitutions, the shift operator, and the mark operator. To complete the definition of $\to_{\text{El}}$, figure 20.12 contains the elimination rules for the shift operator and figure 20.13 contains the elimination rules for the mark operator (see DEP-J and DEP-K).

in figure 20.12, the rules (ShiftId) and (ShiftLocalId) explain shifting for identifiers. Both rules first compare the level associated with the identifier with the level of the shift operator. If the level of the identifier is smaller than the level of the operator, the variable is a local identifier from the point of view of the shift operator. In this case, the rule (ShiftLocalId) matches and does not alter the level; otherwise (ShiftId) increments the level. Accordingly, rule (ShiftLam) increments the level of the shift operator as it applies it to the body of the λ-abstraction. For the *letrec-syn* form, the rule (ShiftLetSyn) increments the level of the shift operator both for the transformer and for the body, as *letrec-syn* is a recursive binding construct. There is no rule for macro applications because its the parser's responsibility to care of this case.

Figure 20.13 contains the elimination rules for the mark operator (needed by $\to_{\text{El}}$, see DEP-K). The operator is unchanged as it propagates to the components of the various forms. The only interesting case is rule (MarkId), which describes the elimination of the mark operator for identifiers. The rule adds the mark to the set of marks of the identifier.

$$\to_{\sigma} \subseteq c\sigma^k \times c$$

$$a\sigma^n \to_{\sigma} a \qquad\qquad\qquad\text{(MarkConst)}$$

$$x^n\sigma^m \to_{\sigma} x^n \qquad\qquad\qquad\text{(MarkId)}$$

$$(\lambda x.lse)\sigma^n \to_{\sigma} (\lambda x.lse\sigma^n) \qquad\qquad\text{(MarkLam)}$$

$$(letrec\text{-}syn\ x\ lse_{tf}\ lse)\sigma^n \to_{\sigma} (letrec\text{-}syn\ x\ lse_{tf}\sigma^n\ lse\sigma^n) \qquad\text{(MarkLetSyn)}$$

$$(@\ lse_1\ lse_2 \ldots)\sigma^n \to_{\sigma} (@\ lse_1\sigma^n\ lse_2\sigma^n \ldots) \qquad\qquad\text{(MarkApp)}$$

Figure 20.13: Elimination of the σ operator

Now all the reductions that make up $\to_{El}$ are in place (see DEP-I). To place the redex inside the three expansion substitutions, a re-definition of the elimination contexts EL is necessary as well:

$$\to_{El} = \to_{\uparrow} \cup \to_{\sigma} \cup \to_{(\!\mid\!)}$$

$$EL \quad ::= EL(\!\mid\! t\!\mid) \mid EL\uparrow^n \mid EL\sigma^k \mid [\ ]$$

The unshift operator is the final operator left to define the expansion process (see DEP-N). Unlike expansion substitutions, it is not applied to unexpanded terms but merely serves as a post-processor on expressions to decrement the level of variables after the removal of a *letrec-syn* form. Figure 20.14 contains the rules for its elimination. They are identical to the rules for the $\uparrow$ operator except, of course, for the identifier case where (UnshiftId) decrements the level of the identifier if it is not smaller than the level of the operator.

The parser from the previous section needs extensions to handle the terms generated by the macro expander and to produce *letrec-syn* forms and macro applications. The author's dissertation [45] contains the augmented parser; hence, this chapter does not contain further information about DEP-P.

We can now define the standard expansion reduction, written $c \mapsto_{\text{Expand}} c'$, iff for some parsing context EP, $c \equiv EP[c_1], c' \equiv EP[c_2], c_1 \to_{\text{Expand}} c_2)$. We let $\mapsto^*_{\text{Expand}}$ denote its reflexive, transitive closure. Likewise we define the standard unshift reduction, written $c \mapsto_{\downarrow} c'$, if for some parsing context EP, $c \equiv EP[e_1], c' \equiv EP[e_2], e_1 \to_{\downarrow} e_2)$ and let again $\mapsto^*_{\downarrow}$ denote the reflexive, transitive closure.

Macro expansion is then defined as the union of parsing, expansion, and unshifting:

$$\rightarrow_\downarrow \,\subseteq e\!\downarrow^n \times c$$

$$(a\!\downarrow^n) \rightarrow_\downarrow a \hspace{5cm} \text{(UnshiftConst)}$$

$$(x^n\!\downarrow^m) \rightarrow_\downarrow x^{n-1} \text{ iff } n \geq m \hspace{3cm} \text{(UnshiftId)}$$

$$(x^n\!\downarrow^m) \rightarrow_\downarrow x^n \text{ iff } n < m \hspace{3cm} \text{(UnshiftIdLocal)}$$

$$((\lambda x.e)\!\downarrow^n) \rightarrow_\downarrow (\lambda x.(e\!\downarrow^{n+1})) \hspace{2.7cm} \text{(UnshiftLam)}$$

$$((@\,e_1\,e_2\ldots)\!\downarrow^n) \rightarrow_\downarrow (@\,(e_1\!\downarrow^n)\,(e_2\!\downarrow^n)\ldots) \hspace{1.5cm} \text{(UnshiftApp)}$$

Figure 20.14: Elimination of the $\downarrow$ operator

$$expand : se \rightarrow e$$

$$expand(se) = e \text{ iff } se(\!(^{\varnothing}\lambda^0/\texttt{lambda})\!)(\!(^{\varnothing}\star^0/\star)\!) \longmapsto^*_{\text{ParseExpandUnshift}} e$$

where

$$\longmapsto_{\text{ParseExpandUnshift}} = \longmapsto_{\text{Parse}} \cup \longmapsto_{\text{Expand}} \cup \longmapsto_\downarrow$$

20·5 Outlook.

At this point the description of the core macro expander is complete. For a full macro expansion facility, however, we still need a parser that handles letrec-syntax via the production of *letrec-syn* forms as well as the description of the actual transformers.

A definition of a transformer needs to provide three definitions:

1. Reduction rules for macro applications, which extend $\rightarrow_{\text{Expand}}$.

2. A definition of the parsing reduction for transformers, $\rightarrow_{\text{PT}}$, which is used by the rule (ExpandParseTransformer).

3. A definition of the $\rightarrow_{\text{El-Tf}}$ reduction to eliminate expansion substitutions for transformers.

The author's dissertation [45] contains such definitions for two transformers: a syntax-rules transformer and a computational transformer similar to syntax-case. The transformer built on the expansion substitutions defined in this chapter. Both transformers allow the user to bind parts of the macro arguments to so-called *meta-variables*. The user may then specify the macro output using s-expressions that contain meta-variables (so-called *templates*), and the transformers hygienically replace the meta-variables by the macro argument in the template. To specify this process, the semantics introduce *meta-substitutions*, a new kind of explicit substitutions, and corresponding elimination rules that extend the elimination reduction $\longmapsto_{El}$. In addition, the dissertation extends the parser to recognize meta-variables.

For the semantics of the computational macro expander, the dissertation also needs to describe the evaluation of the meta-language. As the elimination of the expansion substitutions takes place during the evaluation of the meta-language, the elimination becomes part of the evaluation, which is a unique feature of this semantics. The dissertation also describes the combination of this macro system with a fully-parameterized, first-class module system. The resulting specification covers over two hundred reduction rules, and its development would have been impossible without the ability to experiment and test with the system using PLT Redex.

Acknowledgments. This work was partially carried out while the author was a research associate at Universität Tübingen.

21 · A Model of Java/Scheme Interoperability
Kathryn E. Gray, University of Utah

The Java + `dynamic` language supports programs that consist of interoperating Java and Scheme modules without sacrificing safety. In this chapter, we present a formal model of this interoperability using PLT Redex and discuss errors in our formalization discovered through trace executions.

21·1 Java—Scheme Interoperability.

Increasingly, software developers use multiple programming languages for single projects. Combining multiple languages provides added flexibility and expressivity over using either in isolation. When these languages utilize different value representations and different levels of statically assured safety guarantees (such as types), the combination additionally requires data conversions and dynamic safety checks that preserve the static guarantees as values pass back and forth between components in different languages.

Including these checks manually can be error prone; we therefore produced a compiler for a combined system, called Java + `dynamic`, that automatically inserts these runtime checks into programs written in Java and PLT Scheme [51]. Our technique requires extensions to Java that support interacting with Scheme, including a `dynamic` type specification. While we provide an implementation for our language, this cannot be used to prove the safety of the system. The first requirement in proving safety is a model of the language and its static and dynamic semantics. Building the model as an executable system, as is possible with Redex, aids in understanding the model, finding its faults, and experimenting with extensions and different semantics.

The rest of this chapter presents a model of a language, $j+s$ that represent the core constructs from Java and Scheme as well as necessary additions to support interoperation. We then outline the static analysis requirements of the system followed by the reduction rules. Using example programs and Redex reduction tracing facilities, we discuss discovering and correcting errors within our model, to improve confidence in the formalization.

```
class TreeBranch extends TreeNode {
  Entry e;
  TreeNode left,right;

  TreeNode filter(dynamic pred) {
    if ( pred(e) )
      ....
  }
}
class Data {
  TreeNode curBranch = ...
.... curBranch.left = scheme.reader.readData();
.... curBranch.filter(scheme.reader.printableP)
}


(define (readData)
  ...)
(define (printable? e)
  ... (send e to-string) ...
  )
```

Figure 21.1: Sample Java + dynamic program

$21 \cdot 2$ **Background on Java + dynamic.** In the Java + dynamic language, Java programms may import values from Scheme modules. Since these values do not have a Java type, programmers may use dynamic in lieu of a type specification. That is, fields, method parameters, and method returns may all be declared dynamic. A sample Java program using dynamic and a Scheme function appears in figure 21.1.

The sample program includes a dynamic parameter, two direct uses of Scheme values, and a call to a Java object within Scheme. During compilation, type-driven analysis determines the expected runtime types for the use of any dynamic parameter or Scheme value. In this program, the pred function must return a boolean when used within an if condition; the readData function must return a TreeNode when used to assign to the left field. Checks are inserted to ensure these expectations dynamically.

Transferring objects between the languages requires higher-order style wrappings that delay checks and conversions until access events take place. In our sample, the Scheme function readData must generate a TreeNode object; this value is wrapped so that field accesses and method calls perform runtime type-checks based on the TreeNode specification. Conversely, the call to pred passes an Entry object to Scheme. This transfer requires a wrapper that checks Scheme values provided as method parameters and similarly wraps the returned values from field and method accesses. With these wrappers, Scheme values may be indiscriminately used as Java values and vice-versa while limiting type-errors to the boundaries of the two languages.

21·3 Modeling Interoperability.

Providing fine-grained, type-safe interoperation between Java and Scheme requires preserving a Java program's static guarantees without constraining the form of Scheme programs unnecessarily. Java + dynamic supports this style of interoperability by guarding Java objects, checking Scheme values, and translating values where necessary.

A model of a programming language need not support all features, only those that express and reflect interoperability in its core. Therefore, we reduce the features of both languages to create a statically typed object-oriented language with booleans, j, and a dynamically-checked functional language with booleans, s. Neither language supports mutation, although the design could accommodate mutable fields. A program in our language, $j+s$, consists of j or s program fragments.

Ensuring that values originating in an s fragment adhere to the type expectations of a j fragment requires runtime access to the type requirements. Local type information, deduced during type-checking, informs the expectations of an untyped value. Our analysis inserts annotations around the value that record the type expectation and guides the dynamic check or data conversion.

Our model uses a rewriting relation to insert type annotations around expressions within a j fragment. This rewriting relation only annotates j fragments that satisfy the j type system, thereby representing the type-checking phase of compilation as well as recording the information necessary for interacting with s fragments. Program points where a value passes from a j fragment to an s fragment (or vice-versa) receive annotations that indicate the transfer and direction.

A properly typed j expression either reduces to a value from j or generates an infinite sequence of evaluations. An s expression either reduces to a value from s, generates an infinite sequence of evaluations, or encounters a state with no possible reductions—a dynamic type error.

The $j+s$ language conservatively extends the evaluations of the original languages. Reductions in a program utilizing $j+s$ functionality can encounter a distinguishing dynamic error indicating that an s value does not meet the type expectations, based on the j fragments of the program.

21·4 **The Language.** The *j+s* language, presented in figure 21.2, combines the features of *j* and *s* outlined above. A subset of *j+s* comprises the *j* language, and another comprises *s*. Both subsets require extensions to support interoperability between program fragments written in the two languages. The grammar definition separates the language specification into appropriate subsets.

A program in the combined language consists of a sequence of definitions followed by one expression. As seen in figure 21.3, the main expression can be an expression from *j* or *s*. The language includes four identifier forms with distinct roles in the grammar; an individual program can use the same symbol, i.e. word, as an identifier in multiple categories, i.e. a *fid* and a *cid*.

Within the PLT-Redex implementation of our model, we represent the distinct language subsets through parameterized grammar definitions. This strategy allows us to investigate either *j* or *s* in isolation as well as the full language. Although the *j+s* language combines *j* and *s* values, we utilize syntactic restrictions to prohibit a source program from freely intermingling values across the sub languages.

Our language model does not include a representation of Object or null. Requiring that all classes descend from a single source places additional restrictions on an extension to *j+s* that includes untyped classes; however, the omission does not impact the general model as it does support general inheritance. The null value provides limited utility in modeling interoperability. Programs that directly access null statically fail, and so would not impact our model, and in all other circumstances the dynamic check and failure reside within the typed interaction and so does not impact interoperability.

The *j* Subset. Our model for the Java-like language encodes a simple class-based language with overridable methods and shadowable fields, seen in the left column of figure 21.2. The *j* syntax follows many Java conventions, but includes several simplifications that improve our rule presentation. We merge statements and expressions into one form, *expr*. We provide distinct operators for field and method access (**call**, **super**, and **get-field**), instead of following the Java dot notation. Similarly **instanceof** follows the format of our method call. The two primitive values, **trueT** and **falseT**, use a trailing **T** as a visual tag denoting their origin in the statically typed language. All field definitions precede all method definitions in order to simplify lists of class members within annotation and reduction rules.

We omit special local access forms for fields and methods, instead these forms must utilize the special **this** variable. We further omit constructor specifications and default field values. Object instantiation binds the given values to the field names of the class, with the first value bound to the first

j constructs

def ::=
| **class** *cid* { *field** *method** }
| **class** *cid$_i$* **extends** *cid$_p$* { *field** *method** }

field ::=
| *type fid* ;

method ::=
| *type$_i$ mid$_i$* (*type$_a$ id$_a$* , .. , *type$_n$ id$_n$*) { *expr* }

type ::=
| *baseType*
| *cid*

baseType ::=
| **boolean**

expr ::=
| **new** *cid* (*expr$_1$* , .. , *expr$_n$*)
| **get-field**(*expr*,*fid*)
| **call**(*expr$_i$* , *mid* , *expr$_a$* .. *expr$_n$*)
| **super**(*mid* , *expr$_1$* .. *expr$_n$*)
| **instanceof**(*expr* , *type*)
| **if** (*expr$_c$*) *expr$_t$ expr$_e$*
| **this**
| *id*
| *value*

value ::=
| **trueT**
| **falseT**

s constructs

def ::=
| . . .
| (**defineU** *id exprU*)

exprU ::=
| (**ifU** *exprU$_c$ exprU$_t$ exprU$_e$*)
| (*exprU$_f$ exprU$_a$* .. *exprU$_n$*)
| *id*
| *value*

value ::=
| . . .
| (λ (*id$_1$* .. *id$_n$*) *exprU*)
| **trueU**
| **falseU**

j extensions

baseTypes ::=
| . . .
| **dynamic**

expr ::=
| . . .
| **app**(*expr$_i$* , *expr$_a$* , .. , *expr$_n$*)

s extensions

exprU ::=
| (**get-fieldU** *fid exprU*)
| (**callU** *exprU$_i$ mid exprU$_a$* .. *exprU$_n$*)

Figure 21.2: The *j+s* language

prog ::=
| *def$_1$* .. *def$_n$ exprM*

exprM ::=
| *expr*
| *exprU*

Figure 21.3: Full program

field specified. When the ancestor classes of the instantiated object contain fields, values are first bound to each ancestor class's fields beginning with the most distant ancestor. Field names can shadow ancestor fields; accessing a field retrieves the most recently introduced field with the specified identifier.

Although not visibly evident from the language specification, this model contains one notable defect when compared to Java expressibility—forward type references may only refer to base classes, prohibiting some cyclic type references. Our annotation technique, described in section 21.5, requires the full type information for a class (including the entire inheritance tree) for a variety of type references. With cyclic type references involving a class and its children, this information may not be available during the annotation phase. Cyclic type references are supported among classes that do not form an inheritance hierarchy.

We could regain the full expressibility with an additional pass that first expands class-specific type information for all class hierarchies. This matches the implementation technique allowing such cyclic references. However, our current experiments do not require examples combining inheritance and cyclic references, therefore we have not extended the model to support an initial expansion pass.

The s Subset. Our model for the Scheme-like language encodes a variant of the λ-calculus including conditionals, booleans, and named definitions, seen in the upper right column of figure 21.2. As in the j language, the primitive boolean values are represented with **U**, to denote that the values originated in an untyped fragment. Further, the conditional operator is also distinguished with a **U** suffix. Unlike the other expressions, function application does not utilize a keyword operator.

Using s Values Within j. Extending the statically-typed j language to interact with s values requires adding untyped values and function application. The lower right portion of figure 21.2 contains these extensions. The primitive type, **dynamic**, may appear in any location that an ordinary type can appear. Any field or parameter may be **dynamic** and uses of these variables are not statically checked. Methods may declare a **dynamic** return value; however, overriding methods must return the same type as the original. The **dynamic** type can be the subject of an **instanceof** query, which always produces **trueT** regardless of the value.

The **app** form statically requires that $expr_i$, the function argument, refer to an expression with type **dynamic**. Statically typed values cannot produce function values. The arguments can be of any type; the return type of the expression is **dynamic**.

Additionally, the j fragment may explicitly refer to a **defineU** entity by its *id*. The usage automatically receives a **dynamic** type expectation. Expressions with the **dynamic** type can be used in any expression position in j, including positions with explicit class type expectations. Multiple uses of a variable with type **dynamic** do not place type restrictions on other uses, for example a **dynamic** variable *tree* can be used as both a boolean and an object within the same program without any static errors.

Using j Values Within s. Extending the untyped s language to interact with j values adds support for accessing fields and methods of object values, as seen in lowest right column of figure 21.2. As with the original s language, the operators contain a trailing **U** that distinguishes them from the respective j expressions. The grammar specifies that a field lookup use a *fid* and a method call use a *mid*; no static requirements enforce any class in the program to contain appropriate fields or methods.

If desired, object instantiation requires knowledge of the j types within the s fragment and could be modeled with a special instantiation construct. The $j+s$ language does not include support for object instantiation within an s fragment because this operation does not address the core issues in interoperability.

21·5 Adding Type Annotations.
Type-checking within our model proceeds by translating a $j+s$ program into an annotated $j+s$ program. In an annotated program, all j expressions are annotated with type information and class definitions contain full hierarchy information, following the type-checking style outlined by Kuan et al. [67]. To benefit from Redex's visualization abilities, we define our translation function via reduction relations that insert annotations and utilize the current type information to generate dynamic checks and interoperable data-wrappers.

The annotated $j+s$ language, presented in figure 21.4, extends the j portion of the $j+s$ language that receive annotations. The left column introduces one new definition form, one method form, and several expression forms that each replace the corresponding forms of $j+s$. The s portions of $j+s$ are unaffected by annotations and therefore do not require modifications. The j portion of the annotated $j+s$ language also includes two new annotation forms that project j values into s and s values in j—**guard** and **mimic**.

We utilize two relations in translating a $j+s$ program into its annotated version. The first, $prog \leadsto_a progA$, rewrites a $j+s$ program into an annotated $j+s$ program without protecting untyped values. The second, $progA \leadsto_{aD} progA'$, rewrites annotated portions of an annotated j fragment to insert dynamic checks and appropriate wrappers. These annotation relations reduce concurrently and jointly comprise the $prog \leadsto progA$ annotation relation.

Annotation types

Annotated *j* grammar

$aType ::=$
    | *type*
    | **classT** *cid* (
        extendT , *fieldT*[*] , *methodT*[*])

defA ::=
    | **class** *cid* { *extendT field*[*] *methodA*[*] }

methodA ::=
    | $type_i$ mid_i ($type_a$ id_a , .. , $type_n$ id_n) {
        ant }

extendT ::=
    | [cid_0 , .. , cid_n]

fieldT ::=
    | [*fid type cid*]

aExpr ::=
    | **new** *cid* ($aExpr_1$, .. , $aExpr_n$)
    | **get-field**(*aExpr*, *fid*)
    | **call**($aExpr_i$, *mid* , $aExpr_a$ .. $aExpr_n$)
    | **super**(*mid* , $aExpr_1$ .. $aExpr_n$)
    | **instanceof**(*aExpr* , *type*)
    | **if** ($aExpr_c$) $aExpr_t$ $aExpr_e$
    | *ant*
    | **this**
    | *id*
    | *value*

methodT ::=
    | *mid* $type_r$ [id_1 $type_1$, .. , id_n $type_n$]

dynamic annotation extensions

ant ::=
    | . . .
    | **guard** *aExpr* $|_{aType}$
    | **mimic** *aExpr* $|_{aType}$

ant ::=
    | *aExpr* $|_{aType}$

aType ::=
    | . . .
    | **dynamicObjT** *fid*[*] *methodI*[*]

methodI ::=
    | *mid* (id_1 .. id_n)

Figure 21.4: Annotated *j+s*

$$expC ::=$$
$$| \; \textbf{new} \; cid \, (\, ant_1 \, , \, .. \, ant_n \, , \, expC \, , \, expr_1 \, , \, .. \, , \, expr_m \,)$$
$$| \; \textbf{get-field}(expC, fid)$$
$$| \; \textbf{call}(\, expC \, , \, mid \, , \, expr_a \, .. \, expr_n \,)$$
$$| \; \textbf{call}(\, ant_o \, , \, mid \, , \, ant_a \, .. \, ant_n \, expC \, expr_m \, .. \, expr_o \,)$$
$$| \; \textbf{instanceof}(\, expC \, , \, type \,)$$
$$| \; \textbf{if} \; (\, expC \,) \, expr_t \, expr_e$$
$$| \; \textbf{if} \; (\, ant_c \,) \, expC \, expr_e$$
$$| \; \textbf{if} \; (\, ant_c \,) \, ant_t \, expC$$
$$| \; [\,]$$

Figure 21.5: Annotation context for j

The $\leadsto$ relation produces an annotated $j+s$ program when the j program fragments are well typed. Both the $\leadsto_a$ and $\leadsto_{aD}$ relations apply to any redex in the hole of an annotation context, presented as the $expC$ grammar in figure 21.5. We do not provide rules to produce an alternate reduction in the event of a static type error; instead the reduction becomes stuck and applications of $\leadsto$ do not produce a program.

During translation, annotations surrounding expressions provide the context and type-information for subsequent annotations. An annotation on an expression derives from bottom-up program analysis for the expression. Transforming an annotation into either a **guard** or **mimic** derives from top-down analysis of the program context as well as existing annotations.

The type within an annotation can refer to a cid as a class type as well as the **classT** form. Most annotations with a class type initially contain the cid form; this enables the relation to utilize a generalized type look-up rule and supports a simplified member-type representation within a **classT**. Any reduction rule using a class value requires the **classT** type expansion.

Annotating j Fragments. The relation $prog \leadsto_a progA$ translates a j fragment into an annotated j fragment, using two subrelations: $def \leadsto_{def} defA$ and $aExpr \leadsto_{exp} ant$. The first performs the translation on class definitions, while the second performs the translation on individual expressions.

Each **class** definition in a $j+s$ program expands into an updated **class** form that contains summary inheritance information for all ancestors and methods containing annotated bodies, using $\leadsto_{def}$. Specifically, for a class with no ancestors, the resulting **class** contains only rewritten methods. For a class with a parent, the resulting **class** lists all ancestors, their fields, and

$$\boxed{\mathcal{E}_e[aExpr] \leadsto_{exp} \mathcal{E}_e[ant]}$$

$$\mathcal{E}_e[\textbf{trueT}] \leadsto_{exp} \mathcal{E}_e[\textbf{trueT} \mid_{\textbf{boolean}}] \quad \text{TRUEA}$$

$$\mathcal{E}_e[\textbf{instanceof}(aExpr_o, type_o)] \leadsto_{exp} \mathcal{E}_e[\textbf{instanceof}(aExpr_o, type_o) \mid_{\textbf{boolean}}] \quad \text{INSTANCEOFA}$$

$$\mathcal{E}_e[aExpr_f] \leadsto_{exp} \mathcal{E}_e[aExpr_f \mid_{type_c}]$$

WHERE

$aExpr_f = \textbf{get-field}(aExpr_o \mid_{aType_o}, fid_c)$ \hfill FIELDA

$aType_f = \textbf{classT}\, cid_n\, (\, extendT, \overline{fieldT_i}^{\,i}\, [\, fid_c\, type_c\, cid_c\,]\, \overline{fieldT_j'}^{\,j}, methodT^*\,)$

Figure 21.6: Annotation rules using local information

it includes their non-overridden methods. During annotation, forward type information can be extracted from **class** forms without **extends** while backward type information can be extracted from any definition.

The rules of the $\leadsto_{exp}$ relation examine the redex and use local knowledge to derive an appropriate annotation for the reduction. Three representative rules are presented in figure 21.6. Where necessary for space preservation, a rule internally uses a shorthand with the full expansion presented below. Side conditions also appear below the reduction.

The rule for annotating a method call expression directly follows the pattern for field access in FIELDA, extracting the return type from the *methodT* portion of the class type. The method call rule additionally ensures that the argument values are subtypes of the parameter types before annotating the full expression. The **classT** specification simplifies object access rules by placing the class's signature within the expression instead of requiring a lookup from the definitions.

Since the **classT** specification does not contain embedded **classT** specifications, the result of extracting type information from an object access is either a **boolean** or *cid*. Before further annotations occur, any *cid* types are translated into appropriate **classT** specification. This requires a type-lookup rule. The type-lookup rule transforms any annotation containing an *cid* into one containing the appropriate class type specification.

The object instantiation rule requires an examination of the class definition, to confirm field argument annotations. Therefore, this rule, presented in figure 21.7, combines instantiation and type expansion. The INSTA definition examines the preceding *defAs* for an equivalent *cid*, and extracts the

$$\boxed{progA \rightsquigarrow_{exp} progA'}$$

$$\overline{defA_i}^{\,i}\, defA_c\, \overline{defA_j'}^{\,j}\, \mathcal{E}_e[aExpr_n] \rightsquigarrow_{exp} \overline{defA_i}^{\,i}\, defA_c\, \overline{defA_j'}^{\,j}\, \mathcal{E}_e[aExpr_n\,|_{aType_c}]$$

WHERE

$$defA_c = \textbf{class}\, cid_c\, \{\, extendT\, \overline{type_f\, fid_f\,;}^{\,f}\, \overline{type_m'\, mid_m'\, (\, \overline{type_a''\, id_a''}^{\,a}\,)\, \{\, ant_m'\, \}}^{\,m}\, \}$$ INSTA

$$aExpr_n = \textbf{new}\, cid_c\, (\, ant_1\, ,\, ..\, ,\, ant_n\,)$$

$$aType_c = \textbf{classT}\, cid_c\, (\, extendT\, ,\, \overline{[\, fid_f\, type_f\, cid_f\,]}^{\,f}\, ,\, \overline{mid_m'\, type_m'\, [\, \overline{id_a''\, type_a''}^{\,a}\,]}^{\,m}\,)$$

Figure 21.7: Rule inserting **classT** annotation during allocation

inheritance, field, and method information from the definition. The independent type-lookup rule is a simplified version of this rule.

Any rule that examines the surrounding definitions requires multiple versions, depending on the placement of the redex hole—a rule in which the class definition occurs prior to the current hole, a rule for usage within the current class, and a rule for subsequent definitions.

An Annotated Program. The rules of the $\rightsquigarrow_a$ relation are used to transform a j fragment into an annotated j fragment without inserting dynamic checks. To illustrate the use of the rules, we provide both a source program and an annotated program produced by a Redex trace. As Redex performs best with fully parenthesized syntax, any trace example utilizes a Scheme-like syntax for j as well as s. Additionally, annotated expressions are wrapped in an annotate form instead of tagging the expression.

The top of figure 21.8 presents a set of three class definitions implementing a boolean list with an *and-map* method. The bottom of the figure presents the fully annotated translation of this program, in the Scheme-like presentation. In the annotated program, the ancestor classes and any inherited fields are listed following the name of the class.

Inserting Mimics. Allowing j expressions to access and interact with s values and vice-versa requires evaluation-time access to type information and the origin of a value. In addition, untyped values from s program fragments must first be checked and then transformed into values that mimic j values.

The $progA \rightsquigarrow_{aD} progA'$ relation contains rules that transform existing annotations with type **dynamic** into **mimic**s with the type information informed by the program context. Concretely, the annotation on an expression is rewritten to a **mimic** when the expression's type is **dynamic** and its context

```
class list { boolean all() { falseT } }
class empty extends list { boolean all() { trueT } }
class cons extends list {
  boolean car; list cdr;
  boolean all() {
   if (get-field(this, car))
      call(get-field(this,cdr),all)
      falseT }
}
call(new cons(trueT, new empty()), all)
```

```
(((class list () () ((boolean all () (annotate boolean falseT))))
  (class empty (list) () ((boolean all () (annotate boolean trueT))))
  (class cons (list) ((boolean car) (list cdr))
    ((boolean all ()
        (annotate boolean
          (if (annotate boolean
                (get-field
                  (annotate
                    (classT cons (list) ((car boolean cons) (cdr list cons))
                      ((all boolean ())))
                    this)
                  (car cons)))
            (annotate boolean
              (call
                (annotate (classT list () () ((all boolean ())))
                  (get-field
                    (annotate
                      (classT cons (list) ((car boolean cons) (cdr list cons))
                        ((all boolean ())))
                      this)
                    (cdr cons)))
                all))
            (annotate boolean falseT)))))))
  (annotate boolean
    (call
      (annotate
        (classT cons (list) ((car boolean cons) (cdr list cons)) ((all boolean ())))
        (new cons (annotate boolean trueT)
          (annotate (classT empty (list) () ((all boolean ()))) (new empty))))
      all)))
```

Figure 21.8: Annotating a *j+s* program

$$\boxed{\mathcal{E}_e[aExpr] \leadsto_{aD} \mathcal{E}_e[aExpr']}$$

$$\mathcal{E}_e[\textbf{if}\,(\,aExpr_c\,|_{\textbf{dynamic}}\,)\,expr_t\,expr_e] \leadsto_{aD} \mathcal{E}_e[\textbf{if}\,(\,\textbf{mimic}\,aExpr_c\,|_{\textbf{boolean}}\,)\,expr_t\,expr_e] \qquad \text{DynIfA}$$

$$\boxed{progA \leadsto_{aD} progA'}$$

$$\overline{defA_i}^{\,i}\;defA_c\;\overline{defA'_j}^{\,j}\;\mathcal{E}_e[aExpr_n] \leadsto_{aD} \overline{defA_i}^{\,i}\;defA_c\;\overline{defA'_j}^{\,j}\;\mathcal{E}_e[aExpr_g]$$

Where

$defA_c = \textbf{class}\,cid_c\,\{\,\text{extend}T\,\overline{type_b\,fid_b}^{\,b};\,\textbf{dynamic}\,fid_c;\,\overline{type'_a\,fid'_a}^{\,a}\,methodA_c^*\,\}$ GNew

$aExpr_n = \textbf{new}\,cid_c\,(\,\overline{ant_b}^{\,b},\,aExpr_c\,|_{aType_c},\,\overline{expr_a}^{\,a}\,)$

$aExpr_g = \textbf{new}\,cid_c\,(\,\overline{ant_b}^{\,b},\,\textbf{guard}\,aExpr_c\,|_{aType_c},\,\overline{expr_a}^{\,a}\,)$

$$\overline{defA_i}^{\,i}\;defA_c\;\overline{defA'_j}^{\,j}\;\mathcal{E}_e[aExpr_n] \leadsto_{aD} \overline{defA_i}^{\,i}\;defA_c\;\overline{defA'_j}^{\,j}\;\mathcal{E}_e[aExpr_g]$$

Where

$defA_c = \textbf{class}\,cid_c\,\{\,\text{extend}T\,\overline{type_b\,fid_b}^{\,b};\,type_c\,fid_c;\,\overline{type'_a\,fid'_a}^{\,a}\,methodA_c^*\,\}$ MNew

$aExpr_n = \textbf{new}\,cid_c\,(\,\overline{ant_b}^{\,b},\,aExpr_c\,|_{\textbf{dynamic}},\,\overline{expr_a}^{\,a}\,)$

$aExpr_g = \textbf{new}\,cid_c\,(\,\overline{ant_b}^{\,b},\,\textbf{mimic}\,aExpr_c\,|_{type_c},\,\overline{expr_a}^{\,a}\,)$

Figure 21.9: Rules for translating annotations into guards and mimics

---

requires a known type. These situations represent locations where an s value enters a j fragment. For example when in an annotation context containing an **if** expression and $aExpr_c\,|_{\textbf{dynamic}}$ in the condition position, the $\leadsto_{aD}$ relation rewrites the condition into **mimic** $aExpr_c\,|_{\textbf{boolean}}$. Figure 21.9 presents this rule (and others) for rewriting annotations into **mimic**s and **guard**s.

In **call** expressions, the translation between annotations and mimics requires knowledge of the specified types for a particular parameter as well as the derived types for the corresponding argument. For a **new** expression, the specified class's fields correspond to the parameters of a method. Translating the annotation for a **dynamic** argument requires matching the number of previously fully annotated expressions as well as the number of expressions remaining to annotate. When the expected type for a parameter is **dynamic**, the mimic records this requirement as well, although no checks are performed.

During annotation, programs first contain *aExpr*s with the dynamic type, where the subsequent annotation step transforms this into a mimic position.

```
(class cons (list)                       (class cons (list)
  ((dynamic car cons) (list cdr cons))     ((dynamic car cons) (list cdr cons))
  ((boolean all ()                         ((boolean all ()
    (if (annotate dynamic                    (if (mimic boolean
         (get-field                               (get-field
          (annotate                                (annotate
           (classT cons (list)                      (classT cons (list)
            ((car dynamic cons)                      ((car dynamic cons)
             (cdr list cons))                         (cdr list cons))
            ((all boolean ())))                       ((all boolean ())))
          this)                                     this)
         (car cons)))                             (car cons)))
        (call (get-field this cdr) all)         (call (get-field this cdr) all)
        falseT))))                              falseT))))
```

Insert boolean check

Figure 21.10: Insertion of boolean check

Figure 21.10 provides a trace of three steps in annotating a list of dynamic items, containing the *and-map* function from our previous example. The highlighted region indicates the transformation that introduces the **mimic** form.

As with annotation rules introducing types, mimicking a class type requires an additional type lookup rule that follows directly from the annotation type lookup rules demonstrated in figure 21.6 to expand the identifier type into a **classT**. Figure 21.11 demonstrates the steps in annotating a binary tree instantiation with appropriate run-time guards for the two field values. The highlighted portion indicates the transformation into a mimic, and the subsequent step expands the expected type for the values.

An extended rule supporting annotating an **if** expression examines dynamic annotations of the two branches. When both are dynamic, the dynamic annotation propagates up. When one branch is dynamic and the other is t ($t \neq$ **dynamic**), the dynamic annotation translates into a mimic of t. Resolving this rule may require non-determinism within the relation, as the proper resolution of the first branch of the **if** may or may not depend on the proper resolution of the **else** branch.

When an expression with a dynamic annotation is used as an object, without specifying a type, the relation rule generates a **mimic** annotation with an **dynamicObjT** type specification to indicate the field or method accessed without introducing additional (unknown) type constraints. The resulting expression annotation has the **dynamic** type.

Inserting Guards. The rules of the $progA \leadsto_{aD} progA'$ relation rewrite an annotation into a **guard** when the resulting value must be prepared to enter an s fragment. In a program where a method parameter uses a **dynamic** type (such as *List insert*(**dynamic** e) { $\cdots$ }), the corresponding argument at the

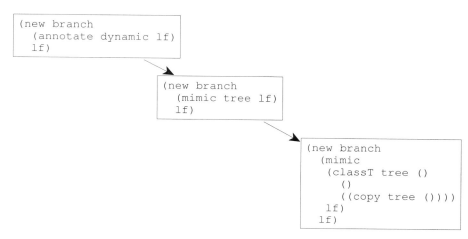

Figure 21.11: Insertion of an object check

call-site must be guarded. A call to *insert* with an object from the *Entry* class wraps the value in a guard for this class. Parameters and fields with explicit **dynamic** types direct the placement of guards, as do **app** expressions. Each argument to an **app** function is guarded with the derived type.

Individual rules for transforming annotations into guards resemble those for mimics; however, the **dynamic** type specification drives the transformation and the type within the annotation informs the guarded type, as seen in figure 21.9. Since guard transformations expand fully expanded annotations, the guard type is always either a primitive type or a **classT**, and no type look-up is required.

Two steps in adding a guard to a *j* object are outlined in figure 21.12. As visible within the highlighted portion, the annotated expression becomes a **guard**, leaving the type in place.

21·6 **Evaluation.** Our model of evaluation reduces the main expression of an annotated *j+s* program to a value using the reduction relation →$_r$. This relation uses a standard left-to-right evaluation context, where the expression position within an annotation is a context hole.

The set of values for a *j+s* program includes the four primitive boolean values, a representation of objects, and mimics and guards with embedded values—seen in figure 21.13. Programs in the *j* and *s* subset languages reduce to the values that belong to the *j* expression and *s* expression sets respectively.

```
(app
  (mimic dynamicT id)
  (annotate
    (classT tree ()
    ()
    ((prune tree ()))))
  (new tree)))
```

```
(annotate dynamic
  (app
    (mimic dynamicT id)
    (guard
      (classT tree ()
      ()
      ((prune tree ()))))
    (new tree))))
```

Figure 21.12: Guarding a *j* object

$$value ::=$$
$$\mid \ \cdots$$
$$\mid \ \textbf{obj}(\ cid_c\ (\ cid_0 .. cid_p\ )\ [\ fid_0\ value_0\ ] .. [\ fid_n\ value_n\ ]\ )$$
$$\mid \ \textbf{guardV}\ |_{aType}\ value$$
$$\mid \ \textbf{mimicV}\ |_{aType}\ value$$

Figure 21.13: Value specifications

In particular, they do not reduce to guard or mimic values, or to values that contain guards or mimics.

Reducing *j*. The $\rightarrow_r$ relation rules remove annotations and reduce boolean expressions. Figure 21.14 presents three local rules reducing *j* expressions. Annotations can be removed once they decorate values as the type information no longer impacts the program, except within **guard**s and **mimic**s. Object instantiation and field access operate locally, with object instantiation utilizing the annotation information to connect field names with values. The annotation proves convenient in this circumstance but is not necessary.

Reducing a method call requires examination of the appropriate class definition to extract the method body and perform substitution, which modifies *ids* and skips other names. The call reduction matches the implementation of the method with the name of the current object's class, as shown in CALLR— see figure 21.15. Calls to super methods resolve using the class hierarchy recorded in the current **this** expression.

Reducing *s*. The reduction rules for *s* are the standard call-by-value relations, combined with relations for boolean operations. Reduction of the *s* subset does not introduce error messages when evaluation cannot proceed; we rely on the halted evaluation to represent the error.

$\boxed{\mathcal{E}_e[aExpr] \rightarrow_{re} \mathcal{E}_e[aExpr']}$

$$\mathcal{E}_e[value_c \mid_{aType_c}] \rightarrow_{re} \mathcal{E}_e[value_c] \quad \text{UNANNOTATER}$$

$$\mathcal{E}_e[\textbf{instanceof}(\, \textbf{trueT}\, ,\, cid\,)] \rightarrow_{re} \mathcal{E}_e[\textbf{falseT}] \quad \text{INSTANCEOFTR}$$

$$\begin{array}{l} \mathcal{E}_e[\textbf{get-field}(value_o, fid_f)] \rightarrow_{re} \mathcal{E}_e[value_f] \\ \quad \text{WHERE} \\ \qquad value_o \;=\; \textbf{obj}(\, cid_c\, (\, cid_0 \,..\, cid_n\,)\, \overline{[fid_i value_i]}^{\,i}\, [fid_f\; value_f\,]\, \overline{[fid'_j value'_j]}^{\,j}\,) \end{array} \quad \text{FIELDACCESSR}$$

Figure 21.14: Reduction rules for *j*

$\boxed{progA \rightarrow_r progA'}$

$$\begin{array}{l} defAs_n\, \mathcal{E}_r[aExpr_c] \rightarrow_r defAs_n\, \mathcal{E}_r[ant_m\, \{\, \textbf{this} := value_c\, \}\, \overline{\{id'_a{:=}value_a\}}^{\,a\in 1\ldots n}] \\ \quad \text{WHERE} \\ \qquad defAs_n \;=\; \overline{defA_i}^{\,i}\, defA_c\, \overline{defA'_j}^{\,j} \\ \qquad defA_c \;=\; \textbf{class}\; cid_c\, \{\, extendT \\ \qquad\qquad\qquad field^*_f \\ \qquad\qquad\qquad \overline{methodA_i}^{\,i}\, type_m\; mid_m\, (\, \overline{type'_a id'_a}^{\,a\in 1\ldots n}\,)\, \{\, ant_m\, \}\, \overline{methodA'_j}^{\,j}\, \} \\ \qquad aExpr_c \;=\; \textbf{call}(\, value_c\, ,\, mid_m\, ,\, \overline{value_a}^{\,a\in 1\ldots n}\,) \\ \qquad value_c \;=\; \textbf{obj}(\, cid_c\, (\, \overline{cid_o}^{\,o}\,)\, \overline{[fid_f value'_f]}^{\,f}\,) \end{array} \quad \text{CALLR}$$

Figure 21.15: Reduction rule for call

$$\boxed{\mathcal{E}_e[aExpr] \rightarrow_{rD} \mathcal{E}_e[aExpr']}$$

$$\mathcal{E}_e[\textbf{mimic trueU} \,|_{\textbf{boolean}}] \rightarrow_{rD} \mathcal{E}_e[\textbf{trueT}] \quad \text{MIMICB}$$

$$\mathcal{E}_e[\textbf{guard trueT} \,|_{\textbf{boolean}}] \rightarrow_{rD} \mathcal{E}_e[\textbf{trueU}] \quad \text{GUARDB}$$

$$\mathcal{E}_e[\textbf{mimic obj}(\, cid\,(\, \overline{cid_i}^{\,i}\,)\, \overline{[fid_j value_j]}^{\,j}\,) \,|_{\textbf{boolean}}] \rightarrow_{rD} \mathcal{E}_e[\textbf{mimicError}] \quad \text{MIMICF}$$

Figure 21.16: Boolean transforming reduction rules

Reductions with Guards and Mimics. Unlike the rules for s, the reduction rules of $\rightarrow_r$ that encounter mimicked and guarded values may introduce a specific error value that indicates a failed transformation.

A **mimic** (or **guard**) containing a boolean value requires a representation transformation. The reduction relation MIMICB and GUARDB in figure 21.16 remove the annotation and translates a boolean into the alternate form. The final rule in the figure demonstrates the introduction of a **mimicError** when an object value is supposed to mimic a boolean.

In general, the dynamic role of guards and mimics is to prepare j and s values to migrate to s and j program fragments, respectively. The mimics must also assess whether a given value satisfies the embedded type requirement. Modifications to object representations, naming conventions, etc., are also the dynamic responsibility of these forms when required.

A **guard** wrapping an **obj** value manages access to the object via the interjection of further **mimic**s and **guard**s. When accessing a field via the **get-fieldU** expression, the **guard** evaluation ensures that the resulting value is wrapped with an appropriate guard, as shown in figure 21.17. The resulting **guard** requires a type lookup when extracting another object to transform a *cid* into the corresponding **classT**. Method calls similarly require that the returned value be embedded in an appropriate guard. The argument values for the method must be embedded in type-directed **mimic**s prior to substitution.

Rules for accessing embedded objects through a **mimic** follow a similar strategy to the one for **get-fieldU**, with an additional check performed when embedding the value. The rule for accessing an object through a **mimic** where the dynamic check of the static type expectation fails appears in figure 21.18. This rule ensures that the value contains all necessary fields and methods with checks of the types of these values delayed until access.

A **mimic** does not ensure that the embedded object descends from the named class. The role of the **mimic** is to prepare data that may not originate

$$\boxed{\mathcal{E}_e[aExpr] \rightarrow_{rD} \mathcal{E}_e[aExpr']}$$

$$\mathcal{E}_e[(\textbf{get-fieldU guardV}\,|_{aType_g}\,value_g\,fid_c)] \rightarrow_{rD} \mathcal{E}_e[\textbf{guard}\,value_c\,|_{type_c}]$$

WHERE

$$aType_g = \textbf{classT}\,cid_a\,(\,extendT_p,$$
$$\overline{fieldT_i}^{\,i}\,[\,fid_c\,type_c\,cid_c\,]\,\overline{fieldT_j'}^{\,j}, \qquad\qquad \text{GETFIELDUG}$$
$$methodT_n^*\,)$$

$$value_g = \textbf{obj}(\,cid_m\,(\overline{cid_o}^{\,o})\,\overline{[fid_a value_a]}^{\,a}\,[\,fid_c\,value_c\,]\,\overline{[fid_b' value_b']}^{\,b}\,)$$

Figure 21.17: Rule for accessing a guarded object

---

in j to act within the program without error, marshaling data as necessary. This can obscure the origin of the object, and enforcing inheritance can reduce the ability of two languages with differing object layouts to interoperate even though both representations containing the necessary functionality.

Tracing Reductions to Debug a Model. To examine our model for defects, we utilized the PLT Redex tracing facility to examine the performance of our reduction rules on $j+s$ programs. Snapshots of these traces illustrate the translation of values between s and j program fragments.

The program in figure 21.19 combines a class implementing a standard boolean operation, not, and an s function negating an s boolean. The main expression combines the two definitions to produce true from false. A snapshot of the reduction trace, in the bottom of figure 21.19, outlines the step that converts a mimicked boolean into a j-value. The trace elides the type information for surrounding expressions.

Guarded values receive orthogonal transformations in untyped reduction contexts. The program in figure 21.20 returns a j object from a function before performing a method call. This sequence removes the static type information for the j object and therefore the call interacts with a guarded object. The reduction step of performing a call within a **guard** embedding appears in the trace snapshot at the bottom of figure 21.20.

When untyped values satisfy the static type requirements, reduction proceeds with the rules translating value representations and embedding values as required. However, the untyped fragment may not satisfy the requirements, generating a **mimicError**. The program in figure 21.21 performs multiple operations with a method accepting a **dynamic** parameter. This parameter must behave identically to an object of the b class; however, on the

$$\boxed{progA \rightarrow_{rD} progA'}$$

$$defAs_n \; \mathcal{E}_r[\mathbf{mimicV} \mid_{aType_m} value_m] \rightarrow_{rD} defAs_n \; \mathcal{E}_r[\mathbf{mimicError}]$$

WHERE

$$defAs_n = \overline{defA_i}^{\,i} \; defA_c \; \overline{defA'_j}^{\,j}$$

$$defA_c = \mathbf{class}\, cid_c \, \{\, extendT$$

$$\overline{type_f \, fid_f \,;}^{\,f}$$

$$\overline{type'_m \, mid'_m \, (\,\overline{type''_a id_a}^{\,a}\,)\, \{\, ant_m \,\}}^{\,m} \; \}$$

$$aType_m = \mathbf{classT}\, cid \, (\, extendT_p \,,$$

$$\overline{[\, fid'_g \, type'''_g \, cid'_g \,]}^{\,g} \,,$$

$$\overline{type''''_e \, mid_e \, [\,\overline{id'_b type'''''_b}^{\,b}\,]}^{\,e} \,)$$

$$value_m = \mathbf{obj}(\, cid_c \, (\,\overline{cid_o}^{\,o}\,) \, \overline{[fid''_n value_n]}^{\,n}\,)$$

$$\overline{fid''_n}^{\,n} \notin \overline{fid'_g}^{\,g}$$

$$\overline{(\, mid'_m \, (\,\overline{id_a}^{\,a}\,)\,)}^{\,m} \notin \overline{(\, mid_e \, (\,\overline{id'_b}^{\,b}\,)\,)}^{\,e}$$

MIMICERROR

Figure 21.18: Rule introducing mimic errors

```
class Not {
  boolean n;
  Not negate ((boolean c)) {
    if (c)
       new Not(falseT)
       new Not(trueT)
  } }
(defineU f (lam (o) (callU o negate trueU)))
app(f, new Not(falseT))
```

```
(mimic dynamicT
 (guard not
  (if (annotate boolean
       (mimic boolean trueU))
     (annotate .
     (new not
       (annotate . falseT)))
     (annotate .
     (new not
       (annotate . trueT))))))
```

```
(mimic dynamicT
 (guard not
  (if (annotate boolean trueT)
     (annotate .
     (new not
       (annotate . falseT)))
     (annotate .
     (new not
       (annotate . trueT))))))
```

Figure 21.19: Translation of a boolean

```
class Tree {
  Tree prune() { new Tree() }
}
(defineU id (lam (x) x))
call( app( id, new Tree()), prune)
```

```
(mimic dynamicT
 (call
  (guardV
   (classT tree () ()
    ((prune tree ())))
   (objT tree () ()))
  prune))
```

guard method call

```
(mimic dynamicT
 (guard tree
  (call
   (objT tree () ())
   prune)))
```

Figure 21.20: A guarded method call

```
class b {
  boolean not (boolean n) { if (n) falseT trueT }
}
class c {
  boolean f (b o) { call(o, not, trueT) }
  dynamic ex (dynamic o) { call(this, f, o) }
}
call( new c(), ex, call( new c(), ex, new b()))
```

```
(mimic dynamicT                          (mimic dynamicT
 (annotate boolean                        (annotate boolean
  (call                                    (call
   (objT c () ())                           (objT c () ())
   f                                        f
   (mimic                      ➤            mimic-error)))
    (classT bool ()
     ()
     ((not boolean
       ((n boolean)))))
     falseU))))
```

Figure 21.21: Failed mimic of an object

outermost method call, the programmer provides a boolean value instead. The introduction of the **mimicError** appears at the bottom of figure 21.21. At the point of reducing the inner call into a value, the type expectations of the outer call require that the value match the type expectations of a *b* object. Since they do not, the **mimicError** value is produced and reduction ends.

Tracing this program uncovered two errors within our model that jointly led to the creation of an illegal value: **mimic falseT** $|_{\mathbf{boolean}}$. This illegal value arose due to an error in interacting with guarded values where an instantiation of *b* is first embedded in a **guard** and a **mimic** as it passes between untyped and typed expressions. When the call to *not* returned **falseT** to the surrounding **guard**, the **guard** reduction rule did not inject a **guard** around the return value allowing **falseT** to propagate into untyped expressions. A test evaluation demonstrated two omissions within the reduction rules.

The first mistake allowed a **falseT** value to return through a guarded object without transformation. In response, we updated the method call reduction to insert the appropriate guard on the return value, thus removing the insertion of a plain *j* value into an *s* expression. Although an unguarded *j* value should never be passed to an *s*-expression, the acceptance of the illegal value demonstrated a weakness in our mimic checks, which is the second mistake. To avoid the generation of further illegal values, we generalized our rule for mimicking booleans to produce a **mimicError** for any value other than **trueU** or **falseU** with type **boolean**.

21·7 Related Work.
Prior work explored models of the Java language, models combining statically and dynamically typed functional languages, and semantics exploring the type safety of combining static and dynamic types within one language.

Models of Java. Previous models of Java and other object-oriented calculi encode the features of pure OO interactions with varying numbers of operations. Two of these models, ClassicJava [41] and Featherweight Java [59], provided direct inspiration for the form of the j model.

Models of Dynamic/Static Combinations. Matthews and Findler [74] propose models of combining multiple languages using guards to protect the type expectations of the different languages. Their semantics follows similar techniques as those presented in our model; however, neither language represented in this work supports object-oriented computations.

Siek and Taha [99] present a calculus for incorporating static types and dynamic checks within an object language utilizing casts to inferred types, similar to our mimics, but lacking distinct representations of transformation and guards. This system has been proven statically type-safe when fully annotated. Their early work [98] connects the simply typed lambda calculus to the untyped variant and proves that their fully annotated calculus is equivalent to the simply typed lambda calculus.

Tobin-Hochstadt and Felleisen [106] also present a formal model of integrating a statically typed functional language with dynamically typed scripts, utilizing contracts to preserve higher-order type safety. This work proves soundness for the system; i.e., that the statically typed programs do not result in type errors.

A proposed extension to ML allows for a `Dynamic` type constructor [2, 29], which is similar to the `dynamic` declaration. The `Dynamic` operators allow the explicit extraction of untyped data into programmer-specified types; guards are not supported. This work demonstrates that within one language, such operations are sound.

Mixing Dynamic and Static Types. Other implementations also provide combinations of static and dynamic types.

Strongtalk [13] adds an optional static type system to Smalltalk [47]. On the boundary between typed and untyped expressions, the compiler either assumes a type or relies on an annotation from the programmer.

The Amber programming language [15] also mixes static and dynamic type checking. Values from statically type-checked expressions can be placed into `Dynamic` wrappers, in which the static type information is disregarded. During program execution, interaction with these values is checked to conform to the static type knowledge. Like the `Dynamic` ML language, the programmer must explicitly cast the type.

Work on embedding languages by Benton [9] and Ramsey [88] provides connections between statically typed languages and embedded dynamically typed languages. For both systems, when a value from the dynamically typed language is passed into the statically typed language, the system performs an immediate check of the value but does not check higher-order properties. The expected type is derived from a specification either written by the programmer or provided by the system library.

21·8 Conclusions and Supporting More Java Features. The $j+s$ language illustrates the semantics of merging programming languages with different static expectations and linguistic constructs. The constructs of these two languages represent the core features involved in interoperation and provide support for the safety of interoperating the base languages; however, additional features may provide relevant insights in guiding further implementation choices.

Neither j nor s support mutation, although both Java and Scheme do. Still, the reduction rules for wrapped field accesses should only require modifications related to accessing a store. Since these field accesses specifically delegate to the embedded object, the rule already ensures that the current value of the field is retrieved. Rules for updating wrapped fields must inject **mimic**s or **guards** around the stored values.

Java access restrictions may require extending the data stored within a **classT** for use by wrappers. This information should include the specified visibility of each member. Accesses through the wrapper would require additional dynamic checks to ensure that the member could be accessed within the current location. This, in turn, may require additional information to represent the current location of an object with regard to class and package visibility. However, the dynamic checks continue to reside within accesses to the guards and mimics.

22 · Implementing Hidden Type Variables in Fortress

Joe Hallett, Boston University
Eric Allen, Sun Microsystems, Inc.
Sukyoung Ryu, Sun Microsystems, Inc.

Hidden type variables enable programmers to express relationships between types that cannot be expressed in conventional object-oriented languages. However, they also significantly complicate subtype checking and dynamic dispatch. To help ensure that the semantics of a language including hidden type variables is sound and has other desirable properties, we have mechanized their semantics using PLT Redex. Our mechanization serves as a proof of concept of a formal semantics of hidden type variables in the Fortress programming language and has been useful in drawing out subtle bugs. Our mechanization is available online, along with a type checker over it, allowing readers to experiment with it interactively.

22·1 Hidden Type Variables.

Many object-oriented programming languages with static typing allow the programmer to parameterize a type definition by a set of type parameters. A type that is parameterized in this way effectively becomes a function, mapping instantiations of its type parameters to a new type with more precise information. In this way, programmers are able to define more precise types while keeping a single point of control over the definition of a collection of types with a similar form. In the Fortress programming language [4], a class-based object-oriented language with multiple inheritance, programmers define classes via *trait definitions*, and *object definitions*. Trait definitions are parameterized types that exist in a multiple-inheritance hierarchy with nominal subtyping. Traits define methods (but not fields); they are similar to interfaces in the Java[TM] Programming Language [48], except methods in a trait are allowed to be concrete. Object definitions exist at the leaves of the type hierarchy; although they extend trait definitions, they are not themselves extended. An object definition may be a singleton (defining a single runtime value) or parameterized (declaring a constructor that produces a new value each time it is called, like a final class in the Java Programming Language).

For example, we walk through the following definition of a trait List:

```
trait List⟦X⟧ extends {Collection, Object}
    append(other: List⟦X⟧) : List⟦X⟧
end
```

The reserved word `trait` is followed by the name of the defined trait, List, which is followed by a type parameter X enclosed in white square brackets (indicating the type of the elements in a list), and an extends clause that lists the set of types extended by each instantiation of List: Collection and Object, enclosed in braces. Trait List also includes an abstract method *append*, which takes one parameter, *other* (with type List⟦X⟧). In Fortress, the type of a parameter is declared following the name of the parameter (preceded by a colon). After the list of parameters (and a colon), the return type of the method is provided: List⟦X⟧. In Fortress, abstract methods are distinguished simply by the fact that they have no body.

We extend trait List⟦X⟧ with a parametric object definition Cons:

```
object Cons⟦X⟧(hd: X, tl: List⟦X⟧) extends {List⟦X⟧}
    append(other: List⟦X⟧): List⟦X⟧ = Cons⟦X⟧(hd, tl.append(other))
end
```

This definition is parameterized with respect to a type parameter, X, and two *value parameters*, *hd* and *tl*. Each value parameter implicitly defines a field. The object definition as a whole implicitly defines a constructor that takes an instantiation of each parameter and produces a new value, with each field initialized to the value of its respective constructor argument. For example, the constructor call Cons⟦String⟧("hello", Empty) produces a new value of type Cons⟦String⟧, whose *hd* field is initialized to "hello" and whose tail is initialized to Empty (defined below). After the declared value parameters, an `extends` clause lists the set of traits that type Cons⟦X⟧ extends (that is, List⟦X⟧), and a concrete definition of the *append* method is provided. The body of this method is provided after an $=$ sign following the method header. This method returns the result of calling constructor Cons⟦X⟧ with two arguments: *hd*, and the result of recursively calling *append*(*other*) on field *tl*.

By parameterizing List by its element type, we are able to define the form of lists of every conceivable element type, all at once, while allowing clients to precisely type the elements put into and taken out of a list. This use of type parameters is similar to what can be done in the Java Programming

Language or C#. In Fortress, we further extend the expressive power of generic object-oriented programming languages by allowing the programmer to declare additional type variables in a *where clause* that is separate from ordinary type parameter declarations. As with ordinary type parameters, the type variables in a where clause are universally quantified. But unlike ordinary type parameters, the parameterized type is not a function of these *hidden type variables*. For example, in Fortress we can write the following definition of a singleton object named Empty:

```
object Empty extends {List⟦Y⟧}
    where {Y extends Object}
    append(other: List⟦Y⟧): List⟦Y⟧ = other
end
```

This definition starts with the reserved word object, followed by the name of the defined object, Empty, the set of traits it "extends," and a where clause binding the hidden type variable Y. Unlike with parametric object definitions, a singleton object definition in Fortress such as the one above has no parameters and defines no constructor; instead, it defines a single runtime value. This single object Empty (with its own type, also named Empty) extends type List⟦Y⟧, where the type variable Y is bound in a where clause. This where clause is interpreted as asserting that Empty extends *every instantiation* of List⟦Y⟧. It is important to emphasize that Empty itself has no type parameters; we can understand the type variable Y as being universally quantified over the definition of Empty. Thus, the single Empty value can be used in any context requiring a List⟦Y⟧ for any type Y. Moreover, because the definition of *append* in Empty takes a parameter with type List⟦Y⟧, we understand this definition as actually defining infinitely many methods, one for each instantiation of Y.

Hidden type variables are first-class types in the sense that they can be used in type-dependent operations such as **instanceof** testing or run-time type casting. Their scope is the header of the definition in which they are introduced. If they appear in the signature of an inherited method definition, that definition actually states that there are infinitely many methods, one for each instantiation of the hidden type variables. For example, because Empty extends every instantiation of List⟦Y⟧, it inherits infinitely many abstract methods named *append*, each with a distinct return type. Concrete definitions for all of these abstract methods are provided by the infinitely many *append* methods defined in Empty.

We have found hidden type variables to be an important tool in designing the Fortress libraries, especially when modeling relationships among mathematical objects in Fortress [4]. In order to explore and refine the semantics of hidden type variables, we have mechanized a core language in PLT Redex. This mechanization serves as a proof of concept of the formal semantics of hidden type variables. In addition, the implementation was useful in drawing out subtle bugs in the semantics. Our mechanization can be queried online [52]: one can run the evaluator on some existing programs or enter a new program. A detailed description of the semantics of hidden type variables is available [4]. In this chapter, we describe the challenges involved in defining the semantics, along with our solutions, and share our experiences in mechanizing the semantics in PLT Redex.

22·2 Applications of Hidden Type Variables. Although simple, the idea of hidden type variables provides surprisingly rich expressive power. It enables us to elide redundant type parameters from definitions and encode many-to-one relationships among instantiations of multiple parametric types. It also allows us to express complex subtyping relationships among various instantiations of a single parametric type; in particular, we can encode covariance and contravariance without additional language primitives.

Variance Types. Hidden type variables allow us to express subtype relationships between various instantiations of a single parametric type directly in the language. Such relationships are often useful but are typically allowed only through special-purpose language features. For example, if we wish to define an immutable list type that is covariant in its element type, we need some way to express that some instantiations of type List are subtypes of other instantiations.

This property cannot be expressed directly in most object-oriented languages. Languages that do allow expression of covariance typically do so via a mechanism designed specifically for this purpose, such as variance annotations in Scala [81] or wildcards in the Java Programming Language [109]. Using hidden type variables, we are able to express covariance without additional language features:

```
trait CoList⟦X extends Y⟧
  extends {CoList⟦Y⟧, Collection, Object}
  where {Y extends Object}
end
```

The definition of trait CoList⟦X⟧ declares a hidden type variable Y, which serves as the bound of type parameter X. Effectively, this definition expresses that an instantiation of CoList⟦X⟧ is a subtype of every instantiation of CoList⟦Y⟧, such that X is a subtype of Y (i.e., CoList is covariant).

Notice that, unlike variance annotations or Java wildcards, hidden type variables can be used to define relationships between two different types. That is, one type may extend an entirely different type, whose type arguments are in some variance relation. For example, consider the following trait definition:

```
trait RedBlack⟦X extends Y⟧
    extends {BinaryTree⟦Y⟧}
    where {Y extends Object}
end
```

This definition expresses that an instantiation of RedBlack⟦X⟧ is a subtype of every instantiation of BinaryTree⟦Y⟧, such that X is a subtype of Y. More concretely, a RedBlack⟦String⟧ is a BinaryTree⟦Object⟧.

Many-to-One Relationships. Hidden type variables allow us to express new subtype relationships: a single type can be a subtype of another type instantiated with hidden type variables, which admits an infinite number of instantiations. For example, the None type of an Option type need not be parameterized because it does not use the type parameter:

```
trait Option⟦X⟧ end
object None
        extends Option⟦X⟧
        where {X extends Object}
end
object Some⟦X⟧(x: X)
        extends Option⟦X⟧
end
```

The resulting program captures the desired specification and enjoys the performance benefits of sharing a single value None among all instantiations of Option⟦X⟧.

Elimination of Extraneous Parameters. In conventional object-oriented languages such as the Java Programming Language (or C#, or Eiffel, etc.), we must sometimes include type parameters that obscure the interpretation of the class. The following example illustrates how hidden type variables can avoid such parameterization.

Suppose we want to represent measurements in a particular unit, such as 5 meters or 12.4 seconds. A straightforward approach is to define a type Unit that represents all units of a measurement, such as Meter:

```
trait Unit end
trait Meter extends Unit end
```

and then define a measurement as a parametric object Measurement, parameterized by a type U (corresponding to its unit) and a value mag (corresponding to its magnitude):

```
object Measurement⟦U extends Unit⟧(mag : ℝ) end
```

We define the type of mag as $\mathbb{R}$ (which is the type of arbitrary-precision floating point numbers in Fortress). Using these definitions, the measurement "5 meters" can be denoted as Measurement⟦Meter⟧(5).

Now, suppose that we wish to augment our system of measurements by capturing the dimension of a unit. For example, the dimension of a meter is length and the dimension of a second is time. To do this we define a type Dimension that represents all dimensional values, such as Length:[1]

```
trait Dimension end
trait Length extends Dimension end
```

Now, units are encoded as:

```
trait Unit⟦D extends Dimension⟧ end
trait Meter extends Unit⟦Length⟧ end
```

and measurements as:

```
object Measurement⟦U extends Unit⟦D⟧,
                   D extends Dimension⟧(mag : ℝ) end
```

A particular measurement, such as "5 meters," is written as:

Measurement⟦Meter, Length⟧(5)

But the type Length is redundant: its value can be inferred from Meter. With hidden type variables, we can instead put the declaration of D into a where clause:

```
object Measurement⟦U extends Unit⟦D⟧⟧(mag : ℝ)
   where {D extends Dimension}
end
```

The where clause allows us to omit the dimension, with the intention that it is derived from the unit parameter, making the resulting program more readable. For example, the measurement "5 meters" can be written as:

Measurement⟦Meter⟧(5)

---

[1]Note that this toy encoding ignores the algebraic properties of units. For a thorough treatment of the problem of encoding units in an object-oriented languages, see Allen et al. [5].

```
trait List⟦X extends Object⟧
    extends {Collection, Object}
    cons(x : X) : List⟦X⟧ = Cons⟦X⟧(x, self)
    size() : ℤ
end

object Cons⟦X extends Object⟧(hd : X, tl : List⟦X⟧)
    extends {List⟦X⟧}
    size() = 1 + tl.size()
end

object Empty
    extends List⟦Y⟧
    where {Y extends Object}
    size() = 0
end
```

Figure 22.1: List example

22·3 Challenges When Implementing Hidden Type Variables.
Unlike the Java Programming Language, Fortress preserves types at run time. That is, type parameters and type arguments are not erased at compile time. This allows Fortress to avoid the shortcomings associated with type erasure [3]. Namely, Fortress can allow type-dependent operations, such as instanceof tests or run-time casts to type variables.

Type-dependent operations require concrete types, however. A type variable must be instantiated before a type-dependent operation can be performed on it. Because hidden type variables cannot be explicitly instantiated by the programmer, as ordinary type parameters can, it is necessary to infer instantiations of hidden type variables, which we refer to as *witnesses*.

Witnesses are inferred during subtype checking and method dispatch. To illustrate this, we modify the definitions of a list presented previously. The new definitions are shown in figure 22.1.

The occurrence of a hidden type variable in a type in an extends clause indicates that infinitely many types are extended. For example, the definition of the Empty object declares that a single object Empty extends infinitely many types (i.e., each instantiation of List⟦Y⟧). Therefore, to verify that Empty is a subtype of List⟦String⟧, we must check that String is a valid witness for Y. That is, we must check that String meets the bounds on Y.

Similarly, an inherited method definition with a hidden type variable in its type denotes infinitely many methods (all with the same name); we must determine which of these methods is called at each call site. For example, because Empty extends *every* instantiation of List⟦Y⟧, it inherits infinitely many methods named *cons*, each with a distinct type. Thus, for the following method invocation:

Empty.*cons*(5)

the type checker must decide which of these infinitely many methods to call. This method call could produce one of several different types, including[2] Cons⟦ℤ⟧(5, Empty), Cons⟦Number⟧(5, Empty), Cons⟦Object⟧(5, Empty).

Note that due to type-dependent operations, this decision can affect the observable behavior of a program. For example, if this method call is embedded within the following type-depended operation:

typecase x = Empty.*cons*(5) of
    List⟦ℤ⟧ ⟹ "Integer List"
    List⟦Number⟧ ⟹ "Number List"
    List⟦Object⟧ ⟹ "Object List"
    else ⟹ "Other List"
end

then the choice of the witness will determine the result of the expression. Note that typecase is an expression in Fortress that evaluates the test expression (the method call in this case) and then executes the top-most branch whose guarding type is a supertype of the test expression.

22·4 Selecting Witnesses for Hidden Type Variables.

Witnesses for hidden type variables are automatically inferred by the compiler and run-time system. Any witness that satisfies the bounds on the corresponding hidden type variable will produce a well-typed program. However, as we have seen in the previous section, oftentimes there are several such witnesses.

The lack of unique witnesses presents a problem for the semantics of hidden type variables. If witnesses are chosen non-deterministically, then the programmer will not be able to determine the type of a program. In a language with type-dependent operations, the witnesses for hidden type variables can influence the result of the program. In this case, if witnesses are chosen non-deterministically, then the programmer will not be able to determine the result of a program.

To address this issue, *most-specific witnesses* for hidden type variables are inferred. Most-specific witnesses provide the most information possible about a hidden type variable. The increase in type information provided by

---

[2] ℤ is the type of integers in Fortress.

```
trait Printable extends Object end
trait Serializable extends Object end

object PSFile(name: String) extends {Printable, Serializable} end
object PDFFile(name: String) extends {Printable, Serializable} end

trait List⟦X extends Y⟧
    extends {List⟦Y⟧, Collection, Object} where {Y extends Object}
    cons(y: Y) : List⟦Y⟧ = Cons⟦Y⟧(y, self)
end
object Cons⟦X extends Object⟧(hd: X, tl: List⟦X⟧)
    extends List⟦X⟧
end
object Empty
    extends List⟦Z⟧
    where {Z extends Object}
end

Cons⟦PSFile⟧(PSFile("myPSFile"),
            Empty).cons(PDFFile("myPDFFile"))
```

Figure 22.2: Union type example

---

a most-specific witness enlarges the set of contexts in which it is safe to use an expression whose type is the witness.

Most-specific witnesses do not always exist. If a hidden type variable has no lower bounds then a most-specific witness exists only if the programmer defines one. In case the programmer did not define such a trait or object, we introduce the type Bottom, which is a subtype of every other type.

Even with the type Bottom, most-specific witnesses do not necessarily exist. Consider the program shown in figure 22.2. Notice that the type of the method call is $List⟦Y⟧$, for some instantiation of Y. In fact, Y must be a supertype of both PSFile and PDFFile. However, both Printable and Serializable are supertypes of both PSFile and PDFFile, and neither is more specific than the other. In other words, the least upper bound of PSFile and PDFFile is not unique. This is a consequence of multiple extensions and a nominal type hierarchy.

To ensure that least upper bounds are always unique, we introduce union types into the language. In the above example, the witness PSFile ∪ PDFFile would be inferred for Y. Informally, a value of this type either has type PSFile or has type PDFFile.

22·5 Annotating Programs with Witnesses.

There are programs in which hidden type variables are not statically evident but appear during dynamic dispatch. For example, consider the following method call in the context of figure 22.1:

l : List⟦Object⟧ = Empty
$l.cons(5)$

The static type of the receiver l is List⟦Object⟧, but l evaluates to the value Empty. Therefore, when evaluating the method call, a witness is needed for the hidden type variable Y. This method call could return one of

Cons⟦$\mathbb{Z}$⟧(5, Empty),
Cons⟦Number⟧(5, Empty) or
Cons⟦Object⟧(5, Empty),

depending on the witness. In fact, if Bottom is chosen as the witness then the method call returns Cons⟦Bottom⟧(5, Empty), violating type soundness.

To account for this situation, witnesses are added to a program as annotations. To annotate a program with witnesses, we have developed the notion of a *path* in the type hierarchy. A path is a list of types such that each type is an immediate subtype of its successor. That is, a path is a step-by-step traversal between two types in the type hierarchy. As an example:

Empty List⟦Number⟧ Collection

is a valid path in the type hierarchy created by the declarations in figure 22.1.

If each method call is annotated with a path from the type of the receiver to the type defining the method, the run-time semantics can simply follow this path when dispatching to a method. Because each type in the path will be fully instantiated at run time, the path provides witnesses for hidden type variables. At compile time, a path from the static type of the receiver to the type defining the method is inferred. At run time, the path is extended from the dynamic type of the receiver to the static type of the receiver.

For example, consider the method call

l : List⟦Object⟧ = Empty
$l.size()$

in the context of figure 22.1. Its receiver expression has type List⟦Object⟧. At compile time, the method call is annotated with the single element path:

List⟦Object⟧

as follows:

l path List⟦Object⟧.*size*()

At run time, before the method is dispatched, the receiver is fully evaluated:

Empty path List⟦Object⟧.*size*()

The current path does not begin with the type of the receiver. In particular, the type of the receiver, Empty, is a strict subtype of the first (and only) type in the path, List⟦Object⟧. If the current path is used to dispatch the method, the definition of the method in trait List⟦Object⟧ (which is abstract) would be invoked instead of the definition in object Empty. Therefore, the path annotation must be extended to the dynamic type of the receiver:

Empty path Empty List⟦Object⟧.*size*()

22·6 A Redex Model for Hidden Type Variables.

We have mechanized the semantics of hidden type variables in PLT Redex to help us understand it better, and to decide what semantics we should ultimately adopt for Fortress. This chapter presents the formalization of one of our semantics, specifically HTV1. In this section, we describe the Redex model for the HTV1 language. Implementation of the type checking algorithm and inference procedures are described in the following section. The resulting system can be queried online [52].

It is important to note that the semantics of HTV1 diverges from the semantics of hidden type variables in the Fortress language specification in the following ways:

- hidden type variables are not allowed to occur in method definitions;

- both ordinary type parameters and hidden type variables can have lower bounds (this allows programs that have hidden type variables in method definitions to be encoded); and

- overloading is forbidden but overriding is allowed (in Fortress, both overloading and overriding are allowed).

Syntax. The syntax of the Redex model for HTV1 is presented in figure 22.3. A program p in HTV1 consists of a list of definitions (d...) followed by a single expression e. All programs in HTV1 are purely functional.

A definition is either a trait defintion td or an object definition od. Trait definitions are represented as a list of: the keyword trait, a trait name T, a list of bounds (bnd...) corresponding to ordinary type parameters, a list of extended types (M...), a list of bounds (bnd...) corresponding to hidden type

$$
\begin{aligned}
p &::= (d \; ... \; e) \\
d &::= td \\
  &\quad \mid od \\
td &::= (\text{trait } T \; (bnd \; ...) \; (M \; ...) \; (bnd \; ...) \; (md \; ...)) \\
od &::= (\text{object } O \; (bnd \; ...) \; ((x \; A) \; ...) \; (M \; ...) \; (bnd \; ...) \; (md \; ...)) \\
md &::= (m \; (bnd \; ...) \; ((x \; A) \; ...) \; A \; e) \\
bnd &::= (X \; \text{extends} \; K) \\
    &\quad \mid (X \; \text{bounds} \; K) \\
e &::= x \\
  &\quad \mid \text{self} \\
  &\quad \mid (O \; (A \; ...) \; (e \; ...)) \\
  &\quad \mid (e \; x) \\
  &\quad \mid (e \; m \; (A \; ...) \; (e \; ...)) \\
  &\quad \mid (e \; (A \; ...) \; m \; (A \; ...) \; (e \; ...)) \\
  &\quad \mid ((x \; e) \; ((A \; e) \; ...) \; e) \\
  &\quad \mid (e \; \text{as} \; A) \\
A &::= (O \; (A \; ...)) \\
  &\quad \mid K \\
  &\quad \mid \text{Bottom} \\
  &\quad \mid (A \; \text{union} \; A) \\
K &::= X \\
  &\quad \mid M \\
M &::= (T \; (A \; ...)) \\
  &\quad \mid \text{Object}
\end{aligned}
$$

Figure 22.3: Syntax of HTV1

variables, and a list of method definitions $(md...)$. Object definitions are similar, except the keyword `object` is used and a list of parameters $((x\ A)...)$ corresponding to field declarations is included. For simplicity, abstract methods are not included in HTV1.

Both traits and objects may extend multiple traits; they inherit the methods provided by the extended traits. For simplicity, we allow a trait or object to inherit only one method definition for each method name. However, a trait or object can override the definition of an inherited method.

Bounds are either upper bounds on type variables (X `extends` K) or lower bounds on type variables (X `bounds` K).

A method definitions is represented as a list of a method name m, a list of bounds $(bnd...)$ corresponding to method type parameters, a list of parameters $((x\ A)...)$, a return type A, and an expression e for the method body.

An expression is either: a variable x; the special identifier `self`; a constructor call $(O\ (A...)\ (e...))$, which includes an object name, type arguments, and value arguments; a field access $(e\ x)$, which includes a receiver and a field name; a method call $(e\ (A...)\ m\ (A...)\ (e...))$, which includes a receiver, a list of types denoting the path annotation, a method name, type arguments, and value arguments; a typecase expression $((x\ e)\ ((A\ e)...)\ e)$, which includes a variable bound to the test expression, a list of guarding types and branch bodies, and the body of the else branch; or a type annotation $(e$ `as` $A)$.

Recall that typecase expressions are type-dependent operations that evaluate the test expression, assigning the result to the specified variable, and then evaluate the first clause whose guarding type is a supertype of the test expression's type. For each clause, the static type of the variable is the guarding type of that clause.

A type A is either an object type $(O\ (A...))$, a non-object type K, the special type `Bottom`, or a union type $(A$ `union` $A)$. Non-object types are either a type variable X or a trait type M. A trait type is either an instance of a trait $(T\ (A...))$ or the special type `Object`.

In figure 22.4, we define values and evaluation contexts. Values are fully evaluated object instances, i.e., object constructor invocations whose value arguments are themselves values. The definition of evaluation contexts defines a left-most, inner-most evaluation strategy for expressions.

Dynamic Semantics. Figure 22.5 shows two of the redex evaluation rules for HTV1. The field access redex evaluation rule looks up the receiver object and the field name (using `obj-lookup` and `fld-lookup`, respectively). The corresponding value argument of the object instance is returned.

The method call rule looks up the receiver object and the method name with the auxiliary functions `obj-lookup` and `md-lookup`, respectively. The

$$v ::= (O\ (A\ ...)\ (v\ ...))$$
$$EC ::= [\,]$$
$$\mid (O\ (A\ ...)\ (v\ ...\ EC\ e\ ...))$$
$$\mid (EC\ x)$$
$$\mid (EC\ (A\ ...)\ m\ (A\ ...)\ (e\ ...))$$
$$\mid (v\ (A\ ...)\ m\ (A\ ...)\ (v\ ...\ EC\ e\ ...))$$
$$\mid ((x\ EC)\ ((A\ e)\ ...)\ e)$$

Figure 22.4: Values and evaluation contexts of HTV1

$$((O_0\ (A\ ...)\ (v_0\ ...))\ x_i) \rightsquigarrow v_i \qquad\qquad\qquad\qquad \text{[R-Field]}$$
$$\text{where } \mathsf{obj\text{-}def} = \mathsf{obj\text{-}lookup}[\![\mathsf{p},\ O_0]\!],$$
$$v_i = \mathsf{fld\text{-}lookup}[\![\mathsf{obj\text{-}def},\ (v_0\ ...),\ x_i]\!]$$

$$((O_0\ (A_0\ ...)\ (v_0\ ...))\ (A_1\ ...)\ m_0\ (A_2\ ...)\ (v_1\ ...)) \qquad\qquad \text{[R-Method]}$$
$$\rightsquigarrow \mathsf{substs}[\![(v_0\ ...\ v_1\ ...\ A_2\ ...\ (O_0\ (A_0\ ...)\ (v_0\ ...))),$$
$$(x\ ...\ \mathsf{y}\ ...\ X\ ...\ \mathsf{self}),$$
$$e]\!]$$
$$\text{where } ((bnd_0\ ...)\ ((x\ A)\ ...)\ (M\ ...)\ (bnd_1\ ...)\ (md\ ...)) = \mathsf{obj\text{-}lookup}[\![\mathsf{p},\ O_0]\!],$$
$$(((X\ \ K)\ ...)\ ((\mathsf{y}\ A)\ ...)\ \mathsf{B}\ e) = \mathsf{md\text{-}lookup}[\![\mathsf{p},\ m_0,\ (A_1\ ...)]\!]$$

Figure 22.5: Some evaluation rules of HTV1

Path update: $\boxed{path_p(e) = e}$

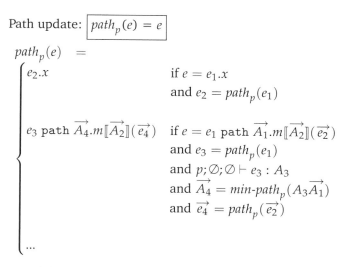

$$path_p(e) =$$
$$\begin{cases} e_2.x & \text{if } e = e_1.x \\ & \text{and } e_2 = path_p(e_1) \\ \\ e_3 \text{ path } \overrightarrow{A_4}.m[\![\overrightarrow{A_2}]\!](\overrightarrow{e_4}) & \text{if } e = e_1 \text{ path } \overrightarrow{A_1}.m[\![\overrightarrow{A_2}]\!](\overrightarrow{e_2}) \\ & \text{and } e_3 = path_p(e_1) \\ & \text{and } p;\varnothing;\varnothing \vdash e_3 : A_3 \\ & \text{and } \overrightarrow{A_4} = min\text{-}path_p(A_3\overrightarrow{A_1}) \\ & \text{and } \overrightarrow{e_4} = path_p(\overrightarrow{e_2}) \\ \\ \dots \end{cases}$$

Figure 22.6: Some of the path update function

type and value arguments of the call are substituted into the body of the method and the result is returned.

Figure 22.6 shows the path update function, $path_p(e)$, which extends path annotations at run time. Specifically, for each method call in e, the path update function calls $min\text{-}path_p(A_3\overrightarrow{A_1})$, where A_3 is the type of the receiver and $\overrightarrow{A_1}$ is the existing path annotation. This function returns the minimal path that contains each of its input types. The result of $min\text{-}path_p(A_3\overrightarrow{A_1})$ becomes the new, extended path annotation of the method call.

22·7 Type Checking HTV1.

The most interesting and novel aspect of HTV1 is its type system. Even the run-time implementation requires the type checker. As discussed in the previous section, path annotations must be extended at run time. We have used PLT Redex to rapidly prototype our dynamic semantics, allowing us to focus our efforts on the type checker.

In this section, we describe the path annotation inference and the constraint solving algorithm, which was the most challenging part of the type checker to implement. More details about the implementation of HTV1 can be found in the first author's Ph.D. thesis [53]. PLT Redex proved useful for testing other aspects of the type checker, and we describe our experiences in the next section.

Inferring Path Annotations. Inferring path annotations on method calls is a matter of searching the hierarchy of trait and object definitions for a path between the definition corresponding to the static type of the receiver and the definition enclosing the method. This search is done in a breadth-first manner to ensure that the shortest path is found. During this search, the constraints on hidden type variables are collected. When the trait or object definition enclosing the method definition is found, the constraint solving algorithm (described later in this section) is used to find witnesses for all hidden type variables that occur in the path.

Constraint Solving. The core of the type checker is a constraint solving algorithm. The constraint solving algorithm is given a set of subtype constraints, possibly containing free type variables, and returns a path in the type hierarchy for each constraint, substituting for free type variables along the way. The implementation of the constraint solving algorithm is shown in the appendix section (22.10). The constraint solving algorithm is used to extend path annotations, infer path annotations, check the well-formedness of types, check valid overriding, and perform many more tasks.

For each constraint $A_1 <: A_2$, the constraint solver executes a breadth-first search of the trait and object hierarchy starting from A_1. When the constraint solver finds A_2, it returns the path that led to this type. The type hierarchy traversal algorithm is presented in Appendix 0.2. During this traversal, constraints of hidden type variables are collected. After A_2 is found, these constraints are solved and the witnesses for the hidden type variables are substituted into the path. If a constraint does not contain free type variables, the algorithm simply performs subtype checking.

However, there is a theoretical difficulty: the problem of determining whether two types are in a subtype relation of HTV1 is undecidable. This follows from a result by Kennedy and Pierce [61], who showed that subtype checking in a simple language with nominal inheritance and variance for generic types is undecidable. The language of Kennedy and Pierce consists of class declarations of the form:

$$T\langle \overrightarrow{vX} \rangle \quad <:: \quad M_1 \dots M_n$$

where v is a variance annotation used to indicate covariant, invariant, and contravariant type parameters. Note that we renamed the metavariables used by Kennedy and Pierce [61] according to our naming convention. Such classes can be encoded in HTV1 as:

```
trait T[[X₁, X₂ extends Y₂, X₃]] extends {T[[X₁, Y₂, Y₃]], M₁, ..., Mₙ}
      where {Y₂ extends Object, Y₃ extends X₃}
end
```

$$p; \Delta \vdash S[\![\overrightarrow{Y}]\!] \overrightarrow{C} \text{ path-ok}$$

$$method_p(m, \overrightarrow{C}) = \{m[\![\overrightarrow{bnd'}]\!](\overrightarrow{\_:A'}):B'\_\}$$

$$\overrightarrow{bnd} = \overrightarrow{X\_} \qquad \overrightarrow{bnd'} = \overrightarrow{X'\_}$$

$$convert(\overrightarrow{bnd}) = \overrightarrow{K}_1 <: \overrightarrow{K}_2 \qquad \Delta' = \Delta \, convert(\overrightarrow{bnd'})$$

$$p; \Delta' \vdash [\overrightarrow{X'}/\overrightarrow{X}] \overrightarrow{K}_1 <: [\overrightarrow{X'}/\overrightarrow{X}] \overrightarrow{K}_2$$

[OVERRIDE]

$$\frac{p; \Delta' \vdash \overrightarrow{A'} <: [\overrightarrow{X'}/\overrightarrow{X}] \overrightarrow{A} \qquad p; \Delta' \vdash [\overrightarrow{X'}/\overrightarrow{X}]B <: B'}{p; \Delta; S[\![\overrightarrow{Y}]\!] \vdash override(m[\![\overrightarrow{bnd}]\!](x:\overrightarrow{A}):B = e)}$$

Figure 22.7: Valid overriding in HTV1

where each of $\overrightarrow{X_1}$ is invariant, each of $\overrightarrow{X_2}$ is covariant, and each of $\overrightarrow{X_3}$ is contravariant. This encoding preserves the validity of the subtype relation, and it therefore implies the undecidability of our type system.

As a result of this undecidability, a naive constraint solving algorithm may fail to terminate. Various restrictions, such as a limit on the nesting depth of generic types, can ensure termination. However, using PLT Redex we have shown that many programs terminate without any such restriction. We have developed a test suite of approximately 180 tests that exercise the constraint solving algorithm, none of which loop infinitely. This evidence supports the conjecture that a nesting depth limit will not be a serious impediment to expressiveness in practice.

22·8 Testing with PLT Redex. In this section, we describe our experiences using PLT Redex to test the implementation of HTV1. First, we describe how PLT Redex allowed us to test the constraint solver. Next, we discuss two experiences using PLT Redex to test changes in the semantics of HTV1.

Testing the Constraint Solver. It is not difficult to develop test inputs for the constraint solving algorithm. For example,

$$\text{Integer} <: \text{Object}$$

or

$$\text{Float} <: X \text{ for } X <: \text{Float}$$

It is even fairly easy to make the constraint solver work hard. For example,

$$T <: S[\![T]\!]$$

where

```
trait CoListWithCons⟦X extends Y⟧ extends {CoListWithCons⟦Y⟧}
    where {Y extends Object}
    cons⟦Z bounds X⟧(z : Z) : CoListWithCons⟦Z⟧ =
        CoConsWithCons⟦Z⟧(z, self)
end
```

Figure 22.8: Covariant lists with *cons* methods in HTV1

```
trait ContraListWithCons⟦X extends Y⟧ extends {ContraListWithCons⟦Y⟧}
    where {Y extends Object}
    cons⟦Z bounds X⟧(z : Z) : ContraListWithCons⟦Z⟧ =
        ContraConsWithCons⟦Z⟧(z, self)
end
```

Figure 22.9: Contravariant lists with *cons* methods in HTV1

```
trait T extends {S⟦X⟧} where {X extends S⟦T⟧} end
```

Note that solving the constraint $T <: S⟦T⟧$ generates the same constraint, and thus causes an infinite regression (assuming no memoization).

It is much more difficult, however, to judge whether a set of test constraints would occur in practice, but PLT Redex can help with this task. In the course of evaluating a program, our PLT Redex model must invoke the constraint solving algorithm. That is, our PLT Redex model generates constraints during its execution. These constraints help to test the constraint solving algorithm. If the PLT Redex model is given a practical program, we can be assured that the constraints are realistic. In short, the model reduces the problem of finding practical constraints to finding practical programs.

Testing Overriding. This particular experience concerns checking if an overriding method is valid. Figure 22.7 shows the rule to judge valid overriding in HTV1. The specifics of this rule are unimportant here. The only purpose of showing it is to illustrate its complexity.[3]

This complexity has led to subtle bugs. For example, at one point, the semantics allowed the definition of covariant lists shown in figure 22.8, but

---

[3]The interested reader can see the first author's Ph.D. thesis for the details of the rule [53].

it rejected the dual definition of contravariant lists shown in figure 22.9. Notice that the method in each definition overrides an occurrence of itself.

This discrepancy was a result of the semantics constructing a type variable environment that included only the ordinary type parameters of a trait but failed to include the hidden type variables. With the ability to test the rule against our suite of examples, this bug was quickly discovered and fixed.

$$\cdots$$

$$[\text{T-TRAITDEF}] \dfrac{inherited_p(M_i) \cap inherited_p(M_j) = \varnothing \quad i \neq j \quad i,j \in \{1 \ldots |\overrightarrow{M}|\}}{p \vdash \text{trait } T[\![\overrightarrow{bnd_1}]\!] \text{ extends } \{\overrightarrow{M}\} \text{ where } [\![\overrightarrow{bnd_2}]\!] \overrightarrow{md} \text{ end ok}}$$

Figure 22.10: Correct trait well-formedness rule in HTV1

$$\cdots$$

$$[\text{T-TRAITDEF}] \dfrac{inherited_p(M_1) \cap \ldots \cap inherited_p(M_{\overrightarrow{|M|}}) = \varnothing}{p \vdash \text{trait } T[\![\overrightarrow{bnd_1}]\!] \text{ extends } \{\overrightarrow{M}\} \text{ where } [\![\overrightarrow{bnd_2}]\!] \overrightarrow{md} \text{ end ok}}$$

Figure 22.11: Invalid trait well-formedness rule in HTV1

Testing Single Inheritance The semantics of HTV1 imposes a single inheritance requirement on all traits. The relevant parts of the rule to judge well-formed traits are given in figure 22.10, where $inherited_p(M)$ is a set of all method names that are defined or inherited by type M. At one point, however, the rule appeared as it is written in figure 22.11. Upon inspection, we can see that this formulation is incorrect. Using this rule, it would be possible to inherit multiple methods of the same name as long as those methods are not inherited by every supertype.

Fortunately, formalization in PLT Redex requires more precision. While defining and testing the trait well-formedness rule, we were able to catch and fix this bug early in the formalization process.

22·9 Conclusion.

The stories in section 22.8 illustrate a key advantage of designing a formal semantics with PLT Redex. By first testing and refining our semantics, we were able to use a test-driven approach, ensuring that our calculus was reasonable and relatively stable before investing the effort involved in proving theorems about it. Moreover, because the formulation of the dynamic semantics of HTV1 in PLT Redex was straightforward, we were able to focus our efforts on implementing and refining the static semantics. In short, mechanizing the semantics of HTV1 in PLT Redex has helped to ensure that the semantics of Fortress are sound, and we are eager to make use of it in exploring other language features.

22·10 Implementation of Constraint Solving Algorithm. This appendix contains a skeleton of the code for the constraint solving algorithm. The constraint solving algorithm is an integral part of the type checker. See section 22.7 for more details.

```
;; constraints solving
;;   input: a set of declarations
;;          a type variable environment
;;          a set of constraints
;; output: a list of paths for each constraint
;;         a substitution for free type variables in the constraints
(define (solve ds d c)
  (with-handlers
      ((exn:fail:user? (lambda (exn)
                         (let ((s (string-append
                                    "constraint solving failed: \n"
                                    "constraint set = \n"
                                    (print-constraints c))))
                           (error s)))))
    (let*
        ((result (simplify ds d c empty-table))
         (sub1 (construct-witnesses ds d (simp-result-constraints result)))
         (c (apply-sub-env sub1 (simp-result-constraints result)))
         (paths (map (lambda (p) (apply-sub-path sub1 p))
                     (simp-result-paths result)))
         ; check that witnesses are valid
         (_ (map (lambda (pair) (traverse ds d pair)) c))
         (sub2 (append (simp-result-sub result) sub1)))
      (make-solve-result paths sub2))))

;; simplifying constraints
;;   input: a set of declarations
;;          a type environment
;;          a set of constraints
;;          a memotable
;; output: a path betwen each of the types in the constraint set
;;         a set of simplified constraints satisfied by valid paths
;;         a substitution replacing hidden type variables found on the paths
(define (simplify ds d c t) #| ... |# )
```

```
;; construct witnesses
;;   input: a set of declarations
;;          a type variable environment
;;          a set of constraints
;; output: a substitution
(define (construct-witnesses ds d c) #| ... |# )


;; applying a substitution to an environment
;;   input: a substitution
;;          an environment
;; output: a substituted environment
(define (apply-sub-env s env) #| ... |# )


;; applying a substitution to a path
;;   input: a substitution
;;          a path
;; output: a substituted path
(define (apply-sub-path sub path) #| ... |# )
```

22·11 Implementation of Type Hierarchy Traversal Algorithm.

The type hierarchy traversal algorithm in this appendix is used by the constraint solving algorithm. See section 22.7 for more details.

```
;; traversing the type hierarchy
;;   input: a set of declarations
;;          a type environment
;;          a pair of types
;; output: a path betwen the given two types
;;          a set of simplified constraints for valid paths
;;          a substitution replacing some hidden type vars found on the path
(define (traverse ds d pair)
  (traverse-aux ds d '((((,(first pair)) ())) (second pair)))


;; type unification
;;   input: a type environment
;;          a type
;;          a type
;; output: a substitution that unifies two types or false
(define (unify d A1 A2) #| ... |# )


;; construct a queue for traversing the type hierarchy based on a supertypes
;;   input: a set of declarations
;;          a type variable environment
;;          a trait or object name
;;          a list of types
;;          a path
;;          a set of constraints
;; output: a queue of types
(define (super-paths ds d S As restPath c) #| ... |# )
```

```
;; upper bounds of a type variable
;;  input: a type variable environment
;;          a type variable
;; output: a list of upper bounds of the given type variable
(define (upper-bounds d X) #| ... |# )

;; auxiliary function for type hierarchy traversal
(define (traverse-aux ds d queue A2)
  (match (list queue A2)
    ; queue empty
    [(() A2) (raise-user-error "traverse failed")]
    ; queue not empty
    [((((A1 rstPth ...) c) rstQu ...) A2)
     (let ((sub1 (unify d A1 A2)))
       (if sub1
           ; A1 = A2 ...
           (match A2 ; A2 = Object ... & A2 = A3 union A4 ...
             [_
              (match A1
                ; A1 = A3 union A4 ...
                ; A1 = Bottom ...
                ; A1 = Object ...
                [(S (As ...))  ; A1 = S[As ...]
                 ; check whether A1 has upper bounds
                 (let* ((nwQu1 (super-paths ds S As rstPth c))
                        (As1 (upper-bounds d A1))
                        (nwQu2 (map (lambda (A)
                                      (list (cons A (cons A1 rstPth)) c))
                                    As1)))
                   (traverse-aux ds d (append rstQu nwQu1 nwQu2) A2))]
                [X  ; A1 = X
                 (let* ((As (upper-bounds d X))
                        (nwQu (map (lambda (A)
                                     (list (cons A (cons X rstPth)) c))
                                   As)))
                   (traverse-aux ds d (append rstQu nwQu) A2))])])))]))
```

23 · Type Checking and Inference via Reductions
George Kuan, University of Chicago

Type systems are usually presented as collections of declarative logical inference rules. Algorithmic presentations of type systems describe type checking and type inferencing algorithms as procedures, functions, and methods. Reduction semantics provides an alternative presentation of type systems that bridges the gap between the declarative and algorithmic presentations. In this chapter, we describe reduction semantics analogues for the simply typed λ-calculus and System F. We extend the reduction semantics with Curry-Hindley inference and later Hindley-Milner inference.

23·1 Introduction.
The intuition behind type checking via a reduction semantics is that expressions are progressively reduced to their types. We present reduction systems for type checking the simply typed λ-calculus; type inference for a similar, but untyped λ-calculus; type checking System F [94]; and inference for a let-bound polymorphic language (*à la* Hindley-Milner) [25, 77].

In two previous papers [66, 67], we have investigated the use of reduction systems to express type checking algorithms and Hindley-Milner–style type inference. This chapter summarizes these results and expands on them. Specifically, it adds recursion, primitive operations, termination theorems, and a λ-depth annotation reduction system. Furthermore, it contributes an implementation of System F using a reduction system similar to the SLC.

23·2 Notation.
Throughout the chapter, we discuss four main languages, each with a few varieties. A language may come in simple, hybrid, annotated, and hybrid ranked varieties. When a language name such as ULC (Untyped λ-calculus) is modified by H, A, or HR, it refers to the hybrid, annotated, and hybrid ranked varieties of the language, respectively. For example, ULC-HR refers to the hybrid ranked untyped λ-calculus. Furthermore, context grammars CTX can be modified by V, P, and R, indicating

SLC-H $e ::= n \mid x \mid (\lambda (x\ \tau)\ e) \mid (@\ e\ e) \mid (\to\ \tau\ e) \mid \mathsf{num}$

CTX $T ::= (@\ T\ e) \mid (@\ \tau\ T) \mid (\to\ \tau\ T) \mid \square$

TYPE $\tau ::= \mathsf{num} \mid (\to\ \tau\ \tau)$

        $n ::= \mathbf{number}$

(a) Language and Type Checking Context

$$T[n] \mapsto_t T[\mathsf{num}] \qquad\qquad [\text{tc-const}]$$
$$T[(\lambda (x\ \tau)\ e)] \mapsto_t T[(\to\ \tau\ \{\tau/x\}e)] \qquad [\text{tc-lam}]$$
$$T[(@\ (\to\ \tau_1\ \tau_2)\ \tau_1)] \mapsto_t T[\tau_2] \qquad\qquad [\text{tc-}\tau\beta]$$

(b) Type Checking Reduction Rules

Figure 23.1: Type checking (TC) reduction system

---

whether the context might contain unification type variables, polymorphic bound type variables, and ranking. Details are specified in subsequent sections.

The symbols $\xi, \zeta, \phi,$ and ψ represent unification variables (i.e., type variables subject to unification constraints). Types are written in sans-serif font to distinguish them from other program text. Furthermore, auxiliary functions (i.e., Scheme functions) are indicated by **bold face**. The $\{\tau/x\}$ notation is standard capture-avoiding substitution. The notation is extended to work for lists of variables. For example, $\{\bar{\alpha}/\bar{\xi}\}$ will replace the ith ξ in $\bar{\xi}$ with the ith α in $\bar{\alpha}$ for all i. It is assumed that $\bar{\alpha}$ and $\bar{\xi}$ contain the same number of elements. We use the substitution notation to denote type substitutions, i.e., substituting types for type variables $\{\tau/\xi\}$. The ftv function obtains the list of free type variables in a type τ. We extend ftv to work over type environments Γ in the intuitive way: $\text{ftv}(\Gamma) = \text{ftv}(\tau_1) \cup \text{ftv}(\tau_2) \cup \ldots \cup \text{ftv}(\tau_n)$ where $\Gamma = [x_1 : \tau_1][x_2 : \tau_2] \ldots [x_3 : \tau_n]$. The $\mathcal{E}$ function erases type annotations from simply typed λ-calculus expressions.

23.3 **A Simple Type Checker.** We start with the simply typed λ-calculus (SLC) in figure 23.1. As shown in the example in figure 23.2, the type checker reduces λs into arrow types and applications by matching the function position's domain type with the argument type to the function's range type. Number literals reduce to the num type.

The reduction system introduces a type checking context T that imposes a left-to-right order of type checking. Variable occurrences are replaced by their types as soon as we reduce the binding λ ([tc-lam]). This kind of substitution produces hybrid terms (SLC-H) that are neither entirely program expressions nor types. The [tc-lam] also introduces the arrow type constructor.

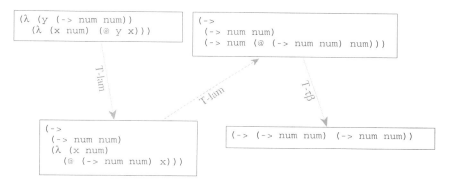

Figure 23.2: Simple reduction sequence

$$\Gamma \vdash \mathit{number} : \mathsf{num} \qquad\qquad \frac{(x : \tau \in \Gamma)}{\Gamma \vdash x : \tau} \text{ [t-var]}$$

$$\frac{\Gamma \vdash e_1 : (\to\ \tau_1\ \tau_2) \qquad \Gamma \vdash e_2 : \tau_1}{\Gamma \vdash (@\ e_1\ e_2) : \tau_2} \text{ [t-app]} \qquad \frac{\Gamma[x : \tau_1] \vdash e : \tau_2}{\Gamma \vdash \lambda x : \tau_1.e : (\to\ \tau_1\ \tau_2)} \text{ [t-lam]}$$

Figure 23.3: Traditional type system for the simply typed λ-calculus

The [tc-$\tau\beta$] rule checks that the function formal parameter type and the argument type match. This check is purely syntactic.

Theorem 1 (Termination of type checking Reductions). *For all* $e \in SLC\text{-}H$, *either* $e \mapsto_t^* \tau$ *or* $e \mapsto_t^* e'$ *and* e' *is irreducible.*

Proof. Every reduction rule eliminates some SLC expression constructs. No rule introduces SLC expressions. Let the hybrid expressions be ordered by the number of SLC expression constructs. Because this ordering is well-founded, the reductions must terminate in a finite number of steps. □

When the type checking reduction gets stuck, the reduction system has discovered a type error. In this simple language, the only possible type errors are the application of an expression of a non-function type and a type mismatch between function parameter and the argument of the application. The stuck reduction sequence for an ill-typed program corresponds to the non-existence of a complete type derivation for the same program under the traditional type judgments (see figure 23.3).

A complete type checking reduction is one that reduces to a type (i.e., does not reduce to an error). Complete type checking reduction sequences correspond to complete type derivation proof trees. We can construct a complete type checking reduction sequence from a complete derivation and vice versa.

Theorem 2 (Soundness and Completeness for $\mapsto_t$).
For any e and τ, $\emptyset \vdash e : \tau$ if and only if $e \mapsto_t^* \tau$.

Proof Sketch. In the left-to-right direction, the proof is by straightforward induction on the derivation of $\emptyset \vdash e : \tau$. In the reverse direction, the proof requires a CEK machine analogue of the reduction system in order to reconstruct the type environment for the typing derivation during reduction. □

Type Soundness Proofs from First Principles. The point of type checking is the existence of type soundness theorems that guarantee that a well-typed program does not go wrong. Whenever we design new type systems, our first goal must be to prove the type soundness theorem. Let us explore what type soundness theorems and proofs look like under type checking reduction semantics.

Type soundness relates well-typing to the evaluation semantics. Because we have well-typing in terms of a reduction semantics, the theorems must relate the type checking reduction relation to the evaluation reduction relation. Since we are relating two reduction relations, at first glance it may appear that preservation is some confluence result. This intuition is incorrect, however. Let $\mapsto_e$ be the conventional call-by-value β reduction relation. We can combine the evaluation and type checking reduction relations and then try to obtain a confluence result for the resulting reduction relation.

Definition 1 (Combined reduction relation $\mapsto$). $\mapsto = \mapsto_e \cup \mapsto_t$.

The confluence of the combined reduction relation seems to hold for naive examples such as in figure 23.4. It is easy, however, to construct a counterexample to confluence. Ill-typed subexpressions get stuck by the type checking reduction, but application of a function that ignores its argument to an ill-typed subexpressions fully reduces to a value.

An expression e is said to be stuck under $\mapsto$ if

1. e is not a type, and

2. there does not exist an expression e' such that $e \mapsto e'$.

This definition specifies exactly those states that Tofte [108] would have reduced to wrong states.

Proposition 1 (Non-confluence of $\mapsto$). *There exists an expression e, such that $e \mapsto e_h$, $e \mapsto e'_h$, $e_h \neq e'_h$, and both e_h and e'_h are either types or stuck under $\mapsto$.*

Figure 23.4: Confluent example for the combined reduction relation

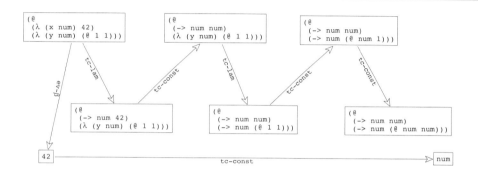

Figure 23.5: Non-confluent counterexample for the combined reduction relation

Proof. The program (@ (λ (x num) 42) (λ (y num) (@ 1 1))) rewrites to both num and an expression that decomposes into a type checking context with the stuck state (@ num num) in the hole. See figure 23.5.   □

Now that we have shown that ↦ is not confluent, what does preservation look like in this reduction system? The preservation theorem predicates a confluence-like result on the existence of a complete type checking reduction for the program in question. The fact that the program is well-typed ensures the type checking reduction does not get stuck. If all steps in the evaluation of the program reduce down to the same type, type preservation must hold.

Theorem 3 (Preservation). *If $e \mapsto_t^* \tau$ & $e \mapsto_e e'$, then $e' \mapsto_t^* \tau$.*

Proof Sketch. This follows from the observation that, once a term takes a type checking step, it can never again take an evaluation step. That, plus theorem 2 and a standard type preservation argument for the traditional type system tells us that the relation produces the correct type when the original term is well-typed, and thus the theorem holds.   □

$$e \ ::= \ x \mid (\lambda \ (x \ \tau) \ e) \mid (\Lambda \ X \ e) \mid (@_T \ e \ \tau) \mid (@ \ e \ e) \mid (\rightarrow \ \tau \ e)$$
$$\tau \ ::= \ (\rightarrow \ \tau \ \tau) \mid (\Pi \ X \ \tau) \mid X$$
$$T_F \ ::= \ (@ \ T_F \ e) \mid (@ \ \tau \ T_F) \mid (@_T \ T_F \ \tau) \mid (\rightarrow \ \tau \ T_F) \mid (\Pi \ X \ T_F) \mid \square$$

(a) Language

$$
\begin{array}{ll}
T_F[(\lambda \ (x \ \tau) \ e)] \ \longmapsto_F \ T_F[(\rightarrow \ \tau \ (\{\tau/x\}e))] & [\text{f-}\lambda] \\
T_F[(\Lambda \ X \ e)] \ \longmapsto_F \ T_F[(\Pi \ X \ e)] & [\text{f-}\Lambda] \\
T_F[(@ \ (\rightarrow \ \tau_1 \ \tau_2) \ \tau_1)] \ \longmapsto_F \ T_F[\tau_2] & [\text{f-app}] \\
T_F[(@_T \ (\Pi \ X \ \tau_1) \ \tau_2)] \ \longmapsto_F \ T_F[\{\tau_2/X\}\tau_1] & [\text{f-tapp}]
\end{array}
$$

(b) Type Checking Reductions

Figure 23.6: System F

The progress theorem does not change much. Its proof is essentially the same as it is under the traditional system [118].

23·4 System F.
System F is an approach to explicit polymorphism independently discovered by Girard [46] and Reynolds [94]. It features full parametric polymorphism by means of type abstraction and type application. This section presents a type checking reduction semantics for System F.

Figure 23.6 gives a reduction semantics for System F. The language extends the SLC with type abstractions (universal abstraction in Girard's terminology) over type variables $(\Lambda \ X \ e)$ and type applications (universal application) $(@_T \ e \ \tau)$. The types must be extended with type variables X and type function type $(\Pi \ X \ \tau)$.

Type checking System F programs is fairly straightforward. We treat Λs much like we do λs. As soon as the type checker gets to a $(\Lambda \ X \ e)$, it rewrites that Λ to a Π (universal type), whose domain is the type variable X and whose range is the body of the Λ. Unlike with λ-abstractions, the type checker does not do any substitutions for X in the body because X is already a type, and until the universal is applied we do not know what to substitute. Π binds the type variable X in the type language, just as Λ bound it in the expression (value) language. The range of Π is potentially hybrid at this point, much like with the arrow types to which λs reduce. The Λ rule, however, does not apply any environment substitution (types for program variables). The range of Π is only hybrid if the body of Λ was hybrid from before the Λ reduction. Type application $(@_T \ (\Pi \ X \ \tau_1) \ \tau_2)$ is responsible for eliminating the type variable X by substituting the type argument τ_2 for X in τ_1.

$$\frac{\Gamma, X \vdash_F e : \tau}{\Gamma \vdash_F (\Lambda\ X\ e) : (\Pi\ X\ \tau)} \text{ [t-tabs]} \qquad \frac{\Gamma \vdash_F e : (\Pi\ X\ \tau_1)}{\Gamma \vdash_F (@_T\ e\ \tau_2) : \{\tau_2/X\}\tau_1} \text{ [t-tapp]}$$

All rules in figure 23.3 are inherited.

Figure 23.7: System F-specific type rules

This reduction system is consistent with the traditional System F type judgments in figure 23.7.

Theorem 4 (Soundness and Completeness for $\mapsto_F$).
For any e and τ, $\varnothing \vdash_F e : \tau$ if and only if $e \mapsto_F^* \tau$.

Proof Sketch. This proof is a straightforward extension of theorem 2's proof. The new cases for the [t-tabs] and [t-tapp] are similar to the cases for [t-lam] and [t-app], respectively. □

23·5 Adding Nondeterministic Inference.
Programs in the SLC usually have many type annotations, one for each λ-abstraction. It would be much better if the type checker could infer these annotations. In practice, the programmer would manually annotate interesting λs and leave uninteresting ones to type inference. As a first cut, we can infer the type annotations by trying all possible annotations. We ultimately choose the annotation that makes the expression type check. In many cases, there may be more than one annotation that does so. If all attempts fail, then the expression is untypeable. If at least one guess succeeds, then the expression is well-typed.

To summarize, there are three possibilities when inferring an annotation by this guess-and-check method:

1. There is exactly one annotation that works. For example, x can only be type num for (@ (λx.x) 1).

2. There is an infinite number of annotations that work. For some expressions such as $\lambda x.x$, every type annotation for x works. For others, such as (@ (λx.x) λy.y), an infinite subset of all type annotations work.

3. No annotation works, e.g., the expression ($\lambda x.x$ 1) 2 is untypeable.

The inference reduction system (ND) using the nondeterministic reduction relation in figure 23.8 is simply the TC system with the λ type annotations erased. The only significant change concerns the [nd-lam] rule, where an arbitrary parameter type τ must be substituted for the parameter of the

ULC	$e ::= x \mid (\lambda\ (x)\ e) \mid (@\ e\ e)$
ULC-H	$e_n ::= x \mid (\lambda\ (x)\ e_n) \mid (@\ e_n\ e_n) \mid number \mid (\to \tau\ e_n) \mid \text{num}$
CTX	$T_n ::= (@\ T_n\ e_n) \mid (@\ \tau\ T_n) \mid (\to \tau\ T_n) \mid \square$
TYPE	$\tau ::= \text{num} \mid (\to \tau\ \tau)$

$$T_n[number] \mapsto_n T_n[\text{num}] \qquad\qquad [\text{nd-num}]$$
$$T_n[(\lambda\ (x)\ e_n)] \mapsto_n T_n[(\to \tau\ \{x \mapsto \tau\}\ e_n)] \qquad\qquad [\text{nd-lam}]$$
$$T_n[(@\ (\to \tau_1\ \tau_2)\ \tau_1)] \mapsto_n T_n[\tau_2] \qquad\qquad [\text{nd-}\tau\beta]$$

Figure 23.8: Nondeterministic (ND) inference system

abstraction. For the remaining rules, only the type checking context changes in order to admit the unannotated λs.

The type inference reduction system should reduce only the well-typed programs into their types. That is to say, the ND system should type check exactly the programs that the TC system type checked, which are the well-typed simply typed λ-calculus programs. Put differently, the TC and ND reduction relations ought to be related by type erasure ($\mathcal{E}$). Because type erasure is not a one-to-one function, the relationship between TC and ND reductions is asymmetric. Whereas multiple SLC programs map to a single ND reduction sequence by erasure, a single ND reduction sequence corresponds only to a unique SLC program by a type annotation.

Theorem 5 (Completeness of nondeterministic reduction). *For any SLC expression e and type τ,*

$$e \mapsto_t^* \tau \Rightarrow \mathcal{E}(e) \mapsto_n^* \tau$$

Proof Sketch. Given the complete TC reduction sequence $e \mapsto_t^* \tau$, simply erase the type annotations to get the equivalent ND reduction sequence. $\square$

Let the notation Γe_h (i.e., the juxtaposition of a type environment and a hybrid expression) denote that hybrid expression e_h with all program variables x_i replaced by $\Gamma(x_i)$.

Theorem 6 (Soundness of nondeterministic reduction). *For any ULC expression e and type τ, if $e \mapsto_n^* \tau$ then there exists a SLC expression e' such that $\mathcal{E}(e') = e$ and $e' \mapsto_t^* \tau$.*

Proof Sketch. This theorem follows from a substitution lemma: for all e_n, type environments Γ, and τ, $\Gamma e_n \mapsto_n^* \tau$ implies that there exists e_h such that $\mathcal{E}(e_h) = e_n$ and $\Gamma e_h \mapsto_t^* \tau$. The proof is by induction on e_n. $\square$

23·6 Unification-Based Inference.

Obviously, inference by trying all possible type assignments is impossible to implement. The most common technique[1] for implementing inference uses *unification variables* (*univariables*) to act as placeholders for unconstrained types. The reduction semantics in figs. 23.9, 23.10, and 23.11 is inspired by Curry and Hindley's technique. Whenever the type checker initially reaches a λ-abstraction, the parameter type is assigned a fresh univariable because at first the entire parameter type is unconstrained. The [ch-τβ] rule introduces a unification constraint that unifies the function position type with a function type scheme whose domain is the argument type and whose range is a fresh univariable representing the return type. The system uses a separate reduction system to solve the unification constraint introduced by the [τβ] reductions, and thus eliminates univariables (though not necessarily all the univariables).

Univariables are eliminated by instantiation during unification to some type, which may in turn contain other univariables. Those univariables that are instantiated at some point in a reduction sequence are said to be **constrained** univariables. A univariable that is never instantiated is called **unconstrained**. There are two kinds of unconstrained univariables. Some unconstrained univariables are dropped in the reduction sequence by τβ steps. For example, $(@ (\rightarrow \xi \text{ num}) \xi)$ drops the univariable ξ, which is neither instantiated nor in the final type in the reduction sequence. Others survive the entire reduction sequence and occur in the final type. We call this latter kind of univariable **residual**. This phenomenon means that we cannot determine the type assignment for all λ-abstractions in an expression solely based on the final type of that expression. In particular, dropped univariables may be either constrained by unification or completely unconstrained.

Type variables in System F differ somewhat from the univariables used in this section. Unlike univariables, type variables in System F are in the surface language. In the Curry-Hindley system, the surface language is the ULC, which contains neither univariables nor bound type variables. The programmer can write down type variables in System F whereas unification variables and bound type variables are internal to the type checking algorithm except when an expression fully reduces down to a type that may contain some residual univariables under the Curry-Hindley reduction system.

The hybrid language in figure 23.9 introduces univariables ξ and unify terms p that eliminate (i.e., instantiate) those univariables. Types may now contain univariables. A unify terms consists of a unify prefix (i.e., a context) enclosing a unification subterm, which may be just an expression, i.e., a degenerate unification subterm. The nested unify prefixes must ultimately enclose an expression; indeed, it is the program being type checked because

---

[1]Curry and Hindley devised this technique early on [23, 56].

$$
\begin{array}{ll}
& p ::= (\text{unify } \tau_u \ \tau_u \ p) \mid e \\
\text{ULC-HV} & e ::= number \mid x \mid (\lambda(x) \ e) \mid (@ \ e \ e) \mid \text{num} \mid (\rightarrow \ \tau_u \ e) \mid \xi \\
\text{CTX-V} & T_u ::= (@ \ T_u \ e) \mid (@ \ \tau_u \ T_u) \mid (\rightarrow \ \tau_u \ T_u) \mid \square \\
\text{TYPE-V} & \tau_u ::= \text{num} \mid (\rightarrow \ \tau_u \ \tau_u) \mid \xi \\
\text{Univariables} & \xi, \zeta, \phi, \psi
\end{array}
$$

Figure 23.9: Curry-Hindley system language

$$
\begin{array}{ll}
T_u[number] \longmapsto_u T_u[\text{num}] & [\text{ch-const}] \\
T_u[(\lambda(x) \ e)] \longmapsto_u T_u[(\rightarrow \ \xi \ \{\xi/x\}e)] & [\text{ch-lam}] \\
\quad \text{where } \xi \notin \text{ftv}(T_u[(\lambda(x) \ e)]) & \\
T_u[(@ \ \tau_1 \ \tau_2)] \longmapsto_u (\text{unify } \tau_1 \ (\rightarrow \ \tau_2 \ \xi) \ T_u[\xi]) & [\text{ch-}\tau\beta] \\
\quad \text{where } \xi \notin \text{ftv}(T_u[(@ \ \tau_1 \ \tau_2)]) &
\end{array}
$$

Figure 23.10: Curry-Hindley system inference reductions

---

unification affects the entire program. For example, the unify prefixes of the term $(\text{unify } \tau_1 \ \tau_2 \ (\text{unify } \tau_3 \ \tau_4 \ \lambda x.x))$ are $(\text{unify } \tau_1 \ \tau_2 \ \square)$ and $(\text{unify } \tau_3 \ \tau_4 \ \square))$, which ultimately encloses the expression $\lambda x.x$. The first and second argument of a unify prefix are the types to be unified.

In the Curry-Hindley-style reduction system in figure 23.10, the [ch-lam] rule introduces a fresh univariable instead of a ground type in place of the bound λ-variable. The [ch-$\tau\beta$] rule introduces unify prefixes to instantiate univariables. Because the effect of unification is global, the [ch-$\tau\beta$] puts the unify prefix around the current type checking context. The result of the unification is applied to all occurrences of the instantiated univariables in the type checking context. Also, the type in the function position is not necessarily an arrow type before unification. For example, $(\lambda(x) \ (@ \ x \ 1))$ reduces to $(\rightarrow \ \xi \ (@ \ \xi \ \text{num}))$ and the type in the function position is ξ. Consequently, the [ch-$\tau\beta$] rule unifies the type of the function position with a function scheme, i.e., an arrow type whose domain is the argument type and whose range is some fresh univariable representing the result type.

The unification reduction rules (figure 23.11) are straightforward. The instantiation rule, [ch-u-inst], performs an occurs check. The number of univariables monotonically decreases during a unification reduction sequence. There is some bias in the rules as indicated by the [ch-u-orient] rule. Unification as implemented prefers to instantiate from left to right.

With the introduction of unification, the termination of the reduction system now hinges on the termination of the unification reduction rules. Fur-

$$(\text{unify } \tau_1 \ \tau_1 \ p) \mapsto_f \ p \qquad\qquad\qquad \text{[ch-u-const]}$$

$$(\text{unify } (\rightarrow \ \tau_1 \ \tau_2) \ (\rightarrow \ \tau_3 \ \tau_4) \ p) \mapsto_f (\text{unify } \tau_1 \ \tau_3 \ (\text{unify } \tau_2 \ \tau_4 \ p)) \qquad \text{[ch-u-dist]}$$

$$\text{where } \tau_1 \neq \tau_3 \text{ or } \tau_2 \neq \tau_4$$

$$(\text{unify } \tau \ \xi \ p) \mapsto_f (\text{unify } \xi \ \tau \ p) \qquad\qquad \text{[ch-u-orient]}$$

$$\text{where } \tau \text{ is not a univariable}$$

$$(\text{unify } \xi \ \tau \ p) \mapsto_f \ \{\tau/\xi\}p \qquad\qquad\qquad \text{[ch-u-inst]}$$

$$\text{where } \tau \neq \xi \text{ and } \xi \notin \text{ftv}(\tau)$$

Figure 23.11: Curry-Hindley system unification reductions

thermore, the correctness of unification also depends on the fact that unification always terminates. To formalize correctness of unification, we define **unifiable** and the **most general unifier** (definition 2).

Definition 2 (Unifiable and Most General Unifier). *τ_1 and τ_2 are unifiable if there exists a substitution σ such that $\sigma(\tau_1) = \sigma(\tau_2)$. A most general unifier is a substitution θ such that for all unifiers σ, there exists a substitution δ, $\sigma = \delta\theta$.*

Lemma 1 (Termination of Unification). *If τ_u^1 and τ_u^2 are unifiable, then the reduction $\mapsto_f$ terminates for term* (unify $\tau_u^1 \ \tau_u^2 \ p$) *in a finite number of steps.*

Proof. Let the unification expressions be ordered according to the free univariable subset ordering and the size of the types being unified in all prefixes (whenever the unification expression is equivalent according to free unvariable subset ordering). Because this ordering is well-founded and each unification reduction shrinks the unification expression according to this ordering, unification reductions must terminate. □

The unification reductions yield the most general unifier of two types. The most general unifier may contain univariables wherever unification underconstrains univariables. Consequently, the Curry-Hindley reduction relation produces type schemes for the principal type that gets the program to type check rather than some arbitrary instance type that happens to satisfy the type checker.

Lemma 2 (Correctness of Unification). *If τ_u and τ_u' are unifiable and σ is a most general unifier of τ_u and τ_u', then* (unify $\tau_u \ \tau_u' \ p$) $\mapsto_f^* \sigma p$.

Proof Sketch. This proof is by induction on the number of univariables and the size of the types being unified in the whole unification expression, i.e., the measure for the ordering given above. The interesting case is the [ch-u-inst] rule, which relies on the definition of unifier, the occurs check, and most general unifier. □

Whereas the Curry-Hindley reduction relation gives type schemes for the principal type of a program, the ND reduction relation gives every ground type that satisfies well-typing. This means that the ND ground types are simply all the possible ground type instantiations of the Curry-Hindley type scheme. Curry-Hindley reduction sequences are related to their analogous ND reduction sequence by the composition of all the substitutions produced by unification and an arbitrary instantiating substitution that gives an arbitrary ground type instantiation to all unconstrained univariables. Note that it is insufficient to instantiate only residual univariables because [nd-lam] must give **all** λ-bound variables a ground type, regardless of whether its type is unconstrained by use and does not appear in the final type. Nonresidual univariables must be instantiated in order to give the ND reduction sequence complete instructions for how to proceed at each λ because the ND reduction relation has to give a ground type for every λ-bound variable.

Theorem 7 (Nondeterministic & Curry-Hindley typing relationship).
Let $e \in$ ULC and $\mapsto_c = \mapsto_u \cup \mapsto_f$.
Completeness *If $e \mapsto_n^* \tau$ then there exists a τ_u and a type substitution γ such that $e \mapsto_c^* \tau_u$ and $\gamma\tau_u = \tau$.*

Soundness *If $e \mapsto_c^* \tau_u$ then for all ground types τ that are instantiations of τ_u, $e \mapsto_n^* \tau$.*

Proof Sketch. For the completeness direction, construct a substitution that maps all λ-variables associated with each [nd-lam] step in the complete CH reduction to ground types. Using this instantiating substitution, conduct a case analysis on the ND reduction relation. The $\tau\beta$ case of this proof relies on lemma 2.

For the soundness direction, construct the complete unification substitution, comprised of all the substitutions introduced by unification instantiation steps, and an arbitrary instantiating substitution for instantiating **all** the unconstrained univariables. Because lemma 2 already established the soundness of the unification reductions, there is no need to establish anything about the unification reductions. Instead, for the purpose of this proof, fold the unification step into the [ch-$\tau\beta$] rule. The key step of this proof is to show that the complete unification substitution and an arbitrary instantiating substitution eliminates all the univariables in each CH reduction step. Similar to the completeness direction, this proof is by case analysis on the CH reduction relation. □

23·7 Let-Bound Polymorphism. To support local, polymorphic definitions, we add let-expressions to our language in section 23.6.

ULCL $e ::= number \mid \textbf{true} \mid \textbf{false} \mid x \mid (\lambda(x)\ e) \mid (@\ e\ e) \mid (\textbf{let}\ (x\ e)\ e) \mid (\textbf{pair}\ e\ e)$

TYPE-V $\tau ::= \textsf{num} \mid \textsf{bool} \mid (\rightarrow\ \tau \ldots\ \tau) \mid (\textsf{pair}\ \tau\ \tau) \mid \alpha \mid \xi$

PTYPE $\sigma ::= (\forall \bar{\alpha}\ \tau)$

Type Env. $\Gamma ::= \varnothing \mid \Gamma[x : \tau] \mid \Gamma[x : \sigma]$

(a) Hindley-Milner Language

$$\frac{}{\Gamma \vdash number : \textsf{num}}\ [\textsf{hm-dec-num}] \qquad \frac{(b \in \{\textsf{true}, \textsf{false}\})}{\Gamma \vdash b : \textsf{bool}}\ [\textsf{hm-dec-bool}]$$

$$\frac{\Gamma \vdash e_1 : \tau_1 \qquad \Gamma \vdash e_2 : \tau_2}{\Gamma \vdash (\textbf{pair}\ e_1\ e_2) : (\textsf{pair}\ \tau_1\ \tau_2)}\ [\textsf{hm-dec-pair}] \qquad \frac{(x : \tau \in \Gamma\ \text{or}\ \tau = \mathcal{I}(\sigma)\ x : \sigma \in \Gamma)}{\Gamma \vdash x : \tau}\ [\textsf{hm-dec-var}]$$

$$\frac{\Gamma \vdash e_1 : (\rightarrow\ \tau_1\ \tau_2) \qquad \Gamma \vdash e_2 : \tau_1}{\Gamma \vdash (@\ e_1\ e_2) : \tau_2}\ [\textsf{hm-dec-app}] \qquad \frac{\Gamma[x : \tau_1] \vdash e : \tau_2}{\Gamma \vdash \lambda x.e : (\rightarrow\ \tau_1\ \tau_2)}\ [\textsf{hm-dec-lam}]$$

$$\frac{\Gamma \vdash e_1 : \tau_1 \qquad \Gamma[x : \sigma] \vdash e_2 : \tau_2 \qquad \sigma = (\forall \bar{\alpha}\ \{\bar{\alpha}/\textbf{Gen}_\Gamma(\tau_1)\}\tau)}{\Gamma \vdash (\textbf{let}\ (x\ e_1)\ e_2) : \tau_2}\ [\textsf{hm-dec-let}]$$

$$\textbf{Gen}_\Gamma(\tau) = \{\xi \in \tau \mid \xi \notin \textsf{ftv}(\Gamma)\}$$

(b) Declarative Hindley-Milner Type System

Figure 23.12: Traditional Hindley-Milner presentation

The dynamic semantics of let expressions substitutes the definien for every occurrence of the let-bound variable in the let-expression's body. Naively, we can therefore type check let-expressions by eliminating all occurrences of let via substitution and type checking the result. Unfortunately, this simple method has the substantial drawback of duplicating much work during type checking. After substitution for all the occurrences of the let-bound variable, the type checker would have to type check the definien multiple times. It is far more efficient to type check the definien once and reuse the resultant type at each use in the body of the let-expression. The declarative Hindley-Milner type system in figure 23.12 takes advantage of this optimization.

Damas and Milner's Algorithm $\mathcal{W}$ (figure 23.13) provides the means to efficiently type check let-expressions. We cannot naively reuse the definien type in the body because then univariables in that type are instantiated by the first unification encountered. For example, $(\textbf{let}\ (f\ (\lambda(x)\ x))\ (@\ (@\ f\ (\lambda(y)\ y))\ (@\ f1)))$ ought to type check, but replacing the occurrences of f with the definien type $(\rightarrow\ \xi\ \xi)$ leads to a type error because the definien type instantiates to $(\rightarrow\ (\rightarrow\ \zeta\ \zeta)\ (\rightarrow\ \zeta\ \zeta))$ when type checking $(@\ f\ (\lambda(y)\ y))$. The application rule fails for $(@\ f\ 1)$ because f's type $(\rightarrow\ (\rightarrow\ \zeta\ \zeta)\ (\rightarrow\ \zeta\ \zeta))$

$$
\begin{aligned}
\mathcal{W}(\Gamma, x) \quad\;\; &= \quad (id, \mathcal{I}(\Gamma(x))) \\
\mathcal{W}(\Gamma, \lambda x.e) \quad\;\; &= \;\text{let} \quad (\theta, \tau) = \mathcal{W}(\Gamma[x : \xi], e) \qquad \xi \text{ fresh} \\
&\;\;\;\text{in} \quad\; (\theta, \theta\xi \rightarrow \tau) \\
\mathcal{W}(\Gamma, e\; e') \quad\;\; &= \;\text{let} \quad (\theta, \tau) = \mathcal{W}(\Gamma, e) \\
&\qquad\qquad (\theta', \tau') = \mathcal{W}(\theta\Gamma, e') \\
&\qquad\qquad \theta'' = \mathcal{U}(\theta'\tau, \tau' \rightarrow \xi) \qquad \xi \text{ fresh} \\
&\;\;\;\text{in} \quad\; (\theta''\theta'\theta, \theta''\xi) \\
\mathcal{W}(\Gamma, (\mathbf{let}\; x = e\; e')) &= \;\text{let} \quad (\theta, \tau) = \mathcal{W}(\Gamma, e) \\
&\qquad\qquad (\theta', \tau') = \mathcal{W}(\theta\Gamma[x : \sigma], e') \\
&\;\;\;\text{in} \quad\; (\theta'\theta, \tau') \qquad\quad \sigma = \forall\bar{\alpha}.\{\bar{\alpha}/\mathbf{Gen}_\Gamma(\tau)\}\tau
\end{aligned}
$$

$$
\begin{aligned}
\mathcal{U}(\tau, \tau) = \varepsilon \quad & \mathcal{U}(\tau, \xi) = \mathcal{U}(\xi, \tau) \\
& \text{where } \tau \text{ is not a univariable} \\
\mathcal{U}(\xi, \tau) = \{\tau/\xi\} & \text{ if } \xi \notin \mathrm{ftv}(\tau) \\
\mathcal{U}(\tau_1 \rightarrow \tau_2, \tau_3 \rightarrow \tau_4) = \mathcal{U}(\theta(\tau_2), \theta(\tau_4)) \circ \theta \\
& \text{where } \theta = \mathcal{U}(\tau_1, \tau_3)
\end{aligned}
$$

Figure 23.13: Algorithm $\mathcal{W}$ from Lee and Yi [69]

is incompatible with the num argument type. The problem is that at every let definien, some univariables in the definien type can be reused independently of other uses of the definien type. These independently reusable univariables are exactly those that are local to the definien, i.e., the univariables were not introduced in the context of the let-expression. We call these univariables **generic**. If τ is the definien type and Γ is the type environment at the let definien (not inside the let definien), then the generic univariables comprise the set $\mathrm{ftv}(\tau) - \mathrm{ftv}(\Gamma)$. Algorithm $\mathcal{W}$ replaces the generic univariables with distinct polymorphic type variables $\alpha, \beta, \ldots$. We call this step **polymorphic generalization**, or simply **generalization**. Whenever we use this resultant polymorphic type scheme (usually denoted σ), we have to replace each polymorphic type variable with a distinct fresh univariable. This step is called **generic instantiation**. In the above example, we generalize the definien type to $(\forall\alpha(\rightarrow \alpha\; \alpha))$ and instantiate it twice, once for the occurrence of f in $(@\; f\; (\lambda(y)\; y))$ and once for the f in $(@\; f\; 1)$.

Generalization by Type Environment. Milner, in his original presentation of Algorithm $\mathcal{W}$ tested for membership of univariables in the type environment to determine whether to generalize those univariables. The intuition is that if a given univariable is in the type environment when the type checker encounters a let definien, then that univariable must be constrained outside of the let-expression, and thus it may have a specific type that the type checker determines at a later point. Generalization of this univariable is unsound because this univariable, in general, cannot be instantiated to any arbitrary type. Consider the following example.

Example 1. $(\lambda\ (x)\ (@\ (let\ (f\ (\lambda\ (y)\ (@\ y\ x)))\ f)\ (\lambda\ (z)\ (+\ x\ 1))))$

In the example, the type of f before generalization is $\xi \to \phi$, where ξ is the univariable introduced for x and ϕ is the univariable introduced for the return type of the application $(@\ y\ x)$. ξ cannot be generalized at the let because it is constrained at $\lambda(x)$.

Type environments have an implicit order to them, namely the order in which its constituent bindings are introduced. Environments can contain two kinds of bindings, those introduced by λ-abstractions, called λ-bindings, and those by let-expressions, called let-bindings. Generalizable univariables are those that are constrained by bindings in the let-binding against which the algorithm should generalize. A binding b **precedes** another binding b' in a type environment if b occurs to the left of b'. We can exploit the definition of sound generalization and the ordering of type environments to derive a reduction semantics for the Hindley-Milner type system.

Direct Reduction Semantics. The reduction semantics for the Hindley-Milner type system follows the Curry-Hindley semantics. The key addition is a reduction rule and a context for let-expressions as shown in figure 23.15. The key to Algorithm $\mathcal{W}$ is the search through the type environment $\xi \notin \mathrm{ftv}(\Gamma)$ for each univariable in the definien type. By definition, $\mathrm{ftv}(\Gamma)$ is the union of all the free univariables in the type component of the bindings in Γ. Because generic univariables are generalized (and therefore bound) in let-bindings, any free univariables in a let-binding must occur in a λ-binding preceding this let-binding. The types in λ-bindings are the types of λ-bound variables. As in the previous reduction systems, those types appear as the left subtrees of $\to$ in partially reduced programs. Let the **spine** of the context be the path from the root of the program to the hole including the (left) subtrees of $\to$ that are on the path. As shown in figure 23.14, spines exclude the subtrees of @- and let- nodes that are not on the path. The types in the λ-bindings in a type environment are those in the spine of a partially reduced program. Because univariables never occur first in a let-binding in a type environment, we can safely ignore the fact that the [hm-let] rule eagerly substitutes the generalized definien type and thus potentially drops that type.

Generalization by Depth Ranking. In practice, repeatedly searching the environment or the spine is too expensive. There are two main practical alternatives: λ depth ranking and let depth ranking. Both are used in production

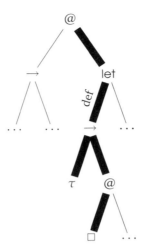

The spine for the context of □ is the bold path.

Figure 23.14: An example of a spine

compilers. The intuition is that these schemes rank univariables according to the depth of their outermost binding λs and lets according to their depths respectively. By comparing the ranks, the type checking algorithm can determine whether the univariable in question would have been in the type environment for the given let. This chapter covers only the λ-depth ranking scheme. Our earlier paper [66] provides an abstract machine for the let-depth ranking scheme that can easily be adapted to a reduction semantics.

The metafunction $\mathcal{A}$ in figure 23.16 provide the λ-nesting depth annotations for all the λs and let-expressions in an unannotated program. λ-nesting depth is formally defined in definition 3. $\mathcal{A}$ takes unannotated ULCL expressions to annotated ULCL-A expressions. The annotation starts at 0. Any lets that are not nested inside at least one λ receive an annotation of 0. The first λ receives a depth annotation of 1 because it is exactly one λ in.

This reduction system yields a correct λ-depth annotation of the program. An annotation is correct if nested λs and lets have annotations that are equal to the number of enclosing λs. This is essential for correct generalization.

CTX-V $T_h ::= (@ \ \tau \dots T_h \ e \dots) \mid (\to \ \tau \dots T_h \ e \dots) \mid (\text{let } (x \ T_h) \ e) \mid (\text{pair } T_h \ e) \mid (\text{pair } \tau \ T_h) \mid \square$

TYPE-VP $\tau_h ::= \text{num} \mid \text{bool} \mid (\to \ \tau \ \tau) \mid (\text{pair } \tau \ \tau) \mid \xi \mid \alpha$

$$T_h[number] \mapsto_h T_h[\text{num}] \qquad\qquad [\text{hm-const}]$$
$$T_h[true] \mapsto_h T_h[\text{bool}]$$
$$T_h[false] \mapsto_h T_h[\text{bool}]$$
$$T_h[(\text{let } (x \ \tau_h) \ e)] \mapsto_h T_h[\{(\forall(\bar{\alpha})\{\bar{\alpha}/\bar{\xi}\}\tau_h)/x\}e] \qquad [\text{hm-let}]$$
$$\text{where } \bar{\alpha} \text{ is a set of } n \text{ bound type variables}$$
$$\text{not in } T_h[(\text{let } (x \ \tau_h) \ e)]$$
$$\text{where } \bar{\xi} = \mathbf{Gen}_{\text{spine}(T_h)}(\tau_h)$$
$$\text{where } n = |\bar{\xi}| \ (\# \text{ of generalizable univars})$$
$$T_h[\forall(\bar{\alpha})\tau_h] \mapsto_h T_h[\{\bar{\xi}/\bar{\alpha}\}\tau] \qquad\qquad [\text{hm-inst}]$$
$$\text{where } \bar{\xi} \text{ is a set of } |\bar{\alpha}|$$
$$\text{generic univariables not in } T_h[\forall(\bar{\alpha})\tau_h]$$
$$T_h[(\lambda \ (x) \ e)] \mapsto_h T_h[(\to \ \xi \ \{\xi/x\}e)] \qquad\qquad [\text{hm-lam}]$$
$$\text{where } \xi \notin \text{ftv}(T_h[(\lambda \ (x) \ e)])$$
$$T_h[(@ \ \tau_1 \ \tau_2 \dots)] \mapsto_h (\text{unify } \tau_1 \ (\to \ \tau_2 \dots \ \xi) \ T_h[\xi]) \qquad [\text{hm-}\tau\beta]$$
$$T_h[primid] \mapsto_h T_h[(\mathbf{lookup} \ primid)]$$

The unify clauses are reduced using the ch-u reductions rules from the Curry-Hindley section plus the usual unify rule for the pair type.

Figure 23.15: Hindley-Milner reduction system

Definition 3 (λ-nesting Depth). *For any context* c,

$$\text{lampath}(c) = \begin{cases} 0 & c = \square \\ 1 + \text{lampath}(c') & c = (\lambda \ m \ (x) \ c') \\ \text{lampath}(c') & c = (@ \ e\# \ c') \\ \text{lampath}(c') & c = (@ \ c' \ e\#) \\ \text{lampath}(c') & c = (\textbf{let } m \ (x \ c') \ e\#) \\ \text{lampath}(c') & c = (\textbf{let } m \ (x \ e\#) \ c') \\ \text{lampath}(c') & c = (\text{pair } c' \ e\#) \\ \text{lampath}(c') & c = (\text{pair } e\# \ c') \\ 0 & otherwise \end{cases}$$

Theorem 8 (λ-Annotation Correctness). *For any ULCL expression* e, *let* $e\# = \mathcal{A}(e)$. *For any* $M = (\lambda \ m \ (x) \ e\#_1)$ *or* $M = (\textbf{let } m \ (x \ e\#_1) \ e\#_2)$ *such that there exists a context* c, $c[M] = e\#$, $m = \text{lampath}(c) + 1$.

Proof Sketch. This proof is by induction on the number of λs that surround M. □

$$\mathsf{lamrank}[\![((\lambda\ (x_l)\ e_l)\ d_l)]\!] \quad = (\lambda\ d_l{+}1\ (x_l)\ \mathsf{lamrank}[\![(e_l\ d_l{+}1\ )]\!]\ )$$

$$\mathsf{lamrank}[\![((\mathsf{let}\ (x_l\ e_l)\ e_2)\ d_l)]\!] = (\mathsf{let}\ d_l\ (x_l\ \mathsf{lamrank}[\![(e_l\ d_l)]\!]\ )\ \mathsf{lamrank}[\![(e_2\ d_l)]\!]\ )$$

$$\mathsf{lamrank}[\![((@\ e_l\ e_2)\ d_l)]\!] \quad = (@\ \mathsf{lamrank}[\![(e_l\ d_l)]\!]\ \ \mathsf{lamrank}[\![(e_2\ d_l)]\!]\ )$$

$$\mathsf{lamrank}[\![((primid_l\ e_l\ e_2)\ d_l)]\!] = (primid_l\ \mathsf{lamrank}[\![(e_l\ d_l)]\!]\ \ \mathsf{lamrank}[\![(e_2\ d_l)]\!]\ )$$

$$\mathsf{lamrank}[\![(e_l\ d_l)]\!] \quad\quad = e_l$$

$$\mathcal{A} : \mathsf{ULCL} \rightarrow \mathsf{ULCL\text{-}A}$$

$$\mathcal{A}(e) = (\mathsf{lamrank}\ e\ 0)$$

Figure 23.16: λ-depth annotation metafunction

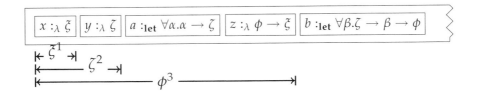

Figure 23.17: Intrinsic ranks of univariables in a environment

The λ-ranking Reduction System. The let-polymorphic language shown in figure 23.18 follows Milner and Damas[2] by adding a let-expression form, let-definien context, polymorphic type schemas ($\forall\ (\alpha)\ \tau$), polymorphic type variables (α), λ-depth annotations for λ and lets, and ranks for univariables, a shortcut to computing $\mathrm{ftv}(\tau) - \mathrm{ftv}(\Gamma)$ that will be explained later. The λs and lets in the language are each annotated with their λ nesting depths. Univariables derive their **intrinsic ranks** from these λ depth annotations but, strictly speaking, depth annotations and intrinsic ranks are different. The former refers to the syntactic property of let and λ-nesting depths, and the latter to ranks that the type checker computes.

The T_p type checking context goes into the definien. To add a wider variety of types, the language includes boolean and tuple types. These additional types gives an opportunity to show how the type checker would handle primitives and multi-arity functions. Similar to how we handle arrow types and applications, T_p goes through both parts of the pair type hybrid expression in order to fully reduce both sides. Pairs and booleans are constructed and eliminated by primitives, whose types are given in a separate lookup table.

---

[2]Luís Damas, private memo, 1984.

ULCL-HVR $e\# ::= number \mid \mathbf{true} \mid \mathbf{false} \mid x \mid (\lambda\ d\ (x)\ e\#) \mid (@\ e\#\ e\#\ldots) \mid (\mathbf{let}\ d\ (x\ e\#)\ e\#)$
                  $\mid (\rightarrow\ \tau\ e\#\ldots) \mid \mathbf{num} \mid \mathbf{bool} \mid \xi^r \mid (\mathbf{pair}\ e\#\ e\#) \mid (\forall(\alpha\ldots)\ \tau_p)$

Unif. constr. $p\ ::= (\mathbf{unify}\ \tau_p\ \tau_p\ p) \mid e\#$

CTX-VR $T_p ::= (@\ \tau\ldots T_p e\#\ldots) \mid (\rightarrow\ \tau\ldots\ T_p\ e\#\ldots) \mid (\mathbf{let}\ d\ (x\ T_p)\ e\#) \mid (\mathbf{pair}\ T_p\ e\#)$
                  $\mid (\mathbf{pair}\ \tau\ T_p) \mid \square$

Depth $d\ ::= number$

Rank $r\ ::= d \mid \infty$

TYPE-VPR $\tau_p ::= nt \mid pt$

Primitive $at ::= \mathbf{num} \mid \mathbf{bool}$

Compound $ct ::= (\rightarrow\ \tau\ldots\ \tau) \mid (\mathbf{pair}\ \tau\ \tau)$

Non-primitive $nt ::= ct \mid \xi^r \mid \alpha$

PTYPE $\sigma_p ::= (\forall\overline{\alpha}\ \tau_p)$

Figure 23.18: Hindley-Milner system language

To support multi-arity primitive operators such as **if**, the arrow type, application, and the associated contexts have been extended. To make the unification error reduction rules compact, we partition the grammar for types. Types can either be primitive (at) or non-primitive (nt). There are now two kinds of primitive types, num and bool. Non-primitive types, in turn, may be compound types (ct), polymorphic bound type variables (α), or univariables. We now have two kinds of compound types, arrow types and pair (tuple) types.

Of the new features, polymorphic type schemas (polytypes) are the most interesting. These type schemas explicitly bind polymorphic type variables and such bindings distinguish polymorphic type variables from univariables. Univariables can exist free even in the final type in a reduction sequence. Polymorphic type variables in types **must** be bound by a universal quantifier that quantifies over that whole type. Moreover, polytypes are short-lived. They only exist after generalization up until the algorithm reaches those polytypes in the body, when [hm-rank-inst] generically instantiates the polytype immediately.

In figure 23.19, the first three rules reduce literals to their types. The [hm-rank-let] rule computes the set of generalizable univariables using the helper function **Gen**, replaces all those univariables with fresh polymorphically bound type variables, and wraps the resulting type with a universal quantifier binding those bound type variables. If no univariables are generalizable, the quantifier is omitted. The [hm-rank-inst] rule instantiates all the polymorphic bound type variables with fresh generic univariables, stripping away the quantifier in the result. Both the [hm-rank-let] and [hm-rank-inst] need to obtain univariables fresh in the entire program. The [hm-rank-lam] rule

$$T_p[number] \longmapsto_p T_p[\text{num}] \qquad\qquad\qquad\qquad \text{[hm-rank-const]}$$
$$T_p[\text{true}] \longmapsto_p T_p[\text{bool}]$$
$$T_p[\text{false}] \longmapsto_p T_p[\text{bool}]$$
$$T_p[(\text{let } d \ (x \ \tau_p) \ e\#)] \longmapsto_p T_p[\{(\forall(\bar{\alpha})\{\bar{\alpha}/\bar{\xi}\}\tau_p)/x\}e\#] \qquad \text{[hm-rank-let]}$$
$$\text{where } \bar{\alpha} \text{ is a set of } n \text{ bound type variables}$$
$$\text{not in } T_p[(\text{let } d \ (x \ \tau_p) \ e\#)]$$
$$\text{where } \bar{\xi} = \mathbf{Gen}_d(\tau_p)$$
$$\text{where } n = |\bar{\xi}| \ (\# \text{ of generalizable univars})$$
$$T_p[\forall(\bar{\alpha})\tau_p] \longmapsto_p T_p[\{\overline{\xi^{\infty}}/\bar{\alpha}\}\tau] \qquad\qquad\qquad \text{[hm-rank-inst]}$$
$$\text{where } \bar{\xi^{\infty}} \text{ is a set of } |\bar{\alpha}|$$
$$\text{generic univariables not in } T_p[\forall(\bar{\alpha})\tau_p]$$
$$T_p[(\lambda \ d \ (x) \ e)] \longmapsto_p T_p[(\to \ \xi^d \ \{\xi^d/x\}e)] \qquad\qquad \text{[hm-rank-lam]}$$
$$\text{where } \xi \notin \text{ftv}(T_p[(\lambda \ d \ (x) \ e)])$$
$$T_p[(@ \ \tau_1 \ \tau_2 \dots)] \longmapsto_p (\text{unify } \tau_1 \ (\to \ \tau_2 \dots \xi^{\infty}) \ T_p[\xi^{\infty}]) \qquad \text{[hm-rank-}\tau\beta]$$
$$T_p[primid] \longmapsto_p T_p[(\mathbf{lookup} \ primid)]$$
$$\mathbf{Gen}(\tau, d) \text{ returns a list of all univariables in } \tau \text{ with rank greater than the current depth } d.$$

Figure 23.19: Hindley-Milner system reductions (not including unification rules)

reduces the λ to an arrow, just as before, except now the fresh univariable introduced for the bound parameter is given a rank of the current λ-depth. The [hm-rank-$\tau\beta$] rule is similar to [ch-$\tau\beta$] except the fresh result type univariable is given rank ∞. The [hm-rank-prim] rule uses a **lookup** helper function to look up a table mapping primitive identifiers to the types of those primitives. For example, (if e_1 e_2 e_3) $\longmapsto_p$ (@ $(\forall(\alpha)(\to \ \text{bool } \alpha \ \alpha))$ e_1 e_2 e_3). Figure 23.20 significantly modifies the unification instantiation rule [hm-u-inst] to adjust ranks appropriately.[3] The limit substitution ($\mathbf{Limit}(\tau_p, r)$) ensures that the maximum rank for any univariable in τ_p would be the given depth r. Limiting the ranks of the univariables prevents high ranked (i.e., local) univariables from remaining high ranked when they are introduced into the context and the type environment in place of low ranked ξ^r by substitution. Figure 23.21 shows why the limit substitution is necessary. ζ is promoted because the instantiation substitution introduced a new occurrence of ζ that precedes the old first occurrence binding. The [hm-u-dist-pr] and [hm-u-dist] distributes unification across pair and arrow types. Most importantly, [hm-u-err-occurs] is the occurs check that guarantees that there will be no cycle in the unification and thus unification must terminate. The [hm-u-const] and [hm-u-orient] rules are identical to the analogous rules in the CH system. The remaining unification rules flag unification errors, which are type errors.

---

[3]Although [hm-u-inst] promotes univariable ranks via a substitution, in practice, ML compilers promote ranks via an update to a ref cell containing the rank.

$$(\text{unify } \tau \ \tau \ p) \mapsto_p \ p \qquad\qquad\qquad\qquad\qquad \text{[hm-u-const]}$$

$$(\text{unify } at \ at \ p) \mapsto_p \ \text{error} \qquad\qquad\qquad\qquad \text{[hm-u-err-at]}$$
$$\text{where } at \neq at$$

$$(\text{unify } ct \ at \ p) \mapsto_p \ \text{error} \qquad\qquad\qquad\qquad \text{[hm-u-err-ct1]}$$

$$(\text{unify } at \ ct \ p) \mapsto_p \ \text{error} \qquad\qquad\qquad\qquad \text{[hm-u-err-ct2]}$$

$$(\text{unify } \xi^r \ \tau_p \ p) \mapsto_p \ \mathbf{Limit}(\tau_p, r) \circ \{\tau_p / \xi^r\} p \qquad \text{[hm-u-inst]}$$
$$\text{where } \xi^r \notin \text{ftv}(\tau_p)$$

$$(\text{unify } \tau_p \ \xi^r \ p) \mapsto_p \ (\text{unify } \xi^r \ \tau_p \ p) \qquad\qquad \text{[hm-u-orient]}$$
$$\text{where } \xi^r \notin \text{ftv}(\tau)$$

$$(\text{unify } (\text{pair } \tau_{p1} \ \tau_{p2}) \ (\text{pair } \tau_{p3} \ \tau_{p4}) \ p) \mapsto_p \ (\text{unify } \tau_{p1} \ \tau_{p3} \ (\text{unify } \tau_{p2} \ \tau_{p4} \ p)) \qquad \text{[hm-u-dist-pr]}$$
$$\text{where } (\text{pair } \tau_{p1} \ \tau_{p2}) \neq (\text{pair } \tau_{p3} \ \tau_{p4})$$

$$(\text{unify } \tau_p \ \tau'_p \ p) \mapsto_p \ (\text{unify } \tau_{p1} \ \tau_{p3} \ \ldots (\text{unify } \tau_{p2} \ \tau_{p4} \ p)) \qquad \text{[hm-u-dist]}$$
$$\text{where } \tau_p = (\rightarrow \ \tau_{p1} \ldots \ \tau_{p2})$$
$$\text{and } \tau'_p = (\rightarrow \ \tau_{p3} \ldots \ \tau_{p4})$$
$$\tau_p \neq \tau'_p$$
$$\text{and } \tau_p \text{ and } \tau'_p \text{ have the same arity}$$

$$(\text{unify } (\rightarrow \ \ldots \ ) \ (\rightarrow \ \ldots) \ p) \mapsto_p \ \text{error} \qquad\qquad \text{[hm-u-err-arr]}$$
$$\text{where the two arrow types have different arities}$$

$$(\text{unify } nt_1 \ nt_2 \ p) \mapsto_p \ \text{error} \qquad\qquad\qquad \text{[hm-u-err-occurs]}$$
$$\text{where } nt_1 \neq nt_2 \text{ and } nt_1 \in \text{ftv}(nt_2) \text{ or } nt_2 \in \text{ftv}(nt_1)$$

$$\mathbf{Limit}(\tau_p, r) = \{\xi^r / \xi^{r'} \mid \xi^{r'} \in \text{ftv}(\tau_p) \text{ and } r < r'\}$$

Figure 23.20: Hindley-Milner system unification reductions

Simulating Virtual Type Environment by Depth Ranking. Depth ranking simulates the salient information for generalization that we would have obtained from the environment. Let the *virtual environment* be this environment that we are simulating constructed as a list. We build this list by consing new bindings to the right of a preexisting list. Figure 23.22 shows how a small virtual environment is constructed. Generalizability of a univariable boils down to when that univariable is first introduced into the type environment. More precisely, generalizability is determined by when the outermost enclosing λ abstraction that constrains the given univariable introduced a binding into the virtual environment. This information is manifested in the current type environment as the position of the first (reading the environment from left to right, counting only λ-bindings) λ binding in the environment that has an occurrence of the univariable in question. This position is what we call the intrinsic rank. The intrinsic rank is the crucial bit of information that determines generalizability. The correctness of the depth ranking scheme hinges on whether the type checking and unification reduc-

$$\boxed{x :_\lambda \xi}\ \boxed{y :_\lambda \zeta}\ \boxed{a :_{\text{let}} \forall \alpha.\alpha \to \zeta}\ \boxed{z :_\lambda \phi \to \xi}\ \boxed{b :_{\text{let}} \forall \beta.\zeta \to \beta \to \phi}$$

$$\Big\downarrow\ \theta = \{\zeta / \xi\}$$

$$\boxed{x :_\lambda \zeta}\ \boxed{y :_\lambda \zeta}\ \boxed{a :_{\text{let}} \forall \alpha.\alpha \to \zeta}\ \boxed{z :_\lambda \phi \to \zeta}\ \boxed{b :_{\text{let}} \forall \beta.\zeta \to \beta \to \phi}$$

Figure 23.21: Unification instantiation can promote univariables

1.	$(\lambda\, 1\ (v)\ (\text{let}\, 1\ f = (\lambda\, 2\ (u)\ (@\ u\ v))$ $\text{in}\ (@\ f\ (\lambda\, 2\ (z)\ 1))))$	
2.	$(\to\ \xi^1\ (\text{let}\, 1\ f = (\lambda\, 2\ (u)\ (@\ u\ \xi^1))$ $\text{in}\ (@\ f\ (\lambda\, 2\ (z)\ 1))))$	$v : \xi$
3.	$(\to\ \xi^1\ (\text{let}\, 1\ f = (\to\ \phi^2\ (@\ \phi^2\ \xi^1))$ $\text{in}\ (@\ f\ (\lambda\, 2\ (z)\ 1))))$	$v : \xi, u : \phi$
4.	$(\text{unify}\ \phi^2\ (\to\ \xi^1\ \psi^\infty)$ $(\to\ \xi^1\ (\text{let}\, 1\ f = (\to\ \phi^2\ \psi^\infty)$ $\text{in}\ (@\ f\ (\lambda\, 2\ (z)\ 1)))))$	$v : \xi, u : \phi$
5.	$(\to\ \xi^1\ (\text{let}\, 1\ f = (\to\ (\to\ \xi^1\ \psi^2)\ \psi^2)$ $\text{in}\ (@\ f\ (\lambda\, 2\ (z)\ 1))))$	$v : \xi, u : (\to\ \xi\ \psi)$

Figure 23.22: Example reduction sequence

tions keep track of the intrinsic ranks of univariables, because unification reductions can alter intrinsic ranks.

Initially in figure 23.22, each λ and let-expression is annotated with its λ-depth. The univariable introduced by each λ is initially given a rank corresponding to that λ-abstraction's λ-nesting depth (steps 2 and 3). For more intuition, consider figure 23.23, which shows what abstract syntax looks like after an $\mathcal{A}$ annotation . The key observation is that when [hm-rank-lam] reduces a λ, at that point, the intrinsic rank equals the λ-nesting depth, i.e., the univariable rank must necessarily correspond to the position (with respect to other λ bindings) of its first binding occurrence in the virtual environment. This is the case because the number of λ-bindings in the type environment is always equal to the number of λ-abstractions traversed to get to the current redex. After all, we only push a new λ-binding onto the type environment when we are inside the scope of the corresponding λ-abstraction.

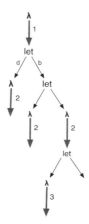

Figure 23.23: λ-nesting depth annotation and the abstract syntax

In step 4, the [hm-$\tau\beta$] rule introduces a unification prefix and a result type univariable ψ. The univariable ψ is not in the virtual environment; thus it gets a rank of ∞, indicating that it is not constrained by any λ. In step 5, the [hm-u-inst] rule instantiates ϕ to $(\rightarrow \quad \xi \ \psi)$. Occurrences of ϕ in the virtual environment must be instantiated. Thus, ψ is introduced into the u λ-binding in the virtual environment, i.e., the second λ-binding in the environment. The first occurrence of ξ is still the first λ-binding. It follows that ψ must be given ϕ's rank while ξ's rank remains unchanged.

The general principle is that whenever the type checker instantiates a univariable ϕ to a type, any univariable ψ in that type with a rank greater than ϕ's will inherit ϕ's rank. This arrangement corresponds to what happens in the virtual environment. The first occurrence of ϕ becomes the first occurrence of any ψ, whose first occurrence used to be to the right of ϕ's first occurrence.

Generalization and Generic Instantiation. We generalize the definien type using [hm-let], which generalizes all univariables with rank greater than the let us λ depth.

Figure 23.24 shows how the [hm-let] reduction plays out with respect to the virtual type environment. The reduction rules shift the redex out of what was formerly λu to the entire let expression. Thus, the virtual environment has to pop off the u binding. Based on this environment, ξ should not be generalized, but ψ should be. Correspondingly, ψ's rank is greater than the

$$\dfrac{(\to \ \xi^1 \quad (\text{let } 1\ f = (\to\ (\to\ \xi^1\ \psi^2)\ \psi^2)}{(\to\ \xi^1 \quad (@\ (\forall\alpha(\to\ (\to\ \xi^1\ \alpha)\ \alpha))\ (\lambda^2 z.1)))} \ \Big| \ \begin{matrix} v:\xi \\ v:\xi \end{matrix}$$

Figure 23.24: Generalization and virtual type environment

$\texttt{let}$'s λ-depth, but ξ's rank is equal to the λ-depth. The reduction, therefore, generalizes ψ but not ξ.

The [hm-let] rule substitutes the generalized type for the let-bound program variable in the body of the $\texttt{let}$ expression. Generalized types are polymorphic type schemas, which the type checking context distinguishes from ordinary monomorphic type schemas (e.g., $(\to\ \ \xi^1\ \text{num})$). In particular, whereas monomorphic type schemas are the final forms with respect to the reduction relation (analogous to how values are final forms for evaluation reduction relations), polymorphic type schemas are not. Polymorphic type schemas can be further reduced by the [hm-inst] rule, which replaces bound polymorphic type variables with fresh univariables with rank ∞. The fresh univariables are given rank ∞ so that they can be re-generalized because they are fully generic. Having the [hm-inst] rule instantiate all bound polymorphic type variables for every occurrence of the polymorphic type schema to fresh univariables ensures that the polymorphic program variable can be reused independently at each occurrence.

Since Milner proved the soundness of $\mathcal{W}$, we show that this reduction system is equivalent to Algorithm $\mathcal{W}$. The key lemma for this proof shows that the λ-depth bookkeeping technique generalizes exactly the same univariables the environment search technique would have.

Theorem 9 (HM Reduction Soundness and Completeness relative to $\mathcal{W}$).
For any closed ULCL-A expression $e\#$, $e\# \mapsto_p^* \tau$ iff $\mathcal{W}(\emptyset, e\#) = (\theta, \tau_u)$.

Proof Sketch. The proof of this theorem[4] relies on a standard transformation into an abstract machine with four registers, the redex as the control, an environment Γ mapping program variables to types, the cumulative unification substitution, and the stack (continuation) of the rest of the expression to type check. The stack is similar to the type checking context. We derive the rules for the abstract machine from the rules in the reduction semantics. An important requirement for this machine is that when the machine is leaving for a shallower context (e.g., leaving the body of a λ), then any environment binding specific to the deeper context must be popped out the environment.

---

[4]This is only a high-level sketch. For a complete proof, consult the author's MS thesis [65].

Let $\mathcal{R}(\xi^m, \Gamma)$ be the index of the first occurrence of ξ^m in Γ if we index only bindings introduced by [hm-lam]. Let $\mathcal{D}(\Gamma)$ be the total number of bindings in the environment introduced by [hm-lam].

The following four properties are invariants of the abstract machine:

Property 1. For all $\xi^m \in \text{ftv}(\Gamma)$, $\mathcal{R}(\xi^m, \Gamma) = m$.

Property 2. For all $\xi^m \in \text{ftv}(e\#)$ such that $m \leq \mathcal{D}(\Gamma)$, $\xi^m \in \text{ftv}(\Gamma)$.

Property 3. $\mathcal{D}(\Gamma) = \#$ of $(\rightarrow \ \tau \ \Box)$s on the stack.

Property 4. For all $\xi^m \in \text{ftv}(k)$ such that $m \leq r$ where r is the number of $(\rightarrow \ \tau \ \Box)$ frames below the frame with the occurrence of ξ^m in the stack, $\xi^m \in \text{ftv}(\Gamma)$.

Properties 1 and 2 show that $\mathbf{Gen}(\tau, d)$ equals $\text{ftv}(\tau) - \text{ftv}(\Gamma)$. With this fact, it is straightforward to show that the machine is indeed equivalent to $\mathcal{W}$, and therefore the reduction system is also equivalent to $\mathcal{W}$. Property 3 says that the number of λ-bindings in Γ is equal to the λ depth. This statement follows from the fact that by construction, we push on a λ-binding for each λ-abstraction we enter and then pop off a λ-binding for each λ-abstraction we leave. This property shows that property 1 holds initially when a univariable is first introduced into the environment. Property 4 ensures that what may seem to be low ranked univariables were actually high ranked at the time we reached it and will reach it when we pop back up through the stack (and therefore decrease the current λ-depth). This fact ensures that when a type is popped off the stack and is the new control, no univariable in this new control is low ranked and yet not bound in the environment. $\Box$

Because Damas and Milner proved the soundness and completeness of Algorithm $\mathcal{W}$ with respect to the declarative Hindley-Milner type system [25, 26, 77], this ranked Hindley-Milner reduction system is also sound and complete with respect to the declarative type system.

Acknowledgments. We thank David MacQueen of the University of Chicago for the many insightful discussions and his helpful feedback.

24 · Topsl: DSEL as Multi-language System
Jacob Matthews, University of Chicago

We present Topsl, a domain-specific embedded language (DSEL) for writing online surveys suitable for use in social science studies. After a discussion of the surprising difficulties that arise in designing such a language, we reframe the problem as one of designing a formal multi-language system in the style of Matthews and Findler. This approach leads us to a design that is both clearer and more powerful than the design we began with, lending support to the view that domain-specific language can be usefully thought of as instances of multi-language systems.

24·1 Introduction.

The demand for web-based surveys has grown significantly in recent years as social scientists have become more aware of the practical and theoretical benefits of gathering information online [10]. Unfortunately, this growing demand has not been met by correspondingly mature technologies. While many domain-specific languages (DSLs) and wizards exist for online surveys—for instance SuML [7] and QPL [110]—every one we have found falls into the common trap for DSLs of being "80% solutions," with rich facilities for asking individual questions but only rudimentary support for the other tasks a programming language must perform, such as controlling flow and performing arbitrary computations. Simple surveys are easy to implement, but sometimes even seemingly minor extensions are impossible.

When studies run into these limitations, programmers resort to implementing them in a general-purpose language, such as PHP or Perl, that allows them to express anything they want (as evidence that this is a popular approach, Fraley recently published a how-to guide on the subject for psychologists [44]). Unfortunately, if they make that choice, they become responsible for handling HTML generation, CGI, and data storage, all are unrelated to the specific survey being written. In the author's direct experience, online surveys are plagued by bugs in this non-domain-specific code. For instance, my introduction to the problems with online surveys was as a student in a sociology class. The class designed an online survey and hired independent consultants to implement it in ColdFusion; unfortunately, after a few hundred participants had already completed the survey, the class discovered that the program had a major bug in its answer-saving routines that caused it to lose all answers to about half of the questions on the survey. When the bug was discovered, the class had to contact all the participants and ask them to fill out the survey again; only about 10% of the original participants actually did. Such incidents are common, but they are an unacceptable risk in expensive research.

It is natural that these two general strategies for solving the survey problem should emerge. Survey programs exist to collect answers to questions that will then be put into rows in a database or analyzed by a statistics program, and that might be printed out for copy-editing or for handing out to off-line survey participants. To make those operations possible, it must be possible to identify (before runtime) every question that a particular survey could possibly ask. Of course, if a survey program had complete freedom at runtime to generate questions, that identification would be impossible. So, the problem must be made easier, and two simple ways to make it easier are to restrict the language in which programmers write surveys to the point where questions are statically identifiable, or to restrict analysis to one particular survey and do the analysis by hand.

Both available options have serious problems, though: current domain-specific languages afford too little flexibility in their models of flow control, and general-purpose languages make programmers implement substantial amounts of non-domain-specific code for each survey. In this chapter, we demonstrate a way to take the middle path with Topsl, a domain-specific language for writing online surveys embedded into the general-purpose language PLT Scheme. We follow the tradition of domain-specific embedded languages (DSELs) [57,58,96] by embedding a domain-specific sublanguage for survey-specific tasks into a general-purpose language, PLT Scheme, whose full power is available when necessary. We depart from tradition, however, in that rather than approaching the problem as one of programming appropriate combinators, we approach it instead as a multi-language system [74] operational-semantics design problem. Specifically, we design a small-step operational semantics that combines a calculus for a special-purpose survey language with a variant of the untyped lambda calculus that also models web interaction using ideas from webL by Krishnamurthi et al. [49,63]. After motivating our design with a description of some non-obvious design requirements we have found (section 24.2), we step back and develop a new design for Topsl by repeatedly refining a basic model of a domain-specific survey language into a full-featured multi-language system (sections 24.3,

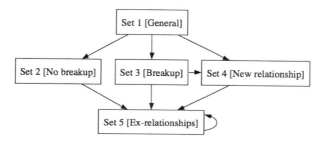

Figure 24.1: Finkel's survey

24.4, 24.5, 24.6, and 24.7). These models presented an unusual challenge for PLT Redex in that they require two kinds of nondeterminism; we discuss how we addressed that problem in section 24.8. Finally, in section 24.9 we recount how the development we present here led us to a much simpler and more flexible version of Topsl than we had found in previous work [70].

24·2 Web Surveys.
The author was introduced to the problem of designing a language for online surveys by Dr. Eli Finkel, assistant professor of psychology at Northwestern University, in Fall 2003. At that time Finkel had written a paper-and-pencil design for a recurring online survey that he intended to use as a key component in a year-long longitudinal study.[1] Figure 24.1 shows a simplified version of his survey, which works for our purposes. At each two-week interval, every participant answered set 1, a set of general questions that assessed the status of his or her relationship. Then, depending on the answers the participant gave, he or she was categorized as either having entered a relationship, exited a relationship, both, or neither since the last time he or she completed the survey. Depending on the answer, the participant was guided to answer some relevant set of questions, some subset of question sets 2 through 4. Finally, all participants, no matter their status, were asked to answer the questions in set 5 once for *each* relationship they had been involved in during the study.

To his surprise, Finkel found that while he could easily find survey authoring services that would suffice to implement almost his entire design, none would implement set 5's looping behavior because none of them could han-

---

[1]A longitudinal study is a study in which the researcher tracks a group of participants over time; in Finkel's study, this meant asking a group of freshmen to complete a survey once every two weeks for a year.

dle surveys in which a question was asked once for each distinct way another question had been answered in the past, effectively creating a loop whose iteration count grew over the course of the study. Hearing about Finkel's problem, we immediately thought that it could be solved with a simple use of *map* in an implementation based around PLT Scheme's continuation-based web server [50,64], a technology we were eager to gain practical experience with anyway. So, we decided to solve his problem by building an embedded domain-specific language for constructing online surveys using the PLT Scheme web server, based on two guiding design principles:

1. The system had to be easy to use correctly. Specifically, we wanted it to be impossible for a programmer to write a buggy survey that fails to save a participant's responses to questions, in the same way that a traditional type system makes it impossible for a programmer to write a buggy program that can cause a segmentation fault.

2. The system had to be flexible enough to handle unforeseen designs. It would not be a particularly robust general solution if we just implemented another domain-specific language that added a new construct to allow us to write Finkel's loop, since the next survey that came along might have some new twist that would put us back at the drawing board. Instead, we wanted a language that would be flexible enough to allow Finkel's loop but also new experimental designs that we had not even heard of yet.

At first blush this did not seem to be a hard problem. However, as we worked on the problem, we uncovered several non-obvious requirements that could not all be met simultaneously using a naive design strategy. The next three subsections discuss them in turn.

Row-passing Style. A basic question that our implementation needed to answer was how to arrange the basic plumbing that receives user answers, allows them to be inspected and used during the program, and eventually saves them as completed survey answers. Unfortunately, this brings up a subtle implementation problem. Consider the function *ask*, a hypothetical function that Topsl could use to ask questions of a user and receive their answers. How should we arrange for it to store those answers so that they cannot be lost? An obvious choice would be to use mutation of global state, but unfortunately mutation does not have quite the right semantics for our needs in the presence of *send/suspend*. When a participant, in the middle of some long multi-page survey, realizes she has made a mistake, say, three pages back, she may well press the back button to get back to the page with the error, resubmit it with a correct answer, and continue. This might cause

TST	: "The Scheme Type"
page	: *page-element ... → survey*
(**?** *question-type question-id string*)	: syntax[*page-element*]
sequence	: *survey ... → survey*

(**branch** *question-id*
     [(*TST → bool*) *survey*]
     ...)
	: syntax[*survey*]

(**bind** *var symbol survey* *survey*)	: syntax[*survey*]

Figure 24.2: Topsl primitives, attempt 1

---

the survey program to present her with the same two pages she just answered, but it may also cause the program to present some entirely new path
of pages. In the former case, the participant probably expects the old answers from the incorrect path to disappear, and in either case the researcher
looking at the answers later definitely expects answers from paths not finished to disappear always since otherwise the set of survey answers might
not correspond to any legal path through the survey. If *ask* mutates a global
table to record new answers, the continuations that *send/suspend* uses do
capture control information and lexical bindings but not the current values
in the store; thus, when the participant goes back to an old page the global
table will continue to hold now-invalid answers.

To avoid using mutation, though, we would have to make *ask* produce a
row of answers, and make every survey end with a survey-finalization procedure that took a list of answer rows that represented all answers that had
been given over the entire survey and blessed them as a complete set of answers ready for data analysis. This causes another problem: left to their own
devices, programmers could easily write a buggy program that received a row
of answers from *ask* and then simply ignored them, never including them in
the final result set at the end of the program. In effect, programmers would
have to write surveys in a monadic "result-row-passing style" that would be
easy to get wrong. To alleviate that burden, we wrote several combinators
(see figure 24.2) that consumed and produced surveys of which pages were
the ground elements, and threaded row-passing through automatically.

Abstraction. While implementing Finkel's survey, we found that function
abstractions play a more interesting role than we had initially thought they

would. We had expected to write functions that abstracted over pages, since often pages needed to be dynamically generated: in Finkel's survey, many questions took the form "When is the last time you talked to *[name]*?" where *[name]* was the answer to a question on a previous page, or drawn from a previous session. In particular, his set 5, the set that had caused him so many problems, relied on this ability.

Another use of abstraction that we had not anticipated was to satisfy the need to define a standard, repetitive group of questions that appeared with variations many times on a survey. For instance, Finkel's survey included many 4-question blocks of the form, "How do you predict you will feel about *[subject]* in . . . one week? . . . two weeks? . . . one month? . . . two months?" where *[subject]* varied and each question was answered separately. For this pattern, we found it very useful to write question-producing functions that factored out the repeated elements.[2]

Static Analysis. A requirement that might at first seem innocuous, but in fact has become the major technical challenge of Topsl's development, is the need to know all of the pages and questions that could be asked of a participant independently of any participant taking the survey and answering the questions (and in fact before participants even saw the survey at all). We have encountered this need in two ways: first, to build a database back-end laid out with one table per page, each table column corresponding to a particular question and each row corresponding to a particular submission of answers, it is necessary to know each possible question and a SQL type that can hold answers to that question before the survey executes. Second, Finkel and his colleagues wanted documentation that was in principle derivable from the program itself: a printed, paper copy of the entire survey for proofreading, and a "code book" listing the ID of each question, question type (*e.g.*, Likert-type[3] or free-response), and question text.[4] To meet these needs, we needed

---

[2]In fact, after completing the survey we learned that this form of abstraction was even more important than we had realized, since researchers in the social sciences take great pains to ensure that question types are standard from use to use and from survey to survey. They do this to cut down potential sources of imprecision in data analysis: for instance, if some questions asked about how the participant would feel in "four weeks" and others asked how the participant would feel in "one month," analyses that used answers from both sets would need to take into account that the participant might—perhaps subconsciously—think of "four weeks" and "one month" as significantly different durations.

[3]A Likert-type question is the technical name for a question in which respondents are presented with a scale from 1 to 7, 1 labeled "strongly disagree" and 7 labeled "strongly agree," and are asked to rank where they fall on that scale with respect to some particular proposal. Likert-type questions are probably the most common question type in surveys conducted by social scientists due to their quantitative nature and broad applicability.

[4]Every survey of any substantial size requires a code book. Surveys often comprise many hundreds of questions and researchers often share datasets with their colleagues or make them

to know all possible questions a survey could produce, independently of any actual participant taking the survey.

This requirement is incompatible with using abstractions as a way to build up surveys and their answers. All of the previous requirements we have discussed tend to suggest that a survey ought be built up by composing functions that produce pages and questions. Some of these functions could be provided by a standard library, and some of them were intended to be written directly by the Topsl programmer; some could be evaluated statically to predict their runtime effect, but some could not even in principle be applied until a participant actually responded to some questions to produce inputs—without having any way to look inside these abstractions other than running them, we cannot not possibly perform a useful static analysis. Even applying them to dummy data was not workable, because a page's question set, or the particular phrasings of questions, could depend on the input data, and pages could produce or rely on effects—for instance, many pages in Finkel's survey took a participant ID and queried a database for information about that participant's responses in previous iterations of the survey.

It is possible to solve this problem by building a function-like mechanism that also supported some kind of inspection, for instance an object that had a *run* method and an *analyze* method. These abstractions could behave like a function when encountered at survey runtime by the other Topsl primitives. The construct could evaluate its body to a list of questions before survey runtime, allowing string constants in question text to be substituted with survey runtime arguments; static analysis could then simply read this list of questions without substituting arguments. Since the body is evaluated, we could use native Scheme functions to abstract over common question patterns. This is the solution documented previously [70]. That approach has a limitation too, however, in that not only functions but also every other way of putting functions together—**if**, **let**, *for-each*, and so on must be reimplemented so that they also support both *run* and *analyze* methods, or we will not be able to properly pipe the static analysis of their subparts to the top level. For instance, the survey

(**define-page** (*page1*)
    (? likert q_1 "Text 1 ...")
    (? free q_2 "Text 2 ...")
    (? likert q_3 "Text 3 ..."))

(**define-page** (*page2 txt*)
    (? free q_4 "Question pertaining to " *txt*))

---

publically available, and a code book is the most compact and useful way to record all the information about a survey that a researcher would need to interpret its dataset.

```
(bind ([txt 'q₂] [pivot 'q₃]) (page1)
  (if (= pivot 7)
      (sequence (page2 txt))
      (sequence)))
```

would generate two database tables, one for *page1* and one for *page2*; the table for *page1* would contain columns q_1 of type number, q_2 of type text, and q_3 of type number; the table for *page3* would contain a single column for question q_4 of type text. The only information relevant to the decision of how to construct tables is the **define-page** statements and their contents; any survey flow control code (for instance the last expression in the above code fragment, which controls evaluation of the survey) is completely ignored when generating the static summary of a survey. The control information does, however, need to implement row-passing style, and each construct in the control is responsible for gathering up any rows produced by its subexpressions and delivering them in a reasonable way. For that reason, the **if** clause's second alternative has to be an empty **sequence** instead of a call to Scheme's built-in *void*—if we had put a call to *void* in that position, then since (*void*) does not return a row the program would not observe row-passing style and thus the survey would not save its results. We could provide a replacement for the built-in *void*, but that would only offer limited protection; for instance, it would not help us if we wanted to use a one-armed **if** instead.

While this system is workable, and in fact we and others implemented two more large-scale surveys using variations of it, it retains little of the simplicity of our initial idea. Ironically, the idea that had led us to take on the project in the first place—the idea that Finkel's set 5 loop corresponded to Scheme's *map*—did not make it into the final implementation, because Scheme's built-in *map* did not conform to row-passing style and did not work with our static analysis technique; instead we had to implement our own *map*-like construct. In fact, the impact of this design choice rippled through the entire language design, essentially requiring us to implement a Topsl version of every control construct we wanted to use. Furthermore, the language we had designed did not match our initial design goals very well: while we offered support for building surveys in row-passing style, in practice computations that needed to access an answer during survey runtime often had to deal with row-passing style manually, leading to the possibility of data loss errors; and while the system was flexible enough allow us to write Finkel's loop, the set of control constructs we provided was somewhat ad-hoc and limited to those constructs we could analyze statically, giving us no guarantee that we could implement the next survey we encountered without a major rebuilding effort—in the worst case possibly even requiring us to build a sophisticated analysis framework.

These problems left us unsatisfied with our solution, so we decided to go back to the drawing board. Our goal is to ensure that our new language is flexible enough to write arbitrary surveys, no matter how complicated, and furthermore that the language was safe by construction, in that participants' responses can never be dropped by a bug in the survey, mixed up in an inconsistent state in the final result file, or mixed in a way that the participant did not intend when he (or she) uses the browser's back button. Our strategy for achieving that goal is to take a formal approach to what we had previously articulated only informally: we revised our design through several permutations, at each step of the way formally articulating the critical safety properties as theorems and proving that they hold for our designs.

We call these properties the *analysis*, *consistency*, and *coherence* theorems. Analysis and consistency, taken together, say that every run of the survey must result in all the participant's responses, stored in a database whose layout can be determined ahead of time: analysis says that we can safely approximate the set of possible pages and questions a survey could produce, and consistency says that the responses to every page and question will be remembered. The coherence property is only relevant to the web-based Topsl model, and it guarantees any web-based interaction (including normal page-to-page interaction but also possibly uses of the back button or cloned browser windows) always leads to a set of answers that could have been the result of a single, linear traversal through a survey.

This methodical way of building up a domain-specific language is an unusual approach, but the most novel aspect of the development that follows is that we use boundaries [74] as a simple technique to allow us to partition our design into the domain-specific survey part of the language and the general-purpose computational part of the language. Thinking about the problem as a multilanguage problem gives us the insight required to see how we can borrow Scheme's existing control and binding constructs as a way of extending Topsl's power.

24.3 Base Topsl.

We start with a model of as simple a survey language as we can (though our model itself is slightly more complicated than at first appears necessary, allowing us to extend it into a multi-language system later). Figure 24.3 presents the grammar for "base Topsl," a language with no features other than the ability to ask a sequence of pages, each of which may contain any number of Likert-scale and free-response questions. The *s* (for "survey") nonterminal generates a sequence of survey elements (nonterminal *s-elt*), which in turn may be a page (nonterminal *p*) or another survey. Furthermore, because we want to think of base Topsl as a small-step semantics, we need a term representation for partially-completed

$$
\begin{aligned}
\textit{complete-survey} &::= s \\
s &::= (\text{seq } \textit{s-elt} \dots) \\
\textit{s-elt} &::= p \mid r \mid s \mid a \\
p &::= (\text{page } x \; q \dots) \\
r &::= (\text{response } x \; (x \; \textit{rty} \; \textit{ans}) \dots) \\
a &::= (r \dots) \\
q &::= (?\; x \; \textit{rty} \; \textit{q-elt} \dots) \\
\textit{rty} &::= \text{likert} \mid \text{free} \\
\textit{q-elt} &::= \text{string} \\
\textit{ans} &::= \text{string} \mid \textit{number}
\end{aligned}
$$

Figure 24.3: Base Topsl grammar

surveys as well; for this reason a survey element may also be a page response (nonterminal r) corresponding to a page that has been asked and answered, and an answer sequence (nonterminal a) that corresponds to a sequence of such page responses. Evaluation reduces a survey down to flat sequence of answers that we interpret as a completed response to the survey.

A page is straightforward: every page has a name x, which we represent as an arbitrary symbol with the side constraint that no name may be used on more than one page, and a sequence of questions (nonterminal q). Each question has a name, a question type (nonterminal rty), and a sequence of elements, each of which must be a string.

Base Topsl's value terms, evaluation contexts, and reductions are shown in figure 24.4. We include several notions of values as nonterminals here that we do not yet use, but which become important later on: the qv ("question value") and $q\text{-}eltv$ ("question element value") nonterminals, which represent fully evaluated, ready-to-ask questions and strings within question text, respectively. Here, they only serve to distinguish uses of nonterminals q and $q\text{-}elt$, respectively, that we consider "fully-evaluated;" by making this distinction we can extend q and $q\text{-}elt$ in subsequent sections to introduce new ways to generate a question without also extending what constitutes a question that is ready to be printed on a web page. Also note that a survey contains two notions of a completely evaluated page: a page that is ready to be presented to a user (an element of pv), and a page that has actually been asked and answered and has become a set of responses (an element of r).

A top-level Topsl evaluation context (TE) is simply a sequence evaluation context ($SeqE$); a sequence evaluation context can be a hole seq, corresponding to direct evaluation of a sequence by either the (seq demotion 1) or (seq demotion 2) reduction (explained below), or a survey to which a participant has partially responded, allowing evaluation on the left-most uncompleted

$$pv ::= (\text{page } x \ qv \ ...)$$
$$qv ::= (? \ x \ rty \ q\text{-}eltv \ ...)$$
$$q\text{-}eltv ::= \text{string}$$
$$TE ::= SeqE$$
$$SeqE ::= [\,]_{\text{seq}} \mid (\text{seq } r \ ... \ PE \ s\text{-}elt \ ...)$$
$$PE ::= [\,]_{\text{page}} \mid SeqE \mid (\text{page } x \ qv \ ... \ QE \ q \ ...)$$
$$QE ::= [\,]_{\text{q}}$$

$$TE_1[\,(\text{page } x_1 \ (? \ x_q \ rty_q \ q\text{-}eltv_q \ ...) \ ...)\,]_{\text{page}} \longrightarrow \quad (\text{page response})$$
$$TE_1[\,(\text{response } x_1 \ (x_q \ rty_q \ A[\![\,(x_1 \ (? \ x_q \ rty_q \ q\text{-}eltv_q \ ...))\,]\!]\,) \ ...)\,]_{\text{page}}$$

$$TE_1[\,(\text{seq } r_1 \ ...)\,]_{\text{seq}} \longrightarrow \qquad\qquad\qquad (\text{seq demotion 1})$$
$$TE_1[\,(r_1 \ ...)\,]_{\text{seq}}$$

$$TE_1[\,(\text{seq } r_1 \ ... \ (r_2 \ ...) \ s\text{-}elt_3 \ ...)\,]_{\text{seq}} \longrightarrow \qquad (\text{seq demotion 2})$$
$$TE_1[\,(\text{seq } r_1 \ ... \ r_2 \ ... \ s\text{-}elt_3 \ ...)\,]_{\text{seq}}$$

Figure 24.4: Base Topsl reductions

---

page element. A page element evaluation context is either a hole labeled page, corresponding to direct evaluation of a page by the (page response) reduction (explained below) or evaluation of a page element. While the evaluation contexts further subdivide pages, allowing left-to-right evaluation of page elements by use of a hole q, these productions are not yet useful because there are no reductions that make use of them.

The reductions themselves are very simple. Rule (page response) represents a survey participant answering a page; we model that participant as an unspecified relation A (for "answers") that maps a question and the ID of the page it came from to an answer of the appropriate result type (string for free response questions, number between 1 and 7 for Likert-type questions). It is important that A can be a general relation, rather than needing to be a function, to represent the fact that the same question can be freely answered in many different ways.

With all these rules in place, surveys do something quite simple: from left to right, the rewriting system applies the page response rule and the two demotion rules, which do nothing but flatten nested responses. These rules successively replace each page of questions with a response, flattening response sequences as it goes, until the entire survey has been rewritten into a single, flat answer sequence which we interpret as the survey's final result.

Theorem 24.1 (base Topsl safety). *For each survey cs in base Topsl, cs* $\longmapsto^*$ *(r . . .).*

Proof. Similar to standard type-soundness theorems, though here preservation is trivial and only progress (*i.e.*, that every term either reduces to another term or is an element of $(r \ldots)$) needs to be established. This holds by induction on the structure of the term.   □

Furthermore, static analysis of the flavor we described in section 24.2 is extremely simple: all pages and all questions asked during the execution of the survey must correspond to some page that syntactically appears in the source survey term.

Definition 24.2 (Topsl contexts). An unrestricted Topsl context, written *TC*, is a Topsl term with a hole in an arbitrary position.

With this definition in place, we establish the first of what we call our "analysis theorems," theorems that give us a simple, sound static analysis technique; the analysis theorem is the critical property we need to hold for all of the languages we introduce in order for static analysis to work. Theorem 24.3 is the simplest of these theorems; it establishes the entirely straightforward fact that under the semantics we have defined, if during execution the survey asks a question, that question appeared textually in the original source code.

Theorem 24.3 (base Topsl analysis). *For each survey cs in base Topsl, if cs* $\longmapsto^*$ *TE*$[(\textbf{page } x_p \ (? \ x_q \ rty \ qv \ldots) \ldots)]$ *then there exists some context TC such that* $cs = TC[(\textbf{page } x_p \ (? \ x_q \ rty \ qv \ldots) \ldots)]$.

Proof. It suffices to show the related claim that if $cs \longmapsto TC[(\textbf{page } x_p \ (? \ x_q \ rty \ qv \ldots) \ldots)]$ for any *TC* then there exists some context *TC′* such that $cs = TC'[(\textbf{page } x_p \ (? \ x_q \ rty \ qv \ldots) \ldots)]$. This holds by inspection of the reduction rules.   □

Because this theorem holds, we can implement static analysis for a given base Topsl survey very simply by just reading off every page that appears syntactically within it.

24·4 Imperative Topsl.

At this point, we can understand the final design we settled on in section 24.2 as an attempt to scale the language to more complex systems by adding new forms to base Topsl—a branch form, a binding form, and so on. We take this as our departure point from that solution. Instead, we will explore the possibility of making Topsl as small as possible, letting programmers reuse Scheme's flow control and binding constructs instead of building new, redundant ones. By taking a semantic approach, we can (for the moment) ignore the problems we described in the obvious implementation strategy. We proceed in two steps. First, we define

$$complete\text{-}survey ::= ((survey: s) (answers: a))$$
$$TE ::= ((survey: SeqE) (answers: a))$$

$((survey: PE_1[(page\ x_1\ (?\ x_q\ rty_q\ q\text{-}eltv_q\ ...)\ ...)]_{page}) \longrightarrow$ (page response)
$\quad (answers: (r_1\ ...)))$
$((survey: PE_1[(response\ x_1\ answer\ ...)]_{page})$
$\quad (answers: (r_1\ ...\ (response\ x_1\ answer\ ...))))$
$\qquad where\ (answer\ ...) = (term\ A[(page\ x_1\ (?\ x_q\ rty_q\ q\text{-}eltv_q\ ...)\ ...)])$
$TE_1[(seq\ r_1\ ...)]_{seq} \longrightarrow$ (seq demotion 1)
$TE_1[(r_1\ ...)]_{seq}$
$TE_1[(seq\ r_1\ ...\ (r_2\ ...)\ s\text{-}elt_3\ ...)]_{seq} \longrightarrow$ (seq demotion 2)
$TE_1[(seq\ r_1\ ...\ r_2\ ...\ s\text{-}elt_3\ ...)]_{seq}$

Figure 24.5: Figures 24.3 and 24.4 modified for imperative Topsl

---

imperative Topsl, a variant on base Topsl that stores page results in a global store in addition to returning them as values. Second, we use the technical devices introduced by that refinement to make a convenient Scheme interface; with the Scheme interface in place, we can use its native control-flow and binding constructs rather than needing to implement special-purpose forms for Topsl.

Figure 24.5 shows how we extend base Topsl to form imperative Topsl. Only two nonterminals need to change. First, a complete survey must now consist of two parts: a program and an accumulated store of results with the invariant that all pages that have been asked and answered during a survey's execution have their results contained in this store. Second, the top-level evaluation context must now allow for the store as well.

The changes to base Topsl's reduction rules are similarly small. The only rule that differs from its base Topsl counterpart is (page response), which now puts the participant's answers in the survey's top-level results section in addition to making it the result of a page's evaluation. (One might reasonably wonder at this point why we reduce a page to any meaningful value, rather than void or a unit value, since the results are stored in a global store anyway—more on this shortly.)

Those changes complete imperative Topsl. We can establish a straightforward soundness property for it: for any program, all responses that occur during a run are included in the store and all inclusions in the store (except those that were already in the store at the beginning of the program's execution) arise because they were responses to questions asked at some point. More formally, if a survey term reduces to a term that represents a page being asked and answered, then any further term to which it reduces will contain the supplied answer in its store, and similarly every answer contained in the store is the result of the survey asking a question that yielded that answer at some point.

Theorem 24.4 (Imperative Topsl consistency). *For any Topsl program plus store* $cs = ((survey: s) \, (answers: a))$ *and any* $r \notin a$,

$$cs \mapsto^* TE[pv_i] \mapsto TE'[r] \mapsto^* ((survey: s') \, (answers: a'))$$

iff

$$a' \supseteq a + r$$

Proof. It suffices to prove the related claim that for all s, a, s', and a',

$$((survey: s) \, (answers: a)) \mapsto ((survey: s') \, (answers: a'))$$

holds if and only if either:

1. $a = a'$ and there do not exist any qv and r such that $s = TE[qv]$ and $s' = TE[r]$, and $a' = a, r$; or

2. there exists some qv and r such that $s = TE[qv]$, $s' = TE[r]$, and $a' = a, r$.

This claim holds by inspection of the cases of the reduction relation. Note that the restriction in the theorem statement that $r \notin a$ is necessary for the "only if" part of the theorem, because if the desired response is already in the response set in the initial term, then it will also appear in the final term even if it is never asked during the rest of the survey's execution. □

In addition, we prove that any question that is asked during any execution of a survey appeared textually in the survey's source.

Theorem 24.5 (Imperative Topsl analysis). *For each complete survey* cs *in imperative Topsl, if* $cs \mapsto^* TE[(\textbf{page}\, x_p \, (?\, x_q \, rty \, qv \ldots) \ldots)]$ *then there exists some context* TC *such that* $cs = TC[(\textbf{page}\, x_p \, (?\, x_q \, rty \, qv \ldots) \ldots)]$.

Proof. As the proof of theorem 24.3. □

24·5 **Topsl + Scheme.** At this point we can easily add Scheme constructs by introducing Scheme as a separate language that interacts with imperative Topsl through boundaries. (It is important that we use imperative Topsl rather than base Topsl for the embedding; otherwise any Scheme fragment that ran embedded Topsl code but did not return the answers produced would lose data.) First we define a model for a simple Scheme-like language; it is presented on its own in figure 24.6. The model

$$e ::= (e\ e) \mid x \mid (\text{if } e\ e\ e) \mid (\text{eq? } e\ e)$$
$$\mid (\lambda\ (x)\ e) \mid number \mid \text{string} \mid \text{\#t} \mid \text{\#f} \mid \text{null} \mid (\text{cons } e\ e) \mid \text{car} \mid \text{cdr}$$
$$v ::= (\lambda\ (x)\ e) \mid number \mid \text{string} \mid \text{\#t} \mid \text{\#f} \mid \text{null} \mid (\text{cons } v\ v) \mid \text{car} \mid \text{cdr}$$
$$SE ::= [\,]_S \mid (SE\ e) \mid (v\ SE) \mid (\text{eq? } SE\ e)$$
$$\mid (\text{eq? } v\ SE) \mid (\text{if } SE\ e\ e) \mid (\text{cons } SE\ e) \mid (\text{cons } v\ SE)$$

$$TE_1[((\lambda\ (x_1)\ e_1)\ v_1)]_S \longrightarrow \quad \text{(beta)}$$
$$TE_1[\text{SUBST}[[(x_1\ v_1\ e_1)]]\ ]_S$$
$$TE_1[(\text{if \#f } e_1\ e_2)]_S \longrightarrow \quad \text{(if \#f)}$$
$$TE_1[e_2]_S$$
$$TE_1[(\text{if } v_1\ e_1\ e_2)]_S \longrightarrow \quad \text{(if \#t)}$$
$$TE_1[e_1]_S$$
$$\text{where } v_1 \neq \text{\#f}$$
$$TE_1[(\text{eq? } v_1\ v_1)]_S \longrightarrow \quad \text{(eq? \#t)}$$
$$TE_1[\text{\#t}]_S$$
$$TE_1[(\text{eq? } v_1\ v_2)]_S \longrightarrow \quad \text{(eq? \#f)}$$
$$TE_1[\text{\#f}]_S$$
$$\text{where } v_1 \neq v_2$$
$$TE_1[(\text{car} (\text{cons } v_1\ v_2))]_S \longrightarrow \quad \text{(car)}$$
$$TE_1[v_1]_S$$
$$TE_1[(\text{cdr} (\text{cons } v_1\ v_2))]_S \longrightarrow \quad \text{(cdr)}$$
$$TE_1[v_2]_S$$

Figure 24.6: Simple Scheme model

we have chosen is just the call-by-value λ-calculus extended with booleans, numbers, strings, and cons cells as base values and if and eq? as new syntactic forms. Its grammar, evalation contexts, and reductions are standard with the exception that we use a hole S for holes in which Scheme reductions may occur, and we use a TE top-level evaluation context rather than an SE evaluation context in the definitions of our reduction rules because in a multi-language setting Scheme evaluation now occurs within Topsl programs, whose top-level is not Scheme (we discuss this point in more detail in prior work [74]).

With Scheme defined, we can consider how to define appropriate boundaries between it and the imperative Topsl language. Figure 24.7 shows extensions to the grammars of our models of Scheme and imperative Topsl to add cross-language boundaries, and figure 24.8 shows the new reduction rules. There are two essential extensions: a survey element may now be a TS ("Topsl-to-Scheme") boundary—in other words, a syntactic marker that indicates a switch from Topsl to Scheme— which allows Topsl to run a Scheme expression that can perform arbitrary computation, and an ST ("Scheme-to-

$$
\begin{aligned}
s &::= \quad .... \mid (\text{TS Ans } e) \\
q\text{-}elt &::= \quad .... \mid (\text{TS str } e) \\
SeqE &::= \quad .... \mid (\text{TS Ans } SE) \\
QEltE &::= \quad .... \mid (\text{TS str } SE)
\end{aligned}
$$

$$
\begin{aligned}
e &::= \quad .... \mid (\text{ST } \tau\ s) \\
v &::= \quad .... \mid (\text{ST Ans } a) \\
\tau &::= \quad (\text{from } x\ x) \mid \text{Ans}
\end{aligned}
$$

$$
\begin{aligned}
SeqE &::= \quad .... \mid (\text{TS Ans } SE) \\
QEltE &::= \quad .... \mid (\text{TS str } SE) \\
SE &::= \quad .... \mid (\text{ST } \tau\ SeqE)
\end{aligned}
$$

Figure 24.7: Extensions to figures 24.5 and 24.6 to form Topsl + Scheme grammar

Topsl") boundary that allows Scheme to call back into Topsl to ask further questions.

TS boundaries may appear in two different places in Topsl code: first, they may be survey elements, in which case the Scheme value produced will be converted to an answer by one of the (TS ans) rules. Since all answers are recorded whenever they are submitted, it is not particularly important for a Scheme fragment that asks questions to gather up all of its answers and return them here. In fact, generally speaking, Scheme code will not return any particularly useful answer and the default empty answer sequence produced by rule (TS ans 2) (which converts any non-answer value that Scheme produces to an empty answer sequence) will appear here, though if Scheme wants to return a particular answer sequence it may do so using rule (TS ans 1) (which converts Scheme answer values to their Topsl representations). Second, they appear as question elements (where in base and imperative Topsl only strings were allowed), in which case Scheme's result will be converted to a string by rule (TS question). This feature allows us to make questions whose text varies programmatically based on runtime input but that are still amenable to static analysis in the sense that we can separate out the parts of a question that never change from those that depend on "survey-taking time" computation. (We will revisit the other kind of programmatically generated questions we identified in section 24.2, questions that are programmatically generated purely to take advantage of abstraction to factor out common patterns, in section 24.7.) Notice here that since we were careful to make a distinction between question elements and question element values, and between questions and question values in base Topsl, we do not have to rework those definitions here. Instead we can simply extend what constitutes a ques-

$$TE_1[\![(\text{TS str } \textit{string}_1)]\!]_{\text{qelt}} \longrightarrow \quad (\text{TS question})$$
$$TE_1[\![\textit{string}_1]\!]_{\text{qelt}}$$

$$TE_1[\![(\text{TS Ans } (\text{ST Ans } a_1))]\!]_{\text{seq}} \longrightarrow \quad (\text{TS ans 1})$$
$$TE_1[\![a_1]\!]_{\text{seq}}$$

$$TE_1[\![(\text{TS Ans } v_1)]\!]_{\text{seq}} \longrightarrow \quad (\text{TS ans 2})$$
$$TE_1[\![(\,)]\!]_{\text{seq}}$$
$$\text{where } v_1 \neq (\text{ST Ans } a) \text{ for any } a$$

$$TE_1[\![(\text{ST (from } x_1 \ x_3) \qquad\qquad\qquad \longrightarrow \quad (\text{ST from})$$
$$\qquad (r \ ...$$
$$\qquad\quad (\text{response } x_1$$
$$\qquad\qquad\qquad (x_2 \ \textit{rty}_2 \ \textit{ans}_2) \ ...$$
$$\qquad\qquad\qquad (x_3 \ \textit{rty}_3 \ \textit{ans}_3)$$
$$\qquad\qquad\qquad (x_4 \ \textit{rty}_4 \ \textit{ans}_4) \ ...)$$
$$\qquad r \ ...))]\!]_{\text{s}}$$
$$TE_1[\![\textit{ans}_3]\!]_{\text{s}}$$

Figure 24.8: Topsl + Scheme boundary reduction rules

---

tion without extending what constitutes a question value, and the rest of the system, including the reduction rules we have already written, is able to properly distinguish between questions with unevaluated portions and those that are fully evaluated.

ST boundaries can appear in Scheme as normal expressions, each of which is intended to evaluate the survey element to an answer. They may be annotated with either of two different conversion strategies (identified by the τ nonterminal), either (from x_p x_a) or Ans. A boundary with conversion strategy (from x_p x_a) evaluates the embedded Topsl program to an answer sequence, then finds the answer to the question x_a on the page named x_p in that answer sequence and returns the answer to the question named x_a on that page as a string or number as appropriate to the question. (It is an error to select the answer from a page if that page is represented multiple times in the same answer sequence.) A boundary with conversion strategy Ans also evaluates its embedded survey element to an answer sequence, but then simply holds it in its entirety as a Scheme value. These two conversion strategies work together to allow a Scheme program to extract multiple values from the same page: for instance (relying on **let** and *max*, two very straightforward extensions to our Scheme model), the Scheme fragment

```
(let ((a (ST (page p (? likert q₁ ...) (? likert q₂ ...))))))
   (max (ST (from p q₁) (TS Ans a))
            (ST (from p q₁) (TS Ans a))))
```

extracts the answers to both q_1 and q_2 from the same answer sequence and computes their maximum. More generally, in this model we can consider the **bind** mechanism we discussed in section 24.2 as syntactic sugar: (**bind** ((($[x_p$ $x_q]$ ...) s) e) becomes

```
(let ((ans (ST Ans s)))
   (let ((x_q (ST (from x_p x_q) (TS Ans ans))) ... )
      e))
```

Many other idioms are conveniently expressible in this language as well. For instance, a branching survey can be written using Scheme's **if**:

```
(let ((pivot (ST (from x_p xpivot) s)))
   (if (eq? pivot [some value])
      s1
      s2))
```

A survey that iterates over arbitrary input is also easy to build:

```
(let ((strings [arbitrary Scheme computation]))
   (for-each
      (lambda (s) (ST Ans (page P (? free "question about " (TS str s)))))
      strings))
```

In fact, at this point the system is sufficiently powerful to express the entire survey suggested by figure 24.1. Figure 24.9 is a sketch of how it would be implemented.

Since we record the answers to every question on every page in a global register, we could have designed a different semantics for *from* that drew from that global store and ignored the answer sequence provided by Topsl altogether. We chose this design instead because we like to think of Topsl programs as essentially functional programs that have an imperative backup system that programmers trust to save answers but otherwise ignore. In practical terms, we expect that because of this decision a Topsl programmer will have to reason not about the global state of a survey ("Am I guaranteed that page p1 has been asked at this point?") which depends on whole-program reasoning, but instead only about its local value flow ("Must the expression inside this boundary evaluate to an answer sequence that includes page p1?"), which is a local property.

Owing to the unrestricted computation Scheme allows, this combined language is powerful enough to let us create surveys that loop and have interesting runtime behavior without giving up on the guarantees we want. In fact, the consistency theorem does not need to be changed at all:

```
;; gets initials of person the participant reported seeing last week; #f if none
(define (get-last-partner-inits-from-db participant) ··· )

;; gets initials of all previous partners of the given participant
(define (get-all-partners name) ··· )

;; gets initials of person the participant reported seeing last week; #f if none
(define (get-last-partner-inits-from-db participant) ··· )

;; gets the initials of all previous partners of the given participant
(define (get-all-partners name) ··· )
(define (general-set)
  (ST Ans (page Set1
                (? free name "Your name?")
                (? yes/no seeing-anyone? "Currently seeing anyone?")
                (? free partner-inits "Current partner's intials?"))))
(define (no-breakup-set) (ST Ans ··· ))
(define (breakup-set) (ST Ans ··· ))
(define (new-relationship-set) (ST Ans ··· ))
(define (ex-relationship name) (ST Ans ··· ))

(bind ([[(Set1 name)
         (Set1 seeing-anyone?)
         (Set1 partner-inits)]
        (general-set))
  (let ((old-partner-inits (get-last-partner-inits-from-db name)))
    (cond [(and seeing-anyone? (eq? old-partner-inits partner-inits))
           (no-breakup-set)]
          [(and seeing-anyone? (not (eq? old-partner-inits partner-inits)))
           (breakup-set)
           (new-relationship-set)]
          [(and (not seeing-anyone?) old-partner-inits)
           (breakup-set)]
          [(and (not seeing-anyone?) (not old-partner-inits)) (void)]))
    (for-each ex-relationship (get-all-partners name)))
```

Figure 24.9: Sketch implementation of the survey described in figure 24.1

Theorem 24.6 (Topsl + Scheme consistency). *For any Topsl + Scheme program* $cs = ((survey{:}\, s)\ (answers{:}\, a))$ *where* $r \notin a$,

$$cs \mapsto^* TE[pv_i] \mapsto TE'[r] \mapsto^* ((survey{:}\, s')\ (answers{:}\, a'))$$

if and only if $a' \supseteq a + r$.

Proof. As the proof of theorem 24.4.   □

The analysis theorem needs to be weakened slightly, because Topsl questions may now contain Scheme code that evaluates to an arbitrary string at runtime rather than appearing literally in the source. So, instead of demanding that any question asked a runtime appear literally in the source text, we demand that some source question *describes* any question posed at runtime.

Definition 24.7. The describes relation holds if:

- (**page** $x_p\ q_1\ \ldots\ q_n$) describes (**page** $x_p'\ q_1'\ \ldots\ q_m$) if $x_p = x_p'$, $n = m$, and for each $i \in \{1 \ldots n\}$, q_i describes q_i'.

- (? $x_q'\ rty\ q\text{-}elt_1\ \ldots\ q\text{-}elt_n$) describes (? $x_q'\ rty'\ q\text{-}elt_1'\ \ldots\ q\text{-}elt_m'$) if $x_q = x_q'$, $rty = rty'$, $n = m$, and for each $i \in \{1 \ldots n\}$, if $q - elt_i = str$ for any string str, then $q - elt_i' = str$.

Theorem 24.8 (Topsl + Scheme analysis). *For each complete survey cs in imperative Topsl, if* $cs \mapsto^* TE[pv]$ *then there exists some context TC such that* $cs = TC[p]$ *and p describes pv.*

Proof. As the proof of theorem 24.3.   □

24·6 Web Topsl.
Up to this point, we have only been dealing with sequential surveys. This is a reasonable model for surveys that take place in person or over the phone. It is not, however, a good model of our intended application domain, surveys conducted over the web, because web users may use the back button or clone browser windows and submit answers multiple times to the same page of questions. These features are of particular concern to us because they correspond to re-entering a continuation, and since our Topsl + Scheme model makes important use of state we are obligated to extend it in such a way that submitting a page twice does not violate our assumptions about that state.

To do so, we borrow aspects of the webL model of client/server web interaction [49, 63], adapting it and paring it down as we go to focus on the aspects of web interaction that concern us here. In particular, webL models the client as well as the server; since we are not interested in the client, we

$$
\begin{aligned}
\textit{complete-survey} ::= &\ ((\text{survey: } s) \\
&\ (\text{answers: } a) \\
&\ (\text{resumption-points: } (\textit{rp} \dots))) \\
\textit{rp} ::= &\ (\textit{pv } s\ a) \\
\textit{TE} ::= &\ ((\text{survey: } \textit{SeqE}) \\
&\ (\text{answers: } a) \\
&\ (\text{resumption-points: } (\textit{rp} \dots)))
\end{aligned}
$$

Figure 24.10: Modifications to figure 24.7 to form web Topsl grammar

replace it with a rule that nondeterministically chooses to submit answers to any survey page it has seen.

Concretely, we extend a complete survey so that in addition to a survey program and a list of answers already recorded, it also holds a set of resumption points, as shown in figure 24.10. Conceptually, a resumption point is a "save point" in a survey; it contains the entire state of the survey saved at the moment the survey sent a particular page of questions to the participant, which is necessary to back up the survey exactly where it left off when (and if) the participant submits answers to that page. Each resumption point (rp) contains three items: the first, pv, represents the page value sent to the participant. The second, s, is the code representing the continuation to run should the user submit answers. The third, a, is a record of the current value of answers at the point when the program sent this page to the participant. To understand its role, it is helpful to look at web Topsl's reduction rules; see figure 24.11.

Web Topsl adds two reduction rules beyond the ones we have seen before. Essentially, they break the process of asking and answering a question into two reductions: (page to web) for asking questions and (web to page) for answering them. The former applies as before whenever a page appears in an evaluation context. However, instead of rewriting directly to an answer, it rewrites to a new configuration in which there is no survey or current sequence of answers, only the set of resumption points. Furthermore, to that set of resumption points it adds a new one corresponding to the page just asked; the new point has the page to ask, the evaluation context in which the page appeared (which corresponds to its continuation [37]). No reduction rules apply to this configuration except (web to page).

The (web to page) rule selects a resumption point arbitrarily, chooses some arbitrary set of answers to the questions on the page it represents, and then starts the survey running again, restoring the suspended evaluation context and replacing its hole with those answers. Furthermore, it sets answers: to be the answers sequence stored by the selected resumption point. By fol-

$$((\text{survey: } PE_{\text{l}}[(\text{page } x_1 (? x_{\text{q}} rty_{\text{q}} q\text{-}eltv_{\text{q}} \ldots) \ldots)]_{\text{page}}) \longrightarrow \quad (\text{page to web})$$
$$(\text{answers: } (r_1 \ldots))$$
$$(\text{resumption-points: } (rp_1 \ldots)))$$
$$(\text{resumption-points: } (rp_1 \ldots$$
$$((\text{page } x_1 (? x_{\text{q}} rty_{\text{q}} q\text{-}eltv_{\text{q}} \ldots) \ldots)$$
$$PE_{\text{l}}[(\text{TS Ans } x)]$$
$$(r_1 \ldots))))$$

where x fresh

$$(\text{resumption-points: } (rp_1 \ldots \qquad\qquad \longrightarrow \quad (\text{web to page})$$
$$((\text{page } x_i (? x_{\text{q}} rty_{\text{q}} q\text{-}eltv_{\text{q}} \ldots) \ldots)$$
$$PE_{\text{l}}[(\text{TS Ans } x_k)]_{\text{page}}$$
$$(r_{i1} \ldots))$$
$$rp_{i+1} \ldots))$$
$$((\text{survey: } PE_{\text{l}}[(\text{response } x_i (x_{\text{q}} rty_{\text{q}} \text{A}[[(x_i (? x_{\text{q}} rty_{\text{q}} q\text{-}eltv_{\text{q}} \ldots))]]) \ldots)]_{\text{page}})$$
$$(\text{answers: } (r_{i1} \ldots (\text{response } x_i (x_{\text{q}} rty_{\text{q}} \text{A}[[(x_i (? x_{\text{q}} rty_{\text{q}} q\text{-}eltv_{\text{q}} \ldots))]]) \ldots)))$$
$$(\text{resumption-points: } (rp_1 \ldots$$
$$((\text{page } x_i (? x_{\text{q}} rty_{\text{q}} q\text{-}eltv_{\text{q}} \ldots) \ldots)$$
$$PE_{\text{l}}[(\text{TS Ans } x_k)]$$
$$(r_{i1} \ldots))$$
$$rp_{i+1} \ldots)))$$

Figure 24.11: Web Topsl reductions

lowing this procedure, the reduction rules maintain the invariant that the answers sequence in answers: always corresponds to some sequential path through the program, or, more precisely, to a state that could be reached by an interaction with the same survey run with sequential Topsl + Scheme semantics.

Definition 24.9.

$$s_1 \mapsto_{st} s_2 \quad\overset{\text{def}}{=}\quad s_1 \mapsto s_2 \text{ under the rules of section 24.5}$$
$$s_1 \mapsto_{wt} s_2 \quad\overset{\text{def}}{=}\quad s_1 \mapsto s_2 \text{ under the rules of section 24.6}$$

Theorem 24.10 (web Topsl coherence). *For any survey element s, if*

$$((\text{survey: } s) (\text{answers: } ()) (\text{resumption-points: } ()))$$
$$\mapsto^*_{wt} ((\text{survey: } s') (\text{answers: } a) (\text{resumption-points: } (rp \ldots)))$$

then there exists some s'' such that

$$((\text{survey: } s) (\text{answers: } ()))$$
$$\mapsto^*_{ts} ((\text{survey: } s'') (\text{answers: } a))$$

This theorem's proof is slightly more complicated than the proofs of prior theorems. First, we observe that all web Topsl reduction sequences that do not involve the (page to web) or (web to page) reduction rules correspond to reduction sequences in Topsl + Scheme:

Lemma 24.11. *If*

$$\mapsto^*_{wt} \quad \begin{array}{l} ((\textit{survey: } s) \ (\textit{answers: } a) \ (\textit{resumption-points: } (rp \ \ldots)) \\ ((\textit{survey: } s') \ (\textit{answers: } a') \ (\textit{resumption-points: } (rp \ldots))) \end{array}$$

and no reduction used in the reduction sequence is generated by (page to web) or (web to page), $((\textit{survey: } s) \ (\textit{answers: } a)) \mapsto^*_{ts} ((\textit{survey: } s') \ (\textit{answers: } a'))$.

Proof. By induction on the length of the reduction sequence. The base case is immediate; for the inductive case, observe that each rule $\mapsto_{wt}$ other than the two excluded rules is also present in $\mapsto_{ts}$. □

Using this lemma we can establish that any resumption point contains an answer sequence and a continuation that could be found on a valid Topsl + Scheme reduction sequence.

Lemma 24.12. *Suppose*

$$\mapsto^*_{wt} \quad \begin{array}{l} ((\textit{survey: } s) \ (\textit{answers: } ()) \ (\textit{resumption-points: } ()) \\ ((\textit{survey: } s') \ (\textit{answers: } a) \ (\textit{resumption-points: } (rp_1 \ldots rp_n))) \end{array}$$

Then for each $i \in \{1 \ldots n\}$, if $rp_i = (pv_i \ s_i \ a_i)$ then

$$\mapsto^*_{ts} \quad \begin{array}{l} ((\textit{survey: } s) \ (\textit{answers: } ()) \\ ((\textit{survey: } TE_i[pv_i]) \ (\textit{answers: } a_i)) \end{array}$$

where $TE_i[(\textbf{TS Ans } x)] = s_i$.

Proof. Observe that since each reduction using rule (page to web) increases the number of resumption points in the subsequent term by exactly one and no other rules modify resumption points, the number of resumption points in any term in the sequence is equal to the number of uses of the rule (page to web) in the subsequence that precedes it. Now we can use induction on the number of such uses in the reduction sequence. If it is zero, the theorem trivially holds. Otherwise, consider subsequence that ends with the last use of (page to web) and begins with the rightmost use of (web to page) that precedes it (or the beginning of the entire sequence if no use of (web to page) precedes it). By induction, that use of (web to page) restores some resumption point — say, $(pv_i \ s_i \ a_i)$—that corresponds to a sequential trace. Furthermore, by inspection the contents of the survey: and answers: fields in the term produced by rule (web to page) correspond to a step from

$((\text{survey: } TE_i[pv_i]) \, (\text{answers: } a_i))$ using the Topsl + Scheme rule (page response).

Now, by appealing to lemma 24.11 and the straightforward fact that Topsl + Scheme reduction sequences compose, we have that the term immediately to the left of the last use of the rule (page to web) corresponds to an Topsl + Scheme sequence. Thus, the resumption point (web to page) adds has the desired property; by induction all the others do as well, so the lemma holds.   □

Now the proof of the main theorem is straightforward:

Proof. Consider the last use of rule (page to web) in the reduction sequence. By lemma 24.12, that use results in a term that corresponds to a legal Topsl + Scheme reduction sequence. Then the theorem holds by application of lemma 24.11 to that term and the final term in the sequence.   □

Theorem 24.13 (web Topsl analysis). *For each complete survey cs in web Topsl, if cs $\longmapsto^*$ TE[pv] then there exists some context TC such that cs = TC[p] and p describes pv.*

Proof. As the proof of theorem 24.3.   □

24.7 User + Core Topsl.

At this point we have established some reasonable safety properties for a language that seems reasonably close to what we had in mind from the outset. The one feature on our desiderata that we have not yet modeled is the ability to programmatically generate questions purely so that we can abstract out repeated question patterns. In fact we will not do so at all. By using Scheme as our host language and decomposing the problem as we have in the previous sections, we have made such a feature unnecessary.

As the analysis theorems have shown, it is sound for our static analysis to consist of simply reading out every page that syntactically occurs in the initial web Topsl source term. However, since we are embedding our survey language in Scheme and thus have access to its rich macro system, we are free to use them to programmatically compute the Topsl source code itself at compile time. The analysis theorems along with our ability to compute dynamic text for questions using boundaries draws a bright line: questions generated by abstractions for convenience that should appear separately in static analysis must be computed at compile time using macros, and questions generated by abstractions in order to account for information acquired at run time must be generated by boundaries.

We call this the line between user Topsl and core Topsl. User Topsl is a version of Topsl that a programmer will actually interact with, and it allows arbitrary computation in generating a survey to allow the programmer to abstract commonalities in questions or to do anything else he or she wants to do; for instance, to automatically generate unique page and question names for the dozens or hundreds of pages and questions that do not play any special role in computation and whose names are thus a nuisance to have to write by hand. When a user Topsl program is executed, it does not go to the web or do any interaction with a user; instead, it produces a core Topsl program. A core Topsl program is a Topsl program as in the previous sections; all of its static computation has already been performed and it can be statically analyzed or executed to interact with a survey participant.

For instance, a survey writer might want to abstract out common patterns in asking questions while still having all the computed questions appear in the survey's static summary. For this purpose, regular Scheme functions are unsuitable: for one thing, it is not grammatically possible in the language we have defined for questions to appear outside the lexical context of a page, and for another, even if it were possible, those questions would not be able to appear in the survey's static summary, because they would not be computed until after the static summary were already final. So instead, the programmer can compute them before runtime the same way Scheme programmers always compute things before runtime, using macros. Here, for instance, is how a programmer could abstract a series of two related questions:

```
(define-syntax related-questions
  (syntax-rules ()
    [(related-questions (id1 id2) shared-text)
     (begin
       (? free id1 shared-text)
       (? free id2 shared-text " ... part 2"))]))
```

This macro can be used like any Scheme macro:

```
(page P
   ...
  (related-questions (q1 q2) "shared text 1")
  (related-questions (q3 q4) "shared text 2")
  ...)
```

As this example shows, our method allows Topsl to reuse Scheme's macro facilities in a meaningful manner for survey construction in the same way it connects Scheme control and binding mechanisms to intuitively similar survey tasks. This is not automatic, and in fact it did not hold of our previous design: just as new Scheme binding and control constructs could not be used to extend Topsl survey binding and control, Scheme macros had no particularly useful interaction with static analysis.

$24{\cdot}8$ **Using PLT Redex.** We have implemented all of the reduction systems discussed in the preceeding sections as PLT Redex programs. This presents an unusual challenge, since PLT Redex is designed to be good at nondeterministically matching input terms against patterns and infinitely long chains of reductions, but not to be good at handling rules that nondeterministically select different outputs based on the same input or reductions in which a term reduces in a single step to infinitely many successors.

Our semantics depend on both kinds of nondeterminism. They use the former to represent a survey participant's ability to go back to any previously asked web page and resubmit answers (see the ambiguous evaluation context grammar in the web-to-page rule in figure 24.11), and the latter to represent the participant's ability to answer any question with an arbitrary response (via the unspecified A relation). For that reason, we have to make a compromise to implement our semantics as Redex programs by giving a concrete, function representation for A.

Here we have a few choices. The first and easiest option is to make A a constant function that maps every question to a constant dummy answer. This is actually more effective than it might at first seem, since when we design test cases we can arrange to test all of the rules of the operational semantics by knowing what the dummy variables are, and most automated tests that we might want to perform do not depend critically on particular answer values anyway.

The second option is a variant on the first: rather than using a single constant function, design a test harness that reruns the same test case with many different functions for A in successive runs. By changing A itself rather than working around it behaving like a constant, we can directly test programs that do interesting things based on the answers to a question. It is also useful to have a function that returns two different answers to the same question during the same test, for instance to test the web coherence property (theorem 24.10). Since PLT Redex is embedded in PLT Scheme, we are not really limited to pure mathematical functions for our implementation of A—we can use any Scheme function we like—so we can use state in conjunction with this strategy to make functions that behave this way.

The final option we have explored is to exploit the connection between PLT Redex in PLT Scheme even further by having the A function present the user with a page of questions and take his or her answers as its result. Since this option requires user supervision, it is not a good choice for automatic

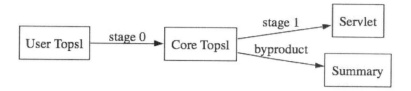

Figure 24.12: Macro-expansion stages for combining static analysis with question abstraction

---

testing, but it works well as an interactive frontend for experimenting. In fact, by using the PLT web server we can even have the user interact with Redex through a web browser, making our model of Topsl into a makeshift implementation, providing an excellent sense of how the language might work in practice.

24·9 Implementation.
After languishing for a year and a half, our Topsl implementation effort has been revitalized due to the semantic exploration of the last section, which we conducted by building and refining PLT Redex models. The analysis in section 24.7 indicates our overall compilation strategy, which we have summarized in figure 24.12: a user Topsl program is a module that compiles down to a core Topsl program, which in turn compiles to a PLT Scheme web server-compatible servlet that additionally provides static analysis information.

Static Analysis. We perform the static analysis when transforming a core Topsl program into a servlet. A sound and simple static analysis technique is to record the compilation of each **page** and **?** form that appears in a survey, generating a list of all pages and questions that textually appear anywhere. Because of the way we have built the language, and in particular because it satisfies the static analysis theorems (theorems 24.3, 24.5, 24.8, and 24.13), we know this method is sound.

Imperative State. The implementation-analogue of our models' answers: sections is less obvious. Here again, though, formal methods indicate a simple solution: as long as a survey saves the current answers sequence with the continuation whenever it asks the participant to respond to a page, restores that saved answers sequence when it returns, the current answers sequence will remain consistent with sequential ordering. So the following implementation sketch has the proper behavior, which we hope the reader will appreciate our calling the "caller-save strategy" in analogy to the assembly-level function calling convention it resembles:

```
(define *current-answers* '())
(define (ask-page p)
  (let ((saved-current-answers *current-answers*))
    (let ((results (request→results
                      (send/suspend (html-derived-from-page p)))))
      (begin
        (set! *current-answers* (cons results saved-current-answers))
        results))))
```

In fact, at one point we used this strategy. However, recent versions of the PLT Scheme web server have introduced a more general facility called web cells [75] that serve our purpose; the current implementation uses those instead.

Our implementation effort is ongoing, particularly with regard to user Topsl. However, preliminary results are very encouraging: when we rewrote our existing implementation using the new design, we were able to reduce the total size of the implementation by a third (1410 lines versus 2198) while continuing to be able to run a large, complicated survey that had been developed and deployed for use in a psychologist's research project.

24·10 Related Work.

There are many mechanisms for creating online surveys apart from implementing them in a general-purpose language. In particular, two domain-specific languages, SuML [7] and QPL [110], stand out as being the closest to the goals the authors set for Topsl.

SuML is an XML/Perl-based survey language in which the programmer describes a survey in an XML document that follows the SuML Schema. The SuML Schema has a *question* element that contains question text and a sequence of allowable responses, much like Topsl. The root *survey* element contains any number of questions and a *routing* element that describes control flow. The *routing* element contains any number of **if** and *ask* elements that are composed to ask questions in the survey and branch on their responses.

The programmer creates two files in addition to the content of the survey: an XSLT stylesheet and a front-end Perl CGI program. The style sheet is responsible for describing what a survey will look like when presented on the web to a participant, and multiple stylesheets can be written for different media. The front end is a Perl CGI program that acts as the entry point to the survey.

SuML's most significant problem, for our purposes, is that owing to its need for static analysis, its notion of control-flow is limited, providing its users with only an **if** statement with which to branch to different parts of the survey. Furthermore, the test position of the **if** is written in a domain-specific language that only allows access to the results of the current survey execution, which makes it unsuitable for longitudinal studies or other more exotic study designs.

In addition, SuML is somewhat too generic for our purposes. The user-written Perl CGI is in charge of driving the survey by using SuML's Perl API to get the next questions to be asked and then present them, as well as storing the results of the questions asked. Putting the burden on the programmer makes survey development more difficult, time-consuming, and error-prone.

QPL is another domain-specific language for creating surveys that offers static analysis by restricting what programmers can express, and as a result it suffers from problems similar to SuML's. QPL's semantics are reminiscent of BASIC: it is an imperative language using **if** and **goto** for control flow along with a large set of built-in predicates used for conditional testing. Current distributions provide users with a large set of comparison functions for use with **if**; however, it lacks any means of growing to meet programmers' changing needs.

Finally, Queinnec's library for quizzes [85] is similar to Topsl in that it provides a library of combinators for generating questionnaires in a high-level way, with implementation based on a continuation-based web server. Queinnec's library is quite a bit lighter-weight than Topsl and offers neither Topsl's safety guarantees nor its static analysis, but a design close to Queinnec's is probably appropriate for some lighter-weight social science surveys.

24·11 Conclusions.
In this chapter we have explained some surprising challenges in designing a robust language for writing online surveys suitable for use in social science research, and we have used a semantic approach to arrive at a design that we believe meets those challenges. Our intent has been two-fold: first, to report on an interesting problem domain for continuation-based web servers, but, second, to propose by example a semantic approach to thinking about embedded domain-specific languages. We put forth that it is worthwhile to depart from the traditional view of embedded domain-specific languages as a library of domain-specific combinators, and instead think of them as tiny multi-language systems. This lets us focus first on reasonable semantics, and then move over to implementation once we are sure that the language we are implementing behaves as we want.

Acknowledgments. Though this chapter was written by one person, it reflects the combined experience of three people gathered over the course of implementing three large psychology studies: Mike MacHenry and I implemented the Northwestern University Freshman Dating Study; I implemented the Northwestern University Speed Dating Study myself; and Dave Herman and Mike MacHenry implemented the George Mason University Repatriation Study. Mike and Dave's input has been essential. I would also like to thank Jeff Herman, Paul Eastwick, and especially Eli Finkel for entrusting their research to us.

25 · Prototyping Nested Schedulers
Mike Rainey, University of Chicago

Multicore processors expose many different forms of parallelism: SIMD instructions, simultaneous multi-threading, multiple cores and multiple chips. To utilize this type of parallelism, language implementations need sophisticated infrastructure for scheduling and process synchronization. Because scheduling and synchronization code contains many subtle protocols, however, it is especially prone to race conditions, deadlock, and other concurrency bugs. Concurrency bugs are notoriously hard to diagnose, in part, because actual language implementations are subject to outside forces. For instance, the OS scheduler prevents the majority of possible thread interleavings, thereby making it harder to detect concurrency bugs. For this and several other reasons, it is thus desirable to test some of our scheduling and synchronization code from within an abstract machine. In this chapter, we describe our efforts to prototype our scheduling and synchronization algorithms, using PLT Redex as a host for our abstract machine.

25.1 Introduction.
Commodity processor architects can no longer improve uniprocessor performance by increasing frequency or by increasing instruction-level parallelism. As a result, new multi-core processors are bringing parallelism to the masses. These processors support parallelism at multiple levels, including SIMD instructions, simultaneous multi-threading, multiple cores, and even multiple chips. Applications with the potential of utilizing multi-core processors, such as 3-d games and multimedia applications, exhibit parallelism at different granularities, often at the same time during execution. We refer to parallelism at multiple levels in hardware and different granularities in software as *heterogeneous parallelism*. Supporting heterogeneous parallelism requires mapping parallelism expressed in software efficiently onto hardware.

Programming languages need a variety of mechanisms to support heterogeneous parallelism. Consider, for example, a networked flight simulator.

Such an application might use data-parallel computations for particle systems to model natural phenomena such as rain, fog, and clouds. At the same time, it might use parallel threads to preload terrain data and compute level-of-detail refinements, and use SIMD parallelism in its physics simulations. Finally, it might also use explicit concurrency for user interface and network components. Programming these heterogeneous applications will be challenging without language support for different parallel programming mechanisms.

Compilers and runtime systems for heterogeneous languages must meet the diverse scheduling requirements of their different parallel mechanisms. Data-parallel computations need mechanisms to keep processors busy and to throttle parallelism when it is overabundant, e.g., workcrews [112]. On the other hand, threads need load balancing to encourage parallelism, e.g., work stealing [11, 16]. Threads also need timed preemption to simulate concurrency for GUI and network applications. When threads and data-parallel constructs coexist, the language must provide mechanisms for their scheduling policies to coordinate. For example, suppose a thread launches a data-parallel computation across several processors. Some of the data-parallel processes might be subject to timed preemption if they share a processor with other threads.

In previous work, we presented the design of a compiler and runtime-system framework for heterogeneous parallelism [43, 86]. This framework takes a microkernel approach with a minimal set of process abstractions and a small compiler internal representation (IR). This framework allows us to implement a wide variety of schedulers, supporting thread migration and asynchronous events like timed preemption. We also use this framework for rapidly developing and experimenting with different scheduling disciplines.

Implementing correct and efficient schedulers is a challenging task, as schedulers in our framework are low-level programs. They make heavy use of continuations and have only basic atomic operations for concurrency, e.g., compare-and-swap. Scheduler implementations must handle non-determinism from asynchronous events and from parallel execution, making them tricky to debug. To make matters worse, different scheduler implementations must run together, requiring further testing to check for composability.

Prototyping and debugging scheduler implementations in our production compiler can be difficult because

- bugs will often crash the entire application;

- tracing errors often requires stepping through assembly code; and

- implementation details, i.e., how the runtime handles asynchronous signals, can hide subtle bugs.

In this chapter, we ease these difficulties by building a prototyping and debugging framework for our scheduler language. This framework is based in
PLT Redex and contains a formal model of our scheduler language. Using
Redex, we can prototype scheduling code entirely in our formal model and
benefit from Redex's unit-testing framework and visualization support. There
are, however, challenges to using this framework effectively, and we discuss
those challenges and our solutions in detail in section 25.7.

This chapter proceeds as follows. In section 25.2, we present our scheduling framework. We present our formal model of this framework in section 25.3. We give two key scheduler examples in sections 25.5 and 25.6.
These examples demonstrate the power and expressiveness of our framework
but also demonstrate the subtleties of implementing schedulers. Finally, we
describe our prototyping framework in PLT Redex and experience prototyping schedulers.

25·2 Our Scheduling Framework. Process schedulers perform the
crucial duty of responding to an event, e.g., process termination
or preemption, and choosing the next process to run. Nested schedulers
are a natural extension of process schedulers in which a nested scheduler
inherits CPU cycles from its parent, and thus inherits its parent's scheduling
policy. Nested schedulers are known to improve modularity and simplify
development of complex scheduling regimes [90].

Our framework is a low-level substrate for programming nested schedulers and consists of a few process abstractions and a Scheme-like language
extended with new scheduling primitives. We treat schedulers and regular computations equally: both run as normal programs, except schedulers
make use of special control primitives. Despite this simplicity, our framework allows us to encode a wide variety of scheduling policies and parallel-
programming mechanisms in a single runtime environment. The novel aspect of our design is that we use nested schedulers as the glue for connecting
uniprocessor and multi-processor scheduling policies.

In this section, we first describe continuations as a building block for
concurrency. We then describe our process abstractions and our scheduling
primitives. Finally we give examples that show how to use this framework to
build mechanisms for concurrency and mechanisms for parallel dispatch.

Continuations. Continuations are a well-known language-level mechanism
for expressing concurrency [55, 91, 97, 113]. Continuations come in a number of different strengths or flavors.

1. *First-class* continuations, like those provided by Scheme and SML/NJ,
   have unconstrained lifetimes and may be used more than once.

2. *One-shot* continuations [14] have unconstrained lifetimes but may be used only once. In practice, most concurrency operations (but not thread creation) can be implemented using one-shot continuations.

3. *Escaping* continuations have a scope-limited lifetime and can only be used once, but they also can be used to implement many concurrency operations [38, 89].

Our scheduling framework works with any one of these kinds of continuations. We use first-class continuations in this chapter because they simplify our formal semantics.

Process Abstractions. Our framework has three distinct notions of process abstraction. At the lowest level, a *fiber* is an unadorned thread of control. We use continuations to represent the state of suspended fibers.

Surface-language *threads*, e.g., CML threads, correspond to programmer-created threads. These threads, in contrast to more traditional threads, can execute data-parallel computations or futures on multiple processing elements, and thus consist of a *group* of fibers. We identify each thread with a unique group identifier (gid).

Lastly, a *virtual processor* (vproc) is an abstraction of a hardware processor. A vproc runs at most one fiber at a time, and, furthermore, is the only means of running fibers. The vproc that is currently running a fiber is called the *host vproc* of the fiber. Each vproc has a state that consists of a stack of signal actions, a queue of threads, and a signal mask bit. We discuss vprocs in more detail in the sequel.

The Scheduler Language. The collected syntax of this language is given in figure 25.1. We partition the syntax into a sequential core, vproc operations, and multi-vproc operations. The sequential syntax is standard except for four forms. The fix operator evaluates the fixpoint of a function. The fun operator is a binding form for functions. The handle operator performs a case analysis on a signal. The letcont operator binds the continuation k with arguments x ... and body e_1 in the expression e_2.

$$(\text{letcont } k\, x \ldots e_1\, e_2)$$

We describe the remaining syntax in more detail in section 25.3.

Although this chapter presents the framework as a high-level language, we intend it to be part of an intermediate representation. Thus, only compiler writers have access to the scheduling operations and process abstractions.

The Scheduler-action Stack. The heart of our framework is the scheduler action. Scheduler actions are continuations that handle synchronous and

$$
\begin{array}{rl}
signal ::= & (\text{stop}) \mid (\text{preempt } e) \\
v ::= & number \mid (\lambda \ (x \ ...) \ e) \mid (\text{unit}) \mid signal \\
e\text{-}sequential ::= & x \mid v \mid (e \ e \ ...) \mid (\text{if } e \ e \ e) \mid (\text{begin } e \ e \ ...) \mid (\text{let } ((x \ e)) \ e) \mid (\text{letrec } ((x \ e)) \ e) \\
& \mid (\text{fix } e) \mid (\text{fun } (x \ x \ ...) \ e \ e) \\
& \mid (\text{abort } e) \mid (\text{letcont } x \ x \ ... \ e \ e) \\
& \mid (\text{handle } e \ (\text{stop-handler } e) \ (\text{preempt-handler } e)) \\
e\text{-}vproc\text{-}ops ::= & (\text{run } e \ e) \mid (\text{forward } e) \\
& \mid (\text{deq-vp}) \\
& \mid (\text{mask-preemption}) \mid (\text{unmask-preemption}) \mid (\text{host-vp}) \\
e\text{-}multiproc\text{-}ops ::= & (\text{enq-on-vp } e \ e) \\
& \mid (\text{gid}) \mid (\text{provision } e) \mid (\text{release } e \ e) \\
& \mid (\text{ref } e) \mid (\text{deref } e) \mid (\text{cas } e \ e \ e)
\end{array}
$$

Figure 25.1: Syntax for the scheduler language.

---

asynchronous signals. An action takes a signal and performs the appropriate scheduling activity in response to that signal. For our purposes we use only two signals: stop, which signals the termination of the current fiber, and preempt, which is used to asynchronously preempt the current fiber. Preemption signals could come from hardware events like timer interrupts or from another thread; we only consider the former type of event here. When the runtime system preempts a fiber, it reifies the fiber's state as a continuation k that is carried by the preempt signal (preempt k).

Each vproc has its own stack of scheduler actions to support nesting of schedulers. The top of a vproc's stack is called the *current* scheduler action. When a vproc receives a signal, it handles it by popping the current action from the stack, setting the signal mask, and throwing the signal to the current action. Figure 25.2 illustrates the effect of a preemption signal. Here we use black in the mask box to denote when signals are masked. Masking signals is necessary to protect some scheduler implementations. The oval contains the the expression that the vproc is evaluating.

There are two expression forms in the IR that scheduling code can use to affect a vproc's scheduler stack directly. The run operation executes a fiber under a scheduler. The expression (run *act'* k) pushes *act'* onto the host vproc's action stack, clears the vproc's signal mask, and invokes the continuation k (see figure 25.3). The run operation requires that signals be masked, since it manipulates the vproc's action stack. The other form is the expression (forward *sig*), which sets the signal mask and invokes the current action with the argument *sig* (see figure 25.4). The forward operation is used both in scheduling code to propagate signals up the stack of actions and in user code to signal termination, thus allowing signals to be masked or unmasked. For example, a thread exit function can be defined as below.

$$(\text{fun } (exit) \ (\text{forward } (\text{stop})))$$

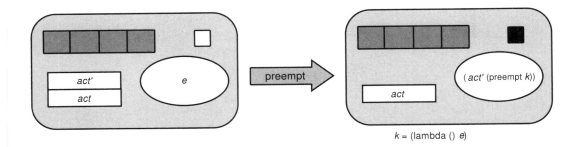

Figure 25.2: The effect of preemption on a vproc

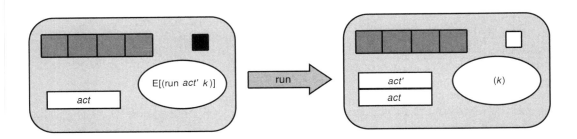

Figure 25.3: The effect of the run operation on a vproc

Another example is the implementation of a yield operation that causes the current fiber to yield control of the processor. This function captures the current continuation k, packages it in a preemption signal, and forwards the signal.

```
(fun (yield)
    (letcont k x (unit)
        (forward (preempt k))))
```

Scheduling Queues. In addition to the scheduler stack, each vproc has a queue of ready fibers that is used for scheduling. The enq-on-vp operation takes a suspended fiber and adds it to the scheduler queue, while the deq-vp operation removes the next fiber from the queue. If the queue is empty, the deq-vp operation causes the vproc to go idle until there is work for it. At this point, only other vprocs can fill the queue and wake up the idling vproc.

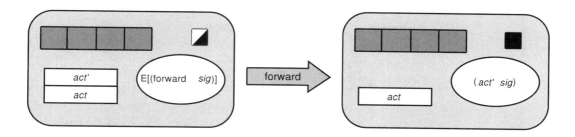

Figure 25.4: The effect of the *forward* operation on a vproc

Implementing Language-level Threads. Given that our framework includes first-class continuations, it is easy to implement language-level thread mechanisms [87, 92, 113]. We start with a function for turning a function into a fiber (i.e., continuation). When applied to a function, *fiber* constructs a continuation that will invoke the function and then exit to the current scheduler.

$$
\begin{array}{l}
(\text{fun } (\textit{fiber } f) \\
\qquad (\text{letcont } k\ x\ (\text{begin } (f) \\
\qquad\qquad\qquad\qquad\quad (\textit{exit}))) \\
\quad k)
\end{array}
$$

The code below takes an initial function f and spawns a thread, which consists of creating a fiber and placing it on the vproc's queue.

$$(\text{fun } (\textit{spawn } f)\ (\text{enq-on-vp } (\textit{fiber } f)))$$

Synchronization and communication mechanisms are supported via atomic operations, such as *compare-and-swap* (cas), and a concurrent-queue abstraction [76] supported by the compiler and runtime.

For language-level threads we use a simple round-robin scheduler built on top of the per-vproc scheduling queues. Before this scheduler runs the next thread, it always pushes itself on the action stack to handle future signals. We install this scheduler at the bottom of each action stack and we call it the *default scheduler*.

$$
\begin{array}{l}
(\text{letcont } \textit{switch } \textit{sig} \\
\qquad (\text{handle } \textit{sig} \\
\qquad\qquad (\textit{stop-handler } (\lambda\ ()\ (\text{run } \textit{switch } (\text{deq-vp})))) \\
\qquad\qquad (\textit{preempt-handler } (\lambda\ (k) \\
\qquad\qquad\qquad\qquad\qquad (\text{begin } (\text{enq-vp } k) \\
\qquad\qquad\qquad\qquad\qquad\qquad (\text{run } \textit{switch } (\text{deq-vp}))))))))
\end{array}
$$

On a stop signal, it runs the next fiber in the queue, and on a preempt signal it enqueues the preempted fiber and then runs the next fiber.

Provisioning Parallel Computations. The last part of our framework is the operations that threads use to map a parallel computation across multiple vprocs. The (enq-on-vp *vp k*) operation enqueues the fiber represented by the continuation *k* on the vproc named by *vp*. Using this operation, we can implement an explicit migration function that moves the calling computation to a specific vproc.

$$\text{(fun } (migrate\ vp)$$
$$\text{(letcont } k\ x \text{ (unit)}$$
$$\text{(begin (enq-on-vp } vp\ k)$$
$$(exit))))$$

We also provide a mechanism for assigning vprocs to computations. The basic parallel computation is a group of fibers running on separate vprocs; the scheduling framework provides the mechanism of *group IDs* to distinguish between different parallel computations. When initiating a parallel computation, threads use gid operation to create a unique group ID for the computation. Threads pass this ID to the provision operation to request additional vprocs. This operation either returns a vproc that is not already assigned to the computation or else halts the thread to indicate that no additional vprocs are available for the group. When a computation is finished with a vproc, it uses the release operation to signal to the runtime that it is done with the vproc.

25·3 Formal Semantics.
This section lays out the formal model for our scheduler framework using an abstract machine and an operational semantics.

We define sequential evaluation of an expression by

$$e \Rightarrow e,$$

a state transition. To support scheduling infrastructure, we lift the expression language to a *vproc machine*. The vproc machine includes the state necessary for the management of a single virtual processor (i.e., a stack of scheduler actions, a set of ready fibers, etc.) and evaluates according to

$$VP \Longrightarrow VP,$$

a simple state transition. Finally, we lift a collection of vproc machines to a *multi-proc machine*. The multi-proc machine adds a global state that all vproc machines share (e.g., mutable store), and it evaluates according to

$$MP \longmapsto MP .$$

$$E_1[((\lambda\ (x_1\ ...)\ e_1)\ v_1\ ...)] \Rightarrow E_1[\text{MULTI-SUBST}[\![((x_1\ ...)\ (v_1\ ...)\ e_1)]\!]\ ] \qquad \text{(beta)}$$

$$E_1[(\text{fix}\ (\lambda\ (x_1)\ e_1))] \Rightarrow E_1[\text{SUBST}[\![(x_1\ (\text{fix}\ (\lambda\ (x_1)\ e_1))\ e_1)]\!]\ ] \qquad \text{(fix)}$$

$$E_1[(\text{abort}\ e_1)] \Rightarrow e_1 \qquad \text{(abort)}$$

$$E_1[(\text{letcont}\ x_1\ x_2\ ...\ e_1\ e_2)] \Rightarrow E_1[(\text{letrec}\ ((x_1\ (\lambda\ (x_2\ ...)\ (\text{abort}\ E_1[e_1]))))\ e_2)] \quad \text{(letcont)}$$

$$E_1[(\text{let}\ ((x_1\ v_1))\ e_2)] \Rightarrow E_1[\text{SUBST}[\![(x_1\ v_1\ e_2)]\!]\ ] \qquad \text{(let)}$$

$$E_1[(\text{letrec}\ ((x_1\ e_1))\ e_2)] \Rightarrow E_1[(\text{let}\ ((x_1\ (\text{fix}\ (\lambda\ (x_1)\ e_1))))\ e_2)] \qquad \text{(letrec)}$$

$$E_1[(\text{fun}\ (x_f\ x_1\ ...)\ e_1\ e_2)] \Rightarrow E_1[(\text{letrec}\ ((x_f\ (\lambda\ (x_1\ ...)\ e_1)))\ e_2)] \qquad \text{(fun)}$$

$$E_1[(\text{if}\ number_1\ e_1\ e_2)] \Rightarrow E_1[e_1] \qquad \text{(if-t)}$$
$$\text{where}\ number_1 \neq 0$$

$$E_1[(\text{if}\ 0\ e_1\ e_2)] \Rightarrow E_1[e_2] \qquad \text{(if-f)}$$

$$E_1[(\text{begin}\ v_1\ e_1\ e_2\ ...)] \Rightarrow E_1[(\text{begin}\ e_1\ e_2\ ...)] \qquad \text{(begin-many)}$$

$$E_1[(\text{begin}\ e_1)] \Rightarrow E_1[e_1] \qquad \text{(begin-one)}$$

$$E_1[(\text{handle}\ (\text{stop})\ (\text{stop-handler}\ v_s)\ (\text{preempt-handler}\ v_k))] \Rightarrow E_1[(v_s)] \qquad \text{(handle-stop)}$$

$$E_1[(\text{handle}\ (\text{preempt}\ v_k)\ (\text{stop-handler}\ v_s)\ (\text{preempt-handler}\ v_{\text{ph}}))] \Rightarrow E_1[(v_{\text{ph}}\ v_k)] \qquad \text{(handle-preempt)}$$

Figure 25.5: Sequential state transitions

Sequential Evaluation. Figure 25.5 defines the sequential state-transition function $e \Rightarrow e$. The language is a standard λ-calculus with recursive-function binding, first-class continuations, and primitive operators. The evaluator uses the evaluation contexts given in figure 25.6. We define first-class continuations with the letcont operator, which uses the the abort operator to escape the surrounding context. Note, however, that letcont is a recursive binding, which is helpful later for defining scheduler actions.

VProc Machine. We give definitions for the vproc machine VP in figure 25.7. A vproc machine state VP contains a vproc identifier, an expression, a queue of ready threads, a stack of scheduler actions, and a signal mask. The queue contains a list of fibers that are ready to execute on a vproc, but we leave open the possibility of different thread orderings in an implementation. The stack of scheduler actions supports nested schedulers. The signal mask determines whether the vproc can receive asynchronous signals: masked masks signals and unmasked unmasks signals.

Figure 25.8 gives the core of our semantics, the state-transition function for the vproc machine. The primary function of the vproc is to host sequential evaluation; the first transition steps forward a sequential evaluation. This

$$E ::= [] \mid (v \dots E \, e \dots) \mid (\text{if } E \, e \, e) \mid (\text{begin } E \, e \, e \dots) \mid (\text{let } ((x \, E)) \, e)$$
$$\mid (\text{enq } E \, e) \mid (\text{enq } v \, E) \mid (\text{deq } E)$$
$$\mid (\text{run } E \, e) \mid (\text{run } v \, E) \mid (\text{forward } E)$$
$$\mid (\text{enq-on-vp } E \, e) \mid (\text{enq-on-vp } v \, E)$$
$$\mid (\text{provision } E) \mid (\text{release } E \, e) \mid (\text{release } v \, E)$$
$$\mid (\text{ref } E) \mid (\text{deref } E) \mid (\text{fix } E)$$
$$\mid (\text{cas } E \, e \, e) \mid (\text{cas } number \, E \, e) \mid (\text{cas } number \, v \, E)$$
$$\mid (\text{handle } E \, (\text{stop-handler } e) \, (\text{preempt-handler } e))$$
$$\mid (\text{handle } v \, (\text{stop-handler } E) \, (\text{preempt-handler } e))$$
$$\mid (\text{handle } v \, (\text{stop-handler } v) \, (\text{preempt-handler } E))$$

Figure 25.6: Evaluation contexts

transition occurs under an arbitrary signal mask, as the sequential machine evaluates user computations and scheduler code.

The vproc machine is responsible for evaluating the scheduling operations: run and forward. The (run) transition rule installs a new scheduling action on the scheduler stack and begins evaluating a computation. Note that this rule begins with masked signals but leaves signals unmasked. This corresponds to the fact that run is used both to install nested scheduling actions with signals masked and to initiate the evaluation of user computations with signals unmasked.

The (forward) transition rule forwards a signal to the current scheduler action, in this case v_{act}. Note that the forward operation may only make a transition when the stack of scheduler actions is non-empty. This transition rule masks signals, thus ensuring that the scheduler action is evaluated without being preempted.

The (preempt) transition rule simulates the preemption of the vproc machine. This rule applies to any unmasked state and thus adds a source of non-determinism. When it applies, this rule packages the current expression e_1 into the preemption signal and forwards the signal to the vproc.

The (deq-vp) transition rule returns the next ready fiber, but note that it only applies when the set of ready fibers is non-empty. In our implementation, attempting to dequeue from an empty set of ready fibers places the vproc in an idle state, which may affect its priority to be selected for provisioning; however, this level of detail is immaterial for the formal semantics. The (mask-preemption) and (unmask-preemption) primitives explicitly set the signal mask. The (host-vp) transition rule simply returns the vproc identifier of the vproc to the underlying sequential computation.

Multiproc Machine. A multi-proc machine state MP (see figure 25.7) contains a set of vprocs, a global store, and a global provisioning map. Each vproc must have a unique, positive, and non-zero integer identifier. The pro-

$$
\begin{aligned}
MP &::= ((\text{vps } VP \dots) \textit{ global-store provision-map}) \\
\textit{provision-map} &::= (\text{pmap } (\textit{group-id vproc-id} \dots) \dots) \\
\textit{group-id} &::= \textit{number} \\
\textit{vproc-id} &::= \textit{number} \\
\textit{global-store} &::= (\text{store } (\textit{store-location } v) \dots) \\
\textit{store-location} &::= \textit{number} \\
VP &::= (\text{vproc } \textit{vproc-id actions fiber-queue mask } e) \\
\textit{actions} &::= (\text{action-stack } v \dots) \\
\textit{fiber-queue} &::= (\text{queue } v \dots) \\
\textit{mask} &::= (\text{masked}) \mid (\text{unmasked})
\end{aligned}
$$

Initial multi-proc machine state for program e with n vprocs and initialization e-init:

```
((vps (vproc 1 (action-stack) (queue) (masked) e)
      (vproc 2 (action-stack) (queue) (masked) e-init)
      ...
      (vproc n (action-stack) (queue) (masked) e-init)
  (store (0 0))
  (pmap))
```

Figure 25.7: The abstract machine definitions.

---

visioning map keeps a record of each vproc currently allocated to a group id. Finally, the store models shared, mutable state. We use the store to build concurrent data structures for our scheduler examples.

Figure 25.7 also shows the initial machine state for a program e. If the target multi-proc machine has n vprocs, one vproc begins executing the program e, while the remaining vprocs begin executing an initialization expression e-inint. Note that we initialize each vproc with an empty queue of ready fibers, an empty stack of scheduler actions, and signals masked. The initialization expression is customizable but normally installs a default scheduler that tries to run a fiber from the queue. The program e should also contain similar initialization code. The initial provision map and store are empty.

The primary job of the multi-processor machine is to host all the vprocs in the system. The transition rule in figure 25.9 steps forward one of the vprocs. The remaining multi-processor rules manage provisioning, vproc queues, and store operations.

The transition rules in figure 25.10 manipulate the global provision map, which maps group identifiers to the vproc identifiers that have *not* been allocated to the group. The (provision) transition rule tries to find an available vproc; if one exists, the rule updates the provision map and passes the vproc id to the underlying sequential computation. The (release) transition rule returns a vproc identifier to the provision map for a specified group identifier.

Hosting sequential evaluation:

$$(\text{vproc } number_1 \text{ } actions_1 \text{ } fiber\text{-}queue_1 \text{ } mask_1 \text{ } e_1) \Longrightarrow$$
$$(\text{vproc } number_1 \text{ } actions_1 \text{ } fiber\text{-}queue_1 \text{ } mask_1 \text{ } e_2)$$
$$\text{where } e_1 \Rightarrow e_2$$

(vproc $number_1$ (action-stack v_{act1} ...) $fiber\text{-}queue_1$ (masked) $E_1[(\text{run } v_{act2} (\lambda \; () \; e_1))]) \Longrightarrow$ (run)
(vproc $number_1$ (action-stack v_{act2} v_{act1} ...) $fiber\text{-}queue_1$ (unmasked) e_1)

(vproc $number_1$ (action-stack v_{act} v_{acts} ...) $fiber\text{-}queue_1$ $mask_1$ $E_1[(\text{forward } v_{sig})]) \Longrightarrow$ (forward)
(vproc $number_1$ (action-stack v_{acts} ...) $fiber\text{-}queue_1$ (masked) $(v_{act} \; v_{sig}))$

(vproc $number_1$ (action-stack v_{act} v_{acts} ...) $fiber\text{-}queue_1$ (unmasked) $e_1) \Longrightarrow$ (preempt)
(vproc $number_1$ (action-stack v_{acts} ...) $fiber\text{-}queue_1$ (masked) $(v_{act} \; (\text{preempt } (\lambda \; () \; e_1))))$

(vproc $number_1$ $actions_1$ (queue v_{ks} ... v_k) $mask_1$ $E_1[(\text{deq-vp})]) \Longrightarrow$ (deq-vp)
(vproc $number_1$ $actions_1$ (queue v_{ks} ...) $mask_1$ $E_1[v_k])$

(vproc $number_1$ $actions_1$ $fiber\text{-}queue_1$ $mask_1$ $E_1[(\text{mask-preemption})]) \Longrightarrow$ (mask-preemption)
(vproc $number_1$ $actions_1$ $fiber\text{-}queue_1$ (masked) $E_1[(\text{unit})])$

(vproc $number_1$ $actions_1$ $fiber\text{-}queue_1$ $mask_1$ $E_1[(\text{unmask-preemption})]) \Longrightarrow$ (unmask-preemption)
(vproc $number_1$ $actions_1$ $fiber\text{-}queue_1$ (unmasked) $E_1[(\text{unit})])$

(vproc $number_1$ $actions_1$ $fiber\text{-}queue_1$ $mask_1$ $E_1[(\text{host-vp})]) \Longrightarrow$ (host-vp)
(vproc $number_1$ $actions_1$ $fiber\text{-}queue_1$ $mask_1$ $E_1[number_1])$

Figure 25.8: VProc state transitions

$$((\text{vps } VP_1 \ldots vp_1 \text{ } VP_2 \ldots) \text{ } global\text{-}store_1 \text{ } provision\text{-}map_1) \longmapsto$$
$$((\text{vps } VP_1 \ldots vp_2 \text{ } VP_2 \ldots) \text{ } global\text{-}store_1 \text{ } provision\text{-}map_1)$$
$$\text{where } vp_1 \Longrightarrow vp_2$$

Figure 25.9: Hosting multiple vprocs

Invoking the release primitive should indicate that the task for which the vproc was provisioned has completed. Thus the provision map approximates the computational demand placed on the vprocs; while the formal semantics does not depend on this, an implementation is likely to be faster under this assumption. The (gid) transition rule generates a unique group identifier for a parallel computation; the fresh group identifier is returned to the underlying sequential computation and the provision map is updated to map the group identifier *number-gid* to all of the vproc identifiers (*all-vp-ids*).

The transition rules in figure 25.11 manipulate the vproc queues. The (enq-on-self) rule enqueues a fiber on the host vproc's queue. The (enq-on-vp-l) rule enqueues a fiber on another vproc's queue that is on the left side of the host vproc, and the (enq-on-vp-r) rule handles the right-side case.

The transition rules in figure 25.12 manipulate the store *global-store*. The (ref) rule allocates and initializes a new store location. The (deref) rule simply

((vps VP_1 ...
        (vproc $number_1$ $actions_1$ $fiber$-$queue_1$ $mask_1$ E_1[(provision $number_{gid}$)]) $\longrightarrow$ (provision)
        VP_2 ...)
 global-store$_1$
 (pmap ($number_{p1}$ $number_{p2}$ ...) ...
        ($number_{gid}$ $number_{vp}$ $number_{vps}$ ...)
        ($number_{p3}$ $number_{p4}$ ...) ...))
((vps VP_1 ...
        (vproc $number_1$ $actions_1$ $fiber$-$queue_1$ $mask_1$ E_1[$number_{vp}$])
        VP_2 ...)
 global-store$_1$
 (pmap ($number_{p1}$ $number_{p2}$ ...) ...
        ($number_{gid}$ $number_{vps}$ ...)
        ($number_{p3}$ $number_{p4}$ ...) ...))
((vps VP_1 ...
        (vproc $number_1$ $actions_1$ $fiber$-$queue_1$ $mask_1$ E_1[(release $number_{gid}$ $number_{vp}$)]) $\longrightarrow$ (release)
        VP_2 ...)
 global-store$_1$
 (pmap ($number_{p1}$ $number_{p2}$ ...) ... ($number_{gid}$ $number_{vps}$ ...) ($number_{p3}$ $number_{p4}$ ...) ...))
((vps VP_1 ...
        (vproc $number_1$ $actions_1$ $fiber$-$queue_1$ $mask_1$ E_1[(unit)])
        VP_2 ...)
 global-store$_1$
 (pmap ($number_{p1}$ $number_{p2}$ ...) ...
        ($number_{gid}$ $number_{vp}$ $number_{vps}$ ...)
        ($number_{p3}$ $number_{p4}$ ...) ...))
                                                                    where (not (memq $number_{vp}$($number_{vps}$ ...)))
((vps VP_1 ... $\longrightarrow$ (gid)
        (vproc $number_1$ $actions_1$ $fiber$-$queue_1$ $mask_1$ E_1[(gid)])
        VP_2 ...)
 global-store$_1$
 (pmap ($number_{p1}$ $number_{p2}$ ...) ...))

((vps VP_1 ...
        (vproc $number_1$ $actions_1$ $fiber$-$queue_1$ $mask_1$ E_1[number-gid])
        VP_2 ...)
 global-store$_1$
 (pmap ($number_{p1}$ $number_{p2}$ ...) ... (number-gid all-vp-ids ...)))
where number-gid = (fresh-gid (term ($number_{p1}$ ...))), (all-vp-ids ...) = (cons (term $number_1$) (map get-vp-id (term (VP_1 ... VP_2 ...))))

Figure 25.10: Multiproc state transitions for provisioning

$((\text{vps } VP_1 \dots$
    $(\text{vproc } number_1 \ actions_1 \ (\text{queue } v_{ks} \dots) \ mask_1 \ E_1[(\text{enq-on-vp } number_1 \ v_k)])$ $\longrightarrow$ (enq-vp-self)
    $VP_3 \dots)$
 $global\text{-}store_1 \ provision\text{-}map_1)$
$((\text{vps } VP_1 \dots$
    $(\text{vproc } number_1 \ actions_1 \ (\text{queue } v_k \ v_{ks} \dots) \ mask_1 \ E_1[(\text{unit})])$
    $VP_3 \dots)$
 $global\text{-}store_1 \ provision\text{-}map_1)$

$((\text{vps } VP_1 \dots$
    $(\text{vproc } number_1 \ actions_1 \ fiber\text{-}queue_1 \ mask_1 \ E_1[(\text{enq-on-vp } number_2 \ v_k)])$ $\longrightarrow$ (enq-on-vp-l)
    $VP_2 \dots$
    $(\text{vproc } number_2 \ actions_2 \ (\text{queue } v_{ks2} \dots) \ mask_2 \ e_2)$
    $VP_3 \dots)$
 $global\text{-}store_1 \ provision\text{-}map_1)$
$((\text{vps } VP_1 \dots$
    $(\text{vproc } number_1 \ actions_1 \ fiber\text{-}queue_1 \ mask_1 \ E_1[(\text{unit})])$
    $VP_2 \dots$
    $(\text{vproc } number_2 \ actions_2 \ (\text{queue } v_k \ v_{ks2} \dots) \ mask_2 \ e_2)$
    $VP_3 \dots)$
 $global\text{-}store_1 \ provision\text{-}map_1)$

$((\text{vps } VP_1 \dots$ $\longrightarrow$ (enq-on-vp-r)
    $(\text{vproc } number_2 \ actions_2 \ (\text{queue } v_{ks2} \dots) \ mask_2 \ e_2)$
    $VP_2 \dots$
    $(\text{vproc } number_1 \ actions_1 \ fiber\text{-}queue_1 \ mask_1 \ E_1[(\text{enq-on-vp } number_2 \ v_k)])$
    $VP_3 \dots)$
 $global\text{-}store_1 \ provision\text{-}map_1)$
$((\text{vps } VP_1 \dots$
    $(\text{vproc } number_2 \ actions_2 \ (\text{queue } v_k \ v_{ks2} \dots) \ mask_2 \ e_2)$
    $VP_2 \dots$
    $(\text{vproc } number_1 \ actions_1 \ fiber\text{-}queue_1 \ mask_1 \ E_1[(\text{unit})])$
    $VP_3 \dots)$
 $global\text{-}store_1 \ provision\text{-}map_1)$

Figure 25.11: Multiproc state transitions for queues

$$((\text{vps } VP_1 \ldots \qquad\qquad\qquad\qquad\qquad\qquad\qquad\qquad \longrightarrow \quad \text{(ref)}$$
$$\quad (\text{vproc } number_1 \; actions_1 \; fiber\text{-}queue_1 \; mask_1 \; E_1[(\text{let } ((x_1 \; (\text{ref } v_1))) \; e_1)])$$
$$\quad VP_2 \ldots)$$
$$(\text{store } (number_1 \; v_s) \ldots (number_r \; v_r)) \; provision\text{-}map_1)$$
$$((\text{vps } VP_1 \ldots$$
$$\quad (\text{vproc } number_1 \; actions_1 \; fiber\text{-}queue_1 \; mask_1 \; E_1[(\text{let } ((x_1 \; (\texttt{add1 } number_r))) \; e_1)])$$
$$\quad VP_2 \ldots)$$
$$(\text{store } (number_1 \; v_s) \ldots (number_r \; v_r) \; ((\texttt{add1 } number_r) \;\; v_1)) \; provision\text{-}map_1)$$

$$((\text{vps } VP_1 \ldots \qquad\qquad\qquad\qquad\qquad\qquad\qquad\qquad \longrightarrow \quad \text{(deref)}$$
$$\quad (\text{vproc } number_1 \; actions_1 \; fiber\text{-}queue_1 \; mask_1 \; E_1[(\text{deref } number_1)])$$
$$\quad VP_2 \ldots)$$
$$(\text{store } (number_{s1} \; v_{s1}) \ldots (number_1 \; v_1) \; (number_{s2} \; v_{s2}) \ldots) \; provision\text{-}map_1)$$
$$((\text{vps } VP_1 \ldots$$
$$\quad (\text{vproc } number_1 \; actions_1 \; fiber\text{-}queue_1 \; mask_1 \; E_1[v_1])$$
$$\quad VP_2 \ldots)$$
$$(\text{store } (number_{s1} \; v_{s1}) \ldots (number_1 \; v_1) \; (number_{s2} \; v_{s2}) \ldots) \; provision\text{-}map_1)$$

$$((\text{vps } VP_1 \ldots \qquad\qquad\qquad\qquad\qquad\qquad\qquad\qquad \longrightarrow \quad \text{(cas)}$$
$$\quad (\text{vproc } number_1 \; actions_1 \; fiber\text{-}queue_1 \; mask_1 \; E_1[(\text{cas } number_1 \; v_o \; v_n)])$$
$$\quad VP_2 \ldots)$$
$$(\text{store } (number_{s1} \; v_{s1}) \ldots (number_1 \; v_1) \; (number_{s2} \; v_{s2}) \ldots) \; provision\text{-}map_1)$$
$$((\text{vps } VP_1 \ldots$$
$$\quad (\text{vproc } number_1 \; actions_1 \; fiber\text{-}queue_1 \; mask_1 \; E_1[v_1])$$
$$\quad VP_2 \ldots)$$
$$(\text{store } (number_{s1} \; v_{s1}) \ldots (number_1 \; (\texttt{if } (\texttt{equal? } v_1 v_o)$$
$$\qquad\qquad\qquad\qquad\qquad\qquad\qquad v_n$$
$$\qquad\qquad\qquad\qquad\qquad\qquad\qquad v_1))$$
$$\qquad (number_{s2} \; v_{s2}) \ldots)$$
$$provision\text{-}map_1)$$

Figure 25.12: Multiproc state transitions for the store

reads the machine value at the specified store location. Finally, the (cas) rule performs a compare-and-swap operation. The first argument to the cas primitive is the store location, the second argument is the expected old value at the location, and the third argument is the new value to be stored at the location. The store is updated with the new value if and only if the location's current value is equal to the expected old value. Other atomic operations, such as test-and-set and fetch-and-add, can be built using cas.

25·4 Scheduler Utility Functions.
Here we extend the scheduler language with variable-arity functions and a match operation.

There are a number of operations that are common to many schedulers. These include

$$(\textit{provision-n id n})$$

which takes a group ID and a desired number of vprocs and returns a list of vprocs from the runtime system (note that the result does *not* include the host vproc). We also use the function

$$(\text{fun } (\textit{atomic-yield}) \text{ (begin } (\textit{yield}) \text{ } (\textit{mask-preemption})))$$

for passing preemptions up the action stack that remasks signals when it resumes. The *sched-fiber* function creates a fiber that will run the function *f* with a given signal action.

$$(\text{fun } (\textit{sched-fiber switch } f)$$
$$(\textit{fiber } (\lambda \text{ () (run } \textit{switch } (\textit{fiber } f)))))$$

The *dispatch-on* function invokes a scheduler on another vproc. It takes a vproc and a scheduler action, which creates a fiber that immediately exits the thread in action, and then enqueues the fiber on the vproc.

$$(\text{fun } (\textit{dispatch-on vp switch})$$
$$(\text{enq-on-vp } \textit{vp } (\textit{sched-fiber switch exit})))$$

By using the *exit* function as the function to run, we cause the stop signal to be sent to the *switch* action on the remote vproc. The *finish* function is used to release a vproc and terminate the computation.

$$(\text{fun } (\textit{finish id})$$
$$(\text{begin } (\text{release } \textit{id } (\textit{host-vp})) \text{ } (\textit{exit})))$$

We also need concurrent queues to schedule work between vprocs, with this interface

$$(\textit{empty-q})$$
$$(\textit{add-q q elt})$$
$$(\textit{rem-q q})$$

```
(fun (workcrew n-jobs n-workers job)
    (letcont done-k (unit)
        (let ((id (gid))
              (n-started (ref 1))
              (n-done (ref 0))
              (vprs (provision-n id n-workers))
              (n (length vprs)))
            (letcont switch sig
                (handle sig
                    (handle-stop
                        (λ ()
                            (let ((next-job (fetch-and-inc n-started)))
                                (if0 (< next-job n-jobs)
                                    (run switch
                                        (fiber (λ () (job next-job))))
                                    (if0 (= (fetch-and-inc n-done) n)
                                        (begin (release id (host-vp))
                                            (done-k))
                                        (finish id))))))
                    (handle-preempt
                        (λ (k)
                            (begin (atomic-yield)
                                (run switch k)))))
                (begin (for-each (λ (vp) (dispatch-on vp switch)) vprs)
                    (run switch (fiber (λ () (job 0)))))))))
```

Figure 25.13: Workcrews for data-parallel computations

25·5 **Scheduling Data-parallel Fibers.** Data-parallel computations require multiple fibers running on multiple vprocs. There are many ways to organize this computation, but this example uses the *workcrew* approach [112]. A workcrew consists of some number of workers, each running on a separate processor, and a global pool of functions that perform work. Workers iterate taking a job from the work pool and executing it. The function in figure 25.13 creates a workcrew of up to *n-workers* to compute a job that has been partitioned into *n-jobs* pieces. The *job* parameter is a function that takes an integer argument i and computes the ith job.

The implementation begins by provisioning a group of processors. It then installs the its scheduler (*switch*) on each of the vprocs. Once initialized on a vproc, *switch* begins running jobs from the work pool. Since jobs run in fibers, they generate stop signals upon completion. The stop signal indicates

```
(fun (time-sharing f₀ fuel0)
    (let ((q (empty-q)))
        (fun (fill fuel) (cons fuel fuel))
            (fun (te-switch fuel)
                (letcont switch sig
                    (handle sig
                        (handle-stop
                            (λ () (run-next)))
                        (handle-preempt
                            (λ (k)
                                (let ((curr-fuel (car fuel))
                                      (capacity (cdr fuel)))
                                    (if (= curr-fuel 0)
                                        (begin (add-q q (cons capacity k))
                                            (run-next))
                                        (run (te-switch (cons (sub1 curr-fuel) capacity)) k))))))
                    switch)
                (fun (run-next)
                    (match (rem-q q)
                        ('() (exit))
                        ('(,fuel-cap ,k) (run te-switch (fill fuel-cap) k)))
                    (fun (spawn-fe f fuel) (add-q q (cons fuel (fiber f)))
                        (fiber (λ ()
                            (run (te-switch (fill fuel0))
                                (fiber (λ () (f₀ spawn-fe)))))))))))))))
```

Figure 25.14: A time-sharing scheduler that uses flat engines.

the completion of a job. If another job is available, the scheduler creates a fiber for the job and runs it. Otherwise, it releases the host vproc. The last vproc to finish will return control to *done-k*.

When the scheduler receives a preempt signal, it yields control to the current scheduler, which effectively lets us inherit the preemption policy of the parent scheduler. This practice of immediately yielding the vproc allows the parent scheduler to decide whether to resume this scheduler or to perform other computations before resuming this scheduler.

25·6 Engines.
Engines are an abstraction of computations that are subject to timed preemption [54]. Engines consist of a processor state and a quantity of *fuel* to measure processor time. When either their fuel runs out or their computations are finished, active engines are responsible

```
(fun (ne-switch cell)
    (let ...
        (letcont switch sig
            (handle sig
                (handle-stop (λ () (run-next)))
                (handle-preempt
                    (λ (k)
                        (begin (atomic-yield)
                                (if (empty? (charge-cell cell))
                                    (begin
                                        (add-q q (cons k cell))
                                        (run-next))
                                    (run (ne-switch cell) k))))))))
        switch)))
```

Figure 25.15: Nested-engine scheduler action.

---

for invoking the next computations. As such, engines provide a minimal and efficient representation for customizable time-sharing schedulers.

Engines typically come in two types, flat or nested. A flat engine only accounts for its own fuel, so it cannot properly run within another engine. A nested engine [30], on the other hand, can run in a tree of engines. The standard implementation technique is called *fair nesting*, in which every unit of fuel charged to an engine is also charged to its ancestors. Nested engines provide a convenient abstraction for finer-grain division of processor time and improve modularity of scheduling code.

Compilers such as Chez Scheme have successfully incorporated engines to implement a virtualizable, proportional-share threading system and to simulate parallelism on a uniprocessor, e.g., in the implementation of the *parallel-or* operator. For an efficient implementation of engines, the host language only needs first-class continuations and timer interrupts [30], both of which are available in the scheduler framework. Our framework, as shown in this section, supports particularly elegant implementations of engines, demonstrating the power and expressiveness of our scheduling primitives. Section 25.6 first presents a simple implementation of flat engines, and then section 25.6 presents an extension to nested engines.

Flat Engines. Proportional-share schedulers keep a ready queue of engines and periodically switch between them until all are finished computing. In our implementation, such schedulers export a spawning function that, when given an initial function value and some fuel, creates an engine and adds it to the ready queue.

Example The example below spawns three engines from different functions and with different amounts of fuel. If the fuel amounts are $t_1 = t_2 = t_3 = 1$, then the behavior is the same as a round-robin scheduler. But assigning $t_1 = 2$, $t_2 = 3$, and $t_3 = 5$ allocates about 20%, 30%, and 50% of the processor time to f_1, f_2, and f_3, respectively.

$$(\text{fun } (f_1) \ldots$$
$$(\text{fun } (f_2) \ldots$$
$$(\text{fun } (f_3) \ldots$$
$$(\text{fun } (f_0 \; \textit{spawn-fe})$$
$$(\text{begin } (\textit{spawn-fe } f_1 \; 5)$$
$$(\textit{spawn-fe } f_2 \; 2)$$
$$(\textit{spawn-fe } f_3 \; 3))$$
$$(\textit{init})))))$$

The *time-sharing* function in figure 25.14 creates a new instance of this scheduler. It takes an initial engine f_0 that is given access to the spawn function, f_0's fuel *fuel0*, and returns a fiber that wil start the engines. The following function creates the scheduler fiber and then enqueues it on its vproc.

$$(\text{fun } (\textit{init})$$
$$(\text{let } ((k \; (\textit{time-sharing } f_0 \; 1)))$$
$$(\text{enq-on-vp } (\textit{host-vp}) \; k)))$$

Implementation Figure 25.14 shows the proportional-share scheduler *time-sharing* for a uniprocessor. The scheduler initializes itself by creating a fiber that, when invoked, applies the initial function f_0 to its *spawn-fe* operator. During execution, the scheduler maintains a ready queue q of engines that are swapped in and out by the *te-switch* function. When *te-switch* receives a stop signal, it tries to run the next engine. If there are no engines left to run, the scheduler exits. A preempt signal, the more interesting case, causes *te-switch* to check if the active engine is out of fuel. If so, it is put on the ready queue, and the next engine is run; if not, the active engine is charged a unit of fuel before being resumed. Notice how this behavior precludes proper nesting of engines: the proportional-share scheduler does not relinquish control to a parent engine if its fuel runs out.

Nested Engines. In this section, we augment the implementation of engines to support fair nesting. The interface for nested engines differs from flat nesting in that it has two types of engines.

- *Leaf engines* run actual computations and are created from an initial function *f* and an amount of fuel.

$$\text{(fun } (leaf\ f\ fuel)\ \ldots\ )$$

- *Nested engines* run other engines and are created from a spawning function *spawn-fn* and an amount of fuel.

$$\text{(fun } (engine\ spawn\text{-}fn\ fuel)\ \ldots\ )$$

There is also an initialization function for creating the root engine and initializing the scheduler.

$$\text{(fun } (init\text{-}engines\ spawn\text{-}fn)\ \ldots\ )$$

Example The example below spawns a root engine that gives its thread 80% of the processor time and gives the remainder to a nested engine containing three threads. The nested engine e_1 is essentially the same as the example in the previous section, except e_1 runs within another engine.

```
(fun (e₁ spawn-ne)
     (begin
        (spawn-ne (leaf f₁ 5))
        (spawn-ne (leaf f₂ 2))
        (spawn-ne (leaf f₃ 3))))
```

The root engine contains the engine e_1 and the leaf engine *f4*. The leaf is given 80% of the processor time, but the engines spawned by e_1 share only the remaining 20%.

```
(fun (e₀ spawn-ne)
     (begin
        (spawn-ne (engine e₁ 2))
        (spawn-ne (leaf f4 8))))
```

The *init* function initializes these engines and enqueues them on the host vproc.

```
(fun (init)
     (let ((k (engines-init e₀)))
        (enq-on-vp (host-vp) k)))
```

Implementation   The implementation has special data constructors to represent fuel cells and engines. A fuel cell contains the amount of remaining fuel and the capacity of the cell. There are two constructors for engines: leaf engines contain a function for evaluation and a fuel cell, and nested engines contain an initial function *init-fn* for evaluation and a fuel cell *fuel-cell*. The implementation applies this initial function to a spawn function for the enclosing engine. We implement the *spawn-ne* function that creates values for engines and adds them to the appropriate ready queue.

- When spawning a leaf, the spawn function initializes it with the *leaf-engine* function. This leaf initializer wraps the leaf fiber in a trivial scheduler that stops when leaf stops and always yields to the parent scheduler when preempted.

- When spawning a nested engine, the spawn function simply makes a recursive call to initialize the subtree of engines.

```
(fun (spawn-ne engine)
    (match
            ('(leaf ,f ,cell) (add-q q (leaf-engine f cell)))
            ('(engine ,init-fn ,fuel-cell)
                (add-q q (init-engines init-fn fuel-cell)))))
```

The scheduler action *ne-switch*, given in figure 25.15, is the heart of our implementation. When it receives a stop signal, the scheduler runs the next engine. When it receives a preempt signal, the scheduler yields to its parent and, once control returns, charges the running engine a tick of fuel. If the engine is empty, the scheduler picks the next engine but otherwise resumes the preempted engine.

Notice how the preemption signal propagates on a path from the active engine upward to the root engine. Only when another scheduler, e.g., the thread scheduler from section 25.2, resumes the root engine, can the engine proceed downwards to the active engine.

The function for running the next engine checks to see if the ready queue is empty; if it is, the scheduler terminates. Otherwise, the scheduler picks the next engine, refills its fuel cell, and runs the engine.

```
(fun (run-next)
    (match (rem-q q)
        ('() (exit))
        ('(,k, ,fuel) (begin (refill-cell fuel)
                            (run ne-switch fuel k)))))
```

The *init-engines* function is the entry point for our nested-engines implementation. It allocates a queue for one level of nesting, then it runs the initial function under the scheduler action.

```
(fun (init-engines init-fn)
    (let ((q (empty-q)))
        (sched-fiber (ne-switch (fuel-cell 1)
                        (λ () (init-fn spawn-ne)))))))
```

25·7 Prototyping in PLT Redex.

In this section, we describe our scheduler prototyping framework based in PLT Redex. This framework consists of a faithful transcription of our semantics from section 25.3, a collection of utility code for writing schedulers, and functions for testing scheduler code. Redex allows us to encode the non-deterministic preemption rule directly in the model. When running a program, each regular state transition is thus paired with delivery of a preemption signal.

We chose to prototype our schedulers using a unit-testing framework based on SchemeUnit. In this framework, the programmer writes scheduler code, checks it on several example programs, and continues the cycle until all checks succeed. To make tests, the programmer needs only provide a suite of expressions in our scheduler framework and their sets of expected outputs (recall that a scheduler is a non-deterministic program and should in some cases produce multiple correct answers).

In prototyping several schedulers, including thread, data-parallel, and work-stealing schedulers, we have found that error messages should contain detailed information to help track down a problem, e.g., printing the final state is usually not enough. Upon encountering an error, our unit tester dumps the faulty reduction sequences to the Redex Stepper, which can be an effective tool for tracking bugs in schedulers. If the error is unclear from viewing just the faulty reduction path, the programmer can also step through alternate paths in the reduction graph for comparison.

Even with the unit-testing framework, debugging even simple programs in our scheduling language poses several challenges. We discuss these issues below, along with our solutions, and note where outstanding problems remain.

Large Reduction Graphs. One key difficulty in protyping in Redex is the large number of states our schedulers generate. With a preemptive scheduler on a single processor, each unmasked state has a corresponding branch for handling preemption. For two fibers with each making n state transitions under the thread scheduler, the reduction graph will contain $O(n^2)$ unique states, and for m fibers it will contain $O(n^m)$ unique states. Running fibers in parallel on separate vprocs has similar growth of states.

Even small scheduler examples, e.g., one using the fiber scheduler from section 25.2, generate about a hundred states. The data-parallel scheduler, with its complex initialization, contains several hundred to thousands of states for simple examples. Computing the reduction sequences for these larger examples takes several minutes, even on a modern PC. Often though, evaluating the full reduction graph is an overkill for prototyping schedulers.

Instead of always evaluating the entire reduction graph, we chose to experiment with a randomized approach. We found that this approach often yields similar results with much fewer system resources. To support randomized checking, we implemented the *random-reduction-path* function that, similar to *apply-reduction-relation*, takes a maximum number of reductions, a reduction relation, and an expression and then returns a random reduction path to a terminal state. We use the maximum number of reductions to cut an execution short, as errors in schedulers sometimes manifest themselves as infinite reduction sequences.

Detecting Infinite Reduction Sequences. Our most basic scheduler, the fiber scheduler from section 25.2, generates infinite reduction sequences in its regular operation. When the fiber scheduler's queue contains a single fiber, a preemption triggers a series of reductions that puts the fiber back on the queue, takes it off, and then resumes the fiber where it left off. Since preemption is non-deterministic, this scheduler will have reduction paths that make no progress, even for multiple threads. For building our test suites, we modified implementation of *apply-reduction-relation*∗ and *random-reduction-path* to drop previously visted states, thus avoiding these useless scheduler operations.

Large States. Machine states contain a surplus of bookkeeping information that, while important to the semantics, impedes debugging. Depending on the reduction path, the store might assign different locations to different variables, or the provisioning map might contain different vproc assignments. We solve this issue by having programs put their final results into the first store location. In this way, a multithreaded program has a single answer that we can compare to a suite of checks.

25·8 Conclusions.
In this chapter we describe our framework for supporting heterogeneous parallelism in a language and runtime system, with an emphasis on programming bug-free scheduler implementations. We begin by describing the basic design of our framework, giving a formal semantics that we model directly in PLT Redex. We give example implementations for workcrew and nested engine schedulers, demonstrating

the expressiveness and programming style of our framework. Finally, we describe a scheduler prototyping system that we implemented using our Redex model.

Acknowledgments. This work is a part of the Manticore project, which investigates the design and implementation of programming languages for multi-core processors. Thanks to the other project members, in particular Matthew Fluet and John Reppy, who contributed to the design of our scheduling framework.

Bibliography

[1] Abadi, M., L. Cardelli, P.-L. Curien and J.-J. Lévy. Explicit substitutions. *Journal of Functional Programming*, 1(4):375–416, 1991.

[2] Abadi, M., L. Cardelli, B. Pierce and G. Plotkin. Dynamic typing in a statically typed language. *ACM Transactions on Programming Languages and Systems*, 13(2):237–268, 1991.

[3] Allen, E. and R. Cartwright. The case for run-time types in Generic Java. In *Proc. Inaugural Conference on the Principles and Practice of Programming in Java*, pages 19–24, 2002.

[4] Allen, E., D. Chase, J. Hallett, V. Luchangco, J.-W. Maessen, S. Ryu, G. L. Steele Jr. and S. Tobin-Hochstadt. The Fortress language specification version 1.0 beta. `http://research.sun.com/projects/plrg/fortress.pdf`, 2007.

[5] Allen, E., D. Chase, V. Luchangco, J.-W. Maessen and G. L. Steele Jr. Object-oriented units of measurement. In *Proc. ACM Conference on Object-Oriented Programming, Systems, Languages, and Applications*, pages 384–403, 2004.

[6] Appel, A. *Compiling with Continuations*. Cambridge University Press, Cambridge, England; New York, New York, 1992.

[7] Barclay, M. W., W. B. Lober and B. T. Karras. SuML: A survey markup language for generalized survey encoding. In *Proc. AMIA Annual Symposium*, 2002.

[8] Barendregt, H. P. *The Lambda Calculus: Its Syntax and Semantics*. North-Holland, Amsterdam, the Netherlands, 1984.

[9] Benton, N. Embedded interpreters. *Journal of Functional Programming*, 15(4):503–542, 2005.

[10] Birnbaum, M., editor. *Psychological Experiments on the Internet*. Academic Press, Amsterdam, the Netherlands, 2000.

[11] Blumofe, R. D. and C. E. Leiserson. Scheduling multithreaded computations by work stealing. *Journal of the ACM*, 46(5):720–748, 1999.

[12] Bove, A. and L. Arbilla. A confluent calculus of macro expansion and evaluation. In *Proc. ACM Conference on Lisp and Functional Programming*, pages 278–287, 1992.

[13] Bracha, G. and D. Griswold. Strongtalk: Typechecking Smalltalk in a production environment. In *Proc. ACM Conference on Object-Oriented Programming, Systems, Languages, and Applications*, pages 215–230, 1993.

[14] Bruggeman, C., O. Waddell and R. K. Dybvig. Representing control in the presence of one-shot continuations. In *Proc. ACM Conference on Programming Language Design and Implementation*, pages 99–107, 1996.

[15] Cardelli, L. Amber. In *Combinators and Functional Programming Languages : Thirteenth Spring School of the LITP, Val d'Ajol, France, May 6-10, 1985*, volume 242 of *Lecture Notes in Computer Science*, pages 21–47. Springer-Verlag, 1986.

[16] Carlisle, M. C. and A. Rogers. Software caching and computation migration in Olden. In *Proc. ACM Symposium on Principles and Practice of Parallel Programming*, pages 29–38, 1995.

[17] Chase, D. R. Safety considerations for storage allocation optimizations. In *Proc. ACM Conference on Programming Language Design and Implementation*, pages 1–10, 1988.

[18] Church, A. A formulation of the simple theory of types. *Journal of Symbolic Logic*, 5:56–68, 1940.

[19] Church, A. *The Calculi of Lambda Conversion. (AM-6) (Annals of Mathematics Studies)*. Princeton University Press, Princeton, New Jersey, 1941.

[20] Clinger, W., D. P. Friedman and M. Wand. A scheme for a higher-level semantic algebra. In Reynolds, J. and M. Nivat, editors, *Algebraic Methods in Semantics*, pages 237–250. Cambridge University Press, 1985.

[21] Clinger, W. D. Proper tail recursion and space efficiency. In *Proc. ACM Conference on Programming Language Design and Implementation*, pages 174–185, 1998.

[22] Clinger, W. D. and J. Rees. Macros that work. In *Proc. ACM Symposium on Principles of Programming Languages*, pages 155–162, 1991.

[23] Curry, H. Modified basic functionality in combinatory logic. *Dialectica*, 23:83–92, 1969.

[24] Curry, H. and R. Feys. Combinatory logic I. Amsterdam, the Netherlands, 1958.

[25] Damas, L. *Type assignment in programming languages*. PhD thesis, University of Edinburgh, 1985.

[26] Damas, L. and R. Milner. Principal type-schemes for functional programs. In *Proc. ACM Symposium on Principles of Programming Languages*, pages 207–212, 1982.

[27] de Bruijn, N. G. Lambda calculus notation with nameless dummies, a tool for automatic formula manipulation, with application to the Church-Rosser theorem. *Indagationes Mathematicae*, 75(5):381–392, 1972.

[28] Demers, A. and J. Donahue. Making variables abstract: an equational theory for Russell. In *Proc. ACM Symposium on Principles of Programming Languages*, pages 59–72, 1983.

[29] Duggan, D. Dynamic typing for distributed programming in polymorphic languages. *ACM Transactions on Programming Languages and Systems*, 21(1):11–45, 1999.

[30] Dybvig, R. K. and R. Hieb. Engines from continuations. *Computer Languages*, 14(2):109–123, 1989.

[31] Dybvig, R. K., R. Hieb and C. Bruggeman. Syntactic abstraction in Scheme. *Lisp and Symbolic Computation*, 5(4):295–326, 1992.

[32] Felleisen, M. *The Calculi of Lambda-v-CS-Conversion: A Syntactic Theory of Control and State in Imperative Higher-Order Programming Languages*. PhD thesis, Indiana University, 1987.

[33] Felleisen, M. On the expressive power of programming languages. *Science of Computer Programming*, 17:35–75, 1991.

[34] Felleisen, M. and D. P. Friedman. Control operators, the SECD-machine, and the λ-calculus. In *Formal Description of Programming Concepts III*, pages 193–217. Elsevier Science Publishers B.V. (North-Holland), 1986.

[35] Felleisen, M. and D. P. Friedman. A syntactic theory of sequential state. *Theoretical Computer Science*, 69:243–287, 1989.

[36] Felleisen, M., D. P. Friedman, E. Kohlbecker and B. Duba. A syntactic theory of sequential control. *Theoretical Computer Science*, 52:205–237, 1987.

[37] Felleisen, M. and R. Hieb. The revised report on the syntactic theories of sequential control and state. *Theoretical Computer Science*, 103:235–271, 1992.

[38] Fisher, K. and J. Reppy. Compiler support for lightweight concurrency. Technical memorandum, Bell Labs, 2002. Available from `http://moby.cs.uchicago.edu/`.

[39] Flatt, M. *Programming Languages for Reusable Software Components*. PhD thesis, Rice University, 2000.

[40] Flatt, M. and M. Felleisen. Units: cool modules for HOT languages. In *Proc. ACM Conference on Programming Language Design and Implementation*, pages 236–248, 1998.

[41] Flatt, M., S. Krishnamurthi and M. Felleisen. A programmer's reduction semantics for classes and mixins. In *Formal Syntax and Semantics of Java*, volume 1523 of *Lecture Notes in Computer Science*, pages 369–388. Springer-Verlag, 1999. Preliminary version appeared in POPL'98. Revised version is Rice University Technical Report TR 97-293, June 1999.

[42] Flatt, M., G. Yu, R. B. Findler and M. Felleisen. Adding delimited and composable control to a production programming environment. In *Proc. ACM International Conference on Functional Programming*, pages 165–176, 2007.

[43] Fluet, M., M. Rainey, J. Reppy, A. Shaw and Y. Xiao. Manticore: A heterogeneous parallel language. In *Proc. Workshop on Declarative Aspects of Multicore Programming*, pages 37–44, 2007.

[44] Fraley, R. C. *How to Conduct Behavioral Research over the Internet: A Beginner's Guide to HTML and CGI/Perl*. Guilford Press, New York, NY, 2004.

[45] Gasbichler, M. *Fully-parameterized Higer-order Modules with Hygienic Macros*. PhD thesis, Universität Tübingen, 2006.

[46] Girard, J. Une extension de l'interprétation de Gödel à l'analyse, et son application à l'élimination des coupures dans l'analyse et la théorie des types. In Fenstad, J., editor, *Proc. Scandinavian Logic Symposium*, pages 63–92. North-Holland, 1971.

[47] Goldberg, A. and D. Robson. *Smalltalk-80: The Language and its Implementation*. Addison-Wesley, Reading, MA, USA, 1983.

[48] Gosling, J., B. Joy, G. L. Steele Jr. and G. Bracha. *Java^{TM} Language Specification, The 3rd Edition (Java Series)*. Addison-Wesley Professional, Reading, MA, USA, 2005.

[49] Graunke, P., R. B. Findler, S. Krishnamurthi and M. Felleisen. Modeling web interactions. In *Proc. European Symposium on Programming*, 2003.

[50] Graunke, P., S. Krishnamurthi, S. Van Der Hoeven and M. Felleisen. Programming the web with high-level programming languages. In *Proc. European Symposium on Programming*, 2001.

[51] Gray, K. E., R. B. Findler and M. Flatt. Fine-grained interoperability through mirrors and contracts. In *Proc. ACM Conference on Object-Oriented Programming, Systems, Languages, and Applications*, pages 231–245, 2005.

[52] Hallett, J. Evaluator for a simple language with hidden type variables and conditional extension. http://cs-people.bu.edu/jhallett/thesis/demo/.

[53] Hallett, J. Hidden type variables and conditional extension for more expressive generic programs. Technical Report BUCS-TR-2007-012, CS Department, Boston University, 2007.

[54] Haynes, C. T. and D. P. Friedman. Engines build process abstractions. In *Proc. ACM Conference on Lisp and Functional Programming*, pages 18–24, 1984.

[55] Haynes, C. T., D. P. Friedman and M. Wand. Continuations and coroutines. In *Proc. ACM Conference on Lisp and Functional Programming*, pages 293–298, 1984.

[56] Hindley, J. R. The principal type scheme of an object in combinatory logic. *Transactions of the American Mathematical Society*, 146:29–40, 1969.

[57] Hudak, P. Building domain-specific embedded languages. *ACM Computing Surveys*, 28(4es):196, 1996.

[58] Hudak, P. Modular domain specific languages and tools. In *Proc. International Conference on Software Reuse*, pages 134–142, 1998.

[59] Igarashi, A., B. Pierce and P. Wadler. Featherweight Java: A minimal core calculus for Java and GJ. In *Proc. ACM Conference on Object-Oriented Programming, Systems, Languages, and Applications*, pages 396–450, 1999.

[60] Kaufmann, M., J. S. Moore and P. Manolios. *Computer-Aided Reasoning: An Approach*. Kluwer Academic Publishers, Norwell, MA, USA, 2000.

[61] Kennedy, A. and B. Pierce. On decidability of nominal subtyping with variance. In *Proc. International Workshop on Foundations and Developments of Object-Oriented Languages*, 2007.

[62] Kohlbecker, E., D. P. Friedman, M. Felleisen and B. Duba. Hygienic macro expansion. In *Proc. ACM Conference on Lisp and Functional Programming*, pages 151–161, 1986.

[63] Krishnamurthi, S., R. B. Findler, P. Graunke and M. Felleisen. Modeling web interactions and errors. In Goldin, D., S. Smolka and P. Wegner, editors, *Interactive Computation: The New Paradigm*, chapter 11. Springer-Verlag, 2006.

[64] Krishnamurthi, S., P. W. Hopkins, J. McCarthy, P. Graunke, G. Pettyjohn and M. Felleisen. Implementation and use of the PLT Scheme web server. *Journal of Higher-Order and Symbolic Computation*, 20(4):431–460, 2007.

[65] Kuan, G. A rewriting semantics for type inference. Technical Report TR-2007-01, University of Chicago, 2007.

[66] Kuan, G. and D. MacQueen. Efficient ML type inference using ranked type variables. In *Proc. Workshop on ML*, 2007.

[67] Kuan, G., D. MacQueen and R. B. Findler. A rewriting semantics for type inference. In *Proc. European Symposium on Programming*, volume 4421 of *Lecture Notes in Computer Science*, pages 426–440, 2007.

[68] Landin, P. J. The mechanical evaluation of expressions. *Computer Journal*, 6:308–320, 1964.

[69] Lee, O. and K. Yi. Proofs about a folklore let-polymorphic type inference algorithm. *ACM Transactions on Programming Languages and Systems*, 20(4):707–723, 1998.

[70] MacHenry, M. and J. Matthews. Topsl: a domain-specific language for on-line surveys. In *Proc. Workshop on Scheme and Functional Programming*, pages 33–39, 2004.

[71] MacQueen, D. Modules for Standard ML. In *Proc. ACM Conference on Lisp and Functional Programming*, pages 198–207, 1984.

[72] Mason, I. A. *The Semantics of Destructive Lisp*. PhD thesis, Stanford University, 1986.

[73] Mason, I. A. and C. Talcott. Inferring the equivalence of functional programs that mutate data. *Theoretical Computer Science*, 105:167–215, 1992.

[74] Matthews, J. and R. B. Findler. Operational semantics for multi-language programs. In *Proc. ACM Symposium on Principles of Programming Languages*, 2007. Extended version to appear in TOPLAS 2009.

[75] McCarthy, J. and S. Krishnamurthi. Interaction-safe state for the web. In *Proc. Workshop on Scheme and Functional Programming*, pages 137–146, 2006.

[76] Michael, M. M. and M. L. Scott. Simple, fast, and practical non-blocking and blocking concurrent queue algorithms. In *Proc. ACM Symposium on Principles of Distributed Computing*, pages 267–275, 1996.

[77] Milner, R. A theory of type polymorphism in programming. *Journal of Computer and System Sciences*, 17(3):348–375, 1978.

[78] Moggi, E. Computational lambda-calculus and monads. In *Proc. Fourth Annual Symposium on Logic in Computer Science*, pages 14–23, 1989.

[79] Morris, J. H. *Lambda-Calculus Models of Programming Languages*. PhD thesis, Massachusetts Institute of Technology, 1968.

[80] Morrisett, G., M. Felleisen and R. Harper. Abstract models of memory management. In *Proc. Conference on Functional Programming Languages and Computer Architecture*, pages 66–77, 1995.

[81] Odersky, M. *The Scala Language Specification, Version 2.6*. http://scala.epfl.ch/docu/files/ScalaReference.pdf, Programming Methods Laboratory, Ecole Polytechnique Federale Lausanne, Lausanne, Switzerland, 2007.

[82] Owens, S. and M. Flatt. From structures and functors to modules and units. *Proc. ACM International Conference on Functional Programming*, pages 87–98, 2006.

[83] Plotkin, G. D. Call-by-name, call-by-value, and the lambda calculus. *Theoretical Computer Science*, 1:125–159, 1975.

[84] Plotkin, G. D. LCF considered as a programming language. *Theoretical Computer Science*, pages 223–255, 1977.

[85] Queinnec, C. A library for quizzes. In *Proc. Workshop on Scheme and Functional Programming*, 2002.

[86] Rainey, M. The Manticore runtime model. Master's thesis, University of Chicago, 2007. Available from `http://manticore.cs.uchicago.edu`.

[87] Ramsey, N. Concurrent programming in ML. Technical Report CS-TR-262-90, Dept. of C.S., Princeton University, 1990.

[88] Ramsey, N. Embedding an interpreted language using higher-order functions and types. In *Proc. Workshop on Interpreters, Virtual Machines and Emulators*, pages 6–14, 2003.

[89] Ramsey, N. and S. Peyton Jones. Featherweight concurrency in a portable assembly language. Unpublished paper available at `http://www.cminusminus.org/abstracts/c--con.html`, 2000.

[90] Regehr, J. *Using Hierarchical Scheduling to Support Soft Real-Time Applications on General-Purpose Operating Systems*. PhD thesis, University of Virginia, 2001.

[91] Reppy, J. H. First-class synchronous operations in Standard ML. Technical Report TR 89-1068, Dept. of CS, Cornell University, 1989.

[92] Reppy, J. H. *Concurrent Programming in ML*. Cambridge University Press, Cambridge, England; New York, New York, 1999.

[93] Reynolds, J. C. Definitional interpreters for higher-order programming languages. In *Proc. ACM Annual Conference*, pages 717–740, 1972.

[94] Reynolds, J. C. Towards a theory of type structure. In *Programming Symposium, Proceedings Colloque sur la Programmation*, volume 19 of *Lecture Notes in Computer Science*, pages 408–425, London, UK, 1974. Springer-Verlag.

[95] Rose, K. H. *Operational Reduction Models for Functional Programming Languages*. PhD thesis, DIKU, University of Copenhagen, 1996. also DIKU Report 96/1.

[96] Shivers, O. A universal scripting framework or Lambda: the ultimate 'little language'. *Concurrency and Parallelism, Programming, Networking, and Security, Lecture Notes in Computer Science*, 1179:254–265, 1996.

[97] Shivers, O. Continuations and threads: Expressing machine concurrency directly in advanced languages. In *Proc. Continuations Workshop*, 1997.

[98] Siek, J. G. and W. Taha. Gradual typing for functional languages. In *Proc. Workshop on Scheme and Functional Programming*, pages 81–92, 2006.

[99] Siek, J. G. and W. Taha. Gradual typing for objects. In *Proc. European Conference on Object-Oriented Programming*, pages 2–27, 2007.

[100] Sitaram, D. Handling control. In *Proc. ACM Conference on Programming Language Design and Implementation*, pages 147–155, 1993.

[101] Sperber, M., K. Dybvig, M. Flatt and A. van Straaten (Eds.). Revised[6] report of the algorithmic language Scheme, 26 September 2007. http://www.r6rs.org.

[102] Steele Jr., G. L. *Common LISP: the Language*. Digital Press, Newton, MA, USA, 1984.

[103] Stone, J. D. SRFI 8: receive: Binding to multiple values. http://srfi.schemers.org/srfi-8/, 1999.

[104] Sussman, G. L. and G. L. Steele Jr. Scheme: An interpreter for extended lambda calculus. Technical Report 349, MIT Artificial Intelligence Laboratory, 1975.

[105] Talcott, C. *The Essence of Rum—A Theory of the Intensional and Extensional Aspects of Lisp-type Computation*. PhD thesis, Stanford University, 1985.

[106] Tobin-Hochstadt, S. and M. Felleisen. Interlanguage migration: From scripts to programs. In *Proc. Dynamic Languages Symposium*, pages 964–974, 2006.

[107] Tobin-Hochstadt, S. and M. Felleisen. The design and implementation of Typed Scheme. In *Proc. ACM Symposium on Principles of Programming Languages*, pages 395–407, 2008.

[108] Tofte, M. *Operational Semantics and Polymorphic Type Inference*. PhD thesis, University of Edinburgh, 1987.

[109] Torgersen, M., C. P. Hansen, E. Ernst, P. von der Ahé, G. Bracha and N. Gafter. Adding wildcards to the Java Programming Language. In *Proc. ACM Symposium on Applied Computing*, pages 1289–1296, 2004.

[110] U.S. General Accounting Office. QPL. Software: `http://www.gao.gov/qpl/`.

[111] Vaillancourt, D., R. Page and M. Felleisen. ACL2 in DrScheme. In *Proc. International Workshop on the ACL2 Theorem Prover and its Applications*, pages 107–116, 2006.

[112] Vandevoorde, M. T. and E. S. Roberts. Workcrews: an abstraction for controlling parallelism. *International Journal of Parallel Programming*, 17(4):347–366, 1988.

[113] Wand, M. Continuation-based multiprocessing. In *Proc. ACM Conference on Lisp and Functional Programming*, pages 19–28, 1980.

[114] Welsh, N., F. Solsona and I. Glover. SchemeUnit and SchemeQL: Two little languages. In *Proc. Workshop on Scheme and Functional Programming*, 2002.

[115] Wirth, N. Modula: a language for modular multiprogramming. *Software Practice and Experience*, 7(1):3–35, 1977.

[116] Wirth, N. The module: A system structuring facility in high-level programming languages. In Tobias, J. M., editor, *Language Design and Programming Methodology*, volume 79 of *Lecture Notes in Computer Science*, pages 1–24. Springer-Verlag, 1979.

[117] Wirth, N. *Programming in Modula-2*. Springer-Verlag, Berlin, Germany, second edition, 1983.

[118] Wright, A. K. and M. Felleisen. A syntactic approach to type soundness. *Information and Computation*, 115(1):38–94, 1994.

Index